A GUIDE TO
AMERICAN
SCREENWRITERS

GARLAND REFERENCE LIBRARY
OF THE HUMANITIES
(VOL. 501)

A GUIDE TO AMERICAN SCREENWRITERS
The Sound Era, 1929–1982

Vol. I: Screenwriters

Larry Langman

GARLAND PUBLISHING, INC. · NEW YORK & LONDON
1984

Library of Congress Cataloging in Publication Data

Langman, Larry.
A guide to American screenwriters.

(Garland reference library of the humanities ;
vol. 501)
Contents: v. 1. Organized by screenwriter—v. 2.
Organized by title.
Bibliography: p.
1. Screen writers—United States—Registers.
I. Title.   II. Series: Garland reference library of the
humanities ; v. 501.
PN1998.L24   1984   011'.37   84-48018
ISBN 0-8240-8927-8 (set : alk. paper)

Cover design by Mirta Vian

CONTENTS

Preface   vii
Sources   xi
Abbreviations   xiii
A Guide to American Screenwriters   1

PREFACE

These volumes present the complete works of American screen-writers—their features, full-length documentaries, and animated films from 1929 through 1982. The author has attempted to make this list as complete as possible. However, to keep this book man-ageable, short subjects, one- and two-reel cartoons, X-rated films, movies made for television, and features for which no specific screenwriter is listed have been omitted.

X-rated films were excluded on technical, not moral, grounds. These works are not widely distributed or known, their lengths often fall short of what is generally accepted as "feature-length," and in many cases the screenwriters are not provided. So, this genre was omitted.

Since sound films did not start abruptly in 1929, this book lists the screenwriters of those transitional years (1927–1928) in which many features were part sound and part silent and the writers were known as "scenario writers," "scenarists," or "dialogue writers." In many instances, to take advantage of the new market and public demand, the studios added sound tracks to their silent films long after the works had been completed. It is difficult to estimate to what degree a writer in this period contributed to the story and/or to the screenplay. For historical reasons, however, we felt we should in-clude these writers.

In the process of compiling this work, certain discrepancies were discovered. Many names were misspelled (Reisner, Riesner); first names varied from film to film (Bill–William, Bob–Robert); and middle initials came and went at random. These anomalies were corrected wherever possible. Misspelled surnames were cross-refer-enced for the reader's convenience. In the case of pseudonyms, both names were listed and cross-referenced with the film titles under the more popular appellation.

Names beginning with "Mac" and "Mc" appear alphabetically

within the "M" listing. Those starting with "von" or "Von" may be located under "V." The dates preceding film titles refer to the year of release.

A large number of films are the creative effort of more than one screenwriter, often the result of three or four contributors. This is not necessarily unique to "A" features or big-budget productions; many "B" musicals and pedestrian comedies list a trio or quartet of collaborators. If a film had only one co-writer, that name was listed in parentheses following the title within the filmography. In general, only the initial of the co-writer's first name was provided. When this conflicted with other writers having the same surname, the full Christian name was furnished. An asterisk denotes films with more than one collaborator. However, a complete list of co-writers of each film may be found in the second volume, the title index.

To those who decide to search the title index first and discover a missing movie, a note of explanation is needed. As stated earlier, a number of features, some rather famous, list no screenwriter; e.g., the 1943 version of "The Desert Song," "A Long Day's Journey into Night" (1962), certain works based on Shakespeare's plays and various documentaries such as "Pumping Iron" (1977). Therefore, the titles were not included.

On the other hand, the researcher may be surprised to find a screenwriter listed for a particular film which has generally gone uncredited on screen ("Friendly Persuasion"), has been attributed to another screenwriter, or simply credits the original author ("The Bridge on the River Kwai"). These situations occurred frequently during the blacklist period of the 1950s. Fortunately, recent books such as *The Hollywood Writers' Wars* by Nancy Lynn Schwartz reveal many of the actual writers, including those who used an assortment of "fronts" during that oppressive decade. These films are listed in this work with a notation that the screenwriter went "uncredited."

The compiler of these volumes hopes that they will serve as a basis for further research. The number of screenplays contributed by women has yet to be explored. The works of various writing teams need to be studied, as do the films of major authors who occasionally wrote for the screen. Another uncharted area concerns those screenwriters who have taken their skills abroad to start entirely new careers. A case in point is Richard Maibaum, who has gone from Broadway in the early 1930s to Hollywood, to television in the

1950s, and then to England in the 1960s to pen most of the James Bond films.

A book of this nature and scope (almost 5,000 screenwriters and more than 20,000 titles) could never have been completed without the knowledge and assistance of others. I would like to thank Alan Barbour for his help in ferreting out the screenwriters of the serials of the 1950s and William K. Everson for his editorial suggestions.

Also, my deepest appreciation goes to librarian Rita Kaikow for her generosity concerning certain reference materials; to Kathleen, Michael, and Dawn Eberts for their clerical assistance; to Gary Kuris for his encouragement; and to the following staff members of the Queensboro Public Library, Art and Music Division, for their patience and understanding: Dorothea Wu, Claire Kach, Wendy Wiederhorn, Lucille Vener, Richard Slapsys, and Samuel Powers.

SOURCES

Blum, Daniel, ed. *Screen World*. New York: Greenberg, (annual).

Catalog of Copyright Entries: Cumulative Series: Motion Pictures. Washington, D.C.: Copyright Office, Library of Congress, 1951.

Corliss, Richard, *Talking Pictures*. New York: Penguin Books, 1975.

Film Daily Year Book of Motion Pictures (annually from 1930). New York: Distributed by Arno Press, 1970.

Munden, Kenneth, ed. *American Film Institute Catalogue of Motion Pictures in the United States*. New York: R. R. Bowker Company, 1971.

Schwartz, Nancy Lynn. *The Hollywood Writers' Wars*. New York: Alfred A. Knopf, 1982.

Willis, John, ed. *Screen World*. New York: Crown Publishers (annually through 1983).

ABBREVIATIONS

alt.   alternate title

anim.   animation

doc.   documentary film

orig.   original title

ret.   retitled

ser.   serial

unc.   uncredited

unr.   unreleased

(*)   denotes more than one collaborator

A

DENNIS AABERG

1978: Big Wednesday (J. Milius)

SIDNEY AARON

1980: Altered States (P. Chayefsky)

GEORGE ABAGNALO

1977: Andy Warhol's Bed (P. Hackett)

SAM X. ABARBANEL

1951: Prehistoric Women (G. Tallas)

GEORGE ABBOTT (1887–   ) director, producer

1929: Why Bring That Up?; Half Way to Heaven
1930: All Quiet on the Western Front*; Fall Guy
       (J. Gleason); Manslaughter; Sea God
1931: Secrets of a Secretary (D. Taylor)
1957: The Pajama Game*
1958: Damn Yankees

W. J. ABBOTT

1947: Scared to Death
1951: Stop That Cab (L. MacFarlane)

ACHMED ABDULAH

1935:   Lives of a Bengal Lancer*

ALAN & JEANNE ABEL

1971:   Is There Sex After Death?
1976:   The Faking of the President

ROBERT ABEL

1952:   Breakdown

JIM ABRAHAMS

1977:   The Kentucky Fried Movie*
1980:   Airplane!*

GOODMAN ACE

1958:   I Married a Woman

RODNEY ACKLAND

1944:   Uncensored (T. Rattigan)

ALLEN J. ACTOR

1976:   Terror House (orig. Terror at Red Wolf Inn)

CLAY ADAMS

1939:   The Honeymoon's Over*
1940:   Girl in 313 (B. Trivers)

ERNIE ADAMS

1937:   Stars over Arizona (R. Tansey)

FRANK R. ADAMS

```
1933:  Peg O' My Heart (F. Marion)
1934:  She Made Her Bed (C. Robinson)
1935:  The Virginia Judge*
1938:  Trade Winds*
```

GERALD DRAYSON ADAMS (1904-   ) Can.

```
1942:  Duke of the Navy (W. Beaudine); The Miracle
       Kid*
1948:  The Gallant Legion (J. Butler); Old Los
       Angeles (ret. California Outpost; C. Riley);
       The Plunderers (G. Geraghty)
1949:  The Big Steal (G. Homes)
1950:  Armored Car Robbery (E. Felton); The Desert
       Hawk*
1951:  The Lady from Texas (C. Bennett); Flame of
       Araby; The Golden Horde; The Prince Who Was
       a Thief (A. MacKenzie); The Sea Hornet;
       Flaming Feather (F. Gruber)
1952:  The Battle at Apache Pass; The Duel at
       Silver Creek (J. Hoffman); Son of Ali Baba;
       Steel Town (L. Breslow); Untamed Frontier
       (G. Bagni)
1954:  Tarza, Son of Cochise; Three Young Texans;
       The Gambler from Natchez (I. Wallace);
       Princess of the Nile
1955:  Chief Crazy Horse (F. Coen); Duel on the
       Mississippi
1956:  Gun Brothers (R. Schayer); Three Bad Sisters
1957:  War Drums
1961:  Gun Fight (R. Schayer)
1962:  The Wild Westerners
1964:  Kissin' Cousins
1965:  Harum Scarum
```

MAX ADAMS

```
1951:  Let's Go Navy
```

RICHARD L. ADAMS

```
1973:  I Escaped from Devil's Island; The Slams
```

ROBERT ADAMS

3

1936:   The Walking Dead*

EWART ADAMSON

1928:   Blindfold (R. Horwood)
1929:   Barnum Was Right (A. Ripley)
1930:   Inside the Lines
1935:   Circumstantial Evidence; False Pretenses;
        The Girl Who Came Back
1936:   Below the Deadline; The Dark Hour; In Paris,
        A.W.O.L. (Matty Brooks); The Walking Dead*
1937:   Rhythm Wranglers (C. Roberts)
1938:   Long Shot
1940:   Earl of Puddlestone (V. Burton); Meet the
        Missus*
1941:   The Gay Vagabond (T. Craven); Petticoat
        Politics (T. Craven)
1942:   House of Errors (E. Davis)

VICTOR ADAMSON (1890-1972) director

1930:   Sagebrush Politics
1939:   Roll, Wagons, Roll*

ALAN ADLER

1982:   Parasite*; The Concrete Jungle

FELIX ADLER

1930:   Feet First
1936:   Our Relations*
1937:   Way Out West*
1938:   Block-Heads*; Swiss Miss*
1940:   A Chump at Oxford*; Saps at Sea*
1944:   Cowboy Canteen (P. Gangelin)

ED ADLUM

1976:   Invasion of the Blood Farmers (E. Kelleher)

4

FRANKLYN ADREON (1902–   ) director

1937:   Zorro Rides Again (ser.)*; S.O.S. Coast
        Guard (ser.)*
1938:   The Lone Ranger (ser.)*; Dick Tracy Returns
        (ser.)*; The Fighting Devil Dogs (ser.)*
1939:   The Lone Ranger Rides Again (ser.)*; Zorro's
        Fighting Legion (ser.)*; Daredevils of the
        Red Circle (ser.)*; Dick Tracy's G-Men
        (ser.)*
1940:   Adventures of Red Ryder (ser.)*; King of the
        Royal Mounted (ser.)*; Drums of Fu Manchu
        (ser.)*; The Mysterious Dr. Satan (ser.)*
1942:   The Yukon Patrol
1947:   Son of Zorro (ser.)*; Jesse James Rides
        Again (ser.)*; The Black Widow (ser.)*
1948:   Dangers of the Canadian Mounted (ser.)*;
        Adventures of Frank and Jesse James (ser.)*;
        Sons of Adventure (S. Shor); G-Men Never
        Forget (ser.)*

JAMES AGEE (1910–1955) critic

1951:   The African Queen (J. Huston)
1952:   Face to Face (A. Mackenzie)
1955:   The Night of the Hunter

FRANCES AGNEW

1929:   Syncopation; Rainbow Man

THOMAS AHEARN

1948:   Disaster

ZOE AKINS (1886–1958)

1930:   Sarah and Son; Anybody's Woman (D.
        Anderson); Right to Love
1931:   Once a Lady (S. Hoffenstein); Women Love
        Once; Working Girls
1933:   Christopher Strong
1934:   Outcast Lady
1936:   Accused (G. Barraud); Camille*; Lady of

```
                Secrets (J. Anthony)
1938:   The Toy Wife
1939:   Zaza
1947:   Desire Me (M. Roberts)
```

EDWARD ALBEE (1928-   ) playwright

1973:   A Delicate Balance

KATHERINE ALBERT

```
1951:   On the Loose (D. Eunson)
1953:   The Star (D. Eunson)
```

MARVIN H. ALBERT

```
1966:   Duel at Diablo (M. Grilikhes)
1967:   Rough Night in Jerico (S. Boehm)
1968:   Lady in Cement (J. Guss); A Twist of Sand
1973:   The Don Is Dead
```

RON W. ALCORN

1961:   Armored Command

ALAN ALDA

```
1979:   The Seduction of Joe Tynan
1981:   The Four Seasons
```

JEROME ALDEN

1978:   Bully

CHARLES ALDERSON

1941:   The Pioneers

ROBERT ALDRICH (1918-   ) director

```
1959:    Ten Seconds to Hell (T. Sherman)
1963:    Four for Texas (T. Sherman)
1970:    Too Late the Hero (L. Heller)
```

J. GRUBB ALEXANDER

```
1929:    The Gamblers; Evidence
1930:    Murder Will Out; A Notorious Affair; General
         Crack (W. Anthony); Moby Dick (O. Garrett);
         Sweet Kitty Bellairs; Outward Bound
1931:    Mad Genius (H. Thew); Road to Singapore;
         Svengali; Hatchet Man
1932:    So Big (J. Jackson)
```

LARRY ALEXANDER

```
1972:    The Stoolie*
```

RONALD ALEXANDER

```
1961:    Return to Peyton Place
1965:    Billie; The Bounty Killer (Leo Gordon);
         Requiem for a Gunfighter
```

SIDNEY ALEXANDER

```
1949:    The Pirates of Capri (Ital.)
```

ALBERT ALEY

```
1960:    The Hound That Thought He Was a Racoon
1966:    The Ugly Dachshund)
```

JAMES ALGAR (1912-   ) director

```
1953:    The Living Desert (doc.)*
1954:    The Vanishing Prairie (doc.)
1955:    The African Lion (doc.)*
1956:    Secrets of Life (doc.)
1958:    White Wilderness (doc.)
1960:    Jungle Cat (doc.)
1962:    The Legend of Lobo
```

1963:   The Incredible Journey (Can.)

WILLIAM ALLAND

1958:   As Young As We Are (M. Dolinsky)

JAMES ALLARDICE

1951:   Sailor Beware (M. Rackin)

COREY ALLEN (1934-   ) director

1971:   Pinocchio
1978:   Avalanche (C. Pola)

ERIC ALLEN

1975:   Smoke in the Wind

EUGENE ALLEN

1942:   Rodeo Rhythm (G. Tuttle)

IRWIN ALLEN (1916-   ) director

1953:   The Sea Around Us (doc.)
1956:   The Animal World (doc.)
1957:   The Story of Mankind (C. Bennett)
1959:   The Big Circus*
1960:   The Lost World (C. Bennett)
1961:   Voyage to the Bottom of the Sea (C. Bennett)
1962:   Five Weeks in a Balloon*

JAY B. ALLEN

1964:   Marnie

JAY PRESSON ALLEN

1972:   Cabaret; Travels with My Aunt

8

```
1975:   Funny Lady (A. Schulman)
1980:   Just Tell Me What You Want
1981:   Prince of the City (S. Lumet)
1982:   Deathtrap
```

R. S. ALLEN

```
1964:   Honeymoon Hotel (H. Bullock)
1965:   Girl Happy (H. Bullock)
1966:   The Man Called Flintstone (anim.; H.
        Bullock)
1967:   Who's Minding the Mint? (H. Bullock)
1968:   With Six You Get Eggroll*
1969:   Don't Drink the Water (H. Bullock)
```

WOODY ALLEN (1935-   )

```
1965:   What's New Pussycat?
1966:   What's Up, Tiger Lily?*
1969:   Take the Money and Run (M. Rose)
1971:   Bananas (M. Rose)
1972:   Play It Again, Sam; Everything You Always
        Wanted to Know About Sex* But Were Afraid to
        Ask
1973:   Sleeper
1975:   Love and Death
1977:   Annie Hall (M. Brickman)
1978:   Interiors
1979:   Manhattan (M. Brickman)
1980:   Stardust Memories
1982:   A Midsummer Night's Sex Comedy
```

MICHAEL ALLIN

```
1973:   Enter the Dragon
1974:   Truck Turner (O. Williams)
1978:   Checkered Flag or Crash
```

CHARLES GRAY ALLISON

```
1977:   Fraternity Row
```

ROGER ALLMON

```
1935:   Hong Kong Nights (N. Houston)
1936:   Feud of the West*
```

ARTHUR ALSBERG

```
1976:   No Deposit, No Return (Don Nelson); Gus (D.
        Nelson)
1977:   Herbie Goes to Monte Carlo (D. Nelson)
1978:   Hot Lead and Cold Feet*
```

HENRY ALTIMUS

```
1938:   Crime Takes a Holiday*
```

HERBERT S. ALTMAN

```
1970:   Dirtymouth
```

ROBERT ALTMAN (1925–   ) director

```
1957:   The Delinquents
1971:   McCabe and Mrs. Miller (B. McKay)
1972:   Images
1974:   Thieves Like Us*
1976:   Buffalo Bill and the Indians (A. Rudolph)
1977:   Three Women
1978:   A Wedding*
1979:   Quintet*; A Perfect Couple (A. Nicholls)
1980:   Health*
```

WILLIAM ALTMAN

```
1956:   That Certain Feeling*
```

ALICE ALTSCHULER

```
1939:   Sabotage (L. Houser)
```

ROD AMATEAU (1923–   ) director

```
1952:   The Bushwackers (T. Gries)
1969:   Hook, Line and Sinker
1970:   Pussycat, Pussycat, I Love You
1972:   Where Does It Hurt? (B. Robinson)
1975:   The Wilby Conspiracy (H. Nebenzal)
```

DAVID AMBROSE

```
1980:   The Final Countdown*
```

WALTER C. AMENT

```
1950:   Fifty Years Before Your Eyes (doc.; A.
        Butterfield)
```

MARTIN AMIS

```
1980:   Saturn 3
```

MARINO AMORUSO

```
1982:   Beach House (J. Gallagher)
```

ROBERT AMRAM

```
1975:   Pacific Challenge
1979:   The Late Great Planet Earth
```

LEWIS AMSTER

```
1942:   Tough As They Come (B. Weisberg)
1943:   Mug Town*
```

MOREY AMSTERDAM

```
1943:   The Ghost and the Guest
1966:   Don't Worry, We'll Think of a Title (J.
        Hart)
```

DORIS ANDERSON

```
1929:   Wolf of Wall Street; Charming Sinners;
        Marriage Playground (J.W. Ruben)
1930:   Anybody's Woman (Z. Akins); Grumpy; Fast and
        Loose; True to the Navy
1931:   The Gay Diplomat; Men Call It Love; Woman
        Pursued (B. Levy)
1932:   Wild Girl (E. Mayer)
1934:   Glamour (G. Unger); I Give My Love (M.
        Krims); Love Birds
1935:   Straight from the Heart; Without Regret (C.
        Brackett)
1936:   And So They Were Married*
1937:   Girl from Scotland Yard (D. Schary); King of
        Gamblers; Sophie Lang Goes West*
1938:   Give Me a Sailor (F. Butler)
1939:   Beauty for the Asking (P. Jarrico)
1940:   Women in War (F. Herbert)
1942:   Mrs. Wiggs of the Cabbage Patch*
1943:   Salute for Three*
1946:   That Brennan Girl
1950:   Never a Dull Moment (L. Breslow)
```

EDGAR C. ANDERSON, JR.

```
1952:   Gold Fever (C. Lancaster)
```

GERRY & SYLVIA ANDERSON

```
1968:   Thunderbirds Are Go
1969:   Journey to the Far Side of the Sun (Donald
        James)
```

HESPER ANDERSON

```
1980:   Touched by Love
```

KEN ANDERSON

```
1967:   The Jungle Book (anim.)*
```

MAXWELL ANDERSON (1888-1959) playwright

```
1930:   All Quiet on the Western Front*
1932:   Rain
1934:   Death Takes a Holiday*; We Live Again (alt.
        Resurrection)*
1935:   So Red the Rose*
1948:   Joan of Arc (A. Solt)
1957:   The Wrong Man (A. MacPhail)
```

ROBERT ANDERSON (1917-   )

```
1956:   Tea and Sympathy
1957:   Until They Sail
1959:   The Nun's Story
1965:   The Sand Pebbles
1970:   I Never Sang for My Father
```

SYLVIA ANDERSON (see GERRY ANDERSON)

CLARK ANDREWS

```
1940:   Manhattan Heartbeat*; Pier 13 (S. Rauh)
```

DEL ANDREWS

```
1930:   All Quiet on the Western Front*
1935:   The Outlaw Deputy (F. Beebe)
```

JACK ANDREWS

```
1940:   Maryland (E. Hill)
1941:   Marry the Boss' Daughter
1942:   Berlin Correspondent (S. Fisher)
1943:   Chetniks
1945:   The Caribbean Mystery (L. Praskins)
1946:   Johnny Comes Flying Home (G. Bricker)
1947:   Dark Delusion (H. Ruskin)
1949:   Johnny Holiday*
1959:   Subway in the Sky
```

ROBERT D. ANDREWS

```
1935:   I Live for Love*; Little Big Shot*
```

13

```
1936:   Jailbreak (J. Hoffman); The Longest Night;
        Isle of Fury (W. Jacobs)
1938:   Gangster's Boy (Karl Brown)
1939:   I Was a Convict (B. Markson); Mutiny in the
        Big House; Streets of New York
1940:   Babies for Sale; Before I Hang; Dreaming Out
        Loud*; Girls of the Road; Island of Doomed
        Men; Men Without Souls (J. Carole)
1941:   The Devil Commands (M. Gunzberg); Sweetheart
        of the Campus (E. Hartmann); Under Age
1942:   Road to Happiness; Sherlock Holmes and the
        Voice of Terror*; Smith of Minnesota
1943:   Bataan; The Cross of Lorraine*; Power of the
        Press
1944:   The Hairy Ape (D. Dunning)
1948:   The Man from Colorado (B. Maddow)
1949:   Bad Boy
```

ROBERT HARDY ANDREWS

```
1949:   Bagdad; I Married a Communist (C. Grayson)
1950:   The Kid from Texas (K. Lamb); The Woman on
        Pier 13 (C. Grayson)
1951:   Best of the Badmen (J. Twist); Mark of the
        Renegade (L. Solomon); The Tanks Are Coming
1962:   Tarzan Goes to India (J. Guillermin)
```

JAMES ANDRONICA

```
1978:   Nunzio
```

MIKE ANGEL

```
1975:   Psychic Killer*
```

BUCKLEY ANGELL

```
1957:   The Hired Gun (D. Lang)
```

MAYA ANGELOU

```
1972:   Georgia, Georgia
```

EDNA ANHALT

1947: Bulldog Drummond Strikes Back (Edward
      Anhalt)
1948: Embraceable You
1949: The Younger Brothers
1950: Sierra; Return of the Frontiersman; Panic in
      the Streets*
1952: The Member of the Wedding (Edward Anhalt);
      The Sniper (Edward Anhalt)
1955: Not As a Stranger (Edward Anhalt)
1957: The Pride and the Passion (Edward Anhalt)

EDWARD ANHALT (1914-   )

1946: Avalanche (A. Holt)
1947: Bulldog Drummond Strikes Back (Edna Anhalt)
1949: Crime Doctor's Diary
1950: Panic in the Streets*
1952: The Member of the Wedding (Edna Anhalt); The
      Sniper (Edna Anhalt)
1955: Not As a Stranger (Edna Anhalt)
1957: The Pride and the Passion (Edna Anhalt)
1958: The Young Lions; The Restless Years; In Love
      and War
1961: The Sins of Rachel Cade; The Young Savages
      (J. P. Miller)
1962: A Girl Named Tamiko; Girls! Girls! Girls!
      (A. Weiss)
1963: Wives and Lovers
1964: Becket
1965: Boeing Boeing; The Satan Bug (J. Clavell)
1967: Hour of the Gun
1968: The Boston Strangler; In Enemy Country
1969: The Madwoman of Chaillot
1972: Jeremiah Johnson (J. Milius); The Salzburg
      Connection
1974: Luther
1975: The Man in the Glass Booth
1979: Escape to Athena (R. Lochte)

JEFF ANJAN

1950: Joe Palooka in Humphrey Takes a Chance

JOE ANSEN

1950:   The Golden Gloves Story (F. Feist)
1952:   Babes in Bagdad (F. Feist)
1958:   South Seas Adventure*

DANIEL ANSLEY

1977:   Moonshine County Express (Hugh Smith)

EDWARD ANTHONY

1933:   The Big Cage (F. Reyher)

EDWIN ANTHONY

1937:   Mile-a-Minute Love
1938:   Crime Afloat

JOSEPH ANTHONY

1935:   Crime and Punishment (S. Lauren); One Way
        Ticket*
1936:   And So They Were Married*; Lady of Secrets
        (Z. Akins); Meet Nero Wolfe*; Wedding
        Present
1937:   Woman Chases Man*

STUART ANTHONY

1931:   Desert Vengeance; The Fighting Sheriff;
        Border Law
1932:   Whistlin' Dan; The Vanishing Frontier;
        McKenna of the Mounted; End of the Trail;
        Lena Rivers (W. Duff); Police Court;
        Strangers of the Evening (W. Duff)
1933:   Silent Men*; The Whirlwind; Life in the Raw;
        The Last Trail; Smoky (P. Perez); Love Is
        Dangerous (alt. Love Is Like That); State
        Trooper
1934:   Frontier Marshal (W. Counselman); Ever Since
        Eve (H. Johnson); Happy Landing; Pursued (L.

Cole)

1935: Border Brigands; Wanderer of the Wasteland; Nevada (G. Weston); Charlie Chan in Paris (E. Lowe); Motive for Revenge; Mutiny Ahead

1936: Drift Fence (alt.: Texas Desperadoes; R. Yost); Desert Gold (R. Yost); Arizona Mahoney (R. Yost); Border Flight (A. Beckhard); Girl of the Ozarks (M. Simmons)

1937: Forlorn River (R. Yost); Thunder Trail (R. Yost); Born to the West (R. Yost)

1938: Highway Patrol (R. Kent); Illegal Traffic*; Prison Farm*; Tip-Off Girls*

1939: Saga of Death Valley (K. DeWolf)

1940: The Ranger and the Lady (G. Geraghty); The Biscuit Eater (L. Hayward)

1941: The Shepherd of the Hills (G. Jones); The Monster and the Girl

WALTER ANTHONY

1930: Courage; Golden Dawn; General Crack (J. Alexander); Scarlet Pages; Old English (M. Howell)

MICHELANGELO ANTONIONI (1912-   ) director Ital.

(American films only)
1970: Zabriskie Point*

LEAH APPEL

1981: Separate Ways

MAX APPLE

1981: Smokey Bites the Dust

CHRIS APPLEY

1958: The Fearmakers (E. West)

THEODORE APSTEIN

1969:   Whatever Happened to Aunt Alice?

WILLIAM ARCHIBALD

1953: I Confess (G. Tabori)

ROBERT ARDREY (1908-1980)

1940:   They Knew What They Wanted
1943:   A Lady Takes a Chance
1946:   The Green Years (S. Levien)
1947:   Song of Love
1948:   The Three Musketeers
1949:   The Secret Garden; Madame Bovary
1955:   Quentin Durward
1956:   The Power and the Prize
1959:   The Wonderful Country
1962:   The Four Horsemen of the Apocalypse (J. Gay)
1966:   Khartoum

ROBERT ARKLESS

1975:   The Man Who Would Not Die*

DAVID ARLEN

1940:   Broken Strings*

MICHAEL ARLEN

1943:   The Heavenly Body (W. Reisch)

A. ARMBAND

1935:   Yiddish King Lear

GEORGE ARMITAGE

1970:   Gas-s-s-s!
1972:   Hit Man; Private Duty Nurses

```
1974:  Night Call Nurses
1975:  Darktown Strutters
1976:  Vigilante Force
```

SAM ARMSTRONG

```
1934:  Sequoia*
```

DANNY ARNOLD

```
1953:  The Caddy*
1955:  Desert Sands*; Fort Yuma
1956:  Outside the Law; Rebel in Town
1958:  The Lady Takes a Flyer
1972:  The War Between Men and Women (M. Shavelson)
```

ELLIOT ARNOLD

```
1963:  Kings of the Sun (James Webb)
1964:  Flight from Ashiya (W. Salt)
1966:  Alvarez Kelly (F. Coen)
```

NEWTON ARNOLD

```
1962:  Hands of a Stranger
```

JOHN ARNOLDY

```
1978:  Disco Fever
1979:  The Young Cycle Girls
1980:  The Last of the Blue Devils (B. Ricker)
```

ART ARTHUR

```
1937:  Love and Hisses (Curtis Kenyon)
1938:  Kentucky Moonshine*
1939:  Day-Time Wife (R. Harari); Everything
       Happens at Night (R. Harari)
1941:  Sailors on Leave (M. Boylan); Tight Shoes
       (L. Spigelgass)
1942:  Dr. Broadway; Priorities on Parade (F.
       Loesser); Sleepytime Gal*; True to the Army
```

(B. Ropes)
1943: Lady Bodyguard (E. Hartmann); Riding High*
1947: Heaven Only Knows (ret. Montana Mike; R. Leigh); The Fabulous Dorseys*
1948: Northwest Stampede (L. Hayward)
1949: The Song of India (K. Perkins)
1964: Flipper's New Adventure; Rhino! (A. Weiss)
1965: Zebra in the Kitchen
1966: Around the World Under the Sea (A. Weiss); Birds Do It (A. Kogen)

HELENE ARTHUR

1975: Inside Amy

ROBERT ARTHUR

1940: New Moon (J. Deval)
1957: Edge of the City

VICTOR ARTHUR

1950: Trail of the Rustlers; Hills of Oklahoma (O. Cooper); Lightning Guns
1951: Ridin' the Outlaw Trail

MARK L. ARYWITZ

1982: Just Before Dawn (G. Irving)

HERBERT ASBURY

1934: Among the Missing*; Fugitive Lady (F. Niblo); Name the Woman (F. Niblo)

WILLIAM ASHER (1919-   ) director

1964: Bikini Beach*
1965: Beach Blanket Bingo (L. Townsend); How to Stuff a Wild Bikini (L. Townsend)
1966: Fireball 500 (L. Townsend)

RAY ASHLEY

1953: Little Fugitive*

WILSON ASHLEY

1962: The Seducers

JAMES ASHTON

1975: The Devil's Rain*

HERBERT ASMODI

1977: Cross of Iron (J. Epstein)

LEOPOLD ATLAS

1935: Mystery of Edwin Drood*; A Notorious
       Gentleman (R. Tasker)
1944: Tomorrow the World (R. Lardner)
1945: The Story of G.I. Joe*
1946: Her Kind of Man (G. Kahn)
1948: Raw Deal (J. Higgins)

DUKE ATTEBERRY

1937: Double or Nothing*; Mountain Music
1939: I'm from Missouri (J. Moffitt)
1940: Comin' Round the Mountain*

GLADYS ATWATER

1937: Criminal Lawyer; The Man Who Found Himself*
1938: Crashing Hollywood (P. Yawitz); Crime Ring
       (J. Bren); This Marriage Business (J. Bren)
1939: Parents on Trial*
1942: American Empire*
1953: The Great Sioux Uprising

JAMES AUBREY

1930:   Under Montana Skies (B. Cohen)

GEORGE AUERBACH

1935:   The Bishop Misbehaves (Leon Gordon)

HELEN & TOM AUGUST

1964:   The Misadventures of Merlin Jones
1965:   The Monkey's Uncle

JEAN AURENCHE (1904-   ) Fr.

(American films only)
1960:   Is Paris Burning? (U.S./Fr.)*

ROBERT ALAN AURTHUR (1922-1978) novelist

1957:   Edge of the City
1959:   Warlock
1964:   Lilith (unc.; A. Rossen)
1966:   Grand Prix
1968:   For Love of Ivy
1969:   The Lost Man
1979:   All That Jazz (B. Fosse)

ISLEN AUSTER

1933:   Cheating Blondes (L. Foster)

EDWARD R. AUSTIN

1939:   Death Goes North

IRVING AUSTIN

1982:   Warlords of the 21st Century*

MICHAEL AUSTIN

1982:   Five Days One Summer

RONALD AUSTIN

1967:   The Happening*
1969:   Midas Run (J. Buchanan)
1973:   Harry in Your Pocket (J. Buchanan)

WILLIAM AUSTIN

1945:   Allotment Wives (H. Gates)

HIKMET AVEDIS

1973:   The Stepmother
1974:   The Teacher
1975:   The Specialist*; Dr. Minx
1976:   Scorchy
1978:   Texas Detour

HOWARD AVEDIS

1980:   The Fifth Floor

RUTH AVERGON

1981:   Night School

STEPHEN MOREHOUSE AVERY

1934:   Pursuit of Happiness*; Wharf Angel*
1935:   The Gay Deception (D. Hartman); Our Little
        Girl*
1936:   The Gorgeous Hussy (A. Morgan); One Rainy
        Afternoon (M. Hanline)
1939:   Rio*
1941:   Four Mothers
1942:   The Male Animal*
1947:   Deep Valley (S. Viertel)
1948:   Every Girl Should Be Married (D. Hartman)

JOHN G. AVILDSEN (1937-   ) director

1970:   Guess What We Learned in School Today? (E. Price)
1971:   Okay Bill

DAVID AXELROD

1981:   Charlie Chan and the Curse of the Dragon Queen (S. Burns)

GEORGE AXELROD (1922-   ) director, producer, playwright

1954:   Pffft
1955:   The Seven Year Itch (B. Wilder)
1956:   Bus Stop
1961:   Breakfast at Tiffany's
1962:   The Manchurian Candidate
1964:   Paris When It Sizzles
1965:   How to Murder Your Wife
1966:   Lord Love a Duck (L.H. Johnson)
1968:   The Secret Life of an American Wife
1980:   The Lady Vanishes

JONATHAN AXELROD

1972:   Every Little Crook and Nanny (Cy Howard)

DAN AYKROYD

1980:   The Blues Brothers (J. Landis)

GERALD AYRES

1980:   Foxes
1981:   Rich and Famous

LEW AYRES

1955:   Altars of the East (doc.)

B

DWIGHT D. BABCOCK

1944:   Dead Man's Eyes
1945:   Jungle Captive (M. Webster); Road to
        Alcatraz (J. Sackheim)
1946:   So Dark the Night (M. Berkeley)
1947:   Bury Me Dead (K. DeWolf); The Corpse Came
        C.O.D. (G. Bricker)
1951:   FBI Girl (R. Landau)
1953:   SavageFrontier (G. Geraghty)
1955:   Jungle Moon Men (J. Pagano)

RICHARD BACH

1973:   Jonathan Livingston Seagull (H. Bartlett)
1975:   Nothing by Chance

GORDON BACHE

1947:   Blonde Savage

LAWRENCE P. BACHMANN

1935:   Jalna*
1942:   Dr. Gillespie's New Assistant*; Fingers at
        the Window (R. Caylor)
1943:   Dr. Gillespie's Criminal Case*

NICHOLAS E. BAEHR

1968:   The Incident

25

GEORGE BAER

1940:   One Million BC*

MAX BAER

1974:   Macon County Line (R. Compton)
1975:   The Wild McCullochs

RICHARD BAER

1958:   Life Begins at 17

SAM BAERWITZ

1948:   Bungalow 13 (R. Hubler)
1950:   The Great Plane Robbery (R. Hubler)

GWEN BAGNI

1949:   Captain China (L. Foster)
1952:   Untamed Frontier (G. Adams)
1953:   Law and Order (D. Beauchamp)
1968:   With Six You Get Eggroll*

RICHARD BAILEY

1975:   Win, Place or Steal (A. Monaco)

GARY L. BAIM

1978:   Ice Castles (D. Wrye)

BETTY BAINBRIDGE

1933:   Secrets of Hollywood

JOHN V. BAINES

1953: I'll Get You

ROBERT BAIRD

1979: Seven (W. Driskill)

ELLIOT BAKER

1966: A Fine Madness
1967: Luv (H. Baker)
1979: Viva Max!
1975: Breakout*

FRED BAKER

1970: Events

GRAHAM BAKER

1928: Singing Fool; Air Circus*
1929: Sonny Boy; Conquest; Fancy Baggage; Glad Rag
       Doll; Honky Tonk
1933: The Billion Dollar Scandal (G. Towne);
       Broadway Through a Keyhole (G. Towne); I
       Love That Man (G. Towne)
1935: Every Night at Eight (G. Towne); Mary Burns,
       Fugitive*; Shanghai*
1936: The Case Against Mrs. Ames (G. Towne)
1937: History Is Made at Night (G. Towne);
       Stand-In (G. Towne); You Only Live Once (G.
       Towne)
1938: Joy of Living*
1939: Eternally Yours (G. Towne)
1940: Swiss Family Robinson*; Tom Brown's School
       Days
1943: Crime Doctor (L. Lantz)
1945: Danger Signal (A. Comandini)
1946: Shadow of a Woman (W. Chambers)
1947: Ramrod*
1948: Four Faces West (T. Sherman)

HERBERT BAKER

1948: So This Is New York (C. Foreman)
1952: Jumping Jacks*
1953: Dream Wife*; Scared Stiff (W. DeLeon); The
       Big Leaguer
1955: Artists and Models*
1956: Thegirl Can't Help It (F. Tashlin)
1957: Loving You (H. Kanter)
1958: King Creole (M. Gazzo)
1959: Don't Give Up the Ship*
1966: Murderers' Row
1967: Luv (E. Baker); The Ambushers
1968: Hammerhead (William Bast)
1979: Sextette
1980: The Jazz Singer

JANE & PIP BAKER

1970: Captain Nemo and the Underwater City (R. W.
       Campbell)

MELVILLE BAKER

1928: Circus Kid
1929: Fashions in Love; Darkened Rooms (Pat
       Kearney)
1930: One Romantic Night
1931: His Woman (A. Heilbron)
1932: Downstairs (L. Coffee)
1936: Ladies in Love; Next Time We Love (M. Baker)
1937: Seventh Heaven
1938: The First Hundred Years
1939: Joe and Ethel Turp Call on the President
1943: Above Suspicion*

RALPH BAKSHI (1939-   ) director, etc.

1972: Fritz the Cat (anim.)
1973: Heavy Traffic (anim.)
1975: Coonskin (anim.)
1977: Wizards (anim.)
1982: Hey Good Lookin' (anim.)

NIGEL BALCHIN (1908-1970) Brit. novelist, etc.

(American films only)
1961:   Circle of Deception (R. Musel)

JOHN L. BALDERSTON (1899-1954) playwright, etc.

1932:   The Mummy
1933:   Berkeley Square (S. Levien)
1935:   Bride of frankenstein (W. Hurlbut); Lives of
        a Bengal Lancer*; Mad Love*; Mystery of
        Edwin Drood*
1936:   Beloved Enemy*; Last of the Mohicans*
1937:   The Prisoner of Zenda*; Romance and Riches
1940:   Victory
1941:   Scotland Yard (S. Engel); Smilin' Through
        (D. Stewart)
1942:   Stand By for Action*; Tennessee Johnson (W.
        Root)
1944:   Gaslight*
1952:   The Prisoner of Zenda (N. Langley); Red
        Planet Mars (A. Veiller); Red Ball Express*

EARL BALDWIN

1928:   Brotherly Love
1929:   Red Hot Rhythm (W. DeLeon)
1930:   Sweet Mama (F. Brennan); The Widow from
        Chicago
1931:   Naughty Flirt (R. Weil); Tip Off; The Big
        Shot (J. Fields)
1932:   Central Park (W. Morehouse); The Crash (L.
        Barretto); Doctor X (R. Tasker); Life
        Begins; The Mouthpiece; The Tenderfoot*
1933:   Blondie Johnson; Havana Widows; Wild Boys of
        the Road
1934:   Here Comes the Navy (B. Markson); Six-Day
        Bike Rider; A Very Honorable Guy; Wonder Bar
1935:   Devil Dogs of the Air (M. Boylan); Go into
        Your Dance; The Irish in Us
1937:   Ever Since Eve*
1938:   The Cowboy from Brooklyn; Gold Diggers in
        Paris (W. Duff); A Slight Case of Murder (J.
        Schrank)
1939:   Off the Record*
1940:   Brother Orchid; My Love Came Back*
1941:   Honeymoon for Three; She Couldn't Say No (C.
        Grayson); Unholy Partners*

```
1944:  Pin-Up Girl*; Greenwich Village (W.
       Bullock); Irish Eyes Are Smiling (J. Battle)
1945:  Hold That Blonde*
1946:  Breakfast in Hollywood
1949:  Africa Screams
1951:  The Lullaby of Broadway
1959:  Juke Box Rhythm
```

JOHN BALLARD

```
1979:  The Orphan
```

BILL BALLINGER

```
1964:  The Strangler
1965:  Operation C.I.A. (P. Oppenheimer)
```

ANNE BANCROFT (1931-   ) actress, etc.

```
1980:  Fatso
```

HENRY BANCROFT

```
1941:  I Killed That Man
```

ALBERT BAND (1924-   )

```
1957:  Footsteps in the Night (E. Ullman)
1966:  The Tramplers
1979:  She Came to the Valley (F. Perilli)
```

MONTY BANKS (1897-1950) Brit.

```
(American films only)
1932:  The Tenderfoot*
```

MILT BANTA

```
1953:  Peter Pan*
1959:  Sleeping Beauty*
```

BEATRICE BANYARD

1931: Reducing (W. Mack)
1933: Strictly Personal (W. Mack)

JACK BARAN

1971: Roommates

ELOISE BARANGON

1938: Spring Fever*

BOB BARBASH

1960: The Plunderers
1967: Tarzan and the Great River
1979: Target: Harry

ROWLAND BARBER

1959: The Thirty Foot Bride of Candy Rock (A.
        Ross)

JOSEPH BARBERA (1911-   )

1964: Hey There, It's Yogi Bear (anim.)*
1979: C.H.O.M.P.S.*
1982: Heidi's Song (anim.)*

GORDON BARCLAY

1974: The Last of the American Hoboes

RICHARD BARE (1909-   ) director, etc.

1939: Two-Gun Troubador (P. Dunham)
1973: Wicked, Wicked

FRANK BARHYDT

1979:   Quintet*
1980:   Health*

MILDRED BARISH

1939:   The Phantom Creeps (ser.)*

H.E. BARNE

1958:   Frankenstein's Daughter

FORREST BARNES

1935:   Valley of Wanted Men (B. Barringer)
1937:   Western Gold

HENRY BARNES

1976:   Ebony Ivory and Jade

PETER BARNES

1966:   Not with My Wife, You Don't!*

KEN BARNETT

1964:   Diary of a Bachelor

JOHN BARNSWELL

1959:   Surrender Hell!

ALLEN BARON

1961:   Blast of Silence
1965:   Terror in the City

MEL BARR

1960: Murder, Inc. (I. Tunick)

GEORGE BARRAUD

1938: Dark Sands

JAMES LEE BARRETT (1929-   )

1957: The D.I.
1965: The Greatest Story Ever Told (G. Stevens);
      Shenandoah; The Truth About Spring
1968: The Green Berets; Bandolero!
1969: The Undefeated
1970: tick...tick...tick...; The Cheyenne Social
      Club
1971: Fools' Parade; Something Big
1977: Smokey and the Bandit*

TONY BARRETT

1967: Good Times

LARRY BARRETTO

1932: The Crash (E. Baldwin)

H.E. BARRIE

1958: She Demons (R. Cunha)
1961: The Girl in Room 13 (R. Cunha)

BARRY BARRINGER (-1938)

1929: Bye, Bye Buddy;
1931: Graft; Lightning Flyer
1932: The Death Kiss (G. Kahn); Dynamite Ranch (F.
      Sheldon); The Face on the Barroom Floor (B.
      Bracken); Murder at Dawn
1933: Daring Daughter (F. Herbert)
1934: The Dude Ranger; The Way of the West; The

33

Return of Chandu (ser.); 16 Fathoms Deep (N. Houston); What's Your Racket
1935: Northern Frontier; The Red Blood of Courage; Valley of Wanted Men (F. Barnes); Men of Action*
1936: Song of the Trail*; Federal Agent
1938: Held for Ransom

LOWELL BARRINGTON

1967: Valley of Mystery (R. Neal)

CHUCK BARRIS

1980: The Gong Show Movie (R. Downey)

JERRY R. BARRISH

1982: Dan's Motel

ARTHUR BARRON

1973: Jeremy

FRED BARRON

1977: Between the Lines
1979: Something Short of Paradise

NICHOLAS T. BARROWS

1932: Million Dollar Legs*
1937: Dangerous Holiday; Swing It, Professor (R. St. Clair)
1938: I'm from the City*
1944: That's My Baby! (W. Tunberg)

JULIAN BARRY

1974: Rhinoceros; Lenny

KEVIN BARRY

1962:   Saintly Sinners

TOM BARRY

1929:   In Old Arizona; The Valiant (J. Booth); Thru
        Different Eyes (alt. Guilty; Public Opinion;
        M. Gropper)
1930:   Song O' My Heart (S. Levien); Under
        Suspicion
1931:   East Lynne (B. King); Over the Hill (J.
        Furthman)

DICK BARRYMORE

1969:   The Last of the Ski Bums

LEON BARSHA

1942:   The Devil's Trail

JEAN BART

1935:   The Man Who Reclaimed His Head
1939:   The Mad Empress*

PETER BART

1971:   Making It

PAUL BARTEL

1968:   The Secret Cinema
1976:   Cannonball (D. Simpson)
1982:   Eating Raoul (R. Blackburn)

HALL BARTLETT (1922-   ) director, producer, etc.

1953:   Crazylegs, All-American

```
1955:   Unchained
1957:   Drango; Zero Hour*
1960:   All the Young Men
1963:   The Caretakers (H. Greenberg)
1969:   Changes (B. Kelly)
1972:   The Wild Pack
1973:   Jonathan Livingston Seagull (R. Bach)
1978:   The Children of Sanchez
```

JEANNE BARTLETT

```
1945:   Son of Lassie
1946:   Gallant Bess
1948:   Man Eater of Kumaon (L. Meltzer)
```

RICHARD (DICK) BARTLETT
```
1955:   The Silver Star (I. MacDonald)
1956:   Two Gun Lady (N. Jolley)
1971:   Wanda*
1972:   The Gentle People
```

SY BARTLETT (1909-1978) producer

```
1933:   The Big Brain
1934:   Kansas City Princess (M. Seff)
1935:   Going Highbrow (E. Kaufman)
1936:   Boulder Dam (R. Block); The Murder of Dr.
        Harrington*
1937:   Danger Patrol; The Man Who Cried Wolf (C.
        Grayson)
1938:   Cocoanut Grove (O. Cooper)
1939:   The Amazing Mr. Williams*
1940:   Sandy Gets Her Man (J. Storm)
1941:   Road to Zanzibar*
1942:   Two Yanks in Trinidad*
1944:   The Princess and the Pirate*
1946:   13 Rue Madeleine (J. Monks)
1949:   Down to the Sea in Ships (J. Mahin); Twelve
        O'Clock High (B. Lay)
1955:   That Lady (A. Veiller); The Last Command (W.
        Duff)
1958:   The Big Country
1959:   Beloved Infidel
1969:   Che! (M. Wilson)
```

WILLIAM BARTLETT

1938: Call of the Yukon (G. Orr)

CHARLES BARTON

1946: The Ghost Steps Out

JOACHIM J. BARTSCH

1966: Desperado Trail (H. Peterson)

HAL BARWOOD

1974: The Sugarland Express (M. Robbins)
1976: The Bing Long Traveling All-Stars and Motor
       Kings (M. Robbins)
1977: MacArthur (M. Robbins)
1978: Corvette Summer (M. Robbins)
1981: Dragonslayer (M. Robbins)

BEN BARZMAN (1911-   ) Can.

1943: You're a Lucky Fellow, Mr. Smith*
1945: Back to Bataan (R. Landau)
1948: The Boy with Green Hair (A. Levitt)
1949: Give Us This Day (Brit.)
1950: Salt to the Devil
1957: Time Without Pity
1958: He Who Must Die (Fr.;J. Dassin)
1960: Chance Meeting (M. Lampell)
1963: The Ceremony
1964: The Fall of the Roman Empire*; The Visit

SARA WARE BASSETT

1935: Captain Hurricane (J. Lovett)

EILEEN & ROBERT BASSING

1958: Home Before Dark

37

WILLIAM BAST

1968:   Hammerhead (H. Baker)
1969:   The Valley of Gwangi
1978:   The Betsy (W. Bernstein)

KENT BATEMAN

1978:   The Land of No Return (F. Perilli)

GARRIE BATESON

1970:   The Traveling Executioner

ALFRED BATSON

1941:   Jungle Girl (ser.)*

GORDON BATTLE

1933:   Treason

JOHN TUCKER BATTLE

1944:   Irish Eyes Are Smiling (E. Baldwin)
1945:   Captain Eddie
1948:   So Dear to My Heart
1951:   The Frogmen
1955:   A Man Alone
1956:   Lisbon
1957:   Shoot-Out at Medicine Bend (D. Beauchamp)

NORMAN BATTLE

1932:   Widow in Scarlet

FRED BAUER

1981:   Under the Rainbow*

TOM BAUM

1976: Hugo the Hippo
1980: Carny

J. L. BAYONAS

1970: Madigan's Millions (J. Henaghan)

PETER S. BEAGLE

1974: The Dove (A. Kennedy)
1978: The Lord of the Rings (anim.; C. Conkling)
1982: The Last Unicorn (anim.)

CHARLES BEAHAN

1930: Ladies in Love
1935: Sweet Surrender*
1938: Dynamite Delaney (J. Rothman)

SCOTT E. BEAL

1938: Convicts at Large (W. James)

GEORGE BEATTY

1941: You're in the Army Now (P. Smith)

ROGER BEATTY

1978: The Billion Dollar Hobo*

WARREN BEATTY (1937-   ) actor, producer

1975: Shampoo (R. Towne)
1978: Heaven Can Wait (E. May)
1981: Reds (Trevor Griffiths)

D. D. BEAUCHAMP

1948: Feudin', Fussin' and A-Fightin'; River Lady
      (W. Bowers)
1949: Leave It to Henry
1950: Father's Wild Game; Father Makes Good
1951: Father Takes the Air; Belle le Grande
1952: The San Francisco Story
1953: Gunsmoke; Abbott and Costello Go to Mars
      (John Grant); Law and Order (G. Bagni); The
      Man from the Alamo (S. Fisher); The
      All-American; Son of Belle Star (W. Raynor)
1954: Jesse James' Women; Rails into Laramie (J.
      Hoffman)
1955: Man Without a Star (B. Chase); Tennessee's
      Partner (M. Krims)
1956: Massacre; Yaqui Drums (J. Pagano)
1957: Shoot-Out at Medicine Bend (J. Battle)
1959: Alias Jesse James (W. Bowers)
1960: For the Love of Mike
1969: A Man Called Gannon*

LANE BEAUCHAMP

1949: Henry, the Rainmaker

WILLIAM BEAUDINE (1890-1970) director, etc.

1942: Duke of the Navy (G. Adams)

CHARLES BEAUMONT (1930-1967)

1958: Queen of Outer Space
1962: Burn Witch Burn (Brit.; R. Matheson); I Hate
      Your Guts; Premature Burial (Ray Russell);
      The Wonderful World of the Brothers Grimm*;
      The Intruder
1963: The Haunted Palace
1964: Masque of the Red Death (R. W. Campbell);
      Seven Faces of Dr. Lao
1965: Mister Moses (M. Danischewsky)

DAN BEAUMONT

1964: For Those Who Think Young*

ROBERT BECHE

1942: The Secret Code (ser.)*

GEORGE BECK

1951: Behave Yourself

ARNOLD BECKER

1954: Go, Man, Go

VERNON P. BECKER

1969: The Funniest Man in the World (doc.)

BARRY BECKERMAN

1973: Shamus
1976: St. Ivesane)

EDWARD BECKHARD

1935: Curly Top (P. McNutt); West Point of the Air
       (F. Wead)
1936: Border Flight (S. Anthony); The Sky Parade*

RICHARD BEE

1929: Seven Footprints to Satan; House of Horror

FORD BEEBE (1888-   ) director

1929: Overland Bound (J. Kane)
1930: Oklahoma Cyclone; The Indians Are Coming (G.
       Plympton)
1931: The Vanishing Legion (ser.)*; Lightning
       Warrior (ser.)*; King of the Wild (ser.)*;

41

```
              The Phantom of the West (ser.)*
1932:   The Last of the Mohicans (ser.)*; Pride of
        the Legion; The Shadow of the Eagle (ser.)*
1934:   The Prescott Kid
1935:   Law Beyond the Range; The Revenge Rider;
        Fighting Shadows; Justice of the Range; The
        Outlaw Deputy (D. Andrews); Riding Wild; The
        Man from Guntown (T. Ince); Tumbling
        Tumbleweeds; Gallant Defender
1936:   The Mysterious Avenger; Code of the Range
1938:   Trouble at Midnight (M. Geraghty)
1939:   Oklahoma Frontier
1940:   Riders of Pasco Basin
1946:   My Dog Shep
1949:   The Dalton Gang; Bomba on Panther Island;
        Shep Comes Home
1950:   The Girl from San Lorenzo; The Lost Volcano
1951:   Bomba and the Elephant Stampede; The Lion
        Hunters
1952:   African Treasure; Bomba and the Jungle Girl
1953:   Safari Drums
1954:   Killer Leopard; The Golden Idol
1955:   Lord of the Jungle
1959:   King of the Wild Stallions
```

JOHN BEECH

```
1982:   Warlords of the 21st Century*
```

ELIZABETH BEECHER

```
1941:   Underground Rustlers*
1942:   The Lone Rider in Cheyenne (O. Drake); The
        Silver Bullet; Little Joe the Wrangler (S.
        Lowe)
1943:   Tenting Tonight on the Old Camp Ground;
        Haunted Ranch; Land of Hunted Men; Wild
        Horse Stampede; Cowboy Commandos; Bullets
        and Saddles; Death Valley Rangers*; Cowboy
        in the Clouds
1944:   Swing in the saddle*; Cyclone Prairie
        Rangers; Saddle Leather Law
1945:   Sing Me a Song of Texas (J. Cheney); Rough
        Ridin' Justice; Rough Riders of Cheyenne
```

42

MAC BEHM

1971:   Someone Behind the Door (J. Robert)

MARC BEHM

1982:   Hospital Massacre

HARRY BEHN

1929:   Sin Sister
1930:   Hell's Angels (H. Estabrook)

S. N. BEHRMAN (1893-1973) playwright

1930:   Liliom*; Lightnin' (S. Levien)
1931:   The Brat (S. Levien); Surrender (S.Levien)
1932:   Rebecca of Sunnybrook Farm (S. Levien); Tess
        of the Storm Country*
1933:   Hallelujah, I'm a Bum
1934:   As Husbands Go (S. Levien)
1935:   Anna Karenina*; A Tale of Two Cities
        (W.Lipscomb)
1937:   Conquest*; Parnell (J. Van Druten)
1938:   Cowboy and the Lady (S. Levien)
1940:   Waterloo Bridge*
1941:   Two-Faced Woman*
1951:   Quo Vadis*
1958:   Me and the Colonel (G. Froeschel)

ALBERT BEICH

1943:   Girls in Chains; The West Side Kid (A.
        Coldeway); You Can't Beat the Law
1946:   Gay Blades
1948:   The Bride Goes Wild
1950:   The Milkman*; The Yellow Cab Man (D.
        Freeman)
1956:   The Lieutenant Wore Skirts (F. Tashlin)
1964:   Dead Ringer (O. Millard)
1967:   The Perils of Pauline

ALBERT BEIN

1938:   Boy Slaves (B. Orkow)

PERCY BEKROFF

1931:   Soldiers' Plaything

NICHOLAS BELA

1938:   The Headleys at Home (C. North)

CHARLES BELDEN

1934:   15 Wives; Fugitive Road*; The Ghost Walks
1935:   Port of Lost Dreams; A Shot in the Dark;
        Sons of Steel; Symphony of Living; Widow
        from Monte Carlo*; The World Accuses
1936:   Charlie Chan at the Opera (W. Darling); The
        Murder of Dr. Harrigan*
1937:   Charlie Chan at Monte Carlo (J. Cady);
        Charlie Chan on Broadway (J. Cady)
1938:   Charlie Chan in Honolulu; Mr. Moto's Gamble
        (J. Cady); One Wild Night (J. Cady)
1939:   Kid Nightingale (R. Schrock); On Dress
        Parade (T. Reed); Torchy Plays with Dynamite
        (E. Snell)
1940:   Tear Gas Squad*
1946:   The Gay Cavalier
1947:   The Marauders; South of Monterey; Beauty and
        the Bandit; The Strange Mr. Gregory
1948:   Silent Conflict; Million Dollar Weekend
1950:   Double Deal (L. Berman)

ARNOLD BELGARD

1938:   Bar 20 Justice (H. Jacobs); Block-Heads*
1941:   My Life with Caroline (J. Van Druten); Road
        Show*
1943:   Calaboose; Praire Chickens (E. Snell)
1947:   The Hal Roach Comedy Carnival*; The
        Invisible Wall; Second Chance; The Tender
        Years (J. Jungmeyer)
1948:   Dangerous Years; Half-Past Midnight; Night
        Wind (R. North); Trouble Preferred

44

1949:   Miss Mink of 1949; Tucson
1950:   Tarzan and the Slave Girl (H. Jacoby)
1957:   Bop Girl; Panama Sal

MONTA BELL (1891-1958) director, producer

1929:   The Bellamy Trial
1933:   The Worst Woman in Paris (M. Dix)

TOM BELL

1936:   Kelly the Second*

JAMES WARNER BELLAH

1955:   The Sea Chase (J. Twist)
1960:   Sergeant Rutledge (W. Goldbeck)
1961:   A Thunder of Drums; X-15 (T. Luzzarino)
1962:   The Man Who Shot Liberty Valance (W.
        Goldbeck)

GEORGE BELLAK

1958:   Invisible Avenger (B. Jeffries)

EDMUND BELOIN (1910-   )

1940:   Buck Benny Rides Again (W. Morrow); Love Thy
        Neighbor*
1945:   Lady on a Train (R. O'Brien)
1946:   The Harvey Girls*; Because of Him
1947:   Ladies' Man*; My Favorite Brunette (J.
        Rose); Road to Rio (Jack Rose)
1949:   A Connecticut Yankee in King Arthur's Court;
        The Great Lover*; Top o' the Morning (R.
        Breen)
1957:   Sad Sack (N. Monaster)
1958:   Paris Holiday (D. Riesner)
1959:   Don't Give Up the Ship*
1960:   G.I. Blues (H. Garson); Visit to a Small
        Planet (H. Garson)
1961:   All in a Night's Work*

JERRY BELSON

1968: How Sweet It Is (G. Marshall)
1970: The Grasshopper (G. Marshall)
1975: Smile
1977: Fun with Dick and Jane*
1978: The End
1980: Smokey and the Bandit II (B. Yates)
1982: Jekyll and Hyde Together Again*

NATHANIEL BENCHLEY

1956: The Great American Pastime

PETER BENCHLEY

1975: Jaws (C. Gottlieb)
1977: The Deep (T. Wynn)
1980: The Island

ROBERT BENCHLEY (1889-1945) journalist, critic, actor

(Feature-length films only)
1935: Murder on a Honeymoon (S. Miller)

RUSS BENDER

1957: Voodoo Woman (V. Voss)
1961: Woman-Hunt (E. Lakso)

TONY BENEDICT

1970: Santa and the Three Bears (anim.)

STEPHEN VINCENT BENET (1898-1943) poet, short story writer, playwright

1930: Abraham Lincoln (G. Lloyd)
1941: All That Money Can Buy (alt. The Devil and Daniel Webster; D. Totheroh)

BEN BENGAL

1946:   Crack-Up*
1949:   The Mutineers (J. Carole)

BURTON BENJAMIN

1953:   Below the Sahara (J. Brondfield)

RICHARD BENNER

1980:   Happy Birthday, Gemini

CHARLES BENNETT

1935:   The Clairvoyant
1936:   King of the Damned (S. Giliat); Secret Agent
1937:   King Solomon's Mines*; The Woman Alone
1938:   The Young in Heart (P. Osborn)
1939:   Balalaika*
1940:   Foreign Correspondent*
1941:   They Dare Not Love (E. Vajda)
1942:   Joan of Paris (E. St. Joseph); Reap the Wild
        Wind*
1943:   Forever and a Day*
1944:   The Story of Dr. Wassell (A. Le May)
1947:   Ivy; Unconquered*
1948:   The Sign of the Ram
1949:   Black Magic
1950:   Where Danger Lives
1951:   Kind Lady*
1952:   The Green Glove (Fr.)
1953:   No Escape
1954:   Dangerous Mission*
1957:   The Story of Mankind (I. Allen)
1958:   Curse of the Demon (H. Chester)
1959:   The Big Circus*
1960:   The Lost World (I. Allen)
1961:   Voyage to the Bottom of the Sea (I. Allen)
1962:   Five Weeks in a Balloon*
1965:   War Gods of the Deep (L. Leyword)

CONNIE LEE BENNETT

1951:   The Lady from Texas (G. Adams)
1953:   The Last Posse*

DOROTHY BENNETT

1943:   When Johnny Comes Marching Home (O.
        Brodney); Follow the Band (W. Wilson); It
        Comes Up Love (Charles Kenyon); Mr. Big (J.
        Pollexfen)
1944:   Show Business (J. Quillan); Sensations of
        1945 (alt. Sensations; A.L. Stone)
1945:   Patrick the Great (B. Millhauser)

EDWARD BENNETT

1941:   Criminals Within

KEN BENNETT

1953:   Terror on a Train

SEYMOUR BENNETT

1947:   The Macomber Affair (C. Robinson)
1953:   The Last Posse*

STEVE BENNETT

1964:   Madmen of Mandoras (R. Miles)

WALLACE C. BENNETT

1974:   Welcome to Arrow Beach
1979:   Silent Scream*

ANDREW BENNISON

1928:   Air Circus*
1929:   Strong Boy; Captain Lash (J. Stone); Chasing

```
          Through Europe (J. Stone)
1935:  The Affair of Susan*
1936:  Undercover Man
1937:  Lawless Land
1939:  Desperate Trails; Chip of the Flying U (L.
       Rhine)
```

MAC BENOFF

```
1944:  Take It or Leave It*
1949:  Love Happy*
1977:  Bless the Beasts and the Children
```

RICHARD BENSON

```
1977:  God Bless Mr. Shagetz (L. Spiegel)
```

ROBBY BENSON

```
1977:  One on One (J. Segal)
1980:  Die Laughing*
```

SALLY BENSON

```
1943:  Shadow of a Doubt*
1946:  Anna and the King of Siam (T. Jennings)
1949:  Come to the Stable (O. Millard)
1950:  Conspirator; No Man of Her Own (C. Turney)
1953:  The Farmer Takes a Wife*
1963:  Summer Magic
1964:  Viva Las Vegas
1965:  Joy in the Morning*
1966:  The Singing Nun (J. Furia)
```

JACK BENTON   (see J. BENTON CHENEY)

ROBERT BENTON (1932-   ) director

```
1967:  Bonnie and Clyde (D. Newman)
1970:  There Was a Crooked Man*
1972:  What's Up, Doc?*; Bad Company (D. Newman);
       Oh! Calcutta!
```

```
1977:  The Late Show
1978:  Superman*
1979:  Kramer vs. Kramer
1982:  Still of the Night
```

CLARA BERANGER (1886-1956)

```
1929:  The Idle Rich
1930:  This Mad World (A. Caesar)
1933:  His Double Life (A. Hopkins)
1934:  Social Register*
```

ERIC BERCOVICI

```
1963:  Square of Violence (L. Bercovici)
1968:  Hell in the Pacific (A. Jacobs); Day of the
       Evil Gun (C.Warren)
1969:  Change of Habit*
1972:  The Culpepper Cattle Company (G. Prentiss)
1974:  Three the Hard Way (J. Ludwig)
1975:  Take a Hard Ride (J. Ludwig); Out of Season
       (Reuben Bercovitch)
```

LEONARDO BERCOVICI

```
1938:  Racket Busters (R. Rossen)
1947:  The Bishop's Wife (R. Sherwood); The Lost
       Moment
1948:  Kiss the Blood off My Hands
1953:  Monsoon*
1963:  Square of Violence (E. Bercovici)
1970:  The Story of a Woman
```

CHERNEY BERG

```
1967:  Come Spy with Me
```

DICK BERG

```
1976: Shoot
```

GERTRUDE BERG

1937: Make a Wish*
1950: The Goldbergs (R. Nash)

JUDITH & SANDRA BERG

1978: Almost Summer*

ANDREW BERGMAN

1979: The In-Laws
1981: So Fine

HELMER BERGMAN

1931: The Vanishing Legion (ser.)*

ERIC BERGREN

1982: Frances*

ELEANOR BERGSTEIN

1980: It's My Turn

IVO BERILLI

1954: Ulysses (Ital.; I. Shaw)

HOWARD BERK

1966: Bikini Paradise
1967: A Witch Without a Broom

WILLIAM BERKE (1903-1958) director

1949: Deputy Marshal
1950: Gunfire (V. West); I Shot Billy The Kid*;
      Border Rangers (V. West)

MARTIN BERKELEY

1943: Dr. Gillespie's Criminal Case*; Harrigan's Kid (A. Friedman)
1944: Three Men in White (H. Ruskin)
1945: Out of the Depths (T. Thomas)
1946: The Notorious Lone Wolf (E. Dein); So Dark the Night (D. Babcock)
1948: Green Grass of Wyoming
1949: Will James' Sand (alt. Sand; J. Cady)
1953: War Paint (R. Simmons); The Nebraskan (D. Lang)
1954: Gypsy Colt
1955: Revenge of the Creature; Tarantula
1956: Red Sundown
1957: The Deadly Mantis; The Big Caper

REGINALD BERKELEY (—1935)

1932: Broken Lullaby (alt. The Man I Killed)*
1933: Cavalcade (S. Levien)
1934: Carolina; Marie Galante*; The World Moves On
1936: Wanted Men

RALPH BERKEY

1957: Time Limit (H. Denker)

TED BERKMAN

1957: Fear Strikes Out (R. Blau); Short Cut to Hell (R. Blau)
1960: Girl of the Night (R. Blau)

LEE BERMAN

1950: Double Deal (C. Belden)

IAN BERNARD

1965: Synanon (S. Pogostin)
1967: Oh Dad, Poor Dad, Mama's Hung You in the

Closet and I'm Feelin' So Sad

EDWARD BERNDS (1911–   ) director

1946:   Blondie Knows Best (A. Martin)
1948:   Blondie's Reward
1951:   Gasoline Alley; Corky of Gasoline Alley
1952:   Harem Girl (E. Ullman)
1953:   Loose in London (E. Ullman)
1954:   The Bowery Boys Meet the Monster (E.
        Ullman); Jungle Gents (E. Ullman); Paris
        Playboys*
1955:   Bowery to Bagdad (E. Ullman); Jail Busters
        (E. Ullman)
1956:   Calling Homicide; World Without End
1957:   The Storm Rider (Don Martin); Reform School
        Girl
1958:   Escape from Red Rock
1959:   Alaska Passage; The Return of the Fly
1961:   Valley of the Dragons
1963:   Gunfight at Comanche Creek
1965:   Tickle Me (E. Ullman)

J. BERNE

1939:   Mirele Efros (O. Dymov)

PETER BERNEIS

1948:   Portrait of Jenny (P. Osborn)
1950:   The Glass Menagerie (T. Williams)
1957:   My Man Godfrey*
1959:   Stranger in My Arms
1963:   Escape from East Berlin*

JACK BERNHARD

1940:   West of Carson City*

CURTIS BERNHARDT (1899–   ) director

1951:   Payment on Demand (B. Manning)

ARMYAN BERNSTEIN

1982:   One from the Heart (F. Coppola)

BARRY A. BERNSTEIN

1978:   Thank God It's Friday

HERMAN BERNSTEIN

1929:   Her Private Affair (F. Faragoh)

ISADORE BERNSTEIN

1929:   Broken Barriers; Dream Melody; Daughters of
        Desire; Montmarte Rose (S. Bernstein); One
        Splendid Hour (S. Bernstein); George
        Washington Cohen; Lucky Boy
1932:   Destry Rides Again (R. Schayer); By Whose
        Hand? (S. Roe)
1936:   For the Service; Shadow of Chinatown (B.
        Dickey)

RICHARD BERNSTEIN

1957:   From Hell It Came
1959:   Speed Crazy (G. Waters)
1963:   Terrified

SYLVIA BERNSTEIN

1929:   Montmarte Rose (I. Bernstein); One Splendid
        Hour (I. Bernstein)

WALTER BERNSTEIN (1920-   )

1959:   That Kind of Woman
1960:   A Breath of Scandal (Ital.; R. Lardner);
        Heller in Pink Tights (D. Nichols)
1961:   Paris Blues*
1964:   Fail Safe

```
1965:   The Train*
1966:   The Money Trap
1970:   The Molly Maguires
1976:   The Front
1977:   Semi-Tough
1978:   The Betsy (W. Bast)
1979:   An Almost Perfect Affair (D. Peterson);
        Yanks (Colin Welland)
1980:   Little Miss Marker
```

DANIEL BERRIGAN

```
1972:   The Trial of the Catonsville Nine (S.
        Levitt)
```

JOHN BERRY (1917-   ) director

```
1955:   Ca va barster (Fr.)*; Je suis un sentimental
        (Fr.)*
1957:   Pantaloons (Fr.;J. Barden)
1958:   Tamango (Fr.)*
```

ALVAH BESSIE (1904-   ) journalist, novelist

```
1943:   Northern Pursuit*
1944:   The Very Thought of You (D. Daves)
1945:   Hotel Berlin (J. Pagano)
1948:   Smart Woman*
```

RALPH BETTINSON

```
1938:   Rose of the Rio Grande
1940:   Doomed to Die (M. Jacoby)
1945:   South of the Rio Grande (V. Hammond)
```

ERNEST BETTS

```
1936:   Love in Exile (R. Burford)
```

RICHARD BEYMER (1939-   ) actor, director

```
1974:   The Innerview
```

A. I. BEZZERIDES

1942:   Juke Girl
1943:   Northern Pursuit*
1949:   Thieves' Highway
1951:   On Dangerous Ground; Sirocco (H. Jacoby)
1952:   Holiday for Sinners
1953:   Beneath the 12 Mile Reef
1954:   Track of the Cat
1955:   A Bullet for Joey (G. Homes); Kiss Me Deadly
1959:   The Angry Hills; The Jayhawkers*

HERBERT J. BIBERMAN (1900-1971) director, producer

1939:   King of Chinatown*
1944:   Action in Arabia (P. MacDonald); The Master
        Race*
1947:   New Orleans*
1969:   Slaves*

WILLIAM BICKLEY

1976:   Hawmps (M. Warren)

JOE BIGELOW

1938:   Wide Open Faces*
1942:   Here We go Again (P. Smith)
1944:   Take It Big (Howard Green)

ELIOT BIGGONS

1947:   Code of the Saddle

HAL BILLER

1957:   Domino Kid (K. Gamet)
1964:   Panic Button

LARRY BILLMAN

1969:   Five the Hard Way (T. Huston)

GEORGE R. BILSON

1942:   Busses Roar (A. Coldeway)
1943:   Adventure in Iraq (R. Kent)

JOHN BINDER

1980:   Honeysuckle Rose*
1982:   Endangered Species (A. Rudolph)

CLAUDE BINYON (1905-1978) director

1932:   If I Had a Million*
1933:   College Humor (F. Butler); Gambling Ship*;
        Girl Without a Room (F. Butler)
1934:   Ladies Should Listen*; Many Happy Returns*;
        Search for Beauty*
1935:   The Bride Comes Home; Accent on Youth (H.
        Fields); The Gilded Lily; Mississippi*;
        Stolen Harmony*
1936:   Valiant Is the Word for Carrie
1937:   I Met Him in Paris; True Confession
1938:   Sing You Sinners
1939:   Invitation to Happiness
1940:   Arizona; Too Many Husbands
1941:   You Belong to Me
1942:   Holiday Inn; Take a Letter, Darling
1943:   No Time for Love; This Is the Army (C.
        Robinson); Dixie*
1945:   Incendiary Blonde (F. Butler)
1946:   The Well-Groomed Bride (R. Russell)
1947:   Suddenly It's Spring (P. Wolfson)
1948:   The Saxon Charm
1950:   Emergency Wedding (N. Perrin); My Blue
        Heaven (L. Trotti); Stella; Mother Didn't
        Tell Me
1952:   Aaron Slick from Punkin Crick; Dreamboat
1953:   Down Among the Sheltering Palms*
1954:   Woman's World*
1956:   You Can't Run Away From It (R. Riskin)
1958:   Sing, Boy, Sing; Rally 'Round the Flag Boys!
        (L. McCarey)

```
1960:   North to Alaska*; Pepe (D. Kingsley)
1962:   Satan Never Sleeps (L. McCarey)
1964:   Kisses for My President
```

LEO BIRINSKI

```
1929:   Love and the Devil
1932:   Mata Hari (B. Glazer)
1933:   Song of Songs (H. Hoffenstein)
```

ANDREW BIRKIN

```
1981:   The Final Conflict
```

LAJOS BIRO (1880-1948) playwright (Hung.)

```
(American films only)
1930:   Women Everywhere (F. Gay)
```

LARRY BISCHOF

```
1979:   Dreamer (J. Proctor)
```

RON BISHOP

```
1970:   Underground
```

WES BISHOP

```
1972:   The Thing with Two Heads*
1975:   Race with the Devil (L. Frost); The Black
        Gestapo (L. Frost)
1976:   Dixie Dynamite (L. Frost)
```

RICHARD BISSELL

```
1957:   The Pajama Game*
```

JEROME BIXBY   science fiction writer

1958:   It! the Terror from Beyond Space; Curse of
        the Faceless Man; The Lost Missile (J.
        McPartland)

JOHN D. F. BLACK

1967:   Gunfight in Abilene (B.Giler)
1968:   Nobody's Perfect: Three Guns for Texas
1971:   Shaft (E. Tidyman)
1972:   Trouble Man

RALPH BLACK

1930:   The Sea Wolf

RICHARD BLACKBURN

1982:   Eating Raoul (P. Bartel)

THOMAS W. BLACKBURN

1949:   Killer at Large (F. Earnshaw)
1950:   Colt 45; Short Grass
1951:   Sierra Passage (W. Wandberg); Raton Pass (J.
        Webb); Cavalry Scout (D. Ullman)
1952:   Cattle Town
1953:   Cow Country (A. Buffington)
1954:   Riding Shotgun
1955:   Davy Crockett, King of the Wild Frontier (N.
        Foster)
1956:   Davy Crockett and the River Pirates (N.
        Foster); Westward Ho the Wagons; The Wild
        Dakotas
1957:   Johnny Tremain
1965:   Mara of the Wilderness
1973:   Santee

IRWIN BLACKER

1962:   Brushfire! (Jack Warner)

CHARLES BLACKWELL

1977:   A Piece of the Action

ANTHONY BLAKE

1972:   Pickup on 101

RICHARD BLAKE

1937:   The Devil Is Driving (J. Milward)
1953:   Invaders from Mars
1959:   Counterplot

HENRY BLANKFORT

1942:   Klondike Fury; Rubber Racketeers; Tales of
        Manhattan*
1943:   I Escaped from the Gestapo (W. Sullivan);
        She's for Me
1944:   The Singing Sheriff (E. Conrad); Night Club
        Girl (D. Hyland); Reckess Age (G. Purcell)
1945:   The Crimson Canary (P. Phillips); Easy to
        Look At; I'll Tell the World; Swing Out,
        Sister
1948:   The Open Secret*
1949:   Joe Palooka in the Counterpunch (C.
        Endfield)
1950:   Joe Palooka Meets Humphrey; The Underworld
        Story

MICHAEL BLANKFORT (1907-   ) playwright, novelist

1939:   Blind Alley*
1941:   Texas*; Adam Had Four Sons (W. Hurlbut)
1942:   Flight Lieutenant
1948:   An Act of Murder (R. Thoeren); The Dark
        Past*
1950:   Broken Arrow; Halls of Montezuma
1952:   Lydia Bailey (P. Dunne); My Six Convicts
1953:   The Juggler
1955:   Untamed*
1956:   Tribute to a Badman
1957:   The Vintage
1966:   The Plainsman

JERRY BLATT

1980:   A Divine Madness

WILLIAM PETER BLATTY (—   ) novelist

1963:   The Man from the Diner's Club
1964:   John Goldfarb, Please Come Home; A Shot in
        the Dark (B. Edwards)
1966:   Promise Her Anything; What Did You Do in the
        War, Daddy?
1967:   Gunn (B. Edwards)
1969:   The Great Bank Robbery
1970:   Darling Lili (B. Edwards)
1973:   The Exorcist
1980:   Twinkle, Twinkle, "Killer" Kane

RAPHAEL BLAU

1957:   Fear Strikes Out (T. Berkman); Short Cut to
        Hell (T. Berkman)
1960:   Girl of the Night (T. Berkman)

ROBERT BLEES

1950:   Paid in Full (C. Schnee)
1953:   All I Desire (J. Gunn); The Glass Web (L.
        Lee)
1954:   Magnificent Obsession*; Play Girl; Catttle
        Queen of Montana (H. Estabrook); The Yellow
        Mountain*
1955:   One Desire (L. Roman)
1956:   Autumn Leaves*; Slightly Scarlet
1957:   The Black Scorpion (D. Duncan)
1958:   Screaming Mimi; High School Confidential!
        (L. Meltzer); From the Earth to the Moon (J.
        Leicester)
1971:   Who Slew Auntie Roo? (J. Sangster)
1972:   Frogs (R. Hutchison)
1981:   Savage Harvest (Robert Collins)

WILLIM BLEICH

1980:   The Hearse

BERT BLESSING

1982:   Jinxed (D. Newman)

JOHN W. BLOCH

1964:   One Man's Way (E. Griffin)

ROBERT BLOCH (1917-   ) novelist

1962:   The Cabinet of Dr. Caligari; The Couch
1964:   The Night Walker; Strait-Jacket
1966:   The Psychopath
1967:   The Deadly Bees (A. Marriott)
1968:   Torture Garden
1971:   The House That Dripped Blood
1972:   Asylum

WALTER BLOCH

1978:   Born Again

ALFRED BLOCK

1930:   Way Out West

HAL BLOCK

1940:   I'm Nobody's Sweetheart Now*

LARRY BLOCK

1981:   The Funhouse

RALPH BLOCK

1930:   The Arizona Kid (J. Wright); The Sea Wolf

1931:   A Holy Terror
1933:   Before Dawn*
1934:   Dark Hazard (B. Holmes); Gambling Lady (D.
         Malloy); I Am a Thief (D. Malloy); Massacre
         (S. Gibney)
1935:   The Melody Lingers On (P. Dunne); The Right
         to Live
1936:   Boulder Dam (C. Bartlett); Nobody's Fool (B.
         Markson)

ERIC BLOOM

1981:   Eyes of the Stranger

GEORGE ARTHUR BLOOM

1974:   A Knife for the Ladies
1980:   The Last Flight of Noah's Ark*

HAROLD JACK BLOOM

1953:   The Naked Spur (S. Rolfe); Arena
1955:   Land of the Pharaohs*
1956:   Behind the High Wall; Pillars of the Sky (S.
         Rolfe)
1971:   A Gunfight

JEFFREY BLOOM

1974:   11 Harrowhouse
1976:   Swashbuckler
1981:   Blood Beach

GEORGE BLOOMFIELD

1970:   Jenny (M. LaVut)
1972:   To Kill a Clown (I. Rapaport)
1975:   Child Under a Leaf

RICHARD BLUEL

1971:   Raid on Rommel

EDWIN HARVEY BLUM

1935: New Adventures of Tarzan (C. Royal)
1938: Kidnapped*
1940: Young People (D. Ettlinger); Adventures of
       Sherlock Holmes (W. Drake)
1941: The Great American Broadcast*
1942: The Boogie Man Will Get You
1943: Henry Aldrich Gets Glamour (A.Leslie)
1944: The Canterville Ghost
1945: Man Alive
1946: Down to Earth (D. Hartman)
1953: South Sea Woman (S. Shapiro)
1954: The Bamboo Prison (J. DeWitt)
1957: The Midnight Story (J. Robinson)

JUDY & RALPH BLUM

1975: Mysteries from Beyond the Earth (doc.; D.
       Scioli)

LEN BLUM

1981: Stripes*; Heavy Metal (D. Goldberg)

RALPH BLUM (see JUDY BLUM)

JAMES BLUMGARTEN

1957: Mister Rock and Roll

DON BLUTH

1982: The Secret of N.I.M.H. (anim.)*

SAMUEL BLYTHE

1932: Washington Masquerade (J. Meehan)

JEFFREY BOAM

1978:   Straight Time*

TRUE BOARDMAN

1942:   Ride 'Em, Cowboy (John Grant); Between Us
        Girls (M. Connolly); Pardon My Sarong*
1951:   The Painted Hills

AL BOASBERG

1929:   So This Is College; It's a Great Life; The
        Hollywood Revue of 1929 (R. Hopkins)
1931:   Cracked Nuts (D. MacLean)
1934:   Murder in the Private Car*; Myrt and Marge
1935:   The Nitwits (F. Guiol)
1936:   Sill Billies (J. Townley)

SAM BOBRICK

1976:   Norman...Is That You?*
1982:   Jimmy the Kid

STEVE BOCHCO

1968:   The Counterfeit Killer (H. Clemens)
1972:   Silent Running*

EDWARD BOCK

1946:   The Man Who Dared
1947:   The Crime Doctor's Gamble; Key Witness; The
        Thirteenth Hour (R. Schrock)
1948:   The Return of the Whistler (M. Tombragel)

ROBERT BODANSKY

1930:   Rogue Song*

DeWITT BODEEN (1908-   )

```
1942:   Cat People
1943:   The Seventh Victim (C. O'Neal)
1944:   The Curse of the Cat People; The Yellow
        Canary
1945:   The Enchanted Cottage*
1948:   I Remember Mama
1949:   Mrs. Mike*
1960:   Twelve to the Moon
1962:   Billy Budd (P. Ustinov)
```

AL BODIAN

```
1971:   Jack Johnson (doc.)
```

JAMES BODRERO

```
1934:   White Heat (L. Weber)
```

DAVID BOEHM

```
1933:   Ex-Lady; Grand Slam (E. Gelsey); Life of
        Jimmy Dolan (E. Gelsey)
1934:   The Personality Kid*; Search for Beauty*
1935:   The Raven*
1936:   Florida Special*
1937:   A Doctor's Diary
1938:   Peck's Bad Boy with the Circus*
1942:   Powder Town
1944:   Knickerbocker Holiday (R. Leigh)
```

SYDNEY BOEHM (1908-   )

```
1947:   The High Wall (L. Cole)
1949:   Side Street; The Undercover Man
1950:   Branded (C.Hume); Mystery Street (R.
        Brooks); Union Station
1951:   When Worlds Collide
1952:   The Atomic City; The Savage
1953:   Second Chance (O. Millard); The Big Heat (D.
        Harmon)
1954:   The Siege at Red River (L. Townsend); Secret
        of the Incas (R. MacDougall); The Raid;
        Black Tuesday; Rogue Cop
```

1955: Hell on Frisco Bay (M. Rackin); Six Bridges
to Cross; The Tall Men (F. Nugent); Violent
Saturday
1956: The Bottom of the Bottle; The Revolt of
Mamie Stover
1958: Harry Black and the Tiger; A Nice Little
Bank That Should Be Robbed
1959: A Woman Possessed
1960: One Foot in Hell (A. Spelling); Seven
Thieves
1964: Shock Treatment
1965: Sylvia
1967: Rough Night in Jericho (M. Albert)

BUDD BOETTICHER (1916-   ) director

1971: A Time for Dying; Arruza (doc.)*

JOSEF BOGDANOVICH

1982: Boxoffice

PETER BOGDANOVITCH (1939-   ) director, producer
1968: Targets
1971: The Last Picture Show (L. McMurtry)
1975: At Long Last Love
1976: Nickelodeon (W. D. Richter)
1979: Saint Jack*
1981: They All Laughed

BENEDICT BOGEAUS

1947: Christmas Eve (L. Stallings)

ANDRE BOHEM

1929: Desert Nights
1936: Girl from Mandalay (W. Totman); The House of
a Thousand Candles (H. Hanemann)
1937: Larceny on the Air (R. English)
1954: Bengazi
1957: Pawnee*
1958: Cattle Empire (E. Norden); Desert Hell

V. BOKRIS

1979: Cocaine Cowboys*

BRIDGET BOLAND

1962: Damon and Pythias

JAMES BOLOGNA

1971: Made for Each Other (Renee Taylor)

JOSEPH BOLOGNA

1970: Lovers and Other Strangers*

A. J. BOLTON

1940: The Marines Fly High (J. Cady)

GUY BOLTON (1885-1979) playwright, novelist

1929: The Love Doctor
1930: The Love Parade
1931: Ambassador Bill; Delicious (S. Levien);
       Transatlantic; The Lady Refuses (W. Smith);
       The Yellow Ticket (J. Furthman)
1932: Careless Lady; Devil's Lottery; Painted
       Woman; Woman in Room 13; Pleasure Cruise
1934: Along Came Sally*; The Lady Is Willing;
       Ladies Should Listen*
1935: The Morals of Marcus*; Strauss' Great Waltz
       (A. Reville); Murder Man*
1936: Mister Hobo
1964: Adorable Julia (Fr.)

MURIEL ROY BOLTON

1942: Henry Aldrich, Editor (V. Burton); This Time
       for Keeps*

```
1943:   Henry Aldrich Haunts a House (V. Burton);
        Henry Aldrich Swings It (V. Burton)
1944:   Passport to Adventure (V. Burton); Henry
        Aldrich, Boy Scout; Henry Aldrich Plays
        Cupid (V. Burton); She's a Sweetheart; Meet
        Miss Bobby Socks
1945:   Grissly's Millions; My Name Is Julia Ross
1948:   Mickey (A. Johnston); The Spiritualist (I.
        Hunter)
```

WHITNEY BOLTON

```
1932:   If I Had a Million*
1939:   Spirit of Culver (N. West)
```

ANSON BOND

```
1949:   The Judge*
1958:   Unwed Mother (A. Nash)
```

PETER BONERZ

```
1971:   Funnyman (J. Korty)
```

JAMES P. BONNER

```
1972:   The Carey Treatment
```

JAMES BONNET

```
1970: The Cross and the Switchblade (D. Murray)
```

BOB BONNEY

```
1981:   The Night the Lights Went Out in Georgia
```

SONNY BONO

```
1969:   Chastity
```

CHARLES G. BOOTH

1941:   Sundown (B. Lyndon)
1945:   The House on 92nd Street*
1946:   Behind Green Lights (W. Darling)
1948:   Fury at Furnace Creek

DELORES BOOTH

1934:   Riding Speed

ERNEST BOOTH

1938:   Penrod's Double Trouble (C. Wilbur)
1942:   Men of San Quentin

JAMES BOOTH

1979:   Sunburn*

JOHN HUNTER BOOTH

1929:   The Valiant (T. Barry)

JON BOOTHE

1971:   The Pursuit of Happiness (G. L. Sherman)

ETHEL B. BORDEN

1935:   I Live My Life*
1937:   They Wanted to Marry (P. Yawitz); The Woman
        I Love

LON BORDEN

1935:   Unconquered Bandit (Rose Gordon)

ALVIN BORETZ

1978:   Brass Target

ALLEN BORETZ

1943:   It Ain't Hay (John Grant)
1944:   Bathing Beauty*; Up in Arms*
1947:   Copacabana*; Where There's Life (M.
        Shavelson)
1948:   My Girl Tisa; Two Guys from Texas (I.
        Diamond)

ROBERT BORIS

1982:   Some Kind of Hero (James Kirkwood)

MARVIN BOROWSKY

1941:   Free and Easy
1942:   Reunion in France*
1949:   Big Jack*
1950:   Gambling House (A. Rivkin)

ROBERT BORIS

1973:   Electra Glide in Blue

ORIN BORSTEN

1961:   Angel Baby*

NED BOSNICK

1970:   Imago
1972:   To Be Free

BETTY BOTLEY

1970:   Tropic of Cancer (J. Strick)

FRANK BOTTAR

1968:   The Young, the Evil and the Savage (A. Dawson)

SERGE BOURGUIGNON

1965:   The Reward (O. Millard)

PAMELA BOWER

1954:   Laughing Anne

JESS BOWERS (see ADELE BUFFINGTON)

WILLIAM BOWERS (1916-   )

1942:   Seven Days' Leave*; My Favorite Spy (S. Herzig)
1943:   Higher and Higher*
1945:   Sing Your Way Home
1946:   Night and Day*
1947:   Something in the Wind (H. Kurnitz); The Web*
1948:   Black Bart*; River Lady (D. Beauchamp); The Countess of Monte Cristo; Larceny*
1949:   The Gal Who Took the West (O. Brodney)
1950:   TheGunfighter (W. Sellers); Convicted*; Mrs. O'Malley and Mr. Malone
1951:   Cry Danger; The Mob
1952:   Assignment Paris
1953:   Split Second (I. Wallace)
1954:   She Couldn't Say No
1955:   Five Against the House (S. Silliphant); Tight Spot
1956:   The Best Things in Life Are Free (P. Ephron)
1957:   My Man Godfrey*
1958:   The Sheepman (James Grant); The Law and Jack Wade; Imitation General
1959:   Alias Jesse James (D. Beauchamp; -30-
1961:   The Last Time I Saw Archie
1964:   Advance to the Rear (S. Peeples)
1966:   Way...Way Out (L. Vadnay)
1967:   The Ride to Hangman's Tree*
1969:   Support Your Local Sheriff!

JOHN BOWLES

1957:   That Night (R. Wallace)

MALCOLM STUART BOYLAN

1929:   Masquerade (F. Brennan)
1931:   Hell Divers (H. Gates)
1932:   Cheaters at Play; If I Had a Million*;
        Madame Racketeer (H. Gates)
1933:   A Lady's Profession (W. DeLeon)
1934:   Flaming Gold (J. Goodrich)
1935:   Devil Dogs of the Air (E. Baldwin)
1936:   Dangerous Waters*
1937:   When's Your Birthday?*
1938:   A Yank at Oxford*
1939:   The Lady's from Kentucky; St. Louis Blues
        (J. Moffitt)
1941:   Sailors on Leave (A. Arthur); Red River
        Valley; The Devil Pays Off (L. Kimble);
        Mercy Island; Mr. District Attorney (K.
        Brown)
1942:   Remember Pearl Harbor (I. Dawn)
1944:   Alaska*
1945:   Bedside Manner (F. Jackson)
1946:   The Unknown (J. Harmon)
1947:   For the Love of Rusty; Keeper of the Bees
        (L. Watkin); Son of Rusty
1949:   The Lone Wolf and His Lady
1950:   One Too Many
1951:   Soldiers 3*
1952:   And Now Tomorrow

GEORGE BOYLE

1935:   Convention Girl

MARIA BOYLE

1930:   The Big Trail*

CHARLES BRABIN

1930:   The Great Meadow (E. Ellis)

BERT BRACKEN

1932:   The Face on the Barroom Floor (B. Barringer)

CHARLES BRACKETT (1892-1969) producer

1934:   Enter Madame (G. Lehman)
1935:   College Scandal*; The Last Outpost*; Without
         Regret (D. Anderson)
1936:   Piccadilly Jim*; Rose of the Rancho*
1937:   Live, Love and Learn*
1938:   Bluebeard's Eighth Wife (B. Wilder)
1939:   Midnight (B. Wilder); Ninotchka*; What a
         Life (B. Wilder)
1940:   Arise, My Love (B. Wilder)
1941:   Ball of Fire (B. Wilder); Hold Back the Dawn
         (B. Wilder)
1942:   The Major and the Minor (B. Wilder)
1943:   Five Graves to Cairo (B. Wilder)
1944:   Double Indemnity*
1945:   The Lost Weekend (B. Wilder)
1946:   To Each His Own*
1948:   The Emperor Waltz (B. Wilder); A Foreign
         Affair*; Miss Tatlock's Millions (R. Breen)
1950:   Sunset Boulevard*
1951:   The Mating Season*; The Model and the
         Marriage Broker*
1953:   Niagara*; Titanic*
1955:   The Girl in the Red Velvet Swing (W. Reisch)
1956:   Teenage Rebel (W. Reisch)
1959:   Journey to the Center of the Earth (W.
         Reisch)

LEIGH BRACKETT (1915-1978) novelist

1945:   The Vampire's Ghost (J. Butler)
1946:   The Big Sleep*; Crime Doctor's Man Hunt
1959:   Rio Bravo (J. Furthman)
1961:   Gold of the Seven Saints (L. Freeman)
1962:   Hatari!
1967:   El Dorado
1970:   Rio Lobo (B. Wohl)
1973:   The Long Goodbye

1980:   The Empire Strikes Back (L. Kasdan)

JACOB BRACKMAN

1972:   The King of Marvin Gardens (B. Rafelson)
1980:   Times Square

RAY BRADBURY

1956:   Moby Dick (J. Huston)

ROBERT NORTH BRADBURY (1885-   ) director

1931:   Dugan of the Badlands; Son of the Plains
1932:   Law of the West; Man from Hell's Edges;
         Texas Buddies; The Gallant Fool (H. Fraser)
1933:   Riders of Destiny
1934:   The Lucky Texan; West of the Divide; Blue
         Steel; The Star Packer; Lawless Frontier
1935:   Texas Terror; The Dawn Rider; Kid
         Courageous; Smokey Smith; Tombstone Terror;
         Trail of Terror; Western Justice
1936:   Valley of the Lawless; The Kid Ranger; Last
         of the Warrens; Sundown Saunders

SUE BRADFORD

1956:   The Indestructable Man (V. Russell)

PAT BRADLEY

1981:   Under the Rainbow

FRED BRADY

1950:   Champagne for Caesar (H. Jacoby)

A. BRAGADIN

1954:   Hell Raiders of the Deep

MELVYN BRAGG

1973:   Jesus Christ Superstar (N. Jewison)

MALCOLM BRALY

1979: On the Yard

BILL BRAME

1970:   Cycle Savages

HOUSTON BRANCH

1929:   Square Shoulders (G. Drumgold); Sioux Blood;
        Shanghai Lady
1930:   Captain of the Guard (A. Ripley)
1931:   I Like Your Nerve
1932:   Alias the Doctor; Heart of New York (A.
        Caesar); Manhattan Parade (R. Lord); The
        Match King (S. Sutherland)
1933:   Silk Express (B. Markson)
1934:   She Had to Choose
1936:   Don't Get Personal*
1937:   Public Wedding (R. Chanslor); Wallaby Jim of
        the Islands (B. Cohen)
1938:   Mr. Wong, Detective
1941:   Mystery Ship (D. Silverstein)
1943:   Klondike Kate (M. Webster); Headin' for
        God's Country (E. Meehan); Women in Bondage
1944:   Block Busters
1945:   Girls of the Big House
1952:   Bal Tabarin
1953:   Sweethearts on Parade
1955:   City of Shadows; The Fighting Chance
1956:   A Strange Adventure
1957:   The Wayward Girl (F.L. Fox)
1958:   Sierra Baron

HARRY BRAND

1929:   Making the Grade (E. Kaufman); Masked
        Emotions

MAX BRAND (1892-1944) writer, poet

1944:   Uncertain Glory (L. Vadnay)

MILLEN BRAND

1948:   The Snake Pit*

JOHN BRASCIA

1980:   The Baltimore Bullet (R. V. O'Neil)

MICHAEL BRAUM

1978:   The Secret Life of Plants*

MORTIMER BRAUS

1942:   The Postman Didn't Ring
1946:   Strange Triangle
1951:   The Son of Dr. Jekyll (J. Pollexfen)

STEVE BRAXTON (also SAM ROBINS)

1939:   Range War
1940:   Bad Man from Red Butte; Black Diamonds (C.
        Young); Enemy Agent (E. Hartmann)
1941:   Bowery Blitzkrieg (C. Foreman)
1942:   The Lone Rider and the Bandit; The Lone
        Rider in Texas Justice (alt. Texas Justice);
        Law and Order; The Mysterious Rider; Outlaws
        of Boulder Pass; Overland Stagecoach; Jungle
        Siren*; Lady from Chungking; Mr. Wise Guy*

A. LAURIE BRAZEE

1936:   And So They Were Married*
1937:   Behind Prison Bars; The Outer Gate

GEORGE BREAKSTON (1920-1973) actor, director,
       producer

1948:   Urubu
1954:   The Scarlet Spear (R. Stahl)

IRVING S. BRECHER (1914-   ) director

1937:   New Faces of 1937*; Fools for Scandal*
1939:   At the Circus
1940:   Go West; Broadway Melody of 1940*
1941:   Shadow of the Thin Man (H. Kurnitz)
1943:   Best Foot Forward (F. Finklehoffe); DuBarry
        Was a Lady
1944:   Meet Me in St. Louis (F. Finklehoffe)
1945:   Yolanda and the Thief
1948:   Summer Holiday*
1949:   The Life of Riley
1952:   Somebody Loves Me
1961:   Cry for Happy
1962:   Sail a Crooked Ship*
1963:   Bye Bye Birdie

BERTOLT BRECHT (1898-1956) playwright   Germ.

(American films only)
1943:   Hangmen Also Die*

RICHARD L. BREEN (1919-1967)

1948:   Isn't It Romantic?*; Miss Tatlock's Millions
        (C. Brackett); A Foreign Affair*
1949:   Top of the Morning (E. Beloin)
1951:   Appointment with Danger (W. Duff); The
        Mating Season*; The Model and the Marriage
        Broker*
1952:   O. Henry's Full House*
1953:   Niagara*; Titanic*
1954:   Dragnet
1955:   Pete Kelly's Blues; Seven Cities of Gold (J.
        Higgins)
1957:   Stopover Tokyo (W. Reisch)
1959:   The FBI Story (J. Twist)
1960:   Wake Me When It's Over
1962:   State Fair

1963: Captain Newman, M.D.*; Mary, Mary; PT 109
1965: Do Not Disturb (M. Rosen)
1966: A Man Could Get Killed (T.E.B. Clarke)
1967: Tony Rome

J. ROBERT BREN

1936: Without Orders (E. Hartmann)
1937: Behind the Headlines (E. Hartmann); China
       Passage (E. Hartmann); Hideaway (E.
       Hartmann); The Man Who Found Himself*
1938: Crime Ring (G. Atwater); Double Danger (A.
       Horman); Everybody's Doing It*; This
       Marriage Business (G. Atwater)
1939: Parents on Trial*
1942: American Empire*; Underground Agent
1945: First Yank in Tokyo; The Gay Senorita (E.
       Eliscu)
1953: The Great Sioux Uprising*
1954: Overland Pacific

MILTON H. BREN

1952: Three for Bedroom C

F. H. BRENNAN (also Fred Hazlitt)

1929: Speakeasy (E. Burke); The Ghost Talks;
       Protection; Masquerade (M. Boylan); Song of
       Kentucky
1930: Sweet Mama (E. Baldwin)
1936: Wives Never Know (E. Mayer)
1940: Sailor's Lady; Untamed (F. Butler)
1942: American Empire*
1945: Adventure*
1951: Follow the Sun
1953: Devil's Canyon

JAY BRENNAN

1937: Expensive Husbands

ALFRED BRENNER

1960:   Key Witness (S. Michaels)

WILLIAM BRENT

1942:   The Spirit of Stanford*

LOU BRESLOW

1932:   No Greater Love; Rackety Rax (B. Markson)
1933:   Sitting Pretty*
1934:   Gift of Gab*; No More Women (D. Daves)
1935:   Music Is Magic (E. Eliscu); Paddy O'Day (E.
        Eliscu); Silk Hat Kid*; Ten Dollar Raise (H.
        Johnson)
1936:   15 Maiden Lane*; High Tension*; Little Miss
        Nobody*; 36 Hours to Kill (J. Patrick
1937:   Big Town Girl*; Dangerously Yours (J.
        Patrick); The Holy Terror (J. Patrick);
        Midnight Taxi (J. Patrick); Sing and Be
        Happy*; Time Out for Romance (J. Patrick);
        One Mile from Heaven (J. Patrick)
1938:   The Battle of Broadway (J. Patrick); City
        Streets (F. Niblo); Five of a Kind (J.
        Patrick); International Settlement (J.
        Patrick); Mr. Moto Takes a Chance*; Up the
        River (J. Patrick)
1939:   It Could Happen to You (A. Rivkin); Pack Up
        Your Troubles (O. Francis); 20,000 Men a
        Year (O. Francis)
1940:   Shooting High (O. Francis)
1941:   Great Guns; Sleepers West (S. Rauh)
1942:   A-Haunting We Will Go; Blondie Goes to
        College; Whispering Ghosts
1943:   Good Luck, Mr. Yates (A. Comandini);
        Something to Shout About (E. Eliscu)
1944:   Follow the Boys (G. Purcell)
1945:   Abbott and Costello in Hollywood (N.
        Perrin); Murder, He Says
1947:   Merton of the Movies (G. Wells)
1948:   Don't Trust Your Husband (J. Hoffman)
1949:   And Baby Makes Three (J. Hoffman)
1950:   Never a Dull Moment (D. Anderson)
1951:   Bedtime for Bonzo (V. Burton); You Can Never
        Tell (D. Chandler)
1952:   Back at the Front*; Steel Town (G. Adams)

1955:   The Crooked Web

MARTIN BREST

1979:   Going in Style

JAMESON BREWER

1947:   Sweet Genevieve (A. Dreifuss); Two Blondes
        and a Redhead (V. McLeod)
1948:   French Leave (J. Rubin)
1952:   Okinawa (A. Ross)
1955:   Ghost Town
1957:   Jungle Heat
1961:   Mary Had a Little (R. Kent)
1962:   Swingin' Along
1964:   The Incredible Mr. Limpet (Jack Rose)
1973:   Arnold (J. Murray); Terror in the Wax Museum

1976:   The Making of a Lady*
1982:   Heidi's Song (anim.)*

MONTE BRICE

1933:   Take a Chance*
1937:   Merry-Go-Round of 1938 (D. Otvos); You're a
        Sweetheart (C. Grayson)
1939:   Night Work*
1942:   Mexican Spitfire Sees a Ghost (C. Roberts);
        Sing Your Worries Away
1943:   Is Everybody Happy?
1944:   Beautiful but Broke; Stars on Parade
1945:   Eadie Was a Lady; A Guy, a Gal and a Pal;
        Mama Loves Papa (C. Roberts);
Radio   Stars on Parade (R. Kent)
1946:   Genius at Work (R. Kent); Singin' in the
        Corn (I. Dawn)
1947:   Variety Girl*

ELSIE BRICKER

1946:   Gas House Kids (G. Bricker)

GEORGE BRICKER

1935: Broadway Hostess; The Pay-Off (J. Sayre);
Widow from Monte Carlo*
1936: The Big Noise (W. Jacobs); Freshman Love (E.
Felton); King of Hockey; The Law in Her
Hands (L. Ward)
1937: Fugitive in the Sky; Melody for Two*; Sh!
the Octopus
1938: Accidents Will Happen (A. Coldeway); The Kid
Comes Back; Little Miss Thoroughbred (A.
DeMond); Mr. Chump; Over the Wall
(C.Wilbur); Torchy Blane in Panama
1939: King of the Underworld (V. Sherman); Missing
Daughters (M. Simmons); Torchy Blane in
Chinatown
1940: Buried Alive; A Fugitive from Justice; Hold
That Woman: I Take This Oath; Marked Men
1941: The Blonde from Singapore; Murder by
Invitation
1942: Frisco Lil (M. Jacoby); North to the
Klondike*; Law of the Jungle; Little Tokyo,
U.S.A.; Lure of the Islands*; Meet the Mob
(E. Kelso); So's Your Aunt Emma (E. Kelso)
1944: The Mark of the Whistler
1945: Pillow of Death
1946: Blonde Alibi; House of Horrors; If I'm
Lucky*; Inside Job (J. Warner); Johnny Comes
Flying Home (J. Andrews); Meet Me on
Broadway (J. Henley); She Wolf of London;
Gas House Kids (E. Bricker)
1947: The Big Fix (A. Wisberg); The Brute Man (M.
Webster); The Corpse Came C.O.D. (D.
Babcock); Heartaches
1949: Alimony*
1950: The Tougher They Come; Beauty on Parade (A.
Orloff); Bodyhold; Mary Ryan, Detective
1951: Roadblock (S. Fisher); Al Jennings of
Oklahoma; The Whip Hand (F. Moss)
1952: Arctic Flight (R. Hill)
1953: Man in the Dark (J. Leonard); Tangier
Incident; Mexican Manhunt
1954: Ketchikan (W. Douglas); Cry Vengeance (W.
Douglas)

MARSHALL BRICKMAN

```
1977:   Annie Hall (W. Allen)
1979:   Manhattan (W. Allen)
1980:   Simon
```

PAUL BRICKMAN

```
1977:   Handle With Care (alt. Citizen's Band); The
        Bad News Bears in Breaking Training
```

JAMES BRIDGES (—   ) director

```
1966:   The Appaloosa (R. Kibbee)
1970:   The Forbin Project; The Baby Maker
1972:   Limbo (J. Silver)
1973:   The Paper Chase
1978:   September 30, 1955
1979:   The China Syndrome*; Agatha (J. Lemmon)
1980:   Urban Cowboy (A. Latham)
```

JOHN BRIGHT   (also HAL CRAVES)

```
1931:   Blonde Crazy (K. Glasmon); Larceny Lane (K.
        Glasmon); Smart Money *
1932:   The Crowd Roars*; If I Had a Million*; Taxi
        (K. Glasmon)
1933:   She Done Him Wrong (H. Thew)
1936:   The Accusing Finger*
1938:   Frankie*
1939:   Back Door to Heaven (R. Tasker)
1940:   Glamour for Sale
1942:   Broadway (Felix Jackson)
1948:   Close-Up (M. Wilk); Fighting Mad
1949:   The Kid from Cleveland
1951:   The Brave Bulls
1954:   Rebellion of the Hanged (Mex.)
```

JOHN BRILEY

```
1980:   Eagle's Wing
```

LEIGHTON BRILL

```
1942:   The Secret Code(ser.)*
```

1944:   Black Arrow (ser.)*; The Desert Hawk (ser.)*

MORT BRISKIN

1951:   The Magic Face (Robert Smith)
1973:   Walking Tall
1975:   Framed

LOUIS BROCK
1933:   Flying Down to Rio
1945:   Enchanted Forest*

W. W. BROCKWAY

1939:   Everybody's Hobby (K. Gamet)

ROBERT STEPHEN BRODE

1946:   Sing While You Dance

JOHN C. BRODERICK

1977:   Maniac (R. Silkosky)

OSCAR BRODNEY (1907-   )

1942:   Moonlight in Havana
1943:   Rhythm of the Islands (M. Musselman); When
        Johnny Comes Marching Home (D. Bennett);
        Always a Bridesmaid (M. Ronson)
1945:   On Stage Everybody (W. Wilson)
1946:   She Wrote the Book (W. Wilson)
1948:   Are You With It; If You Knew Susie (W.
        Wilson); Mexican Hayride (John Grant); For
        the Love of Mary
1949:   Arctic Manhunt (J. Malone); The Gal Who Took
        the West (W. Bowers); Yes Sir, That's My
        Baby
1950:   South Sea Sinner*; Harvey (M. Chase); Double
        Crossbones
1951:   Frenchie; Francis Goes to the Races; Little
        Egypt (D. Gilbert)

1952: Back at the Front*; Francis Goes to West
       Point; Scarlet Angel
1953: Francis Covers the Big Town; Walking My Baby
       Back Home (D.McGuire)
1954: The Black Shield of Falworth; Sign of the
       Pagan (B. Lyndon); The Glenn Miller Story
       (V. Davies)
1955: Captain Lightfoot (W. Burnett); Lady Godiva
       (H. Ruskin); The Purple Mask; The Spoilers
       (C. Hoffman)
1956: A Day of Fury (J. Edmiston); Star in the
       Dust
1957: Tammy and the Bachelor
1958: When Hell Broke Loose
1960: Bobbikins
1961: Tammy Tell Me True; The Right Approach*; All
       Hands on Deck*
1963: Tammy and the Doctor
1964: The Brass Bottle; I'd Rather Be Rich
1965: The Sword of Ali Baba (E. Hartmann)
1971: One Thousand Convicts and a Woman

JEROME BRONDFIELD

1953: Below the Sahara (B. Benjamin); Louisiana
       Territory

HUGH BROOKE

1954: This Is My Love (H. Wilde)

PETER R. BROOKE

1951: The Basketball Fix (C. Peck)

ALBERT BROOKS

1979: Real Life*
1981: Modern Romance (M. Johnson)

ARTHUR BROOKS

1937: Dark Manhattan

GEORGE BROOKS

1930:   Double Cross Roads

HARRY BROOKS

1952:   Bugles in the Afternoon*

JAMES L. BROOKS

1979:   Starting Over

JOSEPH BROOKS

1977:   You Light Up My Life
1978:   If Ever I See You Again (M. Davidson)
1980:   Headin' for Broadway*

MATTY BROOKS

1936:   In Paris, A.W.O.L. (E. Adamson)
1938:   Radio City Revels*

MEL BROOKS (1926-   ) director, comedian

1954:   New Faces*
1967:   The Producers
1970:   The Twelve Chairs
1974:   Blazing Saddles*; Young Frankenstein (G.
        Wilder)
1976:   Silent Movie*
1977:   High Anxiety*
1981:   History of the World, Part I

RICHARD BROOKS (1912-   ) director

1942:   Men of Texas (H. Shumate); Sin Town*
1943:   White Savage
1944:   Cobra Woman (G. Lewis)
1946:   Swell Guy

```
1947:  Brute Force
1948:  Key Largo (J. Huston); To the Victor
1949:  Any Number Can Play
1950:  Crisis; Mystery Street (S. Boehm); Storm
       Warning (D. Fuchs)
1951:  The LIght Touch
1952:  Deadline U.S.A.
1953:  Battle Circus
1954:  The Last Time I Saw Paris*
1955:  The Blackboard Jungle
1956:  The Last Hunt
1957:  Something of Value
1958:  The Brothers Karamazov; Cat on a Hot Tin
       Roof (J. Poe)
1960:  Elmer Gantry
1962:  Sweet Bird of Youth
1965:  Lord Jim
1966:  The Professionals
1967:  In Cold Blood
1969:  The Happy Ending
1971:  Dollars
1975:  Bite the Bullet
1977:  Looking for Mr. Goodbar
1982:  Wrong Is Right
```

WALTER BROUGH

```
1969:  The Desperadoes
```

BARRY BROWN

```
1970:  The Way We Live Now (D. Tamkus)
```

BRUCE BROWN

```
1971: On Any Sunday (doc.)
```

CECIL BROWN

```
1977:  Which Way Is Up? (C. Gottlieb)
```

CHARLES BROWN

1937:   Assassin of Youth (E. Clifton)

GEORGE CARLETON BROWN

1941:   Angels with Broken Wings (B. Ropes)
1942:   Youth on Parade
1943:   Chatterbox (F. Gill); Sleepy Lagoon (F.
        Gill)
1944:   Atlantic City
1945:   The Tiger Woman
1948:   Here Comes Trouble (E. Seabrook)
1964:   McHale's Navy (F. Gill)

GILSON BROWN

1937:   Boy of the Streets (W. Darling)
1938:   Little Tough Guy (B. Weisberg)

HARRY BROWN (1917-   ) novelist

1947:   The Other Love (L. Fodor)
1948:   Arch of Triumph   (L. Milestone); Wake of the
        Red Witch (K. Gamet)
1949:   Sands of Iwo Jima (James Grant); The Man on
        the Eiffel Tower
1950:   Kiss Tomorrow Goodbye
1951:   Only the Valiant (E. North); A Place in the
        Sun (M. Wilson)
1952:   Bugles in the Afternoon*; Eight Iron Men
1953:   All the Brothers Were Valiant
1955:   Many Rivers to Cross (G. Trosper); The
        Virgin Queen (M. Lord)
1956:   Between Heaven and Hell; D-Day the Sixth of
        June (I. Moffat)
1958:   The Deep Six*; The Fiend Who Walked the West
        (P. Yordan)
1960:   Ocean's Eleven (C. Lederer)

HARRY JOE BROWN, JR.

1968:   Duffy (D. Cammell)

KARL BROWN (1895?-   ) director

1930: Under Fiesta Stars (E. Gibbons)
1933: Fast Workers (R. Wheelwright)
1934: City Park; The Curtain Falls; One in a
Million (R. Ellis); Stolen Sweets
1935: Calling of Dan Matthews*; Tarzan Escapes*
1936: In His Steps (Hinton Smith); The White
Legion
1937: Federal Bullets
1938: Port of Missing Girls; Numbered Woman (J.
Neville); Barefoot Boy (J. Neville); Under
the Big Top (M. Orth); Gangster's Boy (R.D.
Andrews)
1939: The Man They Could Not Hang; A Woman Is the
Judge
1940: Gangs of Chicago; Girl from Havana; The Man
with Nine Lives; Military Academy (D.
Silverstein)
1941: I Was a Prisoner on Devil's Island; Mr.
District Attorney (M. Boylan); Rookies on
Parade*
1942: Phantom Killer
1943: Hitler — Dead or Alive (S. Neuman); The Ape
Man (B. Sarecky)

KENNETH G. BROWN

1951: Korea Patrol (W. Shenson)
1966: The Brig

LEW BROWN

1938: Straight, Place and Show*

MARTIN BROWN

1930: Virtuous Sin
1934: Uncertain Lady (D. Evans)
1935: Java Head (G. Wellesley)

RHOZIER T. BROWN

1973: Holidays...Hollow Days

RITA MAE BROWN

1982:   The Slumberparty Massacre

ROWLAND BROWN (1900-1963) director

1929:   Points West
1931:   Quick Millions (C. Terrett
1932:   Hell's Highway*; State's Attorney (G.
        Fowler); What Price Hollywood?*
1933: Blood Money (H. Long)
1940:   Johnny Apollo (P. Dunne)

WILLIAM O. BROWN

1969:   The Witchmaker

ARTHUR BROWNE, JR.

1967:   Clambake

HOWARD BROWNE

1961:   Portrait of a Mobster
1967:   The St. Valentine's Day Massacre
1975:   Capone

REG BROWNE

1947:   Gunsmoke

RICOU BROWNING

1975:   Salty

ROD BROWNING

1980:   Oh! Heavenly Dog (J. Camp)

TOD BROWNING (1882-1962) director

1962:   The Devil Doll*

GEORGE BRUCE (1898-   )

1937:   Navy Blue and Gold; (She's No Lady (F.
        Partos)
1938:   The Crowd Roars*; The Duke of West Point
1939:   King of the Turf; The Man in the Iron Mask
1940:   Kit Carson; The Son of Monte Cristo; South
        of Pago Pago
1941:   The Corsican Brothers (H. Estabrook)
1942:   A Gentleman After Dark (P. McNutt); Miss
        Annie Rooney; Stand By for Action*
1943:   Salute to the Marines
1945:   Keep Your Powder Dry (M. McCall)
1946:   Little Mr. Jim; The Return of Monte Cristo
        (A. Newmann); Two Years Before the Mast (S.
        Miller)
1947:   Fiesta (L. Cole); Killer McCoy*
1948:   Walk a Crooked Mile
1950:   Rogues of Sherwood Forest
1951:   Valentino; Lorna Doone*
1952:   Kansas City Confidential (H. Essex); The
        Brigand (J. Lasky)
1955:   Fury in Paradise
1959:   Solomon and Sheba*
1962:   Beauty and the Beast (O. Hampton)

LENNY BRUCE

1954:   The Rocket Man (J. Henley)

CLYDE BRUCKMAN (1894-1955) director

1943:   Honeymoon Lodge; So's Your Uncle (M. Leo)
1944:   Swingtime Johnny; Weekend Pass; Twilight on
        the Prairie; Moon over Las Vegas; South of
        Dixie
1945:   Under Western Skies (S. Roberts); Her Lucky
        Night; She Gets Her Man (W. Wilson)

WILLIAM BRUCKNER

1942: Sundown Jim (R. Metzler); Dr. Renault's
Secret (R. Metzler)

KATHERIN BRUSH

1929: Footlights and Fools (T. Geraghty)

JAMES BRUNER

1981: An Eye for an Eye (W. Gray)

JOHN BRYAN

1957: The Spanish Gardener (L. Storm)

CHRIS BRYANT

1974: The Girl from Petrovka (Allan Scott)

BILL BRYDEN

1980: The Long Riders*

JAMES D. BUCHANAN

1967: The Happening*
1969: Midas Run (R. Austin)
1973: Harry in Your Pocket (R. Austin)

LARRY BUCHANAN

1963: Free, White and 21 (H. Dwain)
1965: The Eye Creatures
1976: Goodbye, Norma Jean (L. Schubert)
1978: Hughes and Harlow: Angels in Hell (L.
Schubert)

WILLIAM BUCHANAN

```
1936:   Rip Roarin' Buckaroo
1937:   Two Minutes to Play
1938:   Silks and Saddles
```

HAROLD BUCHMAN

```
1935:   Case of the Missing Man (L. Loeb)
1936:   Blackmailer*; Don't Gamble with Love (L.
        Loeb); Trapped by Television (L. Loeb); Come
        Closer, Folks (L. Loeb)
1937:   Counsel for Crime*; It Can't Last Forever
        (L. Loeb)
1939:   The Forgotten Woman (L. Houser); Hero for a
        Day (R. S. Allen); North of Shanghai (M.
        Rapf)
1940:   Double Alibi (R. Chanslor); Manhattan
        Heartbeat*; On Their Own (V. Burton)
1941:   The Perfect Snob (L. Loeb)
1942:   A Gentleman at Heart (L. Loeb); It Happened
        in Flatbush (L.Loeb)
1943:   Dixie Dugan (L. Loeb); Paris After Dark
1944:   Take It or Leave It*
1945:   Snafu (L. Solomon)
1947:   Cynthia (C. Kaufman)
1954:   The Sleeping Tiger (Brit.; C. Foreman)
1965:   Opereration Snafu
1970:   The Lawyer (S. Furie)
```

SIDNEY BUCHMAN (1902-1975) producer

```
1931:   Daughter of the Dragon*; Beloved Bachelor*
1932:   If I Had a Million*; No One Man*; The Sign
        of the Cross (W. Young); Thunder Below (J.
        Lovett)
1933:   From Hell to Heaven (P. Heath); Right to
        Romance (H. McCarty)
1934:   All of Me (T. Mitchell); His Greatest Gamble
        (H. Hervey); Whom the Gods Destroy (F.
        Niblo); Broadway Bill (unc.; R. Riskin)
1935:   I'll Love You Always (V. Caspary); Love Me
        Forever (J. Swerling); She Married Her Boss
1936:   Adventure in Manhattan; The King Steps Out;
        Theodora Goes Wild
1937:   The Awful Truth (unc.)*; Lost Horizon (unc.;
        R. Riskin)
1938:   Holiday (D. Stewart)
```

```
1939:   Mr. Smith Goes to Washington
1940:   The Howards of Virginia
1941:   Here Comes Mr. Jordan (S. Miller)
1942:   The Talk of the Town (I. Shaw)
1943:   Sahara (unc.)*
1945:   Over 21; A Song to Remember
1946:   The Jolson Story (unc.)*
1948:   To the Ends of the Earth (unc.; J. Kennedy)
1949:   Jolson Sings Again
1951:   Saturday's Hero (M. Lampell)
1961:   The Mark (S. Mann)
1963:   Cleopatra*
1966:   The Group
1972:   The Deadly Trap*
```

PEARL S. BUCK

```
1962:   The Big Wave (T. Danielewski)
1965:   The Guide (T. Danielewski)
```

RONALD BUCK

```
1971:   Clay Pigeon (B. Ruskin)
```

TOM BUCKINGHAM (-1934)

```
1930:   Officer O'Brien; Her Man
1931:   The Painted Desert (H. Higgin); Bad Company
        (T. Garnett)
1932:   Tom Brown of Culver
1933:   Destination Unknown
1934:   He Was Her Man (N. Busch)
1935:   Secret Bride*
1936:   Stage Struck (P. Flick)
```

HAROLD BUCKLEY

```
1936:   The California Mail (R. Chanslor); Public
        Enemy's Wife (A. Finkel)
1937:   Guns of the Pecos; Idol of the Crowds (G.
        Waggner); Carnival Queen (J. Mulhauser)
1938:   Air Devils (G. Waggner); The Black Doll;
        Sinners in Paradise*
```

JOHN BUCKLEY

1978:   Hitchhike to Hell
1979:   Malibu High (Tom Singer)

R. BUCKLEY

1973:   Summertime Killer (B. Degas)

NATHALIE BUCKNALL

1939:   Five Little Peppers and How They Grew (J.
        Parker)

ROBERT BUCKNER (1906-   ) producer

1938:   Gold Is Where You Find It (W. Duff); Comet
        over Broadway (M. Hellinger); Love, Honor
        and Behave*; Jezebel*
1939:   You Can't Get Away with Murder*; Oklahoma
        Kid*; Dodge City; Angels Wash Their Faces*
1940:   Virginia City; Santa Fe Trail; Knute Rockne,
        All American; My Love Came Back*
1941:   Riders of the Purple Sage (R. Metzler); Dive
        Bomber (F. Wead)
1942:   Yankee Doodle Dandy (E. Joseph)
1945:   Confidential Agent
1948:   Rogue's Regiment (R. Florey)
1949:   Free for All; Sword in the Desert
1950:   Deported
1951:   Bright Victory
1952:   The Man Behind the Gun (J. Twist)
1955:   A Prize of Gold (J. Paxton); To Paris with
        Love
1956:   Love Me Tender; Safari (Brit.; A. Veiller)
1957:   Triple Deception (B. Forbes)
1958:   From Hell to Texas (W. Mayes)
1966:   Return of the Gunfighter

AVERY BUDDY

1981:   On the Right Track*

JED BUELL

1942:　　Professor Creeps*

ADELE BUFFINGTON (also JESS BOWERS) (1900-1973)

1928:　　River Woman (H. Shumate); Times Square
1929:　　Phantom City
1930:　　Swellhead (R. Cahoon); Just Like Heaven;
　　　　　Extravagance*
1931:　　Freighters of Destiny; Aloha
1932:　　A Man's Land; Ghost Valley; Haunted Gold;
　　　　　Forgotten Women (W. Totman); High Speed
1933:　　The Eleventh Commandment (K. Kempler); The
　　　　　Iron Master; West of Singapore
1934:　　Beggar's Holiday; The Moonstone; Picture
　　　　　Brides; When Strangers Meet; Cheaters
1935:　　Powdersmoke Range; Keeper of the Bees (G.
　　　　　Waggner)
1936:　　Hi, Gaucho
1937:　　Circus Girl (B. Ropes); The Duke Comes Back
　　　　　(E. Seward); Michael O'Halloran; The Sheik
　　　　　Steps Out (G. Kahn); Any Man's Wife
1941:　　Arizona Bound; The Gunman from Bodie;
　　　　　Forbidden Trails
1942:　　Below the Border;　Ghost Town Law; Down
　　　　　Texas Way; Riders of the West; West of the
　　　　　Law; Dawn on the Great Divide
1943:　　The Ghost Rider; The Stranger from Pecos;
　　　　　Six Gun Gospel (E. Repp); Outlaws of
　　　　　Stampede Pass; The Texas Kid
1944:　　Raiders of the Border
1945:　　The Navajo Trail; Flame of the West; Bad Men
　　　　　of the Border; The Lost Trail; Frontier Feud
1946:　　Drifting Along; Wild Beauty; Shadows on the
　　　　　Range
1948:　　Overland Trails; Crossed Trails; The Valiant
　　　　　Hombre
1949:　　Crashing Thru; Shadows of the West; West of
　　　　　Eldorado; Haunted Trails; Western Renegades;
　　　　　Riders of the Dusk (R. Tansey); Range Land
1950:　　West of Wyoming; Gunslingers; Jiggs and
　　　　　Maggie Out West (B. Gerard); Six Gun Mesa;
　　　　　Arizona Territory
1951:　　Overland Telegraph
1953:　　Cow Country (T. Blackburn)

1958:   Bullwhip

RAY BUFFUM

1952:   Girls in the Night
1954:   The Black Dakotas
1955:   Teen-Age Crime Wave (H. Essex)
1959:   Island of Lost Women

KITTY BUHLER

1958:   China Doll

AL BUKZIN

1976:   The Amorous Adventures of Don Quixote and
         Sancho Panza*

HARVEY BULLOCK

1964:   Honeymoon Hotel (R. S. Allen)
1965:   Girl Happy (R. S. Allen)
1966:   The Man Called Flintstone (anim.; Ray Allen)
1967:   Who's Minding the Mint? (R. S. Allen)
1968:   With Six You Get Eggroll*
1969:   Don't Drink the Water (R. S. Allen)

WALTER BULLOCK

1941:   The Cowboy and the Blonde; For Beauty's
         Sake*; Moon over Her Shoulder
1942:   Right to the Heart; Springtime in the
         Rockies (K. Englund)
1943:   The Gang's All Here
1944:   Greenwich Village (E. Baldwin)
1947:   Out of the Blue*; Repeat Performance
1948:   Adventures of Casanova*
1951:   Golden Girl*
1952:   O. Henry's Full House*
1953:   The I Don't Care Girl; The Farmer Takes a
         Wife*

97

ROBERT BUNDY

1979:   The Visitor (L. Comici)

EDWARD BUNKER

1978:   Straight Time*

ALFRED BUNN

1936:   The Bohemian Girl

JOYCE BUNUEL

1981:   Tattoo

BETTY BURBRIDGE

1931:   Law of the Rio Grande (B. Cohen); Mounted
        Fury; Between Fighting Men (F. Sheldon);
        Neck and Neck; Chinatown After Dark;
        Anybody's Blonde; Is There Justice?
1932:   Hellfire Austin (F. Sheldon); The Racing
        Strain (W. Kent); Sin's Pay Day (G. Morgan)
1933:   Dance Hall Hostess; Phantom Thunderbolt*
1934:   Rawhide Mail (Rose Gordon); Boss Cowboy;
        Redhead (J. Lasky)
1935:   Tracy Rides (Rose Gordon); The Singing
        Vagabond (O. Drake); Get That Man; Honeymoon
        Limited (D. Reid); Reckless Roads; Rescue
        Squad (G. Morgan); Calling All Cars (G.
        Morgan)
1936:   The Crime Patrol
1937:   Come On, Cowboys; Springtime in the Rockies
        (G. Wright); Paradise Express (J. Natteford)

1938:   The Purple Vigilantes (O. Drake); Outlaws of
        Sonora (E. Kelso); Under Western Stars *;
        Wild Horse Rodeo; Riders of the Black Hills;
        Gold Mine in the Sky (J. Natteford); Heroes
        of the Hills (S. Roberts); Man from Music
        Mourntain (L. Ward); Pals of the Saddle (S.
        Roberts); Prairie Moon (S. Roberts); Santa
        Fe Stampede (L. Ward); Red River Range*

1939:   The Night Riders (S. Roberts); Three Texas
        Steers (S. Roberts); Wyoming Outlaw (J.
        Natteford); Colorado Sunset (S. Roberts);
        New Frontier (L. Ward); The Kansas Terrors
        (J. Natteford); Rovin' Tumbleweeds (alt.
        Washington Cowboy)*
1940:   Rancho Grande*; Gaucho Serenade (B. Ropes);
        Under Texas Skies (A. Coldeway)
1941:   Thunder over the Prairie; Riders of the
        Badlands
1942:   Stardust on the Stage
1943:   Santa Fe Scouts (M. Grant); Frontier Fury;
        Robin Hood of the Range
1944:   Oklahoma Raiders; West of the Rio Grande;
        Song of the Range
1945:   The Cisco Kid Returns; In Old New Mexico;
        Oregon Trail; The Cherokee Flash
1946:   Alias Billy the Kid (E. Snell); Home on the
        Range; Man from Rainbow Valley; Out
        California Way
1947:   Where the North Begins (L. Swabacker); Trail
        of the Mounties
1948:   The Return of Wildfire (C. Hittleman)
1949:   The Daring Caballero

ROGER BURFORD

1936:   April Romance*; Love in Exile (E. Betts)
1937:   Dr. Syn

PAUL BURGER

1936:   Little Miss Nobody*

EDWIN J. BURKE

1929:   Speakeasy (F. Brennan)
1930:   The Dancers; Happy Days (S. Lanfield)
1931:   Bad Girl; The Man Who Came Back; Sob Sister;
        Young As You Feel
1932:   Call Her Savage; Dance Team; Down to Earth
1933:   Paddy the Next Best Thing
1934:   Now I'll Tell
1935:   The Farmer Takes a Wife; The Littlest Rebel
        (H. Tugend); One More Spring

ADDISON BURKHART

1928:   Home Towners
1929:   Queen of the Night Clubs

DANA BURNET

1929:   Love, Live and Laugh
1939:   The Great Commandment

W. R. BURNETT (1899-1982) novelist

1931:   The Finger Points*
1932:   Scarface*
1941:   The Get-Away (W. Root); High Sierra (J.
        Huston)
1942:   This Gun for Hire (A. Maltz); Wake Island
        (F. Butler)
1943:   Background to Danger
1945:   San Antonio (A. LeMay)
1946:   Nobody Lives Forever
1948:   Belle Starr's Daughter
1950:   Vendetta
1951:   The Racket (W. Haines)
1954:   Dangerous Mission*
1955:   Captain Lightfoot (O. Brodney); I Died a
        Thousand Times; Illegal (J. Webb)
1956:   Accused of Murder (B. Williams)
1960:   September Storm
1962:   Sergeants 3
1963:   The Great Escape (J. Clavell)

STEPHEN C. BURNHAM

1982:   Soggy Bottom U.S.A.*

ALLAN BURNS

1979:   A Little Romance; Butch and Sundance: the
        Early Days

100

JACK BURNS

1979:   The Muppet Movie (J. Juhl)

STAN BURNS

1981:   Charlie Chan and the Curse of the Dragon
        Queen (D. Axelrod)

WALTER NOBLE BURNS

1941:   Billy the Kid

NORMAN BURNSIDE

1940:   Dr. Ehrlich's Magic Bullet*

NORMAN BURNSTINE

1938:   Arson Gang Busters (A. Gottlieb)

ABE BURROWS (1910-   ) playwright

1956:   The Solid Gold Cadillac

FRANK BURT

1949:   Flame of Youth*; Law of the Barbary Coast
        (R. Libott); Air Hostess (R. Libott);
        Barbary Pirate (R. Libott)
1950:   Chinatown at Midnight (R. Libott); Fortunes
        of Captain Blood*; State Penitentiary*;
        Tyrant of the Sea (R. Libott)
1951:   Stage to Tucson*; The Groom Wore Spurs*; The
        Lady and the Bandit (R. Libott)
1952:   Captain Pirate*
1955:   The Man from Laramie (P. Yordan)

THOMSON BURTIS

1932:   Under-Cover Man*

VAL BURTON

1939: Two Bright Boys (E. Hartmann)
1940: Earl of Puddlestone (E. Adamson); Meet the
       Missus*; On Their Own (H. Buchman);
       Scatterbrain (J. Townley)
1941: Glamour Boy (B. Ropes); Henry Aldrich for
       President
1942: Henry Aldrich, Editor (M. Bolton); Henry and
       Dizzy
1943: Henry Aldrich Haunts a House (M. Bolton);
       Henry Aldrich Swings It (M. Bolton)
1944: Passport to Adventure (M. Bolton); You Can't
       Ration Love (H. Fimberg); Henry Aldrich
       Plays Cupid (M. Bolton); Pardon My Rhythm
       (E. Conrad); Henry Aldrich's Little Secret
       (A. Leslie)
1945: Honeymoon Ahead (E. Ullman)
1946: The Time of Their Lives*
1951: Bedtime for Bonzo (L. Breslow)

NIVEN BUSCH (1903-   ) novelist

1932: Miss Pinkerton (L. Hayward); Scarlet Dawn
       (E. Gelsey); The Crowd Roars*
1933: The College Coach (M. Seff)
1934: Babbitt*; He Was Her Man (T. Buckingham);
       The Man with Two Faces (T. Reed); The Big
       Shakedown
1935: Three Kids and a Queen*; Lady Tubbs (B.
       Trivers)
1939: Angels Wash Their Faces*; Off the Record*
1940: The Westerner (J. Swerling)
1946: The Postman Always Rings Twice (H. Ruskin)
1947: Pursued
1950: The Capture
1951: Distant Drums (M. Rackin)
1953: The Moonlighter
1955: The Treasure of Pancho Villa

L. BUS-FEKETE

1948: Casbah (A. Manoff)

JOSEF BUSH

1970: Barbara

WILLIAM H. BUSHNELL, JR.

1975: Prisoners (J. Marley)

CARL A. BUSS

1934: Wagon Wheels*

DAVID BUTLER (1894-1979) director

1929: Sunny Side Up
1930: Just Imagine
1933: My Weakness (B. Ryan)
1934: Bottoms Up*; Have a Heart*

DAVID BUTLER

1976: Voyage of the Damned (S. Shagan)
1980: Bear Island*

FRANK BUTLER (1890-1967) actor,

1929: Untamed
1930: Montana Moon; Strictly Unconventional;
       Remote Control; Those Three French Girls
1931: New Moon (S. Thalberg); This Modern Age*
1932: When a Feller Needs a Friend (S. Thalberg);
       Prosperity*
1933: College Humor (C. Binyon); Girl Without a
       Room (C. Binyon); The Way to Love*
1934: Ladies Should Listen (C. Binyon); Search for
       Beauty*; Babes in Toyland (N. Grinde)
1935: Coronado (D. Hartman); Vagabond Lady; Bonnie
       Scotland (J. Moffit)
1936: The Milky Way*; The Princess Comes Across*;
       Strike Me Pink*
1937: Champagne Waltz (D. Hartman); Waikiki
       Wedding*

1938: Give Me a Sailor (D. Anderson); Tropic
      Holiday (D. Hartman)
1939: Never Say Die*; Paris Honeymoon (D.
      Hartman); The Star Maker (D. Hartman)
1940: Rangers of Fortune; I Want a Divorce; Road
      to Singapore (D. Hartman); Untamed (F.
      Brennan)
1941: Aloma of the South Seas*; Road to Zanzibar*
1942: Wake Island (W. Burnett); Beyond the Blue
      Horizon; My Favorite Blonde (D. Hartman)
      Road to Morocco (D. Hartman)
1943: China; Hostages (L. Cole)
1944: Going My Way (F. Cavett)
1945: Incendiary Blonde (C. Binyon); A Medal for
      Benny
1946: California (T. Strauss); The Kid from
      Brooklyn*
1947: Golden Earrings*; The Perils of Pauline
1948: Whispering Smith (K. Lamb)
1952: Road to Bali*
1955: Strange Lady in Town
1959: The Miracle

HUGO BUTLER (1914-1968) Can.   (also H.B. ADDIS;
      HUGO MOZO)

1937: The Big City (D. Schary)
1938: A Christmas Carol
1939: The Adventures of Huckleberry Finn; Society
      Lawyer*
1940: Wyoming (J. Jevne); Young Tom Edison*
1941: Barnacle Bill (J. Jevne)
1942: The Omaha Trail (J. Lasky); A Yank on the
      Burma Road*
1943: Lassie Come Home
1945: Miss Susie Slagle's (A. Froelick); The
      Southerner (J. Renoir)
1946: From This Day Forward (C. Schnee)
1949: Roughshod (G. Homes)
1950: Eye Witness (I. Hunter)
1951: He Ran All the Way (G. Endore); The Prowler
      (D. Trumbo); The Big Night*
1952: The First Time*
1953: The Adventures of Robin Crusoe (Mex.)*
1956: Torero (doc.)
1958: How Tall Is a Giant? (Mex.; doc.)*; Cowboy
      (unc.)*

1961:   The Young One (Mex.; L. Bunuel)
1963:   A Face in the Rain (J. Rouverol); Sodom and
        Gomorrah
1965:   Eva (Evan Jones)
1968:   The Legend of Lylah Clare (J. Rouverol)

JOHN K. BUTLER

1943:   The Blocked Trail (J. Frank); Silver Spurs
        (J. Cheney); Beyond the Last Frontier (M.
        Grant); Raiders of Sunset Pass
1944:   Pride of the Plains (R. Williams); Hidden
        Valley Outlaws (R. Williams); The Girl Who
        Dared
1945:   Utah (J. Townley); The Man from Oklahoma;
        Don't Fence Me In*; The Phantom Speaks; Tell
        It to a Star; The Vampire's Ghost (L.
        Brackett); Sunset in El Dorado
1946:   My Pal Trigger (J. Townley); Affairs of
        Geraldine; G.I. War Brides; One Exciting
        Week (J. Townley)
1947:   Robin Hood in Texas (E. Snell)
1948:   Secret Service Investigator; California
        Firebrand (J. Cheney); The Gallant Legion
        (C. Adams); Lightnin' in the Forest; Out of
        the Storm
1949:   Susanna Pass (S. Nibley); Rim of the Canyon;
        Down Dakota Way (S. Nibley); The Blonde
        Bandit; Flaming Fury; Post Office
        Investigator; Streets of San Francisco;
        Hideout
1950:   Rodeo King and the Senorita; Utah Wagon
        Train; Missing Women; Pride of Maryland;
        Secrets of Monte Carlo; Harbor of Missing
        Men; Tarnished
1952:   Toughest Man in Arizona
1954:   Drums Across the River; The Outcast (R.
        Wormser)
1955:   Headline Hunters (F. Fox); I Cover the
        Underworld; No Man's Woman
1956:   Terror at Midnight; When Gangland Strikes
        (F. Fox)
1957:   Hell's Crossroads (B. Shipman); Affair in
        Reno
1958:   Ambush at Cimarron Pass (R. C. Taylor)

MICHAEL BUTLER

1975: Brannigan*
1977: The Car*; The Gauntlet (D. Shryack)

ALFRED BUTTERFIELD

1950: Fifty Years Before Your Eyes (doc.; W. Ament)
1956: Secrets of the Reef (doc.)*

WALTON BUTTERFIELD

1929: Fast Company

FRANK BUXTON

1966: What's Up, Tiger Lily?*

EDWARD BUZZELL (1897-   ) director

1933: Love, Honor and Oh Baby! (N. Krasna)
1935: Transient Lady*
1954: Ain't Misbehavin'*

JOHN BYRNE

1953: Guerrilla Girl (B. Parker)

JOHN BYRUM

1975: Mahogany
1976: Harry and Walter Go to New York (R. Kaufman)
1980: Heart Beat
1981: Sphynx

C

CHRISTY CABANNE (1888–1950) director

1941:   Scattergood Pulls the Strings (B. Schubert)

JERRY CADY

1937:   Charlie Chan at Monte Carlo (C. Belden);
        Charlie Chan on Broadway (C. Belden); The
        Great Hospital Mystery*
1938:   Inside Story; Mr. Moto's Gamble (C. Belden);
        One Wild Night (C. Belden); Time Out for
        Murder
1939:   Five Came Back*; Full Confession; The
        Arizona Wildcat (B. Trivers); Two Thousand
        Thoroughbreds (J. Fields)
1940:   Anne of Windy Poplars (M. Kanin);
        Cross-Country Romance (B. Granet); Laddie
        (B. Granet); The Marines Fly High (A.
        Bolton); Sued for Libel; You Can't Fool Your
        Wife
1941:   Play Girl; Repent at Leisure; The Saint in
        Palm Springs; They Met in Argentina; Mexican
        Spitfire's Baby (C. E. Roberts)
1942:   Mexican Spitfire at Sea (C. E. Roberts);
        What's Cooking? (S. Roberts)
1943:   Silver Skates
1944:   The Purple Heart; Roger Touhy, Gangster (C.
        Wilbur); Wing and a Prayer
1947:   Bob – Son of Battle; Thunder in the Valley
1948:   Call Northside 777 (J. Dratler)
1949:   Will James' Sand (alt. Sand; M. Berkeley)

ARTHUR CAESAR

1929:   The Aviator; So Long Letty (R. Lord)
1930:   This Mad World (C. Beranger); Wide Open;

Three Faces East (O. Garrett); Life of the
Party; She Couldn't Say No (R. Lord)
1931: Divorce Among Friends; Her Majesty, Love (R.
Lord)
1932: Fireman, Save My Child*; Heart of New York
(H. Branch); The Tenderfoot*
1933: The Chief (R. Hopkins); No Marriage Ties (S.
Mintz); Obey the Law
1934: Their Big Moment (M. Dix)
1935: McFadden's Flats*; Transient Lady (H. Thew)
1940: Little Men (M. Kelly)
1941: Adventure in Washington (L. Foster)
1944: Three of a Kind (E. Snell)
1951: Anne of the Indies (P. Dunne)

G. M. CAHILL

1980: Survival Run (L. Spiegel)

RICHARD CAHOON

1930: Swellhead (A. Buffington)

ALAN CAILLOU

1965: Clarence, the Cross-Eyed Lion; Village of
the Giants
1970: The Losers
1971: Evel Knievel (J. Milius)
1976: Assault on Agathon
1977: Kingdom of the Spiders (Richard Robinson)

GUILLERMO CAIN

1971: Vanishing Point

JAMES M. CAIN (1892-1977)

1938: Algiers (J. Lawson)
1939: Stand Up and Fight*
1944: Gypsy Wildcat*; The Bridge of San Luis Rey
(H. Estabrook)

RORY CALHOUN (1922–   ) actor

1955:   Shotgun (C. E. Reynolds)

GEORGE CALLAHAN

1944:   Charlie Chan in the Secret Service; Black
        Magic*; Call of the Jungle; The Chinese Cat
1945:   Adventures of Kitty O'Day* Captain Tugboat
        Annie; The Jade Mask; The Red Dragon; The
        Scarlet Clue; The Shanghai Cobra (G. Milton)
1946:   Behind the Mask; Dark Alibi; The Missing
        Lady; The Shadow Returns
1948:   The Babe Ruth Story (B. Considine)
1949:   Red Light
1950:   Bunco Squad
1951:   Lucky Nick Cain (W. Rose)

JEAN PAUL CALLEGARI

1955:   Mystery of the Black Jungle (Ralph Murphy)

JOSEPH CALLEIA (1897–1975) actor

1935:   Robin Hood of Eldorado*

JOSEPH CALVELLI

1963:   My Six Loves*
1969:   Death of a Gunfighter

DONALD CAMMELL

1970:   Performance

ANNE CAMERON

1981:   Ticket to Heaven (R. C. Thomas)

SEAN CAMERON

1972:   The Limit

DONALD CAMMELL

1968:   Duffy (H. J. Brown)
1979:   Tilt (R. Durand)

JOE CAMP

1974:   Benji
1977:   For the Love of Benji
1979:   The Double McGuffin
1980:   Oh! Heavenly Dog (R. Browning)

ALAN CAMPBELL

1936:   Lady Be Careful*; The Moon's Our Home*;
        Suzy*; Three Married Men (D. Parker
1937:   A Star Is Born*
1938:   Sweethearts (D. Parker); Trade Winds*
1941:   Week-End for Three (D. Parker)
1942:   Tales of Manhattan*
1943:   Forever and a Day*
1950:   Woman on the Run (N. Foster)

R. WRIGHT CAMPBELL

1955:   Five Guns West
1957:   Gun for a Coward; Man of a Thousand Faces*;
        Quantes
1958:   Machine Gun Kelly; Teen Age Caveman
1960:   The Night Fighters (Ir.)
1963:   The Young Racers
1964:   Masque of the Red Death (C. Beaumont); The
        Secret Invasion
1967:   Hell's Angels on Wheels
1970:   Captain Nemo and the Underwater City*

MARK CANFIELD

1960:   Crack in the Mirror

DORAN WILLIAM CANNON

1968: Skidoo
1970: Brewster McCloud

RAYMOND CANNON (—   ) director

1935: Tailspin Tommy in the Great Air Mystery
       (ser.)*

EDDIE CANTOR (1892-1964) singer, actor

1931: Mr. Lemon of Orange*; Palmy Days*;

LEON CAPETANOS

1974: Summer Rain
1976: The Gumball Rally
1982: Tempest (P. Mazursky)

TRUMAN CAPOTE (1924—   ) author

1954: Beat the Devil (J. Huston)
1961: The Innocents (Brit.)
1969: Trilogy (E. Perry)

FRANK CAPRA (1897—   ) director

1946: It's a Wonderful Life*

HAL CAPTAIN

1970: Suppose They Gave a War and Nobody Came? (D.
       McGuire)

JAMES CARABATSOS

1977: Heroes
1981: Underground Aces*; Beyond the Reef (L.

LaRusso)

STEVEN CARABATSOS

1970: El Condor (L. Cohen)
1980: The Last Flight of Noah's Ark*

RICHARD CARDELLA

1977: The Crater Lake Monster (W. Stromberg)

J. S. CARDONE

1982: The Slayer (W. R. Ewing)

ANTHONY CARDOZA

1980: Smokey and the Hotwire Gang

REX CARLETON

1969: Blood of Dracula's Castle; Nightmare in Wax

CLANCY CARLILE

1982: Honkytonk Man

LEWIS JOHN CARLINO

1966: Seconds
1967: The Fox (H. Koch)
1968: The Brotherhood
1972: The Mechanic
1974: Crazy Joe
1976: The Sailor Who Fell from Grace with the Sea
1979: The Great Santini
1980: Resurrection

RODNEY CARLISLE

1948: Let's Live Again (R. Smalley)

JOHN CARMODY

1977: The Farmer*

JOSEPH CAROLE

1940: Convicted Woman; Men Without Souls (R.
       Andrews); My Son Is Guilty (H. Shumate);
       Scandal Sheet
1944: I'm from Arkansas (M. Klauber)
1945: How Do You Do? (H. Sauber)
1948: Racing Luck*; Triple Threat (D. Martin)
1949: The Mutineers (B. Bengal); Ladies of the
       Chorus (H. Sauber)

A. J. CAROTHERS

1963: Miracle of the White Stallions
1967: The Happiest Millionaire
1968: Never a Dull Moment
1980: Hero at Large

DON CARPENTER

1973: Payday

EDWARD CHILDS CARPENTER

1935: The Perfect Gentleman

JOHN CARPENTER (—   ) director

1953: Son of the Renegade
1954: The Lawless Rider
1956: I Killed Wild Bill Hickok
1974: Dark Star (D. O'Bannon)
1976: Assault on Precinct 13
1977: Eyes of Laura Mars (D. Goodman)
1978: Halloween (Debra Hill)
1980: The Fog (Debra Hill)

1981:   Escape from New York (N. Castle); Halloween
         II (Debra Hill)

JOSEPH CARPENTER

1953: Shark River (L. Meltzer)

STEPHEN CARPENTER

1982:   Pranks*

ALLAN CARR

1980:   Can't Stop the Music (B. Woodward)

RICHARD CARR

1956:   Man from Del Rio
1962:   Hell Is for Heroes (R. Pirosh); Too Late
        Blues (J. Cassavetes)
1969:   Heaven with a Gun

ROBERT CARR

1929:   Hot Stuff; Why Leave Home?

MICHAEL CARRERAS

1971:   Creatures the World Forgot

RICK CARRIER

1962:   Strangers in the City

JANE-HOWARD CARRINGTON

1966:   Kaleidoscope (R. Carrington)
1967:   Wait Until Dark (R. Carrington)

ROBERT CARRINGTON

1966: Kaleidoscope (J. Carrington)
1967: Wait Unti Dark (J. Carrington)
1973: Fear Is the Key
1982: Venom

J. LARRY CARROLL

1979: Tourist Trap (D. Schmoeller)
1980: The Day Time Ended*

JUNE CARROLL

1945: An Angel Comes to Brooklyn (S. Paley)

KENT CARROLL

1975: Abduction

MABEL Z. CARROLL

1930: Convict's Code
1937: Lash of the Penitentes

RICHARD A. CARROLL

1940: The Ape (C. Siodmak)
1941: Three Girls About Town
1942: Two Yanks in Trinidad*
1945: Sunbonnet Sue (Ralph Murphy)

SIDNEY CARROLL

1961: The Hustler (R. Rossen)
1966: A Big Hand for the Little Lady

ZELMA CARROLL

1936: The Penitente Murder Case (alt. The Lash of
       the Penitentes)

MILTON CARRUTH

1936:   Love Letters of a Star*

L. M. KIT CARSON

1971:   The Lexington Experience (doc.); The
        American Dreamer (D. Hopper)
1980:   The Last Word*

ROBERT CARSON

1937:   A Star Is Born*
1938:   Men with Wings
1939:   The Light That Failed; Beau Geste
1941:   Western Union
1942:   The Tuttles of Tahiti
1943:   The Desperadoes
1949:   Once More My Darling
1951:   The Groom Wore Spurs*
1952:   Just for You
1956:   Bundle of Joy*
1957:   Action of the Tiger

ARTHUR CARTER

1957:   Operation Mad Ball*

HARRISON CARTER

1940:   Midnight Limited (C. B. Williams)

JAMES CARTHART

1950:   Cry Murder (N. Winter)

DEE CARUSO

1970:   Which Way to the Front? (G. Gardner)
1973:   The World's Greatest Athlete (G. Gardner)

RICHARD CARVER

1930: The Silent Enemy

WILLIAM E. CARVILLE

1977: Poco...Little Dog Lost

ROBERT ORMOND CASE

1942: The Girl from Alaska (E. Lowe)

JOHNNY CASH

1973: The Gospel Road (L. Murray)

VERA CASPARY (1904-   ) novelist

1935: I'll Love You Always (S. Buchman)
1941: Lady from Louisiana*
1946: Bedelia (Brit.)*
1947: Out of the Blue
1950: Three Husbands (E. Eliscu)

JOHN CASSAVETES (1927-   ) actor, director

1962: Too Late Blues (R. Carr)
1968: Faces
1970: Husbands
1971: Minnie and Moskowitz
1974: A Woman Under the Influence
1976: The Killing of a Chinese Bookie
1979: Opening Night
1980: Gloria

TED CASSEDY

1973: The Harrad Experiment (M. Werner)

ALAN CASSIDY

1978:   The Great Brain

JOHN J. CASSITY

1958:   Man or Gun (V. Skarstedt)

JAY CASTLE

1975:   Distance

NICK CASTLE

1979:   Skatetown U.S.A.
1981:   Escape from New York (John Carpenter)

S. CASTLE

1977:   American Matchmaker (Yid.)

SHERLE CASTLE

1939:   Moon over Harlem

WILLIAM CASTLE (1914-1977) director, producer

1945:   Voice of the Whistler (W. Pettitt)
1950:   It's a Small World (O. Schreiber)
1975:   Bug (T. Page)

MATT CAVANAUGH

1971:   Sweet Saviour

TAYLOR CAVEN

1939:   Should Husbands Work (J. Townley)
1940:   Meet the Missus*
1941:   The Gay Vagabond (E. Adamson); Petticoat

```
          Politics (E. Adamson)
1942:  Arizona Terror  (D. Schroeder); Jesse James,
       Jr.*; King of the Mounties (ser.)*
1944:  Silver City Kid
1947:  Untamed Fury (P. Smith)
```

FRANK CAVETT (1907-1973)

```
1939:  Rulers of the Sea*
1940:  Tom Brown's School Days*; Second Chorus*
1942:  Syncopation (P. Yordan)
1944:  Going My Way (F. Butler)
1945:  The Corn Is Green (C. Robinson)
```

ANN CAWTHORNE

```
1974:  The Single Girls
```

ROSE CAYLOR

```
1942:  Fingers at the Window (L. Bachmann)
```

JON CEDAR

```
1978:  The Manitou*
```

JOHN CERULLO

```
1973:  Sweet Jesus, Preacher Man*
```

DON CERVERIS

```
1962:  The Nun and the Sergeant
```

LEE CHADWICK

```
1932:  Strange Adventure (A. Hoerl)
```

NORMAN C. CHAITIN

1962:   The Small Hours

TERRY CHAMBERS

1977:   Breaker! Breaker!

WHITMAN CHAMBERS

1946:   Shadow of a Woman (G. Baker)
1947:   Big Town After Dark; I Cover Big Town;
         Jungle Flight
1949:   Special Agent (L. Foster); Manhandled (L.
         Foster)
1956:   The Come On (W. Douglas)

ROBERT CHAMBLEE

1976:   The Killer Inside Me (E. Mann)

JOHN C. CHAMPION

1948:   Panhandle (B. Edwards)
1949:   Stampede (B. Edwards)
1954:   Dragonfly Squadron
1957:   Zero Hour*
1966:   The Texican
1972:   Brother of the Wind (J. Mahon)
1976:   Mustang Country

HARRY E. CHANDLEE

1929:   Up the Congo (doc.)
1930:   Reno (D. Churchill)
1936:   Rainbow on the River*
1937:   It Happened Out West*
1940:   Our Town*
1941:   Sergeant York*
1944:   Three Is a Family (M. Pfaelzer)
1946:   The Jolson Story*
1949:   Tale of the Navajos (doc.; J. Hassler);
         Tarzan's Magic Fountain (C. Siodmak)

DAVID CHANDLER

1947:   Winter Wonderland*
1951:   Apache Drums; You Can Never Tell (L.
        Breslow)
1954:   Green Fire‡
1957:   Tomahawk Trail; Calypso Heat Wave; Last of
        the Bad Men
1959:   Face of a Fugitive (D. Ullman)

JOHN CHANDLER

1947:   Pacific Adventure (A. Coppel)

RAYMOND CHANDLER (1888–1959) novelist

1944:   Double Indemnity*; And Now Tomorrow (F.
        Partos)
1945:   The Unseen*
1946:   The Blue Dahlia
1951:   Strangers on a Train (C. Ormonde)

LEE CHANEY

1974:   Vanishing Wilderness (doc.; P. Scott)

WILL CHANEY

1971:   Honky

ROY CHANSLOR

1931:   Shanghaied Love (J. Cunningham)
1934:   Murder in the Clouds (D. Schary)
1935:   Front Page Woman*
1936:   The California Mail (H. Buckley); Bengal
        Tiger (E. Felton); Here Comes Carter; Man
        Hunt; Murder by an Aristocrat (L. Ward);
        Times Square Playboy
1937:   Men in Exile; Public Wedding (H. Branch);
        Wine, Women and Horses
1938:   The Devil's Party; Goodbye Broadway (D.
        Otvos); Nurse from Brooklyn; The Road to

Reno (A. Comandini)
1939:   One Hour to Live
1940:   Double Alibi (H. Buchman); Framed; Honeymoon
         Deferred
1941:   Burma Convoy (S. Rubin); Washington
         Melodrama (M. Parsonnet); Flying Cadets*
1942:   Bombay Clipper (S. Rubin); Drums of the
         Congo (P. Huston); Escape from Hong Kong;
         Mississippi Gambler (A. Martin); The Navy
         Comes Through*; Treat 'Em Rough (R.
         Williams); Unseen Enemy (S. Rubin)
1943:   Idaho (O. Cooper); Tarzan Triumphs (Carroll
         Young)
1944:   Secret Command; Destiny (E. Pascal)
1945:   The Daltons Ride Again (P. Gangelin); The
         House of Fear
1946:   Black Angel; Perilous Holiday; Strange
         Conquest
1947:   The Michigan Kid; The Vigilantes Return
1948:   Hazard (A. Sheekman)

DAVID T. CHANTLER

1962:   Cash on Demand (Brit.; B. Greifer)
1963:   Follow the Boys (D. Osborn)
1965:   She (Brit.)

ANNE MORRISON CHAPIN

1934:   Dangerous Corner (M. Ruthven)
1937:   The Soldier and the Lady*
1938:   Listen, Darling (E. Ryan); Romance in the
         Dark (F. Partos)
1941:   Sunset in Wyoming (I. Goff); Dancing on a
         Dime*
1945:   The Sailor Takes a Wife*
1946:   The Secret Heart (W. Cook)
1947:   High Barbaree*
1948:   The Big City (W. Cook)

FREDERICK CHAPIN

1932:   Mark of the Spur

MARTHA CHAPIN

1940:   Lightning Strikes Twice

ROBERT CHAPIN

1937:   Borrowing Trouble (K. DeWolf); The Jones
        Family in Hot Water (alt. Hot Water; K.
        DeWolf)
1938:   Always in Trouble (K. DeWolf); Passport
        Husband (K. DeWolf); Safety in Numbers*
        Walking Down Broadway (K. DeWolf)
1939:   Everybody's Baby*
1940:   Little Orvie*; Bowery Boy*
1942:   Isle of Missing Men; Prisoner of Japan (A.
        Ripley)

CHARLES CHAPLIN (1889-1977) actor, director,
        producer, composer

1931:   City Lights
1936:   Modern Times
1940:   The Great Dictator
1947:   Monsieur Verdoux
1952:   Limelight
1957:   A King in New York
1967:   A Countess from Hong Kong

PRESCOTT CHAPLIN

1933:   Laughing at Life (T. Dugan); Private Jones
        (W. Robson)
1941:   Never Give a Sucker an Even Break (J.
        Neville)

BEN CHAPMAN

1940:   The Devil's Pipeline*; The Leather Pushers*
1941:   A Dangerous Game*; Six Lessons from Madame
        La Zonga*

LEIGH CHAPMAN

1974:   Dirty Mary Crazy Larry (A. Santean)
1975:   How Come Nobody's on Our Side?
1979:   Boardwalk (S. Verona)
1980:   Steel; The Octagon

PRISCILLA CHAPMAN

1981:   The Fan (J. Hartwell)

RICHARD CHAPMAN

1977:   The Amazing Dobermans*

TEDWELL CHAPMAN

1944:   Abroad with Two Yanks*
1946:   The Fabulous Suzanne (R. Faye)

EDWARD CHAPPELL

1970:   Madron (L. Mahon)

ROBERT CHARLES

1944:   Voodoo Man; Return of the Ape Man

LESLIE CHARTERIS (1907-   ) novelist

1933:   Midnight Club (S. Miiller)
1945:   River Gang
1945:   Two Smart People (Ethel Hill)

BORDEN CHASE (1900-1971)

1935:   Under Pressure*
1938:   Trouble Wagon
1943:   Destroyer*
1944:   The Fighting Seabees (A. MacKenzie)
1945:   Flame of the Barbary Coast; This Man's Navy
1946:   I've Always Loved You
1947:   Tycoon (J. Twist)

```
1948:   Red River (C. Schnee)
1950:   Montana*; Winchester '73 (R. Richards); The
        Great Jewel Robbery
1951:   Iron Man (G. Zuckerman)
1952:   Bend of the River; Lone Star (H. Estabrook);
        A World in His Arms
1953:   Sea Devils; His Majesty O'Keefe (James Hill)
1955:   The Far Country; Man Without a Star (D.
        Beauchamp)
1956:   Backlash
1957:   Night Passage
1958:   Ride a Crooked Trail
1965:   Gunfighters of Casa Grande*
1969:   A Man Called Gannon*; Backtrack
```

DAVID CHASE

```
1974:   Grave of the Vampire
```

FRANK CHASE

```
1967:   Sullivan's Empire
```

MARY C. CHASE

```
1950:   Harvey (O. Brodney)
```

PATRICIA CHASE

```
1965:   Gunfighters of Casa Grande*
```

DON CHASTAIN

```
1979:   The Mafu Cage
```

PADDY CHAYEFSKY (1923-1981) playwright

```
1955:   Marty
1957:   The Bachelor Party
1958:   The Goddess
1959:   Middle of the Night
1964:   The Americanization of Emily
```

```
1971:    The Hospital
1976:    Network
1980:    Altered States (S. Aaron)


PIERRE CHENAL

1951:    Native Son (R. Wright)


J. BENTON CHENEY   (also Jack Benton)

1938:    The Marines Are Here (J. Knapp)
1941:    In Old Colorado*; Border Vigilantes; Pirates
         on Horseback (E. LeBlanche); Doomed Caravan
         (J. McCulley); Wide Open Town (H. Jacobs);
         Riders of the Timberline; Twilight on the
         Trail*; Stick to Your Guns; Outllaws of the
         Desert (B. McConville)
1942:    Romance of the Range; Shadows on the Sage;
         Undercover Man; Pirates of the Prairie (D.
         Schroeder)
1943:    Fighting Frontier (N. Parker); King of the
         Cowboys (O. Cooper); The Man from Thunder
         River; Silver Spurs (J. Butler); Man from
         Music Mountain (B. Ropes)
1944:    Hands Across the Border (B. Ropes); The
         Laramie Trail; Mystery Man
1945:    Sing Me a Song of Texas (E. Beecher);
         Rockin' in the Rockies (J. Gray); Return of
         the Durango Kid; Rustlers of the Badlands;
         Blazing the Western Trail; Outlaws of the
         Rockies; Song of the Prairie; Renegade
         Roundup
1946:    Throw a Saddle on a Star; Under Arizona
         Skies; That Texas Jamboree; The Gentleman
         from Texas; Cowboy Blues; Under Nevada Skies
         (P. Gangelin); Singing on the Trail; Silver
         Range
1947:    Raiders of the South; Valley of Fear;
         Trailing Danger; Land of the Lawless; The
         Law Comes to Gunsight; Song of the
         Wasteland; Hoppy's Holiday*; Prairie Express
         (A. Coldeway); Gun Talk
1948:    Phantom Valley ; California Firebrand (J.
         Butler); Frontier Agent; Cowboy Cavalier (R.
         Davidson); Back Trail; Partners of the
         Sunset; Silver Trails; The Sheriff of
```

126

Medicine Bow; Strange Gamble*; Outlaw Brand;
Gunning for Justice; Hidden Danger (E.
Gibbons)
1949: Gun Runner; Law of the West; Trail's End;
Satan's Cradle
1950: Over the Border

CY CHERMAK

1959: The 4-D Man (T. Simonson)

SONIA CHERNUS

1976: The Outlaw Josey Wales (P. Kaufman)

STANLEY Z. CHERRY

1971: Bunny O'Hare (C. Johnson)

GEORGE CHESBRO

1975: The Man Who Would Not Die*

HAL E. CHESTER

1955: Crashout (L. Foster)
1958: Curse of the Demon (C. Bennett)

HECTOR CHEVIGNY

1942: You Can't Escape Forever (F. Niblo)

LUIGI CHIAVINI

1954: Indiscretion of an American Wife

ALICE CHILDRESS

1977: A Hero Ain't Nothin' But a Sandwich

C. C. CHIN

1936:   Desert Guns (J. Jaccard)

ROBERT C. CHIN

1976:   Panama Red

EDWARD CHODOROV (1904-   ) playwright

1933:   Captured; Mayor of Hell; The World Changes
        (S. Gibney)
1934:   Madame DuBarry
1936:   Craig's Wife; Snowed Under*
1938:   Spring Madness; Woman Against Woman; Yellow
        Jack
1946:   Undercurrent
1948:   Road House
1951:   Kind Lady*

JERRY CHODOROV (1911-   ) playwright

1935:   Case of the Lucky Legs*
1936:   Dancing Feet*
1937:   All over Town (J. Townley); Devil's
        Playground*; Reported Missing (J. Fields)
1938:   Rich Man, Poor Girl (J. Fields)
1939:   Conspiracy; The Mad Empress*
1940:   Dulcy*; Two Girls on Broadway (J. Fields)
1941:   Louisiana Purchase :(J. Fields)
1942:   My Sister Eileen (J. Fields)
1945:   Those Endearing Young Charms
1948:   The Man from Texas (J. Fields)
1957:   Oh Men! Oh Women! (N. Johnson)
1959:   Happy Anniversary (J. Fields)

TOMMY CHONG

1978:   Up in Smoke (Cheech Marin)
1980:   Cheech and Chong's Next Movie (Cheech Marin)
1981:   Cheech and Chong's Nice Dreams (Cheech
        Marin)
1982:   Things Are Tough All Over (C. Marin)

H. R. CHRISTIAN

1973:   Black Mama, White Mama
1974:   Act of Vengeance (B. Conklin)
1981:   King of the Mountain

FRANK & THERESA CHRISTINA

1971:   Billy Jack
1974:   The Trial of Billy Jack*

BLANCHE CHURCH

1936:   The Millionaire Kid (J. Natteford)

CLAIRE CHURCH

1935:   The Headline Woman (J. Natteford); $1,000 a
        Minute*

DOUGLAS W. CHURCHILL

1930:   Reno (H. Chandlee)

EDWARD CHURCHILL

1934:   Rocky Rhodes
1941:   Forced Landing (M. Shane); Power Dive (M.
        Shane)

ROBERT CHURCHILL

1946:   Lighthouse
1947:   West to Glory (E. Clifton); The Fighting
        Vigilantes; Born to Speed*

MATT CIMBER

1982:   Butterfly (J. Goff)

MICHAEL CIMINO (1943-   ) director

1972:   Silent Running*
1973:   Magnum Force (J. Milius)
1974:   Thunderbolt and Lightning
1978:   The Deer Hunter
1980:   Heaven's Gate (re-edited, 1981)

RENE CLAIR (1898-   ) director (Fr.)

(American films only)
1944:   It Happened Tomorrow (D. Nichols)

BARRY CLARK

1976:   Escape from Angola

BENJAMIN CLARK

1974:   Children Shouldn't Play with Dead Things

BOB CLARK

1982:   Porky's

BRIAN CLARK

1981:   Whose Life Is It Anyway? (Reginald Rose)

BRUCE CLARK

1971:   The Ski Bum (M. Siegler)
1981:   Galaxy of Terror (M. Siegler)

CHRIS CLARK

1972:   Lady Sings the Blues*

COLBERT CLARK

1931:   Lightning Warrior (ser.)*
1932:   The Last of the Mohicans (ser.)*; The Shadow
        of the Eagle (ser.)*; The Hurricane Express
        (ser.)*
1933:   Fighting with Kit Carson (ser.)*; Mystery
        Squadron (ser.)*; The Three Musketeers
        (ser.)*; The Whispering Shadow (ser.)*; The
        Wolf Dog (ser.)*
1934:   In Old Santa Fe (J. Gruen); Young and
        Beautiful*

DENNIS LYNTON CLARK

1978:   Comes a Horseman

FRANK CLARK

1929:   Pals of the Prairie (R. Tansey); The
        Fighting Marshal; Come and Get It; Freckled
        Rascal; Amazing Vagabond; Laughing at Death;
        The Little Savage
1930:   Shadow Ranch; The Utah Kid
1932:   The Fighting Fool; Wild Horse Mesa (H.
        Shumate); Rustler's Roundup (J. Cunningham);
        Tangled Fortunes
1936:   O'Malley of the Mounted (D. Jarrett); Two in
        Revolt*

GREYDON CLARK

1973:   Tom (A. Fast)
1975:   Psychic Killer*
1976:   Black Shampoo (A. Fast); The Bad Bunch (A.
        Fast)
1977:   Satan's Cheerleaders (A. Fast)
1978:   Hi-Riders
1980:   Angels Brigade (A. Fast

JANET CLARK

1953:   Hollywood Thrill Makers

RON CLARK

1976:   Silent Movie*; Norman...Is That You?*
1977:   High Anxiety*
1978:   Revenge of the Pink Panther*

DONALD HENDERSON CLARKE

1937:   Women Men Marry*
1943:   The Ghost Ship

SHIRLEY CLARKE   (1925-   ) director

1964:   The Cool World (Carl Lee)

T.E.B. CLARKE (1907-   ) Brit.

(American films only)
1966:   A Man Could Get Killed (R. Breen)

JAMES CLAVELL (1924-   ) director, producer
        (Austral.)

1958:   The Fly
1959:   Watusi; Five Gates to Hell
1960:   Walk Like a Dragon (G.Homes)
1962:   The Sweet and the Bitter (Can.)
1963:   The Great Escape (W. Burnett)
1964:   633 Squadron (H. Koch)
1965:   The Satan Bug (Edward Anhalt)
1967:   To Sir, with Love (Brit.)
1971:   The Last Valley (Brit.)

ELIZABETH CLAWSON

1929:   Sal of Singapore*; Flying Fool; High Voltage

ELLIOT CLAWSON

1929:   The Leatherneck; The 13th Chair; The Flying
        Fool (T. Garnett)

132

LEWIS CLAY

1942: The Valley of VanishingMen (ser.)*
1946: Son of the Guardsman (ser.)*
1947: The Vigilante (ser.)*; Brick Bradford
      (ser.)*; Jack Armstrong (ser.)*; The Sea
      Hound (ser.)*
1948: Tex Granger (ser.)*; Congo Bill (ser.)*;
      Superman (ser.)*
1949: Adventures of Sir Galahad (ser.)*; Bruce
      Gentry — Daredevil of the Skies (ser.)*
1950: Cody of the Pony Express (ser.)*
1951: Mysterious Island (ser.)*

MELVIN CLAY

1973: The Spook Who Sat by the Door (S. Greenlee)

JON CLEARY

1961: The Green Helmet
1975: Sidecar Racers

SCOTT E. CLEETHORPE

1935: Just My Luck (W. Sullivan)

BRIAN CLEMENS

1966: The Corrupt Ones
1971: See No Evil
1980: The Watcher in the Woods*

HAROLD CLEMENS

1968: The Counterfeit Killer (S. Bochco)
1969: Kenner (J. Loring)
1973: Lady Ice (A. Trustman)

RENE CLEMENT

1958:   This Angry Age (I. Shaw)

CALVIN CLEMENTS

1968:   Firecreek
1971:   The Wild Country (P. Savage)
1972:   Kansas City Bomber (T. Rickman)

COLIN CLEMENTS

1930:   Call of the West (F. Ryerson); Sweethearts
        on Parade

ROY CLEMENTS

1942:   Professor Creeps*

LARRY CLEMMONS

1941:   The Reluctant Dragon (anim.)*
1967:   The Jungle Book (anim.)*
1973:   Robin Hood (anim.)

VAL CLEVELAND

1929:   Wolves of the City

JAMES CLIFDEN

1946:   So Goes My Love (B. Manning)

DENISON CLIFT

1944:   Secrets of Scotland Yard; End of the Road
        (Gertrude Walker)

ELMER CLIFTON (1892-1949) director

1935:   Cyclone of the Saddle (G. Merrick); Pals of

                the Range (G. Merrick); Fighting Caballero
                (G. Merrick); Rough Riding Ranger (G.
                Merrick); Captured in Chinatown (A. Durlam)
1937:   Assassin of Youth (Charles Brown)
1938:   Wolves of the Sea; The Secret of Treasure
                Island (ser.)*
1941:   I'll Sell My Life (G. Rosener)
1942:   The Old Chisholm Trail; The Rangers Take
                Over
1943:   Bad Men of Thunder Gap; Cheyenne Roundup (B.
                McConville); Raiders of San Joaquin (M.
                Cox); The Return of the Rangers ; Frontier
                Law; Boss of Rawhide; Swing, Cowboy, Swing
1944:   Gunsmoke Mesa; Outlaw Roundup; Guns of the
                Law; The Pinto Bandit; Spook Town; Brand of
                the Devil; Gangsters of the Frontier; Seven
                Doors to Death; Teen Age
1945:   Marked for Murder; Three in the Saddle;
                Frontier Fugitives; Youth Aflame
1946:   Lightning Raiders; Ambush Trail; Outlaw of
                the Plains (F. Evans)
1947:   Rainbow over the Rockies; West to Glory (R.
                Churchill); Song of the Sierras (O. Drake)
1948:   Sunset Carson Rides Again; Quick on the
                Trigger
1949:   The Judge*
1950:   Red Rock Outlaw; The Kid from Gower Gulch;
                The Silver Bandit

EDDIE CLINE

1948:   Jiggs and Maggie in Court (B. Gerard); Jiggs
                and Maggie in Society (B. Gerard)
1949:   Jackpot Jitters (B. Gerard)

EDWARD CLINTON

1981:   Honky Tonk Freeway

HARRY CLORK

1935:   Diamond Jim*; His Night Out (D. Malloy);
                King Solomon of Broadway*; Mister Dynamite
                (D. Malloy); Princess O'Hara (D. Malloy);
                Remember Last Night*

                            135

1936:   Absolute Quiet; Flying Hostess*; The Man I
         Marry
1937:   New Faces of 1937*; Oh, Doctor (Brown
         Holmes); When's Your Birthday?*
1938:   Flirting with Fate*
1939:   Laughing It Off (L. Loeb)
1940:   And One Was Beautiful; The Captain Is a
         Lady; La Conga Nights*; Moon over Burma*
1941:   Down in San Diego (F. Spencer); Las Vegas
         Nights (E. Pagano); Whistling in the Dark*
1942:   Born to Sing (F. Spencer); Ship Ahoy
1944:   Broadway Rhythm (D. Kingsley)
1946:   The Mighty McGurk*; The Thrill of Brazil*
1948:   The Sainted Sisters
1950:   Tea for Two
1951:   Painting the Clouds with Sunshine (R.
         Kibbee)
1955:   Ma and Pa Kettle at Waikiki (E. Ullman)

ROBERT CLOUSE

1970:   Dreams of Glass
1973:   Happy Mother's Day — Love, George
1976:   The Ultimate Warrior
1978:   The Pack; The Amsterdam Kill (G. Teifer)
1980:   The Big Brawl
1981:   Force: Five

G. H. CLUTSAM

1936:   April Romance*

JOHN CLYMER

1929:   College Love (P. Coudere); The Love Trap;
         His Lucky Day
1930:   What Men Want
1931:   A House Divided (D. Van Every)
1933:   Emergency Call (J. Mankiewicz)

LEWIS COATES

1979:   Starcrash (Nat Wachsberger)

HUMPHREY COBB

1937: San Quentin (P. Milne)

IRWIN S. COBB

1953: The Sun Shines Bright (L. Stallings)

JONATHAN COBBLER

1977: The Lincoln Conspiracy

DORCAS COCHRAN

1941: Fighting Bill Cochran*; Swing It, Soldier
       (A. Jones)
1942: Juke Box Jenny*
1943: Swing Out the Blues
1944: Girl in the Case (J. Hoffman)
1946: Girl on the Spot (J. Warner); The Wife of
       Monte Cristo

NAN COCHRANE

1929: Girl on the Barge; It Can Be Done

FRANCIS COCKRELL

1932: Age of Consent (S. Mason); The Sports
       Parade*
1942: Lady in a Jam*
1951: The Family Secret (A. Solt); Rhubarb (D.
       Reid)
1953: Inferno
1956: On the Threshold of Space (S. Wincelberg)

MARION COCKRELL

1944: Dark Waters*

FRED COE (1914—1979) director, producer

1966:   This Property Is Condemned*

FRANKLIN COEN

1936:   'Til We Meet Again*
1937:   Living on Love; We're on the Jury
1938:   Exposed (C. Kaufman); Quick Money*
1939:   Forged Passport (L. Loeb)
1953:   The Glory Brigade
1954:   Johnny Dark
1955:   Chief Crazy Horse (G. Adams); Kiss of Fire
        (R. Collins); This Island Earth (E.
        O'Callaghan)
1957:   Interlude (D. Fuchs)
1959:   Night of the Quarter Moon (F. Davis)
1965:   The Train*
1966:   Alvarez Kelly (E. Arnold)
1972:   Black Gunn

LENORE J. COFFEE (1900—   )

1929:   Desert Nights
1930:   Bishop Murder Case; Mothers Cry
1931:   The Squaw Man (L. Hubbard); Possessed
1932:   Downstairs (M. Baker); Night Court (B.
        Veiller); Arsene Lupin*
1933:   Torch Singer (L. Starling)
1934:   All Men Are Enemies (S. Hoffenstein); Evelyn
        Prentice; Four Frightened People (B.
        Cormack); Such Women Are Dangerous*
1935:   Vanessa, Her Love Story (H. Walpole)
1936:   Suzy*
1938:   Four Daughters (J. Epstein); White Banners*
1940:   My Son, My Son; The Way of All Flesh
1941:   The Great Lie
1942:   The Gay Sisters
1943:   Old Acquaintance (J. Van Druten)
1944:   'Til We Meet Again; Marriage Is a Private
        Affair
1946:   Tomorrow Is Forever
1947:   Escape Me Never (T. Williamson)
1949:   Beyond the Forest
1951:   Lightning Strikes Twice
1952:   Sudden Fear (R. Smith)

1954:   Young at Heart (J. Epstein)
1955:   The End of the Affair (Brit.); Footsteps in
        the Fog (Brit.;D. Reid)
1959:   Cash McCall (M. Hargrove)

ALBERT J. COHEN

1935:   King Solomon of Broadway*; A Night at the
        Ritz*; Times Square Lady (R. Shannon)
1938:   Invisible Enemy (A. Gottlieb)
1948:   Let's Live a Little (J. Harvey)
1951:   The Lady Pays Off (F. Gill)
1965:   The Naked Brigade (A. Wolf)

BARNEY COHEN

1977:   Stunts (Dennis Johnson)
1978:   French Quarter (D. Kane)

BENNETT R. COHEN

1930:   The Fighting Legion (L. Mason); Mountain
        Justice; Song of the Caballero; Bar L Ranch
        (C. Krusada); Sons of the Saddle; Under
        Montana Skies (J. Aubrey); Parade of the
        West
1931:   West of Cheyenne (O. Drake); In Old
        Cheyenne; Law of the Rio Grande (B.
        Burbridge); Air Police
1932:   The Sunset Trail; Texas Gun-Fighter
1934:   Nevada Cyclone; Mystery Mountain (ser.; A.
        Schaefer); Rainbow Riders
1935:   Wilderness Mail (R. Dillon); Stormy (G.
        Plympton); Swifty; Skull and Crown (C.
        Krusada)
1936:   The Border Patrolman (D. Jarrett); Ambush
        Valley
1937:   Melody of the Plains; The Law Commands; Raw
        Timber (J. Neville); Wallaby Jim of the
        Islands (H. Branch)
1938:   South of Arizona; The Renegade Ranger; West
        of the Santa Fe; Female Fugitive (J.
        Neville);
1939:   Thundering West; North of the Yukon; Western
        Caravans; Riders of Black River

1940:   Pioneer Days; Ghost Valley Raiders; One
        Man's Law (J. Natteford); Frontier Vengeance
        (B. Shipman)
1941:   Wyoming Wildcat (A. Coldeway); Desert Bandit
        (E. Gibbons); Man from Montana
1942:   Bandit Ranger (M. Grant)
1943:   Sagebrush Law; Red River Robin Hood; False
        Colors; Riders of the Deadline
1944:   Trail to Gunsight (P. Harper)
1945:   Sheriff of Cimarron; Beyond the Pecos; Santa
        Fe Saddlemates; Lawless Empire
1946:   Frontier Gun Law
1947:   Six Gun Serenade; Hoppy's Holiday*; Robin
        Hood of Monerey; Ridin' Down the Trail; King
        of the Bandits (G. Roland)
1948:   Oklahoma Blues; Strange Gamble*

HERMAN COHEN

1958:   How to Make a Monster (K. Langtry)
1959:   Horrors of the Black Museum (A. Kandel)
1961:   Konga (Brit.; A. Kandel)
1963:   Black Zoo (A. Kandel)
1967:   Berserk (A. Kandel)
1974:   Craze (A. Kandel)

HOWARD R. COHEN

1972:   Unholy Rollers
1973:   The Young Nurses
1975:   Cover Girl Models
1978:   Vampire Hookers; Death Force
1981:   Saturday the 14th

LARRY COHEN

1966:   Return of the Seven; I Deal in Danger
1969:   Daddy's Gone A-Hunting (L. Semple)
1970:   El Condor (S. Carabatsos)
1972:   Bone
1973:   Black Caesar; Hell Up in Harlem
1974:   It's Alive
1976:   God Told Me To
1977:   Demon
1978:   The Private Files of J. Edgar Hoover; It

Lives Again
1980: The American Success Company (W. Richert)
1982: I, the Jury; Q: Quetzalcoatl (orig. Winged
Serpent)

LAWRENCE D. COHEN

1976: Carrie
1981: Ghost Story

LAWRENCE J. COHEN

1970: Start the Revolution Without Me (F. Freeman)
1974: S*P*Y*S* (F. Freeman)
1976: The Big Bus (F. Freeman)

LESTER COHEN

1933: One Man's Journey (S. Ornitz); Sweepings*
1934: Of Human Bondage

MARTIN B. COHEN

1970: Rebel Rousers*

RONALD M. COHEN

1968: Blue (Meade Roberts)
1969: The Good Guys and the Bad Guys (D. Shryack)
1977: Twilight's Last Gleaming (E. Huebsch)

ALFRED A. COHN (-1951) (also AL COHN)

1929: The Last Warning; Carnation Kid; Divorce
Made Easy
1930: Numbered Men
1931: Cisco Kid
1932: Mystery Ranch
1934: Harold Teen (P. Smith)

ART COHN (-1958)

1949:   The Set-Up
1951:   The Tall Target*; Tomorrow Is Another Day
        (G. Endore)
1952:   Carbine Williams; Glory Alley
1953:   Down Among the Sheltering Palms*; The Girl
        Who Had Everything
1954:   Men of the Fighting Lady; Tennessee Champ
1957:   Ten Thousand Bedrooms*
1958:   The Seven Hills of Rome

BEN COHN

1933:   The Three Musketeers (ser.)*

BRUCE COHN

1978:   Good Guys Wear Black (M. Medoff)

RALPH COHN

1947:   The Adventures of Don Coyote*

HARLEY COKLISS

1982:   Warlords of the 21st Century*

ANTHONY COLDEWAY

1928:   Glorious Betsy
1929:   Noah's Ark; Greyhound Limited; Frozen River
1934:   Cross Streets
1935:   In Spite of Danger; Men of the Hour
1936:   Trailin' West
1937:   Draegerman Courage; Over the Goal (W.
        Jacobs); White Bondage
1938:   Accidents Will Happen (G. Bricker); When
        Were You Born?
1939:   Smashing the Money Ring (R. Schrock)
1940:   The Tulsa Kid (O. Drake); Under Texas Skies
        (B. Burbridge); Texas Terrors (D. Schroeder)
1941:   Wyoming Wildcat (B. Cohen); The Nurse's
        Secret; Shadows on the Stairs

1942: Busses Roar (G. Bilson); The Gorilla Man;
       The Hidden Hand; Lady Gangster
1943: Calling Wild Bill Elliot; Death Valley
       Manhunt (N. Hall); The West Side Kid (A.
       Beich); A Scream in the Dark (G. Schnitzer)
1944: Tucson Raiders; Marshal of Reno; Code of the
       Prairie (A. DeMond); Vigilantes of Dodge
       City (N. Hall)
1947: Prairie Express (J. Cheney)

LESTER COLE (1904-   )

1932: If I Had a Million*
1933: Charlie Chan's Greatest Case (M. Orth)
1934: Pursued (S. Anthony); Sleepers East; Wild
       Gold (H. Johnson)
1935: Hitch Hike Lady (G. Rigby); Too Tough to
       Kill (G. Jay); Under Pressure*
1936: Follow Your Heart*; The President's Mystery
       (N. West)
1937: The Affairs of Cappy Ricks; The Man in Blue;
       Some Blondes Are Dangerous
1938: The "Crime" of Dr. Hallet (Brown Holmes);
       The Jury's Secret (N. Levy); Midnight
       Intruder (G. Waggner); Secrets of a Nurse
       (T. Lennon); Sinners in Paradise*
1939: Winter Carnival*
1940: The Big Guy; The House of Seven Gables; The
       Invisible Man Returns (C. Siodmak)
1941: Among the Living (G. Fort); Footsteps in the
       Dark (J. Wexley); Midnight Angel (W.
       Lipscomb)
1942: Pacific Blackout (W. Lipscomb)
1943: Hostages (F. Butler); Night Plane from
       Chungking*
1944: None Shall Escape
1945: Blood on the Sun; Objective Burma (R.
       MacDougall)
1947: Fiesta (G. Bruce); The High Wall (S. Boehm);
       The Romance of Rosy Ridge
1965: Born Free (Brit.)

ROYAL K. COLE

1943: Captain America (ser.)*; The Masked Marvel
       (ser.)*; Secret Service in Darkest Africa

```
               (ser.)*
1944:    The Black Arrow (ser.)*; Haunted Harbor
         (ser.)*; The Tiger Woman (ser.)*
1945:    The Monster and the Ape (ser.)*; The Purple
         Monster Strikes (ser.)*
1947:    Blackmail; Exposed (C. Moran); Jack
         Armstrong (ser.)*
1948:    Tex Granger (ser.)*; Superman (ser.)*
1949:    Ghost of Zorro (ser.)*; Batman and Robin
         (ser.)*; Federal Agents vs. Underworld, Inc.
         (ser.)*; King of the Rocket Men (ser.)*
1950:    The James Brothers of Missouri (ser.)*;
         Radar Patrol vs. Spy King (ser.)*
1951:    Capt. Video (ser.)*; Gunfighters of the
         Northwest (ser.)*; Mysterious Island; Roar
         of the Iron Horse (ser.)*
1952:    Blackhawk (ser.)*; Son of Geronimo (ser.)*;
         King of the Congo (ser.)*
```

BILL COLEMAN

1966:   Secret Agent Super Dragon

CARYL COLEMAN

1946:   Don't Gamble with Strangers (H. Gates); Wife
         Wanted (S. Sutherland)

PATRICIA COLEMAN

1943:   Above Suspicion*
1944:   Blonde Fever

CONSTANCE COLLIER

1935:   Peter Ibbetson*

JAMES F. COLLIER

1966:   For Pete's Sake

JOHN COLLIER

```
1935:   Sylvia Scarlett*
1942:   Her Cardboard Lover*
1946:   Deception (J. Than)
1949:   Roseanna McCoy
1953:   The Story of Three Loves*
1954:   I Am a Camera (Brit.)
1965:   The War Lord (M. Kaufman)
```

WILLIAM COLLIER, SR.

```
1929:   Harmony at Home
```

PIERRE COLLINGS

```
1929:   The Hole in the Wall
1930:   Animal Crackers (M Ryskind); Dangerous Nan
        McGrew (P. Smith)
1934:   British Agent (L. Doyle)
1935:   Story of Louis Pasteur (S. Gibney)
```

GUNTHER COLLINS

```
1971:   Judd
```

HAL COLLINS

```
1946:   Freddie Steps Out; High School Hero (A.
        Dreifuss); Junior Prom (E. Lazarus)
1947:   Sarge Goes to College; Vacation Days
1948:   Campus Sleuth
1967:   The Love-Ins (A. Dreifuss)
1968:   For Singles Only (A. Dreifuss)
```

LEWIS D. COLLINS (1899-1954) director

```
1930:   The Devil's Pit
1933:   Via Pony Express (O. Drake); Gun Law (O.
        Drake); Trouble Busters (O. Drake
1947:   Heading for Heaven (O. Mugge)
```

MONTY F. COLLINS

```
1946:   Tangier (M. Musselman)
1949:   The Green Promise
```

RICHARD COLLINS (1914-   )

```
1939:   Rulers of the Sea*
1940:   One Crowded Night (A. d'Usseau)
1941:   Lady Scarface (A. d'Usseau)
1943:   Song of Russia (P. Jarrico); Thousands Cheer
        (P. Jarrico)
1953:   China Venture (G. Yates)
1954:   Riot in Cell Block 11; The Adventures of
        Hajji Baba; The Bob Mathius Story
1955:   Cult of the Cobra*; Kiss of Fire (F. Coen)
1957:   My Gun Is Quick (R. Powell)
1958:   Spanish Affair; The Badlanders
1959:   Edge of Eternity (K. Swenson)
1960:   Pay or Die
```

ROBERT COLLINS

```
1981:   Savage Harvest (R. Blees)
```

JANICE COLSON-DODGE

```
1977:   The Farmer*
```

JOHN COLTON

```
1930:   Rogue Song*
1934:   Laughing Boy (J. Mahin)
1935:   The Werewolf of London
1936:   The Invisible Ray
```

ADELE COMANDINI

```
1929:   The Girl from Woolworth's
1930:   Playing Around; Love Racket (J. Goodrich)
1934:   A Girl of the Limberlost; Jane Eyre
1936:   The Country Beyond (L. Trotti)
1937:   Three Smart Girls (A. Parker)
1938:   The Road to Reno (r. Chanslor)
```

```
1940:   Beyond Tomorrow; Her First Romance
1942:   Always in My Heart
1943:   Good Luck, Mr. Yates (L. Breslow)
1945:   Christmas in Connecticut (L. Houser); Danger
        Signal (G. Baker); Strange Illusion
```

CY COMBERS

```
1952:   Bloodhounds of Broadway
```

BETTY COMDEN (1919-   ) playwright

```
1947:   Good News (Adolph Green)
1949:   The Barkleys of Broadway (Adolph Green); On
        the Town (Adolph Green)
1952:   Singin' in the Rain (Adolph Green)
1953:   The Band Wagon (Adolph Green)
1955:   It's Always Fair Weather (Adolph Green)
1958:   Auntie Mame (Adolph Green)
1960:   Bells Are Ringing (Adolph Green)
1964:   What a Way to Go! (Adolph Green)
```

LOU COMICI

```
1979:   The Visitor (R. Bundy)
```

DAVID COMMONS

```
1969:   The Angry Breed
```

RICHARD COMPTON

```
1974:   Macon County Line (M. Baer)
1975:   Return to Macon County
```

S. COMPTON

```
1979:   Cocaine Cowboys*
```

CHARLES R. CONDON

```
1928:   Caught in the Fog
```

```
1929:   Joy Street (F. Fay); Red Wine
1930:   Brothers (A. Hoerl)
1932:   Get That Girl; Speed Madness
1933:   Soldiers of the Storm; Speed Demon
1937:   Galloping Dynamite*; Death in the Air; Sing
        While You're Able (S. Lowe)
1940:   Winners of the West (ser.)*
1941:   The Iron Claw (ser.)*
```

AL CONDREY

```
1974:   Blood Couple (H. Parker)
```

BETTY CONKLIN

```
1974:   Act of Vengeance (H. Christian)
```

FRANK ROLAND CONKLIN

```
1931:   Mad Parade*
```

HAROLD CONKLIN

```
1928:   The Spieler (T. Garnett)
```

CHRIS CONKLING

```
1978:   The Lord of the Rings (anim.; P. Beagle)
```

CASEY CONLON

```
1977:   Guardian of the Wilderness
```

HARRY CONN

```
1935:   Broadway Melody of 1936*
```

BARBARA CONNELL

```
1971:   Make a Face (K. Sperling)
```

JACK CONNELL

1941:   Riders of Death Valley (ser.)*

RICHARD CONNELL (1893-1949)

1936:   The Milky Way*; Our Relations*
1938:   Dr. Rhythm (J. Swerling); Love on Toast*
1940:   Hired Wife (G. Lehman)
1941:   Nice Girl? (G. Lehman)
1942:   Rio Rita (G. Lehman)
1943   Presenting Lily Mars (G. Lehman)
1944:   Two Girls and a Sailor (G. Lehman)
1945:   Her Highness and the Bellboy (G. Lehman);
        Thrill of a Romance (G. Lehman)
1946:   The Kid from Brooklyn*
1948:   Luxury Liner (G. Lehman)

JOE CONNELLY

1966:   Munster, Go Home*

MARC CONNELLY (1890-   ) playwright

1933:   Cradle Song*
1936:   The Green Pastures (S. Gibney)
1937:   The Good Earth*; Captains Courageous*
1942:   I Married a Witch (R. Pirosh); Reunion in
        France*
1956:   Crowded Paradise

MYLES CONNOLLY

1938:   Wives Under Suspicion; Youth Takes a Fling
1941:   Tarzan's Secret Treasure (P.Gangelin)
1942:   Between Us Girls (T. Boardman); Tarzan's New
        York Adventure (W. Lipman)
1944:   Music for Millions
1946:   Till the Clouds Roll By*; Two Sisters from
        Boston
1947:   The Unfinished Dance
1948:   State of the Union (A. Veiller)

149

1951:   Here Comes the Groom*
1952:   My Son John (L.McCarey)

BARRY CONNORS (-1933)

1931:   Black Camel*; Charlie Chan Carries On (P.
        Klein); Riders of the Purple Sage*; The
        Spider (P. Klein); Women of All Nations
1932:   Rainbow Trail (P. Klein); The Gay Caballero
        (P. Klein); Bachelor's Affairs (P. Klein);
        Chandu the Magician (P. Klein); Charlie
        Chan's Chance (P. Klein); Hat Check Girl (P.
        Klein); Too Busy to Work (P. Klein); Trial
        of Vivienne Ware (P. Klein)
1933:   Hot Pepper (P. Klein); Pilgrimage (P. Klein)

EUGENE CONRAD

1941:   Niagara Falls*; Miss Polly (E. Seabrook)
1942:   About Face (E.Seabrook); Fall In (E.
        Seabrook); Yanks Ahoy (E. Seabrook); Hay
        Foot (E. Seabrook)
1943:   Moonlight in Vermont; Moonlight and Cactus
        (P. G. Smith)
1944:   Pardon My Rhythm (V. Burton); The Singing
        Sheriff (H. Blankford); Hi, Good Lookin'*;
        Sing a Jingle; Chip Off the Old Block (L.
        Townsend); Babes on Swing Street (H.
        Dimsdale); My Gal Loves Music
1947:   Gas House Kids Go West*; Love and Learn*;
        Philo Vance's Gamble (A. St. Claire)
1948:   The Cobra Strikes

MIKEL CONRAD

1950:   The Flying Saucer

BOB CONSIDINE

1948:   The Babe Ruth Story (G. Callahan)
1952:   Hoodlum Empire (B.Manning)

JOHN CONSIDINE

1978: A Wedding*

JOHN W. CONSIDINE, JR. (1898-   ) producer

1930: Puttin' on the Ritz*

RALPH CONSUMANA

1934: The Lone Bandit
1935: The Fighting Pilot

JAMES CONWAY

1976: In Search of Noah's Ark (doc.; C. Seller)

PHILIP CONWAY

1937: Fury and the Woman

RICHARD S. CONWAY

1947: Yankee Fakir
1950: Once a Thief

TIM CONWAY

1978: The Billion Dollar Hobo*; They Went
       That-a-way and That-a-way
1979: The Prize Fighter (J. Myers)
1980: The Private Eyes (J. Myers)

T.S. COOK

1979: The China Syndrome*

WHITFIELD COOK

1945: The Sailor Takes a Wife*
1946: The Secret Heart (A. Chapin)

151

1947: High Barbaree*
1948: The Big City (A. Chapin)
1950: Stage Fright (Brit.; A. Reville)

VIRGINIA COOKE

1948: Shed No Tears (Brown Holmes)
1961: Tomboy and the Champ

SPADE COOLEY

1950: I Shot Billy the Kid*

CARL COOLIDGE

1932: The Last Frontier*

GENE L. COON

1957: The Girl in the Kremlin (Robert Hill); Man
       in the Shadow
1959: No Name on the Bullet
1963: The Raiders
1964: The Killers
1967: First to Fight
1968: Journey to Shiloh

JOHN COONAN

1949: Song of Surrender

C. C. COONS

1941: Riot Squad

CHRIS COOPER

1958: Step Down to Terror*

DENNIS COOPER

1944:   When Strangers Marry (P. Yordan)
1945:   The Woman Who Came Back (L. Willis)
1946:   Fear (A. Zeisler); Sensation Hunters
1949:   City Across the River (M. Shane)

DOROTHY COOPER

1948:   A Date with Judy (D. Kingsley); On an Island
        with You*
1950:   Duchess of Idaho (Jerry Davis)
1951:   Rich, Young and Pretty (S. Sheldon)
1953:   Small Town Girl (D. Kingsley)
1957:   Let's Be Happy
1958:   Flood Tide

IRVING COOPER

1960:   Jet over the Atlantic

JACK COOPER

1982:   Goin' All the Way (R. Stone)

MERIAN C. COOPER (1893–1973) director, producer

1933:   King Kong*

OLIVE COOPER

1935:   Confidential (W. Totman); Hot Tip (H.
        Cummings)
1936:   Dancing Feet*; Happy Go Lucky (R. Schrock);
        Hearts in Bondage (B. Schubert); Laughing
        Irish Eyes*; Navy Born*; The Return of Jimmy
        Valentine (J. Natteford)
1937:   Jim Hanvey – Detective (J. Krumgold); Join
        the Marines (J. Krumgold); Lady Behave (J.
        Krumgold); Rhythm in the Clouds
1938:   Annabel Takes a Tour (B. Granet); Cocoanut
        Grove (S. Bartlett); Orphans of the Street*
1939:   The Mysterious Miss X; She Married a Cop
1940:   Young Bill Hickok (N. Parker); The Border

Legion (Louis Stevens)
1941: Robin Hood of the Pecos; In Old Cheyenne;
      The Singing Hills; Sheriff of Tombstone;
      Down Mexico Way; The Great Train Robbery*;
      Ice-Capades*
1942: Cowboy Serenade; Call of the Canyon; Affairs
      of Jimmy Valentine (R. Tasker)
1943: King of the Cowboys (J. Cheney); Idaho (R.
      Chanslor); Nobody's Darling; Shantytown
1944: Song of Nevada (G. Kahn); My Best Gal (F.
      Fenton); Three Little Sisters
1945: Swingin' on a Rainbow (J. Grey)
1946: Sioux City Sue; The Bamboo Blonde (L.
      Kimble)
1949: The Big Sombrero; Outcasts of the Trail;
      Bandit King of Texas
1950: Hills of Oklahoma (V. Arthur)

RALPH COOPER

1937: Bargain with Bullets (P. Dunham)
1938: Gang Smasher (alt. Gun Moll)
1939: Gang War
1940: Mr. Smith Goes Ghost

WILLIS COOPER

1937: Thank You, Mr. Moto (N. Foster)
1938: Mr. Moto Takes a Chance*
1939: Son of Frankenstein

WYATT COOPER

1962: The Chapman Report (D. Mankiewicz)

JACK L. COPELAND

1958: Hell's Five Hours

ALEC COPPEL

1947: Pacific Adventure (J. Chandler)
1949: The Hidden Room (Brit.; ret. Obsession)

154

```
1951:   No Highway in the Sky (Brit.)*
1953:   The Captain's Paradise (Brit.)
1954:   Hell Below Zero (M. Trell); The Black Knight
1958:   Vertigo (S. Taylor); Appointment with a
        Shadow (N. Jolley)
1968:   The Bliss of Mrs. Blossom (D. Norden)
1971:   The Statue (D. Norden)
```

LEWIS COPPLEY

```
1961:   Operation Eichmann
```

FRANCIS FORD COPPOLA (1939-   ) director

```
1963:   Dementia 13
1966:   This Property Is Condemned*; Is Paris
        Burning?*
1967:   You're a Big Boy Now
1969:   The Rain People
1970:   Patton (E. North)
1972:   The Godfather (M. Puzo)
1974:   The Great Gatsby; The Conversation; The
        Godfather, Part II (M. Puzo)
1979:   Apocalype Now (J. Milius)
1982:   One from the Heart (A. Bernstein); Tonight
        for Sure
```

CECILE CORBY

```
1941:   Twilight on the Trail*
```

GEORGE COREY

```
1944:   Mr.Winkle Goes to War*
```

BARTLETT CORMACK

```
1929:   Gentlemen of the Press:  Greene Murder Case;
        Woman Trap; The Laughing Lady
1930:   The Spoilers;  Benson Murder Case
1931:   The Front Page; Kick In,
1932:   Is My Face Red? (C. Robinson); The Phantom
        of Crestwood*; 13 Women; The Half-Naked
```

```
           Truth (C. Ford)
1933:  This Day and Age
1934:  Cleopatra*; Four Frightened People (L.
       Coffee); The Trumpet Blows (W. Smith)
1935:  Orchids to You*
1936:  Fury (F. Lang)
1938:  The Beachcomber (Brit.)
1941:  Unholy Partners*
```

GENE CORMAN

```
1960:  The Secret of the Purple Reef (H. Yablonsky)
```

GERALD CORMIER

```
1976:  Barn of the Naked Dead
```

HARRY CORNER

```
1974:  Savage Sisters (H. Moon)
```

HUBERT CORNFIELD (1929-   ) director

```
1960:  The Third Voice
1962:  Pressure Point (S. Pogostin)
1969:  The Night of the Following Day
1976:  Les Grands Moyens (Fr.)*
```

HAROLD CORNSWEET

```
1975:  Return to Campus
```

LLOYD CORRIGAN (1900-1969) actor, director

```
1929:  The Mysterious Dr. Fu Manchu; Saturday Night
       Kid; Sweetie
1930:  Anybody's War; The Return of Dr. Fu Manchu;
       Follow Thru
1931:  Dude Ranch*; Daughter of the Dragon*;
       Lawyer's Secret (Max Marcin)
1937:  Hold 'Em Navy (E. Gelsey)
1938:  Campus Confessions (E. Gelsey); Touchdown,
```

```
        Army (E. Gelsey)
1939:   Night Work*


JOHN CORRINGTON

1971:   Von Richthofen and Brown (Joyce Corrington)
1972:   Boxcar Bertha (Joyce Corrington)
1973:   Battle for the Planet of the Apes (Joyce
        Corrington)
1974:   The Arena (Joyce Corrington)


JOYCE H. CORRINGTON

1971:   The Omega Man (J. Williams); Von Richtofen
        and Brown (John Corrington)
1972:   Boxcar Bertha (John Corrington)
1973:   Battle for the Planet of the Apes (John
        Corrington)
1974:   The Arena (John Corrington)


WILL CORRY

1971:   Two Lane Blacktop (R. Wurlitzer)


HARVEY CORT

1963:   The Great Chase (doc.)*


NORMAN CORWIN (1910-     ) playwright, novelist

1943:   Forever and a Day*
1951:   The Blue Veil
1956:   Lust for Life; No Place to Hide
1959:   The Naked Maja
1960:   The Story of Ruth
1962:   Madison Avenue


STAN CORWYN

1970:   The Phynx
```

DON COSCARELLI

1976: Jim -- The World's Greatest (C. Mitchell);
      Kenny & Co.
1979: Phantasm
1982: The Beastmaster (P. Pepperman)

ROBERT JAMES COSGRIFF

1937: Roaring Timber (P. Franklin)

JOSEPH COTTEN (1905-   ) actor

1942: Journey into Fear (O. Welles)

BILL COTTRELL

1941: The Reluctant Dragon (anim.)*

PIERRE COUDERE

1929: College Love (J. Clymer)

JACK C. COUFFER

1956: Running Target*

JARVIS COULARD

1949: Prejudice*

WILLIAM COUNSELMAN (-1940)

1930: Way of All Men; Love Among the Millionaires;
      Whoopee!
1931: Not Exactly Gentlemen (D. Nichols); A
      Connecticut Yankee; Plutocrat; Six Cylinder
      Love (N. Houston); Young Sinners
1932: Business and Pleasure (G. Towne); Stepping
      Sisters; Week-Ends Only; Young America
1933: Arizona to Broadway (H. Johnson); The Mad

Game (H. Johnson)
1934:   Frontier Marshal (S. Anthony); Bright Eyes;
        Handy Andy*; I Believed in You; Love Time*;
        Orient Express*; She Learned About Sailors;
        365 Nights in Hollywood (H. Johnson)
1935:   Doubting Thomas; The Little Colonel
1936:   Pigskin Parade*; Private Number (G. Markey);
        Stowaway*
1937:   Fifty Roads to Town (G. Marion); The Great
        Hospital Mystery*; On the Avenue (G.
        Markey); That I May Live (B. Markson)
1939:   East Side of Heaven; Smiling Along (Brit.);
        That's Right, You're Wrong (J. Kern)
1940:   If I Had My Way*; So This Is London (Brit.);
        Yesterday's Heroes (I. Cummings
1941:   Last of the Duanes (I. Cummings); Ride,
        Kelly, Ride (I. Cummings)
1942:   Lone Star Ranger*

SADA COWAN

1934:   Woman in the Dark*
1936:   Forbidden Heaven
1939:   Stop, Look and Love (H. Tarshis)

AL COWLES

1929:   Unmasked

MORGAN B. COX

1936:   Robinson Crusoe of Clipper Island (ser.)*
1937:   Zorro Rides Again (ser.)*
1938:   Arsene Lupin Returns*
1939:   Overland with Kit Carson (ser.)*; Zorro's
        Fighting Legion (ser.)*
1940:   Deadwood Dick (ser.)*; Drums of Fu Manchu
        (ser.)*; The Green Archer (ser.)*
1941:   White Eagle (ser.)*; Road Agent (ret. Texas
        Road Agent; A. Strawn); Desperate Cargo (J.
        Coyle)
1942:   Gang Busters (ser.)*
1943:   Raiders of San Joaquin (E. Clifton);
        Frontier Badman (G. Geraghty); Adventures of
        Flying Cadets (ser.)*; Adventures of Smilin'

```
               Jack (ser.); The Phantom (ser.)*
1944:   Raiders of Ghost City (ser.; L. Ward)
1945:   Jungle Queen (ser.)*


WILLIAM COX

1953:   Veils of Bagdad


GEORGE HARMON COXE

1945:   The Hidden Eye (H. Ruskin)


ELLEN COYLE

1946:   Ghost of Hidden Valley; Overland Riders


JOHN T. COYLE

1941:   Desperate Cargo (M. Cox)
1942:   The Miracle Kid*


PAUL CRABTREE

1966:   Johnny Tiger (R. J. Hugh)


ANDREW CRADDOCK

1967:   Fort Utah (S. Fisher)


HARRY A. L. CRAIG

1968:   Anzio
1981:   Lion of the Desert


HARRY CRANE

1943:   Air Raid Wardens*
1944:   Lost in a Harem*
```

JOSEPH L. CRANSTON

1972:   The Corpse Grinders (A. Hall)

FRANK CRAVEN (1875-1945) actor, playwright

1932:   Handle with Care (S. Mintz)
1934:   The Human Side (E. Pascal); Sons of the
        Desert (B. Morgan); That's Gratitude
1935:   Annapolis Farewell*
1940:   Our Town*

WES CRAVEN

1982:   Swamp Thing

JOANNA CRAWFORD

1969:   My Side of the Mountain*
1972:   The Little Ark
1976:   Birch Interval

JOHN CRAWFORD

1970:   The Ballad of Cable Hogue (E. Penney)

NANCY VOYLES CRAWFORD

1977:   Sidewinder One (T. McMahon)
1978:   Caravans*

OLIVER CRAWFORD

1954:   The Steel Cage*
1958:   Girl in the Woods (M. Klauber)

WAYNE CRAWFORD

1975:   God's Bloody Acre (R. Woodburn)
1979:   Barracuda

TONY CRECHALES

1975:   Impulse
1980:   The Attic (G. Edwards)

JAMES ASHMORE CREELMAN

1929:   The Last Performance; The Vagabond Lover
1930:   Danger Lights; Half Shot at Sunrise
1931:   Honor of the Family
1932:   The Most Dangerous Game
1933:   King Kong*
1934:   Social Register*
1935:   East of Java (P. Perez)

JOHN CRESSWELL

1956:   Port Afrique (F. Partos)
1957:   Cast a Dark Shadow

MICHAEL CRICHTON (1942-   ) director, novelist

1973:   Westworld; Extreme Close-Up
1978:   Coma
1979:   The Great Train Robbery
1981:   Looker

HARRY P. CRIST (see HARRY FRASER)

JIM CRITCHFIELD

1964   The Nasty Rabbit (ret. Spies a Go-Go; A.
       Hall)

JORDAN CRITTENDEN

1972:   Get to Know Your Rabbit

TOM CRIZER

1932: My Pal, the King (J. Natteford)

EMERSON CROCKER

1952: The Treasure of Lost Canyon (B. Duffield)

DAVID CRONENBERG

1976: They Came from Within
1981: Scaners

ISAAC CRONIN

1982: Chan Is Missing*

BEVERLY CROSS

1963: The Long Ships (B. Mather)
1965: Genghis Khan (C. Reynolds)
1977: Sinbad and the Eye of the Tiger
1981: Clash of the Titans

H. B. CROSS

1958: Country Music Holiday
1961: Teenage Millionaire
1974: Chosen Survivors (J. Moffley)

HENRY CROSS

1962: Air Patrol; Young Guns of Texas
1963: Harbor Lights
1964: The Earth Dies Screaming (Brit.); Night
       Train to Paris (Brit.)

E. B. CROSSWHITE

1934: Murder in the Museum

RACHEL CROTHERS

1935:   Splendor

RUSSELL CROUSE

1937:   Mountain Music*
1938:   Artists and Models Abroad*
1939:   The Great Victor Herbert (R. Lively)

CAMERON CROWE

1982:   Fast Times at Ridgemont High

MARTIN CROWLEY

1970:   The Boys in the Band

WILLIAM X. CROWLEY

1942:   Professor Creeps*
1943:   What a Man (B. Sachs); Spotlight Scandals
        (B. Sachs)
1944:   Follow the Leader (B. Sachs)

JOHN CROWTHER

1981:   Kill and Kill Again

HOMER CROY

1936:   The Harvester*

OWEN CRUMP

1956:   The Amazon Trader
1958:   Manhunt in the Jungle (S. Merwin)

GARY CRUTCHER

1968:   The Name of the Game Is Kill

1973: Stanley

ROBERT RILEY CRUTCHER

1942: Girl Trouble (L. Fodor)
1950: Key to the City

JACK CRUTHER

1952: Here Come the Marines*; No Holds Barred
1953: Jalopy (T. Ryan)

SID CULLER

1940: Melody Ranch*

DWIGHT CUMMINGS

1929: The River; True Heaven
1945: Thunderhead, Son of Flicka (D. Yost)
1946: Smoky*
1948: The Strawberry Roan (D. Yost)
1949: Loaded Pistols (D. Yost); The Cowboy and the
       Indians (D. Yost)

HUGH CUMMINGS

1930: Pardon My Gun
1934: The Big Race
1935: Hot Tip (O. Cooper)
1936: Earthworm Tractors*; Polo Joe (P. Milne)
1937: Penrod and Sam (L. Hayward)
1938: Penrod and His Twin Brother (W. Jacobs)

IRVING CUMMINGS, JR.

1940: Yesterday's Heroes (W. Counselman)
1941: Last of the Duanes (W. Counselman); Ride,
       Kelly, Ride (W. Counselman)
1942: Lone Star Ranger*
1943: He Hired the Boss (B. Markson)

1946:   Dangerous Millions (R. North); Deadline for
        Murder
1947:   Jewels of Brandenburg*

RUTH CUMMINGS

1931:   Daybreak (Z. Sears)
1934:   By Candlelight*

RICHARD CUNHA

1958:   The Demons (H.E. Barrie)
1961:   The Girl in Room 13 (H.E. Barrie)

ANN CUNNINGHAM

1934:   Sequoia*

JACK CUNNINGHAM

1931:   The Deceiver*; Guilty Generation; Shanghaied
        Love (R. Chanslor)
1932:   The Rider of Death Vally; Texas Bad Man; The
        Fourth Horseman; Flaming Guns
1933:   Terror Trail; The Thundering Herd (M.
        Flannery); Silent Men*; Rustler's Roundup
        (F. Clark); Under the Tonto Rim (G.
        Geraghty); Sunset Pass (G. Geraghty); Man of
        the Forest (H. Shumate); To the Last Man
1934:   The Last Roundup; Wagon Wheels*; Double Door
        (G. Lehman); It's a Gift; The Old Fashioned
        Way (G. Weston); Pursuit of Happiness*
1935:   Mississippi*
1939:   Union Pacific*

JOSEPH CUNNINGHAM

1934:   Call It Luck*

TIM CURNEN

1982:   Forbidden World

CHARLES CURRAN

1939:   Adventures of Jane Arden*

VICTOR CURRIER

1928:   Perfect Crime

VALERIE CURTIN

1979:   ...And Justice for All (B. Levinson)
1980:   Inside Moves (B. Levinson)
1982:   Best Friends (B. Levinson)

DAN CURTIS

1976:   Burnt Offerings (W. Nolan)

JACK CURTIS

1930:   The Cheyenne Kid

JAMES CURTIS

1941:   Missing Ten Days (J. Meehan)

NATHANIEL CURTIS

1946:   The Harvey Girls*
1948:   The Time of Your Life
1950:   Please Believe Me
1952:   Jack and the Beanstalk

RAY CURTIS

1930:   The Great Divide*

RON CUTLER

1974:   Willie Dynamite

JOHN CUTTING

1940:   Deadwood Dick (ser.)*; The Green Archer
        (ser.)*
1941:   White Eagle (ser.)*

D

RENEE DAALDER

1976:   Massacre at Central High

DON DaGRADI

1955:   The Lady and the Tramp (anim.)*
1964:   Mary Poppins (Bill Walsh)
1966:   Lt. Robin Crusoe, U.S.N. (Bill Walsh)
1968:   Blackbeard's Ghost (Bill Walsh)
1969:   The Love Bug (Bill Walsh)
1971:   Scandalous John (Bill Walsh); Bedknobs and
        Broomsticks (Bill Walsh)

ROALD DAHL (1916-   ) short story writer Brit.

1971:   Willy Wonka and the Chocolate Factory

DAVID DALIE

1955:   The Living Swamp (doc.)
1971:   The Tender Warrior (S. Raffill)

ARTHUR DALES

1958:   The Sheriff of Fractured Jaw

WALTER DALLENBACH

1975:   An Eye for an Eye
1976:   Las Vegas Lady

HERBERT DALMAS

1938: Flash Gordon's Trip to Mars (ser.)*
1941: Pals of the Pecos (O. Drake); Saddlemates
(A. DeMond)
1942: North of the Rockies
1944: Address Unknown; An American Romance (M.
Ludwig)
1947: Last of the Redmen (G. Plympton)
1956: Star of India

JOHN DALY

1979: Sunburn*

BARBARA DANA

1981: Chu Chu and the Philly Flash

BILL DANA

1980: The Nude Bomb*

NED DANDY

1939: Overland with Kit Carson (ser.)*; Mandrake,
the Magician (ser.)*
1940: The Shadow (ser.)*
1942: Tramp, Tramp, Tramp (H. Sauber)
1949: Trouble at Melody Mesa

ALBERT D'ANNIABLE

1960: Jazz on a Summer's Day (doc.; A. Peri)

CLEMENCE DANE (Brit.)

(American films only)
1935: Anna Karenina*
1936: The Amateur Gentleman

TAD DANIELEWSKI

1962: The Big Wave (Jap.; P. Buck)
1965: The Guide (P. Buck)

GEORGE DANIELS

1951: Blazing Bullets

MONJA DANISCHEWSKY

1965: Mister Moses (C. Beaumont)

HERBERT DANSKA

1967: Sweet Love, Bitter (L. Jacobs)

RAY DANTON (1931-   ) actor

1975: Psychic Killer*

RICHARD C. DANUS

1980: Xanadu*

JOE DARION

1971: Shinbone Alley (anim.)

GRETCHEN DARLING

1949: Mississippi Rhythm

KENNETH DARLING

1962: Stagecoach to Dancer's Rock

W. SCOTT DARLING

1929:	Noisy Neighbors; Trent's Last Case (B.M. Dix)
1930:	Borrowed Wives
1931:	The Pocatello Kid; Caught Cheating; Murder at Midnight (F. Strayer); The Night Beat; Soul of the Slums
1932:	Dragnet Patrol; Gold
1935:	The Church Mouse (Brit.); Forced Landing; The Old Homestead; Sweepstake Annie
1936:	Charlie Chan at the Opera (C. Belden); Frontier Justice
1937:	Atlantic Flight (E. Lazarus); Boy of the Streets (G. Brown); California Straight Ahead
1938:	Telephone Operator
1939:	Mr. Wong in Chinatown; The Mystery of Mr. Wong; Stunt Pilot (J. West)
1940:	The Fatal Hour; I'm Nobody's Sweetheart Now*; Margie*
1941:	Double Date*; Cracked Nuts (E. Lazarus)
1942:	Sin Town*; The Ghost of Frankenstein; The Great Impersonation; Sherlock Holmes and the Secret Weapon*; The Body Disappears (E. Lazarus)
1943:	The Dancing Masters; Jitterbugs
1944:	Bermuda Mystery; The Big Noise
1945:	The Bull Fighters; The Spider (J. Eisinger)
1946:	Behind Green Lights (C. Booth)
1947:	Born to Speed*; The Chinese Ring; The Red Hornet; Bush Pilot (Can.)
1948:	Docks of New Orleans; Kidnapped; The Mystery of the Golden Eye (alt. The Golden Eye); The Shanghai Chest (S. Neuman)
1949:	The Wolf Hunters; Forgotten Women; The Lawton Story; Tuna Clipper
1950:	Blue Grass of Kentucky; County Fair
1951:	According to Mrs. Hoyle (B. Gerard); Blue Blood
1952:	Desert Pursuit

HARRY D'ABBADIE D'ARRAST

| 1930: | Laughter |

JULES DASSIN (1911-   ) director, producer

```
1955:   Rififi (Fr.)*
1958:   He Who Must Die (Fr./Ital.; B. Barzman);
        Where the Hot Wind Blows (Ital./Fr.)*
1960:   Never on Sunday (Gr.)
1962:   Phaedra (Gr./U.S.)*
1966:   10:30 P.M. Summer (U.S./Span.)*
1968:   Uptight*
1970:   Promise at Dawn (Fr./U.S.)
1978:   A Dream of Passion
```

MYRON DATTLEBAUM

```
1934:   Outlaw's Highway
```

DOROTHY DAVENPORT (see DOROTHY REID)

GAIL DAVENPORT

```
1944:   Swing Hostess (L. Rousseau)
```

WILLIAM DAVENPORT

```
1952:   Here Come the Nelsons*
```

DELMER DAVES (1904-1977) director

```
1929:   So This Is College
1931:   Shipmates*
1932:   Divorce in the Family
1934:   Dames (R. Lord); Flirtation Walk; No More
        Women (L. Breslow)
1935:   Page Miss Glory (R. Lord); Shipmates
        Forever; Stranded (C. Erickson)
1936:   The Petrified Forest (C. Kenyon)
1937:   The Go-Getter; The Singing Marine
1938:   Professor Beware; She Married an Artist (G.
        Lehman)
1939:   Love Affair (D. Stewart); $1,000 a Touchdown
1940:   Safari
1941:   Night of January 16*; Unexpected Uncle (N.
        Langley)
1942:   You Were Never Lovelier*
1943:   Destination Tokyo (A. Maltz); Stage Door
```

```
              Canteen
1944:   The Very Thought of You (A. Bessie);
              Hollywood Canteen
1945:   Pride of the Marines (A. Maltz)
1947:   Dark Passage; The Red House
1949:   Task Force
1951:   Bird of Paradise
1953:   Treasure of the Golden Condor
1954:   Drum Beat
1955:   White Feather (L. Townsend)
1956:   Jubal (R. Hughes); The Last Wagon*
1957:   An Affair to Remember (L. McCarey)
1959:   A Summer Place
1961:   Parrish; Susan Slade
1962:   Rome Adventure
1963:   Spencer's Mountain
1964:   Youngblood Hawke
1965:   The Battle of the Villa Fiorita
```

CARSON DAVIDSON

```
1975:   The Wrong Damn Film
```

MARTIN DAVIDSON

```
1974:   The Lords of Flatbush*
1978:   If Ever I See You Again (J. Brooks); Almost
              Summer*
```

RONALD DAVIDSON

```
1937:   Zorro Rides Again (ser.)*
1938:   The Lone Ranger (ser.)*; Dick Tracy Returns
              (ser.)*; The Fighting Devil Dogs (ser.)*
1939:   The Lone Ranger Rides Again (ser.)*; Zorro's
              Fighting Legion (ser.)*; Daredevils of the
              Red Circle (ser.)*; Dick Tracy's G-Men
              (ser.)*
1940:   Adventures of Red Ryder (ser.)*; Drums of Fu
              Manchu (ser.)*; The Mysterious Dr. Satan
              (ser.)*
1941:   King of the Texas Rangers (ser.)*;
              Adventures of Captain Marvel (ser.)*; Dick
              Tracy vs. Crime, Inc. (ser.)*; Jungle Girl
              (ser.)*
```

1942: King of the Mounties (ser.)*; Spy Smasher
      (ser.)*; Perils of Nyoka (ser.)*
1943: Daredevils of the West (ser.)*; G-Men vs.
      the Black Dragon (ser.)*; The Masked Marvel
      (ser.)*; Secret Service in Darkest Africa
      (ser.)*; Captain America (ser.)*
1944: The Tiger Woman (ser.)*
1948: Range Renegades (W. Lively); Triggerman;
      Cowboy Cavalier (J. Cheney); The Fighting
      Ranger; Courtin' Trouble
1949: Across the Rio Grande; Roaring Westward;
      Range Justice
1950: Desperadoes of the West (ser.); The
      Invisible Monster (ser.); Jungle Stampede
1951: Don Daredevil Rides Again (ser.); Flying
      Disc Men from Mars (ser.)*; Government Agent
      vs. Phantom Legion (ser.)*
1952: Black Hills Ambush (M. Webster); Radar Men
      from the Moon (ser.)*
1953: Jungle Drums of Africa (ser.)*; Canadian
      Mounties vs. Atomic Invaders (ser.)
1954: Man with the Steel Whip (ser.)*; Trader Tom
      of the China Seas (ser.)*
1955: King of the Carnival (ser.)*; Panther Girl
      of the Kongo (ser.)*
1958: Satan's Satellites; Missile Monsters

JACK DAVIES

1966: The Cavern (M. Pertwee)

VALENTINE DAVIES (1905-   )

1946: Three Little Girls in Blue
1948: Chicken Every Sunday (G. Seaton); You Were
      Meant for Me (E. Moll)
1949: It Happens Every Spring (S. Smith)
1951: On the Riviera*
1953: Sailor of the King
1954: The Bridges of Toko-Ri; The Glenn Miller
      Story (O. Brodney)
1955: The Benny Goodman Story; Strategic Air
      Command (B. Lay)
1961: Bachelor in Paradise (H. Kanter)

175

ALFRED DAVIS

1936: 'Til We Meet Again*

CHARLES DAVIS

1967: The Violated Ones (D. Wilson)
1973: Happy As the Grass Was Green

DONALD DAVIS

1933: Damaged Lives (E. Ulmer)
1937: The Good Earth*
1942: Hello, Annapolis (T. Reed)
1943: One Dangerous Night

EDDIE DAVIS

1938: Radio City Revels*
1942: House of Errors (E. Adamson); Too Many Women
1944: Leave It to the Irish (Tim Ryan)
1968: Panic in the City (C. Savage)
1969: It Takes All Kinds (C. Savage)

FITZROY DAVIS

1943: The Heat's On*

FRANK DAVIS

1935: One New York Night
1940: Dance, Girl, Dance (T. Slesinger)
1941: Remember the Day*
1942: Are Husbands Necessary? (T. Slesinger)
1945: A Tree Grows in Brooklyn (T. Slesinger)
1947: Woman on the Beach (J. Renoir)
1948: Fighting Father Dunne (M. Rackin)
1951: Ten Tall Men (R. Kibbee)
1952: Springfield Rifle (C. Warren); The Story of
       Will Rogers (S. Roberts)
1953: The Jazz Singer*
1954: The Boy from Oklahoma (W. Miller)
1955: The Indian Fighter (B. Hecht)

1959: Night of the Quarter Moon (F. Coen)
1965: The Train*

GERRY DAVIS

1980: The Final Countdown*

JERRY DAVIS

1950: Duchess of Idaho (Dorothy Cooper); Pagan
       Love Song (R. Nathan)
1951: Kind Lady*
1952: Apache War Smoke; The Devil Makes Three
       (Germ.)
1953: A Slight Case of Larceny
1955: Cult of the Cobra*; The Girl Rush (R.
       Pirosh)

KENN DAVIS

1976: Nightmare in Blood (J. Stanley)

KEVIN DAVIS

1975: Swiss Bank Account

LUTHER DAVIS

1947: The Hucksters (G. Wells)
1948: B. F.'s Daughter
1950: Black Hand
1953: A Lion Is in the Streets
1955: Kismet (C. Lederer)
1958: The Gift of Love
1959: Holiday for Lovers
1961: The Wonders of Aladdin
1964: Lady in a Cage
1972: Across 110th Street

MARY DAVIS

1976: Poor White Trash Part 2 (orig. Scum of the

Earth; G. Ross)
1982:   Mark of the Witch (Martha Peters)

OSSIE DAVIS (1917-   ) actor, director

1963:   Gone Are the Days!
1969:   Cotton Comes to Harlem (A. Perl)
1973:   Black Girl (J.E. Franklin)
1976:   Countdown at Kusini*

OWEN DAVIS

1930:   So This Is London (S. Levien)
1931:   Girl Habit (G. Purcell); My Sin (A.
        Heilbron)
1937:   The Good Earth*

ROBERT C. DAVIS

1981:   The Pilot (C. Robertson)

STANLEY DAVIS

1943:   Here Comes Elmer (J. Townley)
1944:   Murder in the Blue Room (I. Diamond); Hat
        Check Honey (M. Leo); Slightly Terrific (E.
        Dein)

DONN DAVISON

1976:   Secrets of the Gods (W. Sachs)

ISABEL DAWN

1932:   If I Had a Million*
1935:   Don't Bet on Blondes (B. DeGaw)
1936:   The Moon's Our Home*
1937:   Wings over Honolulu (B. DeGaw)
1938:   The Girl of the Golden West (B. DeGaw)
1940:   Behind the News (B. DeGaw)
1941:   Doctors Don't Tell (T. Reeves); Lady for a
        Night (B. DeGaw); a Man Betrayed

1942:   Remember Pearl Harbor (M. Boylan); A Tragedy
        at Midnight; Yokel Boy
1944:   Goodnight, Sweetheart (J. Townley)
1946:   Singin' in the Corn (M. Brice)

ANTHONY DAWSON

1968:   The Young, the Evil and the Savage (F.
        Bottar)

GORDON DAWSON

1974:   Bring Me the Head of Alfredo Garcia (S.
        Peckinpah)

GERRY DAY

1979:   The Black Hole (J. Rosebrook)

RICHARD DAY

1958:   Never Love a Stranger (H. Robbins)

ROBERT DAY (1922-   ) director   Brit.

(American films only)
1963:   Tarzan's Three Challenges (B. Giler)

WILLIAM DAY

1932:   Wayward (G. Unger)

LYMAN DAYTON

1976:   Pony Express Rider*

FRANK M. DAZEY

1935:   When a Man's a Man*

CHARLES DEAN

1954: Devil's Harbor
1958: Blonde Blackmailer (Brit.)

PAUL DEASON

1974: Truck Stop Women (M.L. Lester)

JOHN DeBELLO

1978: Attack of the Killer Tomatoes*

HAL DEBRETT

1956: Shadow of Fear

MARGE DECKER

1950: To Please a Lady (B. Lyndon)

RUBY DEE (1924-   ) actress

1968: Uptight*

DON DEER

1961: The Hoodlum Priest (J. Landon)

FRANK DeFELITTA

1972: Z.P.G. (M. Ehrlich)
1974: The Savage Is Loose (M. Ehrlich)
1977: Audrey Rose

MICHAEL A. DE GAETANO

1974: UFO: Target Earth (orig. Target Earth)

B. DEGAS

1973:   Summertime Killer (R. Buckley)

BOYCE DeGAW

1932:   If I Had a Million*
1935:   Don't Bet on Blondes (I. Dawn)
1936:   The Moon's Our Home*
1937:   Wings over Honolulu (I. Dawn)
1938:   The Girl of the Golden West (I. Dawn)
1940:   Behind the News (I. Dawn)
1941:   Lady for a Night (I. Dawn)

FRED DeGORTER

1968:   Dayton's Devils

MADAME FRED De GRESAC

1929:   She Goes to War (H. Estabrook)
1930:   Hell Harbor

EDWARD DEIN

1942:   Baby Face Morgan (J. Rubin); Boss of Big
        Town; The Pay-Off
1943:   Calling Dr. Death; The Falcon Strikes Back;
        Gals, Inc.; Pistol Packin' Mamma (F.
        Schiller)
1944:   Slightly Terrific (S. Davis); Jungle Woman;
        The Soul of a Monster
1945:   Boston Blackie's Rendezvous; Fighting
        Guardsman (F. Spencer)
1946:   The Cat Creeps (J. Warner); The Notorious
        Lone Wolf (M. Berkeley)
1955:   Shack Out on 101 (M. Dein)
1957:   Calypso Joe (M. Dein)
1958:   Seven Guns to Mesa*
1959:   Curse of the Undead (M. Dein)

MILDRED DEIN

```
1955:   Shack Out on 101 (E. Dein)
1957:   Calypso Joe (E. Dein)
1958:   Seven Guns to Mesa*
1959:   Curse of the Undead (E. Dein)
```

ROBERT DeLAURENTIS

```
1982:   A Little Sex
```

WALTER DeLEON

```
1929:   Big News (J. Jungmeyer); Red Hot Rhythm (E.
        Baldwin)
1930:   Night Work; Big Money
1931:   The Big Gamble (F. Willis); Lonely Wives;
        Meet the Wife (F. Willis)
1932:   Hold 'Em Jail*; If I Had a Million*; Make Me
        a Star*; The Phantom President (H.
        Thompson); Union Depot (K. Nicholson)
1933:   International House (F. Martin); A Lady's
        Profession (M. Boylan); Tillie and Gus (F.
        Martin)
1934:   College Rhythm*; Six of a Kind (H. Ruskin);
        You Belong to Me*
1935:   The Big Broadcast of 1936*; Ruggles of Red
        Gap*
1936:   The Big Broadcast of 1937 (F. Martin);
        Rhythm on the Range*; Collegiate (F.
        Martin); The Princess Comes Across*; Strike
        Me Pink*
1937:   Artists and Models (F. Martin); Waikiki
        Wedding*
1938:   The Big Broadcast of 1938*; College Swing
        (F. Martin)
1939:   Union Pacific*; The Cat and the Canary (L.
        Starling)
1940:   The Ghost Breakers; The Man Who Talked Too
        Much (T. Reed); Tugboat Annie Sails Again
1941:   Birth of the Blues (H. Tugend); Pot o' Gold
1942:   The Fleet's In (S. Silvers)
1943:   Happy Go Lucky*; Riding High*
1944:   Rainbow Island (A. Phillips)
1945:   Delightfully Dangerous (A. Phillips); Hold
        That Blonde*; Out of This World (A.
        Phillips)
```

1946: Little Giant; The Time of Their Lives*
1953: Scared Stiff (H. Baker)

GABRIEL DELL

1975: The Manchu Eagle Murder Caper Mystery (D.
       Hargrove)

JEFFREY DELL

1941: The Saint's Vacation
1960: As the Sea Rages (Yugo.; J. Eisenger); A
       French Mistress (Brit.;R. Boulting)

VINA DELMAR

1937: The Awful Truth; Make Way for Tomorrow

LOUIS DeLOS ARCOS

1964: Pyro (S. Pink)
1965: Finger on the Trigger (S. Pink)

HAMPTON DEL RUTH

1931: Air Eagles; Defenders of the Law (L.
       Heifetz); Mystery Train
1933: Goodbye Love (G. Rosener)

RUDY DeLUCA

1976: Silent Movie*
1977: High Anxiety*
1981: Caveman (C. Gottlieb)

WILLIAM C. De MILLE (1878-1955) director,
       playwright

1929: The Doctor's Secret
1939: Captain Fury*

183

JONATHAN DEMME

1971: Angels Hard As They Come (J. Viola)
1974: Caged Heat
1976: Fighting Mad

ALBERT DeMOND

1930: Cohens and Kellys in Scotland
1933: Above the Clouds; Shadows of Sing Sing;
       Skyway; The Sphinx; Sweetheart of Sigma
       Chi*; Sensation Hunters (P. Schofield)
1934: Lost in the Stratosphere; The Loud Speaker;
       School for Girls; Take the Stand; Two Heads
       on a Pillow; House of Mystery
1935: Death Flies East (F. Niblo); No Ransom; The
       Perfect Clue; Secret of the Chateau; The
       Spanish Cape Mystery; Storm over the Andes*;
       Unknown Woman (F. Niblo)
1936: North of Nome; The Leavenworth Case (S.
       Sutherland); Navy Born*
1937: Woman in Distress
1938: Blondes at Work; Little Miss Thoroughbred
       (G. Bricker); Torchy Gets Her Man
1939: Sweepstakes Winner (J. Krafft); Women in the
       Wind (L. Katz)
1940: Fugitive from a Prison Camp; The Great Plane
       Robbery; Outside the Three-Mile Limit;
       Passport to Alcatraz; Prison Camp
1941: Saddlemates (H. Dalmas); Gangs of Sonora (D.
       Schroeder); Outlaws of th Cherokee Trail;
       West of Cimarron (D. Ryan); Gauchos of
       Eldorado (E. Snell); The Great Swindle
1942: Valley of Hunted Men (M. Grant); Ridin' Down
       the Canyon
1943: Riders of the Rio Grande
1944: Call of the South Seas; Beneath Western
       Skies (R. Williams); Code of the Prairie (A.
       Coldeway); Shadow of Suspicion (E. Snell)
1945: Trail of Kit Carson (J. Natteford); Federal
       Operator 99 (ser.)*; Manhunt of Mystery
       Island (ser.)*; The Phantom Rider (ser.)*;
       The Purple Monster Strikes (ser.)*
1946: King of the Forest Rangers (ser.)*; The
       Crimson Ghost (ser.)*; Daughter of Don Q
       (ser.)*

1947:   The Wild Frontier
1948:   King of the Gamblers (B. Foote); Madonna of
        the Desert
1949:   Alias the Champ; Prince of the Plains (L.
        Rousseau); Duke of Chicago; The Red Menace
        (G. Geraghty)
1950:   Federal Agents at Large; Trial Without Jury;
        Unmasked (N. Hall)
1951:   Pals of the Golden West (E. Taylor); Million
        Dollar Pursuit (B. Foote)
1952:   Border Saddlemates; Desperadoes Outpost (A.
        Orloff); Woman in the Dark
1953:   Marshal of Cedar Creek

JACQUES DEMY

1969:   The Model Shop

FRED DENGER

1968:   The Flaming Frontier

REGINALD DENHAM

1941:   Ladies in Retirement (G. Fort)

HENRY DENKER

1957:   Time Limit (R. Berkey)
1963:   The Hook; Twilight of Honor

WILSTON DENMARK

1975:   Johnny Firecloud

GEOFFREY DENNIS

1957:   The Unearthly (J. Mann)

JOHN DENNIS

1961:   By Love Possessed*

ROBERT C. DENNIS

1956:   Crime Against Joe; The Man Is Armed (R.
        Landau)
1957:   Revolt at Fort Laramie

BRIAN De PALMA (1941-   ) director

1968:   Greetings (C. Hirsch); Murder a la Mod
1969:   The Wedding Party*
1970:   Dionysus in '69*; Hi, Mom
1973:   Sisters (L. Rose)
1974:   Phantom of the Paradise
1980:   Dressed to Kill
1981:   Blow Out

SUZANNA DePASSE

1972: Lady Sings the Blues*

ALBERT de PINA

1946:   Joe Palooka, Champ (C. Endfield)

JOHN DEREK (1926-   ) actor, director

1969:   A Boy...a Girl
1981:   Fantasies

RICHARD DeROY

1973:   Two People

ALBERT DERR

1948:   Manhattan Angel

E. B. DERR

186

1943:   Deerslayer (P. Harrington)

PAUL de SAINTE-COLOMBE

1949:   Outpost in Morocco (C. Grayson)

STEVE De SOUZA

1973:   Arnold's Wrecking Co.
1982:   48 Hours*

B. G. DeSYLVA

1934:   Bottoms Up*
1944:   The Stork Club (John McGowan)

BUDDY DeSYLVA (-1950)

1933:   Take a Chance*

DAVID DETIEGE

1965:   The Man from Button Willow

ANDRE DeTOTH (1900-   ) director

1957:   Hidden Fear (J. Hawkins)
1961:   Morgan the Pirate (Ital.)

KARL DETZER

1935:   Car 99 (C. Sullivan)
1936:   Crash Donovan*

HELEN DEUTCH

1944:   The Seventh Cross; National Velvet (T.
        Reeves)
1947:   Golden Earrings*

1948: The Loves of Carmen
1949: Shockproof (S. Fuller)
1950: Kim*; King Solomon's Mines
1951: It's a Big Country*
1952: Plymouth Adventure
1953: Lili
1954: Flame and the Flesh
1955: The Glass Slipper; I'll Cry Tomorrow (J. R. Kennedy)
1956: Forever Darling
1964: The Unsinkable Molly Brown
1967: Valley of the Dolls (D. Kingsley)

JACQUES DEVAL

1939: Balalaika*
1940: New Moon (R. Arthur)
1942: Her Cardboard Lover*

RALPH DeVITO

1976: Death Collector
1978: Family Enforcer

DON DEVLIN

1963: Thunder Island (J. Nicholson)
1970: Loving

CHRISTOPHER DeVORE

1982: Frances*

GARY DeVORE

1981: Back Roads; The Dogs of War (G. Malko)

JACK DeWITT

1947: The Bells of San Fernando (D. Renaldo); Don Ricardo Returns (D. Renaldo); Louisiana; The Return of Rin Tin Tin

1948:   Rocky
1949:   Bomba, the Jungle Boy; Canadian Pacific (K.
        Gamet)
1952:   Fargo (J. Poland)
1954:   Sitting Bull (S. Salkow); Khyber Patrol; The
        Bamboo Prison (E. Blum)
1955:   Cell 2455, Death Row; Women's Prison (C.
        Wilbur)
1956:   Rumble on the Docks (L. Morheim)
1957:   Portland Expose; Oregon Passage
1958:   Wolf Larsen (Turnley Walker)
1960:   The Purple Gang
1961:   Five Guns to Tombstone (R. Schayer)
1967:   Jack of Diamonds (Sandy Howard)
1970:   A Man Called Horse
1971:   Man in the Wilderness
1973:   The Neptune Factor
1974:   Together Brothers (J. Greene)
1976:   The Return of a Man Called Horse; Sky
        Riders*

KAREN DeWOLF

1934:   By Candlelight*; Countess of Monte Cristo
        (G. Unger); Love Captive
1935:   Public Opinion; Society Fever
1936:   Bulldog Edition (R. English); Doughnuts and
        Society*
1937:   Borrowing Trouble (R. Chapin); The Jones
        Family in Hot Water (alt. Hot Water; R.
        Chapin); Love in a Bungalow*
1938:   Always in Trouble (R. Chapin); Passport
        Husband (R. Chapin); Safety in Numbers*
        Walking Down Broadway (R. Chapin)
1939:   Saga Of Death Valley (S. Anthony);
        Everybody's Baby*
1940:   Pioneers of the West*; Blondie Plays Cupid
        (R. Flourney)
1941:   Go West, Young Lady (R. Flourney); Blondie
        in Society; Blondie Goes Latin (R.
        Flourney); Her First Beau (G. Lehman);
        Tillie the Toiler (F. Martin)
1942:   Shut My Big Mouth*; Meet the Stewarts;
        Blondie for Victory (Connie Lee); Blondie's
        Blessed Event*
1943:   Footlight Glamour (Connie Lee); It's a Great
        Life (Connie Lee); The Darling Young Man

```
           (Connie Lee)
1944:   Nine Girls (Connie Lee)
1945:   Getting Gertie's Garter (A. Dwan)
1946:   The Cockeyed Miracle
1947:   Bury Me Dead (D. Babcock); Stepchild
1948:   Adventures of Casanova*
1949:   Johnny Allegro (G. Endore); Slightly French;
        Make Believe Ballroom (A. Duffy); Holiday in
        Havana*
1950:   When You're Smiling (J. Roberts)
1953:   Count the Hours (D. Hoag); Appointment in
        Honduras
1954:   Silver Lode
```

DAVID DIAMOND

```
1937:   The Adventurous Blonde (R. White); Swing It,
        Sailor (C. Marks)
```

I. A. L. DIAMOND (1920-   )

```
1944:   Murder in the Blue Room (S. Davis)
1946:   Two Guys from Milwaukee (C. Hoffman); Never
        Say Goodbye (J. V. Kern)
1947:   Always Together*; Love and Learn*
1948:   Two Guys from Texas (A. Boretz)
1949:   The Girl from Jones Beach
1951:   Let's Make It Legal (F. Herbert); Love Nest
1952:   Monkey Business*; Something for the Birds
        (B. Ingster)
1956:   That Certain Feeling*
1957:   Love in the Afternoon (B. Wilder)
1958:   Merry Andrew (I. Lennart)
1959:   Some Like It Hot (B. Wilder)
1960:   The Apartment (B. Wilder)
1961:   One, Two, Three (B. Wilder)
1963:   Irma La Douce (B. Wilder)
1964:   Kiss Me, Stupid (B. Wilder)
1966:   The Fortune Cookie (B. Wilder)
1969:   Cactus Flower
1970:   The Private Life of Sherlock Holmes (B.
        Wilder)
1972:   Avanti! (B. Wilder)
1974:   The Front Page (B. Wilder)
1979:   Fedora (B. Wilder)
1981:   Buddy Buddy (B. Wilder)
```

PAUL DIAMOND

1977:   The Chicken Chronicles

BASIL DICKEY

1929:   The Tip-Off
1931:   Fingerprints (ser.)*
1932:   Air Mail Mystery (ser.)*; Heroes of the West
         (ser.)*; Jungle Mystery (ser.)*; The Lost
         Special (ser.)*
1933:   Clancy of the Mounted (ser.)*; Gordon of
         Ghost City (ser.)*; Phantom of the Air
         (ser.; G. Plympton)
1934:   Danger Island (ser.)*; Heroes of the Flames
         (ser.)*; Perils of Pauline (ser.)*; Pirate
         Treasure (ser.)*; The Red Rider (ser.)*;
         Tailspin Tommy (ser.)*; The Vanishing Shadow
         (ser.)*
1935:   Rustlers of Red Dog (ser.)*; The Roaring
         West (ser.)*; Call of the Savage (ser.)*;
         Tailspin Tommy in the Great Air Mystery
         (ser.)*
1936:   The Phantom Rider (ser.)*; Law and Lead; The
         Phantom of the Range; Flash Gordon (ser.)*;
         Adventures of Frank Merriwell (ser.)*;
         Shadow of Chinatown (I. Bernstein)
1937:   Cheyenne Rides Again; The Feud of the Trail;
         Mystery Range; Orphan of the Pecos; Brothers
         of the West; Lost Ranch; Million Dollar
         Racket
1938:   Flaming Frontiers (ser.)*; Flying Fists; The
         Spider's Web (ser.)*
1939:   Outlaw's Paradise; The Oregon Trail (ser.)*;
         Straight Shooter (J. O'Donnell); Trigger
         Fingers; Flying G-Men (ser.)*; Mandrake, the
         Magician (ser.)*; The Phantom Creeps
         (ser.)*; Scouts to the Rescue
1940:   Winners of the West (ser.)*; Flash Gordon
         Conquers the Universe (ser.)*; The Green
         Hornet (ser.)*; The Green Hornet Strikes
         Again (ser.)*; Junior G-Men (ser.)*
1941:   Riders of Death Valley (ser.)*; Holt of the
         Secret Service (ser.)*; The Iron Claw
         (ser.)*

191

1942: Perils of the Royal Mounted (ser.)*; Captain
       Midnight (ser.)*; The Secret Code (ser.)*
1943: Daredevils of the West (ser.)*; Captain
       America (ser.)*; The Masked Marvel (ser.)*;
       Secret Service in Darkest Africa (ser.)*
1944: Zorro's Black Whip (ser.)*; Haunted Harbor
       (ser.)*; The Tiger Woman (ser.)*
1945: Federal Operator 99 (ser.)*; The Phantom
       Rider (ser.)*; The Purple Monster Strikes
       (ser.)*
1946: King of the Forest Rangers (ser.)*; The
       Crimson Ghost (ser.)*; Daughter of Don Q
       (ser.)*
1947: Son of Zorro (ser.)*; The Black Widow
       (ser.)*; Jesse James Rides Again (ser.)*
1948: Dangers of the Canadian Mounted (ser.)*; The
       Rangers Ride; Adventures of Frank and Jesse
       James (ser.)*; G-Men Never Forget (ser.)*
1949: Gun Law Justice; Brand of Fear; Lawless
       Code; Federal Agents vs. Underworld, Inc.
       (ser.)*

JAMES DICKEY (1923-   ) author

1972: Deliverance

PAUL DICKEY

1930: Free and Easy (R. Schayer)

JOAN DIDION

1971: The Panic in Needle Park (J. Dunne)
1972: Play It As It Lays (J. Dunne)
1976: A Star Is Born*
1981: True Confessions (J. Dunne)

HOWARD DIETZ

1934: Hollywood Party (A. Kober)

JOHN DIGHTON

```
1953:   Roman Holiday*
1956:   The Swan
1957:   The Barretts of Wimpole Street
1959:   The Devil's Disciple (R. Kibbee)
1961:   Season of Passion (Austral.)
```

COSTA DILLON

```
1978:   Attack of the Killer Tomatoes*
```

LAURI DILLON

```
1975:   French Connection II*
```

ROBERT DILLON

```
1935:   Wilderness Mail (B. Cohen)
1937:   Crusade Against Rackets
1959:   City of Fear (S. Ritch)
1962:   Safe at Home!
1963:   The Old Dark House; 13 Frightened Girls; "X"
        the Man with the X-Ray Eyes (Ray Russell)
1964:   Bikini Beach*; Muscle Beach Party
1972:   Prime Cut
1974:   99 44/100% Dead
1975:   French Connection II*
```

EDWARD DiLORENZO

```
1980:   The Idolmaker
```

HOWARD DIMSDALE

```
1944:   Babes on Swing Street (E. Conrad)
1945:   Senorita from the West; Penthouse Rhythm (S.
        Roberts)
1946:   Somewhere in the Night (J. Mankiewicz)
1949:   A Kiss for Corliss
1950:   A Lady Without Passport; Curtain Call at
        Cactus Creek (John Grant); Aladdin and His
        Lamp (M. Kaufman); The Traveling Saleswoman
1953:   Captain Scarlett
```

MEL DINELLI

1946:	The Spiral Staircase
1949:	The Window
1950:	House by the River
1951:	Cause for Alarm (Tom Lewis)
1952:	Beware, My Lovely
1953:	Jeopardy
1957:	Lizzie
1958:	Step Down to Terror*

GERALD Di PEGO

1974:	"W" (J. Kelly)
1981:	Sharkey's Machine

LARRY DITILLIO

1974:	The Mad, Mad Moviemaker (orig. The Last Porno Flick)

BEULAH MARIE DIX

1929:	Girls Gone Wild; Trent's Last Case (W. Darling); Black Magic
1930:	Girl of the Port; Midnight Mystery; Conspiracy
1931:	Three Who Loved

MARION DIX

1929:	The Kibitzer; Men Are Like That
1930:	Safety in Numbers; Along Came Youth (G. Marion); Sea Legs
1932:	Ladies of the Jury
1933:	Before Dawn*; The Past of Mary Holmes (E. Doherty); The Worst Woman in Paris (M. Bell)
1934:	Down to Their Last Yacht*; Sing and Like It (L. Doyle); Their Big Moment (A. Caesar)
1936:	Everything Is Thunder; It's Love Again (Brit.; Austin Melford)
1938:	Forbidden Music (Brit.)*

ROBERT DIX

1971: Five Bloody Graves

JAMES DIXON

1973: Your Three Minutes Are Up

PETER DIXON

1939: Down the Wyoming Trail (R. Merton)

FRANK DOBBS

1978: Smokey and the Goodtime Outlaws (Bob Walsh)

FRED C. DOBBS

1965: The Great Sioux Massacre

LARRY DOBKIN

1974: The Life and Times of Grizzly Adams

FRANCES DOEL

1974: Big Bad Mama (W. Norton)

EDWARD J. DOHERTY

1933: The Past of Mary Holmes (M. Dix)

ETHEL DOHERTY

1929: Marquis Preferred; Innocents of Paris;
       Studio Murder Mystery; River of Romance
1931: It Pays to Advertise (A. Kober)
1933: Men Are Such Fools (V. Shore); Sailor Be
       Good (V. Shore)

1935:   Rocky Mountain Mystery (E. Paramore); Home
        on the Range*

DON DOHLER

1982:   Nightbeast

FRANK DOLAN

1932:   Amateur Daddy (D. Malloy)
1937:   Man of the People
1939:   Street of Missing Men (L. Lee)

MEYER DOLINSKY

1957:   Hot Rod Rumble
1958:   As Young As We Are (W. Alland)

FRANK DONAGHUE

1939:   Espionage Agent*

PATRICK G. DONAHUE

1982:   Kill Squad

WALTER DONIGER (1917-   ) director

1941:   Mob Town (B. Weisberg)
1942:   Danger in the Pacific (M. Tombragel)
1943:   Jive Junction*
1949:   Rope of Sand; Tokyo Joe*
1951:   Along the Great Divide (L. Meltzer)
1952:   Desperate Search
1953:   Cease Fire
1954:   Alaska Seas (G. Homes); Duffy of San Quentin
        (B. Swartz); The Steel Cage*
1956:   Hold Back the Night (J. C. Higgins); The
        Steel Jungle
1957:   The Guns of Fort Petticoat

ROBERT MORRIS DONLEY

1959: Andy Hardy Comes Home (E. Hutshing)

BUDD DONNELLY

1976: Jessie's Girls

THOMAS MICHAEL DONNELLY

1980: Defiance

MARTIN DONOVAN

1980: Loving Couples

ANITA DOOHAN

1976: Embryo (J. W. Thomas)

PAUL DOOLEY

1980: Health*

NAT N. DORFMAN

1935: Atlantic Adventure (J. Neville)

NATHANIEL DORSKY

1976: Revenge of the Cheerleaders (T. Greenwald)

RICHARD S. DORSO

1957: Sierra Stranger

DAVID DORTORT

1952: The Lusty Men (H. Mc.Coy)

```
1956:   A Cry in the Night; Reprisal!*
1957:   The Big Land (M. Rackin)
```

JOHN DOS PASSOS (1896-1970) novelist

```
1935:   The Devil Is a Woman
```

JAY DOTEN

```
1944:   The Contender
```

DOUGLAS DOTY

```
1929:   Pleasure Crazed
1930:   College Lovers
1932:   Drifting Souls (N. Houston); Silent Witness
1933:   The Important Witness (L. Simmonds);
        Racetrack (W. Lang)
```

EARLE DOUD

```
1979:   Racquet (S. Michaels)
```

GIL DOUD

```
1953:   Thunder Bay (J. M. Hayes)
1954:   Saskatchewan; Port of Hell*
1955:   To Hell and Back
1956:   Walk the Proud Land (J. Sher)
```

GORDON DOUGLAS (1909-   ) director

```
1939:   The Housekeeper's Daughter (R. James)
1941:   Topper Returns (J. Latimer)
```

JOHN DOUGLAS

```
1975:   Milestones (R. Kramer)
```

MICHAEL DOUGLAS (1944-   ) actor, producer

1979:   The China Syndrome*

NATHAN E. DOUGLAS

1958:   The Defiant Ones (H. J. Smith)
1960:   Inherit the Wind (H. J. Smith)

RITA DOUGLAS

1941:   The Jungle Man

WARREN DOUGLAS

1953:   Northern Patrol; Jack Slade; Torpedo Alley
        (S. Roeca)
1954:   Loophole; Cry Vengeance (G. Bricker); Khikan
        (G. Bricker)
1955:   Finger Man; The Return of Jack Slade
1956:   The Come On (W. Chambers); The Cruel Tower;
        Strange Intruder (D. Evans)
1957:   Dragoon Wells Massacre
1966:   The Night of the Grizzly

NANCY DOWD

1977:   Slap Shot

ALLAN DOWLING

1955:   Hunters of the Deep (T. Gries)

ROBERT DOWNEY (1936-   ) director

1966:   Chafed Elbows
1968:   No More Excuses
1969:   Putney Swope
1970:   Pound
1972:   Greaser's Palace
1976:   Two Tons of Turquoise to Taos Tonight
1979:   Jive
1980:   The Gong Show Movie (C. Barris)

LAIRD DOYLE (-1936)

1932: Phantom Express (E. Johnson)
1933: Hell Below*
1934: British Agent (P. Collings); Finishing
       School (W. Tuchock); The Key; Sing and Like
       It (M. Dix)
1935: Bordertown (W. Smith); Dangerous; Front Page
       Woman*; Oil for the Lamps of China; Special
       Agent (A. Finkel)
1936: Hearts Divided (C. Robinson); Three Men on a
       Horse
1937: Another Dawn; Prince and the Pauper

RAY DOYLE

1929: Madonna of Avenue A
1931: Heaven on Earth

ROBERT DOZIER

1957: The Young Stranger
1963: The Cardinal
1969: The Big Bounce
1972: When the Legends Die

HENRY SINCLAIR DRAGO

1930: The Lotus Lady

STAN DRAGOTI

1972: Dirty Little Billy (C. Moss)

OLIVER DRAKE

1929: Vagabond Cub; Gun Law; Desert Rider
1930: Rogue of the Rio Grande
1931: West of Cheyenne (B. Cohen); Hurricane
       Horseman; Law of the Tongs
1932: The Cheyenne Cyclone; Saddle Buster; Scarlet

Brand (Ethel Hill); Beyond the Rockïes;
Outlaw Justice; Law and Lawless; Battling
Buckaroo; Guns for Hire; Lawless Valley;
Texas Tornado; The Drifter; The Reckless
Rider

1933: When a Man Rides Alone; Via Pony Express (L.
CoLlins); Gun Law (L. Collins); Deadwood
Pass; Trouble Busters (L. Collins); War on
the Range

1935: Six Gun Justice; The Cyclone Ranger; The
Texas Rambler; The Vanishing Riders; The
Sagebrush Troubador (J. Poland); The Singing
Vagabond (B. Burbridge)

1936: Comin' Round the Mountain*; Oh, Susanna!;
Ghost Town Gold (J. Rathmell); Roarin' Lead
(J. Natteford); Undersea Kingdom (ser.)*

1937: Riders of the Whistling Skull*; Hit the
Saddle; Round-Up Time in Texas; Gunsmoke
Ranch; Public Cowboy No. 1; Heart of the
Rockies (J. Natteford); Boots and Saddles;
The Trigger Trio (J. Poland); Nation Aflame

1938: The Purple Vigilantes (B. Burbridge); Gun
Law; Border G-Man (B. McConville); The
Painted Desert (J. Rathmell); Lawless
Valley; Wild Horse Rodeo*

1939: Arizona Legion; Trouble in Sundown*;
Racketeers of the Range; The Fighting
Gringo; Cowboys from Texas

1940: Billy the Kid Outlawed; The Tulsa Kid (A.
Coldeway); Trailing Double Trouble

1941: Pals of the Pecos (H. Dalmas); Kansas
Cyclone (D. Schroeder); The Lone Rider
Ambushed; City of Missing Girls (C.
Rosener); Hard Guy

1942: Shut My Big Mouth*; Raiders of the West;
Billy the Kid Trapped; The Lone Rider in
Cheyenne (E. Beecher); Boss of Hangtown
Mesa; Today I Hang

1943: West of Texas; Border Buckaroos; The Lone
Star Trail; Fighting Valley; Trail of Terror

1945: Springtime in Texas
1946: West of the Alamo (L. Rousseau); Trail to
Mexico

1947: Ginger; Song of the Sierras (E. Clifton)
1948: Deadline; The Feathered Serpent
1949: Trail of the Yukon; Sky Dragon
1957: The Parson and the Outlaw (J. Mantley)

WILLIAM A. DRAKE

1932:   Grand Hotel; Strange Justice
1933:   Goldie Get Along
1939:   The Three Musketeers*
1940:   Adventures of Sherlock Holmes (E. Blum)
1942:   Shut My Big Mouth*

GEORGE DRANEY

1930:   Ex-Flame

JAY DRATLER (1911-1968)

1940:   Girls Under 21 (F. Foss); La Conga Nights*
1941:   Meet Boston Blackie; Where Did You Get That
        Girl?*
1942:   Fly by Night; Get Hep to Love; The Wife
        Takes a Flyer (G. Kaus)
1943:   Higher and Higher*
1944:   Laura*
1945:   It's in the Bag (A. Reville)
1946:   The Dark Corner (B. Schoenfeld)
1948:   Call Northside 777 (J. Cady); That Wonderful
        Urge
1949:   Impact (D. Reid)
1960:   I Aim at the Stars

ARTHUR DREIFUSS (1908-   ) director

1941:   Reg'lar Fellers*
1944:   Ever Since Venus (M. Moore)
1946:   Betty Co-Ed (G. Plympton); High School Hero
        (H. Collins)
1947:   Little Miss Broadway*; Sweet Genevieve (J.
        Brewer)
1948:   An Old-Fashioned Girl (McElbert Moore)
1962:   The Quare Fellow (Ir.)
1967:   The Love-Ins (H. Collins)
1968:   For Singles Only (H. Collins)

HAL DRESNER

```
1969:   The April Fools; The Extraordinary Seaman
        (P. Rock)
1973:   SSSSSSSSS
1975:   The Eiger Sanction*
1981:   Zorro, the Gay Blade
```

JOHN DRINKWATER

```
1936:   April Romance*
```

WILLIAM DRISKILL

```
1957:   Rockabilly Baby (W. George)
1961:   Ada (A. Sheekman)
1979:   Seven (R. Baird)
```

GEORGE DRUMGOLD

```
1928:   Show Folks (J. Jungmeyer)
1929:   Geraldine; Square Shoulders (H. Branch)
```

L. C. DUBLIN

```
1937:   Beware of Ladies
```

PAUL DUBOV

```
1969:   With Six You Get Eggroll*
```

ARTHUR DUBS

```
1978:   The Further Adventures of the Wilderness
        Family
1979:   Mountain Family Robinson
```

WILLIAM DUCEY

```
1930:   The Climax (J. Josephson)
```

MARJORIE DUDLEY

1944:   I Accuse My Parents (H. Fraser)

PAUL DUDLEY

1957:   Monkey on My Back*
1959:   Timbuktu (A. Veiller); Solomon and Sheba*

WARREN B. DUFF

1932:   Hotel Continental*; Lena Rivers (S.
        Anthony); Strangers of the Evening (S.
        Anthony); Uptown New York
1933:   The Constant Woman (F. Herbert); The Deluge*
1934:   The Crosby Case (G. Kahn); Friends of Mr.
        Sweeney*; Heat Lightning (B. Holmes); I've
        Got Your Number (S. Sutherland); Midnight
        Alibi; St. Louis Kid (S. Miller); 20 Million
        Sweethearts (H. Sauber)
1935:   Broadway Gondolier*; The Frisco Kid (S.
        Miller); Sweet Music*
1936:   Gold Diggers of 1937; The Singing Kid (P.
        Flick)
1937:   Back in Circulation; Ready, Willing and
        Able*; Submarine D-1*; Varsity Show*
1938:   Angels with Dirty Faces (J. Wexley); Gold Is
        Where You Find It (R. Buckner; Gold Diggers
        in Paris (E. Baldwin)
1939:   The Oklahoma Kid*; Each Dawn I Die*;
        Espionage Agent*
1940:   Invisible Stripes; 'Til We Meet Again
1941:   Lady from Cheyenne (K. Scola)
1943:   The Fallen Sparrow; The Iron Major (A.
        Kandel)
1944:   Step Lively (P. Milne); Experiment Perilous;
        Marine Raiders
1949:   Chicago Deadline; A Dangerous Profession (M.
        Rackin)
1951:   Appointment with Danger (R. Breen)
1952:   The Turning Point
1954:   Make Haste to Live
1955:   The Last Command (S. Bartlett)

BRAINERD DUFFIELD

204

1952:   The Treasure of Lost Canyon (E. Crocker)

ALBERT (JESSE) DUFFY

1937:   Galloping Dynamite*; The Rangers Step In (J.
        Levering)
1939:   Riders of the Frontier (J. Levering);
        Beware, Spooks!*; Blind Alley*; Coast Guard*
1940:   The Gay Caballero (J. Larkin); The Lone Wolf
        Strikes (H. Segall); The Green Archer
        (ser.)*
1941:   The Roar of the Press; Two Latins from
        Manhattan; The Iron Claw (ser.)*
1942:   Sweetheart of the Fleet (M. Tombragel); The
        Spider Returns (ser.)*; Perils of the Royal
        Mounted (ser.)*; Harvard, Here I Come;
        Sleepytime Gal*
1943:   Reveille with Beverly*; Captain America
        (ser.)*; Secret Service in Darkest Africa
        (ser.)*; The Masked Marvel (ser.)*
1944:   Bordertown Trail (R. Williams); Zorro's
        Black Whip (ser.)*; Haunted Harbor (ser.)*;
        The Tiger Woman (ser.)*
1945:   Federal Operator 99 (ser.)*; The Phantom
        Rider (ser.)*; Manhunt of Mystery Island
        (ser.)*
1946:   King of the Forest Rangers (ser.)*; The
        Crimson Ghost (ser.)*; Daughter of Don Q
        (ser.)*
1947:   Son of Zorro (ser.)*; Jesse James Rides
        Again (ser.)*; The Black Widow (ser.)*
1948:   The Dark Past*; G-Men Never Forget (ser.)*
1949:   Make Believe Ballroom (K. DeWolf)

JESSE DUFFY (see ALBERT DUFFY)

THOMAS DUGAN

1933:   Laughing at Life (P. Chaplin)
1937:   Pick a Star*

WILLIAM FRANCIS DUGAN

1930:   Clancy in Wall Street

LAWRENCE DUKORE

1977:   Greased Lightning*

BOB DUNCAN

1953:   The Marshal's Daughter
1963:   Black Gold (W. Duncan)

DAVID DUNCAN

1953:   Sangaree (F. Moss)
1954:   Jivaro; The White Orchid (R. LeBorg)
1957:   The Black Scorpion (R. Blees)
1958:   The Thing That Couldn't Die; Monster on the Campus
1960:   The Leech Woman; The Time Machine (Brit.)

ELIZABETH DUNCAN

1979:   The War at Home (doc.)

PATRICK DUNCAN

1982:   Beach Girls (Phil Groves)

RENAULT DUNCAN (see DUNCAN RENALDO)

SAM DUNCAN

1936:   White Fang (H. Long); White Hunter (K. Earle)

WANDA DUNCAN

1963:   Black Gold (B. Duncan)

PHIL DUNHAM

1933: Rainbow Ranch
1936: Feud of the West*; I'll Name the Murderer
1937: Bargain with Bullets (R. Cooper)
1938: Fury Below; Life Goes On (alt. His Harlem
       Wife)
1939: Two-Gun Troubador (R. Bare)
1940: Ridin' the Trail

WINIFRED DUNN

1930: Mamba (T. Miranda); Free Love
1931: Mother's Millions; The She-Wolf
1932: Impatient Maiden (R. Schrayer)
1933: I Have Lived; Rainbow over Broadway

JOHN GREGORY DUNNE

1971: The Panic in Needle Park (J. Didion)
1972: Play It As It Lays (J. Didion)
1976: A Star Is Born*
1981: True Confessions (J. Didion)

PHILIP DUNNE (1908-   ) director, producer

1934: Count of Monte Cristo*; Student Tour (R.
       Spence)
1935: The Melody Lingers On (R. Block);
       Helldorado*
1936: The Last of the Mohicans*
1937: The Lancer Spy
1938: Suez (J. Josephson)
1939: The Rains Came (J. Josephson); Stanley and
       Livingstone (J. Josephson); Swanee River (J.
       Foote)
1940: Johnny Apollo (Rowland Brown)
1941: How Green Was My Valley
1942: Son of Fury
1947: Forever Amber (R. Lardner); The Ghost and
       Mrs. Muir; The Late George Apley
1948: Escape; The Luck of the Irish
1949: Pinky (D. Nichols)
1951: Anne of the Indies (A. Caesar); David and
       Bathsheba
1952: Lydia Bailey (M. Blankfort); Way of a Gaucho

```
1953:   The Robe*
1954:   The Egyptian (C. Robinson); Demetrius and
        the Gladiators
1955:   The View from Pompey's Head
1956:   Hilda Crane
1957:   Three Brave Men
1958:   Ten North Frederick
1959:   Blue Denim (E. Sommers)
1965:   The Agony and the Ecstasy
1966:   Blindfold (W. Menger)
```

DECLA DUNNING

```
1944:   The Hairy Ape (R.D. Andrews)
1946:   Tars and Spars*
```

E. A. DUPONT (1891-1956) director

```
1951:   The Scarf
1956:   Magic Fire*
```

MICHEL DURAN

```
1946:   Heartbeat*
```

RUDY DURAND

```
1979:   Tilt (D. Cammell)
```

GEORGE ARTHUR DURLAM

```
1930:   The Lonesome Trail; Beyond the Law; Under
        Texas Skies; Code of Honor
1931:   Riders of the North; Partners of the Trail;
        The Montana Kid; The Man from Death Valley;
        Near the Trail's End; Oklahoma Jim;
        Two-Fisted Justice; In Line of Duty
1932:   South of Santa Fe; Aces and Eights
1935:   Captured in Chinatown (E. Clifton)
1936:   Custer's Last Stand (ser.)*
1937:   Young Dynamite*
1938:   The Great Adventures of Wild Bill Hickok
        (ser.)*
```

1941:   Swamp Woman
1942:   Boot Hill Bandits

LAWRENCE DURRELL

1966:   Judith (J. M. Hayes)

DAVID DURSTON

1970:   I Drink Your Blood
1972:   Blue Sextet; Stigma

PHIL DUSENBERRY

1973:   Hail to the Chief (L. Spiegel)
1979:   Washington B.C. (L. Spiegel)

ARNAUD D'USSEAU

1940:   One Crowded Night (R. Collins)
1941:   Lady Scarface (R. Collins)
1942:   Just off Broadway; The Man Who Wouldn't Die;
        Who Is Hope Schuyler?

LEON D'USSEAU

1932:   The Girl from Calgary (S. Schlager)
1933:   Wine, Women and Song
1935:   The Lost City (ser.)*
1936:   The Clutching Hand (ser.)*

JACQUES DUVAL

1937:   Cafe Metropole
1939:   Balalaika*

JULIEN DUVIVIER (1896-1967) director

1944:   The Impostor

ALLAN DWAN (1885-1981) director

1945:   Getting Gertie's Garter (K. DeWolfe)

HAROLD DWAIN

1963:   Free, White and 21 (L. Buchanan)

BOB DYLAN

1978:   Renaldo and Clara

OSSIP DYMOV

1936:   Sins of Man*
1939:   Mirele Efros (Yid.; J. Berne)
1940:   Overture to Glory (doc.; Max Nosseck)

E

KENNETH EARLE

1936:   White Hunter (S. Duncan)
1941:   She Knew All the Answers*
1942:   Seven Days' Leave*; Twin Beds*

FENTON EARNSHAW

1947:   Killer at Large (T. Blackburn)
1951:   Savage Drums

B. REEVES EASON (1886-1956) director

1930:   Roaring Ranch; Trigger Tricks; Spurs
1934:   The Law of the Wild (S. Lowe)
1940:   Men with Steel Faces (edit. from 1935 serial
        The Phantom Empire; O. Brower)

CHARLES EASTMAN

1970:   Little Fauss and Big Halsey
1973:   The All-American Boy
1981:   Second-Hand Hearts

GORDON EASTMAN

1970:   The Savage Wild

SPENCER EASTMAN

1980:   Hide in Plain Sight

MILLER EASTON

1935:   Toll of the Desert

ROBERT EASTON

1975:   The Great Spider Invasion (R. Huff)

ROGER EBERT

1970:   Beyond the Valley of the Dolls

LOIS EBY

1937:   Too Many Wives*
1938:   The Lone Ranger (ser.)*

LOU EDELMAN

1931:   Shipmates*

WILLIAM EDELSON

1964:   The Crawling Hand (H. Strock)

WILLIAM EDGAR

1973:   Stacey!

JAMES EDMISTON

1956:   A Day of Fury (O. Brodney)
1957:   The Devil's Hairpin (C. Wilde)
1958:   Wink of an Eye*
1959:   Four Fast Guns (D. Gaultois)

GUS EDSON

1961:   Dondi (A. Zugsmith)

ERIC EDSON

1982: Soggy Bottom U.S.A.*

BLAKE EDWARDS (1922-   ) director, producer

1948: Panhandle (J. Champion)
1949: Stampede (J. Champion)
1952: Sound Off (R. Quine); Rainbow 'Round My
       Shoulder (R. Quine)
1953: All Ashore; Cruisin' Down the River (R.
       Quine)
1954: Drive a Crooked Road*
1955: Bring Your Smile Along; My Sister Eileen (R.
       Quine)
1956: He Laughed Last
1957: Mister Cory; Operation Mad Ball*
1958: This Happy Feeling
1962: The Notorious Landlady (L. Gelbart)
1963: Soldier in the Rain (M. Richlin)
1964: The Pink Panther (M. Richlin); A Shot in the
       Dark (W. Blatty)
1967: Gunn (W. Blatty)
1968: The Party*
1970: Darling Lili (W. Blatty)
1971: Wild Rovers
1974: The Tamarind Seed
1975: The Return of the Pink Panther (F. Waldman)
1976: The Pink Panther Strikes Again (F. Waldman)
1978: Revenge of the Pink Panther*
1979: "10"
1981: S.O.B.
1982: Victor/Victoria; Trail of the Pink Panther*

EDGAR EDWARDS

1938: Convicted; Woman Against the World
1939: Manhattan Shakedown; Special Investigator

GEOFFREY EDWARDS

1982: Trail of the Pink Panther*

GEORGE EDWARDS

1977:   Ruby (B. Schneider)
1978:   Harper Valley P.T.A. (B. Schneider)
1980:   The Attic (T. Crechales)

HENRY EDWARDS

1978:   Sergeant Pepper's Lonely Heart Club Band

PAUL EDWARDS

1976:   Trackdown
1978:   High-Ballin'

WESTON EDWARDS (see HARRY FRASER)

FRED EGGERS

1954:   Port of Hell*; Thunder Pass (T. Hubbard)
1955:   Treasure of Ruby Hills (T. Hubbard)
1958:   Legion of the Doomed (T.Hubbard)
1965:   The Return of Mr. Moto

JAN EGLESON

1979:   Billy in the Lowlands

MAX EHRLICH

1972:   Z.P.G. (F. DeFelitta)
1974:   The Savage Is Loose (F. DeFelitta)
1975:   The Reincarnation of Peter Proud

RICHARD EINFELD

1957:   Ghost Diver

JO EISINGER

1945:   The Spider (W. Darling)

1950: Night and the City (Brit.); The Sleeping
      City
1953: The System
1955: Bedevilled
1957: The Big Boodle; Crime of Passion
1959: The House of the Seven Hawks
1960: As the Sea Rages (Yugo.; J. Dell); Oscar
      Wilde (Brit.)
1966: The Dirty Game; The Poppy Is Also a Flower
1969: They Came to Rob Las Vegas*

RON ELDER III

1972: Melinda; Sounder
1976: Sounder Part 2

MICHAEL ELIAS

1979: The Jerk*; The Frisco Kid (F. Shaw)
1980: Serial (R. Eustis)
1982: Young Doctors in Love (R. Eustis)

JOYCE ELIASON

1980: Tell Me a Riddle (A. Lytle)

GARTH ELIASSEN

1982: Don't Go in the Woods Alone

IRVING ELINSON

1952: The Belle of New York (R. O'Brien)
1953: By the Light of the Silvery Moon (R.
      O'Brien)
1954: Lucky Me*

EDWARD ELISCU

1935: Music Is Magic (L. Breslow); Paddy O'Day (L.
      Breslow); Silk Hat Kid*
1936: Every Saturday Night; High Tension*; Little

```
            Miss Nobody*
1938:  Little Tough Guys in Society (M. Offner);
       His Exciting Night*
1939:  Charlie McCarthy, Detective*
1941:  Sis Hopkins*
1943:  Something to Shout About (L. Breslow)
1944:  Hey, Rookie*
1945:  The Gay Senorita (J. Bren)
1947:  Out of the Blue*
1950:  Three Husbands (V. Caspary)
1951:  Alice in Wonderland (Fr.)*
```

MICHAEL ELKINS

```
1960:  Esther and the King (R. Walsh)
```

SAUL ELKINS

```
1936:  Star for a Night (F. Hyland); Under Your
       Spell (F. Hyland); The Crime of Dr. Forbes
       (F. Hyland)
1938:  Tarnished Angel (J. Pagano); Women in Prison
1939:  Pride of the Navy (B. Markson)
```

STANLEY ELLIN

```
1951:  The Big Night*
```

PAUL C. ELLIOTT

```
1982:  Death Screams
```

PEGGY ELLIOTT

```
1972:  Come Back Charleston Blue
```

ANDERSON ELLIS

```
1940:  The Mortal Storm*
```

ANTHONY ELLIS

1957:   The Ride Back

CHARLES ELLIS

1959:   Vice Raid

EDITH ELLIS

1930:   The Great Meadow (C. Brabin)
1931:   Easiest Way

ROBERT ELLIS

1932:   The Monster Walks
1933:   By Appointment Only; Dance, Girl, Dance; Man
        of Sentiment
1934:   Fugitive Road*; In Love with Life; In the
        Money; One in a Million (K. Brown); Twin
        Husbands; The Quitter
1935:   Charlie Chan in Egypt (H. Logan); Happiness
        C.O.D. (H. Logan); Ladies Love Danger*; The
        Lady in Scarlet (H. Logan)
1936:   Back to Nature (H. Logan); Charlie Chan at
        the Circus (H. Logan); Charlie Chan at the
        Race Track*; Charlie Chan's Secret*; Here
        Comes Trouble*; Hitch Hike to Heaven (H.
        Logan)
1937:   Red Lights Ahead (H. Logan); The Jones
        Family in Big Business (alt. Big Business;
        H. Logan); Big Town Girl*; Born Reckless*;
        Charlie Chan at the Olympics (H. Logan);
        Laughing at Trouble (H. Logan); Off to the
        Races (H. Logan)
1938:   Sharpshooters (H. Logan); Speed to Burn (H.
        Logan); Down on the Farm (H. Logan); Love on
        a Budget (H. Logan); Rascals (H. Logan);
        Road Demon (H. Logan); A Trip to Paris (H.
        Logan)
1939:   The Escape (H. Logan); Chasing Danger (H.
        Logan); Too Busy to Work*; Susanna of the
        Mounties*; Charlie Chan in City in Darkness
        (H. Logan); Pardon Our Nerve (H. Logan)
1940:   Lucky Cisco Kid (H. Logan); The Man Who
        Wouldn't Talk*; Star Dust (H. Logan); Tin

Pan Alley (H. Logan)
1941:   The Great American Broadcast*; Sun Valley
        Serenade (H. Logan)
1942:   Footlight Serenade*; Iceland (H. Logan);
        Song of the Islands*
1943:   Hello, Frisco, Hello*
1944:   Four Jills in a Jeep*; Pin-Up Girl*;
        Something for the Boys*
1946:   Do You Love Me? (H. Logan); If I'm Lucky*

BOB ELLISON

1975:   Bucktown

HARLAN ELLISON

1966:   The Oscar*

JOSEPH ELLISON

1980:   Don't Go in the House*

IRVING ELMAN

1946:   Accomplice (F. Gruber); Strange Journey
        (Charles Kenyon)
1947:   Backlash; The Crimson Key; Jewels of
        Brandenburg*; Roses Are Red
1948:   The Challenge (F. Gruber); 13 Lead Soldiers

GUY ELMES

1953:   Bad Blonde (R. Landau)
1970:   The Night Visitor

JOHN EMERSON (1874-1956) actor, director, producer

1931:   The Struggle*
1934:   Girl from Missouri (A. Loos)

ROBERT J. EMERY

1975: Willie and Scratch

ROBERT EMMETT (see ROBERT E. TANSEY)

ED EMSCHWILLER

1970: Image, Flesh and Voice

CY ENDFIELD (1914-   ) director S. Afr.

(American films only)
1946: Gentleman Joe Palooka; Joe Palooka, Champ
       (A. de Pina); Mr. Hex
1947: Hard-Boiled Mahoney
1948: The Argyle Secrets
1949: Joe Palooka in the Counterpunch (H.
       Blankfort)
1965: Sands of the Kalahari

GUY ENDORE (1900-1970)

1935: Mad Love*; Mark of the Vampire (B.
       Schubert); The Raven*
1936: The Devil-Doll*
1937: The League of Frightened Men (E. Solow)
1938: Carefree*
1941: Lady from Louisiana*
1945: The Story of G. I. Joe*
1948: The Vicious Circle (H. Herald)
1949: Johnny Allegro (K. DeWolfe)
1951: He Ran All the Way (H. Butler); Tomorrow Is
       Another Day (Art Cohn)

MORRIS ENGEL (1918-   ) director, producer

1953: Little Fugitive*
1956: Lovers and Lollipops (R. Orkin)
1958: Weddings and Babies

SAMUEL G. ENGEL (1904-   ) producer

```
1936:   Sins of Man*
1937:   She Had to Eat
1940:   Viva Cisco Kid (H. Long); Earthbound (J.
        Lawson)
1941:   Romance of the Rio Grande (H. Shumate); Ride
        On, Vaquero; Blue, White and Perfect;
        Charlie Chan in Rio (L. Ziffren); Private
        Nurse; Scotland Yard (J. Balderston)
1942:   Through Different Eyes; Young America
1946:   My Darling Clementine (W. Miller)
```

DAVID ENGELBACH

```
1982: Death Wish II
```

OTTO ENGLANDER

```
1950:   Boy from Indiana
1953:   The Diamond Queen
```

RICHARD ENGLISH

```
1936:   Bulldog Edition (K. DeWolf)
1937:   Larceny on the Air (A. Bohem)
1938:   Mr. Boggs Steps Out
1939:   Million Dollar Legs (L. Foster)
1944:   Sweet and Lowdown
1945:   A Thousand and One Nights (W. Pettitt)
1947:   The Fabulous Dorseys*
1949:   Lust for Gold (T. Sherdeman)
1950:   The Flying Missile (J. Gunn); 711 Ocean
        Drive (F. Swann)
1957:   Beyond Mombasa (G. Levitt)
```

KEN ENGLUND (1911-   )

```
1938:   The Big Broadcast of 1938*; Artists and
        Models Abroad*; There's That Woman Again*
1939:   Good Girls Go to Paris (G. Lehman)
1940:   The Doctor Takes a Wife (G. Seaton); No, No
        Nanette; Slightly Honorable*
1941:   Nothing but the Truth (D. Hartman); This
        Thing Called Love*
1942:   Rings on Her Fingers; Springtime in the
```

Rockies (W. Bullock)
1943:   Sweet Rosie O'Grady
1944:   Here Come the Waves*
1945:   The Unseen*
1947:   The Secret Life of Walter Mitty (E. Freeman)
1948:   Good Sam
1951:   A Millionaire for Christy
1952:   Androcles and the Lion (C. Erskine); Never
        Wave at a WAC
1953:   The Caddy*
1956:   The Vagabond King (N. Langley)
1968:   The Wicked Dreams of Paula Schultz*

DON ENRIGHT

1981:   Search and Destroy; Striking Back

RAY ENRIGHT (1896-1965) director

1931:   Gold Dust Gertie (W. Wells)
1932:   Fireman, Save My Child*

HENRY (1912-   ) & PHOEBE (1914-1971) EPHRON

1944:   Black Magic*; Bride by Mistake
1947:   Always Together*
1948:   Wallflower
1949:   John Loves Mary; Look for the Silver Lining
1950:   The Jackpot
1951:   On the Riviera*
1952:   Belles on Their Toes; What Price Glory
1954:   There's No Business Like Show Business
1955:   Daddy Long Legs
1956:   Carousel; The Best Things in Life Are Free*
1957:   The Desk Set
1963:   Captain Newman, M.D.*

JOEL ENSANA

1970:   Meat/Rack

DAVID EPSTEIN

1950:   Of Men and Music*

JEROME EPSTEIN

1969:   The Adding Machine

JULIUS J. EPSTEIN (1909-   )

1935:   Broadway Gondolier*; I Live for Love*; In
        Caliente (J. Wald); Little Big Shot*; Living
        on Velvet (J. Wald); Stars over Broadway (J.
        Wald); The Big Broadcast of 1936 (unc.)*
1936:   Sons o' Guns (J. Wald)
1937:   Confession (M. LeVine)
1938:   Four Daughters (L. Coffee); Secrets of an
        Actress*
1939:   Daughters Courageous (P. Epstein); Four
        Wives*
1940:   No Time for Comedy (P. Epstein); Saturday's
        Children (P. Epstein)
1941:   The Bride Came C.O.D. (P. Epstein); The Man
        Who Came to Dinner (P. Epstein); The
        Strawberry Blonde (P. Epstein)
1942:   The Male Animal*
1943:   Casablanca*
1944:   Arsenic and Old Lace (P. Epstein); Mr.
        Skeffington (P. Epstein)
1948:   Romance on the High Seas (P. Epstein)
1949:   My Foolish Heart (P. Epstein)
1950:   Born Yesterday (unc.; A. Mannhaimer)
1951:   Take Care of My Little Girl (P. Epstein)
1953:   Forever Female (P. Epstein)
1954:   The Last Time I Saw Paris*; Young at Heart
        (L. Coffee)
1955:   The Tender Trap
1957:   Kiss Them for Me
1959:   Take a Giant Step
1960:   Tall Story
1961:   Fanny
1962:   Light in the Piazza
1964:   Send Me No Flowers
1965:   Return from the Ashes
1966:   Any Wednesday
1972:   Pete and Tillie
1975:   Once Is Not Enough
1977:   Cross of Iron (Herbert Asmodi)

1978: House Calls*

PHILIP G. EPSTEIN (-1952)

1936: The Bride Walks Out (P. Wolfson); Grand Jury
       (J. Fields); Love on a Bet (P. Wolfson);
       Mummy's Boys*
1937: New Faces of 1937*
1938: The Mad Miss Manton; There's That Woman
       Again*
1939: Daughters Courageous (J. Epstein); Four
       Wives*
1940: No Time for Comedy (J. Epstein); Saturday's
       Children (J. Epstein)
1941: The Bride Came C.O.D. (J. Epstein); The Man
       Who Came to Dinner (J. Epstein); The
       Srawberry Blonde (J. Epstein)
1942: The Male Animal*
1943: Casablanca*
1944: Arsenic and Old Lace (J. Epstein); Mr.
       Skeffington (J. Epstein)
1948: Romance on the High Seas (J. Epstein)
1949: My Foolish Heart (J. Epstein)
1951: Take Care of My Little Girl (J. Epstein)
1953: Forever Female (J. Epstein)
1954: The Last Time I Saw Paris*

RICHARD ERDMAN (1925-   ) actor, director

1971: Bleep

CARL ERICKSON

1932: Silver Dollar (H. Thew); Stranger in Town
       (H. Thew)
1933: Girl Missing (D. Mullaly); Mystery of the
       Wax Museum (D. Mullaly)
1934: Easy to Love (M. Seff); Fashions of 1934*;
       Smarty (F. Herbert)
1935: Black Fury (A. Finkel); Stranded (D. Daves);
       Sweet Music*

PAUL ERICKSON

```
1954:   White Fire (J. Gilling)
1955:   The Green Buddha; Secret Venture
1956:   Track the Man Down
1958:   Kill Her Gently
```

CHESTER ERSKINE (1905-   ) director, producer

```
1934:   Midnight
1945:   The Sailor Takes a Wife*
1947:   The Egg and I (F. Finklehoffe)
1948:   All My Sons
1949:   Take One False Step (I. Shaw)
1952:   Androcles and the Lion (K. Englund); A Girl
        in Every Port
1954:   Witness to Murder
```

LEE ERWIN

```
1959:   The Flying Fontaines (D. Mullaly)
1970:   Tarzan's Deadly Silence*
```

LEMIST ESLER

```
1951:   The Whistle at Eaton Falls (V. Shaler)
```

HARRY ESSEX (1910-   ) director, playwright

```
1946:   Boston Blackie and the Law
1947:   Desperate; Dragnet (B. Worth)
1948:   Bodyguard (F. Niblo)
1950:   Wyoming Mail*; The Killer That Stalked New
        York; Undercover Girl
1951:   The Fat Man (L. Lee)
1952:   Kansas City Confidential (G. Bruce); The Las
        Vegas Story (E. Felton); Models, Inc. (P.
        Yawitz)
1953:   The 49th Man; It Came from Outer Space; I,
        the Jury
1954:   Southwest Passage; Creature from the Black
        Lagoon (A. Ross)
1955:   Teen-Age Crime Wave (R. Buffum); Mad at the
        World
1956:   Raw Edge (R. Hill)
1957:   The Lonely Man (Robert Smith)
```

1965: The Sons of Katie Elder*
1972: Man and Boy (O. Saul)
1973: Deaf Smith and Johnny Ears (O. Saul)

GABE ESSOE

1975: The Devil's Rain*

HOWARD ESTABROOK (1884–1978)

1929: The Virginian; Shopworn Angel; Four
      Feathers*; She Goes to War (M. DeGresac)
1930: The Bad Man; Slightly Scarlet*; Double Cross
      Roads (G. Brooks); Behind the Makeup; Street
      of Chance; Hell's Angels (M. Behm)
1931: Cimarron; Kismet; The Woman Between; Woman
      Hungry; Are These Our Children? (W. Ruggles)
1932: A Bill of Divorcement (H. Gribble); Roar of
      the Dragon
1933: The Bowery (J. Gleason); The Devil's in
      Love; The Masquerader; Sweepings*
1935: David Copperfield (H. Walpole); Orchids to
      You*; Way Down East (W. Hurlburt)
1941: The Corsican Brothers (G. Bruce);
      International Lady; New Wine (N. Jory)
1943: The Human Comedy
1944: Heavenly Days (D. Quinn); The Bridge of San
      Luis Rey (J. Cain)
1945: Dakota (L. Hazard)
1946: The Virginian
1948: The Girl from Manhattan
1952: Lone Star (B. Chase)
1954: Cattle Queen of Montana (R. Blees); Passion
1959: The Big Fisherman (R. V. Lee)

EDWIN ESTRATE

1947: Shoot to Kill

ROBIN ESTRIDGE

1961: Beware of Children (N. Hudis)
1962: Escape from Zahrain
1963: Drums of Africa

1966: The Boy Cried Murder
1967: Eye of the Devil (D. Murphy)

ALEXANDER ESWAY

1943: The Cross of Lorraine*

JOE ESZTERHAS

1978: F.I.S.T. (S. Stallone)

DON ETTINGER

1937: Life Begins in College (K. Tunberg); The
      Lady Escapes
1938: Hold That Co-ed*; Rebecca of Sunnybrook Farm
      (K. Tunberg)
1940: I Was an Adventuress*; Young People (E.
      Blum)
1941: The Great American Broadcast*
1950: Guilty Bystander

DALE EUNSON

1951: On the Loose (K. Albert)
1953: The Star (K. Albert); Sabre Jet
1957: All Mine to Give (K. Eunson); Eighteen and
      Anxious (K. Eunson)
1963: Gidget Goes to Rome*
1976: Joe Panther

KATHERINE EUNSON

1957: All Mine to Give (D. Eunson); Eighteen and
      Anxious (D. Eunson)
1963: Gidget Goes to Rome*

RICH EUSTIS

1980: Serial (M. Elias)
1982: Young Doctors in Love (M. Elias)

DANIEL EVANS (-1935)

1934:   Uncertain Lady (M. Brown)

DAVID EVANS

1956:   Strange Intruder (W. Douglas)

FREDERIC A. EVANS

1946:   Outlaw of the Plains (E. Clifton)

JERRY EVANS

1970:   Hell's Bloody Devils

JOHN EVANS

1974:   Black Godfather
1978:   Blackjack

JULIUS EVANS

1948:   Sword of the Avenger

ROSS EVANS

1949:   The Fan*

VINCENT EVANS

1950:   Chain Lightning (L. O'Brien)
1956:   Battle Hymn (C. Grayson)

ARTHUR EVERETT

1937:   Rough Riding Rhythm; Roaring Six Guns

JAMES EVERGREEN

1982:   The Love Butcher (Don Jones)

BERNARD EVSLIN

1970:   A.K.A. Cassius Clay (doc.)

WILLIAM R. EWING

1982:   The Slayer (J. Cardone)

DAVID EYRE

1981:   Cattle Annie and Little Britches (Robert
        Ward); Wolfen (M. Wadleigh)

F

JAMES BERNARD FAGAN

1932: Forgotten Commandments (A. Leahy)

DOUGLAS FAIRBANKS, SR. (1883-1939) actor

1931: Around the World in 80 Minutes (R. E.
       Sherwood)

DOUGLAS FAIRBANKS, JR. (1909-   ) actor

1947: The Exile
1949: The Fighting O'Flynn (R. Thoeren)

WILLIAM FAIRCHILD

1968: Star!
1973: Embassy

GERALD FAIRLIE

1935: Charlie Chan in Shanghai (E. Lowe)
1951: Calling Bulldog Drummond

FRITZ FALKENSTEIN

1937: The Perfect Specimen*

JAMAA FANAKA

1975:   Welcome Home, Brother Charles
1979:   Penitentiary
1982:   Penitentiary II

HAMPTON FANCHER

1982:   Blade Runner (D. Peoples)

JOHN FANTE

1944:   Youth Runs Wild
1952:   My Man and I (J. Leonard)
1956:   Full of Life
1957:   Jeanne Eagels*
1962:   The Reluctant Saint (Ital.; J. Petracca) ;
        Walk on the Wild Side (E. Morris)
1963:   My Six Loves*
1966:   Maya

FRANCIS EDWARD FARAGOH (1898-   )

1929:   Her Private Affair (H. Bernstein)
1930:   Back Pay; Broken Dishes; Little Caesar
1931:   Frankenstein (G. Fort); Iron Man; Right of
        Way; Too Young to Marry
1932:   Prestige*; Under-Cover Man*; The Last Man
        (K. Thompson)
1934:   Hat, Coat and Glove
1935:   Becky Sharpe; Chasing Yesterday; The Return
        of Peter Grimm
1936:   Dancing Pirate*
1942:   The Mad Martindales
1943:   My Friend Flicka (L. Hayward)
1946:   The Renegades (M. Levy)
1947:   Easy Come, Easy Go*

GEORGE FARGO

1977:   The Farmer*

JOE FARNHAM

1929:   So This Is College*

1930: The Big House*

DOROTHY FARNUM

1929: The Pagan; The Unholy Night (E. Mayer)
1930: Redemption; Call of the Flesh
1934: Constant Nymph (Brit.)*; Evensong

WALTON T. FARRAR

1936: Feud of the West*

HENRY FARRELL

1965: Hush...Hush, Sweet Charlotte (L. Heller)
1971: What's the Matter With Helen?

JOHN FARRIS

1975: Dear Dead Delilah
1977: The Fury

JOHN FARROW (1904-1963) director

1929: Wolf Song; Dangerous Woman; Wheel of Life
1930: Shadow of the Law; Seven Days' Leave
1931: Common Law; Woman of Experience
1935: Tarzan Escapes*; Last of the Pagans
1949: Red, Hot and Blue (H. Wilde)
1956: Around the World in 80 Days*
1959: John Paul Jones (J. Lasky)

ALVIN L. FAST

1973: Tom (G. Clark); Bummer
1976: Black Shampoo (G. Clark); The Bad Bunch (G. Clark)
1977: Satan's Cheerleaders (G. Clark)
1980: Angels Brigade (G. Clark)

WILLIAM FAULKNER (1897-1962) novelist

```
1936:   The Road to Glory (J. Sayre)
1944:   To Have and Have Not (J. Furthman)
1946:   The Big Sleep*
1955:   Land of the Pharaohs*
```

FRANK FAY

```
1929:   Joy Street (C. Condon)
1938:   Meet the Mayor
```

WILLIAM FAY

```
1962:   Kid Galahad
```

RANDALL FAYE

```
1931:   Branded; Lasa of the Rio Grande
1932:   The Texas Cyclone
1936:   Murder in the Red Barn
1944:   Cheyenne Wildcat; Firebrands of Arizona
1945:   Great Stagecoach Robbery; Scotland Yard
        Investigator
1946:   The Fabulous Suzanne (T. Chapman)
1947:   The Ghost Goes Wild
```

JIM FEAZELL

```
1982:   Psycho from Texas
```

PETER S. FEIBLEMAN

```
1964:   Ensign Pulver (J. Logan)
```

JULES FEIFFER (1927-   ) cartoonist, writer

```
1971:   Little Murders; Carnal Knowledge
1972:   Oh! Calcutta!*
1980:   Popeye
```

MARVE FEINBERG

1966: Ambush Bay (I. Melchior)

FELIX E. FEIST (1906-1965) director

1947: The Devil Thumbs a Ride
1950: The Golden Gloves Story (J. Ansen)
1952: Babes in Bagdad (J. Ansen)
1953: Donovan's Brain

STEVE FEKE
1979: When a Stranger Calls (F. Walton)

MARTY FELDMAN (1938-   ) actor, director Brit.

(American films only)
1977: The Last Remake of Beau Geste

RANDOLPH FELDMAN

1981: Hell Night

ROBERT FELLOWS

1963: The Girl Hunters*

HENRY GREGOR FELSON

1968: Fever Heat

EARL FELTON

1936: Bengal Tiger (R. Chanslor); Freshman Love
       (G. Bricker)
1937: Bad Guy (H. Ruskin)
1938: Extortion; The Night Hawk; Prison Nurse (S.
       Salkow)
1939: Calling All Marines; Smuggled Cargo (M.
       Jacoby); Society Smugglers (A. Horman)
1941: The Pittsburgh Kid; World Premiere; Sierra
       Sue (J. Zimet); The Lone Wolf Keeps a Date

```
                  (S. Salkow); The Lone Wolf Takes a Chance
                  (S. Salkow)
1942:     Sunset Serenade; Heart of the Golden West
1943:     Night Plane from Chungking*
1945:     Pardon My Past (K. Lamb)
1949:     Trapped (G. Zuckerman)
1950:     Armored Car Robbery (G. D. Adams)
1952:     The Happy Time; The Las Vegas Story*; The
                  Narrow Margin
1954:     Twenty Thousand Leagues Under the Sea
1955:     The Marauders (J. Leonard)
1956:     Bandido; The Rawhide Years
1960:     Killers of Kilimanjaro*
```

ANDREW J. FENADY

```
1958:     Stakeout on Dope Street*
1959:     The Young Captives
1966:     Ride Beyond Vengeance
1967:     Hondo and the Apaches
1970:     Chisum
1980:     Sam Marlowe, Private Eye (orig. The Man With
                  Bogart's Face)
```

FRANK FENTON

```
1937:     Angel's Holiday (L. Root); Step Lively,
                  Jeeves! (L. Root); Wild and Woolly (L.
                  Root); Checkers
1939:     The Saint in London (L. Root)
1940:     Little Orvie*; Millionaires in Prison (L.
                  Root); The Saint Takes Over (L. Root)
1941:     A Date with the Falcon (L. Root); The Gay
                  Falcon (L. Root)
1942:     The Falcon Takes Over (L. Root); Highways by
                  Night (L. Root)
1943:     The Sky's the Limit (L. Root)
1944:     My Best Gal (O. Cooper)
1946:     Lady Luck (L. Root)
1947:     Night Song (D. Hyland)
1948:     Station West (W. Miller)
1949:     Malaya
1950:     Walk Softly, Stranger
1951:     His Kind of Woman; The Man with a Cloak
1952:     The Wild North
1953:     Ride, Vaquero; Escape from Fort Bravo
```

```
1954:   River of No Return; Garden of Evil
1955:   Untamed*
1956:   These Wilder Years
1957:   The Wings of Eagles (W. Haines)
1959:   The Jayhawkers*
```

PHILLIP FENTY

1972:   Super Fly

PEG FENWICK

1955:   All That Heaven Allows

GRAEME FERGUSON

1965:   The Love Goddesses (doc.; S. Turell)

RON FERGUSON

```
1938:   Blind Alibi*
1941:   Double Cross (M. Raison)
```

HARVEY FERGUSON

```
1937:   It Happened in Hollywood (E. Hill)
1939:   Stand Up and Fight*
```

JOSE FERRER (1912-   ) actor, director

1956:   The Great Man (Al Morgan)

MEL FERRER (1917-   ) actor, director

1966:   Every Day Is a Holiday (Sp.)

BETH FERRIS

1979:   Heartland

WALTER FERRIS (1886-   )

1934:   Death Takes a Holiday*
1936:   Lloyds of London (E. Pascal); Under Two
        Flags*
1937:   Heidi (J. Josephson); Maid of Salem*
1938:   Four Men and a Prayer*; A Yank at Oxford*
1939:   The Magnificent Fraud (G. Gabriel); Susannah
        of the Mounties*; The Little Princess (E.
        Hill)
1940:   Swiss Family Robinson*; Tom Brown's School
        Days*
1941:   Melody for Three (L. Loeb)
1948:   The Gallant Blade (M. Grant)
1952:   At Sword's Point*

MICHAEL FESSIER

1935:   Only Eight Hours; Society Doctor (S. Marx)
1936:   Exclusive Story; Speed; Women Are Trouble
1937:   Song of the City
1938:   Valley of the Giants (S. Miller)
1939:   Angels Wash Their Faces*; Espionage Agent*;
        Wings of the Navy
1940:   He Stayed for Breakfast*; It All Came True
        (L. Kimble)
1941:   You'll Never Get Rich (E. Pagano)
1942:   You Were Never Lovelier*
1943:   Fired Wife (E. Pagano)
1944:   Her Primitive Man (E. Pagano); San Diego, I
        Love You (E. Pagano); The Merry Monahans (E.
        Pagano)
1945:   Frontier Gal (E. Pagano); That Night with
        You (E. Pagano); That's the Spirit (E.
        Pagano)
1946:   Lover Come Back (E. Pagano)
1947:   Slave Girl (E. Pagano)
1954:   Red Garters

EDWARD I. FESSLER

1957:   Bayou

MARTIN FIELD

1955: Murder Is My Beat (A. Wisberg)

SALISBURY FIELD

1930: In Gay Madrid*
1931: No Limit (V. Shore); Smart Woman
1934: Witching Hour (A. Veiller)

SYDNEY FIELD

1967: Spree (doc.)

PAT FIELDER

1957: The Monster That Challenged the World; The
       Vampire
1958: The Return of Dracula; The Flame Barrier (G.
       Yates)
1962: Geronimo

DOROTHY FIELDS (1905-1974) songwriter

1941: Father Takes a Wife (H. Fields)

HERBERT FIELDS (1897-1958) playwright

1931: The Hot Heiress*
1934: Let's Fall in Love; Down to Their Last
       Yacht*
1935: Hands Across the Table*; Mississippi*;
       People Will Talk; Ship Cafe (H. Thompson);
       Accent on Youth (C. Binyon)
1936: Love Before Breakfast; The Luckiest Girl in
       the World (H. Myers)
1938: Fools for Scandal*
1939: Honolulu (E. Partos)
1941: Father Takes a Wife (D. Fields)

JEANNE FIELDS

1982: Human Highway

JOSEPH FIELDS (1895-1966) playwright

1931:   The Big Shot (E. Baldwin)
1933:   Pick Up*
1935:   Lightning Strikes Twice (J. Gray); $1,000 a
        Minute*
1936:   The Genteman from Louisiana (G. Rigby);
        Grand Jury (P. Epstein); Palm Springs; That
        Girl from Paris*
1937:   Reported Missing (J. Chodorov); When Love Is
        Young (E. Greene)
1938:   Fools for Scandal*; Rich Man, Poor Girl (J.
        Chodorov)
1939:   The Girl and the Gambler (C. Young); The
        Girl from Mexico (L. Houser); Mexican
        Spitfire (C. Roberts); The Spellbinder (T.
        Lennon); Two Thoroughbreds (J. Cady)
1940:   Dulcy*; Two Girls on Broadway (J. Chodorov)
1941:   Louisiana Purchase (J. Chodorov)
1942:   My Sister Eileen (J. Chodorov)
1946:   A Night in Casablanca (R. Kibbee)
1947:   Lost Honeymoon
1948:   The Man from Texas (J. Chodorov)
1953:   The Farmer Takes a Wife*
1958:   The Tunnel of Love
1959:   Happy Anniversary (J. Chodorov)
1961:   Flower Drum Song

LEONARD FIELDS

1933:   The Devil's Mate (D. Silverstein)
1934:   King Kelly of the U.S.A. (D. Silverstein);
        Manhattan Love Song (D. Silverstein); The
        Scarlet Letter (D. Silverstein); Unknown
        Blonde (D. Silverstein)
1935:   Streamline Express (D. Silverstein); Woman
        Wanted (D. Silverstein)

W. C. FIELDS (1879-1946) actor (also MAHATMA KANE
        JEEVES)

1940:   My Little Chickadee (M. West); The Bank Dick

HAL FIMBERG

1941: The Big Store*
1944: National Barn Dance (L. Loeb); In Society*;
      You Can't Ration Love (V. Burton); A Wave, a
      Wac and a Marine
1945: The Naughty Nineties*
1966: Our Man Flint (B. Starr)
1967: In Like Flint

MORTON FINE

1957: Hot Summer Night (D. Friedkin)
1958: Handle with Care (D. Friedkin)
1965: The Fool Killer (D. Friedkin); The
      Pawnbroker (D. Friedkin)
1976: The Next Man*
1978: The Greek Tycoon
1981: Capoblanco (M. Gelman)

WILLIAM FINGER

1976: Track of the Moon Beast (C. Sinclair)

HARRY JULIAN FINK

1965: Major Dundee*
1971: Big Jake (R. Fink); Dirty Harry*
1973: Cahill, U.S. Marshal (R. Fink)

RITA M. FINK

1971: Big Jake (J. Fink); Dirty Harry*
1973: Cahill, U.S. Marshal (J. Fink)

ABEM FINKEL (1889-1948)

1931: The Deceiver*
1934: Hi, Nellie (S. Sutherland)
1935: Black Fury (C. Erickson); Special Agent (L.
      Doyle)
1936: Black Legion (W. Haines); Public Enemy's
      Wife (H. Buckley)

```
1937:   Marked Woman (R. Rossen)
1938:   Jezebel*; White Banners
1941:   Sergeant York*
1942:   The Big Shot*
1945:   Tonight and Every Night (L Samuels)
1947:   Time Out of Mind
```

ROBERT FINKLE

```
1941:   Wrangler's Roost (J. Vlahos); Fugitive
        Valley (J. Vlahos)
```

FRED F. FINKLEHOFFE (1910-1977) playwright

```
1940:   Brother Rat and a Baby*; Strike Up the Band
        (J. Monks)
1941:   Babes on Broadway (E. Ryan)
1942:   For Me and My Gal*
1943:   Best Foot Forward (I. Brecher); Girl Crazy
1944:   Meet Me in St. Louis (I. Brecher)
1946:   Mr. Ace
1947:   The Egg and I (C. Erskine)
1948:   Words and Music
1950:   At War with the Army
1952:   The Stooge (M. Rackin)
```

KEN FINKLEMAN

```
1982:   Grease 2; Airplane II: the Sequel
```

W. FRANKLIN FINLEY

```
1982:   The First Time
```

ROBERT FIORE

```
1970:   Dionysus in 69*
```

MAX FISCHER

```
1982:   The Lucky Star
```

BARNET FISHBEIN

1979:   Jesus

BOB FISHER

1964:   A Global Affair*
1965:   I'll Take Sweden*
1967:   Eight on the Lam*
1972:   Cancel My Reservation (A. Marx)

DAVID FISHER

1982:   Liar's Moon

MICHAEL FISHER

1968:   The Savage Seven; Killers Three; Buckskin
1981:   Earthbound

STEVE FISHER

1942:   Berlin Correspondent (J. Andrews)
1945:   Johnny Angel
1946:   Lady in the Lake
1947:   Song of the Thin Man (N. Perrin); That's My
        Man (B. King)
1948:   The Hunted; I Wouldn't Be in Your Shoes
1951:   Roadblock (G. Bricker)
1952:   Battle Zone; Flat Top; Whispering Smith vs.
        Scotland Yard
1953:   San Antone; The Woman They almost Lynched;
        The Big Frame (J. Gilling); The City That
        Never Sleeps; Sea of Lost Ships; The Man
        from the Alamo (D. Beauchamp)
1954:   Hell's Half Acre
1955:   The Big Tip-Off; Las Vegas Shakedown; Night
        Freight; Toughest Man Alive; Top Gun (R.
        Schayer); Betrayed Women
1957:   The Restless Breed; Courage of Black Beauty
1958:   I, Mobster
1965:   Black Spurs; Young Fury
1966:   Johnny Reno; Waco

```
1967:   Fort Utah (A. Craddock); Hostile Guns (S.
        Nibley); Red Tomahawk
1968:   Arizona Bushwackers; Rogue's Gallery
1973:   The Clones
1977:   The Great Gundown
```

KENNETH H. FISHMAN

```
1974:   Law and Disorder*
```

PAUL FISK

```
1979:   The Evictors*; The Day It Came to Earth
```

JEFFREY ALLADIN FISKIN

```
1970:   Angel Unchained
1981:   Cutter's Way; The Pursuit of D. B. Cooper
```

HUGH FITE

```
1941:   Parachute Battalion (J. Twist)
```

MARGARET FITTS

```
1949:   The Sun Comes Up (W. Ludwig)
1950:   Stars in My Crown
1952:   Talk About a Stranger
1955:   Moonfleet (J. Lustig)
1956:   The King and Four Queens (R. Simmons)
```

BENEDICT FITZGERALD

```
1980:   Wise Blood
```

DALLAS FITZGERALD

```
1936:   The Clutching Hand (ser.)*
```

EDITH FITZGERALD

1933: Today We Live (D. Taylor)
1934: The Painted Veil*
1936: Small Town Girl (J. Mahin)
1939: Within the Law (C. Lederer)

F. SCOTT FITZGERALD (1896-1940) novelist

1938: Three Comrades (E. Paramore)

RUTH FITZGERALD

1935: The Wedding Night

JAMES A. FITZPATRICK

1930: Lady of the Lake
1945: Song of Mexico

CORTLAND FITZSIMMONS

1937: The Mandarin Mystery*
1939: Death of a Champion (S. Palmer)
1941: All-American Co-Ed (K. Higgins)
1942: Fiesta

ROBERT S. FIVESON

1979: The Clonus Horror (M. Schreibman)

PAUL FIX (1901-   ) actor

1944: Tall in the Saddle (M. Hogan)
1954: Ring of Fear*

FRANCIS FLAHERTY

1948: Louisiana Story (doc.; Robert Flaherty)

ROBERT FLAHERTY (1884-1951) director

```
1933:   Tabu* (doc.)
1934:   Man of Aran (doc.)
1942:   The Land (doc.)
1944:   Louisiana Story (doc.; Frances Flaherty)
```

MARY FLANNERY

```
1933:   The Thundering Herd (J. Cunningham)
```

MARTIN FLAVIN

```
1930:   The Big House*; Passion Flower
```

HARVEY FLAXMAN

```
1970:   Interplay
1977:   Grizzly (D. Sheldon)
```

A. S. FLEISCHMAN

```
1955:   Blood Alley
1958:   Lafayette Escadrille
1961:   The Deadly Companions
```

SID FLEISCHMAN

```
1956:   Goodbye, My Lady
1973:   Scalawag (A. Maltz)
```

LUCILLE FLETCHER

```
1948:   Sorry, Wrong Number
```

PAT C. FLICK

```
1936:   The Singing Kid (W. Duff); Stage Struck (T.
        Buckingham)
1937:   Marry the Girl*; Nobody's Baby*
1938:   His Exciting Night*
```

THEODORE J. FLICKER (1930-   )

1964: The Troublemaker (B. Henry)
1966: Spinout (G. Kirgo)
1967: The President's Analyst
1970: Up in the Cellar
1978: Jacob Two-Two Meets the Hooded Fang

RUTH BROOKS FLIPPEN

1952: Love Is Better Than Ever
1961: Gidget Goes Hawaiian
1962: Sail a Crooked Ship*
1963: Gidget Goes to Rome (K.& D. Eunson); A
       Ticklish Affair
1964: looking for Love

SCOTT FLOHR

1960: Squad Car (E. M. Parsons)

ROBERT FLOREY (1900-   )

1933: A Study in Scarlet
1948: Rogue's Regiment (R. Buckner)

RICHARD FLOURNOY

1936: General Spanky*; Mister Cinderella (A.
       Jones); Neighborhood House (A. Jones)
1937: Fit for a King; Pick a Star*; Riding on Air
       (R. Macaulay)
1938: Blondie
1939: Beware, Spooks!*; Blondie Brings Up Baby (G.
       Lehman); Blondie Meets the Boss; Blondie
       Takes a Vacation
1940: Blondie Has Servant Trouble; Blondie on a
       Budget; Blondie Plays Cupid (K. DeWolf); So
       You Won't Talk
1941: Bedtime Story; Go West, Young Lady (K.
       DeWolf)
1942: Blondie's Blessed Event*
1943: Dangerous Blondes (J. Henley); The More the
       Merrier*; A Night to Remember (J. Henley)

1945: The Affairs of Susan*
1949: One Last Fling (W. Sackheim)
1953: Affair with a Stranger

BUCK FLOWER

1982: Drive-In Massacre (J. Goff); Baby Dolls (J.
       Goff)

ERROL FLYNN (1909-1959) actor

1950: Adventures of Captain Fabian

JOHN FLYNN

1973: The Outfit

LADISLAS FODOR

1941: A Very Young Lady (E. Ryan)
1942: Girl Trouble (R. Crutcher); Tales of
       Manhattan*
1947: The Other Love; (H. Brown)
1949: The Great Sinner (R. Fullop-Miller)
1958: Tom Thumb

JACK FOLEY

1934: Perils of Pauline (ser.)*

JANE FONDA (1937-   ) actress

1972: Free the Army (doc.)*

PETER FONDA (1939-   ) actor, director

1969: Easy Rider*

BRADBURY FOOTE

1937: The Bride Wore Red (T. Slesinger)
1938: Of Human Hearts
1940: Edison, the Man (T. Jennings); Young Tom
       Edison*
1946: The Madonna's Secret (W. Thiele)
1948: Homicide for Three; King of the Gamblers (A.
       DeMond)
1950: Prisoners in Petticoats
1951: Million Dollar Pursuit (A. DeMond)

HORTON FOOTE

1956: Storm Fear
1962: To Kill a Mockingbird
1965: Baby, the Rain Must Fall
1967: Hurry Sundown (T. C. Ryan)
1972: Tomorrow

JOHN TAINTOR FOOTE (-1950)

1938: Kentucky (L. Trotti)
1939: Swanee River (P. Dunne)
1949: The Great Dan Patch; The Story of Seabiscuit

HARRY FORBES

1938: Clipped Wings

JAMES FORBES

1930: Their Own Desire (F. Marion)

BRYANT FORD

1944: Strangers in the Night

COREY FORD

1932: The Half-Naked Truth (B. Cormack); The Sport
       Parade*; The Phantom of Crestwood*
1939: Remember? (N. McLeod); Topper Takes a Trip*;
       Zenobia

HARRIET FORD

1936:   I Married a Doctor*

PATRICK FORD

1950:   Wagonmaster (F. Nugent)

CARL FOREMAN (1914–   ) director, producer (also
        DEREK FRYE)

1941:   Spooks Run Wild (C. Marion); Bowery
        Blitzkrieg (S. Braxton)
1942:   Rhythm Parade (C. Marion)
1948:   So This Is New York (H. Baker)
1949:   Champion; The Clay Pigeon; Home of the Brave
1950:   Cyrano de Bergerac; The Men; Young Man with
        a Horn (E. North)
1952:   High Noon
1954:   The Sleeping Tiger (Brit.; H. Buchman)
1957:   The Bridge on the River Kwai (unc.; M.
        Wilson)
1958:   The Key (Brit.)
1961:   The Guns of Navarone
1963:   The Victors
1969:   NcKenna's Gold
1972:   Young Winston
1980:   When Time Ran Out (S. Silliphant)

RICHARD FOREMAN

1981:   Strong Medicine

C. S. FORESTER (1899–1966) novelist

1943:   Forever and a Day*

EDDIE FORMAN

1951:   Skipalong Rosenbloom (ret. The Square
        Shooter; D. Reisner)

MILOS FORMAN (1932-   ) director Czech.

(American films only)
1971: Taking Off*

PAULINE FORNEY

1929: Jazz Heaven (J.W. Ruben)

LARRY FORRESTER

1970: Tora! Tora! Tora!*

JAMES FORSYTH

1961: Francis of Assisi (E. Vale)

WAYNE FORSYTHE

1973: Valley of Blood

GARRETT FORT

1929: The Letter; The Lady Lies (J. Meehan);
       Jealousy; Return of Sherlock Holmes
1930: The Big Pond; Applause*; Roadhouse Nights;
       Dangerous Dan McGrew; Outside the Law; In
       Deep; Lazy Lady; Scotland Yard
1931: Dracula; Frankenstein (F. Faragoh); Beyond
       Victory*
1932: Panama Flo; 70,000 Witnesses*; Under-Cover
       Man*; Young Bride (J. Murfin)
1933: Before Dawn*
1934: The Lost Patrol (D. Nichols); Private
       Scandal
1935: Jalna*; Mills of the Gods
1936: The Devil-Doll*; Dracula's Daughter
1939: Zero Hour
1940: The Mark of Zorro (B. Meredyth)
1941: Among the Living (L. Cole); Ladies in
       Retirement (R. Denham)

1942:   Street of Chance

JAN FORTUNE

1939:   Man of Conquest*
1941:   The Vanishing Virginian
1942:   Mokey (W. Root)

FANYA FOSS

1940:   Girls Under 21 (J. Dratler)
1941:   Richest Man in Town (J. Sackheim); The Stork
         Pays Off (A. Leslie)

BOB FOSSE (1927-   ) director, choreographer

1979:   All That Jazz (R. Aurthur)

LEWIS R. FOSTER (1900-1974) director

1933:   Cheating Blondes (I. Auster)
1934:   Eight Girls in a Boat (C. Robinson)
1935:   Stolen Harmony*
1936:   Love Letters of a Star*; The Magnificent
         Brute*; Two in a Crowd*
1937:   Armored Car (R. N. Lee); She's Dangerous*;
1938:   Illegal Traffic*; Sons of the Legion*
1939:   Million Dollar Legs (R. English); Night
         Work*; Some Like It Hot (W. Mahoney); Sudden
         Money
1940:   Comin' Round the Mountain*; The Farmer's
         Daughter; Golden Gloves (M. Shane)
1941:   Adventure in Washington (A. Caesar)
1942:   I Live on Danger*; The Mayor of 44th Street
         (F. Ryan)
1943:   Hers to Hold; The More the Merrier*
1944:   Can't Help Singing (F. Ryan)
1947:   I Wonder Who's Kissing Her Now
1949:   Captain China (G. Bagni); El Paso; The Lucky
         Stiff; Special Agent (W. Chambers);
         Manhandled (W. Chambers)
1950:   The Eagle and the Hawk (G. Homes)
1951:   Passage West; Crosswinds
1952:   The Blazing Forest (W. Miller)

```
1953:   Jamaica Run; The Vanquished*; Those Redheads
        from Seattle*; Tropic Zone
1955:   Crashout (H. Chester)
1958:   Tonka (L. Hayward)
```

NORMAN FOSTER (1900-1976) director, actor

```
1937:   Fair Warning; Thank You, Mr. Moto (W.
        Cooper); Think Fast, Mr. Moto (H. E. Smith)
1938:   Mysterious Mr. Moto (P. MacDonald)
1939:   Mr. Moto Takes a Vacation (P. MacDonald);
        Mr. Moto's Last Warning (P. MacDonald)
1950:   Woman on the Run (A. Campbell)
1952:   Sky Full of Moon; Navajo (doc.)
1953:   Sombrero (J. Niggli)
1955:   Davy Crockett, King of the Wild Frontier*
1956:   Davy Crockett and the River Pirates (T.
        Blackburn)
1960:   The Sign of Zorro (L. Hawley)
1965:   The Merry Wives of Windsor (Aust.)
1966:   Indian Paint
1967:   Brighty of Grand Canyon
```

ROYAL FOSTER

```
1947:   Bill and Coo (D. Reisner)
```

WARREN FOSTER

```
1964:   Hey There, It's Yogi Bear (anim.)*
```

VINCENT FOTRE

```
1958:   Missile to the Moon
```

GENE FOWLER, JR.

```
1932:   State's Attorney (R. Brown); What Price
        Hollywood?*
1933:   The Way to Love*
1934:   The Mighty Barnum (B. Meredyth)
1935:   Call of the Wild (L. Praskins); Professional
```

Soldier (Howard Smith)
1936: Half Angel*; A Message to Garcia (W. Lipscomb)
1937: Love Under Fire*; Nancy Steele Is Missing (H. Long)
1941: Billy the Kid
1949: Big Jack*
1951: My Outlaw Brother (A. Levitt)
1959: The Oregon Trail (L. Vittens)

FINIS FOX

1929: Evangeline
1931: Resurrection

FREDERIC LOUIS FOX

1955: Headline Hunters (J. Butler)
1956: Dakota Incident; When Gangland Strikes (J. Butler)
1957: Taming Sutton's Gal (T. Williamson); The Wayward Girl (H. Branch)
1969: 80 Steps to Jonah

FRED S. FOX

1980: Oh, God! Book II*

GEORGE FOX

1974: Earthquake (M. Puzo)

MICHAEL FOX

1982: Fox Style Killer (C. Houston)

PAUL HARVEY FOX

1930: Prince of Diamonds

WALLACE FOX (1895-1958) director

1935:   Red Morning (J. Twist)

FREDDY FOY

1928:   Midnight Taxi

JOSEPH FRALEY

1982:   Silent Rage

BASILIO FRANCHINA

1964:   The Fall of the Roman Empire*

OWEN FRANCIS

1936:   The Magnificent Brute*
1937:   Criminals of the Air
1939:   Pack Up Your Troubles (L. Breslow); Twenty
        Thousand Men a Year (L. Breslow)
1940:   Man from Montreal; Shooting High (L.
        Breslow)

CAROLINE FRANCKE

1932:   Misleading Lady (A. Heilbron); The Wiser Sex
        (H. Hervey)

BRUNO FRANK

1939:   The Hunchback of Notre Dame (S. Levien)

FREDERICK M. FRANK

1947:   Unconquered*
1949:   Samson and Delihah (J. Lasky)
1952:   The Greatest Show on Earth*
1956:   The Ten Commandments*
1961:   El Cid (P. Yordan)

HARRIET FRANK, JR.

1948:   Silver River (S. Longstreet); Whiplash (M.
        Geraghty)
1958:   The Long, Hot Summer (I. Ravetch)
1959:   The Sound and the Fury (I. Ravetch)
1960:   The Dark at the Top of the Stairs (I.
        Ravetch); Home from the Hill (I. Ravetch)
1963:   Hud (I. Ravetch)
1967:   Hombre (I. Ravetch)
1969:   House of Cards (I. Ravetch)
1972:   The Cowboys*
1974:   Conrack (I. Ravetch); The Spikes Gang (I.
        Ravetch)
1979:   Norma Rae (I. Ravetch)

JACQUIN FRANK

1943:   The Blocked Trail (J. Butler)

MELVIN FRANK (1913-   ) director, producer

1943:   Happy Go Lucky*; Thank Your Lucky Stars*
1944:   And the Angels Sing (N. Panama)
1945:   Duffy's Tavern (N. Panama); Road to Utopia
        (N. Panama)
1946:   Monsieur Beaucaire (N. Panama); Our Hearts
        Were Growing Up (N. Panama)
1947:   It Had to Be You*
1948:   Mr. Blandings Builds His Dream House (N.
        Panama)
1949:   The Return of October (N. Panama)
1950:   The Reformer and the Redhead (N. Panama)
1951:   Callaway Went Thataway (N. Panama); Strictly
        Dishonorable (N. Panama)
1952:   Above and Beyond*
1954:   Knock on Wood (N. Panama); White Christmas*
1956:   The Court Jester (N. Panama); That Certain
        Feeling*
1959:   The Jayhawkers*; Li'l Abner (N. Panama)
1960:   The Facts of Life (N. Panama)
1962:   The Road to Hong Kong (N. Panama)
1964:   Strange Bedfellows (M. Pertwee)
1966:   A Funny Thing Happened on the Way to the
        Forum*

```
1968:   Buona Sera, Mrs. Campbell*
1973:   A Touch of Class (J. Rose)
1976:   The Duchess and the Dirtwater Fox*
1979:   Lost and Found (J. Rose)
```

ROBERT FRANK

```
1969:   Me and My Brother (S. Sheppard)
```

ROSE FRANKEN

```
1934:   Elinor Norton
1935:   Alias Mary Dow (G. Unger)
1936:   Beloved Enemy*
1946:   Claudia and David (W. Melony)
```

C. Lester Franklin

```
1975:   The Four Deuces
```

DEAN FRANKLIN

```
1939:   Code of the Secret Service (L. Katz)
1940:   The Fighting 69th*
```

ELBERT FRANKLIN

```
1940:   The Villain Still Pursued Her
```

GEORGE FRANKLIN

```
1982:   The Incubus
```

HARRY FRANKLIN

```
1956:   The Brave One (D. Trumbo)
```

J. E. FRANKLIN

```
1973:   Black Girl (Ossie Davis)
```

PAUL FRANKLIN

1937: Outlaws of the Orient (C Royal); Trouble in
       Morocco; Secret Valley*; Roaring Timber (R.
       Cosgriff); Headin' East (E. La Blanche)
1938: Rhythm of the Saddle; Man Hunters of the
       Caribbean (E. La Blanche)
1939: The Man from Sundown; Home on the Prairie
       (C. Powell); Spoilers of the Range; The
       Stranger from Texas
1940: Blazing Six Shooters; The Durango Kid; West
       of Abilene; Thundering Frontier
1941: Across the Sierras; Outlaws of the
       Panhandle; The Return of Daniel Boone (J.
       Hoffman); Hands Across the Rockies; Where
       Did You Get That Girl?*; Fighting Bill
       Fargo*; Thundering Hoofs
1942: Down Rio Grande Way; Riders of the
       Northland; Overland to Deadwood
1948: Ride, Ryder, Ride
1949: Roll, Thunder, Roll; The Fighting Redhead
       (J. Thomas)

IRVING R. FRANKLYN

1944: Waterfront (M. Mooney); Minstrel Man (P.
       Gendron)
1948: The Woman from Tangier
1949: Daughter of the West (R. Schrock)

HARRY FRASER (also HARRY P. CRIST, HARRY O. JONES, WESTON EDWARDS)

1930: Wings of Adventure
1932: Mason of the Mounted; The Night Rider; Law
       of the North; Texas Pioneers (W. Totman);
       Honor of the Mounted; The Diamond Trail (S.
       Lowe); Land of Wanted Men; Ghost City (W.
       Totman); Without Honors (L. Sage); Border
       Devils
1933: The Gallant Fool (R. N. Bradbury); Breed of
       the Border; The Fighting Parson; Galloping
       Romeo; The Ranger's Code; The Fugitive;
       Return of Casey Jones (J. McCarthy)

```
1934:   Fighting Through
1935:   Fighting Pioneers (C. Roberts); Gunfire;
        Saddle Aces; The Tonto Kid; Rustler's
        Paradise; The Last of the Clintons; Wild
        Mustang
1938:   Six-Shootin' Sheriff; Songs and Saddles
1942:   The Valley of Vanishing Men (ser.)*
1943:   The Batman (ser.)*; Captain America (ser.)*
1944:   Dead or Alive; The Whispering Skull; I
        Accuse My Parents (M. Dudley)
1945:   Enemy of the Law; Flaming Bullets; The
        Navajo Kid
1946:   Six Gun Man; Chick Carter, Detective
        (ser.)*; Son of the Guardsman (ser.)*
1948:   Tex Granger (ser.)*
1949:   Stallion Canyon (H. Heath)
1951:   Abilene Trail
```

GEORGE FREEDLAND

1966: Moonwolf

SAM C. FREEDLE

1962: Gun Street

BENEDICT FREEDMAN

1954: The Atomic Kid (J. F. Murray)
1956: Jaguar (J. F. Murray)
1961: Everything's Ducky (J. F. Murray)

DAVID FREEDMAN (-1936)

1931: Palmy Days*

JERROLD FREEDMAN

1980: Borderline (S. Kline)

THORNTON FREELAND (1898-   ) director

257

1930:   Be Yourself
1931:   Terror by Night

AL FREEMAN, JR.

1976:   Countdown at Kusini*

DAVID FREEMAN

1977:   First Love (J. Hitchcock)
1982:   The Border*

DEVERY FREEMAN

1946:   The Thrill of Brazil*
1947:   The Guilt of Janet Ames*
1948:   The Fuller Brush Man (F. Tashlin)
1949:   Miss Grant Takes Richmond*
1950:   Borderline; Watch the Birdie*; The Yellow
        Cab Man (A. Beich)
1951:   Dear Brat
1953:   Three Sailors and a Girl (*R. Kibbee)
1954:   Francis Joins the WACS
1955:   Ain't Misbehavin'*; Francis in the Navy
1956:   Dance with Me Henry; The First Traveling
        Saleslady (S. Longstreet)
1957:   The Girl Most Likely

EVERETT FREEMAN (1911-   ) producer

1937:   Married Before Breakfast (G. Oppenheimer)
1938:   The Chaser*
1939:   You Can't Cheat an Honest Man*
1942:   George Wasdhington Slept Here; Larceny, Inc.
        (E. Gilbert)
1944:   The Princess and the Pirate*
1947:   It Happened on Fifth Avenue; The Secret Life
        of Walter Mitty (K. Englund)
1948:   Lulu Belle (C. MacArthur)
1949:   The Lady Takes a Sailor
1950:   Pretty Baby (H. Kurnitz)
1951:   Jim Thorpe -- All American ((D. Morrow)
1952:   Million Dollar Mermaid
1953:   Destination Gobi

```
1957:   Kelly and Me; My Man Godfrey*
1958:   Marjorie Morningstar
1966:   The Glass Bottom Boat
1968:   Where Were You When the Light Went Out? (K.
        Tunberg)
1969:   The Maltese Bippy (R. Singer)
1970:   How Do I Love Thee (K. Tunberg)
```

FRED FREEMAN

```
1970:   Start the Revolution Without Me (L. Cohen)
1974:   SPYS* (Lawrence Cohen
1976:   The Big Bus (L. J. Cohen)
```

LEONARD FREEMAN

```
1961:   Claudelle Inglish; Gold of the Seven Saints
        (L. Brackett)
1968:   Hang 'Em High (M. Goldberg)
```

HOWARD FREEN

```
1974:   Dirty O'Neil
```

HUGO FREGONESE (1908-   ) director   Arg.

```
(American films only)
1958:   Live in Fear*
1966:   Savage Pampas (Sp./Arg./U.S.)
```

FRED FREIBERGER

```
1947:   Stork Bites Man
1953:   The Beast from 20,000 Fathoms (L. Morheim)
1955:   The Big Bluff
1957:   The Weapon; Beginning of the End (L. Gorn)
1958:   Crash Landing; Blood Arrow
```

ERIC FREIWALD

```
1958:   The Lone Ranger and the Lost City of Gold
        (R. Schaefer)
```

LLOYD FRENCH

1942:   Snuffy Smith, Yard Bird*

JOSEPH FRICKERT

1940:   One Million B.C.*

FRED R. FRIEDEL

1978:   Kidnapped Co-Ed

J. RAYMOND FRIEDGEN

1958:   Hong Kong Affair*

DAVID FRIEDKIN

1957:   Hot Summer Night (M. Fine)
1958:   Handle with Care (M. Fine)
1965:   The Fool Killer (M. Fine); The Pawnbroker
        (M. Fine)

WILLIAM FRIEDKIN (1939-   )

1980:   Cruising

HOWARD FRIEDLANDER

1973: Gordon's War (E. Spielman)

ALAN FRIEDMAN

1943:   Harrigan's Kid (M. Berkeley)
1945:   A Letter for Edie (D. Scott)
1958:   Girls on the Loose*

BRUCE JAY FRIEDMAN

1980:   Stir Crazy

HARRY FRIEDMAN

1935:   Westward Ho*

KEN FRIEDMAN

1975:   White Line Fever (J. Kaplan)
1977:   Mr. Billion (J. Kaplan)

PHILIP FRIEDMAN

1972:   Rage (D. Kleinman)

STANTON FRIEDMAN

1979:   Alien Encounter (E. Hunt)

TOM FRIEDMAN

1982:   Time Walker (K. Levitt)

KETTI FRINGS (1915-1981) novelist, playwright

1944:   Guest in the House
1947:   The Accused
1949:   Thelma Jordan
1950:   The Company She Keeps; Dark City*
1952:   Because of You; Come Back, Little Sheba
1954:   About Mrs. Leslie (H. Kanter)
1955:   Foxfire; The Shrike
1961:   By Love Possessed*
1975:   Mr. Sycamore (P. Kohner)

JOSEPH FRITZ

1960:   The High-Powered Rifle; Walk Tall

JAMES FRITZELL

1964:   Good Neighbor Sam*
1966:   The Ghost and Mr. Chicken (E. Greenbaum)
1967:   The Reluctant Astronaut (E. Greenbaum)
1969:   Angel in My Pocket (E. Greenbaum)

ANNE FROELICK

1941:   Shining Victory (H. Koch)
1944:   The Master Race*
1945:   Miss Susie Slagle's (H. Butler)
1947:   Easy Come, Easy Go*
1950:   Harriet Craig (J. Gunn)

GEORGE FROESCHEL (1891-1979)

1940:   The Mortal Storm*; Waterloo Bridge*
1942:   Mrs. Miniver*; Random Harvest*; We Were
        Dancing*
1944:   The White Cliffs of Dover*
1948:   Command Decision (W. Laidlaw)
1950:   The Miniver Story (R. Millar)
1951:   The Unknown Man (R. Millar)
1952:   Scaramouche (R. Millar)
1953:   The Story of Three Loves*; Never Let Me Go
        (R. Millar)
1954:   Betrayed (R. Millar); Rose Marie (R. Millar)
1955:   Quentin Durward
1956:   Gaby
1958:   Me and the Colonel (S. N. Behrman)

MELVYN FROHMAN

1976:   Black Streetfighter (T. Kelly)
1981:   ...All The Marbles

LEE FROST

1972:   The Thing with Two Heads*
1974:   Policewomen
1975:   Race with the Devil (Wes Bishop); The Black
        Gestapo (Wes Bishop)
1976:   Dixie Dynamite (Wes Bishop)

CHRISTOPHER FRY

1953:   The Beggar's Opera
1962:   Barabbas (Ital.)
1966:   The Bible (Ital.)

DEREK FRYE (pseud. of CARL FOREMAN and HAROLD
        BUCHMAN)

DANIEL FUCHS (1909-   ) novelist, short story
        writer

1942:   The Hard Way (P. Viertel); The Big Shot*
1944:   Between Two Worlds
1947:   The Gangster
1948:   Hollow Triumph
1949:   Criss Cross
1950:   Panic in the Streets*; Storm Warning (R.
        Brooks)
1953:   Taxi (D. Marshman)
1954:   The Human Jungle (W. Sackheim)
1955:   Love Me or Leave Me (I. Lennart)
1957:   Interlude (F. Coen); Jeanne Eagels*

LESTER FULLER

1951:   Three Steps North

SAMUEL FULLER (1911-   ) director, producer

1936:   Hats Off (E. Joseph)
1938:   Gangs of New York*
1949:   I Shot Jesse James; Shockproof (H. Deutsch)
1950:   The Baron of Arizona
1951:   Fixed Bayonets; The Steel Helmet
1952:   Park Row
1953:   Pickup on South Street
1954:   Hell and High Water (J. Lasky); The Command
        (R. S. Hughes)
1955:   House of Bamboo (H. Kleiner)
1957:   China Gate; Run of the Arrow; Forty Guns
1959:   Verboten!; The Crimson Kimono

1961:   Underworld, U.S.A.
1962:   Merrill's Marauders (M. Sperling)
1963:   Shock Corridor
1964:   The Naked Kiss
1970:   Shark (J. Kingsbridge)
1972:   Dead Pigeon on Beethoven Street (Germ.)
1974:   The Klansmen (M. Kaufman)
1980:   The Big Red One

RENE FULLOP-MILLER

1949:   The Great Sinner (L. Fodor)

MAUDE FULTON

1929:   Nix on Dames (F. Gay)
1930:   Captain Applejack; Steel Highway
1931:   Command Performance (G. Rigby); The Maltese
        Falcon*; Other Men's Women; Safe in Hell
1932:   Under Eighteen (C. Kenyon)
1933:   Broadway Bad (A. Kober); Broken Dreams
1936:   The Song and Dance Man

ALLEN FUNT

1970:   What Do You Say to a Naked Lady?

JOHN FURIA, JR.

1966:   The Singing Nun (S. Benson)

SIDNEY J. FURIE (1933-   ) director   Can.

(American films only)
1970:   The Lawyer (H. Buchman)
1978:   The Boys in Company C (R. Natkin)

V. A. FURLONG

1969:   Run, Angel, Run (J. Wish)

JULES FURTHMAN (1888-1960)

1929:   The Case of Lena Smith; Broadway;
        Thunderbolt; Abie's Irish Rose
1930:   New York Nights; Common Clay; Morocco;
        Renegades
1931:   Body and Soul; Merely Mary Ann; Over the
        Hill (T. Barry); The Yellow Ticket (G.
        Bolton)
1932:   Blonde Venus (S. Lauren); Shanghai Express
1933:   Bombshell (J. Mahin)
1935:   China Seas (J. McGuinness); Mutiny on the
        Bounty*
1936:   Come and Get It! (J. Murfin)
1938:   Spawn of the North (T. Jennings)
1939:   Only Angels Have Wings
1941:   The Shanghai Gesture*
1943:   The Outlaw (B. Hecht)
1944:   To Have and Have Not (W. Faulkner)
1946:   The Big Sleep*
1947:   Moss Rose (T. Reed); Nightmare Alley
1957:   Jet Pilot
1959:   Rio Bravo (L. Brackett)

G

GILBERT GABRIEL

1939: Hotel Imperial (R. Thoeren); The Magnificent
       Fraud (W. Ferris)

FRANK GABRIELSON

1944: Something for the Boys*
1945: Don Juan Quilligan (A. Kober)
1946: It Shouldn't Happen to a Dog (E. Ling)

ALAN GADNEY

1974: Moon Child

GEORGE GAGE

1978: Skateboard (R. Wolf)

WALTER GAGE (pseudonym for WILLIAM INGE)

ALBERT GAIL

1962: Five Weeks in a Balloon*

CHARLES GAINES

1976: Stay Hungry

TERRY GALANOY

1971:   Kovacs (doc.)

ALAN GALE

1943:   Harvest Melody
1944:   Trocadero

BOB GALE

1978:   I Wanna Hold Your Hand (R. Zemeckis)
1979:   1941 (R. Zemeckis)
1980:   Used Cars (R. Zemeckis)

TIMOTHY GALFAS

1978:   Matilda (A. Ruddy)
1979:   Sunnyside (J. King)

JOHN GALLAGHER

1982:   Beach House (M. Amoruso)

PAUL & PAULINE GALLICO

1950:   Never Take No for an Answer (Ital.)

LINDSAY GALLOWAY

1963:   Seven Seas to Calais

SAMUEL GALLU

1975:   Give 'Em Hell, Harry!

KENNETH GAMET

1936:   Smart Blonde (D. Ryan)
1937:   The Case of the Stuttering Bishop (D. Ryan);
        Fly-Away Baby (D. Ryan); Midnight Court (D.

                    Ryan); Missing Witness (D. Ryan)
1938:   Broadway Musketeers (D. Ryan); Nancy Drew,
          Detective
1939:   Everybody's Hobby (W. Brockway); Nancy Drew
          and the Hidden Staircase; Nancy Drew --
          Troubleshooter; Nancy Drew - Reporter; You
          Can't Get Away with Murder*
1940:   Devil's Island (D. Ryan); Flowing Gold;
          Granny Get Your Gun; Tear Gas Squad*
1941:   The Great Mr. Nobody (B Markson); Highway
          West*; The Smiling Ghost; Strange Alibi;
          Kisses for Breakfast
1942:   Flying Tigers (B. Trivers); Pittsburgh (T.
          Reed)
1943:   Bomber's Moon (A. Wisberg)
1944:   Tampico*
1945:   Betrayal from the East (A. Wisberg)
1948:   Wake of the Red Witch (H. Brown); Adventure
          in Silverado*; Coroner Creek; Blonde Ice
1949:   Canadian Pacific (J. DeWitt); The Doolans of
          Oklahoma
1950:   The Savage Horde
1951:   Santa Fe (I. Pichel); Man in the Saddle;
          Fighting Coast Guard
1952:   Indian Uprising (R. Schayer); Last of the
          Comanches
1953:   The Stranger Wore a Gun; The Last Posse*
1955:   Hell's Outpost; A Lawless Street; Ten Wanted
          Men (I. Ravetch)
1956:   The Maverick Queen (D. Scott)
1957:   The Lawless Eighties
1958:   Domino Kid (H. Biller)

PAUL GANGELIN

1929:   Office Scandal (J. Jungmeyer); The Racketeer
1932:   Bachelor Mother*; Hell's House*
1934:   Beloved (G. O'Neill)
1941:   Tarzan's Secret Treasure (M. Connolly)
1942:   Nazi Agent (J. Meehan); Junior Army
1943:   Murder in Times Square
1944:   Strangers in the Night; Cowboy Canteen (F.
          Adler); The Big Bonanza*
1945:   The Daltons Ride Again (R Chanslor)
1946:   Under Nevada Skies (J. Cheney); Roll On,
          Texas Moon (M. Grashin)
1948:   Under California Stars (S. Nibley); Son of

                              268

```
              God's Country
1950:    Sons of New Mexico
1957:    The Giant Claw (Samuel Newman)


AL GANNAWAY

1956:    Hidden Guns (S. Roeca)


ERNEST K. GANN

1951:    The Raging Tide
1953:    Island in the Sky
1954:    Soldier of Fortune
1958:    Twilight for the Gods


LOWELL GANZ

1982:    Night Shift (B. Mandel)


ALVIN GANZER

1956:    The Leather Saint (N. Retchin)


BECKY GARDINER

1929:    Trial of Mary Dugan
1930:    War Nurse
1934:    Stingaree


FRED GARDNER

1970:    Zabriskie Point*


GERALD GARDNER

1970:    Which Way to the Front? (D. Caruso)
1973:    The World's Greatest Athlete (D. Caruso)


HERB GARDNER
```

```
1965:   A Thousand Clowns
1971:   Who Is Harry Kellerman and Why Is He Saying
        Those Terrible Things About Me?
1977:   Thieves
```

JOAN GARDNER

```
1963:   Monster from the Surf
```

LEONARD GARDNER

```
1972:   Fat City
```

ROBERT GARDNER

```
1974:   River of Sand (doc.)
```

HENRY GARDON

```
1949:   The Reckless Moment (R. Solderberg)
```

LEO GAREN

```
1973:   Hex
```

JACK GARFEIN (1930-   ) director

```
1961:   Something Wild (A. Karnel)
```

BRIAN GARFIELD

```
1980:   Hopscotch (Bryan Forbes)
```

LOUIS GARFINKLE

```
1956:   The Young Guns
1958:   I Bury the Living
1959:   Face of Fire
1968:   A Minute to Pray, a Second to Die (U.
        Liberatore)
```

1973: Little Cigars (F. Perilli)

ROBERT GARLAND

1979: The Electric Horseman (A. Sargent)

LEE GARMES

1953: Outlaw Territory (J. Irland)

TAY GARNETT (1894-1977) director

1928: The Spieler (H. Conklin)
1929: Flyin' Fool (E. Clawson); Oh, Yeah! (J. Gleason)
1931: Bad Company (T. Buckingham)
1932: Prestige*
1950: The Fireball (H. McCoy)
1970: The Delta Factor
1972: The Mad Trapper*

JOSEPH GAROFALO

1982: Evilspeak (E. Weston)

GEORGE GARRETT

1964: The Young Lovers
1965: Frankenstein Meets the Space Monster

GRANT GARRETT

1934: Cockeyed Cavaliers*
1935: Home on the Range*; The Rainmakers (L. Goodwins)
1937: Clarence (S. Owen); This Way Please*; Thrill of a Lifetime*
1941: Model Wife*
1943: He's My Guy (M. Webster)
1944: Rationing*; Barbary Coast Gent*
1946: Bad Bascomb (W. Lipman); The Mighty McGurk*

OLIVER H. P. GARRETT (-1952)

1929:   Chinatown Nights
1930:   The Texan (D. Rubin); Three Faces East (A.
        Caesar); For the Defense; Moby Dick (J.
        Alexander)
1931:   City Streets (M. Marcin); Night Nurse
1932:   A Farewell to Arms*; If I Had a Million*;
        Man from Yesterday; World and the Flesh
1933:   Night Flight; The Story of Temple Drake
1934:   Manhattan Melodrama (J. Mankiewicz)
1935:   Age of Indiscretion (Leon Gordon); One Way
        Ticket*; O'Shaughnessy's Boy*; She Couldn't
        Take It
1937:   The Hurricane*
1939:   Four Feathers (Brit.; R. C. Sherriff); One
        Third of a Nation (D. Murphy)
1940:   The Man I Married
1942:   Careful, Soft Shoulders
1943:   Flight for Freedom*
1947:   Dead Reckoning

JACK GARISS

1956:   The Ten Commandments*

SERGIO GARRONE

1973:   The Big Bust-Out

HENRY GARSON

1959:   Don't Give Up the Ship*
1960:   G. I. Blues (H. Beloin); Visit to a Small
        Planet (H. Beloin)

EILEEN GARY

1947:   Law of the Canyon

HARVEY GATES

```
1928:   The Terror
1929:   Redeeming Sin; Stark Mad; Desert Song; From
        Headquarters; Hearts in Exile
1930:   In the Next Room; What a Man!
1931:   Hell Divers (M. Boylan); Sky Raiders
1932:   County Fair; If I Had a Million*; Madame
        Racketeer (*M. Boylan)
1933:   The Mysterious Rider (R. Niles)
1934:   The Band Plays On*
1936:   Flying Hostess*; Voice of Bugle Anne (S.
        Hoffenstein)
1937:   The Luck of Roaring Camp; When's Your
        Birthday?*
1939:   Fugitive at Large (E. Taylor); Navy Secrets;
        Meet Dr. Christian*
1941:   Zis Boom Bah (J. Henley)
1942:   Black Dragons; Smart Alecks; The Corpse
        Vanishes; Let's Get Tough!; Mr. Wise Guy*;
        'Neath Brooklyn Bridge
1943:   Clancy Street Boys
1945:   Docks of New York; Mr. Muggs Rides Again;
        Northwest Trail (L. Swabacher); Allotment
        Wives (W. Austin); Divorce (S. Sutherland)
1946:   Below the Deadline (F. Judd); Don't Gamble
        with Strangers (C. Coleman)
1947:   Last Frontier Uprising
1948:   Racing Luck*
```

NATE GATZERT

```
1933:   The Fiddlin' Buckaroo; The Trail Drive;
        Strawberry Roan
1934:   Wheels of Destiny; Honor of the Range;
        Smoking Guns
1935:   Rustlers of Red Dog (ser.)*; The Roaring
        West (ser.)*; Western Frontier; Western
        Courage; Lawless Riders; Heir to Trouble;
        Call of the Savage (ser.)*
1936:   The Cattle Thief; Avenging Waters; Heroes of
        the Range; The Fugitive Sheriff; The Unknown
        Ranger; Rio Grande Ranger
1937:   Ranger Courage; Law of the Ranger; Reckless
        Ranger
1938:   Rolling Caravans; Stagecoach Days; Pioneer
        Trail; Phantom Gold; In Early Arizona;
        Frontiers of '49
1939:   Lone Star Pioneers; The Law Comes to Texas
```

DALLAS GAULTOIS

1959: Four Fast Guns (J. Edmiston)
1961: When the Clock Strikes

DICK GAUTIER

1968: Mary Jane (P. Marshall)
1972: Wild in the Sky (W. Naud)

FRANK GAY

1929: Nix on Dames (M. Fulton)
1930: Women Everywhere (L. Biro); Not Damaged

JOHN GAY

1958: Run Silent, Run Deep; Separate tables (T. Rattigan)
1962: The Four Horsemen of the Apocalypse (R. Ardrey)
1962: The Happy Thieves
1963: The Courtship of Eddie's Father
1965: The Hallelujah Trail
1967: The Last Safari
1968: The Power; No Way to Treat a Lady
1970: Soldier Blue
1971: Sometimes a Great Notion (ret. Never Give an Inch)
1975: Hennessy
1976: A Matter of Time

DON GAZZANIGA

1976: Special Delivery

MICHAEL VINCENTE GAZZO

1957: A Hatful of Rain (A. Hayes)
1958: King Creole (H. Baker)

FRED GEBHARDT

1961:   The Phantom Planet

ELLEN GEER

1974:   Memory of Us

LARRY GELBART

1962:   The Notorious Landlady (B. Edwards)
1966:   The Wrong Box; Not with My Wife, You Don't*
1969:   On My Way to the Crusades, I Met a Girl
        Who...
1977:   Oh, God!
1978:   Movie Movie (S. Keller)
1981:   Neighbors
1982:   Tootsie (M. Schisgal)

JACK GELBER

1962:   The Connection

BRUCE GELLER

1961:   Sail a Crooked Ship*

JOYCE GELLER

1967:   The Cool Ones

STEPHEN GELLER

1972:   Slaughterhouse Five; The Valachi Papers
1979:   Ashanti

MILTON GELMAN

1956:   Ride the High Iron
1981:   Capoblanco (M. Fine)

ERWIN S. GELSEY

1932: Jewel Robbery; Scarlet Dawn (N. Busch); The
Strange Love of Molly Louvain (B. Holmes)
1933: Gold Diggers of 1933 (J. Seymour); Grand
Slam (D. Boehm); Life of Jimmy Dolan (D.
Boehm)
1934: Friends of Mr. Sweeney*; The Personality
Kid*
1935: Sweet Adeline; We're in the Money*; Muss 'Em
Up
1937: Double or Nothing*; Hold 'Em Navy (L.
Corrigan)
1938: Campus Confessions (L. Corrigan); Touchdown,
Army (L. Corrigan)

PIERRE GENDRON

1929: Sal of Singapore*
1944: The Monster Maker; Minstrel Man (I.
Franklyn); Bluebeard
1945: Fog Island

PETER GENT

1979: North Dallas Forty*

ATLAS GEODESIC

1969: Turn On to Love

GEORGE S. GEORGE

1943: The Heat's On*
1956: Abdulla's Harem (B. Insgster)
1962: The 300 Spartans

GEORGE W. GEORGE

1950: The Nevadan (G. Slavin); Mystery Submarine;
Peggy (G. Slavin)

```
1951:   Red Mountain*
1953:   City of Bad Men (G. Slavin)
1955:   Desert Sands*; Smoke Signal (G. Slavin)
1956:   Uranium Boom*
1957:   The Halliday Brand (G. Slavin)
1958:   Fort Dobbs (B. Kennedy); Apache Territory
        (C. Marion)
1959:   The Son of Robin Hood (G. Slavin)
1961:   The Two Little Bears
```

WILLIAM GEORGE

```
1957:   Lure of the Swamp; Rockabilly Baby (W.
        Driskill)
```

L. GEORGIG

```
1942:   Tales of Manhattan*
```

GERALD GERAGHTY (-1953)

```
1933:   Silent Men*; Under the Tonto Rim (J.
        Cunningham); Sunset Pass (J. Cunningham)
1935:   Bar 20 Rides Again (D. Schroeder)
1936:   The Jungle Princess*
1937:   Wells Fargo*
1938:   Come On, Rangers! (J. Natteford); Western
        Jamboree
1939:   Mexicali Rose; Blue Montana Skies; In Old
        Caliente I(N. Houston); Mountain Rhythm;
        Wall Street Cowboy (N.Hall); In Old
        Monterey*; The Arizona Kid (L. Ward)
1940:   Pioneers of the West*; Young Buffalo Bill*;
        Hidden Gold (J. Mersereau); The Carson City
        Kid (R. Yost); The Ranger and the Lady (S.
        Anthony)
1941:   King of Dodge City; Badlands of Dakota;
        Secrets of the Wasteland; South of Tahiti
1942:   Sunset on the Desert; Sin Town*; Riding
        Through Nevada
1943:   Hoppy Serves a Writ; Frontier Badman (M.
        Cox); Hail to the Rangers; The Falcon and
        the Co-Eds (A. Wray)
1944:   The Falcon in Mexico (G. Yates); The Falcon
```

```
        in Hollywood
1945:   Frisco Sal (C. Siodmak); Along the Navajo
        Trail; Shady Lady*
1946:   Rainbow over Texas; Home in Oklahoma;
        Heldorado (J. Zimet)
1947:   Apache Rose; Wyoming (L. Hazard)
1948:   The Plunderers (G. Adams); Grand Canyon
        Trail; Train to Alcatraz
1949:   Riders of the Sky; The Red Menace (A.
        DeMond)
1950:   Mule Train; Cowtown; Trigger, Jr.; Sunset in
        the West; Trail of Robin Hood
1951:   Silver Canyon; Hills of Utah; Valley of Fire
        (E. Snell)
1952:   Wagon Team; Barbed Wire; Blue Canadian
        Rockies; The Old West; The Rough, Tough West
1953:   Goldtown Ghost Riders; Down Laredo Way;
        Bandits of the West; Savage Frontier (D.
        Babcock); Iron Mountain Trail; On Top of Old
        Smoky; Shadows of Tombstone
1954:   Red River Shore (A. Orloff); Phantom
        Stallion
```

MAURICE GERAGHTY

```
1936:   Robinson Crusoe of Clipper Island (ser.)*;
        The Vigilantes Are Coming (ser.)*;
        Adventures of Frank Merriwell (ser.)*;
        Undersea Kingdom (ser.)*
1937:   Hills of Old Wyoming; Westbound Limited
1938:   Law of the Plains; The Mysterious Rider;
        Trouble at Midnight (F. Beebe)
1942:   West of Tombstone
1943:   Apache Trail; Good Morning, Judge (W.
        Wilson)
1948:   Whiplash (H. Frank); Who Killed "Doc"
        Robbin? (D. Davenport)
1949:   Calamity Jane and Sam Bass (M. Levy); Red
        Canyon
1950:   Dakota Lil
1951:   Tomahawk (S. Richards); The Sword of Monte
        Cristo
1952:   Rose of Cimmaron
1955:   Robbers Roost*
1956:   Mohawk (M. Krims)
```

TOM GERAGHTY

1929: Naughty Baby; Synthetic Sin; Smiling Irish
      Eyes; Footlights and Fools (K. Brush);
      Tanned Legs
1932: Mr. Robinson Crusoe
1933: Elmer the Great; Samarang
1937: Wings of the Morning

ANNE GERARD

1982: Love Child (K. Specktor)

BARNEY GERARD

1931: Lady from Nowhere (A. Johnson); The Lawless
      Woman
1948: Jiggs and Maggie in Society (E. Cline);
      Jiggs and Maggie in Court (E. Cline)
1949: Jackpot Jitters (E. Cline)
1950: Jiggs and Maggie Out West (A. Buffington)
1951: According to Mrs. Hoyle (W. Darling)

MERWIN GERARD

1948: The Checkered Coat (S. Lester)
1952: The Winning Team*

PAUL GERARD

1947: It's a Joke, Son (R. Kent)

HAILE GERIMA

1965: Bush Mama (doc.)
1982: Ashes and Embers

WALTER GERING

1943: Cosmo Jones, Crime Smasher (M. Simmons)

VANCE GERRY

1967:   The Jungle Book (anim.)*

LEONARD GERSHE

1957:   Funny Face; Silk Stockings (L. Spigelgass)
1972:   Butterflies Are Free
1973:   Forty Carats

THEODORE GERSHUNY

1974:   Silent Night Bloody Night (J. Konvitz)
1977:   Sugar Cookies (L. Kaufman)

ROBERT GETCHELL

1975:   Alice Doesn't LIve Here Anymore
1976:   Bound for Glory
1981:   Mommie Dearest*

STACEY GIACHINO

1982:   Pranks*

JOE GIANNONE

1982:   Madman

ELIOT GIBBONS

1930:   Under Fiesta Stars (K. Brown)
1939:   Flight at Midnight
1941:   Desert Bandit (P. Cohen); Under Fiesta Stars
        (H. Shumate); The Apache Kid (R. Murphy)
1948:   Hidden Danger (J. Cheney)
1950:   Fence Riders

SHERIDAN GIBNEY (1903-   )

1932:   Two Against the World; Week-End Marriage; I

Am a Fugitive from a Chain Gang*
1933:   House on 56th Street (A. Parker); The World
        Changes (E. Chodorov)
1934:   Massacre (R. Block)
1935:   Story of Louis Pasteur (P. Collings)
1936:   Anthony Adverse; The Green Pastures (M.
        Connelly)
1938:   Letter of Introduction (L. Spigelgass)
1939:   Disputed Passage (A. Veiller)
1941:   Cheers for Miss Bishop (A. Heilbron);
        Honolulu Lu (P. Yawitz)
1942:   Once Upon a Honeymoon
1944:   Our Hearts Were Young and Gay
1946:   The Locket

TOM GIBSON

1935:   Trigger Tom
1936:   Caryl of the Mountains; Romance Rides the
        Range
1937:   The Singing Buckaroo
1940:   The Cheyenne Kid; Covered Wagon Trails; Land
        of the Six Guns; Billy the Kid's Gun Justice
1946:   The Scarlet Horseman (ser.)*; Lost City of
        the Jungle (ser.)*

WILLIAM GIBSON

1962:   The Miracle Worker

NELSON GIDDING

1957:   The Helen Morgan Story*
1958:   Onionhead; I Want to Live! (D. Mankiewicz)
1959:   Odds Against tomorrow (J. Killen)
1962:   Lisa
1963:   The Haunting; Nine Hours to Rama
1966:   Lost Command
1970:   Skullduggery
1971:   The Andromeda Strain
1975:   The Hindenburg
1979:   Beyond the Poseidon Adventure

GWEN BAGNI GIELGUD

1956:   The Last Wagon*

IRWIN GIELGUD

1949:   Abandoned
1950:   I Was a Shoplifter

DORIS GILBERT

1944:   Lake Placid Serenade (D. Hyland); Ladies
        Courageous (N. Raine); Storm over Lisbon;
        Atlantic City*
1951:   Little Egypt (O. Brodney)

EDWIN GILBERT

1942:   All Through the Night (L. Spigelgass);
        Larceny, Inc. (E. Freeman)

FRAN GILBERT

1947:   Buffalo Bill Rides Again (B. Sarecky)

BERNE GILER

1940:   Turnabout*
1949:   C-Man
1956:   Showdown at Abilene
1959:   Westbound; Tarzan's Greatest Adventure
1960:   Tarzan the Magnificent
1963:   Tarzan's Three Challenges (R. Day)
1967:   Gunfight in Abilene (J. D. Black)

DAVID GILER

1970:   Myra Breckinridge (D. Sarne)
1974:   The Parallax View (L. Semple)
1975:   The Black Bird
1977:   Fun with Dick and Jane
1981:   Southern Comfort*

JAY GILGORE

1951:   Canyon Raiders

FRANK GILL, JR.

1943:   Chatterbox (G. C. Brown); Hit Parade of
        1943; Sleepy Lagoon (C. G. Brown); Thumbs
        Up
1944:   Casanova in Burlesque; Altantic City*;
        Brazil (L. Kerr)
1945:   Earl Carroll Vanities; Mexicana
1946:   Earl Carroll's Sketchbook (P. Levy)
1951:   The Lady Pays Off (A. J. Cohen)
1953:   Geraldine (P. Milne); East of Sumatra
1964:   McHale's Navy (G. C. Brown)

STUART GILLARD

1982:   Paradise; If You Could See What I Hear

JOSEPH C. GILLETTE

1959:   Blood and Steel

JOHN GILLING

1953:   The Big Frame (S. Fisher)
1954:   White Fire (P. Erickson)
1958:   Cross-Up (W. Goldbeck)
1960:   Killers of Kilimanjaro*

FRANK D. GILROY

1956:   The Fastest Gun Alive (R. Rouse)
1960:   The Gallant Hours (B. Lay)
1968:   The Subject Was Roses
1970:   The Only Game in Town
1971:   Desperate Characters
1976:   From Noon Till Three
1978:   Once in Paris

BRYAN GINDORFF

1975: Hard Times*

ROBERT EMMETT GINNA

1967: The Last Challenge (J. Sherry)

ABRAM S. GINNES

1969: Gaily, Gaily

MILTON MOSES GINSBERG

1969: Coming Apart
1973: Werewolf of Washington

GEORGE GIPE

1982: Dead Men Don't Wear Plaid*

FRED GIPSON

1957: Old Yeller (W. Tunberg)
1959: Hound Dog Man (W. Miller)
1963: Savage Sam (W. Tunberg)

BERNARD GIRARD (1930-   ) director

1948: The Big Punch; Waterfront at Midnight
1950: Breakthrough (T. Sherdeman)
1958: The Party Crashers
1959: The Rebel Set (L. Vittes)
1962: A Public Affair
1966: Dead Heat on a Merry-Go-Round
1969: The Mad Room (A. Z. Martin)

WILLIAM GIRDLER

1975: Asylum of Satan; Sheba, Baby

1978: The Manitou*

WYNDHAM GITTENS

1931: The Vanishing Legion (ser.)*; Lightning
      Warrior (ser.)*; King of the Wild (ser.)*
1932: The Last of the Mohicans (ser.)*; The Devil
      Horse (ser.)*; The Shadow of the Eagle
      (ser.)*; The Hurricane Express (ser.)*
1933: Fighting with Kit Carson (ser.)*; Mystery
      Squadron (ser.)*; The Three Musketeers
      (ser.)*; The Whispering Shadow (ser.)*; The
      Wolf Dog (ser.)*
1934: The Lost Jungle (ser.)*
1936: Ghost Patrol; Ace Drummond (ser.)*
1937: Wild West Days (ser.)*; Jungle Jim (ser.)*;
      Radio Patrol (ser.)*; Secret Agent X-9
      (ser.)*; Tim Tyler's Luck (ser.)*
1938: Forbidden Valley; Flaming Frontiers (ser.)*;
      Flash Gordon's Trip to Mars (ser.)*
1939: Scouts to the Rescue (ser.)*
1940: Deadwood Dick (ser.)*
1941: Holt of the Secret Service (ser.)*
1942: Pardon My Gun; Captain Midnight (ser.)*

ROBERT GITTLER

1978: The Buddy Holly Story

MAX GLANDBARD

1957: Hell Canyon Outlaws (A. Kaufman)

KUBEC GLASMON

1931: Blonde Crazy (J. Bright); Larceny Lane (J.
      Bright); Smart Money*
1932: The Crowd Roars*; Rockabye (J. Murfin); Taxi
      (J. Bright); False Faces (L. Hughes)
1934: Handy Andy*; Jealousy (J. March)
1935: The Glass Key*; Men Without Names (H.
      Green); Show Them No Mercy (H. Lehrman)
1936: Parole! (H. McCoy)

GASTON GLASS

1931:   Racetrack (D. Doty)

SANDY GLASS

1980:   The Last Flight of Noah's Ark*

BERNARD GLASSER

1961:   The Sergeant Was a Lady

BENJAMIN GLAZER (1887-1958)

1928:   The Barker; Beggars of Life
1929:   The Trail of '98; Dance of Life
1930:   Tol'able David; The Devil to Pay (F.
        Lonsdale)
1931:   Pagan Lady
1932:   A Farewell to Arms*; Mata Hari (L.
        Birinski); Two Kinds of Women
1933:   A Bedtime Story*; The Way to Love*
1934:   She Loves Me Not
1941:   Paris Calling (C. Kaufman)
1942:   Tortilla Flat (J. Mahin)
1947:   Song of My Heart

JAMES GLEASON (1886-1959) actor

1929:   Oh, Yeah! (T. Garnett); The Broadway Melody*
1930:   Fall Guy (G. Abbott); His First Command (J.
        Jungmeyer); What a Widow!
1931:   Beyond Victory*
1933:   The Bowery (H. Estabrook)
1934:   Change of Heart*

MICHAEL GLEASON

1979:   Fast Charlie...the Moonbeam Rider

GAYLE GLECKER

1974:   The Lords of Flatbush*

BERT GLENNON (1895-1967) director

1930:   Second Wife (F. Herbert)
1942:   Deperate Journey (A. Horman)

JAMES GLICKENHAUS

1980:   The Exterminator
1982:   The Soldier

CHARLES GLORE

1967:   Moonshine Mountain

GARY GODDARD

1981:   Tarzan, the Ape Man (T. Rowe)

PETER GODFREY (1900-1970) director

1943:   Forever and a Day*

JOHN E. GODSON

1931:   Alice in Wonderland (A. Miller)

AUGUSTUS & RUTH GOETZ

1949:   The Heiress
1952:   Carrie
1958:   Stage Struck

IVAN GOFF

1940:   My Love Came Back*
1941:   Sunset in Wyoming (A. Chapin)
1949:   Prejudice*; White Heat (B. Roberts)

1951:   Captain Horatio Hornblower*; Come Fill the
        Cup (B. Roberts); Goodbye, My Fance (B.
        Roberts)
1952:   O. Henry's Full House*
1953:   White Witch Doctor (B. Roberts); King of the
        Khyber Rifles (B. Roberts)
1954:   Green Fire*
1956:   Serenade*
1957:   Man of a Thousand Faces*; Band of Angels*
1959:   Shake Hands with the Devil (B. Roberts)
1960:   Midnight Lace (B. Roberts); Portrait in
        Black (B. Roberts)
1981:   The Legend of the Lone Ranger

JOHN GOFF

1982:   Drive-In Massacre (B. Flower); Butterfly (M.
        Cimber); Baby Dolls (B. Flower)

LEO GOLD

1942:   The Affairs of Martha (I. Lennart)
1948:   Glamour Girl (M. Webster)

MYRON J. GOLD

1969:   The Monitors

ZACHARY GOLD

1943:   Top Man
1946:   Humoresque (C. Odets)
1949:   South of St. Louis (J. Webb)

PETER GOLDBAUM

1947:   Winter Wonderland*

WILLIS GOLDBECK (1900-1979) director, producer

1929:   Wild Orchids*; Desert Nights
1932:   Freaks (Leon Gordon); The Penguin Pool

```
            Murder
1934:  Murder on the Blackboard; Wednesday's Child
1936:  The Garden of Allah*
1938:  Young Dr. Kildare (H. Ruskin)
1939:  Calling Dr. Kildare (H. Ruskin); Secret of
       Dr. Kildare (H. Ruskin)
1940:  Dr. Kildare's Crisis (H. Ruskin); Dr.
       Kildare's Strange Case (H. Ruskin)
1941:  Dr. Kildare's Victory (H. Ruskin); Dr.
       Kildare's Wedding Day (H. Ruskin); The
       People vs. Dr. Kildare (H. Ruskin)
1942:  Calling Dr. Gillespie (H. Ruskin); Dr.
       Gillespie's New Assistant*
1949:  Johnny Holiday*
1958:  Cross-Up (J. Gilling)
1960:  Sergeant Rutledge (J. Bellah)
1962:  The Man Who Shot Liberty Valance (J. Bellah)
```

DAN GOLDBERG

```
1981:  Stripes*; Heavy Metal (L. Blum)
```

LOU GOLDBERG

```
1935:  Frankie and Johnnie (M. Hart)
```

MEL GOLDBERG

```
1964:  The Lively Set (William Wood)
1968:  Hang 'Em High (L. Freeman)
```

MICHAEL GOLDBERG

```
1932:  Joseph in the Land of Egypt (Yid.)
```

RUBE GOLDBERG

```
1930:  Soup to Nuts (H.J. Green)
```

LEO V. GOLDEN

```
1969:  All the Loving Couples
```

RAY GOLDEN

1938: Kentucky Moonshine*
1940: Melody Ranch*; Argentine Nights*
1941: The Big Store*
1944: Nothing but Trouble (R. Rouse)

DAVID GOLDENBERG

1975: The Happy Hooker (W. Richert)

MARILYN GOLDIN

1976: Sweet Revenge (B. J. Perla)

BO GOLDMAN

1975: One Flew over the Cuckoo's Nest (L. Hauben)
1976: End of the Game*
1979: The Rose (B. Kerby)
1980: Melvin and Howard
1982: Shoot the Moon

GARY GOLDMAN

1982: The Secret of N.I.M.H. (anim.)*

HAROLD GOLDMAN

1936: Petticoat Fever
1937: The Emperor's Candlesticks*
1939: The Girl Downstairs*
1940: Haunted Honeymoon (Brit.)*
1943: My Kingdom for a Cook (A. Solt)

JAMES GOLDMAN

1971: They Might Be Giants; Nicholas and Alexandra
1976: Robin and Marian

LAWRENCE GOLDMAN

1950:   Kill or Be Killed*
1957:   Kronos; The Viking Women and the Serpent
1958:   War of the Satellites

MARTIN GOLDMAN

1972:   The Legend of Nigger Charley (L. Spangler)

WILLIAM GOLDMAN

1966:   Harper
1969:   Butch Cassidy and the Sundance Kid
1972:   The Hot Rock
1975:   The Stepford Wives; The Great Waldo Pepper
1976:   All the President's Men; Marathon Man
1977:   A Bridge Too Far
1978:   Magic

CLIFFORD GOLDSMITH

1941:   Life with Henry (D. Hartman)

MARTIN M. GOLDSMITH

1945:   Daangerous Intruder; Detour
1947:   Blind Spot; The Lone Wolf in Mexico (M.
        Tombragel)
1950:   Shakedown (A. Levitt)
1953:   Mission over Korea*
1958:   Fort Massacre
1959:   Cast a Long Shadow (J. McGreevey); The
        Gunfight at Dodge City (D. Ullman)

WILLIAM GOLDSTEIN

1977:   The Amazing Dobermans*

RICHARD GOLDSTONE

1962:   No Man Is an Island (J. Monks)

JOSEPH GOLLAMB

1934:   Murder at the Vanities*

SY GOMBERG

1950:   Summer Stock (G. Wells); The Toast of New
        Orleans (G. Wells)
1952:   Bloodhounds of Broadway
1957:   Joe Butterfly*
1958:   Kathy O' (J. Sher)
1959:   The Wild and the Innocent (J. Sher)

JACK GOOD

1974:   Catch My Soul

PLINY GOODFRIEND

1937:   Santa Fe Rides

WILLIAM GOODHART

1969:   Generation
1977:   Exorcist II: the Heretic

DAVID GOODIS

1947:   The Unfaithful (J. Gunn)
1957:   The Burglar

DAVID Z. GOODMAN

1970:   Lovers and Other Strangers*; Monte Walsh (L.
        Heller)
1971:   Straw Dogs (S. Peckinpah)
1974:   Man on a Swing
1975:   Farewell, My Lovely
1976:   Logan's Run

```
1977:   March or Die
1978:   Eyes of Laura Mars (J. Carpenter)
1982:   Fighting Back (T. Hedley)


GEORGE J. W. GOODMAN

1963:   The Wheeler Dealers (I. Wallach)


HAL GOODMAN

1980:   Oh, God! Book II*


FRANCES GOODRICH (1891-      )

1933:   Penthouse (A. Hackett); The Secret of Madame
        Blanche (A. Hackett)
1934:   Fugitive Lovers*; Hide-Out (A. Hackett); The
        Thin Man (A. Hackett)
1935:   Ah, Wilderness (A. Hackett); Naughty
        Marietta*
1936:   Rose Marie*; After the Thin Man (A. Hackett)
1937:   The Firefly*
1939:   Another Thin Man (A. Hackett); Society
        Lawyer*
1944:   Lady in the Dark (A. Hackett); The Hitler
        Gang (A. Hackett)
1946:   It's a Wonderful Life*; The Virginian*
1948:   Easter Parade*; The Pirate (A. Hackett);
        Summer Holiday*
1949:   In the Good Old Summertime*
1950:   Father of the Bride (A. Hackett)
1951:   Father's Little Dividend (A. Hackett); Too
        Young to Kiss (A. Hackett)
1953:   Give a Girl a Break (A. Hackett)
1954:   The Long, Long Trailer (A. Hackett); Seven
        Brides for Seven Brothers*
1956:   Gaby*
1958:   A Certain Smile (A. Hackett)
1959:   The Diary of Anne Frank (A. Hackett)
1962:   Five Finger Exercise (A. Hackett)


JOHN GOODRICH

1929:   Fast Life
```

1930: Lilies of the Field; Flirting Widow; Love
       Racket (A. Comandini)
1931: Riders of the Purple Sage*
1932: Breach of Promise (B. Verschleiser); The
       Son-Daughter (C. West)
1933: The Deluge*
1934: Flaming gold (M. Boylan)
1935: The Healer*; Life Returns (A. Horman)

MARCUS GOODRICH

1936: Navy Born*; Night Waitress
1937: The Mighty Treve*

LESLIE GOODWINS (1889-1969) director

1935: The Rainmakers (B. Garrett)

ALEX GORDON

1956: Bride of the Monster (E. Wood)

ARTHUR HENRY GORDON

1937: Smoke Tree Range

BERNARD GORDON

1952: Flesh and Fury; The Lawless Breed
1963: Cry of Battle; 55 Days at Peking (P. Yordan)
1964: The Thin Red Line
1968: Custer of the West
1969: Krakatoa, East of Java (C. Gould)

BERT I. GORDON (1922-   ) director

1957: Cyclops; The Amazing Colossal Man (M. Hanna)
1970: How to Succeed with Sex
1972: Necromancy
1973: The Mad Bomber; The Police Connection (orig.
       Detective Geronimo)
1976: The Food of the Gods

DAN GORDON

1939:　Gulliver's Travels (anim.)*
1950:　The Showdown*
1975:　Train Ride to Hollywood

EDWIN GORDON

1982:　The Chosen

GORDON GORDON

1965:　That Darn Cat*

HILDA GORDON

1946:　The Truth About Murder*

HOMER KING GORDON

1935:　Kentucky Blue Streak; Rip Roaring Riley
1936:　Suicide Squad
1939:　In Old Montana*

JAMES B. GORDON

1955:　The Gun That Won the West; Inside Detroit
　　　　(R. Kent)
1956:　Cha-Cha-Cha-Boom!; Don't Knock the Rock (R.
　　　　Kent); The Houston Story; Miami Expose; Rock
　　　　Around the Clock (R. Kent); The Werewolf (R.
　　　　Kent)
1957:　Utah Blaine (R. Kent)
1960:　Three Came to Kill
1961:　Twist Around the Clock
1962:　Don't Knock the Twist; Experiment in Terror
　　　　(Leo Gordon); Tower of London*
1963:　Hootenanny Hoot
1966:　Hold On
1969:　The File of the Golden Goose (J. Higgins)

JOHN E. GORDON

1946: Beware; Look Out, Sister

LEO V. GORDON (1922–   ) actor

1957: Black Patch
1958: Hot Car Girl; The Cry Baby Killer (M. Levy)
1959: Escort West (F. Hartsook); Attack of the
       Giant Leeches (alt. The Giant Leeches); The
       Wasp Woman
1960: Valley of the Redwoods (D. Madison)
1961: The Cat Burglar
1962: Experiment in Terror (J. B. Gordon); Tower
       of London*
1965: The Bounty Killer (R. Alexander)
1966: Tobruk
1970: You Can't Win 'Em All (Turk.)

LEON GORDON

1931: Annabelle's Affairs; Don't Bet on Women (L.
       Starling); Heartbreak; Their Mad Moment
1932: Freaks (W. Goldbeck); Kongo; Man About Town
1933: When Ladies Meet (J. Meehan)
1934: Tarzan and His Mate*
1935: Age of Indiscretion (O. Garrett); The Bishop
       Misbehaves (G. Auerback); Stolen Harmony*
1936: His Brother's Wife (J. Meehan); The
       Unguarded Hour (H. Rogers)
1937: The Last of Mrs. Cheyney*
1939: Balalaika*; Society Lawyer*
1940: Broadway Melody of 1940*
1941: They Met in Bombay*
1942: White Cargo
1950: Kim*
1952: The Hour of 13 (H. Rogers); Rogue's March

MICHAEL GORDON (1909–   ) director

1953: Wherever She Goes (Austral.)

MILDRED GORDON

1965: That Darn Cat*

ROBERT B. GORDON

1960: Noose for a Gunman

ROSE GORDON

1934: Mystery Ranch (C. Krusada); Rawhide Mail (B.
      Burbridge); Fighting Hero (C. Krusada);
      Loser's End (C. Krusada)
1935: Unconquered Bandit (L. Borden); Tracy Rides
      (B. Burbridge); The Silver Bullet (C.
      Krusada); Ridin' Thru; Born to Battle (C.
      Krusada); Coyote Trails (C. Krusada); Silent
      Valley (C. Krusada)
1936: Fast Bullets (C. Krusada); Roamin' Wild; The
      Speed Reporter

RUTH GORDON (1896-   ) actress, playwright

1948: A Double Life (G. Kanin)
1949: Adam's Rib (G. Kanin)
1952: The Marrying Kind (G. Kanin); Pat and Mike
      (G. Kanin)
1953: The Actress

STEVE GORDON

1978: The One and Only
1981: Arthur

WILLIAM D. GORDON

1968: Sergeant Ryker (S. Lester)

CHRISTOPHER GORE

1980: Fame

ROBERT GORE-BROWN

1932:   Lily Christine

LESTER GORN

1957:   The Beginning of the End (F. Freiberger)

JAY GORNEY

1936:   College Holiday*
1944:   Hey, Rookie*

LASLO GOROG

1945:   The Affairs of Susan*
1946:   Murder in the Music Hall (F. Hyland)
1956:   The Mole People
1957:   The Land Unknown
1958:   The Spider (G. Yates)
1960:   Too Soon to Love (R. Rush)
1963:   Of Love and Desire (R. Rush)

JEROME GOTTLER

1955:   High Society (B. Lawrence); Spy Chasers (B.
        Lawrence)

ALEX GOTTLIEB

1938:   Arson Gang Busters (N. Burnstine); Gambliing
        Ship; I Stand Accused (G. Kahn); Invisible
        Enemy (Albert Cohen)
1939:   Inside Information; Mystery of the White
        Room
1940:   Dark Streets of Cairo; Meet the Wildcat
1941:   Lucky Devils; Meet the Chump
1954:   Susan Slept Here
1965:   Arizona Raiders*
1966:   Frankie and Johnny

CARL GOTTLIEB

1975: Jaws (P. Benchley)
1977: Which Way Is Up? (C. Brown)
1978: Jaws 2 (H. Sackler)
1979: The Jerk*
1981: Caveman (R. DeLuca)

BERNI GOULD

1962: Twist All Night

CLIFFORD GOULD

1968: Krakatoa, East of Java (Bernard Gordon)
1970: Macho Callahan

HEYWOOD GOULD

1977: Rolling Thunder (P. Schrader)
1978: The Boys from Brazil
1981: Fort Apache, The Bronx

JOHN GOULD

1975: Who?

EDMUND GOULDING (1891-1959) director

1929: The Trespasser
1930: The Grand Parade; Devil's Holiday
1931: Reaching for the Moon; The Night Angel
1934: Riptide
1935: The Flame Within
1937: That Certain Woman

JAMES GOW

1935: I Dream Too Much (E. North)
1936: Bunker Bean*; Murder on a Bridle Path*
1941: Moonlight in Hawaii*

ED GRACZYK

1982: Come Back to the Five and Dime, Jimmy Dean, Jimmy Dean

TOM GRAEFF

1959: Teenagers from Outer Space

CARROLL GRAHAM

1937: Girl Loves Boy (D. Mansfield); Sweetheart of the Navy

GARRETT GRAHAM

1934: Gambling

LEWIS GRAHAM

1935: The Crime of Dr. Crespi (E. Olmstead)

NORMAN GRAHAM

1960: Macumba Love

RODNEY J. GRAHAM

1948: Sundown Riders

RONALD GRAHAM

1974: Shanks

RONNIE GRAHAM

1954: New Faces*

MICHAEL GRAIS

```
1981:   Death Hunt (M.Victor)
1982:   Poltergeist*
```

RICHARD GRAND

```
1976:   The Commitment*
1979:   Fyre (Ted Zephro)
```

EDDIE GRANEMANN

```
1934:   Thunder over Texas
1935:   The Lost City (ser.)*
1936:   Custer's Last Stand (ser.)*; Jaws of the
        Jungle (alt. Jungle Virgin)
```

BERT GRANET

```
1936:   Legion of Terror
1937:   The Big Shot (A. Horman); High Flyer*; Meet
        the Missus*; Speed to Spare (L. Hillyer)
1938:   Affairs of Annabel (P. Yawitz); Annabel
        Takes a Tour (O. Cooper); Go Chase Yourself
        (P. Yawitz); Law of the Underworld (E.
        Hartmann); Maid's Night Out; Mr. Doodle
        Kicks Off; Quick Money*
1939:   Career (D. Trumbo); The Day the Bookies Wept
        (G. Jeske); Fixer Dugan (P. Yawitz)
1940:   Cross-Country Romance (J. Cady); Laddie (J.
        Cady); Millionaire Playboy (C. E. Roberts)
1941:   Footlight Fever (I. Hunter); A Girl, a Guy
        and a Gob (F. Ryan); Obliging Young Lady (F.
        Ryan)
```

BARRA GRANT

```
1978:   Slow Dancing in the Big City
```

JAMES EDWARD GRANT (1902-1966) director

```
1937:   Danger - Love at Work (B. Markson); Women
        Men Marry*
1938:   Josette; There's That Woman Again*
1939:   Miracles for Sale*
```

```
1940:   Music in My Heart
1941:   Johnny Eager (J. Mahin)
1942:   The Lady Is Willing (A. McCleery)
1944:   Belle of the Yukon
1945:   The Great John L
1947:   Angel and the Badman
1949:   Sands of Iwo Jima (H. Brown)
1950:   Father Is a Bachelor (A. Leslie); Surrender
        (S. Nibley); Rock Island Trail; California
        Passage
1951:   The Bullfighter and the Lady; Flying
        Leathernecks
1952:   Big Jim McLain
1953:   Hondo
1954:   Ring of Fear*
1956:   The Last Wagon*; Three Violent People
1958:   The Sheepman (W. Bowers)
1960:   The Alamo
1961:   The Comancheros (C. Huffaker)
1963:   Donovan's Reef(F. Nugent); McLintock!
1971:   Support Your Local Gunfighter
```

JOHN GRANT

```
1941:   Hold That Ghost*; In the Navy (A. Horman);
        Keep 'Em Flying (N. Perrin)
1942:   Ride 'Em Cowboy (T. Boardman); Pardon My
        Sarong*; Who Done It?*
1943:   Hit the Ice*; It Ain't Hay (A. Boretz)
1944:   In Society*; Lost in a Harem*
1945:   Her Come the Co-Eds (A. Horman)
1945:   The Naughty Nineties*; Ten Cents a Dance
1947:   The Wistful Widow of Wagon Gap (F. Rinaldo);
        Buck Privates Come Home*
1948:   Abbott and Costello Meet Frankenstein*;
        Mexican Hayride (O. Brodney); The Noose
        Hangs High (H. Harris)
1949:   Abbott and Costello Meet the Killer Boris
        Karloff*
1950:   Abbott and Costello in the Foreign Legion
        (M. Ragaway); Curtain Call at Cactus Creek
        (H. Dimsdale)
1951:   Abbott and Costello Meet the Invisible Man*
1952:   Abbott and Costello Meet Captain Kidd (H.
        Dimsdale); Ma and Pa Kettle at the Fair (R.
        Morris)
1953:   Abbott and Costello Go to Mars (D.
```

Beauchamp); Abbott and Costello Meet Dr.
Jekyll and Mr. Hyde (L. Loeb)
1954: Fireman, Save My Child (L. Loeb)
1955: Abbott and Costello Meet the Keystone Kops;
Abbott and Costello Meet the Mummy

MORTON GRANT

1937: Love Is on the Air
1938: She Loved a Fireman (C. Sand); His Exciting
Night*
1939: Timber Stampede
1940: Stage to Chino (A. Jones); Triple Justice
(A. Jones); Wagon Train
1941: Moonlight in Hawaii*; Along the Rio Grande
(A. Jones); Robbers on the Range (A. Jones);
Dude Cowboy; Melody Lane*
1942: Riding the Wind (E. Snell); Land of the Open
Range; Westward Ho (D. Schroeder); Bandit
Ranger (B. Cohen); Valley of Hunted Men (A.
DeMond)
1943: Santa Fe Scouts (B. Burbridge); The Avenging
Rider; Beyond the Last Frontier (J. Butler);
Bar 20*
1944: Swing in the Saddle*; The Falcon Out West (B.
Jones)
1946: Song of the South*
1948: The Gallant Blade (W. Ferris)
1949: The Big Cat (D. Yost)

MAURIE GRASHIN

1941: Mountain Moonlight*
1942: Sons of the Pioneer*
1946: Roll On, Texas Moon (P. Gangelin)
1948: Arthur Takes Over

ALEX GRASSHOFF

1967: Young Americans (doc.)

GARY GRAVER

1981: Texas Lightning

303

1982:   Trick or Treats

FRANK GRAVES

1961:   Rebellion in Cuba (Cub.; M. Hanna)

RALPH GRAVES (1900-1977) actor

1932:   Scandal for Sale (R. Keith)
1934:   Born to Be Bad (H. Jacobs)

BARBARA GRAY

1957:   Istanbul*

GEORGE GRAY

1942:   The Valley of Vanishing Men (ser.)*

HUGH GRAY

1955:   Helen of Troy (J. Twist); Ulysses*

JOHN GRAY

1935:   Lightning Strikes Twice (J. Fields)
1942:   Snuffy Smith, Yard Bird*

MIKE GRAY

1979:   The China Syndrome*

WILLIAM GRAY

1980:   Prom Night; The Changeling
1981:   An Eye for an Eye (J. Bruner)
1982:   Humongous

CHARLES GRAYSON

```
1936:   Crash Donovan*
1937:   Breezing Home; The Man Who Cried Wolf (S.
        Bartlett); The Mighty Treve*; Top of the
        Town (Brown Holmes); We Have Our Moments (B.
        Manning); You're A Sweetheart (M. Brice)
1938:   Freshman Year; Personal Secretary*; Reckless
        Living; Swing, Sister, Swing; Swing That
        Cheer (L. Loeb); Young Fugitives (B. Kohn);
        Strange Faces
1939:   For Love or Money (A. Horman); Hawaiian
        Nights (L. Loeb); Risky Business; Unexpected
        Father (L. Spigelgass)
1940:   Alias the Deacon (N. Perrin); The Boys from
        Syracuse (L. Spiegelgass); Ma, He's Making
        Eyes at Me (E. Hartmann); One Night in the
        Tropics (G. Purcell); Private Affairs*;
        Sandy Is a Lady
1941:   Bad Men of Missouri; Law of the Tropics; She
        Couldn't Say No (E. Baldwin); Thieves Fall
        Out (B. Markson); Underground
1942:   Wild Bill Hickok Rides*
1949:   I Married a Communist (R.H. Andrews);
        Outpost in Morocco (P. Sainte-Colombe)
1950:   The Woman on Pier 13 (R.H. Andrews)
1956:   Battle Hymn (V. Evans)
1958:   The Barbarian and the Geisha
```

WILLIAM GREAVES

```
1974:   The Fighters (doc.)
```

ADOLPH GREEN (1918-   ) playwright

```
1947:   Good News (B. Comden)
1949:   The Barkleys of Broadway (B. Comden); On the
        Town (B. Comden)
1952:   Singin' in the Rain (B. Comden)
1953:   The Band Wagon (B. Comden)
1955:   It's Always Fair Weather (B. Comden)
1958:   Auntie Mame (B. Comden)
1960:   Bells Are Ringing (B. Comden)
1964:   What a Way to Go! (B. Comden)
```

ANNE GREEN

1946:   Her Sister's Secret

GEORGE GREEN

1949:   Omoo-Omoo (L. Leonard)

GERALD GREEN

1949:   Apache Chief (L. Picker)
1959:   The Last Angry Man (Richard Murphy)

GUY GREEN (1913-   ) director   Brit.

(American films only)
1965:   A Patch of Blue

HAROLD GREEN

1966:   Texas Across the River*

HOWARD J. GREEN

1929:   The Long, Long Trail; The Faker; Behind
        Closed doors; The Donovan Affair (D.
        Howell); Broadway Scandals (N. Houston);
        Ramblin' Kid; Song of Love; Flight
1930:   High Society Blues; Melody Man; Cheer Up and
        Smile; On Your Back; Princess and the
        Plumber; Soup to Nuts (R. Goldberg); Part
        Time Wife
1931:   A Dangerous Affair; Maker of Men
1932:   Cohens and Kellys in Hollywood; I Am a
        Fugitive from a Chain Gang*; They Call It
        Sin (L. Hayward)
1933:   Morning Glory; Trick for Trick
1934:   The Lemon Drop Kid*; Man of Two Worlds (A.
        Morgan); Shoot the Works; Success at Any
        Price (J. Lawson)
1935:   If You Could Only Cook (G. Purcell); Men
        Without Names (K. Glasmon); Rumba; Star of
        Midnight*
1936:   Devil's Squadron; Meet Nero Wolfe*; They Met

in a Taxi
1937: New Faces of 1937*; This Way Please*
1938: The House of Mystery (J. Parker); Making the
      Headlines (J. Parker)
1940: Dreaming Out Loud*
1941: The Big Boss; Harmon of Michigan; The Mad
      Doctor; Two in a Taxi*
1942: Cadets on Parade; The Spirit of Stanford*
1943: After Midnight with Boston Blackie;
      Doughboys in Ireland; High Explosive (M.
      Shane); Reveille with Beverly*
1944: Take It Big (J. Bigelow); The Racket Man*
1945: George White's Scandals*; Having Wonderful
      Crime*
1946: San Quentin*
1948: The Winner's Circle
1950: Chain Gang; Military Academy with That 10th
      Avenue Gang; State Penitentiary*
1951: My True Story (Brown Holmes)
1952: The Hawk of Wild River

JANET GREEN (1914-   ) playwright Brit.

(American films only)
1966: Seven Women (J. McCormack); Walk in the
      Shadow (J. McCormack)

JOSEPH GREEN

1963: The Brain That Wouldn't Die

MORRIS LEE GREEN

1960: This Rebel Breed

PAUL GREEN (1894-   ) dramatist

1932: Cabin in the Cotton
1933: Doctor Bull; State Fair (S. Levien);
      Voltaire (M. Howell)

WALON GREEN

307

```
1969:   The Wild Bunch (S. Peckinpah)
1977:   Sorcerer
1978:   The Brink's Job; The Secret Life of Plants*
1982:   The Border*
```

EVERETT GREENBAUM

```
1964:   Good Neighbor Sam*
1966:   The Ghost and Mr. Chicken (J. Fritzell)
1967:   The Reluctant Astronaut (J. Fritzell)
1969:   Angel in My Pocket (J. Fritzell)
```

DON GREENBERG

```
1981:   The President's Women*
```

HENRY F. GREENBERG

```
1959:   Al Capone (M. Wald)
1963:   The Caretakers (H. Bartlett)
```

STANLEY R. GREENBERG

```
1972:   Skyjacked
1973:   Soylent Green
```

DAN GREENBURG

```
1968:   Live a Little, Love a Little (M. Hoey)
1972:   Oh! Calcutta!*
1973:   I Could Never Have Sex with Any Man Who Has
        So Little Regard for My Husband
1975:   Foreplay*
1983:   Private Lessons
```

CLARENCE GREENE (1918-   ) producer

```
1944:   The Town Went Wild (R. Rouse)
1949:   D.O.A. (R. Rouse)
1951:   The Well (R. Rouse)
1952:   The Thief (R. Rouse)
1953:   Wicked Woman (R. Rouse)
```

1955: New York Confidential (R. Rouse)
1964: A House Is Not a Home (R. Rouse)
1966: The Oscar*

DAVID GREENE (1924-   ) director   Brit.

(American films only)
1968: Come Back Baby
1973: Godspell (J. Trebelak)

EVE GREENE

1932: Prosperity*
1933: Beauty for Sale (Z. Sears); Day of Reckoning
       (Z. Sears); Tugboat Annie (Z. Sears)
1934: Operator 13*; This Side of Heaven*; You
       Can't Buy Everything (Z. Sears)
1935: The Great Impersonation (F. Wead); Storm
       over the Andes*
1936: Yours for the Asking*
1937: Her Husband Lies (W. Smith); When Love Is
       Young (J. Fields)
1938: Stolen Heaven (Fred Jackson)
1939: Little Accident (P. Yawitz)
1941: Night of January 16th*
1942: Joan of Ozark*; Sweater Girl
1944: Strange Affair (J. Odlum)
1947: Born to Kill (R. Macaulay)

HAROLD R. GREENE

1950: Counterspy Meets Scotland Yard; On the Isle
       of Samoa (B. Weisberg)
1951: China Corsair; Criminal Lawyer

JOE GREENE

1974: Together Brothers (J. DeWitt)

JOHN GREENE

1959: Plunderers of Painted Flats (P. Shuken)

JOSH GREENFIELD

1974: Harry and Tonto (P. Mazursky)
1980: Oh, God! Book II*

SAM GREENLEE

1973: The Spook Who Sat by the Door (M. Clay)

TED GREENWALD

1976: Revenge of the Cheerleaders (N. Dorsky)

DAN GREER

1976: Baker's Hawk (H. Harrison); Pony Express
       Rider*

WILLIAM GREFE

1964: Racing Fever
1969: The Hooked Generation*

FREDDY GREGOR

1975: The Gorilla Gang

FRANK GREGORY

1961: Then There Were Three (A. Lurie)

EDDIE GRENEMANN

1934: Thunder over Texas

ANTHONY GREVILLE-BELL

1972: The Strange Vengeance of Rosalie (J. Kohn)

CLIFFORD GREY

1934:   The Song You Gave Me
1935:   Elizabeth of England (Brit.)*; Girls Will Be
        Boys (Brit.)*

JOHN W. GREY

1929:   Coquette
1930:   Worldly Goods
1936:   The Farmer in the Dell (S. Mintz)
1937:   Forty Naughty Girls; Mysterious Crossing
        (Jefferson Parker); Too Many Wives*
1938:   I'm from the City*
1944:   Sing a Jingle
1945:   Rockin' in the Rockies (J. Cheney); Swingin'
        on a Rainbow (O. Cooper)

HARRY WAGSTAFF GRIBBLE

1932:   A Bill of Divorcement (H. Estabrook)
1933:   Our Betters (J. Murfin)
1934:   Nana (W. Mack)

HOWARD GRIER

1932:   Blessed Event

TOM GRIES (1922-1977) director

1952:   The Bushwackers (R. Amateau)
1955:   Mustang; Hunters of the Deep (A. Dowling);
        Hell's Horizon; King Dinosaur
1968:   Will Penny
1969:   100 Rifles (C. Huffaker)

ELEANORE GRIFFIN

1943:   War of the Wildcats (ret. In Old Oklahoma;
        Ethel Hill)
1948:   Tenth Avenue Angel (H. Ruskin)
1955:   Good Morning, Miss Dove; A Man Called Peter

1959:	Imitation of Life (Allan Scott); Third Man on the Mountain
1961:	Back Street (W. Ludwig)
1964:	One Man's Way (J. W. Bloch)

CHARLES GRIFFITH

1956:	The Gunslinger (M. Hanna)
1957:	Not of This Earth (M. Hanna); Attack of the Crab Monsters; Rock All Night; The Undead (M. Hanna); Flesh and the Spur (M. Hanna); Naked Paradise (M. Hanna); Teenage Doll
1958:	Ghost of the China Sea
1959:	Forbidden Island; A Bucket of Blood
1960:	Creature from the Haunted Sea; The Little Shop of Horrors; Ski Troop Attack
1966:	The Wild Angels
1967:	Devil's Angels
1975:	Death Race 2000 (R. Thom); The Swinging Barmaids
1976:	Eat My Dust!
1980:	Dr. Heckyl and Mr. Hype

D. W. GRIFFITH (1875-1948) director, producer, writer

1931:	The Struggle*

EDWARD H. GRIFFITH (1894-   ) director

1929:	Shady Lady (J. Jungmeyer)

GORDON S. GRIFFITH

1935:	Hot off the Press (V. Potel)

RAYMOND GRIFFITH (1890-1957) actor, director

1931:	Beloved Bachelor*; Bought (C. Kenyon); Girls About Town (B. Marlow); God's Gift to Women (J. Jackson)

LEON GRIFFITHS

1971:   The Grissom Gang

MICHAEL M. GRILIKHES

1966:   Duel at Diablo (M. Albert)

GRICE GRIMES

1971:   The Beguiled (J. Sherry)
1972:   The Possession of Joel Delaney (M. Robinson)

NICK GRINDE (1893-   ) director

1930:   The Divorcee (J. Meehan)
1934:   Babes in Toyland (F. Butler)
1943:   We've Never Been Licked (N. Raine)

DURWOOD GRINSTEAD

1936:   Maid of Salem*

JOHN GRISSMER

1973:   The House That Cried Murder (J. Pelissie)
1978:   Scalpel

FERDE GROFE, JR.

1961:   The Steel Claw*
1962:   Samar (G. Montgomery)
1964:   The Walls of Hell*
1968:   Warkill
1972:   The Proud and the Damned

MILTON H. GROPPER

1929:   Thru Different Eyes (alt. Guilty; Public
        Opinion; T. Barry)
1932:   No Man of Her Own (M. Watkins)

JERRY GROSS

1968:   Teenage Mother

LARRY GROSS

1981:   Headin' for Broadway*
1982:   48 Hours

MILT GROSS

1941:   Puddin'head (J. Townley); Rookies on
        Parade*; Sis Hopkins*

STEPHEN GROSS

1936:   Thank You, Jeeves (J. Hoffman)

BUDD GROSSMAN

1958:   Going Steady
1961:   Bachelor Flat (F. Tashlin)

R. L. GROVE

1972:   The Deathmaster

HERMAN GROVES

1975:   The Strongest Man in the World (J. McEveety)

PHIL GROVES

1982:   Beach Girls (P. Duncan)

FRANK GRUBER (1904-1969) novelist

1943:   Northern Pursuit*

```
1944:   The Mask of Demetrios
1946:   The French Key; Terror by Night; In Old
        Sacramento (ret. Flame of Sacramento; F.
        Hyland); Accomplice (I. Elman)
1947:   Bulldog Drummond at Bay
1948:   The Challenge (I. Elman)
1949:   Fighting Man of the Plains
1950:   The Cariboo Trail
1951:   The Great Missouri Raid; Warpath; Silver
        City; Flaming Feather (G. Adams)
1952:   The Denver and Rio Grande; Hurricane Smith
1961:   Twenty Plus Two
1965:   Town Tamer
```

JAMES GRUEN

```
1929:   Girl in the Glass Cage; Hard to Get; Night
        Parade
1934:   In Old Santa Fe (C. Clark); The Marines Are
        Coming
1935:   Behind the Green Lights
1936:   Wild Brian Kent*
1937:   Windjammer (D. Jarrett)
```

AXEL GRUENBERG

```
1976:   Starbird and Sweet William
1978:   The Adventures of Starbird
```

JERRY GRUSKIN

```
1947:   Tarzan and the Huntress (R. Leigh)
1948:   Slippy McGee (N. Hall)
```

JOHN GUARE

```
1971:   Taking Off*
1981:   Atlantic City
```

JOHN GUEDEL

```
1936:   General Spanky*
```

ROBERT GUENETTE

1976:   The Mysterious Monsters (doc.); The Amazing
        World of Psychic Phenomena (doc.)
1981:   The Man Who Saw Tomorrow

FRANCES GUIHAN

1929:   Midstream
1935:   The Throwback; Bulldog Courage (J.
        O'Donnell)
1936:   The Cowboy and the Kid; Ride 'Em Cowboy;
        Boss Rider of Gun Creek; The Cowboy Star;
        Empty Saddles
1937:   Westbound Mail; Sandflow; Left Handed Law;
        Black Aces; Law for Tombstone; Sudden Bill
        Dorn; Boss of Lonely Valley
1938:   Frontier Scout

LEO GUILD

1962:   The Devil's Messenger

FRED GUIOL

1933:   The Cohens and Kellys in Trouble (A. Smith)
1935:   The Nitwits (A. Boasberg)
1939:   Gunga Din*
1940:   Vigil in the Night*
1956:   Giant (I.Moffat)

CAMPBELL GULLIAN

1930:   Sky Hawk (L. Hughes)

EUGENE GUMP

1974:   The Wrestler

BILL GUNN

1970:   The Landlord; The Angel Levine (R. Ribman)
1973:   Ganja and Hess

JAMES GUNN

1943:   Lady of Burlesque
1947:   The Unfaithful (D. Goodis)
1950:   The Flying Missile (R. English); Harriet
        Craig (A. Froelick)
1951:   The Barefoot Mailman (E. Swann); Two of a
        Kind (L. Kimble)
1952:   Affair in Trinidad (O. Saul)
1953:   All I Desire (R. Blees)
1956:   Over-Exposed (G. Orlovitz)
1959:   The Young Philadelphians
1960:   Because They're Young

MILTON GRUNZBURG

1941:   The Devil Commands (R. D. Andrews)

ROBERT GURNEY, JR.

1957:   Invasion of the Saucer Men (A. Martin)
1958:   Edge of Fury

JACK GUSS

1968:   Lady in Cement (M. Albert)

A. B. GUTHRIE, JR. (1901-   ) newspaperman,
        novelist

1953:   Shane
1955:   The Kentuckian

JAMES GUTMAN

1974:   I'm a Stranger Here Myself (doc.)*

RICHARD A. GUTTMAN

317

1964:   Back Door to Hell (J. Hackett)

H

CHARLES HAAS

1948: Moonrise

CHARLIE HAAS

1982: Tex (Tim Hunter)

HUGO HAAS (1901-1968) actor, director Czech.

(American films only)
1951: The Girl on the Bridge (A. Phillips); Pickup
       (A. Phillips)
1952: Strange Fascination
1953: One Girl's Confession; Thy Neighbor's Wife
1954: The Other Woman
1955: Hold Back Tomorrow
1956: Edge of Hell
1957: Hit and Run
1959: Born to Be Loved
1962: Paradise Alley

HAL HACKADY

1958: Let's Rock!; Senior Prom
1961: Hey, Let's Twist!
1962: Two Tickets to Paris

ALBERT HACKETT (1900-   )

1933: Penthouse (F. Goodrich); The Secret of
       Madame Blanche (F. Goodrich)
1934: Fugitive Lovers*; Hide-Out (F. Goodrich);

```
           The Thin Man (F. Goodrich)
1935:   Ah, Wilderness (F. Goodrich); Naughty
        Marietta*
1936:   After the Thin Man (F. Goodrich); Rose
        Marie*
1937:   The Firefly*
1939:   Another Thin Man (F. Goodrich); Society
        Lawyer*
1944:   Lady in the Dark (F. Goodrich); The Hitler
        Gang (F. Goodrich)
1946:   It's a Wonderful Life*; The Virginian*
1948:   Easter Parade* The Pirate (F. Goodrich);
        Summer Holiday*
1950:   Father of the Bride (F. Goodrich)
1951:   Father's Little Dividend (F. Goodrich); Too
        Young to Kiss (F. Goodrich)
1953:   Give a Girl a Break (F. Goodrich)
1954:   The Long, Long Trailer (F. Goodrich); Seven
        Brides for Seven Brothers*
1956:   Gaby*
1958:   A Certain Smile (F. Goodrich)
1959:   The Diary of Anne Frank (F. Goodrich)
1962:   Five Finger Exercise (F. Goodrich)
```

JOHN HACKETT

```
1964:   Back Door to Hell (R. Guttman)
```

PAT HACKETT

```
1977:   Andy Warhol's Bed (G. Abagnalo)
```

DENNIS HACKIN

```
1979:   Wanda Nevada
1980:   Bronco Billy
```

ROSS HAGEN

```
1973:   Bad Charleston Charlie*
```

WILLIAM HAGENS

1946:   Crime of the Century*; Passkey to Danger (O.
        Rhinehart)

MARK HAGGARD

1974:   Black Eye (Jim Martin)

ARTHUR HAILEY

1957:   Zero Hour!*

OLIVER HAILEY

1979:   Just You and Me, Kid (L. Stern)

FRED HAINES

1967:   Ulysses (J. Strick)

WILLIAM WISTER HAINES

1935:   Alibi Ike; Man of Iron
1936:   Black Legion (A. Finkel)
1937:   Mr. Dodd Takes the Air (E. Ryan); Slim
1938:   The Texans*
1948:   Beyond Glory*
1951:   The Racket (W. Burnett)
1952:   One Minute to Zero (M. Krims)
1957:   The Wings of Eagles (F. Fenton)
1958:   Torpedo Run (R. Sale)

HARVEY HAISLIP

1939:   Thunder Afloat (W. Root)
1940:   Flight Command (W. Root)

GEORGE HALASZ

1947:   Linda Be Good (L. Vale)

SCOTT HALE

1976:   The Shootist (M. Swarthout)

ALEX HALEY

1973:   Superfly...T.N.T.

EARL HALEY

1939:   The Gentleman from Arizona (Jack O'Donnell)

JACK HALEY, JR.

1974:   That's Entertainment (doc.)

ROBERT HALFF

1943:   Swing Shift Maisie (M. McCall)

H. B. HALICKI

1982:   The Junkman

ALLEN HALL

1936:   Gun Grit (G. Phillips)

ARCH HALL

1964:   The Nasty Rabbit (ret. Spies a Go-Go; J. Critchfield)
1972:   The Corpse Grinders (J. Cranston)

CONRAD HALL

1956:   Running Target*

DONCHO HALL

1942: Snuffy Smith, Yard Bird*

DOUGLAS KENT HALL

1974: The Great American Cowboy (doc.)

F. PAUL HALL

1960: Ma Barker's Killer Brood

JANE HALL

1939: These Glamour Girls (M. Parsonnet)

NORMAN S. HALL

1933: Flirting with Danger; The Three Musketeers
(ser.)*; The Whispering Shadow (ser.)*
1934: Tailspin Tommy (ser.)*
1936: Ace Drummond (ser.)*
1937: Wild West Days (ser.)*; Jungle Jim (ser.)*;
Radio Patrol (ser.)*; Secret Agent X-9
(ser.)*; Tim Tyler's Luck (ser.)*
1938: Mars Attacks the World*; Flash Gordon's Trip
to Mars (ser.)*; Hawk of the Wilderness
(ser.)*; Red Barry (ser.)*
1939: Frontier Pony Express; Wall Street Cowboy
(G. Geraghty); Buck Rogers (ser.; R. Trampe)
1940: Adventures of Red Ryder (ser.)*; King of the
Royal Mounted (ser.)*; Drums of Fu Manchu
(ser.)*; the Mysterious Dr. Satan (ser.)*
1941: King of the Texas Rangers (ser.)*;
Adventures of Captain Marvel (ser.)*; Dick
Tracy vs. Crime, Inc. (ser.)*; Jungle Girl
(ser.)*
1942: The Sombrero Kid; Outlaws of Pine Ridge;
Sundown Kid; Perils of Nyoka (ser.)*; Spy
Smasher (ser.)*; Yukon Patrol*
1943: Thundering Trails*; Dead Man's Gulch (R.
Williams); Kansas City Cyclone; Carson City
Cylcone; Days of Old Cheyenne; Fugitive from
Sonora; Black Hills Express; Death Valley
Manhunt (A. Coldeway); Bordertown

Gunfighters; The Man from the Rio Grande;
California Joe
1944:   Mojave Firebrand; Outlaws of Santa Fe; The
San Antonio Kid; Stagecoach to Monterey;
Sheriff of Sundown; Vigilantes of Dodge City
(A. Coldeway); Sheriff of Las Vegas
1945:   The Topeka Terror (P. Harper); Corpus
Christi Bandits
1946:   Red River Renegades
1947:   Buckaroos from Powder River; Last Days of
Boot Hill
1948:   Slippy McGee (J. Gruskin); Whilrlwind
Raiders; Blazing Across the Pecos; Sundown
in Santa Fe; Daredevils of the Clouds
1949:   Law of th Golden West; South of Rio; San
Antone Ambush; Rose of the Yukon
1950:   Beyond the Purple Hills; Indian Territory;
Unmasked (A. DeMond)
1951:   Gene Autrey and the Mounties; Texans Never
Cry; Whirlwind
1952:   Apache Country; Montana Belle (H. McCoy);
Night Stage to Galveston
1953:   Winning of the West; Pack Train
1958:   The Missouri Traveler
1959:   The Young Land

SAM HALL

1970: House of Dark Shadows (G. Russell)
1971: Night of Dark Shadows

HELEN HALLETT

1929: Three Live Ghosts

FRED HALLIDAY

1974: Nine Lives of Fritz the Cat (anim.)*

JEAN HALLOWAY

1946: Till the Clouds Roll By*

EDWARD HALPERIN

1939:   Code of the Cactus
1940:   Yukon Flight; Danger Ahead; Sky Bandits

VICTOR HUGO HALPERIN (1895-   ) director

1936:   Revolt of the Zombies*

ANN & DAVID HALPERN

1941:   Escort Girl

FORREST HALSEY

1929:   Careers; Her Private Life; A Man's Man; A
        Most Immoral Lady; Prisoners; Saturday's
        Children
1930:   The Furies; Sweethearts and Wives; One Night
        at Susie's
1931:   Kept Husbands (A. Jackson); The Lady Who
        Dared (K. Scola)

JULIAN HALVEY

1964:   Circus World (B. Hecht); Psycho '59
1965:   Crack in the World (J. M. White)

ROBERT HAMES

1954:   The Detective (T. Schnee)

HARRY HAMILTON

1936:   I Cover Chinatown

ROY HAMILTON

1954:   Cat Women of the Moon

WALTER HAMILTON, JR.

1974: Black Sampson

WARREN HAMILTON

1976: Kiss of the Tarantula

WILLIAM HAMILTON

1942: Call Out the Marines (F. Ryan)

EARL HAMMER, JR.

1963: Palm Springs Weekend
1973: Charlotte's Web (anim.)
1974: Where the Lillies Bloom

ROBERT HAMMER

1980: Don't Answer the Phone!

OSCAR HAMMERSTEIN II (1895-1960) lyricist,
        librettist

1930: Viennese Nights
1931: Children of Dreams (S. Romberg)
1936: Showboat (J. Kern)
1937: High, Wide and Handsome; Swing High, Swing
        Low (V. Van Upp)
1939: The Story of Vernon and Irene Castle*
1945: State Fair (S. Levien)

DASHIELL HAMMETT (1894-1961) novelist

1943: Watch on the Rhine

ELLEN HAMMILL

1980: Don't Go in the House*

PETE HAMMILL

1971: Doc
1973: Badge 373

VICTOR HAMMOND

1944: The Utah Kid; Marked Trails (J. McCarthy);
       Trigger Law; Detective Kitty O'Day (Tim
       Ryan)
1945: South of the Rio Grande (R. Bettinson);
       Adventures of Kitty O'Day*; Fashion Model
       (T. Ryan)
1946: In Fast Company*

ROBERT HAMNER

1960: Thirteen Fighting Men (J. Thomas)
1961: The Long Rope

ORVILLE HAMPTON

1950: Hi-Jacked (F. Myton); Motor Patrol (M.
       Tombragel); Train to Tombstone (V. West);
       Everybody's Dancing; Experiment Alcatraz
1951: Three Desperate Men; Fingerprints Don't Lie;
       Mask of the Dragon; Sky High; Leave It to
       the Marines
1952: Outlaw Women; Red Snow (T. Hubbard)
1954: Fangs of the Wild
1955: New Orleans Uncensored (L. Meltzer)
1956: Frontier Gambler; The Three Outlaws
1957: The Black Whip
1958: Jet Attack; Toughest Gun in Tombstone;
       Badman's Country; Hong Kong Confidential
1959: Riot in Juvenile Prison; The Four Skulls of
       Jonathan Drake; The Alligator People; Inside
       the Mafia; The Atomic Submarine
1960: Cage of Evil; A Dog's Best Friend;
       Gunfighters of Abilene; Oklahoma Territory;
       A Police Dog Story; Young Jesse James (J.
       Sackheim)
1961: Operation Bottleneck; The Snake Woman
       (Brit.); You Have to Run Fast

327

```
1962:   Beauty and the Beast (G. Bruce); Jack the
        Giant Killer (N. Juran)
1964:   One Potato, Two Potato (R. Hayes)
1967:   Riot on Sunset Strip
1968:   A Time to Sing (R. E. Kent); The Young
        Runaways
1973:   Detroit 9000
1975:   Friday Foster
```

BLANCHE HANALIS

```
1966:   The Trouble with Angels
1968:   Where Angels Go...Trouble Follows
1973:   From the Mixed-up Files of Mrs. Basil E.
        Frankweiler
1981:   Fish Hawk
```

H. W. HANEMANN

```
1933:   Ace of Aces (J. Saunders); The Great Jasper
        (R. Tasker); Sweepings*
1934:   Meanest Gal in Town*; Rafter Romance*;
        Silver Streak (R. Whately); Where Sinners
        Meet
1935:   Riffraff*; Spring Tonic*
1936:   The House of a Thousand Candles (E. Bohem)
1941:   Cadet Girl (S. Rauh)
1943:   Tahiti Honey*
```

GERALD HANLEY

```
1966:   The Blue Max*
```

JACK HANLEY

```
1954:   Roogie's Bump (D. Totheroh)
```

WILLIAM HANLEY

```
1969:   The Gypsy Moths
1982:   Too Far to Go
```

MAURICE HANLINE

1936:   One Rainy Afternoon (S. Avery)
1939:   Four Wives*

BERT HANLON

1936:   Big Brown Eyes (R. Walsh); Spendthrift (R.
        Walsh)

JAMES HANLON

1950:   The Milkman*

MARK HANNA

1956:   The Gunslinger (C. Griffith)
1957:   Not of This Earth (C. Griffith); Attack of
        the Crab Monsters (C. Griffith); The Amazing
        Colossal Man (B.I. Gordon); The Undead (C.
        Griffith); Flesh and the Spur (C. Griffith);
        Naked Paradise (C. Griffith)
1958:   Attack of the 50-Foot Woman
1960:   Raymie
1961:   Rebellion in Cuba (Cub.; F. Graves)
1972:   Slaughter (D. Williams)
1973:   The Gatling Gun (J. Van Winkle

WILLIAM HANNA

1964:   Hey There, It's Yogi Bear (anim.)*

DOROTHY HANNAH

1947:   The Brasher Doubloon

LORRAINE HANSBERRY

1961:   A Raisin in the Sun

CECIL DAN HANSEN

1961: The Second Time Around (O. Saul)

MICHAEL HANSEN

1950: Timber Fury

CURTIS HANSON

1970: The Dunwich Horror*
1973: The Arousers
1979: The Silent Partner

PETER HANSON

1968: Snow Treasure (I. Jacoby)

ROBERT HARARI

1937: Music For Madame (G. Purcell)
1939: Day-Time Wife (A. Arthur); Everything
       Happens at Night (A. Arthur)
1941: Ice-Capades*
1942: Joan of Ozark*
1943: Larceny with Music

OTTO HARBACH

1931: Men of the Sky (J. Kern)

CARL HARBAUGH

1937: The Three Legionnaires (G. Waggner)

HARRY LEE HARBER

1959: Terror Is a Man (alt. Blood Creature)

E. Y. HARBURG

1968: Finian's Rainbow (F. Saidy)

BERTITA HARDING

1956: Magic Fire*

JOHN BRIARD HARDING

1948: The Kissing Bandit (I. Lennart)

RIC HARDMAN

1960: The Big Night
1966: The Rare Breed

BRUNO HARD-WARDEN

1929: Married in Hollywood

LINDSAY HARDY

1954: World for Ransom

RENE HARDY

1958: Bitter Victory*

SAM HARDY (-1935) actor

1935: Man on the Flying Trapeze (R. Harris)

DEAN HARGROVE

1966: One Spy Too Many
1975: The Manchu Eagle Murder Caper Mystery (G.
       Dell)

MARION HARGROVE

```
1957:   Joe Butterfly*
1959:   Cash McCall (L. Coffee)
1962:   Forty Pounds of Trouble; The Music Man
```

DAVID P. HARMON

```
1953:   The Big Heat (S. Boehm)
1956:   Johnny Concho (D. McGuire); Reprisal!*
1957:   Shadow on the Window (L. Townsend)
1958:   The Last of the Fast Guns; The Big Beat
1962:   The Wonderful World of the Brothers Grimm*
1964:   Dark Purpose
```

JULIAN HARMON

```
1946:   The Unknown (M. Boylan)
1951:   Danger Zone; Pier 23 (V. West); Roaring City
        (V. West)
```

SIDNEY HARMON

```
1951:   Drums in the Deep South (P. Yordan)
1952:   Mutiny (P. Yordan)
1954:   Man Crazy (P. Yordan)
```

RALPH HAROLDE

```
1974:   Terror Circus (R. Valenti)
```

EDWARD HARPER

```
1973:   Trader Horn (W. Norton)
```

HENRY HARPER

```
1979:   Scavenger Hunt (S. Vail)
```

PATRICIA HARPER

```
1942:   Prairie Pals
1943:   Western Cyclone; Black Market Rustlers;
```

              Blazing Frontier
1944:   The Drifter; Trigger Trail (E. Repp); Trail
        to Gunsight (B. Cohen)
1945:   The Topeka Terror (N.Hall); Code of the
        Lawless; Secret Agent X-9 (ser.)*
1946:   The Scarlet Horseman (ser.)*
1947:   Range Beyond the Blue; Border Feud (J.
        O'Donnell); Ghost Town Renegades; Frontier
        Fighters

MICHAEL HARRESCHOU

1982:   Safari 3000

CURTIS HARRINGTON (1928-   ) director

1963:   Night Tide
1969:   Queen of Blood

P. HARRINGTON

1943:   Deerslayer (E. Derr)

ALAN M. HARRIS

1973:   The Devil's Wedding Night (R. Zukor)

ANTHONY HARRIS

1972:   Beware! the Blob (J. Woods)

BEN HARRIS

1979:   The Hitter

ELEANOR HARRIS

1938:   Kidnapped*

ELMER HARRIS

```
1929:   Spirit of Youth
1931:   Stepping Out
1932:   Society Girl
1933:   The Barbarian (A. Loos)
1934:   Cross Country Cruise (S. Raugh); Looking for
        Trouble (L. Praskins)
1935:   Let 'Em Have It (J. March)
1936:   The Three Wise Guys
```

HOWARD HARRIS

```
1947:   Copacabana*
1948:   The Noose Hangs High (John Grant)
```

JAMES B. HARRIS

```
1973:   Some Call It Loving
1982:   Fast-Walking
```

JED HARRIS

```
1957:   Operation Mad Ball*
```

MARK HARRIS

```
1973:   Bang the Drum Slowly
```

OWEN HARRIS

```
1959:   Submarine Seahawk (L. Rusoff)
1961:   Frontier Uprising; The Gambler Wore a Gun;
        Secret of Deep Harbor (W. Root)
1962:   Deadly Duo; Incident in an Alley (H.
        Medford); The Underwater City
```

RAYMOND S. HARRIS

```
1929:   Exalted Flapper; Sailor's Holiday; Wedding
        Rings
1930:   Strictly Modern; Bride of the Regiment
1932:   False Madonna (A. Kober); He Learned About
```

Women (H. Thompson)
1933: Three-Cornered Moon (S. Lauren)
1934: Many Happy Returns*; We're Rich Again
1935: Enchanted April (S. Hoffenstein); Hooray for
Love (L. Hazard); Laddie (D. Yost); Man on
the Flying Trapeze (S. Hardy)
1936: Dancing Pirate*
1942: Hillbilly Blitzkrieg

ROBIN HARRIS

1937: City Girl*

TIMOTHY HARRIS

1980: Cheaper to Keep Her (H. Weingrod)

HAL HARRISON, JR.

1976: Baker's Hawk (D. Greer); Pony Express Rider*

JOAN HARRISON (1911-   ) producer   Brit.

(American films only)
1940: Foreign Correspondent*; Rebecca (R. E.
Sherwood)
1941: Suspicion*
1942: Saboteur*
1944: Dark Waters*

PAUL HARRISON

1974: The House of Seven Corpses
1975: Lord Shango
1978: Young Blood

WILLIAM HARRISON

1975: Rollerball

JOHN HART

1966:   Don't Worry, We'll Think of a Title (M.
        Amsterdam)

JUDITH & RALPH HART

1961:   The Flight That Disappeared

LORENZ HART (1895-1943) lyricist

1931:   Hot Heiress*

 MOSS HART (1904-1961) playwright

1935:   Frankkie and Johnnie (L. Goldberg)
1944:   Winged Victory
1947:   Gentleman's Agreement
1952:   Hans Christian Andersen
1954:   A Star Is Born
1955:   Prince of Players

STANLEY HART

1970:   Move (J. Lieber)

JACK HARTFIELD

1942:   Lucky Legs (S. Rubin)
1943:   Forever and a Day*

CARL HARTLE

1932:   Doomed Battalion*

JEAN HARTLEY

1933:   Police Call (N. Keene)

DON HARTMAN (1900-1958) director, producer

336

1935:   Coronado (F. Butler); The Gay Deception (S.
        Avery); Here Comes Cookie; Redheads on
        Parade (R. James)
1936:   The Princess Comes Across*
1937:   Champagne Waltz (F. Butler); Waikiki
        Wedding*
1938:   Tropic Holiday (F. Butler)
1939:   Never Say Die*; Paris Honeymoon (F. Butler);
        The Star Maker (F. Butler)
1940:   Road to Singapore (F. Butler); Those Were
        the Days
1941:   Life with Henry (C. Goldsmith); Nothing but
        the Truth (K. Englund); Road to Zanzibar*
1942:   My Favorite Blonde (F. Butler); Road to
        Morocco (F. Butler)
1943:   True to Life (H. Tugend)
1944:   Up in Arms (R. Pirosh); The Princess and the
        Pirate*
1945:   Wonder Man*
1946:   Down to Earth (E. Blum); The Kid from
        Brooklyn
1947:   It Had to Be You*
1948:   Every Girl Should Be Married (S. Avery)
1951:   Mr. Imperium (E. Knopf)

EDMUND L. HARTMANN (1911-   )

1935:   Helldorado*
1936:   Without Orders (J. Bren)
1937:   Behind the Headlines (J. Bren); China
        Passage (J. Bren); Hideaway (J. Bren); The
        Man Who Found Himself*
1938:   The Last Express; The Last Warning; Law of
        the Underworld (B. Granet)
1939:   Big Town Czar; Two Bright Boys (V. Burton)
1940:   Diamond Frontier (S. Rubin); Enemy Agent (S.
        Braxton); Ma, He's Making Eyes at Me (C.
        Grayson); South to Karanga (S. Rubin)
1941:   The Feminine Touch*; San Francisco Docks (S.
        Rubin); Sweetheart of the Campus (R. D.
        Andrews); Time Out for Rhythm (B. Lawrence)
1942:   Sherlock Holmes and the Secret Weapon*
1943:   Hi Ya, Chum; Lady Bodyguard (A. Arthur)
1944:   Ghost Catchers; Ali Baba and the 40 Thieves;
        The Scarlet Claw (R. Neill); In Society*
1945:   The Naughty Nineties*; Sudan; See My Lawyer
1947:   Variety Girl

```
1948:   The Paleface*
1949:   Sorrowful Jones*
1950:   Fancy Pants (R. O'Brien)
1951:   The Lemon Drop Kid*; My Favorite Spy (J.
        Sher)
1953:   The Caddy*; Here Come the Girls
1954:   Casanova's Big Night
1965:   The Sword of Ali Baba (O. Brodney)
1968:   The Shakiest Gun in the West (F. Tashlin)
```

FRED HARTSOOK

```
1959:   Escort West (Leo Gordon)
```

JOHN HARTWELL

```
1981:   The Fan (P. Chapman)
```

FRANK HARVEY

```
1954:   Crest of the Wave
1962:   World in My Pocket
```

JACK HARVEY

```
1934:   Strictly Dynamite*
1948:   Last of the Wild Horses; Let's Live a Little
        (A. Cohen); Unknown Island (R. Shannon)
1949:   Grand Canyon (M. Luban)
1953:   City Beneath the Sea (R. Romero)
```

RAYMOND HARVEY

```
1978:   Goin' Coconuts
```

H. M. HARWOOD

```
1933:   Looking Forward (B. Meredyth); Queen
        Christina*
```

JOHANNA HARWOOD

338

1963: Call Me Bwana (N. Monaster)

CLAUDE HARZ

1970: Homer

CHARLIE HASS

1979: Over the Edge (Tim Hunter)

JOHN A. HASSLER

1949: Tale of the Navajos (H. Chandlee)

JOHN EUGENE HASTY

1949: There's a Girl in My Heart (A. Hoerl)

ERIC HATCH

1936: My Man Godfrey*
1937: Topper*

MARGERINE HATCHER

1976: In the Rapture (semi-doc.)

FANNY & FREDERIC HATTON

1929: Mister Antonio
1930: Her Unborn Child; Painted Faces
1931: Damaged Love

RAYMOND HATTON (1887-1971) actor

1929: Her Unborn Child*

LAWRENCE HAUBEN

1975: One Flew over the Cuckoo's Nest (B. Goldman)

DANIEL HAUER

1971: Who Says I Can't Ride the Rainbow! (E. Mann)

EBBA HAVEZ

1933: Horseplay (C. Marks)
1934: The Poor Rich (D. Van Every)

EDMUND H. HAWKINS

1978: Sasquatch, the Legend of Bigfoot

JOHN WARD HAWKINS

1957: Hidden Fear (A. DeToth)

HOWARD HAWKS (1896-1977) director, producer

1930: The Dawn Patrol (S. Miller)
1934: Viva Villa! (B. Hecht)
1951: The Thing*
1965: Red Line 7000 (G. Kirgo)

J. G. HAWKS (-1940)

1929: The Drake Case; Melody Lane

LOWELL S. HAWLEY

1960: Swiss Family Robinson (Brit.); The Sign of
      Zorro (N. Foster)
1961: Babes in Toyland*
1962: In Search of Castaways
1964: A Tiger Walks
1967: The Adventures of Bullwhip Griffin
1968: The One and Only Genuine Original Family
      Band

ROCK HAWLEY (see ROBERT "BOB" HILL)

ERNEST HAYCOX (1899-1950) western writer

1947:   Heaven Only Knows (ret. Montana Mike)*

RUSSELL HAYDEN (1912-   ) actor

1941:   In Old Colorado*

ALFRED HAYES

1952:   Clash by Night
1954:   Human Desire
1955:   The Left Hand of God
1957:   Island in the Sun; A Hatful of Rain (M.
        Gazzo)
1959:   These Thousand Hills
1960:   The Mountain Road
1965:   Joy in the Morning*
1968:   The Double Man (F. Tarloff)
1974:   Lost in the Stars
1976:   The Blue Bird (Hugh Whitemore)

JACK HAYES

1931:   Mr. Lemon of Orange

JOHN HAYES

1982:   Boss Lady

JOHN MICHAEL HAYES

1952:   Red Ball Express*
1953:   Thunder Bay (G. Doud); War Arrow; Torch Song
        (S. Lustig)
1954:   Rear Window
1955:   To Catch a Thief; It's a Dog's Life; The
        Trouble with Harry

341

```
1956:   The Man Who Knew Too Much (A. McPhail)
1957:   Peyton Place
1958:   The Matchmaker
1959:   But Not for Me
1960:   Butterfield 8 (C. Schnee)
1962:   The Children's Hour
1964:   The Carpetbaggers; The Chalk Garden (Brit.);
        Where Love Has Gone
1965:   Harlow
1966:   Judith (L. Durrell); Nevada Smith
```

JOHN PATRICK HAYES

```
1961:   Walk the Angry Beach
```

JOSEPH HAYES

```
1955:   The Desperate Hours
1961:   The Young Doctors
```

LEE HAYES

```
1982:   Wasn't That a Time! (doc.)
```

RAPHAEL HAYES

```
1956:   Reprisal!*
1957:   No Time to Be Young (J. McPartland)
1959:   Hey Boy! Hey Girl! (J. West); Have Rocket
        Will Travel
1964:   One Potato, Two Potato (O. Hampton)
```

WENDELL HAYES

```
1979:   Love and Bullets
```

MICHAEL ALLEN HAYNES

```
1971:   Chrome and Hot Leather*
```

WILL H. HAYS, JR.

1949: You're My Everything (L. Trotti)

LILLIE HAYWARD (1892–1971)

1930: On the Border
1932: Big City Blues (W. Morehouse); Miss
        Pinkerton (N. Busch); They Call It Sin (H.
        Green)
1933: Lady Killer (B. Markson)
1934: Bedside*; Big-Hearted Herbert*; Housewife
        (M. Seff); Registered Nurse (P. Milne)
1935: Front Page Woman*; Personal Maid's Secret
        (F. Herbert); The White Cockatoo (B.
        Markson)
1936: The Walking Dead*
1937: Penrod and Sam (H. Cummings); That I May
        Live; Blonde Trouble; Ever Since Eve*;
        Expensive Husbands*; Her Husband's
        Secretary; Night Club Scandal; That Man's
        Here Again
1938: Her Jungle Love*; Sons of the Legion*
1939: Disbarred (R. Presnell); King of Chinatown*;
        Television Spy*; Unmarried (B. Marlow)
1940: The Biscuit Eater (S. Anthony)
1941: Aloma of the South Seas*
1942: Heart of the Rio Grande (W. Miller); On the
        Sunny Side (G. Templeton); The Undying
        Monster
1943: My Friend Flicka (F. Faragoh); Margin for
        Error
1944: My Pal Wolf*
1945: Tahiti Nights
1946: Black Beauty (A. Johnston); Child of
        Divorce; Smoky*
1947: Banjo
1948: Northwest Stampede (A. Arthur); Blood on the
        Moon*
1949: Follow Me Quietly; Strange Bargain
1951: Cattle Drive (J. Natteford)
1952: Bronco Buster (H. McCoy); The Raiders (P.
        James)
1955: Santa Fe Passage
1957: Tarzan and the Lost Safari (M. Pittman)
1958: The Proud Rebel (J. Petracca); Tonka (L.
        Foster)
1959: The Shaggy Dog (Bill Walsh)

1960:   The Boy and the Pirates (J. Sackheim); Toby
        Tyler (B. Walsh)
1962:   Lad: a Dog (R. Hodes)

LAWRENCE HAZARD

1933:   Hello Everybody (D. Yost)
1935:   A Feather in Her Hat; Hooray for Love (R.
        Harris); Maybe It's Love*
1937:   Mannequin; Thoroughbreds Don't Cry
1940:   Strange Cargo
1942:   Jackass Mail; The Spoilers (T. Reed)
1943:   Forever and a Day*
1944:   Gentle Annie
1945:   Dakota (H. Estabrook); She Went to the Races
1947:   Wyoming (G. Geraghty); The Fabulous Texan
        (H. McCoy)

JEAN HAZLETON

1961:   The Secret Ways

MYRON HEALEY

1951:   Colorado Ambush

PAUL F. HEARD

1958:   Hong Kong Affair*

ARCH HEATH

1941:   White Eagle (ser.)*; Adventures of Captain
        Marvel (ser.)*

HY HEATH

1949:   Stallion Canyon (H. Fraser)

IAN McCLOSKY HEATH

```
1929:   Tarzan, the Tiger (ser.)
1931:   Spell of the Circus (ser.)
```

PERCY HEATH

```
1929:   Close Harmony; The Man I Love
1930:   The Border Legion; Let's Go Native; Playboy
        of Paris; Only Saps Work*
1931:   Dude Ranch*; Gang Buster
1932:   Dr. Jekyll and Mr. Hyde (S. Hoffenstein); No
        One Man*
1933:   From Hell to Heaven (S. Buchman)
```

BEN HECHT (1893-1964) director, producer,
        playwright

```
1931:   Unholy Garden (C. MacArthur)
1932:   Back Street (unc.; G. Lehman)
1933:   Design for Living; Topaz (unc.)*; Turn Back
        the Clock; Queen Christina (unc.)*
1934:   Crime Without Passion (C. MacArthur);
        Twentieth Century (C. MacArthur); Viva
        Villa! (H. Hawks)
1935:   Once in a Blue Moon (C. MacArthur); The
        Scoundrel (C. MacArthur); Barbary Coast*
1936:   Soak the Rich (C. MacArthur)
1937:   Nothing Sacred (R. Lardner); The Hurricane
        (unc.)*
1938:   The Goldwyn Follies
1939:   Gunga Din*; It's a Wonderful World; Lady of
        the Tropics; Let Freedom Ring; Wuthering
        Heights (C. MacArthur); Gone with the Wind
        (unc.; Sidney Howard)
1940:   Angels over Broadway; Comrade X (C.
        Lederer); His Girl Friday (unc.; C.
        Lederer); Foreign Correspondent (unc.)*; The
        Shop Around the Corner (unc.; S. Raphaelson)
1941:   Lydia (S. Hoffenstein)
1942:   The Black Swan (S. Miller); China Girl;
        Tales of Manhattan*; Roxie Hart (unc.; N.
        Johnson)
1943:   The Outlaw (unc.; J. Furthman)
1945:   Spellbound
1946:   Notorious; Specter of the Rose; Gilda (unc.;
        M. Parsonnet)
1947:   Dishonored Lady (unc.; E. North); The
```

```
         Paradine Case (unc.)*; Her Husband's Affair
         (C. Lederer); Kiss of Death (C. Lederer);
         Ride the Pink Horse (C. Lederer)
1948:    The Miracle of the Bells (R. Reynolds); Rope
         (unc.; A. Laurents)
1949:    Love Happy (unc.)*
1950:    Where the Sidewalk Ends (O. Trivas)
1951:    The Thing (unc)*
1952:    Actors and Sin; Monkey Business*
1953:    Roman Holiday (unc.)*
1955:    The Indian Fighter (F. Davis); Ulysses*; The
         Court Martial of Billy Mitchell (unc.)*
1956:    Miracle in the Rain; The Iron Petticoat
         (unc.)
1957:    Legend of the Lost (R. Presnell); A Farewell
         to Arms
1959:    Whirlpool (A. Solt)
1964:    Circus World (J. Halvey)
1967:    Casino Royale (unc.; J. Law)
```

TOM HEDLEY

```
1982:    Fighting Back (D. Z. Goodman)
```

VICTOR HEERMAN (1893-   ) director

```
1933:    Little Women (S. Mason)
1934:    Age of Innocence (S. Mason); The Little
         Minister*
1935:    Break of Hearts*; Magnificent Obsession*
1937:    Stella Dallas (S. Mason)
1939:    Golden Boy*
1949:    Little Women*
1954:    Magnificent Obsession*
```

RICHARD HEFFRON

```
1959:    The Great St. Louis Bank Robbery
```

LEONARD HEIDEMAN

```
1955:    Canyon Crossroads (E. Murphy)
1957:    Valerie (E. Murphy)
```

LOUIS HEIFETZ

1931:   Defenders of the Law (H. Del Ruth)
1938:   Love Is a Headache*
1942:   Perils of the Royal Mounted (ser.)*

ADELAIDE HEILBRON

1929:   Children of the Ritz
1930:   Little Johnny Jones
1931:   His Woman (M. Baker); My Sin (Owen Davis);
        Personal Maid
1932:   Misleading Lady (C. Francke)
1941:   Cheers for Miss Bishop (S. Gibney)
1942:   Friendly Enemies

MORTON HEILIG

1974:   Once

JO HEIMS

1960:   The Threat
1962:   The Devil's Hand
1963:   The Gun Hawk
1967:   Double Trouble; Tell Me in the Sunlight
1969:   The First Time (R. Smith)
1971:   Play Misty for Me (D. Riesner)
1972:   You'll Lke My Mother
1973:   Breezy

ROBERT A. HEINLEIN (1907-   ) novelist

1950:   Destination Moon*
1953:   Project Moonbase (J. Seaman)

JOSEPH HELLER

1964:   Sex and the Single Girl (D. Schwartz)
1970:   Dirty Dingus Magee*

LEON HELLER

1982:   The End of August*

LUKAS HELLER (1930-   ) Germ.

(American films only)
1962:   What Ever Happened to Baby Jane?
1965:   The Flight of the Phoenix; Hush...Hush,
        Sweet Charlotte (H. Farrell)
1967:   The Dirty Dozen (U.S./Brit.; Nunnally
        Johnson)
1970:   Monte Walsh (D. Goodman); Too Late the Hero
        (R. Aldrich)
1973:   The Deadly Trackers
1977:   Damnation Alley (A. Sharp)

ROBERT HELLER

1942:   Divide and Conquer (doc.; A. Veiller)
1943:   The Battle of Russia (doc.; A. Veiller)
1944:   The Battle of China (doc.; A. Veiller)

MARK HELLINGER (1903-1947) journalist, producer

1938:   Comet over Broadway (R. Buckner)

LILLIAN HELLMAN (1905-   ) playwright

1935:   The Dark Angel (M. Shairp)
1936:   These Three
1937:   Dead End
1941:   The Little Foxes
1943:   The North Star
1947:   The Searching Wind
1966:   The Chase

SAM HELLMAN

1934:   Good Dame*; Little Miss Marker*; Murder at
        the Vanities*; Search for Beauty*;
        Thirty-Day Princess*
1935:   The County Chairman (G. Lehman); In Old

Kentucky (G. Lehman); It's a Small World (G.
Lehman); Two Fisted*
1936: Captain January*; The Poor Little Rich
Girl*; Reunion*
1937: Slave Ship*
1938: The Baroness and the Butler*; We're Going to
Be Rich (Brit.; R. Siegel)
1939: Frontier Marshal; Here I Am a Stranger (M.
Sperling); The Three Musketeers*
1940: The Return of Frank James; He Married His
Wife*
1945: The Horn Blows at Midnight (J. V. Kern)
1946: The Runaround (A. Horman)
1947: Pirates of Monterey (M. Wilder)

DAVID HELPERN, JR.

1974: I'm a Stranger Here Myself (doc.)*

JAMES HENAGHAN

1967: The Fickle Finger of Fate
1970: Madigan's Millions (J. L. Bayonas)

ERIC HENDERSHOT

1979: Take Down (K. Merrill)

ROBERT HENDERSON

1975: You and Me

FRANK HENENLOTTER

1982: Basket Case

KIM HENKEL

1974: The Texas Chainsaw Massacre (T. Hooper)

JACK HENLEY

1941: Zis Boom Bah (H. Gates)
1942: Mr. Wise Guy*; Snuffy Smith, Yard Bird*
1943: Dangerous Blondes (R. Flournoy); A Night to
       Remember (R. Flournoy); Reveille with
       Beverly*
1945: One Way to Love (J. Hoffman)
1946: It's Great to Be Young; Meet Me on Broadway
       (G. Bricker)
1947: Blondie in the Dough (A. Marx); Blondie's
       Anniversary
1948: Blondie's Secret
1949: Blondie Hits the Jackpot
1950: Beware of Blondie; Blondie's Hero; He's a
       Cockeyed Wonder
1951: Katie Did It; Ma and Pa Kettle Back on the
       Farm; Ma and Pa Kettle on Vacation
1954: The Rocket Man (L. Bruce)

LUCILE WATSON HENLEY

1949: Blondie's Big Deal

PAUL HENNING

1961: Lover Come Back (S. Shapiro)
1964: Bedtime Story (S. Shapiro)

 BUCK HENRY (1930-   )

1964: The Troublemaker (T. Flicker)
1967: The Graduate (C. Willingham)
1968: Candy (T. Southern)
1970: Catch-22; The Owl and the Pussycat
1972: What's Up, Doc?*
1973: The Day of the Dolphin
1980: First Family

LOUISE HENRY

1935: Remember Last Night*

DARYL HENRY

1974: The Crazy World of Julius Vrooder

PAUL HENSLER

1982: Don't Cry, It's Only Thunder

BRUCE HENSTELL

1975: Hard Times*

HEINZ HERALD

1937: The Life of Emile Zola*
1940: Dr. Ehrlich's Magic Bullet*
1945: The Great Flamarion*
1948: The Vicious Circle (G. Endore)

F. HUGH HERBERT (1897-1958)

1928: Air Circus*; Lights of New York (M. Roth)
1929: A Single Man
1930: Murder on the Roof; Vengeance; He Knew Women
       (W. Tuttle); Road to Paradise; The Great
       Gabbo; Second Wife (B. Glennon)
1931: Sin Ship; X Marks the Spot
1932: Hotel Continental*; A Parisian Romance; The
       Penal Code; The Stoker; Those We Love;
       Vanity Fair
1933: The Constant Woman (W. Duff); Daring
       Daughters (B. Barringer); One Year Later;
       The Women in His Life
1934: By Candlelight*; Dragon Murder Case (R. N.
       Lee); Fashions of 1934*; Friends of Mr.
       Sweeney*; Journal of a Crime (C. Kenyon);
       The Personality Kid*; Smarty (C. Erickson)
1935: Personal Maid's Secret (L. Hayward); Secret
       Bride*; Travelng Saleslady*; We're in the
       Money*; Widow from Monte Carlo*
1936: The Case of the Black Cat; Colleen*; Snowed
       Under*
1937: As Good As Married (L. Starling)
1940: Dark Command*; Melody Ranch*; Forgotten
       Girls (J. March); The Hit Parade of 1941;

Three Faces West*; Women in War (D.
Anderson)
1941:   West Point Widow (H. Kraly)
1942:   My Heart Belongs to Daddy
1944:   Together Again (V. Van Upp)
1945:   Kiss and Tell; Men in Her Diary (E. Ullman)
1946:   Home Sweet Homicide; Margie
1948:   Scudda Hoo! Scudda Hay!; Sitting Pretty
1950:   Our Very Own
1951:   Let's Make It Legal (I. Diamond)
1953:   The Girls of Pleasure Island; The Moon Is
Blue
1957:   The Little Hut

FRANK HERBERT

1975:   Threshold — The Blue Angels Experience
(doc.)

JOHN HERBERT

1971:   Fortune and Men's Eyes

GEZA HERCZEG

1937:   The Life of Emile Zola*
1940:   Florian*
1941:   The Shanghai Gesture*
1950:   Rapture (Ital.)*
1954:   The Tiger and the Flame (Ind.; A. Keeka)

LEWIS HELMAR HERMAN

1946:   The Personality Kid (W. Sackheim); The
Return of Rusty (W. Sackheim)

NORMAN T. HERMAN

1959:   Tokyo After Dark (M. Segal)
1967:   Mondo-Teeno

VENABLE HERNDON

1969: Alice's Restaurant (A. Penn)

BRUCE HERSCHENSOHN

1966: John F. Kennedy: Years of Lightning, Days of
       Drums (doc.)

PERETZ HERSHBEIN

1937: Green Fields (Yid.)

ROBERT HERSHON

1935: Tailspin Tommy and the Great Air Mystery
       (ser.)*

ROGER O. HERSON

1977: Demon Seed (R. Jaffe)

DAVID HERTZ

1937: Woman Chases Man*
1938: I Met My Love Again; Three Loves Has Nancy*
1939: Blackmail (W. Ludwig); Stranger Than Desire
       (W. Ludwig)
1941: Love Crazy*
1942: Journey for Margaret (W. Ludwig)
1943: Pilot No. 5
1944: Marriage Is a Private Affair*
1947: Daisy Kenyon

HARRY HERVEY

1931: The Cheat
1932: The Wiser Sex (L. Francke)
1934: His Greatest Gamble (S. Buchman)

JOHN HERZFELD

1979:   Voices

SIG HERZIG

1929:   Lone Wolf's Daughter
1933:   Moonlight and Pretzels
1935:   Broadway Gondolier*; Millions in the Air (J.
        Storm); Old Man Rhythm (E. Pagano)
1936:   Colleen*; Sing Me a Love Song (J. Wald)
1937:   Marry the Girl*; Ready, Willing and Able*;
        Varsity Show*
1938:   Four's a Crowd (C. Robinson); Going Places*
1939:   Indianapolis Speedway (W.Klein); They Made
        Me a Criminal
1941:   I Wanted Wings*; Sunny
1942:   My Favorite Spy (W. Bowers)
1943:   Forever and a Day*; I Dood It (F. Saidy)
1944:   Meet the People (F. Saidy)
1945:   Brewster's Millions*
1953:   My Heart Goes Crazy (E. Paul)

HENRY HESS

1935:   The Pecos Kid

JOHN D. HESS

1961:   A Matter of Morals (Swed.)

FRASER CLARKE HESTON

1980:   The Mountain Man
1982:   Mother Lode

LEW HEWITT

1954:   The Golden Mistress
1956:   Kentucky Rife (C. Hittleman)

DOUGLAS HEYES

1954:   The Battle of Rogue River; Drums of Tahiti;

354

```
           Masterson of Kansas
1966:   Beau Geste
1968:   Ice Station Zebra
```

DuBOSE HEYWARD

1933:   The Emperor Jones

DONALD HEYWOOD

1932:   Black King

LOUIS M. HEYWORD

1957:   The Big Fun Carnival (N. Wilkes)
1964:   Pajama Party
1965:   Sergeant Deadhead; War Gods of the Deep
        (Charles Bennett)
1966:   Ghost in the Invisible Bikini (E. Ullman);
        Dr. Goldfoot and the Girl Bombs (R. Kaufman)

ENID HIBBARD

1928:   Hit of the Show
1929:   The Hurricane

WINSTON HIBLER

1953:   Peter Pan (anim.)*; The Living Desert
        (doc.)*
1955:   The African Lion (doc.)*
1957:   Perri*
1959:   Sleeping Beauty*
1961:   Nikki, Wild Dog of the North (R. Wright)

SEYMOUR HICKS

1930:   Matrimonial Bed

HOWARD HIGGIN (1893-   ) director

1929:   Sal of Singapore*
1931:   The Painted Desert (T. Buckingham)
1932:   Hell's House*
1933:   Marriage on Approval (E. Sinclair)
1936:   I Conquer the Sea (R. Lloyd); Revolt of the
        Zombies*

COLIN HIGGINS

1971:   Harold and Maude
1976:   Silver Streak
1978:   Foul Play
1980:   Nine to Five (P. Resnick)
1982:   The Best Little Whorehouse in Texas*

JOHN C. HIGGINS

1935:   Murder Man*
1939:   They All Came Out
1941:   The Penalty (H. Ruskin)
1942:   Kid Glove Killer (A. Rivkin)
1944:   Main Street After Dark
1947:   Railroaded; T-Men
1948:   He Walked by Night (C. Wilbur); Raw Deal (L.
        Atlas)
1949:   Border Incident
1952:   Pony Soldier
1954:   Shield for Murder (R. A. Simmons); The
        Diamond Wizard
1955:   Big House, U.S.A.; Seven Cities of Gold (R.
        Breen)
1956:   The Black Sheep; The Broken Star; Hold Back
        the Night (W. Doniger); Quincannon, Frontier
        Scout (Don Martin)
1957:   Untamed Youth
1964:   Robinson Crusoe on Mars (I. Melchior)
1969:   Impasse; The File of the Golden Goose (J. B.
        Gordon)
1972:   Daughters of Satan

KENNETH HIGGINS

1941:   All-American Co-Ed (C. Fitzsimmons)
1943:   Ghosts on the Loose; Strictly in the Groove
        (W. Wilson)

356

1957:   The Unknown Terror

NAT HIKEN

1969:   The Love God?

LAWRENCE HILBEN

1979:   No Longer Alone

CECIL B. HILL

1929:   Broken Hearted

DEBRA HILL

1978:   Halloween (John Carpenter)
1980:   The Fog (John Carpenter)
1981:   Halloween II (John Carpenter)

ELIZABETH HILL

1934:   Our Daily Bread*
1938:   The Citadel (Brit.)*
1941:   H. M. Pulham, Esq. (K. Vidor)

ETHEL HILL

1932:   Scarlet Brand (O. Drake)
1933:   Ship of Wanted Men; Fog (D. Schary)
1934:   Blind Date; Fury of the Jungle (D. Schary);
        The Most Precious Thing in Life (D. Schary);
        Whirlpool (D. Howell)
1935:   The Best Man Wins (B. Manning); Eight Bells
        (B. Manning); Party Wire (J. Lawson); The
        Public Menace (L. Houser)
1937:   It Happened in Hollywood (H. Ferguson);
        Let's Get Married
1938:   Just Around the Corner*
1939:   The Little Princess (W. Ferris)
1940:   Maryland (J. Andrews)
1941:   Dance Hall (S. Rauh); For Beauty's Sake*;

Small Town Deb
1943: War of the Wildcats (ret. In Old Oklahoma;
E. Griffin)
1944: Man from Frisco
1945: Twice Blessed
1946: Two Smart People (L. Charteris)

GEORGE W. HILL (1895-1934)

1931: Stolen Heaven

GLADYS HILL

1967: Reflections in a Golden Eye (C. Mortimer)
1970: The Kremlin Letter (J. Huston)
1975: The Man Who Would Be King (J. Huston)

JACK HILL

1966: Track of the Vampire (orig. Blood Bath)
1968: Spider Baby
1969: Pit Stop
1972: The Big Bird Cage
1973: Coffy
1974: Foxy Brown
1979: City on Fire*

JAMES H. HILL

1941: Keeping Company*
1946: The Hoodlum Saint (F. Wead)
1953: His Majesty O'Keefe (B. Chase)

JEROME HILL

1960: The Sand Castle
1964: Open the Door and See All the People

JOHN HILL

1981: Heartbeeps

MAURICE J. HILL

1968: Track of Thunder

ROBERT "BOB" HILL (also ROCK HAWLEY)

1934: Cowboy Holiday
1935: Danger Trails
1936: Too Much Beef; West of Nevada

ROBERT HILL

1952: Arctic Flight (G. Brickner)
1953: Stolen Identity
1955: Female on the Beach (R. A. Simmons)
1956: The Beast of Hollow Mountain; Raw Edge (H.
       Essex); A Woman's Devotion
1957: The Girl in the Kremlin (G. Coon)
1958: The Female Animal
1959: Tarzan, the Ape Man; Desert Desperadoes
1960: The Private Lives of Adam and Eve; Sex
       Kittens Go to College
1962: Confessions of an Opium Eater
1965: Fanny Hill

ROBERT F. HILL (1886-   ) director

1929: Melody Lane
1932: The Last Frontier (ser.)*
1936: Blake of Scotland Yard (ser.; W.L. Wright)

WALTER HILL (1942-   ) director

1972: Hickey and Boggs; The Getaway
1973: The Thief Who Came to Dinner; The Mackintosh
       Man
1975: The Drowning Pool*; Hard Times*
1978: The Driver
1979: The Warriors (D. Shaber)
1981: Southern Comfort*
1982: Forty-Eight Hours

JESSE HILLFORD

1970:   The Liberation of L. B. Jones (S.
        Silliphant)

RICHARD HILLIARD

1964:   The Horror at Party Beach

REBECCA HILLMAN

1976:   Everyday*

LAMBERT HILLYER (1889-   ) director

1930:   The Hide-Out (A. Ripley)
1931:   The Deadline
1932:   One Man Law; Hello Trouble
1933:   Unknown Valley; The Fighting Code; The
        Sundown Rider; The California Trail
1934:   The Man Trailer; Men of the Night;
        Straightaway
1935:   Guard That Girl
1937:   Girls Can Play; Speed to Spare (B. Granet)
1939:   Parents on Trial*
1941:   The Son of Davy Crockett; The Officer and
        the Lady (J. Hoffman)

JAMES HILTON (1900-1954) novelist Brit.

1936:   Camille*
1939:   We Are Not Alone (M. Krims)
1942:   Mrs. Miniver*; The Tuttles of Tahiti*
1943:   Forever and a Day*

ROBERT HINKLE

1961:   Ole Rex

JANE HINTON

1934:   Kiss and Make Up*

360

LOIS HIRE

1979: Half a House

CHARLES HIRSCH

1968: Greetings (B. DePalma)

PERETZ HIRSHBEIN

1943: Hitler's Madman*

ROGER O. HIRSON

1970: Pieces of Dreams

JANE STANTON HITCHCOCK

1977: First Love (David Freeman)

C. KARL HITTLEMAN

1947: The Hat Box Mystery (Don Martin); The Case
       of the Baby Sitter (A. Lamb)
1948: The Return of Wildfire (B. Burbidge)
1956: Kentucky Rifle (L. Hewitt)
1957: The Buckskin Lady (D. Lang)
1966: Billy the Kid vs. Dracula; Jesse James Meets
       Frankenstein's Daughter

WILLIAM HJORTSBERG

1977: Thunder and Lightning

DOANE R. HOAG

1953: Count the Hours (K. DeWolfe)

ROBERT HOBAN

1975: Mr. Ricco

C. FRED HOBBS

1973: Roseland

PATRICK HOBBY

1977: Hollywood Boulevard

LAURA Z. HOBSON

1954: Her Twelve Men (W. Roberts)

ROBERTA O. HODES

1962: Lad: a Dog (L. Hayward)

MIKE HODGES

1974: The Terminal Man
1978: Damien--Omen II (S. Mann)

GEORGE HODGINS

1958: Dragstrip Riot (V. Rhems)

ARTHUR HOERL

1929: In Old California; Peacock Fan; Bride of the
       Desert; When Dreams Come True; Black Pearl;
       Some Mother's Boy; Devil's Chaplain;
       Shanghai Rose; Anne Against the World; Below
       the Deadline; Two Sisters; Campus Knights;
       Phantom in the House; Handcuffed
1930: Midnight Special; Brothers (C. Condon
1931: The Devil Plays; Grief Street; Last Ride;
       Night Life in Rio; Swanee River; Hell Bent
       for Frisco

1932:   Big Town; Cross Examination; They Never Come
        Back; The 13th Guest (F. Hyland)
1933:   Enlighten Thy Daughter; Hotel Variety; The
        Shadow Laughs; Strange Adventure (L.
        Chadwick)
1934:   Drums O'Voodoo (J.A. Smith)
1937:   Spirit of Youth
1938:   Law of the Texan (M. Schaff); California
        Frontier (M. Schaff); Cipher Bureau; Topa
        Topa (H. M. Young)
1939:   Water Rustlers; Ride 'Em, Cowgirl; The
        Singing Cowgirl; Double Deal (F. E. Miller);
        Panama Patrol
1940:   Isle of Destiny*; Mystery in Swing
1941:   Reg'lar Fellers*; Stolen Paradise
1942:   Texas Trouble Shooters; Arizona Stagecoach;
        Texas to Bataan
1943:   The Girl from Monterey; The Mystery of the
        13th Guest*; Sarong Girl (C. Marion)
1947:   The Vigilante (ser.)*; Jack Armstrong
        (ser.)*; The Sea Hound (ser.)*
1948:   Tex Granger (ser.)*; Congo Bill (ser.)*;
        Superman (ser.)*
1949:   Alaska Patrol; The Lost Tribe (D. Martin);
        Shamrock Hill (M.Moore); There's a Girl in
        My Heart (J. Hasty)
1950:   Border Outlaws
1951:   Gunfighters of the Northwest (ser.)*
1952:   Son of Geronimo (ser.)*; King of the Congo
        (ser.)*
1953:   Killer Ape (Carroll Young); The Great
        Adventures of Captain Kidd (ser.)*; The Lost
        Planet (ser.)*
1955:   African Manhunt
1965:   Taffy and the Jungle Hunter

MICHAEL A. HOEY

1965:   The Navy vs. the Night Monsters
1968:   Stay Away, Joe; Live a Little, Love a Little
        (D. Greenburg)

MONCKTON HOFFE

1934:   Mystery of Mr. X*; What Every Woman Knows
        (J. Meehan)

363

1935:   The Runaway Queen (S. Raphaelson)
1937:   The Emperor's Candlesticks*; The Last of
        Mrs. Cheyney*
1938:   Girls in the Street (Brit.; Florence
        Tranter)
1940:   Haunted Honeymoon (Brit.)*

SAMUEL HOFFENSTEIN (1889-1947)

1931:   An American Tragedy (J. Von Sternberg); Once
        a Lady (Z. Akins)
1932:   Dr. Jekyll and Mr. Hyde (P. Heath); Love Me
        Tonight*; Sinners in the Sun*
1933:   Song of Songs (L. Birinski); White Woman*
1934:   All Men Are Enemies (L. Coffee); Change of
        Heart*; The Fountain (J. Murfin); Wharf
        Angel*; Marie Galante*
1935:   Enchanted April (R. Harris); Paris in
        Spring*
1936:   Desire*; Voice of Bugle Ann (H. Gates);
        Piccadilly Jim*
1937:   Conquest*
1938:   The Great Waltz*
1939:   Bridal Suite (G. Reinhardt)
1941:   Lydia (B. Hecht)
1942:   The Loves of Edgar Allan Poe (T. Reed);
        Tales of Manhattan*
1943:   Flesh and Fantasy*; His Butler's Sister (E.
        Reinhardt); The Phantom of the Opera (E.
        Taylor)
1944:   Laura*
1946:   Cluny Brown (E. Reinhardt); Sentimental
        Journey (E. Reinhardt)
1947:   Carnival in Costa Rica*
1948:   Give My Regards to Broadway (E. Reinhardt)

CHARLES HOFFMAN (1911-1972)

1944:   Janie (A. Johnston)
1945:   Pillow to Post
1946:   Cinderella Jones; Night and Day*; One More
        Tomorrow (C. Turney); Two Guys from
        Milwaukee (I. Diamond)
1947:   That Hagen Girl
1950:   The West Point Story*; A Woman of
        Distinction

1953: The Blue Gardenia
1954: So This Is Paris
1955: The Second Greatest Sex; The Spoilers (O.
       Brodney)
1956: Never Say Goodbye
1959: The Sad Horse; The Miracle of the Hills

HERMAN HOFFMAN

1968: Attack on the Iron Coast
1969: Guns of the Magnificent Seven
1970: The Last Escape

JOSEPH HOFFMAN

1935: Your Uncle Dudley (D. Schary)
1936: Charlie Chan's Secret*; Jailbreak (R. D.
       Andrews); Thank You, Jeeves (S. Gross);
       Country Gentlemen (G. Orr)
1937: Hollywood Roundup (M. Schaff); Damaged
       Goods; Under Suspicion (Jefferson Parker)
1938: Safety in Numbers*; Shadows over Shanghai;
       She's Got Everything (M. Shaff); Marriage
       Forbidden
1939: Boy Friend (B. Trivers); Quick Millions (S.
       Rauh)
1940: Young As You Feel (S. Rauh)
1941: The Return of Daniel Boone (P. Franklin);
       The Officer and the Lady (L. Hillyer)
1942: The Living Ghost; The Man with Two Lives;
       One Thrilling Night
1943: Redhead from Manhattan
1944: Girl in the Case (D. Cochran; Carolina Blues
       (A. Martin)
1945: China Sky (B. Weisberg); One Way to Love (J.
       Henley)
1947: That's My Girl
1948: Don't Trust Your Husband (L. Breslow)
1949: And Baby Makes Three (L. Breslow)
1950: Buccaneer's Girl (H. Shumate)
1951: Week-End with Father
1952: Against All Flags (A. Mackenzie); The Duel
       at Silver Creek (G. Adams); No Room for the
       Groom
1953: Lone Hand
1954: Yankee Pasha; Rails into Laramie (D.

                Beauchamp)
1955:   Chicago Syndicate; Tall Man Riding
1967:   The King's Pirate*

LEONARD HOFFMAN

1939:   The Honeymoon's Over*
1940:   Heaven with a Barbed Wire Fence*

RENAUD HOFFMAN (-1952)

1929:   Blaze o' Glory

SAMUEL HOFFMAN

1952:   Has Anybody Seen My Gal?

TAMAR HOFFS

1975:   Lepke (W. Lau)

JAMES HOGAN (-1945)

1931:   The Sheriff's Secret
1944:   Gypsy Wildcat*

MICHAEL HOGAN

1936:   The Passing of the Third Floor Back (A.
        Reville)
1939:   Nurse Edith Cavell
1941:   Lady from Louisiana*
1942:   Arabian Nights
1943:   Appointment in Berlin (H. McCoy); Forever
        and a Day*
1944:   Tall in the Saddle (P. Fix); The Hour Before
        the Dawn
1949:   Bride of Vengeance (C. Hume)
1950:   Fortunes of Captain Blood*

ANTON HOLDEN

1968: Aroused (Ray Jacobs)

LAWRENCE HOLDEN

1975: The Hiding Place (A. Sloane); Not My
       Daughter

GILBERT HOLLAND (see DONALD OGDEN STEWART)

TOM HOLLAND

1982: The Beast Within; Class of 1984*

ALLEN HOLLEB

1974: Candy Stripe Nurses

DON HOLLIDAY

1972: Night of the Lepus (G. Kearney)

GORDON HOLLINGSHEAD

1944: Trial by Trigger

JEAN HOLLOWAY

1966: Madame X
1978: The Magic of Lassie*

BEN HOLMES

1933: Melody Cruise (M. Sandrich)
1934: Cockeyed Cavaliers*
1940: The Saint's Double Trouble

BROWN HOLMES

```
1931:  The Maltese Falcon*
1932:  I Am a Fugitive from a Chain Gang*; Strange
       Love of Molly Louvain (E. Gelsey)
1933:  The Avenger; Ladies They Talk About*; The
       Stranger's Return (P. Stong)
1934:  Dark Hazard (R. Block); Heat Lightning (W.
       Duff); I Sell Anything (S. Sutherland)
1935:  Case of the Curious Bride (T. Reed); Case of
       the Lucky Legs*; The Florentine Dagger (T.
       Reed); We're in the Money*; While the
       Patient Slept*
1936:  Flying Hostess*; Satan Met a Lady; Snowed
       Under*
1937:  The Lady Fights Back (R. Shannon); Oh,
       Doctor (H. Clork); Top of the Town (C.
       Grayson)
1938:  The "Crime" of Dr. Hallet (L. Cole); Three
       Blind Mice (L. Starling)
1940:  Castle on the Hudson (S. Miller)
1941:  Moon over Miami (V. Lawrence)
1948:  Leather Gloves; Shed No Tears (V. Cook)
1951:  My True Story (H. Green)
```

DON HOLMES

```
1934:  Merry Wives of Reno (R. Lord)
```

MILTON HOLMES

```
1943:  Mr. Lucky (Adrian Scott)
1945:  Salty O'Rourke
1952:  Boots Malone
1958:  Naked Earth
1962:  A Matter of Who (Brit.)
```

ANDREW HOLT

```
1945:  Strange Voyage
1946:  Avalanche (Edward Anhalt)
```

ROBERT I. HOLT

```
1963:  Rampage (Marguerite Roberts)
```

WILLIAM DOUGLAS HOME

1958:   The Reluctant Debutante

BOB HOMEL

1973:   The Boy Who Cried Werewolf (L. Foster)
        (Harry Brown)

GEOFFREY HOMES (pseud. of DANIEL MAINWARING: 1902-
) novelist

1942:   Secrets of the Underground (R. Tasker)
1944:   Dangerous Passage
1945:   Tokyo Rose (M. Shane); Scared Stiff (M.
        Shane)
1946:   Hot Cargo; Swamp Fire; They Made Me a
        Killer*
1947:   Big Town (M. Shane); Out of the Past
1949:   The Big Steal (G. D. Adams); Roughshod (H.
        Butler)
1950:   The Eagle and the Hawk (L. Foster); The
        Lawless
1951:   The Last Outpost*; The Tall Target*
1952:   Bugles in the Afternoon*; This Woman Is
        Dangerous (G. Yates)
1953:   Powder River; Those Redheads from Seattle*
1954:   Alaska Seas (W. Doniger); The Desperado;
        Black Horse Canyon
1955:   An Annapolis Story (D. Ullman); A Bullet for
        Joey (A. Bezzerides); The Phenix City Story
        (C. Wilbur)
1956:   Invasion of the Body Snatchers; Thunderstorm
1957:   Baby Face Nelson (I. Shulman)
1958:   Cole Younger, Gunfighter; Space Master X-7
        (G. Yates); The Gun Runners (P. Monash)
1960:   Walk Like a Dragon (J. Clavell)
1961:   Atlantis, the Lost Continent; The Minotaur
        (Ital.)*
1965:   Convict Stage; The Woman Who Wouldn't Die

TOBE HOOPER

1974:   The Texas Chainsaw Massacre (K. Henkel)

EDWARD HOPE

1955: The Long Gray Line; Three for the Show (L.
       Stern)

HARRY HOPE

1978: Death Dimension

ARTHUR HOPKINS

1933: His Double Life (C. Beranger)

ELIZABETH HOPKINS

1941: Sign of the Wolf (E. Kelso)

ROBERT E. HOPKINS

1929: The Hollywood Revue of 1929 (A. Boasberg)
1930: Caught Short
1933: The Chief (A. Caesar)
1937: Saratoga (A. Loos)

GERALD HOPMAN

1975: The Devil's Rain*

DENNIS HOPPER (1936-   ) actor, director

1969: Easy Rider*
1971: The American Dreamer (L. M. Carson); The
       Last Movie

ARTHUR T. HORMAN

1935: Grand Old Girl*; Life Returns (J. Goodrich);
       This Is the Life (L. Trotti); Welcome Home
       (M. Orth)

1936:   Bridge of Sighs; Easy Money; It Couldn't
        Have Happened; Tango; Three of a Kind; Ellis
        Island
1937:   The Big Shot (B. Granet);The Shadow; You
        Can't Buy Luck (M. Mooney)
1938:   Double Danger (J. Bren); The Lone Wolf in
        Paris; Quick Money*; When G-Men Step In
1939:   Behind Prison Gates (L. White); Call a
        Messenger; For Love or Money (C. Grayson;
        Missing Evidence; My Son Is a Criminal;
        Smashing the Spy Ring*; Society Smugglers
        (E.Felton); They Asked for It; Code of the
        Streets
1940:   Argentine Nights*; Give Us Wings (R. Lee); I
        Can't Give You Anything but Love, Baby (P.
        Smith); Oh, Johnny, How You Can Love;
        Slightly Tempted; You're Not So Tough
1941:   Buck Privates; In the Navy (J. Grant); Navy
        Blues*
1942:   Desperate Journey (B. Glennon); Captains of
        the Clouds*
1944:   Bowery to Broadway*; Dark Waters*; The
        Suspect (B. Millhauser)
1945:   Conflict (D. Taylor); Here Come the Co-Eds
        (John Grant)
1946:   The Runaround (S. Hellman)
1949:   Undertow (L. Loeb)
1952:   Gobs and Gals; Tropical Heat Wave; The WAC
        from Walla Walla
1954:   Day of Triumph
1958:   Juvenile Jungle; Young and Wild

MILDRED HORN

1944:   Mom and Dad
1951:   The Prince of Peace (M. Raison)

JAMES W. HORNE (1880-1942) director

1940:   The Green Archer (ser.)*

ROBERT J. HORNER

1931:   Wild West Whoopee
1934:   The Border Menace

ISRAEL HOROVITZ

1970: The Strawberry Statement
1971: Believe in Me
1982: Author! Author!

BERT HORSWELL

1947: West of Dodge City
1951: Bonanza Town (B. Shipman)

LADYE HORTON

1930: The Medicine Man

C. JEROME HORWIN

1930: See America Thirst

ROBERT HORWOOD

1928: Blindfold (E. Adamson)

JOAN HOTCHKIS

1976: Legacy

A. E. HOTCHNER

1962: Hemingway's Adventures of a Young Man

TRACY HOTCHNER

1981: Mommie Dearest*

JOY N. HOUCK, JR.

1982: Soggy Bottom U.S.A.*

E. MORTON HOUGH

1935: Born to Gamble

ALLAN HOUSE

1943: The Meanest Man in the World (G. Seaton)

MAX HOUSE

1968: The Wild Racers

JOHN HOUSEMAN (1902-   ) actor, producer

1944: Jane Eyre*

LIONEL HOUSER

1935: Grand Exit (B. Manning); The Public Menace
       (E. Hill)
1936: The Lone Wolf Returns*
1937: Border Cafe; I Promise to Pay (M. McCall);
       Let Them Live! (B. Manning); She's
       Dangerous*; Love Takes Flight (M. Houser)
1938: Blind Alibi*; Condemned Women; Night Spot;
       Sky Giant; Smashing the Rackets
1939: First Love (B. Manning); The Forgotten Woman
       (H. Buchman); The Girl from Mexico (J.
       Fields); Sabotage (A. Altschuler); Tell No
       Tales; Three Smart Girls Grow Up*
1940: Dark Command*; Third Finger, Left Hand; Wolf
       of New York (G. Kahn)
1941: Design for Scandal
1942: A Yank at Eton*
1943: Three Hearts for Julia
1945: Christmas in Connecticut (A. Comandini)
1946: Courage of Lassie; Faithful in My Fashion;
       Blue Sierra
1949: Adventure in Baltimore
1950: Cargo to Capetown; The Secret Fury

MERVYN HOUSER

1937:   Love Takes Flight (L. Houser)

CLYDE HOUSTON

1982:   Fox Style Killer (Michael Fox)

JAMES HOUSTON

1974:   The White Dawn (T. Rickman)

NORMAN HOUSTON

1929:   College Coquette; Broadway Scandals (H. J.
        Green); Wall Street; The Broadway Melody*
1930:   Royal Romance; Mexicali Rose
1931:   Six Cylinder Love (W. Counselman)
1932:   Drifting Souls (D. Doty); Exposure;
        Manhattan Tower; Midnight Morals; No Living
        Witness
1934:   Monte Carlo Nights; Sixteen Fathoms Deep (B.
        Barringer)
1935:   Frisco Waterfront; Great God Gold (J.
        Parker); Hong Kong Nights (R. Allmon)
1936:   The Riding Avenger; Cavalcade of the West
1937:   Hopalong Rides Again
1938:   Cassidy of Bar 20; Heart of Arizona; The
        Frontiersman (H. Jacobs); Crashin' Thru
        Danger
1939:   Heritage of the Desert (H. Jacobs); In Old
        Caliente (G. Geraghty); Sunset Trail
1940:   Knights of the Range; The Light of Western
        Stars; Stagecoach War; Cherokee Strip (B.
        McConville)
1943:   Buckskin Frontier; Bar 20*
1944:   Texas Masquerade (J. Lait); Lumberjack (B.
        Shipman); Nevada
1945:   West of the Pecos; Wanderer of the
        Wasteland; A Game of Death
1946:   Sunset Pass
1947:   Code of the West; Trail Street; Thunder
        Mountain; Under the Tonto Rim; Wild Horse
        Mesa
1948:   Western Heritage; Guns of Hate (E. Repp);

374

>   The Arizona Ranger; Indian Agent; Gun
>   Smugglers
> 1949:   Brothers in the Saddle; Stagecoach Kid;
>   Masked Raiders; The Mysterious Desperado
> 1950:   Riders of the Range; Dynamite Pass; Border
>   Treasure; Rio Grand Patrol
> 1951:   Pistol Harvest
> 1952:   Road Agent; Target; Desert Passage

CARL HOVEY

1934:   Orient Express*

TAMARA HOVEY

1949:   That Midnight Kiss (B. Manning)

LARRY HOVIS

1966:   Out of Sight

BRUCE HOWARD

1963:   King Kong vs. Godzilla (Jap.; P. Mason)

CAL HOWARD

1939:   Gulliver's Travels (anim.)*

CY HOWARD (1915-   ) director

1949:   My Friend Irma (P. Levy)
1950:   My Friend Irma Goes West (P. Levy)
1951:   That's My Boy
1965:   Marriage on the Rocks
1972:   Every Little Crook and Nanny (J. Axelrod)
1976:   Won Ton Ton, the Dog Who Saved Hollywood (A.
        Schulman)

DAVID HOWARD

```
1933:   Mystery Squadron (ser.)*
1934:   The Lost Jungle (ser.)*
```

MATTHEW HOWARD

1972:   The Groundstar Conspiracy

RANCE HOWARD

1977:   Grand Theft Auto (Ron Howard)

RON HOWARD (1954-   ) actor

1977:   Grand Theft Auto (Rance Howard)

SANDY HOWARD

```
1967:   Jack of Diamonds (J. DeWitt)
1982:   Vice Squad*
```


SIDNEY HOWARD (1891-1939) playwright

```
1929:   Bulldog Drummond (W. Smith); Condemned
1930:   A Lady to Love; Raffles; Queen of Scandal
1931:   Arrowsmith; One Heavenly Night
1932:   The Greeks Had a Word for Them
1936:   Dodsworth
1939:   Gone with the Wind (B. Hecht)
1940:   Raffles (J. Van Druten)
```


WILLIAM K. HOWARD (1899-1954) director

1939:   Back Door to Heaven*

NINA HOWATT

1935:   Mysterious Mr. Wong

DOROTHY HOWELL

```
1929:   The Donovan Affair (H.J. Green)
1930:   Men Without Law; Guilty?; Soldiers and
        Women; Rain or Shine (J. Swerling); The
        Squealer (C. Robinson); Ladies Must Play;
        For the Love o' Lil; The Last of the Lone
        Wolf
1931:   Arizona (R. Riskin); Dirigible (J.
        Swerling); Platinum Blonde (J. Swerling); 50
        Fathoms Deep; Miracle Woman (J. Swerling)
1932:   Behind the Mask (J. Swerling); Big Timer (R.
        Riskin); Final Edition; Love Affair (J.
        Swerling); The Menace (C. Logue)
1934:   Whirlpool (E. Hill)
1954:   Quest for the Lost City
```

JEAN HOWELL

```
1954:   The Fast and the Furious (J. Odlum)
```

MAUDE HOWELL

```
1930:   Old English (W. Anthony)
1931:   Alexander Hamilton (J. Josephson)
1932:   The Expert (J. Josephson); The Man Who
        Played God (J. Josephson); The Successful
        Calamity*
1933:   The King's Vacation (E. Pascal); Voltaire
        (P. Green); The Working Man (C. Kenyon)
1935:   Cardinal Richelieu*
1936:   East Meets West (Brit.; Edwin Greenwood)
```

BRONSON HOWITZER

```
1963:   Showdown
```

ARTHUR T. HOYLE

```
1932:   Discarded Lovers (E. Lowe)
```

HARRY O. HOYT (1891–1961) director

```
1930:   Rampant Age
1931:   Second Honeymoon
```

1932:   The Man from New Mexico
1933:   Clancy of the Mounted (ser.)*; The Thrill
        Hunter; Gordon of Ghost City (ser.)*
1934:   The Fighting Ranger
1937:   Rustler's Valley; Headline Crasher (*S.
        Lowe); Jungle Menace (ser.)*
1938:   The Singing Outlaw; The Last Stand (N.
        Parker)
1943:   Lost Canyon
1944:   Lady in the Death House

JOHN HOYT

1964:   The Glass Cage (ret. Den of Doom; A.
        Santean)

LUCIEN HUBBARD

1929:   Mysterious Island
1930:   Isle of Escape
1931:   The Squaw Man (L. Coffee); The Maltese
        Falcon*; Paid (C. MacArthur); Smart Money*;
        Star Witness
1932:   Three on a Match
1934:   Lazy River
1943:   Gung Ho!

TOM HUBBARD

1950:   Two Lost Worlds
1952:   Red Snow (O. Hampton)
1954:   Port of Hell*; Thunder in the Pass (F.
        Eggers)
1955:   Treasure of Ruby Hills (F. Eggers)
1956:   Daniel Boone, Trail Blazer (J. Patrick)
1957:   The Badge of Marshal Brennan; Raiders of Old
        California (S. Roeca)
1958:   Legion of the Doomed (F. Eggers)
1959:   Arson for Hire

LYNN HUBERT

1976:   Goodbye, Norma Jean (L. Buchanan)

RICHARD C. HUBLER

1947:   The Last Nazi
1948:   Bungalow 13 (S. Baerwitz)
1949:   I Cheated the Law
1950:   The Great Plane Robbery (S. Baerwitz)

NORMAN HUDIS

1956:   High Terrace (A. Shaughnessy)
1957:   Rock Around the World; The Fighting Wildcats
1958:   Mailbag Robbery (Brit.); Menace in the Night
1960:   Please Turn Over (Brit.)
1961:   Beware of Children (Brit.; Robin Estridge)

FRED HUDSON

1974:   The Education of Sonny Carson

EDWARD HUEBSCH

1947:   Millie's Daughter
1948:   Black Eagle (H. Smith); Best Man Wins
1977:   Twilight's Last Gleaming (R. M. Cohen)

RICHARD L. HUFF

1975:   The Giant Spider Invasion (R. Easton)

CLAIR HUFFAKER

1960:   Flaming Star (N. Johnson); Seven Ways from
        Sundown
1961:   The Comancheros (J. E. Grant); Posse from
        Hell
1964:   Rio Conchos (J. Landon)
1967:   The War Wagon
1969:   Hellfighters; One Hundred Rifles (T. Gries)
1970:   Flap
1971:   The Deserter
1976:   Chino

ROY HUGGINS (1914-   )

1948:   I Love Trouble
1949:   The Lady Gambles; Too Late for Tears
1951:   Sealed Cargo (D. Van Every)
1952:   Hangman's Knot; Gun Fury (I. Wallace)
1954:   Pushover; Three Hours to Kill (R. Simmons)
1961:   A Fever in the Blood (H. Kleiner)

R. JOHN HUGH

1957:   Naked in the Sun (F. Slaughter)
1966:   Johnny Tiger (P. Crabtree)
1975:   The Meal
1979:   Deadly Encounter

JOHN HUGHES

1982:   National Lampoon's Class Reunion

KEN HUGHES (1922-   ) Brit.

1966:   Arrivederci, Baby!

LANGSTON HUGHES (1902-1967) poet, novelist,
        playwright

1939:   Way Down South (C. Muse)

LLEWELLYN HUGHES

1930:   Temple Tower; Sky Hawk (C. Gullian)
1932:   False Faces (K. Glasmon)

RUPERT HUGHES

1932:   Tess of the Storm Country*

RUSSELL S. HUGHES

```
1949:   The House Across the Street
1950:   Customs Agent (M. Stuart); This Side of the
        Law
1951:   Sugarfoot
1953:   Thunder over the Plains
1954:   The Command (S. Fuller); The Yellow
        Mountain*
1955:   The Last Frontier (P. Yordan)
1956:   Jubal (D. Daves)
```

THOMAS HUGHES

```
1933:   The Flaming Signal (C. Roberts)
```

GEORGE HULL

```
1932:   Son of Oklahoma (B. Tuttle)
```

CYRIL HUME

```
1932:   Tarzan, the Ape Man
1934:   Affairs of a Gentleman (P. Ruric); Limehouse
        Blues*
1935:   Tarzan Escapes*
1936:   Yellow Dust (J. Twist); The Jungle Princess*
1937:   Live, Love and Learn*; They Gave Him a Gun*;
        The Bad Men of Tombstone (R. Maibaum)
1939:   Tarzan Finds a Son
1940:   Twenty Mule Team*
1941:   The Bugle Sounds
1947:   High Barbaree*
1949:   Bride of Vengeance (M. Hogan); The Great
        Gatsby (R. Maibaum); Tokyo Joe*
1950:   Branded (S. Boehm)
1952:   Tarzan's Savage Fury*
1956:   Bigger Than Life (R. Maibaum); Forbidden
        Planet; Ransom (R. Maibaum)
1957:   The Invisible Boy
```

EDWARD HUME

```
1971:   Summertree (S. Yafa)
1973:   A Reflection of Fear
1976:   Two-Minute Warning
```

BOB HUNT

1982:   The Boogens (D. O'Malley)

EDWARD HUNT

1978:   Starship Invasions
1979:   Alien Encounter (S. Friedman)

ROBERT F. HUNT

1942:   There's One Born Every Minute (B. Weisberg)

EVAN HUNTER (1926-   ) novelist

1960:   Strangers When We Meet
1963:   The Birds
1972:   Fuzz
1979:   Walk Proud

IAN HUNTER

1939:   Fisherman's Wharf*; Meet Dr. Christian*
1940:   The Courageous Dr. Christian (R. Lardner);
        Second Chorus*
1941:   Footlight Fever (B. Granet)
1943:   Young Ideas (B. Noble)
1947:   Mr. District Attorney
1948:   The Spiritualist (M. Bolton)
1950:   Eye Witness (H. Butler)
1953:   Roman Holiday*
1959:   Virgin Island (R. Lardner)
1969:   A Dream of Kings (H. Petrakis)

TIM HUNTER

1979:   Over the Edge (C. Hass)
1982:   Tex (Charlie Haas)

TOM HUNTER

1975:   The Human Factor (P. Powell)
1980:   The Final Countdown*

GLADYS HURLBUT

1936:   Love on the Run*

WILLIAM HURLBUT

1931:   Good Sport
1934:   Secret of the Blue Room; Imitation of Life;
        Madame Spy; One Exciting Adventure (S.
        Ornitz); There's Always Tomorrow
1935:   Bride of Frankenstein (J. Balderston); The
        Daring Young Man; Orchids to You*; Way Down
        East (H. Estabrook)
1936:   Rainbow on the River*
1937:   Make a Wish*
1941:   Adam Had Four Sons (M. Blankfort)

ARTHUR HURLEY

1929:   The Royal Box (E. Joseph)

GENE HURLEY

1949:   Project X (E. Kennedy)

JAMES F. HURLEY

1968:   Something Weird

HARRY HURWITZ

1971:   The Projectionist
1972:   Richard (L. Yerby)
1981:   Under the Rainbow*
1982:   The Comeback Trail

LEO HURWITZ (1900-   )

1935:   The Plow That Broke the Plains (doc.)
1942:   Native Land (doc.)*
1948:   Strange Victory (doc.)

JOHN HUSTON (1906-   ) director, actor

1932:   Law and Order (T. Reed)
1938:   The Amazing Dr. Clitterhouse (J. Wexley);
        Jezebel*
1939:   Juarez*
1940:   Dr. Ehrlich's Magic Bullet*
1941:   High Sierra (W. Burnett); The Maltese
        Falcon; Sergeant York*
1945:   The Battle of San Pietro (doc.)
1946:   Three Strangers (H. Koch); The Killers
        (unc.; A. Veiller); The Stranger (unc.); Let
        There Be Light (doc.)
1948:   The Treasure of Sierra Madre (R. Rossen);
        Key Largo (R. Brooks)
1949:   We Were Strangers (P. Viertel)
1950:   The Asphalt Jungle (B. Maddow)
1951:   The African Queen (J. Agee); The Red Badge
        of Courage
1953:   Moulin Rouge*
1954:   Beat the Devil (T. Capote)
1956:   Moby Dick (Ray Bradbury)
1957:   Heaven Knows, Mr. Allison (J. Mahin)
1964:   The Night of the Iguana (A. Viertel)
1970:   The Kremlin Letter (Gladys Hill)
1975:   The Man Who Would Be King (Gladys Hill)
1981:   Let There Be Light (doc.; C. Kaufman)

PAUL HUSTON

1940:   The Devil's Pipeline*; Ski Patrol
1941:   Sea Raiders (ser.)*; Sky Raiders (ser.)*
1942:   Overland Mail (ser.); Drums of the Congo (R.
        Chanslor); Don Winslow of the Navy (ser.)*;
        Junior G-Men of the Air (ser.)*
1943:   Adventures of Flying Cadets (ser.)*; Don
        Winslow of the Coast Guard (ser.)*
1946:   Lost City of the Jungle (ser.)*; Mysterious
        Mr. M (ser.)*

384

TONY HUSTON

1969: Five the Hard Way (L. Billman); The Hellcats
       (R. Slatzer)

JERRY HUTCHINSON

1936: Two in Revolt*

ROBERT HUTCHINSON

1971: Outside In
1972: Frogs (R. Blees)

EDWARD EVERETT HUTSHING

1958: Andy Hardy Comes Home (R. Donley)

ROBERT HUTTON (1920–   ) actor

1974: The Terror of Sheba (alt. Persecution)

ALDOUS HUXLEY (1894–1963) novelist   Brit.

(American films only)
1940: Pride and Prejudice (J. Murfin)
1944: Jane Eyre*
1947: A Woman's Vengeance

WILLARD HUYCK

1969: The Devil's Eight*
1973: American Graffiti*
1975: Lucky Lady (G. Katz); Messiah of Evil (G.
       Katz)
1979: French Postcards (G. Katz)

PETER HYAMS (1943–   ) director

1971: T. R. Baskin
1974: Busting; Our Time (J. Stanton)

```
1977:   Telefon (S. Silliphant)
1978:   Capricorn One
1979:   Hanover Street
1980:   The Hunter (T. Leighton)
1981:   Outland
```

DANIEL HYATT

```
1958:   Revolt in the Big House (E. Lourie)
1961:   Gorgo (J. Loring)
```

DONALD HYDE

```
1956:   Please Murder Me (A. Ward)
```

DICK IRVING HYLAND

```
1944:   Hi, Beautiful; Lake Placid Serenade (D.
        Gilbert); Night Club Girl (H. Blankfort)
1945:   Love, Honor and Goodbye*
1946:   I Ring Doorbells
1947:   New Orleans*; Night Song (F. Fenton); Kilroy
        Was Here
1949:   The Threat (H. King)
```

FRANCES HYLAND

```
1929:   Two Men and a Maid; The Voice Within
1930:   Peacock Alley*; Lost Zeppelin; Kathleen
        Marouveen; Extravagance*; Third Alarm
1931:   Morals for Women; Single Sin
1932:   Guilty or Not Guilty; The Thirteenth Guest
        (A.Hoerl); Unholy Love
1933:   The Intruder; Officer 13; A Shriek in the
        Night; The Sin of Nora Moran
1934:   Money Means Nothing; A Woman's Man
1935:   Helldorado*; My Marriage; Smart Girl;
        Thunder in the Night (E. Solow)
1936:   Star for a Night (S. Elkins); Under Your
        Spell (S. Elkins); The Crime of Dr. Forbes
        (S. Elkins)
1937:   City Girl*; 45 Fathers (A. Ray)
1938:   Change of Heart (A. Ray); Island in the Sky
        (A. Ray) Keep Smiling (A. Ray); While New
```

York Sleeps (A. Ray)

1939: Charlie Chan in Reno*; Winner Take All (A. Ray); Everybody's Baby*

1940: The Cisco Kid and the Lady; Free, Blonde and 21; Girl from Avenue A

1942: In Old California (G. Purcell); You're Telling Me (B. Weisberg)

1943: Someone to Remember

1945: The Cheaters (A. Ray)

1946: Murder in the Music Hall (L. Gorog); In Old Sacramento (ret. Flame of Sacramento; F. Gruber)

ARTHUR S. HYMAN

1932: Huddle (R. Lee)

I

STEVE IHNAT

1972:   The Honkers (S. Lodge)

LESTER ILFELD

1932:   Come On, Danger

THOMAS H. INCE, JR.

1935:   The Man from Guntown (F. Beebe)

DON INGALLS

1974:   Airport 1975

WILLIAM INGE (1913-1973)   playwright   (also WALTER
        GAGE)

1961:   Splendor in the Grass
1962:   All Fall Down
1965:   Bus Riley's Back in Town

JAY INGRAM

1956:   The Peacemaker (H. Richards)

REX INGRAM (1892-1950) director

1933:   Love in Morocco (alt. Baroud)*

BORIS INGSTER

1935: Last Days of Pompeii (R. Rose)
1936: Dancing Pirate*
1937: Thin Ice (M. Sperling)
1938: Happy Landing (M. Sperling); I'll Give a
       Million (M. Sperling)
1945: Paris Underground (G. Purcell)
1949: The Judge Steps Out (A. Knox)
1950: Southside 1-1000 (L. Townsend)
1952: Something for the Birds (I. Diamond)
1956: Abdullah's Harem (G. S. George)

JOHN IRELAND

1953: Outlaw Territory (L. Garmes)

MARY IRELAND

1937: Old Louisiana; Under Strange Flags

GREGG IRVING

1982: Just Before Dawn (M. Arywitz)

CHARLES IRWIN

1964: He Rides Tall (R. C. Williams)

JACK IRWIN

1931: Lightnin' Smith Returns (alt. Valley of the
       Bad Men); White Renegade (orig. The Empire
       Builders)

CHRISTOPHER ISHERWOOD (1904-   ) novelist,
       playwright Brit.

(American films only)
1934: Little Friend
1941: Rage in Heaven (R. Thoeren)
1943: Forever and a Day*

1955: Diane
1965: The Loved One (T. Southern)

NEIL ISRAEL

1976: Tunnelvision (M. Mislove)
1979: Americathon*

JAMES IVORY (1928–   ) director

1965: Shakespeare Wallah (Ind.; Ruth Jhabvala)
1969: The Guru (Ind.)*
1970: Bombay Talkie (Ind.)*
1972: Savages*
1981: Quartet (Ruth Jhabvala)

J

CEILA JACCARD

1936: Senor Jim

JACQUES JACCARD

1936: Desert Guns (C.C. Chin)

HAROLD JACK

1971: A Gunfight

ALFRED JACKSON

1930: Leathernecking (J. Murfin)

1931: Kept Husbands (F. Halsey); The Runaround (B. Sarecky)

FELIX JACKSON

1938: Mad About Music (B. Manning); The Rage of Paris (B. Manning)
1939: Destry Rides Again*; The Girl Downstairs*; Three Smart Girls Grow Up*
1940: Spring Parade (B. Manning)
1941: Appointment for Love (B. Manning); Back Street (B. Manning)
1942: Broadway (J. Bright)

FRANCES JACKSON

1931:   Yankee Don

FREDERICK JACKSON

1930:   The Jade Box (ser.)
1932:   Bridegroom for Two (Brit.; W. Mycroft)
1937:   Wells Fargo*; The Great Gambini*; She Asked
        for It*
1938:   Say It in French; Stolen Heaven (E. Greene)
1939:   School for Husbands (Brit.)*
1940:   Half a Sinner; A Miracle on Main Street
1941:   This Woman Is Mind (S. Miller)
1943:   Hi Diddle Diddle; Stormy Weather (T.
        Koehler)
1945:   Bedside Manner (M. Boylan)

HORACE JACKSON

1929:   Strange Cargo; Paris Bound; This Thing
        Called Love; The Awful Truth
1930:   Holiday; Lottery Bride; Sin Takes a Holiday
1931:   Beyond Victory*; Devotion (G. John); Rebound
1932:   The Animal Kingdom; Lady with a Past; A
        Woman Commands
1933:   Dangerously Yours; I Loved You Wednesday (P.
        Klein)
1934:   Biography of a Bachelor Girl (A. Loos);
        Bolero; We're Not Dressing*
1935:   No More Ladies (D. Stewart)
1936:   Suzy*
1938:   Men Are Such Fools (N. Raine); Women Are
        Like That
1941:   Model Wife*
1971:   The Bus Is Coming*
1974:   Tough
1977:   Joey

JOSEPH JACKSON

1928:   Tenderloin (E. Lowe)
1929:   Say It with Songs; Is Everybody Happy?; In
        the Headlines
1930:   Second Choice; Man from Blankey's; Second
        Floor Mystery; Those Who Dance; Oh! Sailor

Behave; Dancing Sweeties; Maybe It's Love;
Man to Man; Mammy (G. Rigby)
1931: Fifty Million Frenchmen; God's Gift to Women
(R. Griffith); Smart Money*
1932: Beauty and the Boss; Dark Horse (W. Mizner);
HIgh Pressure; One Way Passage (W. Mizner);
So Big (J. Alexander)

LARRY E. JACKSON

1968: The Destructors (A. C. Pierce)

MARION JACKSON

1929: California Mail; Wagon Master; Cheyenne
1930: Lucky Larkin; Min and Bill (F. Marion)

MARK JACKSON

1981: Eyes of a Stranger (E. Bloom)

ALEXANDER JACOBS

1967: Point Blank*
1968: Hell in the Pacific (E. Bercovici)
1972: Sitting Target
1973: The Seven Ups (A. Ruben)
1975: The French Connection II*
1980: An Enemy of the People

HARRISON JACOBS (1883-1968)

1934: Born to Be Bad (R. Graves)
1935: The Eagle's Brood (D. Schroeder)
1936: Hopalong Cassidy Returns
1937: Borderland; The Barrier*
1938: Partners of the Plains; Bar 20 Justice (A.
Belgard); In Old Mexico; The Frontiersman
(N. Houston)
1939: Heritage of the Desert (N. Houston); Silver
on the Sage; Renegade Trail (J. Rathmell);
Law of the Pampas
1940: Santa Fe Marshal; Young Buffalo Bill*;

Wagons Westward (J. Marsh); Colorado (Louis Stevens)
1941: Wide Open Town (J. Cheney)
1948: False Paradise (D. Schroeder)

JACK JACOBS

1979: In Search of Historic Jesus (M. Wald);
Legend of Sleepy Hollow (M. Wald)

LEWIS JACOBS

1967: Sweet Love, Bitter (H. Danska)

RAY JACOBS

1968: Aroused (A. Holden)
1969: The Minx (H. Jaffey)

SEAMAN JACOBS

1963: It Happened at the World's Fair (S. Rose)
1980: Oh, God! Book II*

WILLIAM JACOBS

1933: Night of Terror (B. Van)
1935: Moonlight on the Prairie; Swell Head
1936: Song of the Saddle; Treachery Rides the
Range; The Big Noise (G. Bricker); Down the
Stretch; Hot Money; Isle of Fury (R.
Andrews)
1937: Dance, Charlie, Dance (C. Wilbur); Over the
Goal (A. Coldeway); Talent Scout
1938: Penrod and His Twin Brother (H. Cummings);
Sergeant Murphy

JOEL JACOBSON

1950: Catskill Honeymoon

LEOPOLD JACOBSON

1929:   Married in Hollywood*

HANS JACOBY

1945:   Tarzan and the Amazons (M. Pfaelzer)
1950:   Champagne for Caesar (F. Brady); Tarzan and
        the Slave Girl (A. Belgard)
1951:   Reunion in Reno (Whirley White); Sirocco (A.
        Bezzirides)
1952:   Tarzan's Savage Fury*
1954:   Carnival Story*
1958:   Portrait of an Unknown Woman; Circus of Love
        (K. Neumann)
1963:   The Good Soldier Schweik (Germ.)

IRVING JACOBY

1968:   Snow Treasure (P. Hanson)

JOHN JACOBY

1943:   The Amazing Mrs. Holliday (F. Ryan)
1945:   She Wouldn't Say Yes*
1946:   Tars and Spars*

JOSEPH JACOBY

1973:   Hurry Up, or I'll Be 30 (D. Wiltse)
1978:   The Great Georgia Bank Hoax (alt. The Great
        Bank Hoax)

MICHEL JACOBY

1936:   The Charge of the Light Brigade (R. Leigh);
        Two Against the World; The White Angel (M.
        Shairp)
1938:   Love, Honor and Behave*
1939:   Smuggled Cargo (E. Felton)
1940:   Doomed to Die) R. Bettinson
1941:   No Greater Sin
1942:   Frisco Lil (G. Bricker); Mystery of Marie

```
          Roget
1944:   Are These Our Parents?
1945:   Youth on Trial
1946:   The Face of Marble; Sweetheart of Sigma Chi
```

ROBERT JAFFE

1977:   Demon Seed (R. Herson)

STEVEN-CHARLES JAFFE

1980: Motel Hell

HERBERT JAFFEY

1969:   The Minx (R. Jacobs)

HENRY JAGLON

```
1971:   A Safe Place
1977:   Tracks
1980:   Sitting Ducks
```


ALAN JAMES (see ALVIN J. NEITZ)

DAN JAMES

1943:   Three Russian Girls (A. Kandel)

DONALD JAMES

1969:   Journey to the Far Side of the Sun*

EDWARD JAMES

```
1942:   Private Buckaroo (E. Kelso); Over My Dead
        Body
1943:   The Adventures of a Rookie; Rookies in Burma
```

FREDERICK JAMES

1980:   Humanoids from the Deep

J. FRANK JAMES

1975:   The Legend of Earl Durand
1979:   The Sweet Creek County War

JASON JAMES

1957:   Fury at Showdown

POLLY JAMES

1944:   Mrs. Parkington (R. Thoeren)
1952:   The Raiders (L. Hayward); The Redhead from
        Wyoming (H. Meadow); The Riding Kid
1958:   Quantrill's Raiders

RIAN JAMES

1932:   Lawyer Man (J. Seymour)
1933:   Best of Enemies; Central Airport (J.
        Seymour); 42nd Street (J. Seymour); Mary
        Stevens, M.D.; Private Detective 62; She Had
        to Say Yes (D. Mullaly)
1934:   Bedside*; Gift of Gab*
1935:   It Happened in New York (S. Miller);
        Redheads on Parade (D. Hartman); To Beat the
        Band; We're Only Human
1936:   Walking on Air*; Witness Chair (G. Purcell)
1937:   Exclusive*; Internes Can't Take Money (T.
        Reeves)
1938:   Submarine Patrol*
1939:   The Gorilla (S. Silvers); The Housekeeper's
        Daughter (G. Douglas)
1941:   Broadway Limited
1942:   Parachute Nurse; Not a Ladies' Man; This
        Time for Keeps*
1947:   Whispering City (L. Lee)

WALTER JAMES

1938:   Convicts at Large (S. Beal)

HAZEL JAMIESON

1936:   Dangerous Waters*
1939:   Reform School (J. O'Donnell)

ORIN JANNINGS

1949:   Mr. Soft Touch
1951:   Force of Arms
1953:   She's Back on Broadway
1958:   A Time to Love and a Time to Die
1959:   The Gene Krupa Story

MICHAEL JANOVER

1981:   Hardly Working (J. Lewis)

ARTHUR JARRETT

1938:   Birth of a Baby (doc.; B. Symon)

DAN JARRETT

1935:   When a Man's a Man*; The Cowboy Millionaire
        (G. Waggner); Thunder Mountain (D. Swift);
        Calling of Dan Matthews*; Hard Rock Harrigan
        (R. Schrock); Whispering Smith Speaks (D.
        Swift)
1936:   O'Malley of the Mounted (F. Clark); The Mine
        with the Iron Door (D. Swift); The Border
        Patrolman (B. Cohen); Daniel Boone; Let's
        Sing Again (D. Swift)
1937:   Secret Valley*; Park Avenue Logger (E.
        Scott); It Happened Out West*; Hollywood
        Cowboy (E. Scott); Roll Along Cowboy;
        Windjammer (J. Gruen)
1938:   Hawaiian Buckaroo; Rawhide (J. Natteford)

PAUL JARRICO

1938: No Time to Marry
1939: Beauty for the Asking (D. Anderson)
1941: The Face Behind the Mask (A. Vincent); Tom,
      Dick and Harry
1943: Song of Russia (R. Collins); Thousands Cheer
      (R. Collins)
1949: Not Wanted (I. Lupino)
1950: The White Tower
1952: The Las Vegas Story*
1969: The Day the Hot Line Got Hot (Fr./Sp.)*
1977: The Day That Shook the World

JAY JASON

1967: Caprice (F. Tashlin)

LEIGH JASON (1904-1979) director

1929: Eyes of the Underworld (Al Jones)
1933: High Gear*

GRIFFIN JAY

1935: Air Hawks (G. Neville); The Hawk; Too Tough
      to Kill (L. Cole)
1937: Bank Alarm (D. Levy)
1940: The Mummy's Hand (M. Shane)
1941: The Kid from Kansas (D. Silverstein); Men of
      the Timberland (M. Tombragel)
1942: The Mummy's Tomb (H. Sucher); Top Sergeant
      (M. Shane); Don Winslow of the Navy (ser.)*;
      Junior G-Men of the Air (ser.)*; Timber
1943: Captive Wild Woman (H. Sucher); Don Winslow
      of the Coast Guard (ser.)*
1944: Two-Man Submarine (L. White); The Return of
      the Vampire; The Mummy's Ghost*; Cry of the
      Werewolf (C. O'Neal)
1946: Devil Bat's Daughter; The Mask of Diijon (A.
      St. Claire)

MAHATMA KANE JEEVES (see W. C. FIELDS)

L. V. JEFFERSON

1933:   The Fighting Cowboy
1934:   Lightning Bill; Lightning Range; The Pecos
        Dandy; Range Riders; Rawhide Romance
1935:   Twisted Trails; $20 a Week; Riddle Ranch (E.
        Thornton)

BETTY JEFFRIES

1958:   Invisible Avenger (G. Bellak)

JAN JEFFRIES

1950:   Joe Palooka in the Squared Circle
1951:   G.I. Jane; The Highwayman; Joe Palooka in
        Triple Cross

AL JENNINGS

1936:   Song of the Gringo*

ELIZABETH JENNINGS

1957:   Gunsight Ridge (T. Jennings))

TALBOT JENNINGS (1905-   )

1935:   Mutiny on the Bounty*;
1936:   Romeo and Juliet
1937:   The Good Earth*
1938:   Spawn of the North (J. Furthman); Marie
        Antoinette*
1939:   Rulers of the Sea*
1940:   Northwest Passage (L. Stallings); Edison,
        the Man (B. Foote)
1941:   So Ends Our Night
1944:   Frenchman's Creek
1946:   Anna and the King of Siam (S. Benson)
1950:   The Black Rose (Brit.)
1951:   Across the Wide Missouri
1953:   Knights of the Round Table*

1955:   Escape to Burma; Pearl of the South
        Pacific*; Untamed*
1957:   Gunsight Ridge (E. Jennings)

WILLIAM DALE JENNINGS

1972:   The Cowboys*

GEORGE JESKE

1932:   Midnight Patrol
1939:   The Day the Bookies Wept (B. Granet)
1944:   Moon over Las Vegas

GEORGE JESSEL (1898-   ) entertainer, producer

1953:   Yesterday and Today

RICHARD JESSUP

1957:   The Young Don't Cry
1967:   Chuka

JACK JEVNE (also JOHN WEST, JACK LEVINE, JACK T. O.
        GEVNE)

1931:   Honeymoon Lane (B. Sarecky)
1933:   Easy Millions
1934:   Palooka*
1935:   The Cowboy and the Bandit; The Ghost Rider;
        Thunderbolt; Trail's End
1936:   Kelly the Second*; Our Relations*
1937:   Way out West*; Topper*
1938:   Merrily We Live (E. Moran); There Goes My
        Heart (E. Moran)
1939:   Captain Fury*; Topper Takes a Trip*
1940:   Wyoming (H. Butler)
1941:   Barnacle Bill (H. Butler)
1943:   Air Raid Wardens*; Wintertime*
1947:   The Hal Roach Comedy Carnival*; The Fabulous
        Joe
1956:   Autumn Leaves*

NORMAN JEWISON

1973:   Jesus Christ Superstar (M. Bragg)

RUTH JHABVALA

1977:   Roseland
1979:   The Europeans
1981:   Quartet (J. Ivory); Jane Austen in Manhattan

THOMAS JOB

1945:   Escape in the Desert
1947:   The Two Mrs. Carrolls

GRAHAM JOHN

1931:   Devotion (H. Jackson)
1933:   The Monkey's Paw (L. Parker)

ADRIAN JOHNSON

1930:   Jazz Cinderella
1931:   Lady from Nowhere (B. Gerard)
1933:   Found Alive
1937:   Killers of the Sea

BEVERLY JOHNSON

1982:   Satan's Mistress (J. Polakoff)

CHARLES JOHNSON

1972:   Hammer
1973:   Slaughter's Big Ripoff; Beyond Atlantis;
        That Man Bolt (P. Stone)
1976:   The Monkey Hustle

COSLOUGH JOHNSON

1971: Bunny O'Hare (S. Cherry)

DENNIS JOHNSON

1977: Stunts (Barney Cohen)

DIANE JOHNSON

1980: The Shining (S. Kubrick)

EMORY JOHNSON

1932: Phantom Express (L. Doyle)

HENRY M. JOHNSON

1930: A Devil with Women (D. Nichols)
1933: Arizona to Broadway (W. Counselman); The Mad
       Game (W. Counselman); Olsen's Big Moment (J.
       Tynan)
1934: Ever Since Eve (S. Anthony); Handy Andy*;
       Love Time*; 365 Nights in Hollywood (W.
       Counselman); Wild Gold (L. Cole)
1935: Fighting Youth*; Ten-Dollar Raise (L.
       Breslow); The Virginia Judge*
1936: F-Man*; Great Guy*

KAY C. JOHNSON

1978: Jennifer

LARRY H. JOHNSON

1966: Lord Love a Duck (G. Axelrod)

LAWRENCE E. JOHNSON

1931: Bachelor Father; It's a Wise Child
1932: The Passionate Plumber; Speak Easily (R.
       Spence)
1933: Christopher Bean (S. Thalberg)

MONICA JOHNSON

1979:   Real Life*; Americathon*
1981:   Modern Romance (A. Brooks)
1982:   Jekyll and Hyde Together Again*

NORA JOHNSON

1964:   The World of Henry Orient (Nunnally Johnson)

NUNNALLY JOHNSON (1897-1977) director, producer

1933:   A Bedtime Story*; Mama Loves Papa (A. Kober)
1934:   Bulldog Drummond Strikes Back; House of
        Rothschild; Moulin Rouge (H. Lehrman); Kid
        Millions*
1935:   Baby Face Harrington (E. Knopf); The Man Who
        Broke the Bank at Monte Carlo (Howard
        Smith); Thanks a Million*
1936:   Banjo on My Knee; The Prisoner of Shark
        Island
1939:   Jesse James; Rose of Washington Square;
        Wife, Husband and Friend
1940:   Chad Hanna; The Grapes of Wrath
1941:   Tobacco Road
1942:   Life Begins at 8:30; The Pied Piper; Roxie
        Hart (B. Hecht)
1943:   Holy Matrimony; The Moon Is Down
1944:   Casanova Brown; The Woman in the Window; The
        Keys of the Kingdom (J. Mankiewicz)
1945:   Along Came Jones
1946:   The Dark Mirror
1948:   Mr. Peabody and the Mermaid
1949:   Everybody Does It
1950:   The Mudlark; Three Came Home
1951:   The Desert Fox; The Long Dark Hall (Brit.)
1952:   My Cousin Rachel; Phone Call from a
        Stranger; We're Not Married; O. Henry's Full
        House*
1953:   How to Marry a Millionaire
1954:   Night People; Black Widow
1955:   How to Be Very, Very Popular
1956:   The Man in the Gray Flannel Suit
1957:   The Three Faces of Eve; Oh, Men! Oh, Women!

```
            (unc.; J. Chodorov)
1959:   The Man Who Understood Women
1960:   The Angel Wore Red (Sp.); Flaming Star (C.
        Huffaker)
1962:   Mr. Hobbs Takes a Vacation
1963:   Take Her, She's Mine
1964:   The World of Henry Orient (Nora Johnson)
1967:   The Dirty Dozen (U.S./Brit.; Lukas Heller)
```

RAYMOND K. JOHNSON

```
1939:   In Old Montana*
```

ROBERT LEE JOHNSON (see ROBERT LEE)

TYLER JOHNSON

```
1940:   Li'l Abner (Charles Kerr)
```

VAN JOHNSON

```
1935:   Desert Mesa
```

AGNES CHRISTINE JOHNSTON

```
1929:   Divine Lady; Man and the Moment; The
        Shannons of Broadway
1932:   Three Wise Girls
1933:   Lucky Devils (B. Markson); Headline Shooter
        (A. Rivkin)
1935:   When a Man's a Man*
1938:   Out West with the Hardys*
1939:   The Hardys Ride High*
1940:   All Women Have Secrets; Seventeen (S.
        Palmer)
1941:   Double Date*; Life Begins for Andy Hardy
1942:   Andy hardy's Double Life; The Courtship of
        Andy Hardy
1944:   Andy Hardy's Blonde Trouble; Janie (C.
        Hoffman)
1946:   Black Beauty (L. Hayward); Janie Gets
        Married; The Time, the Place and the Girl*
1947:   Black Gold
```

1948:   Mickey (M. Bolton); Stage Struck (G. Milton)

CLINT JOHNSTON

1949:   Black Midnight (E. Lazarus)
1950:   David Harding, Counterspy (T. Reed); Young
        Daniel Boone (R. LeBorg)
1951:   Wanted Dead or Alive; Yellow Fin (W.
        Wandberg)
1966:   The Naked Prey (D. Peters)
1967:   Beach Red*

WILL JOHNSTONE

1931:   Monkey Business*

NORMAN JOLLEY

1956:   I've Lived Before (W. Talman)
1957:   Joe Dakota (W. Talman); The Monolith
        Monsters
1958:   Appointment with a Shadow (A. Coppel)

NORMAN JONAS

1971:   Let's Scare Jessica to Death (Ralph Rose)

ABEL JONES

1976:   Death Journey

AL JONES

1929:   Eyes of the Underworld (L. Jason)

ARTHUR VERNON JONES

1936:   Kelly the Second*; Mister Cinderella (R.
        Flourney); Neighborhood House (R. Flourney)
1937:   Pick a Star*
1940:   Prairie Law (D. Schroeder); Stage to Chino

(M. Grant); Triple Justice (M. Grant)
1941: Along the Rio Grande (M. Grant); Robbers of
the Range (M. Grant); Fighting Bill Fargo*;
Sing It, Soldier (D. Cochran)
1942: Stagecoach Express;Juke Box Jenny*
1946: 'Neath Canadian Skies; North of the Border;
Flight to Nowhere
1957: Undersea Girl

BILLY JONES

1944: The Falcon Out West (M. Grant)

CHARLES REID JONES

1931: Enemies of the Law
1932: The King Murder

CHUCK JONES

1963: Gay Purr-ee (anim.; D. Jones)
1970: The Phantom Tollbooth (Sam Rosen)
1979: The Bugs Bunny/Road-Runner Movie (anim.; M. Maltese)

DON JONES

1982: The Love Butcher (J. Evergreen)

DOROTHY JONES

1963: Gay Purr-ee (anim.; Chuck Jones)

GROVER JONES (-1940)

1929: The Mighty (W. McNutt)
1930: The Light of the Western Stars (W. McNutt);
Burning Up; Dangerous Paradise; Young Eagles
(ser.; W. McNutt); Love Among the
Millionaires; Derelict; Tom Sawyer
1931: The Conquering Horde (W. McNutt); Gun Smoke
(W. McNutt); Dude Ranch*; Huckleberry Finn

           (W. McNutt); Rich Man's Folly (E. Paramore);
           Touchdown*
1932:   Broken Wing (W. McNutt); If I Had a
           Million*; Lady and Gent (W. McNutt); Sky
           Bride*; Strangers in Love (W. McNutt);
           Trouble in Paradise (S. Raphaelson)
1933:   Hell and High Water*; One Sunday Afternoon
           (W. McNutt)
1934:   Limehouse Blues*; You Belong to Me*
1935:   Annapolis Farewell*; Behold My Wife (V.
           Lawrence); Lives of a Bengal Lancer*; One
           Way Ticket*
1936:   The Milky Way*; Trail of the Lonesome Pine*
1937:   52nd Street; Souls at Sea (D. Van Every)
1939:   Captain Fury*; Lucky Night (V. Lawrence);
           The Under-Pup
1940:   Abe Lincoln in Illinois (R. E. Sherwood);
           Dark Command*; Captain Caution
1941:   The Shepherd of the Hills (S. Anthony)
1946:   The Kid from Brooklyn*

HARRY O. JONES (see HARRY FRASER)

L. Q. JONES

1975:   A Boy and His Dog

LeROI JONES (also IMAMU BARAKA)

1967:   Dutchman (Brit.)
1971:   A Fable

ROBERT C. JONES

1978:   Coming Home (W. Salt)

NICHOLAS JORY

1941:   New Wine (H. Estabrook)

EDMUND JOSEPH

1929: The Royal Box (A. Hurley)
1935: Women Must Dress (D. Reid)
1936: Hat Off (S. Fuller)
1938: Everybody's Doing It*
1942: Who Done It?*; Yankee Doodle Dandy (R. Buckner)
1944: Make Your Own Bed (F. Swann); Bowery to Broadway*
1945: The Naughty Nineties*

ROBERT JOSEPH

1958: Gunsmoke in Tucson (P. Peil)
1964: The Third Secret
1969: Strategy of Terror; Ski Fever (C. Siodmak)
1976: Echoes of a Summer

JULIAN JOSEPHSON

1929: Disraeli
1930: Green Goddess; The Climax (W. Ducey)
1931: Alexander Hamilton (M. Howell); Hell Bound; Kiss Me Again (P. Perez); The Millionaire; Misbehaving Ladies
1932: The Expert (M. Howell); The Man Who Played God (M. Howell; The Succesful Calamity*
1933: Chance at Heaven (S. Mason)
1937: Heidi (W. Ferris); Wee Willie Winkle (E. Pascal)
1938: Suez (P. Dunne)
1939: The Rains Came (P. Dunne); Stanley and Livingstone (P. Dunne)
1942: The Great Gildersleeve (J. Townley)
1943: Happy Land (K. Scola)

ALVIN JOSEPHY, JR.

1952: The Captive City (K. Lamb)

JAN JUST

1977: Angel City

GARY JULES JOUVENAT

1982:   Out of the Blue (L. Yakir)

ADRIEN JOYCE (also CAROL EASTMAN)

1970:   Five Easy Pieces; Puzzle of a Downfall Child
1975:   The Fortune

FORREST JUDD

1946:   Below the Deadline (H. Gates)
1953:   Monsoon*

JERRY JUHL

1979:   The Muppet Movie (J. Burns)
1981:   The Great Muppet Caper*

MAURICE JULES

1971:   The Velvet Vampire*
1973:   Scream Blacula Scream*

ARTHUR JULIEN

1957:   The Happy Road*
1970:   The Boatniks

MARTIN JULIEN

1975:   Rooster Cogburn

MAX JULIEN

1973:   Cleopatra Jones (S. Keller)
1974:   Thomasine and Bushrod

RAY JUNE

1935:   Barbary Coast*

JACK JUNGMEYER

1929:   Shady Lady (E.H. Griffith); Office Scandal
        P. Gangelin); Big News (W. DeLeon); Show
        Folks (G. Drumgold)
1930:   His First Command (J. Gleason)
1932:   Men of America (S. Ornitz)
1940:   High School*; Manhattan Heartbeat*
1942:   That Other Woman
1947:   The Tender Years (A. Belgard)

NATHAN JURAN (1907-   ) director, art director

1961:   Boy Who Caught a Crook; Flight of the Lost
        Balloon
1962:   Jack the Giant Killer (O. Hampton)

PHILIP JUST

1960:   Caltiki, the Immortal Monster

WILLIAM JUTTE

1930:   He Knew Women (F. Herbert)

K

ELLIS KADISON

1967:   The Gnome-Mobile

JOHN KAFKA

1944:   Johnny Doesn't Live Here Any More (P.
        Yordan)
1960:   Man on a String (V. Shaler)

GORDON KAHN

1932:   The Death Kiss (B. Barringer)
1934:   The Crosby Case (W. Duff)
1935:   Gigolette; The People's Enemy (E. D.
        Sullivan)
1937:   Mama Runs Wild*; Navy Blues (E. Taylor); The
        Sheik Steps Out (A. Buffington)
1938:   I Stand Accused (A. Gottlieb); Tenth Avenue
        Kid
1939:   Ex-Champ; Mickey the Kid (D. Malloy);
        Newsboy's Home; S.O.S. Tidal Wave (M. Shane)
1940:   Wolf of New York (L. Houser)
1941:   Buy Me That Town
1942:   Northwest Rangers (D. Lang); A Yank on the
        Burma Road*
1944:   The Cowboy and the Senorita; Song of Nevada
        (O. Cooper); Lights of Old Santa Fe (R.
        Williams)
1946:   Her Kind of Man (L. Atlas)
1948:   Ruthless (S. Lauren)

RICHARD KAHN

1934:   Children of Loneliness
1939:   The Bronze Buckaroo; Bad Boy

GYLAN KAIN

1971:   Right On!*

BURT KAISER

1956:   Female Jungle

MURRAY KALIS

1976:   Everyday*

AUSTIN & IRMA KALISH

1975:   Keep Off! Keep Off!

STANLEY KALLIS

1958:   The Hot Angel

BERT KALMAR

1931:   Broad-Minded (H. Ruby)
1932:   The Kid from Spain*; Horse Feathers*
1933:   Duck Soup (H. Ruby)
1934:   Hips, Hips, Hooray*; Kentucky Kernels (H.
        Ruby)
1935:   Bright Lights*
1936:   Walking on Air*
1937:   Life of the Party*

STAN KAMBER

1973:   Bad Charleston Charlie

ROBERT M. KAMEN

```
1981:  Taps (D. Poniscan)
1982:  Split Image*
```

BERNIE KAMINS

```
1944:  Forty Thieves (M. Wilson)
```

IRENE KAMP

```
1961:  Paris Blues*
```

ABEN KANDEL

```
1935:  Manhattan Moon*; She Gets Her Man
1937:  They Won't Forget (R. Rossen); Thunder in
       the City (R. Sherwood)
1939:  Rio*
1943:  The Iron Major (W. Duff); Three Russian
       Girls (D. James)
1952:  The Fighter (H. Kline); Kid Monk Baroni
1956:  Timetable
1959:  Horrors of the Black Museum (Herman Cohen)
1960:  The Walking Target
1961:  Konga (Brit.; Herman Cohen)
1963:  Black Zoo (Herman Cohen)
1967:  Berserk (Herman Cohen)
1970:  Trog
1974:  Craze (Herman Cohen)
```

STEPHEN KANDEL

```
1956:  Magnificent Roughnecks
1958:  Frontier Gun
1959:  Battle of the Coral Sea (D. Ullman)
1966:  Chamber of Horrors
1970:  Cannon for Cordoba
```

DENNIS KANE

```
1978:  French Quarter (Barney Cohen)
```

GEORGE KANE

1942: Lone Star Ranger*

HENRY KANE

1958: Cop Hater; The Muggers

JOSEPH KANE

1929: Overland Bound (F. Beebe)

MICHAEL KANE

1979: Hot Stuff (D. Westlake)
1980: Xanadu*; Foolin' Around (D. Swift)
1981: Hard Country; The Legend of the Lone
       Ranger*; Southern Comfort*

ROBERT G. KANE

1979: The Villain

JEFF KANEW

1979: Natural Enemies

FAY KANIN

1942: Sunday Punch*
1952: My Pal Gus (M. Kanin)
1954: Rhapsody (M. Kanin)
1956: The Opposite Sex (M. Kanin)
1958: Teacher's Pet (M. Kanin)
1961: The Right Approach*
1962: Swordsman of Sienna (M. Kanin)

GARSON KANIN (1912-   ) director, playwright

1939: They Made Her a Spy*
1943: The More the Merrier*

415

```
1948:   A Double Life (R. Gordon)
1949:   Adam's Rib (R. Gordon)
1952:   The Marrying Kind (R. Gordon); Pat and Mike
        (R. Gordon)
1954:   It Should Happen to You
1960:   The Rat Race
1969:   Where It's At; Some Kind of Nut
```

MICHAEL KANIN (1910–   )

```
1939:   Panama Lady; They Made Her a Spy*
1940:   Anne of Windy Poplars (J. Cady)
1942:   Sunday Punch*; Woman of the Year (R.
        Lardner)
1943:   The Cross of Lorraine*
1944:   Marriage Is a Private Affair*
1946:   Centennial Summer
1947:   Honeymoon
1951:   When I Grow Up
1952:   My Pal Gus (F. Kanin)
1954:   Rhapsody (F. Kanin)
1956:   The Opposite Sex (F. Kanin)
1958:   Teacher's Pet (F. Kanin)
1961:   The Right Approach*
1962:   Swordsman of Sienna (F. Kanin)
1964:   The Outrage
1969:   How to Commit Marriage (B. Starr)
```

BOB KANTER

```
1965:   Winter A-Go-Go
```

HAL KANTER (1918–   ) director

```
1951:   Two Tickets to Broadway (S. Silvers)
1952:   Road to Bali*
1953:   Off Limits (J. Sher); Money from Home
1954:   About Mr. Leslie (K. Frings); Casanova's Big
        Night*
1955:   Artists and Models*; The Rose Tattoo
        (Tennessee Williams)
1957:   Loving You (H. Baker)
1958:   Once Upon a Horse; Mardi Gras (W. Miller)
1961:   Bachelor in Paradise (V. Davies); Blue
        Hawaii; Pocketful of Miracles (H. Tugend)
```

1963: Move Over, Darling (J. Sher); The Hot Horse
1965: Dear Brigitte

ALBERT KANTOF

1982: Contract: Kill (C. Mulot)

LENARD KANTOR

1957: Jamboree

MacKINLAY KANTOR (1904-   ) novelist

1949: Deadly As the Female (alt. Gun Crazy; M.
       Kaufman)

JONATHAN KAPLAN (1947-   ) director

1975: White Line Fever (K. Friedman)
1977: Mr. Billion (K. Friedman)

LARRY KARDISH

1968: Slow Run

LESLIE KARDOS

1946: No Leave, No Love (C. Martin)

ALEX KARNEL

1961: Something Wild (J. Garfein)

THOMAS KARNOWSKI

1982: The Sword and the Sorcerer*

DAVID KARP

```
1968:   Sol Madrid
1969:   The Young Rebel


ELINOR & STEPHEN KARPF

1970:   Adam at 6 A.M.


MICHAEL KARS

1970:   Rebel Rousers*


LAWRENCE KASDAN

1980:   The Empire Strikes Back (L. Brackett)
1981:   Raiders of the Lost Ark; Body Heat;
        Continental Divide


LEONARD KASTLE

1969:   The Honeymoon Killers


LEO KATCHER

1951:   "M" (N. Raine)
1955:   The Naked Street (M. Shane)
1957:   The Hard Man


NORMAN KATKOV

1959:   It Happened to Jane
1969:   Once You Kiss a Stranger (F. Tarloff)
1977:   Viva Knievel! (A. Santillan)


MONTE KATTERJOHN

1929:   Broadway Babies (H. Pearson)
1930:   Party Girl; Paradise Island
1931:   Daughter of the Dragon*


GLORIA KATZ
```

1973: American Graffiti*
1975: Lucky Lady (W. Huyck); Messiah of Evil (W. Huyck)
1979: French Postcards (W. Huyck)

LEE KATZ

1938: Heart of the North (V. Sherman)
1939: Code of the Secret Service (D. Franklin); The Man Who Dared; No Place to Go*; The Return of Dr. X; Waterfront (A. Ripley); Women in the Wind (A. DeMond)
1940: British Intelligence

JONATHAN KAUFER

1982: Soup for One

ALLAN KAUFMAN

1957: Hell Canyon Outlaws (M. Glandbard)

CHARLES KAUFMAN

1937: Breakfast for Two*; Saturday's Heroes*
1938: Exposed (F. Coen); The Saint in New York (M. Offner); Blonde Cheat*
1941: Model Wife*; Paris Calling (B. Glazer)
1947: Cynthia (H. Buchman)
1953: Return to Paradise
1955: The Racers
1957: The Story of Esther Costello
1958: South Seas Adventure*
1961: Bridge to the Sun (Jap.)
1962: Freud (W. Reinhardt)
1980: Mother's Day (W. Leight)
1981: Let There Be Light (doc.; J. Huston)
1982: Waitress (M. Stone)

DAVID KAUFMAN

1971: Werewolves on Wheels (M. Levesque)

419

EDWARD KAUFMAN

1929: Making the Grade (H. Brand)
1933: Aggie Appleby, Maker of Men (H. Pearson)
1934: Cockeyed Cavaliers*; The Gay Divorcee*;
       Hips, Hips, Hooray*; Romance in Manhattan
       (J. Murfin)
1935: Going Highbrow (C. Bartlett); McFadden's
       Flats*; Star of Midnight*
1941: Affectionately Yours

GEORGE S. KAUFMAN (1889-1961) playwright

1935: A Night at the Opera (M. Ryskind)

LLOYD KAUFMAN

1971: The Battle of Love's Return
1977: Sugar Cookies (Theodore Gershuny)

MILLARD KAUFMAN

1949: Deadly Is the Female (alt. Gun Crazy; M.
       Kantor)
1951: Unknown World
1952: Aladdin and His Lamp (H. Dimsdale)
1953: Take the High Ground
1954: Bad Day at Black Rock
1957: Raintree County
1959: Never So Few
1962: Convicts 4 (orig. Reprieve)
1965: The War Lord (J. Collier)
1972: Living Free
1974: The Klansmen (S. Fuller)

PHIL KAUFMAN (1936-   ) director

1965: Goldstein (B. Manaster)
1970: Fearless Frank
1972: The Great Northfield Minnesota Raid
1976: The Outlaw Josey Wales (S. Chernus)
1979: The Wanderers (Rose Kaufman); Up Your Ladder

ROBERT KAUFMAN

1965: Dr. Goldfoot and the Bikini Machine (E. Ullman); Ski Party
1966: Dr. Goldfoot and the Girl Bombs (L. Heyward)
1970: Getting Straight; I Love My Wife
1974: Freebie and the Bean
1976: Harry and Walter Go to New York (J. Byrum)
1977: The Happy Hooker Goes to Washington
1979: Love at First Bite
1980: Nothing Personal; How to Beat the High Cost of Living
1982: Split Image*

ROSE KAUFMAN

1979: The Wanderers (P. Kaufman)

SIDNEY KAUFMAN

1958: Sorcerers' Village
1959: Behind the Great Wall (T. Orchard)

GINA KAUS

1942: The Wife Takes a Flyer (J. Dratler)
1949: The Red Danube (A. Wimperis)
1953: The Robe*
1958: Tempestuous Love

FRANCES KAVANAUGH

1941: Dynamite Canyon (R. Tansey); The Driftin' Kid (R. Tansey); Riding the Sunset Trail (R. Tansey); Lone Star Lawmen (R. Tansey)
1942: Western Mail (R. Tansey); Where Trails End (R. Tansey); Trail Riders
1943: The Law Rides Again; Blazing Guns; Death Valley Rangers*
1944: Westward Bound; Arizona Whirlwind; Outlaw Trail; Sonora Stagecoach; Harmony Trail
1945: Wildfire; Saddle Serenade; Song of Old

Wyoming
1946:   Romance of the West; God's Country; The
        Caravan Trail; Colorado Serenade; Driftin'
        River; Tumbleweed Trail; Stars over Texas;
        Wild West
1948:   The Enchanted Valley; Prairie Outlaws
1950:   Forbidden Jungle; The Fighting Stallion (G.
        Slavin)

KATHARINE KAVANAUGH

1936:   Educating Father*

JAMES H. KAY III

1975:   The Gardener

JOEL KAYE

1941:   Gambling Daughters (A. Phillips)

JOHN KAYE

1975:   Rafferty and the Gold Dust Twins
1978:   American Hot Wax
1980:   Where the Buffalo Roam

LOUIS S. KAYE

1940:   Opened by Mistake*
1941:   Too Many Blondes (M. Shane)
1942:   Dudes Are Pretty People; Flying with Music
        (M. Webster)

CHRIS KAZAN

1972:   The Visitors

ELIA KAZAN (1909-   ) director

1951:   A Streetcar Named Desire (Tennessee

Williams)
1963: America, America
1969: The Arrangement

NICHOLAS KAZAN

1982: Frances*

JAMES & STACY KEACH

1980: The Long Riders*

E. ARTHUR KEAN

1975: Live a Little, Steal a Lot

GENE KEARNEY

1967: Games
1969: A Man Called Gannon*
1972: Night of the Lepus (D. Holliday)

PAT KEARNEY

1929: Darkened Rooms (M. Baker)

PHILIP KEARNEY

1972: Private Parts (L. Rendelstein)

ADI F. KEEKA

1954: The Tiger and the Flame (G. Herczeg)

CHUCK KEEN

1975: Timber Tramps

NORMAN KEENE

1933: Police Call (H. Hartley)

WILLIAM KEIGHLEY (1889-   ) director

1951: Close to My Heart

CARLOS KEITH (see VAL LEWTON)

JANE KEITH

1944: Sweethearts of the U.S.A.*

LEONARD KEITH

1973: Charlie One-Eye

ROBERT KEITH

1932: Scandal for Sale (R. Graves); The Unexpected
       Father (D. Van Every)

ED KELLEHER

1976: Shriek of the Mutilated; Invasion of the
       Blood Farmers (E. Adlum)

SHELDON KELLER

1968: Buona Sera, Mrs. Campbell*
1973: Cleopatra Jones (M. Julien)
1978: Movie Movie (L. Gelbart)

ALBERT KELLEY

1948: Street Corner

JOHN T. KELLEY

1965: A Rage to Live
1970: Zigzag

ROY KELLINO

1939: I Met a Murderer

BOB KELLJAN

1970: Count Yorga, Vampire
1971: The Return of Count Yorga (Y. Wilder)

MARJORIE KELLOGG

1970: Tell Me That You Love Me, Junie Moon
1979: The Bell Jar

RAY KELLOGG

1960: My Dog Buddy

VIRGINIA KELLOGG

1949: Caged (B. Schoenfeld)

BILL E. KELLY

1969: Changes (H. Bartlett)

GEORGE KELLY

1936: Old Hutch

JAMES KELLY

1974: "W" (G. D. Pego)

MARK KELLY

1936:   One in a Million (L. Praskins)
1940:   Little Men (A. Caesar)

TIM KELLY

1970:   Cry of the Banshee (C. Wicking)
1974:   Sugar Hill
1976:   Black Street Fighter (Melvyn Frohman)
1977:   Black Fist

EDMUND KELSO

1937:   The Mystery of the Hooded Horsemen
1938:   Tex Rides with the Boy Scouts; Frontier
        Town; Outlaws of Sonora (B. Burbridge);
        Rollin' Plains (L. Parsons); Utah Trail
1939:   Sundown on the Prairie (W. Nolte); The
        Oregon Trail (ser.); Roll, Wagons, Roll*
1941:   Ridin' the Cherokee Trail; The Gang's All
        Here; King of the Zombies; Let's Go
        Collegiate; Sign of the Wolf (E. Hopkins);
        Top Sergeant Mulligan; Up in the Air; You're
        Out of Luck
1942:   Lure of the Islands*; Meet the Mob (G.
        Bricker); Police Bullets (A. Lamb); Private
        Buckaroo (E. James); So's Your Aunt Emma
        (G. Bricker); Freckles Comes Home
1943:   Revenge of the Zombies (V. Norcross)
1945:   There Goes Kelly

KURT KEMPLER

1932:   The Riding Tornado; Two-Fisted Law; The Big
        Stampede
1933:   The Telegraph Trail; Eleventh Commandment
        (A. Buffington)

JOSEPH KENAS

1950:   Farewell to Yesterday (doc.)

J. D. KENDIS

1936:   Gambling with Souls

JAMES KENNAWAY

1968:   The Shoes of the Fisherman (J. Patrick)
1970:   Brotherly Love

ADAM KENNEDY

1974:   The Dove (P. Beagle)
1977:   The Domino Principle
1980:   Raise the Titanic!

BURT KENNEDY (1923-   ) director (also Z.X. Jones)

1956:   Gun the Man Down; Man in the Vault; Seven
        Men from Now
1957:   The Tall T; Fort Dobbs (G. W. George)
1959:   Ride Lonesome; Yellowstone Kelly
1960:   Comanche Station
1961:   The Canadians
1962:   Six Black Horses
1964:   Mail Order Bride
1965:   The Rounders
1967:   Welcome to Hard Times
1969:   Young Billy Young
1971:   Hannie Caulder (Brit.)
1973:   The Train Robbers
1979:   Wolf Lake

DOUGLAS KENNEDY

1978:   National Lampoon's Animal House*
1980:   Caddyshack*

EARL KENNEDY

1949:   Project X (G. Hurley)

JAY RICHARD KENNEDY

1948:   To the Ends of the Earth (S. Buchman)
1955:   I'll Cry Tomorrow (H. Deutsch)

LEON I. KENNEDY

1981: Body and Soul

GEORGE KENNET

1966: Boy, Did I Get the Wrong Number!*

TONY KENRICK

1981: Nobody's Perfekt

DONALD KENT

1935: Trails of Adventure

LARRY KENT

1969: Hugh

ROBERT E. KENT

1937: Paid to Dance
1938: Highway Patrol (S. Anthony); Juvenile
       Court*; Who Killed Gail Preston? (H.
       Taylor); The Spider's Web (ser.)*
1939: Charlie Chan in Reno*; Flying G-Men (ser.)*
1940: Always a Bride; Calling All Husbands; Father
       Is a Prince; Gambling on the High Seas;
       Ladies Must Live
1941: The Case of the Black Parrot
1942: Bullet Scars; I Was Framed; Spy Ship
1943: Murder on the Waterfront; Truck Busters (R.
       Schrock); Adventures in Iraq (G. Bilson);
       Find the Blackmailer; Gildersleeve on
       Broadway
1944: Girl Rush; Gildersleeve's Ghost
1945: The Falcon in San Francisco (B. Markson);
       Radio Stars on Parade (M. Brice); Two
       O'Clock Courage
1946: Dick Tracy vs. Cueball (D. Lussier); Genius

at Work (M. Brice)
1947: Gas House Kids Go West*; The Red Stallion
(C. Wilbur); It's a Joke, Son (Paul Gerard);
The Gas House Kids in Hollywood; Philo Vance
Returns
1950: Last of the Buccaneers
1951: When the Redskins Rode
1952: Brave Warrior; California Conquest; The
Golden Hawk; The Pathfinder; Thief of
Damascus
1953: Fort Ti; Siren of Bagdad; Flame of Calcutta;
Serpent of the Nile
1954: Charge of the Lancers; Jesse James vs. the
Daltons; The Miami Story
1955: Inside Detroit (J. B. Gordon); Seminole
Uprising
1956: Don't Knock the Rock (J. B. Gordon); Rock
Around the Clock (J. B. Gordon); The
Werewolf (J. B. Gordon)
1957: Utah Blaine (J. B. Gordon); Guns, Girls and
Gangsters
1961: Mary Had a Little (J. Brewer)
1963: Diary of a Madman; Twice Told Tales
1964: Blood on the Arrow; Get Yourself a College
Girl; The Quick Gun
1965: When the Boys Meet the Girls
1967: The Fastest Guitar Alive; Hot Rods to Hell
1968: A Time to Sing (O. Hampton)
1970: The Christian Jorgensen Story (E. St.
Joseph)

WILLIAM C. KENT

1941: Reg'lar Fellers*

WILLIS KENT

1932: The Racing Strain (B. Burbridge)
1933: Sucker Money
1935: Outlaw Rule; Range Warfare; Circle of Death;
Arizona Bad Man
1940: Mad Youth

CHARLES KENYON

429

```
1929:   Show Boat
1930:   The River's End; The Office Wife; Recaptured
        Love
1931:   Bought (R. Griffith); Millie; My Past; Party
        Husband
1932:   Crooner; Man Wanted; Street of Women (M.
        McCall); Under 18 (M. Fulton)
1933:   I Loved a Woman (S. Sutherland); The Working
        Man (M. Howell)
1934:   Dr. Monica (L. Mayer); The Firebird; Journal
        of a Crime (F. Herbert); Mandalay (A.
        Parker)
1935:   Girl from Tenth Avenue; The Goose and the
        Gander; A Midsummer Night's Dream (M.
        McCall)
1936:   The Golden Arrow; The Petrified Forest (D.
        Daves); Crack-Up (S. Mintz)
1937:   One Hundred Men and a Girl*; The Road Back
        (R. Sheriff)
1940:   Lady with Red Hair (M. Krims)
1941:   Highway West*
1943:   It Comes Up Love (D. Bennett)
1944:   The Man in Half Moon Street; The Unwritten
        Code (L. White)
1945;   Phantom of the Plains (E. Snell)
1946:   Strange Journey (I. Elman)
```

CURTIS KENYON

```
1934:   Woman Who Dared
1937:   Love and Hisses (A. Arthur)
1938:   Thanks for Everything (H. Tugend)
1941:   She Knew All the Answers*
1942:   Seven Days' Leave*; Twin Beds*
1943:   Salute for Three*
1947:   The Fabulous Dorseys*
1949:   Tulsa (F. Nugent)
1957:   The Persuader (D. Ross)
```

BILL KERBY

```
1974:   Gravy Train (D. Whitney)
1979:   The Rose (Bo Goldman)
```

JAMES V. KERN (1909-1966) director

1939: That's Right — Your're Wrong (W. Counselman)
1940: If I had My Way*; You'll Find Out
1941: Look Who's Laughing; Playmates
1943: Thank Your Lucky Stars*
1944: The Doughgirls; Shine On, Harvest Moon
1945: The Horn Blows at Midnight (S. Hellman)
1946: Never Say Goodbye (I. Diamond)

JEROME KERN (1885-1945) composer

1931: Men of the Sky (O. Harbach)
1936: Showboat (O. Hammerstein)

RONNI KERN

1980: A Change of Seasons*
1981: American Pop (anim.)

IRA KERNS

1966: Nashville Rebel (J. Sheridan)

CHARLES KERR

1940: L'il Abner (T. Johnson)

GENE KERR

1942: Girls' Town (V. McLeod)

LAURA KERR

1944: Brazil (F. Gill)
1947: The Farmer's Daughter (A. Rivkin)
1950: Grounds for Marriage (A. Rivkin)

SOPHIE KERR

1934: Big Hearted Herbert*

IRWIN KERSHNER (1923-   ) director

1958: Stakeout on Dope Street*

HENRY S. KESLER

1957: Five Steps to Danger

TED KEY

1978: The Cat from Outer Space

ROLAND KIBBEE

1946: Angel on My Shoulder (H. Segall); A Night in
       Casablanca (J. Fields)
1951: Painting the Clouds with Sunshine (H.
       Clork); Ten Tall Men (F. Davis); Pardon My
       French
1952: The Crimson Pirate
1953: The Desert Song; Three Sailors and a Girl
       (D. Freeman)
1954: Vera Cruz (J. Webb)
1957: Top Secret Affair (Allan Scott)
1959: The Devil's Disciple (J. Dighton)
1965: The Appaloosa (J. Bridges)
1971: Valdez Is Coming (D. Rayfiel)
1974: The Midnight Man (B. Lancaster)

WARREN KIEFER

1971: The Last Rebel

JOHN O. KILLEN

1959: Odds Against Tomorrow (N. Gidding)
1969: Slaves*

PAUL KILLIAM

1963: The Great Chase (doc.)*

432

TOM KILPATRICK

1937: River of Missing Men; Trapped by G-Men
1939: Whispering Enemies (G. Rigby)
1940: Dr. Cyclops
1948: Adventure in Silverado*
1950: The Palomino

WARD KIMBALL

1961: Babes in Toyland*

LAWRENCE KIMBLE

1936: All American Chump
1937: Submarine D1*
1938: Beloved Brat; Love, Honor and Behave*
1939: No Place to Go*; Off the Record*; Adventures
       of Jane Arden*
1940: It All Came True (M. Fessier)
1941: The Devil Pays Off (M. Boylan); Public
       Enemies (E. Lowe)
1942: Johnny Doughboy; Moonlight Masquerade;
       Pardon My Stripes (S. Palmer); Pierre of the
       Plains; Bells of Capistrano
1943: Tahita Honey*
1944: Music in Manhattan; Seven Days Ashore
1945: Pan-America; Zombies on Broadway
1946: The Bamboo Blonde (O. Cooper); Criminal
       Court; San Quentin*; The Truth About Murder*
1947: Beat the Band; The Flame
1948: Angel on the Amazon; I, Jane Doe; Mystery in
       Mexico
1950: The Avengers (Arg.; A. Mackenzie); Hit
       Parade of 1951*; One Way Street
1951: Two of a Kind (J. Gunn)

BRUCE KIMMEL

1976: The First Nudie Musical
1981: The Creature Wasn't Nice

JUD KINBERG

1963: Siege of the Saxons (J. Kohn)

BRADLEY KING

1929: Dark Streets; The Squall; Weary River; Young
      Nowheres
1930: The Lash; Wild Company
1931: East Lynne (T. Barry); Three Girls Lost
1932: A Passport to Hell; Six Hours to Live;
      Westward Passage
1933: Hoopla (J. March); Humanity
1935: Mystery of Edwin Drood*; Under the Pampas
      Moon (E. Pascal)
1937: Maid of Salem*
1947: That's My Man (S. Fisher)

HUGH KING

1938: The Storm*
1949: The Threat (D. Hyland)

JEFF KING

1979: Sunnyside (T. Galfas)

LARRY L. KING

1977: Off the Wall
1982: The Best Little Whorehouse in Texas*

PAUL KING

1958: Wild Heritage (doc.; J. Stone)

STEPHEN KING

1982: Creepshow

WOODY KING

1976:   The Long Wait (J. Mayfield)

LEWIS KINGDON

1936:   Desert Justice (G. Phillips)

JOHN KINGSBRIDGE

1970:   Shark (S. Fuller)

DOROTHY KINGSLEY (1909–   )

1944:   Broadway Rhythm (H. Clork); Bathing Beauty*
1946:   Easy to Wed
1948:   A Date with Judy (D. Cooper); On an Island
        with You*
1949:   Neptune's Daughter
1950:   The Skipper Surprised His Wife; Two Weeks
        with Love (J. Larkin)
1951:   Angels in the Outfield (G. Wells); It's a
        Big Country*; Texas Carnival
1952:   When in Rome (C. Schnee)
1953:   Small Town Girl (Dorothy Cooper); Dangerous
        When Wet; Kiss Me Kate
1954:   Seven Brides for Seven Brothers*
1955:   Jupiter's Darling
1957:   Pal Joey; Don't Go Near the Water (G. Wells)
1959:   Green Mansions
1960:   Can-Can (C. Lederer); Pepe (C. Binyon)
1967:   Valley of the Dolls (H. Deutsch); Half a
        Sixpence (Brit./U.S.)

TERRY KINGSLEY-SMITH

1972:   Molly and Lawless John

ERNEST KINOY

1971:   Brother John
1972:   Buck and the Preacher

435

1976:   Leadbelly

GEORGE KIRGO

1965:   Red Line 7000 (H. Hawks)
1966:   Spinout (T. Flicker)
1967:   Don't Make Waves (I. Wallach)

DAVID KIRKLAND

1931:   Riders of the Cactus

JACK KIRKLAND

1930:   Heads Up (J. McGowan)
1935:   Wings in the Dark (F. Partos)
1936:   Sutter's Gold*
1954:   The Golden Coach

DAVID KIRKPATRICK

1976:   The Great Texas Dynamite Chase

JAMES KIRKWOOD

1982:   Some Kind of Hero (R. Boris)

MIRIAM KISSINGER

1947:   Dangerous Money; The Trap

MARTIN KITROSSER

1982:   Friday the 13th Part 3 (C. Watson)

C. K. KIVARI

1952:   The Steel Fist

RON KIVETT

1975: Blood Waters of Dr. Z (L. Larew)

ROBERT KLANE

1970: Where's Poppa?
1977: Fire Sale

MARCY KLAUBER

1934: Woman in the Dark*
1943: Follies Girl (C. Robison)
1944: I'm from Arkansas (J. Carole)
1953: Code Two
1958: Girl in the Woods (O. Crawford)

LAWRENCE KLEE

1947: The Roosevelt Story (doc.)

HERBERT KLEIN

1938: Love Is a Headache*

JAIME KLEIN

1982: Pandemonium (R. Whitley)

JOHN KLEIN

1971: Taking Off*

LARRY KLEIN

1970: The Adversary

MAX KLEIN

1950: Cassino to Korea (doc.)

437

PHILIP KLEIN (-1935)

1930:   Oh, for a Man (L. Starling)
1931:   Black Camel*; Charlie Chan Carries On (B.
        Connors); Hush Money*; Riders of the Purple
        Sage* The Spider (B. Connors)
1932:   Rainbow Trail (B. Connors); The Gay
        Caballero (B. Connors); Bachelor's Affairs
        (B. Connors); Chandu the Magician (B.
        Connors); Charlie Chan's Chance (B.
        Connors); Hat Check Girl (B. Connors); Too
        Busy to Work (B. Connors); Trial of Vivienne
        Ware (B. Connors)
1933:   Hot Pepper (B. Connors); I Loved You
        Wednesday (H. Jackson); Pilgrimage (B.
        Connors)
1934:   Baby Take a Bow (E. Paramore); Elinor Norton
        (R. Franklin)
1935:   Dante's Inferno (R. Yost)

WALLY KLEIN

1939:   Indianapolis Speedway (S. Herzig)
1942:   They Died with Their Boots On (A. McMahon)

WILLIAM KLEIN (1926-   ) director

1966:   Who Are You Polly Maggoo? (Fr.)
1967:   Far from Vietnam (Fr.)*
1969:   Mister Freedom (Fr.); Float Like a Butterfly
        -- Sting Like a Bee (Fr.); Festival
        Panafricain (Fr.)
1970:   Eldridge Cleaver (doc.; Fr.)
1977:   Le Couple Temoin (Fr.)

HARRY KLEINER (1916-   )

1945:   Fallen Angel
1948:   The Steet with No Name
1952:   Red Skies of Montana; Kangaroo (Austral.)
1953:   Salome; Miss Sadie Thompson
1954:   Carmen Jones
1955:   House of Bamboo (S. Fuller); The Violent Men

438

```
1957:  The Garment Jungle
1959:  Cry Tough
1960:  Ice Palace
1961:  A Fever in the Blood (R. Huggins)
1966:  Fantastic Voyage
1968:  Bullitt (A. Trustman)
1971:  Le Mans
```

DAN KLEINMAN

```
1972:  Rage (P. Friedman)
```

CARL KLEINSCHMITT

```
1980:  Middle Age Crazy
```

RANDALL KLEISER

```
1976:  Street People (E. Tidyman)
1982:  Summer Lovers
```

JOHN KLEMPNER

```
1956:  Three for Jamie Dawn
```

MAX KLEVEN

```
1981:  Ruckus
```

A.A. KLINE

```
1929:  Rich People
```

BRENDA KLINE

```
1941:  Secret Evidence
```

HERBERT KLINE (1909-   ) director

```
1952:  The Fighter (A. Kandel)
```

STEVE KLINE

1980:   Borderline (J. Freedman)

JOHN KLORER

1945:   Guest Wife (B. Manning); This Love of Ours
        (B. Manning)
1951:   Starlift (K. Lamb)
1955:   Top of the World (R. Nash)

JANE KLOVE

1964:   Island of the Blue Dolphins (T. Sherdeman)
1966:   ...And Now Miguel (T. Sherdeman)
1969:   My Side of the Mountain*

JACK KNAPP

1938:   The Marines Are Here (J. Cheney)

JOHN H. KNEUBUHL

1958:   The True Story of Lynn Stuart; The Screaming
        Skull
1965:   Two on a Guillotine (H. Slesar)

ERIC KNIGHT

1943:   Prelude to War (doc.; A. Veiller)

TRACY KNIGHT

1949:   King of the Jungleland (ser.)*

CHRISTOPHER KNOPF

1955:   The King's Thief
1957:   20 Million Miles to Earth (Bob Williams);

```
           The Tall Stranger
1958:  Joy Ride
1960:  Hell Bent for Leather
1973:  Emperor of the North Pole
1975:  Posse (W. Roberts)
1977:  The Choirboys
1978:  Scott Joplin
```

EDWIN H. KNOPF (1899-   ) director

```
1932:  Nice Woman (G. Lehman); The Rebel (Germ.;
       Luis Trenker)
1935:  Baby Face Harrington (N. Johnson)
1936:  Piccadilly Jim*
1951:  Mr. Imperium (D. Hartman)
```

FREDERICK KNOTT

```
1954:  Dial M for Murder
```

ALEXANDER KNOX (1907-   ) actor

```
1946:  Sister Kenny*
1949:  The Judge Steps Out (B. Ingster)
```

ARTHUR KOBER

```
1931:  It Pays to Advertise (E. Doherty); Secret
       Call (E. Unsell); Up Pops the Devil (E.
       Unsell)
1932:  False Madonna (R. Harris); Guilty As Hell
       (F. Partos); Make Me a Star*; Me and My Gal
1933:  Bondage (D. Malloy); Broadway Bad (M.
       Fulton); Informal Machine; Mama Loves Papa
       (N. Johnson)
1934:  Hollywood Party (H. Dietz); Palooka*
1935:  Calm Yourself; Ginger; Great Hotel Murder
1936:  Early to Bed
1938:  Having Wonderful Time
1944:  In the Meantime, Darling (M. Uris)
1945:  Don Juan Quilligan (F. Gabrielson)
```

JERRY KOBRIN

1973:   Frasier, the Sensuous Lion

HOWARD KOCH (1902–   ) (also PETER HOWARD)

1940:   The Letter; The Sea Hawk (S. Miller)
1941:   Sergeant York*; Shining Victory (A.
         Froelick)
1942:   In This Our Life
1943:   Mission to Moscow; Casablanca*
1944:   In Our Time (E. St. Joseph)
1945:   Rhapsody in Blue (E. Pearl)
1946:   Three Strangers (J. Huston)
1948:   Letter from an Unknown Woman
1950:   No Sad Songs for Me
1951:   The Thirteenth Letter
1956:   A Finger of Guilt (Brit.; alt. The Intimate
         Stranger)
1961:   Loss of Innocence (Brit.)
1962:   The War Lover (Brit.)
1964:   633 Squadron (J. Clavell)
1967:   The Fox (L. Carlino)
1974:   The Woman of Otowi Crossing

TED KOEHLER

1943:   Stormy Weather (Fred Jackson)

LAIRD KOENIG

1966:   The Cat (W. Redlin)
1971:   Red Sun (Fr./Ital./Sp.)*
1977:   The Little Girl Who Lives Down the Lane
1979:   Sidney Sheldon's Bloodline
1981:   Inchon (R. Moore)

RAYMOND KOENIG

1972:   Blacula (J. Torres)
1973:   Scream Blacula Scream*

ARNIE KOGEN

1966: Birds Do It (A. Arthur)

ALLEN KOHN

1970: The Wizard of Gore

BEN GRAUMAN KOHN

1935: Manhattan Moon*
1937: Adventure's End; Once a Doctor (R. White)
1938: He Couldn't Say No*; Young Fugitives (C.
       Grayson)
1940: Heaven with a Barbed Wire Fence*
1941: Golden Hoofs
1942: American Empire*

JOHN KOHN

1963: Siege of the Saxons (J. Kinberg)
1972: The Strange Vengeance of Rosalie (A.
       Greville-Bell)
1979: Goldengirl

FREDERICK KOHNER

1936: Sins of Man*
1941: The Men in Her Life*
1943: Tahiti Honey*
1944: The Lady and the Monster (D. Lussier)
1948: Three Daring Daughters*
1951: Hollywood Story

PANCHO KOHNER

1975: Mr. Sycamore (K. Frings)

KENNETH KOLB

1958: The Seventh Voyage of Sinbad

MAX KOLPE

443

1946:   Heartbeat*

MANUEL KOMROFF

1934:   The Scarlet Empress

HANS KONINGSBERGER

1970:   The Revolutionary

FRANK L. KONKLIN

1936:   Forgotten Women (H. McCarthy)

JEFF KONVITZ

1974:   Silent Night Bloody Night (T. Gershuny)
1977:   The Sentinel (M. Winner)
1980:   Gorp

ZOLTAN KORDA (1895-1961) director

1943:   Sahara*

LEN KOROBKIN

1967:   Mad Monster Party (anim.; H. Kurtzman)

FRITZ KORTNER (1892-1970) actor, director   Austr.

(American films only)
1943:   The Strange Death of Adolf Hitler

JOHN KORTY

1966:   The Crazy Quilt
1970:   Riverrun
1971:   Funnyman (P. Bonerz)

1978: Oliver's Story (E. Segal)

JERZY KOSINSKI

1979: Being There

RON KOSLOW

1976: Lifeguard

TED KOTCHEFF

1979: North Dallas Forty*

M. JAMES KOUF, JR.

1982: Pink Motel

FRANK KOWALSKI

1971: A Man Called Sledge (V. Morrow)

WILLIAM KOZLENKO

1943: A Stranger in Town (I. Lennart)

MICHAEL KOZOLL

1982: First Blood*

JOHN W. KRAFFT

1935: Men of Action*; Million Dollar Baby (J.
       Santley); The Mystery Man (R. Lloyd)
1936: Death from a Distance; Arizona Raiders (R.
       Yost); Lady Luck; Missing Girls (M. Mooney);
       Murder at Glen Athol; The House of Secrets
1937: Here's Flash Casey; The Thirteenth Man
1938: I Am a Criminal; Rebellious Daughters;
       Slander House (G. Orr)

1939:   Sweepstakes Winner (A. DeMond); Convict's
        Code
1940:   Laughing at Danger (J. West)
1941:   Mountain Moonlight*
1942:   Foreign Agent (M. Mooney); Man from
        Headquarters (R. Lloyd)
1944:   Smart Guy (C. Marion)

MICHAEL KRAIKE

1977:   The Amazing Dobermans*

HANS KRALY (1885-1950)   Germ.

(American fims only)
1929:   Betrayal; Eternal Love; The Last of Mrs.
        Cheyney*; Wild Orchids*; Devil May Care
1930:   Lady of Scandal; The Soul Kiss (ret. A
        Lady's Morals; C. West)
1931:   Just a Gigolo*; Private Lives*
1933:   My Lips Betray (J. Storm)
1934:   By Candlelight*
1937:   One Hundred Men and a Girl*
1938:   A Desperate Adventure (M. Webster)
1941:   West Point Widow (F. Herbert)
1943:   The Mad Ghoul

CECILE KRAMER

1941:   Twilight on the Trail*
1942:   Silver Queen (B. Schubert)
1944:   Buffalo Bill*
1947:   Ramrod*

LARRY KRAMER

1970:   Women in Love
1973:   Lost Horizon

REMI KRAMER

1977:   High Velocity (M. Parsons)

RUPERT KRAMER

1968: The Edge
1970: Ice
1975: Milestones (J. Douglas)

SEARLE KRAMER

1951: Mr. Universe; Two Gals and a Guy

STEVE KRANTZ

1979: Swap Meet

NORMAN KRASNA (1909-   ) director, producer

1932: Hollywood Speaks (J. Swerling); That's My
      Boy
1933: Love, Honor and Oh Baby! (E. Buzzell);
      Parole Girl; So This Is Africa
1934: The Richest Girl in the World (G. Tryon)
1935: Four Hours to Kill; Hands Across the Table*
1936: Wife Versus Secretary*
1937: The King and the Chorus Girl (G. Marx)
1939: Bachelor Mother
1940: It's a Date
1941: The Devil and Miss Jones; The Flame of New
      Orleans; It Started with Eve (L. Townsend);
      Mr. and Mrs. Smith
1943: Princess O'Rourke
1945: Practically Yours
1950: The Big Hangover
1954: White Christmas*
1956: The Ambassador's Daughter; Bundle of Joy*
1958: Indiscreet
1960: Let's Make Love; Who Was That Lady?
1962: My Geisha
1963: Sunday in New York

HOWARD B. KREITSEK

1969: The Illustrated Man
1970: Rabbit, Run

```
1975:   Breakout*; Walking Tall Part 2
1977:   Final Chapter -- Walking Tall (S. Peeples)
```

ROSE KREVES

```
1950:   Battling Marshal
```

STU KRIEGER

```
1978:   Goodbye Franklin High
```

MILTON KRIMS

```
1931:   Range Feud (G. Plympton)
1932:   South of the Rio Grande; The Western Code;
        Forbidden Trail
1934:   West of the Pecos (J. Twist); Crimson
        Romance (D. Schroeder); I Give My Love (D.
        Anderson)
1935:   Grand Old Girl*; Strangers All
1937:   The Great O'Malley (T. Reed); The Green
        Light
1938:   Secrets of an Actress*; The Sisters
1939:   Confessions of a Nazi Spy (J. Wexley); We
        Are Not Alone (J. Hilton)
1940:   A Dispatch from Reuters; Lady with Red Hair
        (Charles Kenyon)
1948:   The Iron Curtain
1949:   Prince of Foxes
1952:   One Minute to Zero (W. Haines)
1954    Crossed Swords
1955:   Tennessee's Partner (D. Beauchamp)
1956:   Mohawk (M. Geraghty)
```

HARRY KRONMAN

```
1941:   Bowery Boy*
```

JEREMY FOE KRONSBERG

```
1978:   Every Which Way but Loose
1981:   Going Ape!
```

KARL KRUEGER

1956:   Comanche

JOSEPH KRUMGOLD

1936:   Blackmailer*; Lady from Nowhere*; The Lone
        Wolf Returns*
1937:   Jim Hanvey -- Detective (O. Cooper); Join
        the Marines (O. Cooper); Lady Behave (O.
        Cooper)
1939:   Main Street Lawyer
1940:   The Crooked Road (G. Weston)
1941:   The Phantom Submarine
1942:   Seven Miles from Alcatraz

CARL KRUSADA

1930:   Firebrand Jordan; Beyond the Rio Grande;
        Ridin' Law; Bar L Ranch (B. Cohen); Phantom
        of the Desert
1931:   Westward Bound; The Mystery Trooper (ser.);
        The Sign of the Wolf (ser.)
1932:   Forty-Five Calibre Echo
1934:   Mystery Ranch (Rose Gordon); Fighting Hero
        (Rose Gordon); The Cactus Kid; Loser's End
        (Rose Gordon); Terror of the Plains (J.
        Regan)
1935:   The Silver Bullet (Rose Gordon); Born to
        Battle (Rose Gordon); Coyote Trails (Rose
        Gordon); Defying the Law; The Laramie Kid;
        North of Arizona; The Phantom Cowboy; Rio
        Rattler; Silent Valley (Rose Gordon); Skull
        and Crown (B. Cohen); Texas Jack; Wolf
        Riders; Never too Late (J. Natteford)
1936:   Fast Bullets (Rose Gordon); Santa Fe Bound
1939:   Feud of the Range; Riders of the Sage; The
        Pal from Texas; El Diablo Rides
1940:   Wild Horse Valley; Pinto Canyon; The Kid
        from Santa Fe; Riders from Nowhere; Wild
        Horse Range; Broken Strings (B. Ray)

STANLEY KUBRICK (1928-   ) director

449

```
1955:   Killer's Kiss
1956:   The Killing
1957:   Paths of Glory*
1964:   Dr. Strangelove*
1968:   2001 -- a Space Odyssey (A. C. Clarke)
1971:   A Clockwork Orange
1975:   Barry Lyndon
1980:   The Shining (Diane Johnson)
```

IRENE KUHN

```
1932:   The Mask of Fu Manchu*
```

SID KULLER

```
1940:   Argentine Nights*
1941:   The Big Store*
1951:   Slaughter Trail
1960:   Stop! Look! and Laugh!
```

HARRY KURNITZ (1909-1968) novelist, playwright

```
1938:   Fast Company
1939:   Fast and Furious; Fast and Loose
1940:   I Love You Again*
1941:   Shadow of the Thin Man (I. Brecher)
1942:   Pacific Rendezvous*
1943:   They Got Me Covered; The Heavenly Body
1944:   See Here, Private Hargrove
1945:   What Next, Corporal Hargrove?
1947:   Something in the Wind (W. Bowers); The Web*
1948:   Adventures of Don Juan (G. Oppenheimer); One
        Touch of Venus (F. Tashlin)
1949:   The Inspector General (P. Rapp); A Kiss in
        the Dark; My Dream Is Yours (D. Lussier)
1950:   Of Men and Music*; Pretty Baby (E. Freeman)
1953:   Tonight We Sing (G. Oppenheimer); Melba; The
        Man Between
1955:   Land of the Pharaohs*
1957:   The Happy Road*; Witness for the
        Prosecution*
1960:   Once More, with Feeling; Surprise Package
1964:   Goodbye Charlie
1966:   How to Steal a Million
```

HARVEY KURTZMAN

1967:   Mad Monster Party (anim.; L. Korobkin)

RON KURZ

1981:   Friday the 13th Part 2

DONALD KUSEL

1940:   The Showdown (H. Kusel)

HAROLD KUSEL

1937:   Fight for Your Lady*; New Faces of 1937*;
        There Goes the Groom*
1940:   The Showdown (D. Krusel)

PAUL KYRIAZI

1976:   Death Machines (J. Walder)

L

FIDEL LA BARBA

1939: Susannah of the Mounties*

ETHEL LA BLANCHE

1937: Headin' East (P. Franklin)
1938: Flirting with Fate*; Man Hunters of the
       Caribbean (P. Franklin)
1939: Exile Express (E. Mayer)
1941: Pirates on Horseback (J. Cheney)

PAULA LABROT

1976: The Legend of Bigfoot (H. Winer)

GREGORY LA CAVA (1892-1952) director

1931: Laugh and Get Rich (D. McLean)
1932: The Half-Naked Truth*
1935: Private Worlds (L. Starling)
1936: My Man Godfrey*
1940: Primrose Path (Allan Scott)
1947: Living in a Big Way (I. Ravetch)

HARRY LACHMAN (1886-1975) director

1931: The Outsider (Brit.)

MORT LACHMAN

```
1968:   Yours, Mine and Ours (M. Shavelson)
1974:   Mixed Company (M. Shavelson)
```

FRED LADD

```
1974:   Journey Back to Oz (N. Prescott)
```

FRED LADERMAN

```
1965:   Pinocchio in Outer Space
```

BETTY LAIDLAW

```
1934:   Inside Information (R. Lively)
1935:   The Marriage Bargain (R. Lively); St. Louis
        Woman (R. Lively)
1937:   The Girl Said No (R. Lively)
1938:   Danger on the Air (R. Lively); Personal
        Secretary*
```

WILLIAM R. LAIDLAW

```
1948:   Command Decision (G. Froesche)
```

JACK LAIT, JR.

```
1939:   Marshal of Mesa City
1941:   Death Valley Outlaws (D. Ryan); A Missouri
        Outlaw (D. Schroeder)
1944:   Texas Masquerade (N. Houston)
```

EDWARD LAKSO

```
1961:   Womanhunt (R. Bender)
1962:   The Broken Land; Woman-Hunt (R. Bender)
1967:   Gentle Giant (A. White)
1971:   Head On
1973:   Boots Turner
```

FRANK LaLOGGIA

1981: Fear No Evil

ANDE LAMB

1942: Police Bullets (E. Kelso)
1944: Riders of the Santa Fe
1945: Renegades of the Rio Grande; Brenda Starr,
       Reporter (ser.)*; Jungle Queen (ser.)*;
       Jungle Raiders (ser.)*; The Master Key
       (ser.)*; Who's Guilty? (ser.)*; Trouble
       Chasers (G. Plympton)
1946: Moon over Montana (L. Rousseau); Hop
       Harrigan (ser.)
1947: Unexpected Guest; Hoppy's Holiday*; The Case
       of the Baby Sitter (C. Hittleman)
1948: Strange Gamble*
1950: The Texan Meets Calamity Jane

ELEANOR LAMB

1974: Where the Red Fern Grows (Douglas Stewart)
1975: Seven Alone (Douglas Stewart); Against a
       Crooked Sky (Douglas Stewart)

HAROLD LAMB

1935: The Crusades*
1936: The Plainsman*
1938: The Buccaneer*

KARL LAMB

1945: Pardon My Past (E. Felton)
1947: Carnegie Hall
1948: The Pitfall
1949: Whispering Smith (F. Butler)
1950: The Kid from Texas (R. H. Andrews)
1951: Starlift (J. Klorer)
1952: The Captive City (A. Josephy)
1953: Tarzan and the She-Devil (Carroll Young)

MAX LAMB

1966: Apache Uprising (H. Sanford)

GAVEN LAMBERT

1958: Bitter Victory*
1960: Sons and Lovers (Brit.)
1961: The Roman Spring of Mrs. Stone
1965: Inside Daisy Clover
1977: I Never Promised You a Rose Garden

LEONARD LAMENSDORF

1975: Cornbread, Earl and Me

WAYNE B. LAMONT

1931: Secret Menace

MILLARD LAMPELL

1951: Saturday's Hero (S. Buchman)
1960: Chance Meeting (Brit.; B. Barzman)
1962: Escape from East Berlin*
1966: The Idol
1972: Eagle in a Cage

BILL LANCASTER

1976: The Bad News Bears
1978: The Bad News Bears Go to Japan
1982: The Thing

BURT LANCASTER (1913-   ) actor

1974: The Midnight Man (R. Kibbee)

CLIFF LANCASTER

1952: Gold Fever (E. Anderson)

RICHARD LANDAU

1945: Back to Bataan (B. Barzman)
1946: Little Iodine
1949: The Crooked Way; Wild Weed (alt. The Devil's Weed)
1950: Johnny One-Eye
1951: FBI Girl (D. Babcock); The Lost Continent
1953: Sins of Jezebel; The Great Jesse James Raid; Bad Blonde (G. Elmes)
1954: Blackout
1955: Pearl of the South Pacific*
1956: The Creeping Unknown (Brit.); Hot Cars (D. Martin); The Man Is Armed (R. Dennis)
1957: Pharaoh's Curse; Voodoo Island; Hell Bound; The Girl in Black Stockings
1958: Violent Road; Frankenstein -- 1970 (G. Yates)
1959: Up Periscope; Born Reckless
1965: Fort Courageous

SAUL LANDAU

1971: Fidel (doc.)

ADRIAN LANDIS

1939: Everything's on Ice (S. Lowe)

JAMES LANDIS

1957: Under Fire; Young and Dangerous
1958: Thundering Jets
1959: The Lone Texan (Jack Thomas)

JOHN LANDIS

1973: Schlock
1980: The Blues Brothers (D. Aykroyd)
1981: An American Werewolf in London

JOSEPH LANDON

1960: The Rise and Fall of Legs Diamond
1961: The Explosive Generation; The Hoodlum Priest
(D. Deer)
1963: Johnny Cool; Wall of Noise
1964: Rio Conchos (C. Huffaker)
1965: Von Ryan's Express (W. Mayes)
1966: Stagecoach

GEORGE LANDY

1931: Sidewalks of New York (P. Smith)

AL LANE

1934: The Sundown Trail

BURTON LANE

1957: Affair in Havana (M. Zimm)

SIDNEY LANFIELD

1929: Big Time
1930: Happy Days (E. Burke)

CHARLES LANG

1932: A Farewell to Arms*
1950: Call of the Klondike; Killer Shark
1955: The Magnificent Matador
1957: Decision at Sundown
1958: Buchanan Rides Alone
1960: Tess of the Storm Country; Desire in the
Dust

DAVID LANG

1942: Northwest Rangers (G. Kahn); A Yank on the
Burma Road*
1945: Midnight Manhunt; One Exciting Night
1946: People Are Funny (M. Shane); Queen of
Burlesque; Traffic in Crime

```
1947:   The Web of Danger (G. Milton)
1948:   Caged Fury
1951:   Chain of Circumstance
1953:   The Nebraskan (M. Berkeley); Ambush at
        Tomahawk Gap
1954:   The Outlaw Stallion; Massacre Canyon
1955:   Apache Ambush; Wyoming Renegades
1956:   Fury at Gunsight Pass; Screaming Eagles (R.
        Presnell); Secret of Treasure Mountain
1957:   The Phantom Stagecoach; Hellcats of the Navy
        (R. Marcus); The Buckskin Lady (C.
        Hittleman); The Hired Gun (B. Angell)
```

FRITZ LANG (1890-1976) director Austr.

```
(American films only)
1936:   Fury (B. Cormack)
1943:   Hangmen Also Die*
```

OTTO LANG

```
1957:   Search for Paradise (doc.)*
```

WALTER LANG (1898-1972) director

```
1933:   The Warrior's Husband*; Race Track (D. Doty)
```

HARRY LANGDON (1884-1944) comedian

```
1938:   Block-Heads*
1939:   The Flying Deuces*
1940:   A Chump at Oxford*; Saps at Sea*
1941:   Road Show*
```

NOEL LANGLEY (1911-   ) director, playwright S.
        Afr.

```
1937:   Maytime
1939:   The Wizard of Oz*
1940:   Florian*
1941:   Unexpected Uncle (D. Daves)
1952:   Ivanhoe (Brit.); The Prisoner of Zenda (J.
        Balderston)
```

```
1953:   Knights of the Round Table*
1954:   The Pickwick Papers (Brit.)
1956:   The Search for Bridey Murphy; The Vagabond
        King (K. Englund)
1961:   Snow White and the Three Stooges (E. Ullman)
```

KENNETH LANGTRY

```
1957:   I Was a Teen-Age Frankenstein
1958:   How to Make a Monster (Herman Cohen)
```

ROBERT E. LANING

```
1967:   The Hostage
```

JANET LANSBURGH

```
1964:   The Tattooed Police Horse
```

LOUIS LANTZ

```
1943:   Crime Doctor (G. Baker); You're a Lucky
        Fellow, Mr. Smith*
1947:   Violence (S. Rubin)
1950:   Rogue River
1951:   Fort Defiance
1952:   Lure of the Wilderness
```

HAROLD LAPLAND

```
1975:   The Master Gunfighter
```

RING LARDNER, JR. (1915-   ) also PHILLIP RUSH

```
1937:   A Star Is Born (unc.)*; Nothing Sacred
        (unc.; B. Hecht)
1939:   Meet Dr. Christian*
1940:   The Courageous Dr. Christian (I. Hunter)
1942:   Woman of the Year (M. Kanin)
1943:   The Cross of Lorraine*
1944:   Tomorrow the World (L. Atlas); Marriage Is a
        Private Affair (unc.)*; Laura (unc.)*
```

```
1945:   Cloak and Dagger (A. Maltz)
1947:   Forever Amber (P. Dunne)
1949:   The Forbidden Street (Brit.)
1951:   The Big Night*
1959:   Virgin Island (I. Hunter)
1960:   A Breath of Scandal (unc.; W. Bernstein)
1965:   The Cincinnati Kid (T. Southern)
1970:   M*A*S*H*
1972:   The Deadly Trap (unc.; Fr.)*
1977:   The Greatest
```

LEE LAREW

```
1975:   Blood Waters of Dr. Z (R. Kivett)
```

CHRIS LARKIN

```
1974:   A Very Natural Thing (J. Coencas)
```

JOHN FRANCIS LARKIN

```
1933:   Ladies Must Love; Parachute Jumper
1937:   The Mandarin Mystery*
1939:   Charlie Chan at Treasure Island; News Is
        Made at Night
1940:   The Gay Caballero (A. Duffy); Charlie Chan
        at the Wax Museum; Charlie Chan in Panama;
        City of Chance; The Lone Wolf Meets a Lady
1941:   Accent on Love; Dead Men Tell; Murder Among
        Friends; Man at Large
1942:   Castle in the Desert; The Man in the Trunk;
        Manila Calling; Quiet Please, Murder; Secret
        Agent of Japan
1945:   The Dolly Sisters (M. Spitzer)
1947:   Carnival in Costa Rica*
1950:   Two Weeks with Love (D. Kingsley)
```

JEREMY LARNER

```
1971:   Drive, He Said (J. Nicholson)
1972:   The Candidate
```

PETE La ROCHE

1956: Wetbacks

NANCY LARSEN

1978: Coach (S. B. Rose)

CHARLES LARSON

1948: Angel in Exile

GLEN A. LARSON

1979: Buck Rogers in the 25th Century (L.
       Stevens); Battlestar Galactica

LOUIS LA RUSSO II

1981: Beyond the Reef (J. Carabatsos)

ALEX LASKER

1982: Firefox (Wendell Wellman)

ANDREW LASKOS

1975: The Commitment*

GIL LASKY

1971: Blood and Lace
1975: The Night God Screamed; The Manhandlers

JESSE LASKY, JR. (1908-   ) novelist

1934: Coming Out Party (G. Unger); The White
       Parade*; Redhead (B. Burbridge)
1939: Union Pacific*
1940: North West Mounted Police*
1941: Back in the Saddle (R. Murphy)

```
1942:   The Omaha Trail (H. Butler); Reap the Wild
        Wind*
1947:   Unconquered*
1949:   Samson and Delilah (F. Frank)
1951:   Lorna Doone*; Mask of the Avenger; Never
        Trust a Gambler (J. Odlum); The Sickle and
        the Cross
1952:   The Brigand (G. Bruce); The Thief of Venice
1953:   The Silver Whip; Mission over Korea*
1954:   Hell and High Water (S. Fuller); The Iron
        Glove (D. Scott)
1955:   Pearl of the South Pacific*
1956:   Hot Blood; The Ten Commandments*
1958:   The Buccaneer*
1959:   John Paul Jones (J. Farrow)
1960:   The Wizard of Baghdad (P. Silver)
1961:   Pirates of Tortuga*; Seven Women from Hell
        (P. Silver)
1970:   Land Raiders
1975:   An Ace up My Sleeve (Brit.)
1976:   Crime and Passion (P. Silver)
```

LOUISE LASSER

```
1966:   What's Up, Tiger Lily?*
```

AARON LATHAM

```
1980:   Urban Cowboy (J. Bridges)
```

PHILIP LATHROP

```
1958:   Girls on the Loose*; Live Fast, Die Young*
```

JONATHAN LATIMER (1916-   ) director of photography

```
1939:   The Lone Wolf Spy Hunt
1941:   Topper Returns (G. Douglas)
1942:   The Glass Key; A Night in New Orleans
1946:   Nocturne
1947:   They Won't Believe Me
1948:   Beyond Glory*; The Big Clock; Night Has a
        Thousand Eyes (B. Lyndon); Sealed Verdict
```

1949: Alias Nick Beal
1950: Copper Canyon
1951: The Redhead and the Cowboy (L. O'Brien);
       Submarine Command
1953: Plunder of the Sun; Botany Bay
1956: Back from Eternity
1957: The Unholy Wife
1958: The Whole Truth (Brit.)

MICHAEL LATON

1975: Supercock

WESLEY LAU

1975: Lepke (T. Hoffs)

TOM LAUGHLIN (1938-   ) actor, director (also T.
       C. FRANK, DONALD HENDERSON, LLOYD E. JAMES)

1965: The Young Sinner
1967: Born Losers
1971: Billy Jack*
1974: The Trial of Billy Jack*
1978: Billy Jack Goes to Washington (Delores
       Taylor)

S. K. LAUREN

1932: Blonde Venus (J. Furthman); Evenings for
       Sale (A. Leahy)
1933: Jennie Gerhardt*; Pick Up*; Three-Cornered
       Moon (R. Harris)
1934: One Night of Love (E. North); The Party's
       Over
1935: Crime and Punishment (J. Anthony)
1937: A Damsel in Distress*; There Goes the Groom*
1938: Mother Carey's Chickens (G. Purcell)
1939: Our Neighbors the Carters
1940: Married and in Love
1941: Mr. and Mrs. North; When Ladies Meet (A.
       Loos)
1943: Flight for Freedom*
1948: Ruthless (G. Kahn)

KEN LAURENCE

1973: Howzer

ARTHUR LAURENTS (1918-   ) playwright

1948: Rope (B. Hecht); The Snake Pit*
1949: Anna Lucasta (P. Yordan); Caught
1956: Anastasia
1958: Bonjour Tristesse
1973: The Way We Were
1977: The Turning Point

EMMETT LAVERY

1942: Army Surgeon (B. Trivers)
1943: Behind the Rising Sun; Forever and a Day*;
       Hitler's Children
1949: Guilty of Treason
1950: The Magnificent Yankee
1951: The First Legion
1953: Bright Road
1955: The Court Martial of Billy Mitchell*

MARTIN LA VUT

1970: Jenny (G. Bloomfield)

HAROLD LAW

1937: Nobody's Baby*
1948: Variety Time*

JOHN LAW

1967: Casino Royale (B. Hecht)

ANTHONY LAWRENCE

1964: Roustabout (Allan Weiss)

1966:   Paradise, Hawaiian Style (Allan Weiss)
1967:   Easy Come, Easy Go (Allan Weiss)
1979:   Elvis

BERT LAWRENCE

1941:   Time Out for Rhythm (E. Hartmann)
1949:   Angels in Disguise*; Fighting Fools*
1951:   Ghost Chasers
1952:   Feudin' Fools (T. Ryan)
1955:   High Society (J. Gottler); Spy Chasers (J.
        Gottler)
1956:   Dig That Uranium (E. Ullman)

FANYA F. LAWRENCE

1965:   Nightmare in the Sun (T. Thomas)

JEROME LAWRENCE

1981:   First Monday in October (R. E. Lee)

JOHN LAWRENCE

1968:   The Glory Stompers (J. G. White)
1971:   The Incredible Two-Headed Transplant (J. G.
        White)
1972:   The Loners (B. Sanders)
1975:   Savage Abduction

PETER LAWRENCE

1982:   The Burning (B. Weinstein)

VINCENT LAWRENCE

1931:   I Take This Woman; Scandal Sheet (M. Marcin)
1932:   Movie Crazy; Night After Night; Sinners in
        the Sun*
1934:   Cleopatra*; Good Dame*; Now and Forever (S.
        Thalberg)
1935:   Behold My Wife (G. Jones); Hands Across the

465

Table*; One Way Ticket*; Peter Ibbetson*
1937: John Meade's Woman (H. Mankiewicz)
1938: Man-Proof*; Test Pilot (W. Young)
1939: Lucky Night (G. Jones)
1941: Moon over Miami (Brown Holmes)
1942: Gentleman Jim (H. McCoy)
1945: Adventure*
1947: The Sea of Grass (M. Roberts)

JOHN HOWARD LAWSON (1894-1977) playwright

1930: The Sea Bat (B. Meredyth); The Ship from
      Shanghai*; Our Blushing Brides (B. Meredyth)
1934: Success at Any Price (H. Green)
1935: Party Wire (E. Hill)
1938: Algiers (J. Cain); Blockade
1939: They Shall Have Music
1940: Earthbound (S. Engel); Four Sons
1943: Action in the North Atlantic; Sahara*
1945: Counter-Attack
1947: Smash-Up, the Story of a Woman

ROBERT LAX

1948: Siren of Atlantis (R. Leigh)

BIERNE LAY, JR.

1941: I Wanted Wings*
1949: Twelve O'Clock High (S. Bartlett)
1952: Above and Beyond*
1955: Strategic Air Command (V. Davies)
1956: Toward the Unknown
1960: The Gallant Hours (F. Gilroy)
1963: The Young and the Brave

JOHN HUNTER LAY

1940: Slightly Honorable*

G. CORNELL LAYNE

1974: Abby

ASHLEY LAZARUS

1977:   Forever Young, Forever Free

ERNA LAZARUS

1937:   Atlantic Flight (W. Darling)
1940:   I'm Nobody's Sweetheart Now*; Margie*
1941:   Double Date*; Moonlight in Hawaii*; Cracked
        Nuts (W. Darling)
1942:   The Body Disappears (S. Darling)
1944:   Dancing in Manhattan
1945:   Blonde from Brooklyn; Girl of the
        Limberlost; Let's Go Steady
1946:   Junior Prom (H. Collins); Little Miss Big;
        Slightly Scandalous (D. Mathews)
1948:   Michael O'Halloran
1949:   Black Midnight (C. Johnston)
1956:   Hollywood or Bust (F. Tashlin)
1957:   The Spirit of St. Louis*; Tip on a Dead
        Jockey*

MILTON LAZARUS

1944:   When the Lights Go On Again
1955:   Paris Follies of 1956

WILFORD LEACH

1969:   The Wedding Party*

PAUL EVAN LEAHMAN

1935:   Gunsmoke on the Guadalupe

AGNES BRAND LEAHY

1930:   Only the Brave; The Social Lion (J.
        Mankiewicz)
1931:   Fighting Caravans*; Caught (K. Thompson);
        Beloved Bachelor*

1932: Evenings for Sale (S. Lauren); Forgotten
      Commandments (J. Fagan); Night of June 13*;
      No One Man*; Sky Bride*
1933: The Lone Cowboy (B. Vernon); Hell and High
      Water*; Pick-Up*

NORMAN LEAR (1922-   ) director, producer

1963: Come Blow Your Horn
1967: Divorce American Style
1968: The Night They Raided Minsky's*
1971: Cold Turkey

JOHN LEBAR

1945: Enchanted Forest*

REGINALD LE BORG (1902-   ) director

1950: Young Daniel Boone (C. Johnston); Wyoming
      Mail*
1954: The White Orchid (D. Duncan)

LARRY LE BRON

1976: Dr. Black Mr. Hyde
1979: The Watts Monster

HERBERT J. LEDER

1960: Pretty Boy Floyd
1967: The Frozen Dead; It

CHARLES LEDERER (1910-1976) director

1932: Cock of the Air (R. Sherwood)
1933: Topaze (unc.; B. Hecht)
1937: Double or Nothing*; Mountain Music*
1939: Broadway Serenade; Within the Law (E.
      Fitzgerald)
1940: Comrade X (B. Hecht); His Girl Friday (B.
      Hecht); I Love You Again*

```
1941:   Love Crazy*
1943:   Slightly Dangerous; The Youngest Profession*
1947:   Her Husband's Affairs (B. Hecht); Kiss of
        Death (B. Hecht); Ride the Pink Horse (B.
        Hecht)
1949:   I Was a Male War Bride*
1950:   Wabash Avenue (H. Tugend)
1951:   The Thing*
1952:   Fearless Fagan; Monkey Business*
1953:   Gentlemen Prefer Blondes
1955:   Kismet (L. Davis)
1956:   Gaby*
1957:   Tip on a Dead Jockey*
1959:   Never Steal Anything Small; It Started with
        a Kiss  ·
1960:   Can-Can (D. Kingsley); Ocean's Eleven (H.
        Brown)
1962:   Follow That Dream; Mutiny on the Bounty
1964:   A Global Affair*
```

ALAN S. LEE

```
1965:   The Desert Raven (R. Romen)
```

CARL LEE

```
1964:   The Cool World (S. Clarke)
```

CONNIE LEE

```
1942:   Blondie for Victory (K. DeWolf); Blondie's
        Blessed Event*
1943:   Footlight Glamour (K. DeWolfe); It's a Great
        LIfe (K. DeWolfe); The Daring Young Man (K.
        DeWolf)
1944:   Nine Girls (K. DeWolf)
1945:   Leave It to Blondie; Life with Blondie
1946:   Blondie's Lucky Day
1947:   Blondie's Big Moment; Blondie's Holiday
```

DONALD W. LEE

```
1932:   Partners
```

JAMES LEE

1959: Career
1960: The Adventures of Huckleberry Finn
1968: Banning; Counterpoint (J. Oliansky)
1969: Change of Habit*

LEON LEE

1932: Arm of the Law; The Reckoning

LEONARD LEE

1936: Sinner Take All (W. Wise)
1937: Beg, Borrow or Steal*; Espionage*
1939: Street of Missing Men I(F. Dolan)
1940: Adventure in Diamonds (F. Schulz)
1941: The Chocolate Soldier (K. Winter)
1945: Pursuit to Algiers
1946: Dressed to Kill
1947: Whispering City (R. James)
1950: Wyoming Mail*; Spy Hunt (G. Zuckerman)
1951: The Fat Man (H. Essex); Smuggler's Island
1953: The Glass Web (R. Blees)

LESTER LEE

1930: love at First Sight (C. Levison)

ROBERT E. LEE

1981: First Monday in October (J. Lawrence)

ROBERT N. LEE (also ROBERT LEE JOHNSON)

1930: The Dude Wrangler
1932: Huddle (A. Hyman); 70,000 Witnesses*
1933: Kennel Murder Case (P. Milne)
1934: Dragon Murder Case (F. Herbert); Fog over
       Frisco (E. Solow); Gentlemen Are Born (E.
       Solow)
1935: While the Patient Slept*

```
1936:   Down to the Sea (W. Totman); The Harvester*
1937:   Armored Car (L. Foster); The Hoosier
        Schoolboy
1938:   Tarzan's Revenge (J. Vann)
1939:   The Taming of the West (C. Royal); Tower of
        London
1940:   The Return of Wild Bill (F. Myton); Prairie
        Schooners (F. Myton); Girl from God's
        Country (E. Meehan); Give Us Wings (A.
        Horman)
1941:   Roaring Frontiers; Hit the Road (B.
        Weisberg)
1942:   Bullets for Bandits; Atlantic Convoy; Canal
        Zone; Stand By All Networks
1944:   Sergeant Mike
1945:   Enchanted Forest*; The Man Who Walked Alone
1946:   Two Fisted Stranger
```

ROWLAND V. LEE (1891-1975) director

```
1933:   The Zoo in Budapest*; I Am Suzanne (E.
        Mayer)
1934:   The Count of Monte Cristo*
1935:   The Three Musketeers*
1959:   The Big Fisherman (H. Estabrook)
```

ROBERT LEES

```
1940:   Street of Memories (F. Rinaldo)
1941:   Bachelor Daddy (F. Rinaldo); The Black Cat*;
        Hold that Ghost*; The Invisible Woman*
1942:   Juke Box Jenny*
1943:   Crazy House (F. Rinaldo); Hit the Ice*
1947:   Buck Privates Come Home*
1948:   Abbott and Costello Meet Frankenstein*
1949:   Holiday in Havana*
1951:   Abbott and Costello Meet the Invisible Man*;
        Comin' Round the Mountain (F. Rinaldo)
1952:   Jumping Jacks*
```

LOIS LESSON

```
1928:   Broadway Fever
1929:   Molly and Me
```

GEORGE LEFFERTS

1978:   Mean Dog Blues

ERNEST LEHMAN (1920-   ) director, producer

1954:   Executive Suite; Sabrina (B. Wilder)
1956:   The King and I; Somebody Up There Likes Me
1957:   Sweet Smell of Success (C. Odets)
1959:   North by Northwest
1960:   From the Terrace
1961:   West Side Story
1963:   The Prize
1965:   The Sound of Music
1966:   Who's Afraid of Virginia Woolf?
1969:   Hello, Dolly!
1972:   Portnoy's Complaint
1976:   Family Plot
1977:   Black Sunday*

GLADYS LEHMAN

1929:   Broadway Hoofer; The Fall of Eve; Red Hot
        Speed (M. Taylor)
1930:   A Lady Surrenders; The Little Accident;
        Personality; The Cat Creeps; Embarrassing
        Moments (E. Snell)
1931:   Seed; Many a Slip; Strictly Dishonorable
1932:   Back Street (B. Hecht); Nice Women (E.
        Knopf); They Just Had to Get Married (H. M.
        Walker)
1933:   Hold Me Tight; White Woman*
1934:   Death Takes a Holiday*; Double Door (J.
        Cunningham); Enter Madame (C. Brackett);
        Little Miss Marker*
1935:   The County Chairman (S. Hellman); In Old
        Kentucky (S. Hellman); It's a Small World
        (S. Hellman)
1936:   Captain January*; The Poor Little Rich
        Girl*; Reunion*
1937:   Midnight Madonna (D. Malloy); Slave Ship*
1938:   The Lady Objects; She Married an Artist (D.
        Daves); There's Always a Woman (M. Ryskind)
1939:   Blondie Brings Up Baby (R. Flournoy); Good
        Girls Go to Paris (K. Englund)

```
1940:   Hired Wife (R. Connell)
1941:   Her First Beau (K. DeWolfe); Nice Girl? (R.
        Connell)
1942:   Rio Rita (R. Connell)
1943:   Presenting Lily Mars (R. Connell)
1944:   Two Girls and a Sailor (R. Connell)
1945:   Her Highness and the Bellboy (R. Connell);
        Thrill of a Romance (R. Connell)
1947:   This Time for Keeps
1948:   Luxury Liner (R. Connell)
1951:   Golden Girl*
```

LEW LEHR

```
1934:   Devil Tiger*
```

HENRY LEHRMAN (1886-1946) actor, director

```
1930:   The Poor Millionaire*
1934:   Moulin Rouge (N. Johnson)
1935:   Show Them No Mercy (K. Glasmon)
```

JAMES LEICESTER

```
1957:   The River's Edge (H.J. Smith); Enchanted
        Island (H. J. Smith)
1958:   From the Earth to the Moon (R. Blees)
1961:   Most Dangerous Man Alive (Phillip Rock)
```

WILLIAM LEICESTER

```
1964:   The Last Man on Earth (U.S./Ital.; L.
        Swanson)
```

ROWLAND LEIGH

```
1936:   The Charge of the Light Brigade (M. Jacoby)
1937:   First Lady
1938:   Secrets of an Actress*
1940:   Vigil in the Night*
1944:   Knickerbocker Holiday (D. Boehm); Summer
        Storm (D. Sirk); The Master Race*
1945:   A Song for Miss Julie
```

1947: Heaven Only Knows (ret. Montana Mike; A.
       Arthur)
1948: Siren of Atlantis (R. Lax)

WARREN D. LEIGHT

1980: Mother's Day (C. Kaufman)

TED LEIGHTON

1980: The Hunter (P. Hyams)

ABBEY LEITCH

1973: Sweet Jesus, Preacher Man*

ADELINE LEITZBACH

1929: The House of Secrets

GEORGE LE MAIRE

1928: Blockade; Taxi 13

ALAN LE MAY (1899-   ) novelist

1940: North West Mounted Police*
1942: Reap the Wild Wind*
1944: The Story of Dr. Wassell (Charles Bennett);
       The Adventures of Mark Twain
1945: San Antonio (W. Burnett)
1947: The Gunfighters; Cheyenne (T. Williamson)
1948: Tap Roots
1949: The Walking Hills
1950: The Sundowners; High Lonesome; Rocky
       Mountain (W. Miller)
1951: Quebec
1952: Blackbeard the Pirate; I Dream of Jeanie
1953: Flight Nurse
1955: The Vanishing American

KAY LENARD

```
1954:   Ma and Pa Kettle at Home; Ricochet Romance
1956:   The Kettles in the Ozarks; Navy Wife
```

ISOBEL LENNART (1915-1971)

```
1942:   The Affairs of Martha (L. Gold); Once Upon a
        Thursday
1943:   Lost Angel; A Stranger in Town (W. Kozlenko)
1945:   Anchors Aweigh
1946:   Holiday in Mexico
1947:   It Happened In Brooklyn
1948:   The Kissing Bandit (J. Harding)
1949:   East Side, West Side; Holiday Affair
1950:   A Life of Her Own
1951:   It's a Big Country*
1952:   My Wife's Best Friend; Skirts Ahoy!
1953:   The Girl Next Door; Latin Lovers
1955:   Love Me or Leave Me (D. Fuchs)
1956:   Meet Me in Las Vegas
1957:   This Could Be the Night
1958:   Merry Andrew (I. Diamond); The Inn of the
        Sixth Happiness (Brit.)
1960:   Please Don't Eat the Daisies; The Sundowners
        (Austral.)
1962:   Period of Adjustment; Two for the Seesaw
1967:   Fitzwilly
1968:   Funny Girl
```

THOMAS LENNON

```
1936:   Murder on a Bridle Path*; Second Wife;
        Special Investigator*
1937:   The Man Who Found Himself*; Racing Lady (D.
        Yost)
1938:   The Crowd Roars*; Secrets of a Nurse (L.
        Cole)
1939:   The Spellbinder (J. Fields)
1941:   We Go Fast (Adrian Scott)
1947:   Killer McCoy*
```

MALCOLM LEO

```
1981:   This Is Elvis (A. Solt)
```

MAURICE LEO

1937: Hollywood Hotel*
1938: Going Places*; Hard to Get*; Swing Your Lady
      (J. Schrank)
1940: Flight Angels; The Hit Parade of 1941*
1941: Hello Sucker (P. Smith); They Meet Again (P.
      Milne)
1943: So's Your Uncle (C. Bruckman)
1944: Hat Check Honey (S. Davis)

DAVID LEONARD

1933: Victims of Persecution

ELMORE LEONARD

1970: The Moonshine War
1972: Joe Kidd
1974: Mr. Majestyk

JACK LEONARD

1952: My Man and I (J. Fante)
1953: Cry of the Hunted; Man in the Dark (G.
      Bricker)
1955: The Marauders (E. Felton)
1957: Gun Battle at Monterey (L. Resner)

LEON LEONARD

1949: Omoo-Omoo (George Green)

JOHN LEONE

1978: The Great Smokey Roadblock

ALAN JAY LERNER (1918-   ) playwright

1951: An American in Paris; Royal Wedding
1954: Brigadoon

```
1958:  Gigi
1964:  My Fair Lady
1967:  Camelot
1969:  Paint Your Wagon
1970:  On a Clear Day You Can See Forever
1974:  The Little Prince
```

CARL & GERDA LERNER

```
1964:  Black Like Me
```

ALEEN LESLIE

```
1941:  The Stork Pays Off (F. Foss)
1943:  Henry Aldrich Gets Glamour (E. Blum)
1944:  Rosie, the Riveter (J. Townley); Henry
       Aldrich's Little Secret (V. Burton)
1949:  Father Was a Fullback*
1950:  Father Is a Bachelor (J. E. Grant)
```

BUDD LESSER

```
1950:  Bandit Queen (V. West)
```

NORMAN LESSING

```
1965:  Joy in the Morning*
```

MICHAEL LESSON

```
1982:  Jekyll and Hyde Together Again*
```

ELLIOT LESTER

```
1930:  Rough Romance
```

MARK L. LESTER

```
1973:  Steel Arena
1974:  Truck Stop Women (P. Deason)
1982:  Class of 1984*
```

SEELEG LESTER

1948:   The Checkered Coat (M. Gerard)
1952:   The Winning Team*
1957:   The Iron Sheriff
1968:   Sergeant Ryker (W. D. Gordon)
1969:   Change of Mind (R. Wesson)

OSCAR LEVANT

1934:   Orient Express*

FRANK LEVERING

1982:   Parasite*

JOSEPH LEVERING

1937:   The Rangers Step In (A. Duffy)
1939:   Riders of the Frontier (A. Duffy)

MICHAEL LEVESQUE

1971:   Werewolves on Wheels (D. Kaufman)

SONYA LEVIEN (1895-1960)

1929:   The Younger Generation; Trial Marriage; They
        Had to See Paris*; Frozen Justice; South Sea
        Rose
1930:   Song o' My Heart (T. Barry); So This Is
        London (Owen Davis); Liliom*; Lightnin'
        (S.N. Behrman)
1931:   The Brat (S. N. Behrman); Daddy Long Legs;
        Delicious (G. Bolton); Surrender (S. N.
        Behrman)
1932:   After Tomorrow; Rebecca of Sunnybrook Farm
        (S. N. Behrman); Tess of the Storm Country*
1933:   Berkeley Square (J. Balderston); Cavalcade
        (R. Berkeley); Mr. Skitch (R. Spence); State
        Fair (P. Green); Warrior's Husband*

1934: As Husbands Go (S. N. Behrman); Change of Heart*; The White Parade (E. Pascal)
1935: Beauty's Daughter; Here's to Romance (E. Pascal); Navy Wife
1936: Reunion*; The Country Doctor
1938: The Cowboy and the Lady (S. N. Behrman); Four Men and a Prayer*; In Old Chicago (L. Trotti); Kidnapped*
1939: Drums Along the Mohawk (L. Trotti); The Hunchback of Notre Dame (B. Frank)
1941: Ziegfeld Girl (M. Roberts)
1945: The Valley of Decision (J. Meehan); State Fair (O. Hammerstein II)
1946: The Green Years (R. Ardrey)
1947: Cass Timberlane
1948: Three Daring Daughters*
1951: The Great Caruso (W. Ludwig); Quo Vadis (Ital.)*
1952: The Merry Widow (W. Ludwig)
1954: The Student Prince (W. Ludwig)
1955: Hit the Deck (W. Ludwig); Interrupted Melody (W. Ludwig); Oklahoma! (W. Ludwig)
1956: Bhowani Junction (I. Moffat)
1957: Jeanne Eagels*

MEYER LEVIN

1948: The Illegals (doc.)

JACK LEVINE (see JACK JEVNE)

ALBERT LE VINO

1930: A Man from Wyoming (J. Weaver)
1932: Renegades of the West
1933: After Tonight (J. Murfin)
1934: Keep 'Em Rolling
1942: Tombstone -- the Town Too Tough to Die (E. Paramore)

MARGARET LE VINO

1937: Confession (J. Epstein)

479

BARRY LEVINSON

1976:   Silent Movie*
1977:   High Anxiety*
1979:   ...And Justice for All (V. Curtin)
1980:   Inside Moves (V. Curtin)
1982:   Diner; Best Friends (V. Curtin)

RICHARD LEVINSON

1970:   My Sweet Charlie (W. Link)
1977:   Rollercoaster (W. Link)

CHARLES LEVISON

1930:   Love at First Sight (Lester Lee)

ALBERT LEWIS LEVITT

1948:   The Boy with Green Hair (B. Barzman)
1949:   Mrs. Mike*
1950:   Shakedown (M. Goldsmith)
1951:   My Outlaw Brother (G. Fowler)
1953:   Dream Wife*

GENE LEVITT

1957:   The Night Runner; Beyond Mombasa (R. English)
1958:   Underwater Warrior

HELEN LEVITT

1949:   The Quiet One (doc.)*

KAREN LEVITT

1982:   Time Walker (T. Friedman)

SAUL LEVITT

1967: A Covenant with Death (L. Marcus)
1972: The Trial of the Catonsville Nine (D.
       Berrigan)

BENN W. LEVY

1931: Waterloo Bridge (T. Reed); Woman Pursued (D.
       Anderson)
1932: Devil and the Deep; The Old Dark House
1933: Topaze
1934: Melody in Spring
1935: The Dictator (Brit.); Unfinished Symphony
       (Brit.)

DAVID S. LEVY

1937: Bank Alarm (G. Jay); The Gold Racket

MELVIN LEVY

1935: Robin Hood of Eldorado*
1943: First Comes Courage (L. Meltzer); Hitler's
       Madman*
1944: She's a Soldier Too; Sunday Dinner for a
       Soldier (W. Tuchock)
1946: The Bandit of Sherwood Forest (W. Pettitt);
       The Renegades (F. Faragoh)
1949: Calamity Jane and Sam Bass (M. Geraghty)
1953: The Great Sioux Uprising*
1958: The Cry Baby Killer (Leo Gordon)
1961: Pirates of Tortuga*
1974: Who Fears the Devil (ret. The Legend of
       Hillbilly John)

NEWMAN A. LEVY

1938: The Jury's Secret (L. Cole)

PARKE LEVY

1945: George White's Scandals*; Having Wonderful
       Crime*

481

```
1946:   Earl Carroll's Sketchbook (F. Gill)
1949:   My Friend Irma (C. Howard)
1950:   My Friend Irma Goes West (C. Howard)
```

ALBERT LEWIN (1894-1968) director, producer

```
1928:   The Actress (R. Schayer)
1942:   The Moon and Sixpence
1945:   The Picture of Dorian Gray
1947:   The Private Affairs of Bel Ami
1949:   Oh, You Beautiful Doll (Arthur Lewis)
1951:   Alice in Wonderland (Fr.)*; Call Me Mister
        (B. Styler); Pandora and the Flying Dutchman
        (Brit.)
1953:   Down Among the Sheltering Palms*; Saadia
1957:   The Living Idol
1966:   Boy, Did I Get the Wrong Number!*
1967:   Eight on the Lam*
1968:   The Wicked Dreams of Paula Schultz*
1976:   I Will, I Will...for Now (N. Panama)
```

ROBERT LEWIN

```
1956:  The Bold and the Brave
1962:  Third of a Man
```

ALFRED LEWIS

```
1949:   Ma and Pa Kettle*; Mrs. Mike*
1956:   Our Miss Brooks (J. Quillan)
```

ANDY & DAVE LEWIS

```
1971:   Klute
```

ARTHUR LEWIS

```
1949:   Oh, You Beautiful Doll (Albert Lewin)
1953:   Conquest of Cochise (D. Scott)
```

EDWARD LEWIS

1949: The Lovable Cheat (R. Oswald)
1957: The Careless Years
1977: Brothers (M. Lewis)

GENE LEWIS

1944: Cobra Woman (R. Brooks); Gypsy Wildcat*
1945: Song of the Sarong
1948: Albuquerque (C. Young)
1950: Lonely Hearts Bandits; Woman from
       Headquarters

HERBERT CLYDE LEWIS

1939: Fisherman's Wharf*

HERSCHELL G. LEWIS

1964: Color My Blood Red; Two Thousand Maniacs

JACK LEWIS

1950: Outlaw Gold
1951: King of the Bullwhip (I. Webb)
1960: The Amazing Transparent Man
1964: A Yank in Viet-Nam (J. Wardell)

JERRY LEWIS (1926-   ) actor, comedian, director

1960: The Bellboy
1961: The Ladies' Man (B. Richmond)
1962: The Errand Boy (B. Richmond)
1963: The Nutty Professor (B. Richmond)
1964: The Patsy (B. Richmond)
1965: The Family Jewels
1967: The Big Mouth (B. Richmond)
1981: Hardly Working (M. Janover)

JOHEPH H. LEWIS

1942: Bombs over Burma (G. Milton)

MILDRED LEWIS

1977:   Brothers (E. Lewis)

RICHARD WARREN LEWIS

1971:   The Seven Minutes

THERESE LEWIS

1943:   What a Woman! (B. Trivers)

TOM LEWIS

1951:   Cause for Alarm (M. Dinelli)

VAL LEWTON (1904-1951) novelist, producer (also
        CARLOS KEITH)

1945:   The Body Snatcher (P. MacDonald)
1946:   Bedlam

LEO LIBERMAN

1952:   Bonzo Goes to College

ROBERT LIBOTT

1949:   Flame of Youth*; Law of the Barbary Coast
        (F. Burt); Air Hostess (F. Burt); Barbary
        Pirate (F. Burt)
1950:   Chinatown at Midnight (F. Burt); Fortunes of
        Captain Blood*; State Penitentiary*; Tyrant
        of the Sea (F. Burt)
1951:   Stage to Tucson*; The Groom Wore Spurs*; The
        Lady and the Bandit (F. Burt)
1952:   Captain Pirate*; Last Train from Bombay

RALPH LIDDLE

484

1980: Spirit of the Wind

JOEL LIEBER

1970: Move (Stanley Hart)

JEFF LIEBERMAN

1973: Blade (E. Pintoff)
1976: Squirm
1978: Blue Sunshine

LEO LIEBERMAN

1959: Carnival Rock

MAX LIEF

1942: Sleepytime Gal*

EDWARD C. LILLEY

1935: Sweet Surrender*

ALAN LIN

1951: An American in Paris

MITCH LINDEMANN

1967: The Way West (B. Maddow)

NAT S. LINDEN

1955: Yellowneck

HOWARD LINDSAY

1936: Swing Time (Allan Scott)

1938:   Artists and Models Abroad*

EUGENE LING

1945:   Within These Walls (W. Tuchock)
1946:   It Shouldn't Happen to a Dog (F.
        Gabrielson); Shock
1948:   Assigned to Danger; Behind Locked Doors (M.
        Wald)
1949:   Port of New York
1950:   Between Midnight and Dawn
1952:   Scandal Sheet*
1953:   Mission over Korea*; The Man from Cairo*
1962:   Hand of Death

WILLIAM LINK

1970:   My Sweet Charlie (R. Levinson)
1977:   Rollercoaster (R. Levinson)

WILLIAM R. LIPMAN

1934:   Good Dame*; Little Miss Marker*; Million
        Dollar Ransom (B. Ryan)
1937:   On Such a Night (D. Malloy)
1938:   Dangerous to Know (H. McCoy); Hunted Men (H.
        McCoy); Love Is a Headache*
1939:   Island of Lost Men (H. McCoy); Persons in
        Hiding (H. McCoy); Television Spy*;
        Undercover Doctor (H. McCoy)
1940:   Phantom Raiders; Queen of the Mob (H.
        McCoy); Sky Murder; Women Without Names (H.
        McCoy); Texas Rangers Ride Again (H. McCoy);
        Gallant Sons (M. Parsonnet); Parole Fixer
1942:   Tarzan's New York Adventure (M. Connolly)
1944:   Rationing*; Barbary Coast Gent*
1946:   Bad Bascomb (G. Garrett); The Mighty McGurk*
1948:   Alias a Gentleman

W. P. LIPSCOMB (1887-1958) Brit.

(American films only)
1935:   Cardinal Richelieu*; Clive of India (R.
        Minney); Les Miserables; A Tale of Two

Cities (S. N. Behrman)
1936: The Garden of Allah*; A Message to Garcia
(G. Fowler); Under Two Flags*
1939: The Sun Never Sets
1940: Moon over Burma*
1941: Midnight Angel (L. Cole)
1942: Pacific Blackout (L. Cole)
1943: Forever and a Day*

ROBERT LIPSYTE

1975: That's the Way of the World
1977: Shining Star

LAWRENCE LIPTON

1949: Alimony*

LEW LIPTON

1931: Suicide Fleet; Sweepstakes
1935: It's in the Air*

STEVEN LISBERGER

1982: Tron

BEN LITHMAN

1943: THE UNDERDOG

ROBERT LITTELL

1982: The Amateur (D. Maddox)

HERBERT LITTLE, JR.

1957: Trooper Hook*

SCOTT LITTLETON

```
1930:   The Fourth Alarm
1931:   Sea Devils
1942:   Perils of the Royal Mounted (ser.)*; Lure of
        the Islands*
```

ROBERT LIVELY

```
1934:   Inside Information (B. Laidlaw)
1935:   The Marriage Bargain (B. Laidlaw); St. Louis
        Woman (B. Laidlaw)
1936:   Custer's Last Stand (ser.)*
1937:   The Girl Said No (B. Laidlaw)
1938:   Danger on the Air (B. Laidlaw); Personal
        Secretary*
1939:   The Great Victor Herbert (R. Crouse)
1940:   East Side Kids; Isle of Destiny*
1941:   There's Magic in Music (A. Stone)
```

WILLIAM LIVELY

```
1937:   The Fighting Deputy
1938:   Unashamed
1939:   The Fighting Renegade
1940:   Mercy Plane; That Gang of Mine; The
        Sagebrush Family Trails West; Death Rides
        the Range; Phantom Rancher; Frontier
        Crusader; Boys of the City
1941:   Billy the Kid's Range War; The Lone Rider
        Crosses the Rio; The Lone Rider in Ghost
        Town; The Texas Marshal; King of the Texas
        Rangers (ser.)*; Dick Tracy vs. Crime, Inc.
        (ser.)*; Jungle Girl (ser.)*
1942:   Texas Man Hunt; King of the Mounties
        (ser.)*; Perils of Nyoka (ser.)*; Spy
        Smasher (ser.)*
1943:   Daredevils of the West (ser.)*; Arizona
        Trail; Wagon Tracks West; G-Men vs. the
        Black Dragon (ser.)*
1944:   Marshal of Gunsmoke; Boss of Boomtown; The
        Old Texas Trail
1945:   Both Barrels Blazing
1946:   Gun Town; Days of Buffalo Bill (D.
        Schroeder); Gunman's Code
1948:   Tornado Range; Range Renegades (R. Davidson)
1949:   Ghost of Zorro (ser.)*; Daughter of the
```

Jungle; Federal Agents vs. Underworld, Inc.
(ser.)*; King of the Rocket Men (ser.)*
1950: The James Brothers of Missouri (ser.)*
1951: The Dakota Kid; Arizona Manhunt; Hot Lead
1952: Colorado Sundown (E. Taylor); Trail Guide;
Wild Horse Ambush; Texas Marshal

HAROLD LIVINGSTON

1968: The Hell with Heroes (H. Welles)
1979: Star Trek -- The Motion Picture

E. JAMES LLOYD   (pseud. of TOM LAUGHLIN)

1967: Born Losers

FRANK LLOYD

1931: The Age for Love (E. Pascal)

GERRIT J. LLOYD

1930: Abraham Lincoln (S. V. Benet)
1931: Secret Service (B. Schubert)

ROLLO LLOYD

1932: Prestige*
1935: The Mystery Man (J. Krafft)
1936: I Conquer the Sea (H. Higgin); Revolt of the
Zombies*
1942: Man from Headquarters (J. Krafft)

R. LOCHTE

1979: Escape to Athena (Edward Anhalt)

PETER LOCKE

1971: You've Got to Walk It Like You Talk It or
You'll Lose that Beat

GENE LOCKHART (1891-1957) actor

1943: Forever and a Day*

ALYN LOCKWOOD

1951: Badman's Gold (R. Tansey)

JALE LOCKWOOD

1969: The Female Bunch (B. Nimrod)

BARBARA LODEN

1971: Wanda*

STEPHEN LODGE

1972: The Honkers (S. Ihnat)

JANICE LOEB

1949: The Quiet One (doc.)*

LEE LOEB

1935: Case of the Missing Man (H. Buchman)
1936: Blackmailer*; Don't Gamble with Love (H.
       Buchman); Trapped by Television (H.
       Buchman); Come Closer, Folks (H. Buchman)
1937: Counsel for Crime*; It Can't Last Forever
       (H. Buchman)
1938: The Main Event; Swing That Cheer (C.
       Grayson)
1939: Forged Passport (F. Coen); Hawaiian Nights
       (C. Grayson); Laughing It Off (H. Clork)
1940: Remedy for Riches
1941: Melody for Three (W. Ferris); The Perfect
       Snob (H. Buchman)
1942: A Gentleman at Heart (H. Buchman); It

Happened in Flatbush (H. Buchman)
1943: Dixie Dugan (H. Buchman)
1944: National Barn Dance (H. Fimberg)
1945: Love, Honor and Goodbye*
1947: Calendar Girl*; Seven Keys to Baldpate
1949: Undertow (A. Horman)
1951: Sunny Side of the Street
1953: Abbott and Costello Meet Dr. Jekyll and Mr.
        Hyde (John Grant)
1954: Fireman, Save My Child (John Grant)

FRANK LOESSER (1910-1969) composer, songwriter

1942: Priorities on Parade (A. Arthur)

CHARLES LOGAN

1934: Wagon Wheels*

HELEN LOGAN

1935: Charlie Chan in Egypt (R. Ellis); Happiness
        C.O.D. (R. Ellis); Ladies Love Danger*; The
        Lady in Scarlet (R. Ellis)
1936: Back to Nature (R. Ellis); Charlie Chan at
        the Circus (R. Ellis); Charlie Chan at the
        Race Track*; Here Comes Trouble*; Hitch Hike
        to Heaven (R. Ellis); Charlie Chan's
        Secret*
1937: The Jones Family in Big Business (R. Ellis);
        Born Reckless*; Charlie Chan at the Olympics
        (R. Ellis); Laughing at Trouble (R. Ellis);
        Off to the Races (R. Ellis); Red Lights
        Ahead (R. Ellis); Big Town Girl*
1938: Down on the Farm (R. Ellis); Love on a
        Budget (R. Ellis); Rascals (R. Ellis); Speed
        to Burn (R. Ellis); Road Demon (R. Ellis);
        Sharpshooters (R. Ellis); A Trip to Paris
        (R. Ellis)
1939: Susannah of the Mounties*; Chasing Danger
        (R. Ellis); Charlie Chan in City in Darkness
        (R. Ellis); The Escape (R. Ellis); Too Busy
        to Work*; Pardon Our Nerve (R. Ellis)
1940: The Man Who Wouldn't Talk*; Lucky Cisco Kid
        (R. Ellis); Star Dust (R. Ellis); Tin Pan

Alley (R. Ellis)
1941: The Great American Broadcast*; Sun Valley
       Serenade (R. Ellis)
1942: Footlight Serenade*; Iceland (R. Ellis);
       Song of the Islands*
1943: Hello, Frisco, Hello*
1944: Four Jills in a Jeep*; Pin-Up Girl*;
       Something for the Boys*
1946: Do You Love Me? (R. Ellis); If I'm Lucky*

JOSHUA LOGAN (1908-   ) director, playwright

1955: Mister Roberts (F. Nugent)
1964: Ensign Pulver (P. Feibleman)

CHARLES LOGUE

1931: The Deceiver (J. Cunningham)
1932: The Menace (D. Howell)
1933: Black Beauty
1934: Embarrassing Moments (G. Unger); Sing Sing
       Nights (M. Orth); Ticket to a Crime
1935: Home on the Range*; The Hoosier
       Schoolmaster; Make a Million
1936: Conflict (W. Weems)
1937: Renfrew of the Mounted; The Wildcatter
1938: Crime Takes a Holiday*

U. LOMMEL

1979: Cocaine Cowboys*

HAL LONG

1933: Blood Money (R. Brown)
1935: Folies Bergere (B Meredyth)
1936: White Fang (S. Duncan)
1937: Nancy Steele Is Missing (G. Fowler)
1940: Viva Cisco Kid (S. Engel)
1941: That Night in Rio*

LOUISE LONG

1933:   The Zoo in Budapest*

RICHARD LONG

1944:   Sweethearts of the U.S.A.*

SUMNER ARTHUR LONG

1965:   Never Too Late

STEPHEN LONGSTREET

1945:   The Strange Affair of Uncle Harry (alt.
        Uncle Harry)
1946:   The Jolson Story*
1947:   Stallion Road
1948:   Silver River (H. Frank)
1956:   The First Traveling Saleslady (D. Freeman)
1957:   The Helen Morgan Story*
1958:   Outcasts of the City
1962:   Rider on a Dead Horse

FREDERICK LONSDALE

1930:   The Devil to Pay (B. Glazer)
1932:   Lovers Courageous
1943:   Forever and a Day*

ANITA LOOS (1893-   ) novelist, playwright

1931:   The Struggle*
1932:   Red Headed Woman
1933:   The Barbarian (E. Harris); Hold Your Man (H.
        Rogers)
1934:   Biography of a Bachelor Girl (H. Jackson);
        The Girl from Missouri (J. Emerson)
1935:   Riffraff*
1936:   San Francisco
1937:   Mama Steps Out; Saratoga (R. Hopkins)
1939:   The Women*
1940:   Susan and God
1941:   Blossoms in the Dust; They Met in Bombay*;
        When Ladies Meet (S. Lauren)

```
1942:    I Married an Angel
1949:    Father Was a Fullback*


MARY LOOS

1946:    Rendezvous with Annie (R. Sale)
1947:    Calendar Girl*; Driftwood (R. Sale); Hit
         Parade of 1947
1948:    The Dude Goes West (R. Sale); The Inside
         Story (R. Sale)
1949:    Mother Is a Freshman (R. Sale); Mr.
         Belvedere Goes to College*
1950:    When Willie Comes Marching Home (R. Sale);
         Ticket to Tomahawk (R. Sale); I'll Get By
         (R. Sale)
1951:    Meet Me After the Show (R. Sale)
1953:    Let's Do It Again (R. Sale)
1954:    The French Line (R. Sale); Woman's World*
1955:    Gentlemen Marry Brunettes (R. Sale)


INEZ LOPEZ

1935:    The Virginia Judge*


DAVID LORD

1957:    Johnny Trouble (C. O'Neal)


MINDRET LORD

1946:    The Glass Alibi; Strange Impersonation
1955:    The Virgin Queen (H. Brown)


PHILLIPS H. LORD

1955:    Gang-Busters


ROBERT LORD (1902-1976) producer

1928:    Beware of Bachelors; Lion and the Mouse; On
         Trial (Max Pollack); Women They Talk About
1929:    Hardboiled Rose; Kid Gloves; No Defense; On
```

494

with the Show; The Time the Place and the
Girl; Gold Diggers of Broadway; So Long
Letty (A. Caesar); The Million Dollar
Collar; The Sap
1930: The Aviator; Hold Everything; She Couldn't
Say No (A. Caesar)
1931: Big Business Girl; The Finger Points*; Her
Majesty, Love (A. Caesar); Local Boy Makes
Good; The Reckless Hour (F. Ryerson); The
Ruling Voice; Upper Underworld (B. Morgan)
1932: The Conquerors; Fireman, Save My Child*;
It's Tough to Be Famous; Manhattan Parade
(H. Branch); Purchase Price; You Said a
Mouthful (B. Mallory)
1933: Convention City; Frisco Jenny (W. Mizner);
Hard to Handle (W. Mizner); Heroes for Sale
(W. Mizner); The Little Giant (W. Mizner);
The Mind Reader (W. Mizner); 20,000 Years in
Sing Sing (C. Terrett)
1934: Merry Wives of Reno (D. Holmes); Dames (D.
Daves)
1935: Dr. Socrates (M. McCall); Page Miss Glory
(D. Daves)

STEPHEN LORD

1968: Tarzan and the Jungle Boy
1978: Beyond and Back
1979: The Bermuda Triangle; The Fall of the House
of Usher

PARE LORENTZ (1905-   ) filmmaker

1937: The River (doc.)
1940: The Fight for Life (doc.)

HOPE LORING

1931: Father's Son

JANE LORING

1929: Paris
1933: White Woman*

JOHN LORING

1961:   Gorgo (D. Hyatt)
1969:   Kenner (H. Clemens)

RAY LORING

1971:   Wanda*

JOSEPH LOSEY (1909-   ) director

1951:   The Big Night*
1975:   Galileo (Barbara Bray)
1978:   The Roads to the South*
1979:   Don Giovanni*
1982:   The Trout (Monique Lange)

PATRICIA LOSEY

1978:   The Roads to the South*
1979:   Don Giovanni*

CHARLIE LOVENTHAL

1982:   The First Time*

OTHO LOVERING

1942:   Lady in a Jam*

JOSEPHINE LOVETT

1929:   Our Modern Maidens
1931:   Corsair; Road to Reno
1932:   Hot Saturday*; Madame Butterfly (J. March);
        Thunder Below (S. Buchman); Tomorrow and
        Tomorrow
1933:   Jennie Gerhardt*
1934:   Two Alone (J. March)
1935:   Captain Hurricane (S. W. Bassett)

EUGENE LOURIE (1905-   ) art director, director

1958:   Revolt in the Big House (D. Hyatt)
1959:   The Giant Behemoth (Brit.)

EDWARD T. LOWE (1890-1973)

1928:   State Street Sadie; Tenderloin (J. Jackson)
1929:   The Little Wildcat; The Mississippi Gambler;
         One Stolen Night; Stolen Kisses
1930:   The King of Jazz; Night Ride
1932:   Alias Mary Smith; The Crusader; Discarded
         Lovers (A. Hoyle); Escapade; Forbidden
         Company; Hearts of Humanity; Midnight Lady;
         Probation; Red-Haired Alibi; Shop Angel;
         Tangled Destinies; The Thrill of Youth;
         Unwritten Law
1933:   Sing, Sinner, Sing; The Vampire Bat; The
         World Gone Mad
1934:   Curtain at Eight; Three on a Honeymoon*
1935:   Charlie Chan in Paris (S. Anthony); Charlie
         Chan in Shanghai (G. Fairlie)
1936:   Charlie Chan at the Race Track*; Educating
         Father*
1937:   Bulldog Drummond Comes Back; Bulldog
         Drummond Escapes; Bulldog Drummond's
         Revenge; Wild Money*
1941:   Public Enemies (L. Kimble); Scattergood
         Baines (M. Simmons)
1942:   The Girl from Alaska (R. Case); A Man's
         World (Jack Roberts); Sherlock Holmes and
         the Secret Weapon*
1943:   Minesweeper (M. Shane); Tarzan's Desert
         Mystery
1944:   Timber Queen (M. Shane)
1945:   House of Dracula; House of Frankenstein;
         Rough, Tough and Ready

SHERMAN L. LOWE

1932:   The Diamond Trail (H. Fraser)
1934:   The Law of the Wild (ser.)*; Burn 'Em Up
         Barnes (ser.)*
1935:   Melody Trail; Circus Shadows; On Probation;

497

```
              Fighting Marines (ser.; B. Sarecky)
1936:   The Old Corral (J. Poland); Night Cargo;
        With Love and Kisses
1937:   Arizona Days; Galloping Dynamite*; Headline
        Crasher (H. Hoyt); Sing While You're Able
        (C. Condon); Tough to Handle (J. Neville);
        Jungle Menace (ser.)*; Valley of Terror (J.
        Neville)
1938:   The Daredevil Drivers; I Demand Payment;
        Mystery House (R. White)
1939:   Crashing Thru; Everything's on Ice (A.
        Landis)
1940:   Secrets of a Model (A. St. Clair); Flying
        G-Men (ser.)*; West of Carson City*; Ragtime
        Cowboy Joe; Law and Order (N. McLeod); Pony
        Post; The Green Hornet Strikes Again (ser.)*
1941:   Bury Me Not on the Lone Prairie (V. McLeod);
        Riders of Death Valley (ser.)*; The Masked
        Rider (V. McLeod); Arizona Cyclone; Law of
        the Range
1942:   A Yank in Libya (A. St. Clair); The Yanks
        Are Coming (A. St. Clair); King of the
        Stallions (A. St. Clair); Little Joe the
        Wrangler (E. Beecher); A Night for Crime (A.
        St. Clair)
1943:   Miss V from Moscow (A. St. Clair); The
        Phantom (ser.)*
1944:   Black Arrow (ser.)*; Sweethearts of the
        U.S.A.*; The Desert Hawk (ser.)*
1945:   The Monster and the Ape (ser.)*
1946:   The Undercover Woman (J. Sackheim); The
        Desert Horseman; The Catman of Paris; The
        Invisible Informer
1949:   Alimony*; Parole, Inc.
1950:   The Kangaroo Kid
1951:   Captain Video (ser.)*; Roar of the Iron
        Horse (ser.)*
1952:   Blackhawk (ser.)*
1953:   Eyes of the Jungle (B. Shipman)
```

JAN & MARK LOWELL

```
1958:   High School Hellcats
1959:   The Diary of a High School Bride*
```

STANLEY LOWENSTEIN

1937:   Anything for a Thrill (J. O'Donnell)

MILTON LUBAN

1949:   Grand Canyon (J. Harvey); Tough Assignment

ERNST LUBITSCH (1892-1947) director   Germ.

(American films only)
1932:   If I Had a Million*

GEORGE LUCAS (1945-   ) director

1971:   THX 1138 (W. Murch)
1973:   American Graffiti*
1977:   Star Wars

JOHN MEREDYTH LUCAS

1951:   Peking Express; Red Mountain*
1952:   Captain Pirate*
1953:   Tumbleweed
1956:   The Scarlet Hour*

RALPH LUCAS

1977:   The Child
1980:   Planet of Dinosaurs

FELIPE LUCIANO

1971:   Right On!*

ALAN LUDWIG

1932:   Wyoming Whirlwind

EDWARD LUDWIG (1899-   ) director

1952:   Caribbean (F. Moss)

JERRY LUDWIG

1968:   Fade-In
1974:   Three the Hard Way (E. Bercovici)
1975:   Take a Hard Ride (E. Bercovici)

WILLIAM LUDWIG (1912-   )

1938:   Love Finds Andy Hardy; Out West with the
        Hardys
1939:   Blackmail (D. Hertz); The Hardys Ride High*;
        Stronger than Desire (D. Hertz)
1941:   Love Crazy*
1942:   Journey for Margaret (D. Hertz)
1944:   An American Romance (H. Dalmas); Andy
        Hardy's Blonde Trouble*
1946:   Boys' Ranch; Love Laughs at Andy Hardy (H.
        Ruskin)
1948:   Hills of Home; Julia Misbehaves*
1949:   Challenge to Lassie; The Sun Comes Up (M.
        Fitts)
1950:   Shadow on the Wall
1951:   The Great Caruso (S. Levien); It's a Big
        Country*
1952:   The Merry Widow (S. Levien)
1954:   The Student Prince (S. Levien); Athena
1955:   Hit the Deck (S. Levien); Interrupted Melody
        (S. Levien); Oklahoma! (S. Levien)
1957:   Ten Thousand Bedrooms*; Gun Glory
1961:   Back Street (E. Griffin)

KURT LUEDTKE

1981:   Absence of Malice

FELIX LUETZKENDORF

1955:   They Were So Young (K. Neumann)

HERBERT G. LUFT

500

1958:   Hong Kong Affair*

NICK LUKATS

1942:   The Spirit of Stanford*

SIDNEY LUMET (1924-   ) director

1981:   Prince of the City (J. P. Allen)

VICTOR LUNDIN

1976:   Super Seal (Joshua Smith)

IDA LUPINO (1918-   ) actress, director

1949:   Not Wanted (P. Jarrico)
1950:   Never Fear (Collier Young); Outrage*
1953:   The Hitch Hiker
1954:   Private Hell 36 (Collier Young)

TONY LURASCHI

1980:   The Outsider

ALLAN LURIE

1961:   Then There Were Three (F. Gregory)

DANE LUSSIER

1943:   Ladies' Day (C. Roberts); Mexican Spitfire's
        Blessed Event (C. Roberts); Mystery
        Broadcast
1944:   The Lady and the Monster (F. Kohner); The
        Port of Forty Thieves
1945:   A Sporting Chance; Three's a Crowd
1946:   Dick Tracy vs. Cueball (R. Kent); The
        Magnificent Rogue; Smooth as Silk (K. Shaw)
1947:   The Pilgrim Lady
1948:   Family Honeymoon

1949: My Dream Is Yours (H. Kurnitz)
1952: The First Time*
1953: The Lady Wants Mink (R. Simmons); It Happens
       Every Thursday

SAM LUSTIG

1942: Reunion in France*
1944: The White Cliffs of Dover*
1949: That Forsyte Woman*
1953: The Story of Three Loves*; Young Bess (A.
       Wimperis); Knights of the Round Table*;
       Torch Song (J.M. Hayes)
1955: Moonfleet (M. Fitts)
1961: Town Without Pity (Germ.)

LOU LUSTIG

1940: Wildcat Bus

TONY LUZZARINO

1961: X-15 (J. Bellah)

DAVID LYNCH

1977: Eraserhead

JOHN LYNCH

1931: Cuban Love Song (B. Meredyth)

ROLAND LYNCH

1940: The Cowboy from Sundown (R. Tansey); The
       Golden Trail*; Rainbow over the Range*

PAUL LYNDE (1926-   ) actor

1954: New Faces*

BARRE LYNDON (1896-1972) (also ALFRED EDGAR)
        playwright   Brit.

1941:   Sundown (C. Booth)
1944:   The Lodger
1945:   Hangover Square; The House on 92nd Street*
1948:   Night Has a Thousand Eyes (J. Latimer)
1950:   To Please a Lady (M. Decker)
1952:   The Greatest Show on Earth*
1953:   The War of the Worlds
1954:   Man in the Attic (Robert Presnell); Sign of
        the Pagan (O. Brodney)
1957:   Omar Khayyam
1961:   The Little Shepherd of Kingdom Come
1965:   Dark Intruder

GREY LYNELLE

1975:   The Brass Ring

HENRY LYNN

1939:   Mother of Today (Yid.)

HILARY LYNN

1940:   The Great Profile (M. Sperling)
1943:   Where Are Your Children? (G. Milton)

JEFFREY LYNN

1958:   Lost Lagoon (M. Subotsky)

KANE LYNN

1971:   Brain of Blood (Joe Rogers)

EARLE LYON

1978:   The Astral Factor (A. Pierce)

ALEV LYTLE

1980:   Tell Me a Riddle (J. Eliason)

BART LYTTON

1942:   Tomorrow We Live
1943:   Spy Train*
1944:   Bowery to Broadway*

CHARLES MacARTHUR (1895-1956) director, playwright

1930:   Way for a Sailor (L. Stallings); Billy the
        Kid*
1931:   New Adventures of Get Rich Quick
        Wallingford; Paid (L. Hubbard); Sin of
        Madelon Claudet; The Unholy Garden (B.
        Hecht)
1932:   Rasputin and the Empress
1934:   Crime Without Passion (B. Hecht); Twentieth
        Century (B. Hecht)
1935:   Once in a Blue Moon (B. Hecht); The
        Scroundrel (B. Hecht); Barbary Coast*
1936:   Soak the Rich (B. Hecht)
1939:   Gunga Din*; Wuthering Heights (B. Hecht)
1947:   The Senator Was Indiscreet
1948:   Lulu Belle (E. Freeman)

RICHARD MACAULAY

1936:   Earthworm Tractors*
1937:   Hollywood Hotel*; Riding on Air (R.
        Flourney); Varsity Show*
1938:   Brother Rat (J. Wald); Garden of the Moon
        (J. Wald); Hard to Get*
1939:   The Kid from Kokomo (J. Wald); Naughty but
        Nice (J. Wald); On Your Toes (J. Wald); The
        Roaring Twenties*
1940:   Brother Rat and a Baby*; They Drive by Night
        (J. Wald); Three Cheers for the Irish (J.
        Wald); Torrid Zone (J. Wald)
1941:   Manpower (J. Wald); Million Dollar Baby*;
        Navy Blues*; Out of the Fog*
1942:   Across the Pacific; Captain of the Clouds*
1943:   Hello, Frisco, Hello*
1944:   Tampico*
1946:   Young Widow (M. Wilder)

1947:   Born to Kill (E. Greene)

PHILLIP MacDONALD

1934:   Charlie Chan in London; Mystery of Mr. X*
1935:   The Last Outpost*; Mystery Woman
1936:   Yours for the Asking*
1938:   Mysterious Mr. Moto (N. Foster)
1939:   Blind Alley*; Mr. Moto Takes a Vacation (N.
         Foster); Mr. Moto's Last Warning (N. Foster)
1944:   Action in Arabia (H.J. Biberman)
1945:   The Body Snatcher (C. Keith)
1947:   Love from a Stranger
1948:   The Dark Past*
1950:   The Man Who Cheated Himself (S. Miller)
1951:   Circle of Danger (Brit.)
1954:   Ring of Fear*; Tobor, the Great

WALLACE MacDONALD

1936:   Doughnuts and Society*

RANALD MacDOUGALL (1915-1973)

1945:   Objective Burma (L. Cole); Mildred Pierce
         (C. Turney)
1947:   Possessed (S. Richards); The Unsuspected (B.
         Meredyth)
1948:   The Decision of Christopher Blake; June
         Bride
1949:   The Hasty Heart
1950:   The Breaking Point; Bright Leaf
1951:   I'll Never Forget You (Brit.); Mr. Belvedere
         Rings the Bell
1954:   The Naked Jungle*; Secret of the Incas (S.
         Boehm)
1955:   Queen Bee; We're No Angels
1956:   The Mountain
1957:   Man on Fire
1959:   The World, the Flesh and the Devil
1961:   Go Naked in the World
1963:   Cleopatra*
1970:   The Cockeyed Cowboys of Callico County

ROGER MacDOUGALL

1953:   The Gentle Gunman

HAMILTON MacFADDEN (1901-   ) director

1930:   Crazy That Way (M. Orth)
1933:   Second Hand Wife
1935:   Fighting Youth*
1937:   Sea Racketeers
1939:   The Honeymoon's Over*

LOVELLA MacFARLANE

1947:   The Guilt of Janet Ames*
1948:   The Mating of Millie (S. McKelway)
1951:   Stop That Cab (W. Abbott)

JACK MacGOWAN

1933:   Sitting Pretty*
1935:   Broadway Melody of 1936*
1936:   Born to Dance (S. Silver)
1939:   Babes in Arms (K. Van Riper)
1940:   Little Nellie Kelly
1941:   Lady Be Good*
1942:   Panama Hattie (W. Mahoney)

ROBERT MacGOWAN

1947:   Gas House Kids Go West*

ROBERT MacGUNIGLE

1941:   Whistling in the Dark*

GUSTAV MACHATY (1901-1963) director   Czech

(American films only)
1945:   Jealousy (Arnold Phillips)

507

J.B. MACK

1928:   The Big Hop

RICHARD MACK

1939:   Charlie McCarthy, Detective*; You Can't
        Cheat an Honest Man*

RUSSELL MACK (1892-   )

1934:   Meanest Gal in Town*

WILLARD MACK (-1934)

1929:   His Glorious Night; Madame X; The Voice of
        the City
1931:   Reducing (B. Banyard); Sporting Blood (W.
        Tuchock)
1933:   Broadway to Hollywood (E. Woolf); Song of
        the Eagle (C. Robinson); Strictly Personal
        (B. Banyard); What Price Innocence?
1934:   Nana (H. Gribble)

LAWTON MACKALL

1932:   If I Had a Million*

AENEAS MacKENZIE

1939:   Juarez*; The Private Lives of Elizabeth and
        Essex (N. Raine)
1942:   The Navy Comes Through*
1943:   The Woman of the Town
1944:   Buffalo Bill*; The Fighting Seabees (B.
        Chase)
1949:   Reign of Terror (alt. The Black Book; P.
        Yordan)
1950:   The Avengers (Arg.; L.Kimble)
1951:   Captain Horatio Hornblower*; The Thief Who
        Was a Thief (G. Adams)
1952:   Against All Flags (J. Hoffman); Face to Face
        (J. Agee)

1956:   The Ten Commandments*
1967:   The King's Pirate*

JACK MacKENZIE

1935:   Another Face

MARY MACKEY

1974:   Silence

ALLEN MacKINNON

1954:   The Saint's Girl Friday
1957:   Time Is My Enemy

SHIRLEY MacLAINE (1934-   ) actress

1975:   The Other Half of the Sky: A China Memoir
        (doc.; C. Weill)

BARTON MacLANE (1902-1969) actor

1943:   Man of Courage

ALISTAIR MacLEAN

1976:   Breakheart Pass

DOUGLAS MacLEAN (1890-1967) actor, producer

1931: Cracked Nuts (A. Boasberg); Full of Notions;
        Laugh and Get Rich (G. La Cava); Caught
        Plastered (R. Spence)

AENEAS MacMAHON

1942:   They Died with Their Boots On (W. Klein)

ANGUS MacPHAIL

1940:   Haunted Honeymoon*
1956:   The Man Who Knew Too Much (J. M. Hayes)
1957:   The Wrong Man (M. Anderson)

JEANIE MACPHERSON (1884-1946) actress

1929:   The Godless Girl; Dynamite
1930:   Madam Satan
1933:   The Devil's Brother
1938:   The Buccaneer*

EARL MacRAUCH

1977:   New York, New York (M. Martin)
1982:   A Stranger Is Watching (Victor Miller)

ROBERT MADARIS

1976:   The Jaws of Death

M. STUART MADDEN

1973:   Sweet Jesus, Preacher Man*

BEN MADDOW (also DAVID WOLFF) director

1942:   Native Land (doc.)*
1947:   Framed
1948:   The Man from Colorado (R. D. Andrews)
1949:   Intruder in the Dust
1950:   The Asphalt Jungle (J. Huston)
1951:   Shadow in the Sky
1953:   The Stairs
1954:   Johnny Guitar (unc.; P. Yordan); The Naked
        Jungle (unc.)*
1957:   Men in War (unc.; P. Yordan)
1958:   God's Little Acre (unc.; P. Yordan)
1960:   The Unforgiven; The Savage Eye
1961:   Two Loves
1963:   The Balcony; An Affair of the Skin
1967:   The Way West (M. Lindemann)

1969:   The Chairman; The Secret of Santa Vittoria
        (W. Rose)
1970:   Storm of Strangers
1971:   The Mephisto Waltz

DIANA MADDOX

1982:   The Amateur (R. Littell)

DANIEL MADISON

1960:   Valley of the Redwoods (Leo Gordon)

KERRY MAGNUS

1974:   Night of the Cobra Woman (A. Meyer)

JOHN LEE MAHIN (1902-   )

1932:   Beast of the City; Red Dust; Scarface*; The
        Wet Parade (J. Meehan)
1933:   Bombshell (J. Furthman); Eskimo; The
        Prizefighter and the Lady*; Hell Below
1934:   Chained; Laughing Boy (J. Colton); Treasure
        Island
1935:   Naughty Marietta*
1936:   The Devil Is a Sissy (R. Schayer); Love on
        the Run*; Small Town Girl (E. Fitzgerald);
        Wife Versus Secretary*
1937:   Captains Courageous*; The Last Gangster; A
        Star Is Born (unc.)*
1938:   Too Hot to Handle (L. Stallings)
1940:   Boom Town
1941:   Dr. Jekyll and Mr. Hyde; Johnny Eager (James
        Grant)
1942:   Tortilla Flat (B. Glazer)
1943:   The Adventures of Tartu (Brit.)*
1949:   Down to the Sea in Ships (S. Bartlett)
1950:   Love That Brute*
1951:   Quo Vadis (Ital.)*; Show Boat
1953   Mogambo
1954:   Elephant Walk
1955:   Lucy Gallant (W. Miller)
1956:   The Bad Seed

```
1957:   Heaven Knows, Mr. Allison (J. Huston)
1958:   No Time for Sergeants
1959:   The Horse Soldiers (M. Rackin)
1960:   North to Alaska*
1962:   The Spiral Road (N. Paterson)
1966:   Moment to Moment
```

ANTHONY MAHON

```
1976:   The Premonition*
```

JOHN MAHON

```
1973:   Brother of the Wind (J. Champion)
```

RICHARD MAHONEY

```
1965:   House of the Black Death
```

WILKIE C. MAHONEY

```
1939:   Some Like It Hot (L. Foster)
1942:   Panama Hattie (J. MacGowan)
1944:   Abroad with Two Yanks*
1945:   Brewster's Millions*
```

RICHARD MAIBAUM (1909-   ) producer

```
1936:   We Went to College (M. Rapf)
1937:   Live, Love and Learn*; They Gave Him a Gun*;
        The Bad Men of Brimstone (C. Hume)
1938:   Stablemates (L. Praskins)
1939:   The Amazing Mr. Williams*; Coast Guard*; the
        Lady and the Mob (G. Purcell)
1940:   20 Mule Team*; The Ghost Goes Home (H.
        Ruskin)
1941:   I Wanted Wings*
1942:   Ten Gentlemen from West Point
1946:   O.S.S.
1949:   The Great Gatsby (C. Hume); Song of
        Surrender
1954:   The Paratrooper (F. Nugent)
1956:   Bigger Than Life (C. Hume); The Cockleshell
```

                    Heroes (B. Forbes); Ransom (C. Hume)
1957:   Zarak
1958:   Tank Force (T. Young)
1960:   Killers of Kilimanjaro *
1961:   Battle at Bloody Beach (W. Willingham)
1963:   Dr. No*
1964:   From Russia with Love; Goldfinger (P. Dehm)
1965:   Thunderball (John Hopkins)
1969:   On Her Majesty's Secret Service
1971:   Diamonds Are Forever (T. Mankiewicz)
1974:   The Man with the Golden Gun
1977:   The Spy Who Loved Me (Christopher Wood)
1981:   For Your Eyes Only

CECIL MAIDEN

1955:   Cult of the Cobra*

F. X. MAIER

1975:   Switchblade Sisters

NORMAN MAILER (1923-   ) novelist, filmmaker

1968:   Wild 90; Beyond the Law
1969:   Maidstone

CHARLES ERIC MAINE

1960:   The Electronic Monster

DANIEL MAINWARING (see GEOFFREY HOMES)

JULES MAITLAND

1960:   Justice and Caryl Chessman (doc.)

DAVID MALCOLM

1965:   Beach Ball; The Girls on the Beach
1966:   Wild Wild Winter

TERENCE MALICK (1945-   ) director

1972:   Pocket Money
1974:   Badlands
1978:   Days of Heaven

GEORGE MALKO

1981:   The Dogs of War (G. DeVore)

BOLTON MALLORY

1932:   You Said a Mouthful (R. Lord)

DORIS MALLOY

1931:   Mad Parade*
1932:   Amateur Daddy (F. Dolan)
1933:   Bondage (A. Kober)
1934:   Gambling Lady (R. Block); I Am a Thief (R.
        Block)
1935:   Diamond Jim*; His Night Out (H. Clork); King
        Solomon of Broadway*; Mister Dynamite (H.
        Clork); Princess O'Hara (H. Clork); Remember
        Last Night*
1936:   Human Cargo (J. Parker); Too Many Parents
        (V. Van Upp); Two in a Crowd*
1937:   Midnight Madonna (G. Lehman); On Such a
        Night (W. Lipman); Outcast (D. Schary)
1938:   Love on Toast*
1939:   Mickey, the Kid (G. Kahn)
1940:   Nobody's Children
1941:   Ridin' on a Rainbow (B. Ropes)
1942:   Stand By All Networks*
1943:   Corregidor (E. Ulmer); Hitler's Madman*; My
        Son, the Hero (E. Ulmer)

JOEL MALONE

1944:   Crime by Night (R. Weil)
1949:   Arctic Manhunt (O. Brodney); Illegal Entry
1950:   South Sea Sinner*

1952:   Just Across the Street (R. Rogers)

MIKE MALTESE

1979:   The Bugs Bunny/Road-Runner Movie (anim.;
        Chuck Jones)

ALBERT MALTZ (1908-   ) novelist, playwright

1942:   This Gun for Hire (W. Burnett)
1943:   Destination Tokyo (D. Daves); Seeds of
        Freedom (doc.)
1944:   The Man in Half Moon Street
1945:   Pride of the Marines (D. Daves); Cloak and
        Dagger (R. Lardner)
1948:   The Naked City (M. Wald)
1953:   The Robe (unc.)*
1970:   Two Mules for Sister Sara
1971:   The Beguiled (unc.)
1973:   Scalawag (S. Fleishman)

DAVID MAMET

1981:   The Postman Always Rings Twice
1982:   The Verdict

PAUL MANASH

1973:   The Friends of Eddie Coyle

DAVID MANBER

1969:   Hail, Hero!

ALAN MANDEL

1977:   Smokey and the Bandit
1978:   House Calls*; Goin' South*

BABALOO MANDEL

1982:   Night Shift (L. Ganz)

FRANK MANDEL

1930:   Queen High

LORING MANDEL

1968:   Countdown
1979:   Promises in the Dark

ALBERT MANHEIMER

1939:   Dancing Co-Ed; The Kid from Texas*

DON M. MANKIEWICZ

1955:   Trial
1957:   House of Numbers (R. Rouse)
1958:   I Want to Live! (N. Gidding)
1962:   The Chapman Report (W. Cooper)

HERMAN J. MANKIEWICZ (1897-1953)

1929:   Men Are Like That*; The Dummy
1930:   The Vagabond King; Honey; Ladies Love
        Brutes; Royal Family of Broadway (G.
        Purcell)
1931:   Ladies' Man*; Man of the World
1932:   Dancers in the Dark*; Girl Crazy (T.
        Whelan); The Lost Squadron (W. Smith)
1933:   Another Language (G. Purcell); Dinner at
        Eight (G. Marion)
1934:   The Show-Off (G. Wells); Stamboul Quest
1935:   After Office Hours; Escapade; It's in the
        Air (unc.)*
1937:   John Meade's Woman (V. Lawrence); My Dear
        Miss Aldrich; The Emperor's Candlesticks
        (unc.)*
1938:   The Show Goes On (Brit.)
1941:   Citizen Kane (O. Welles); Rise and Shine
1942:   The Pride of the Yankees (J. Swerling);
        Stand By for Action*

516

1944: Christmas Holiday
1945: The Spanish Main (G. Yates); The Enchanted
      Cottage*
1949: A Woman's Secret
1952: The Pride of St. Louis

JOSEPH L. MANKIEWICZ (1909-   ) director, producer

1930: The Social Lion (A. Leahy); Only Saps Work*;
      Slightly Scarlet*; Sap from Sycracuse
      (Unc.)*; Paramount on Parade (unc.)
1931: June Moon (K. Thompson); Newly Rich*; Skippy
      (N. McLeod); Sooky (N. McLeod); Dude Ranch
      (unc.)*; Forbidden Adventure*; Touchdown
      (unc.)*
1932: If I Had a Million*; Sky Bride*; This
      Reckless Age; Million Dollar Legs*
1933: Alice in Wonderland (W. Menzies); Emergency
      Call (J. Clymer); Diplomaniacs*; Too Much
      Harmony*
1934: Forsaking All Others; Manhattan Melodrama
      (O. Garrett); Our Daily Bread*
1935: I Live My Life*
1944: Keys of the Kingdom (N. Johnson)
1945: The Enchanted Cottage*
1946: Dragonwyck; Somewhere in the Night (H.
      Dimsdale)
1948: A Letter to Three Wives
1950: All About Eve; No Way Out (C. Samuels)
1951: People Will Talk; Julius Caesar
1954: The Barefoot Contessa
1955: Guys and Dolls
1958: The Quiet American
1959: Suddenly, Last Summer*
1963: Cleopatra*
1967: The Honey Pot
1970: There Was a Crooked Man*
1972: Sleuth

TOM MANKIEWICZ

1968: The Sweet Ride
1976: Mother, Juggs and Speed
1977: The Cassandra Crossing*; The Eagle Has
      Landed

AARON MANN

1976:   Everyday*

ABBY MANN (1927-   )

1961:   Judgment at Nuremburg
1963:   A Child Is Waiting; The Condemned of Altona
1965:   Ship of Fools
1968:   The Detective
1975:   Report to the Commissioner (E. Tidyman)

ARTHUR MANN

1950:   The Jackie Robinson Story (L. Taylor)

E. B. MANN

1936:   Stormy Trails

ED MANN   (also SANTOS ALCOVER)

1966:   The Hallucination Generation
1971:   Who Says I Can't Ride a Rainbow! (D. Hauer);
        Cauldron of Blood (alt. Blind Man's Bluff;
        Sp./U.S.)
1974:   Seizure (O. Stone); The Mutations
1976:   The Killer Inside Me (R. Chamblee)

JANE MANN

1957:   The Unearthly (G. Dennis)

MICHAEL MANN

1981:   Thief

MILTON MANN

1956:   Scandal, Inc.

STANLEY MANN

1958: Another Time, Another Place
1961: The Mark (Brit.; S. Buchman)
1965: A High Wind in Jamaica*; Rapture; Up from
      the Beach (C. Brule)
1967: The Naked Runner
1968: The Strange Affair (Brit.)
1969: Fraulein Doktor (Ital./Yugo.)*
1975: Russian Roulette*
1976: Sky Riders*; Breaking Point (R. Swaybill)
1978: Damien -- Omen II (M. Hodges)
1979: Meteor (E. North); Circle of Iron (S.
      Silliphant)
1981: Eye of the Needle

HETT MANNHEIM

1933: Gordon of Ghost City (ser.)*
1934: The Vanishing Shadow (ser.)*

ALBERT MANNHEIMER

1940: Dulcy*; Sporting Blood (D. Yost)
1941: Whistling in the Dark*
1944: Song of the Open Road
1948: Three Daring Daughters*
1950: Born Yesterday (J. Epstein)
1951: Her First Romance

BRUCE MANNING

1935: After the Dance (H. Shumate); The Best Man
      Wins (E. Hill); Eight Bells (E. Hill); Grand
      Exit (L. Houser)
1936: The Lone Wolf Returns*; Meet Nero Wolfe*;
      Counterfeit (W. Rankin)
1937: A Girl with Ideas (R. Shannon); Let Them
      Live! (L. Houser); One Hundred Men and a
      Girl*; We Have Our Moments (C. Grayson)
1938: Mad About Music (Felix Jackson); The Rage of
      Paris (Felix Jackson); That Certain Age
1939: First Love (L. Houser); Three Smart Girls

519

Grow Up*
1940: Spring Parade (Felix Jackson)
1941: Appointment for Love (Felix Jackson); Back Street (Felix Jackson)
1945: Guest Wife (J. Klorer); This Love of Ours (J. Klorer)
1956: So Goes My Love (J. Clifden)
1949: Bride for Sale; That Midnight Kiss (T. Hovey)
1951: Payment on Demand (C. Bernhardt)
1952: Hoodlum Empire (B. Considine)
1954: Jubilee Trail
1955: Flame of the Islands
1957: Spoilers of the Forest

MONROE MANNING

1963: Lassie's Greatest Adventure (C. O'Neal)

ARNOLD MANOFF

1944: Man from Prison; My Buddy
1948: Casbah (L. Bus-Fekete); No Minor Vices

DUNCAN MANSFIELD

1937: Girl Loves Boy (C. Graham)

VICTOR MANSFIELD

1935: Here Comes the Band*

JOHN MANTLEY

1957: The 27th Day; The Parson and the Outlaw (O. Drake)
1965: My Blood Runs Cold

GEORGE MANUPELLI

1971: Cry Dr. Chicago

MARC MARAIS

1977:   Crash; House of the Living Dead

ALLEN MARCH

1955:   Pirates of Tripoli

JOSEPH MONCURE MARCH

1930:   Journey's End*
1932:   Hot Saturday*; Madame Butterfly (J. Lovett);
        Sky Devils (E. Sutherland)
1933:   Hoopla (B. King); Jennie Gerhardt*
1934:   Jealousy (K. Glasmon); Transatlantic
        Merry-Go-Round; Two Alone (J. Lovett)
1935:   Let 'Em Have It (E. Harris)
1936:   And Sudden Death
1937:   Hideaway Girl
1938:   Flirting with Fate*; Her Jungle Love*
1939:   Woman Doctor
1940:   Forgotten Girls (F. Herbert); Three Faces
        West*; Wagons Westward (H. Jacobs); Lone
        Star Raiders (B. Shipman)

MAX MARCIN

1931:   City Streets (O. Garrett); Scandal Sheet (V.
        Lawrence); Silence; Lawyer's Secret (L.
        Corrigan)
1932:   Strange Case of Clara Deane
1933:   Gambling Ship*; King of the Jungle*

LARRY MARCUS

1950:   Backfire; Dark City*
1956:   The Unguarded Moment (H. Meadow)
1957:   Witness for the Prosecution (B. Wilder)
1958:   Diamond Safari; Voice in the Mirror
1967:   A Covenant with Death (S. Levitt)
1969:   Justine
1971:   Going Home
1976:   Alex & the Gypsy

1980:   The Stunt Man

RAYMOND T. MARCUS

1956:   Earth vs. the Flying Saucers*
1957:   The Man Who Turned to Stone; Zombies of Mora
        Tau; Hellcats of the Navy (D. Lang); Chicago
        Confidential; Escape from San Quentin
1958:   The Case Against Brooklyn

GLENVILLE MARETH

1964:   Santa Claus Conquers the Martians

LYONEL MARGOLIES

1940:   The Green Hornet (ser.)*

ARNOLD MARGOLIN

1971:   Star Spangled Girl (Jim Parker)
1972:   Snowball Express*
1975:   Russian Roulette*

HERBERT E. MARGOLIS

1948:   Larceny*; Smart Woman*
1949:   Ma and Pa Kettle*
1956:   Francis in the Haunted House (W. Raynor);
        Rock, Pretty Baby (W. Raynor)
1957:   The Kettles on Old MacDonald's Farm (W.
        Raynor)
1958:   Summer Love (W. Raynor)

ANDREW P. MARIN

1981:   Underground Aces*

CHEECH MARIN

1978:   Up in Smoke (T. Chong)

1980: Cheech and Chong's Next Movie (T. Chong)
1981: Cheech and Chong's Nice Dreams (T. Chong)
1982: Things Are Tough All Over (T. Chong)

CHARLES R. MARION

1941: Spooks Run Wild (C. Foreman)
1942: Rhythm Parade (C. Foreman)
1943: Campus Rhythm; Here Comes Kelly; Melody
       Parade (T. Ryan); Mystery of the 13th
       Guest*; Sarong Girl (A. Hoerl)
1944: Smart Guy (J. Krafft); Hot Rhythm (Tim
       Ryan); Goin' to Town (C. Roberts)
1945: Rhythm Round-Up; Hit the Hay (R. Weil)
1946: The Dark Horse (L. Solomon); Idea Girl
1949: Angels in Disguise*; Hold That Baby (G.
       Schnitzer); Master Minds
1950: Blonde Dynamite; Blues Busters; Triple
       Trouble; Lucky Losers
1951: Bowery Battalion
1952: Here Come the Marines*; Hold That Line (T.
       Ryan); Jet Job; Rodeo; The Rose Bowl Story
1953: White Lightning; Hot News (D. Ullman);
       Clip[ped Wings (E. Ullman); Roar of the
       Crowd
1958: Apache Territory (G. W. George)

FRANCES MARION (1887-1973)

1928: Bringing Up Father
1930: Their Own Desire (J. Forbes)
1930: Anna Christie; The Big House*; Rogue Song*;
       Let Us Be Gay; Good News; Min and Bill (M.
       Jackson)
1931: The Secret Six; The Champ (L. Praskins)
1932: Blondie of the Follies; Cynara (L. Starling)
1933: Secrets; Dinner at Eight (H. Mankiewicz);
       Peg o' My Heart (F. Adams); The Prizefighter
       and the Lady*
1935: Riffraff*
1936: Camille*
1937: The Good Earth*; Knight Without Armour
       (Brit.); Love from a Stranger
1940: Green Hell

GEORGE MARION, JR.

1930:   Along Came Youth (M. Dix)
1932:   The Big Broadcast; Love Me Tonight*; This Is
        the Night
1933:   Adorable (J. Storm)
1934:   The Gay Divorcee*; Kiss and Make Up*; We're
        Not Dressing*
1935:   Metropolitan (B. Meredyth)
1937:   Fifty Roads to Town (W. Counselman)
1938:   The Gladiator*
1939:   You Can't Cheat an Honest Man*

TED MARK

1970:   Man from O.R.G.Y.

LARRY MARKES

1963:   For Love or Money (M. Morris)
1964:   Wild and Wonderful*

GENE MARKEY (1895-1980) producer

1929:   The Battle of Paris; Lucky in Love; Mother's
        Boy
1930:   The Floradora Girl
1931:   The Great Lover (E. Woolf); Inspiration
1932:   As You Desire Me; West of Broadway (B.
        Meredyth)
1933:   Baby Face (K. Scola); Female (K. Scola);
        Lady of the Night (K. Scola); Lilly Turner
        (K. Scola); Luxury Liner (K. Scola);
        Midnight Mary (K. Scola)
1934:   Fashions of 1934*; A Lost Lady (K. Scola);
        The Merry Frinks (K. Scola); A Modern Hero
        (K. Scola)
1935:   King of Burlesque*; Let's Live Tonight
1936:   Girls' Dormitory; Private Number (W.
        Counselman)
1937:   On the Avenue (W. Counselman)
1941:   You're the One
1950:   If This Be Sin (Brit.)
1951:   Wonder Boy

FLETCHER MARKLE

1949: Jigsaw (V. O'Connor)

PETER MARKLE

1982: The Personals

ZEKIAL MARKO

1965: Once a Thief

GREGORY MARKOPOULOS

1968: The Illiac Passion

CLARENCE MARKS

1933: Her First Mate*; Horseplay (E. Havez)
1934: Half a Sinner (E. Snell)
1935: The Affair of Susan*
1936: Don't Get Personal*
1937: Swing It, Sailor (D. Diamond)
1938: Wide Open Faces*
1942: Brooklyn Orchid (E. Snell)
1943: Taxi, Mister (E. Snell); That Nazty Nuisance
       (E. Snell)

JOHN MARKS

1953: Trail Blazers (S. Roeca)

WALTON MARKS

1975: The Wild Party

WILLIAM MARKS

1965: War Party (G. Williams)
1957: Kill a Dragon (G. Schenck)

1970:   Barquero (G. Schenck)

BEN MARKSON

1932:   Rackety Rax (L. Breslow)
1933:   Goodbye Again; Lady Killer (L. Hayward);
        Lucky Devils (A. Johnson); Silk Express (H.
        Branch)
1934:   Big-Hearted Herbert*; Case of the Howling
        Dog; Here Comes the Navy (E. Baldwin); Upper
        World
1935:   Bright Lights*; Case of the Lucky Legs*; The
        White Cockatoo (L. Hayward)
1936:   Brides Are Like That; Nobody's Fool (R.
        Block)
1937:   Danger -- Love at Work (J. Grant); Sing and
        Be Happy*; That I May Live (W. Counselman);
        Woman Wise
1939:   I Was a Convict (R. Andrews); Pride of the
        Navy (S. Elkins)
1941:   The Great Mr. Nobody (K. Gamet); Thieves
        Fall Out (C. Grayson)
1943:   He Hired the Boss (I. Cummings)
1945:   The Beautiful Cheat; The Falcon in San
        Francisco (R. Kent); Prison Ship (J.
        Mischel)
1946:   A Close Call for Boston Blackie

DAVID MARKSON

1972:   Count Your Bullets
1974:   Face to the Wind

JOHN MARLEY

1975:   Prisoners (W. Bushell)

BRIAN MARLOW

1931:   Girls About Town (R. Griffith)
1932:   Dancers in the Dark*; Night of June 13*
1933:   Brief Moment; The Crime of the Century (F.
        Ryerson); My Woman; Supernatural (H. Thew)
1934:   Happiness Ahead (H. Sauber)

1936: The Accusing Finger*; Forgotten Faces*;
      Preview Murder Mystery (R. Yost); The Return
      of Sophie Lang (P. McNutt); The Sky Parade*;
      'Til We Meet Again; Woman Trap (E. Walter)
1937: Murder Goes to College*; Sophie Lang Goes
      West*
1939: Beware, Spooks!*; Unmarried (L. Hayward)

MALCOLM MARMORSTEIN

1974: S*P*Y*S*
1975: Whiffs
1977: Pete's Dragon
1978: Return from Witch Mountain

ANTHONY MARRIOTT

1967: The Deadly Bees

GARRY MARSHALL

1968: How Sweet It Is (J. Belson)
1970: The Grasshopper (J. Belson)

PETER L. MARSHALL

1968: Mary Jane (D. Gautier)

ROGER MARSHALL

1970: Hello — Goodbye

D. M. MARSHMAN

1950: Sunset Boulevard*
1953: Taxi (D. Fuchs)

ALPHONSE MARTEL

1933: Gigolettes of Paris

A. Z. MARTIN

1969:   The Mad Room (B. Girard)

AL MARTIN

1933:   Wolf Dog (ser.)*
1934:   Young and Beautiful*; Burn 'Em Up Barnes
        (ser.)*
1935:   Danger Ahead; What Price Crime?
1936:   Rio Grande Romance; The Law Rides; Trail
        Dust; Kelly of the Secret Service; The Last
        Assignment; Prison Shadows; Put on the Spot;
        The Rogues Tavern; A Face in the Fog; Bars
        of Hate; Taming the Wild
1937:   Island Captives; The Shadow Strikes
1938:   Peck's Bad Boy with the Circus*
1940:   The Last Alarm
1941:   Caught in the Act; Flying Wild; The
        Invisible Ghost (H. Martin)
1942:   Stagecoach Buckaroo; The Devil with Hitler;
        Mississippi Gambler (R. Chanslor); Gang
        Busters (ser.)*; The Mad Doctor of Market
        Street
1944:   Carolina Blues (J. Hoffman)
1946:   Blondie Knows Best (E. Bernds); A Guy Could
        Change
1948:   Money Madness; Racing Luck*; The Strange
        Mrs. Crane
1949:   Amazon Quest
1952:   Army Bound
1957:   Invasion of the Saucer Men (R. Gurney)
1958:   In the Money (E. Ullman)

CHARLES MARTIN

1938:   The Missing Guest (P. Perez)
1946:   No Leave, No Love (L. Karkos)
1948:   My Dear Secretary; On an Island with You*
1956:   Death of a Scoundrel
1964:   The Secret Door
1968:   If He Hollers, Let Him Go!
1974:   How to Seduce a Woman
1978:   One Man Jury
1979:   Dead on Arrival

DON MARTIN

1947: The Pretender; The Hat Box Mystery (C.
       Hittleman)
1948: Appointment with Murder; Triple Threat (J.
       Carole); Devil's Cargo
1949: The Lost Tribe (A. Hoerl); Search for Danger
1950: Destination Murder
1954: Arrow in the Dust; The Lone Gun (R. Schayer)

1955: Double Jeopardy; Stranger on Horseback (H.
       Meadow)
1956: The Brass Legend; The Deadliest Sin (Brit.;
       K. Hughes); Emergency Hospital; Hot Cars (R.
       Landau); Quincannon, Frontier Scout (J.
       Higgins)
1957: The Storm Rider (E. Bernds)

DOROTHEA KNOX MARTIN

1947: Hollywood Barn Dance

FRANCIS MARTIN

1933: Disgraced (A. Miller); Her Bodyguard (F.
       Partos); International House (W. DeLeon);
       Tillie and Gus (W. DeLeon)
1934: College Rhythm*; We're Not Dressing*
1935: The Big Broadcast of 1936*: Mississippi*;
       Two Fisted*
1936: Collegiate (W. DeLeon); Rhythm on the
       Range*; Strike Me Pink*
1936: The Big Broadcast of 1937 (W. DeLeon); The
       Princess Comes Across*
1937: Artists and Models (W. DeLeon); Waikiki
       Wedding*
1938: The Big Broadcast of 1938*; College Swing
       (W. DeLeon)
1941: Tillie the Toiler (K. DeWolf)
1942: Shut My Big Mouth*
1956: Unidentified Flying Objects

GEORGE MARTIN

1940:   Pals of the Silver Sage

HELEN MARTIN

1941:   The Invisible Ghost*
1945:   The Lady Confesses

IAN KENNEDY MARTIN

1975:   Mitchell

JIM MARTIN

1974:   Black Eye (M. Haggard)

MARDIK MARTIN

1973:   Mean Streets (M. Scorsese)
1977:   New York, New York (E. MacRauch); Valentino
        (Ken Russell)
1980:   Raging Bull (P. Schrader)

PAUL MARTIN

1934:   Orient Express*

STEVE MARTIN

1979:   The Jerk*
1982:   Dead Men Don't Wear Plaid*

TROY KENNEDY MARTIN

1970:   Kelly's Heroes

CHRIS MARTINO

1972:   Blood of Ghastly Horror (D. Poston)

PIERRE MARTON (see PETER STONE)

TOM MARUZZI

1961:   The Silent Call; Sniper's Ridge

MIKE MARVIN

1982:   Six Pack (A. Matter)

ARTHUR MARX

1947:   Blondie in the Dough (J. Henley); Winter
        Wonderland
1964:   A Global Affair*
1965:   I'll Take Sweden*
1967:   Eight on the Lam*
1972:   Cancel My Reservation (B. Fisher)

GROUCHO MARX (1890-1977) comedian

1937:   The King and the Chorus Girl (N. Krasna)

SAM MARX

1935:   Society Doctor (M. Fessier)
1954:   Duel in the Jungle (T. J. Morrison)

LAURENCE MASCOTT

1958:   Ten Days to Tulara
1961:   Look in Any Window

JOSEPH R. MASEFIELD

1980:   Don't Go in the House*

BASIL MASON

1932:   Aren't We All? (G. Wakefield)

LESLEY MASON

1929:   Senor Americano
1930:   The Fighting Legion (B. Cohen)
1933:   The Man from Monterey

PAUL MASON

1961:   Angel Baby*
1963:   King Kong vs. Godzilla (Jap.; B. Howard)

SARAH Y. MASON

1928:   Alias Jimmy Valentine (A. Younger)
1929:   The Broadway Melody*
1930:   The Girl Said No; Love in the Rough; They
        Learned About Women
1931:   Man in Possession
1932:   Age of Consent (F. Cockrell); Shopworn
1933:   Chance at Heaven (J. Josephson); Little
        Women (V. Heerman)
1934:   Age of Innocence (V. Heerman); The Little
        Minister*
1935:   Break of Hearts*; Magnificent Obsession*
1937:   Stella Dallas (V. Heerman)
1939:   Golden Boy*
1949:   Little Women*
1954:   Magnificent Obsession*

SCOTT MASON

1932:   Ride Him, Cowboy

JOE MASSOT

1971:   Zachariah

PETER MASTERSON

1982:   The Best Little Whorehouse in Texas*

BERKELEY MATHER

1963:   The Long Ships (B. Cross)

JAMES MATHERS

1982:   Dr. Jekyll's Dungeon of Death

RICHARD MATHESON

1957:   The Incredible Shrinking Man
1959:   The Beat Generation (L. Meltzer)
1960:   The House of Usher
1961:   Master of the World; The Pit and the
        Pendulum
1962:   Burn Witch Burn (C. Beaumont); Poe's Tales
        of Terror (alt. Tales of Terror)
1963:   The Comedy of Terrors; The Raven
1965:   Die! Die! My Darling!
1967:   The Young Warriors
1968:   The Devil's Bride
1969:   De Sade
1973:   The Legend of Hell House
1980:   Somewhere in Time

MELISSA MATHISON

1982:   The Escape Artist (S. Zito); E.T. the
        Extra-Terrestrial

THERESA MATHISON

1979:   The Black Stallion*

ALEX MATTER

1967:   The Drifter
1982:   Six Pack (M. Marvin)

DAVID MATTHEWS

1936: Slightly Scandalous (E. Lazarus)
1949: Adventures of Sir Galahad (ser.)*
1950: Cody of the Pony Express (ser.)*; Atom Man
vs. Superman (ser.)*; Pirates of the High
Seas (ser.)*
1951: Hurricane Island; The Magic Carpet

THOMAS MATTHIESEN

1975: Idaho Transfer

JEROME MAX

1977: Tentacles (U.S./Ital.)

LEN MAXWELL

1966: What's Up, Tiger Lily?*

RICHARD MAXWELL

1982: The Challenge (J. Sayles)

ELAINE MAY (1932-   ) actress, director (also
ESTHER DALE)

1971: A New Leaf; Such Good Friends
1976: Mikey and Nicky
1978: Heaven Can Wait (W. Beatty)

CARL MAYER (1894-1944) Aust.

(American films only)
1929: The Four Devils

EDWIN JUSTUS MAYER (1896-1960)

1929: The Unholy Night (D. Farnum)
1930: In Gay Madrid*; Romance (B. Meredyth)
1931: Never the Twain Shall Meet

1932: Merrily We Go to Hell; Wild Girl (D.
       Anderson)
1933: Tonight Is Ours; I Am Suzanne (R.V. Lee)
1934: Here Is My Heart*; Thirty-Day Princess*
1935: Peter Ibbetsen*; So Red the Rose*
1936: Desire*; Give Us This Night (L. Starling);
       'Til We Meet Again*; Wives Never Know (unc.;
       F. Brennan)
1938: The Buccaneers*
1939: Rio*; Exile Express (E. LaBlanche)
1941: They Met in Bombay*
1942: To Be or Not to Be
1945: A Royal Scandal; Masquerade in Mexico (K.
       Tunberg)

LAURA WALKER MAYER

1934: Dr. Monica (C. Kenyon)

WENDELL MAYES

1957: The Spirit of St. Louis*; The Way to the
       Gold (R. Webb); The Enemy Below
1958: From Hell to Texas (R. Buckner); The Hunters
1959: The Hanging Tree (H. Welles); Anatomy of a
       Murder
1962: Advise and Consent
1965: In Harm's Way; Von Ryan's Express (J.
       Landon)
1967: Hotel
1972: The Revengers; The Poseidon Adventure (S.
       Silliphant)
1974: The Bank Shot; Death Wish
1978: Go Tell the Spartans
1979: Love and Bullets
1982: Monsignor (A. Polonsky)

JULIAN MAYFIELD

1968: Uptight*
1976: The Long Wait (Woodie King)

ALBERT & DAVID MAYSLES

1969:   Salesman (doc.)

CHARLES E. MAZIN

1965:   All Men Are Apes (B. Sackett)

PAUL MAZURSKY (1930-   ) actor, director, producer

1968:   I Love You, Alice B. Toklas! (L. Tucker)
1969:   Bob and Carol and Ted and Alice (L. Tucker)
1970:   Alex in Wonderland (L. Tucker)
1973:   Blume in Love
1974:   Harry and Tonto (Josh Greenfield)
1976:   Next Stop, Greenwich Village
1978:   An Unmarried Woman
1980:   Willie and Paul
1982:   Tempest (L. Capetanos)

ROBERT McCAHON

1975:   Deliver Us from Evil

MARY McCALL, JR.

1932:   Street of Women (C. Kenyon)
1934:   Babbitt*; Desirable
1935:   Dr. Socrates (R. Lord); A Midsummer Night's
        Dream (C. Kenyon); Secret Bride*; Woman in
        Red (P. Milne)
1937:   I Promise to Pay (L. Houser); It's All
        Yours; Women of Glamour (L. Starling)
1938:   Breaking the Ice*; Dramatic School (E.
        Vajda)
1939:   Maisie
1940:   Congo Maisie; Gold Rush Maisie (M.
        Reinhardt)
1941:   Kathleen; Maisie Was a Lady (E. Reinhardt);
        Ringside Maisie
1942:   Maisie Gets Her Man (E. Reinhardt)
1943:   Swing Shift Maisie (R. Halff)
1944:   The Sullivans; Maisie Goes to Reno
1945:   Keep Your Powder Dry (G. Bruce)
1949:   Dancing in the Dark; Mr. Belvedere Goes to
        College*

```
1952:   Ride the Man Down; Thunderbirds
1959:   Juke Box Rhythm (E. Baldwin)
```

LEO McCAREY (1898-1969) director, producer

```
1930:   The Shepper-Newfounder*
1931:   Indiscreet
1952:   My Son John (M. Connolly)
1957:   An Affair to Remember (D. Daves)
1958:   Rally Round the Flag Boys! (C. Binyon)
1962:   Satan Never Sleeps (C. Binyon)
```

RAY McCAREY

```
1930:   Swing High
```

HENRY McCARTHY

```
1930:   Sunny (H. Pearson); Top Speed (H. Pearson)
1931:   Bright Lights (H. Pearson); Going Wild (H.
        Pearson);The Mad Parade*
1933:   Right to Romance (S. Buchman)
1936:   Forgotten Women (F. Konklin); Great Guy*
1937:   23 1/2 Hours Leave*
```

JOHN P. McCARTHY

```
1930:   The Land of Missing Men (R. Quigley);
        Headin' North; Cavalier of the West
1933:   Return of Casey Jones (H.O. Jones)
1936:   Song of the Gringo*
1944:   Marked Trails (V. Hammond)
```

MARY McCARTHY

```
1932:   Slightly Married
1934:   I Hate Women; Woman Unafraid
1939:   Irish Luck
1940:   Chasing Trouble
1946:   Sister Kenny*
```

JOHN McCLAIN

```
1940:  Turnabout*
1941:  Lady Be Good*
1942:  Cairo
```

ALBERT McCLEERY

```
1942:  The Lady Is Willing (J. Grant)
```

TERENCE McCLOY

```
1972:  Lady Sings the Blues*
```

BERNARD McCONVILLE

```
1932:  Cannonball Express; Devil on Deck
1936:  King of the Pecos*; The Lonely Trail (J.
       Natteford)
1937:  Riders of the Whistling Skull*
1938:  The Old Barn Dance (C. Royal); Border G-Man
       (O. Drake)
1940:  Cherokee Strip (N. Houston)
1941:  Outlaws of the Desert (J. Cheney)
1943:  Cheyenne Roundup (E. Clifton)
```

JOHN McCORMICK

```
1965:  Seven Women (J. Green)
1966:  Walk in the Shadow (J. Green)
```

PAT McCORMICK

```
1981:  Under the Rainbow*
```

ARCH McCOY

```
1978:  Here Come the Tigers
```

HARRY McCOY (1894-1937) actor

```
1930:  Midnight Daddies
```

```
1932:   Hypnotized*
1934:   Call It Luck*


HOMER McCOY

1965:   Git!


HORACE McCOY (     -1954)

1933:   Dangerous Crossroads; Hold the Press
1934:   Speed Wings
1936:   Fatal Lady (S. Ornitz); Parole! (K.
        Glasmon); Postal Inspector; Trail of the
        Lonesome Pine*
1938:   Dangerous to Know (W. Lipman); Hunted Men
        (W. Lipman)
1939:   Island of Lost Men (W. Lipman); Persons in
        Hiding (W. Lipman); Television Spy*;
        Undercover Doctor (W. Lipman)
1940:   Texas Rangers Ride Again (W. Lipman); Queen
        of the Mob (W. Lipman); Women Without Names
        (W. Lipman)
1941:   Texas*; Wild Geese Calling
1942:   Valley of the Sun; Gentleman Jim (V.
        Lawrence)
1943:   Appointment in Berlin (M. Hogan); There's
        Something About a Soldier (B. Trivers)
1947:   The Fabulous Texan (L. Hazard)
1950:   The Fireball (T. Garnett)
1952:   Bronco Buster (L. Hayward); Montana Belle
        (N. Hall); The Lusty Men (D. Dortort)
1953:   Bad for Each Other (I. Wallace); El Alemein
        (H. Purdum)
1954:   Dangerous Mission*
1955:   Rage at Dawn; The Road to Denver (A.
        Rivkin); Texas Lady


JOHNSTON McCULLEY

1941:   Doomed Caravan (J. Cheney)


JIM McCULLOUGH

1976:   The Creature from Black Lake
```

539

1977: Charge of the Model T's

RUSTY McCULLOUGH

1942: Queen of Broadway (G. Sayre)

JOHN McDERMOTT

1934: College Rhythm*
1947: Three Wise Fools (J. O'Hanlon)

FRANK McDONALD (1899-   )

1954: Security Risk (J. Pagano)

JOSEPH McEVEETY

1970: The Computer Wore Tennis Shoes
1971: The Barefoot Executive
1972: Now You See Him, Now You Don't
1974: Superdad
1975: The Strongest Man in the World (H. Groves)
1978: Hot Lead and Cold Feet*

J. P. McEVOY

1934: The Lemon Drop Kid*; Many Happy Returns*;
       Pursuit of Happiness*; Ready for Love (W.
       McNutt); You're Telling Me
1935: Love in Bloom*
1936: College Holiday*
1938: Just Around the Corner*

WILLIAM F. McGAHA

1972: J. C. (J. Thirty)

JOHN McGEEVEY

1982: Night Crossing

DAVID McGILLIVRAY

1975:   Frightmare; The House of Whipcord
1977:   The Confessional
1978:   Schizo
1979:   Terror

WILLIAM McGIVERN

1965:   I Saw What You Did
1969:   The Wrecking Crew
1975:   Brannigan*

DORRELL & STUART McGOWAN

1936:   Red River Valley; King of the Pecos (B.
        McConville); Comin' Round the Mountain (O.
        Drake); The Singing Cowboy; Ride, Ranger,
        Ride; The Big Show; Guns and Guitars
1937:   A Man Betrayed; Git Along Little Dogies;
        Yodelin' Kid from Pine Ridge (J. Natteford);
        Bill Cracks Down
1938:   Under Western Stars (B. Burbridge); Come On,
        Leathernecks (S. Salkow); Down in
        "Arkansaw"; Hollywood Stadium Mystery (alt.
        The Stadium Murders; S. Palmer); Ladies in
        Distress
1939:   Trouble in Sundown (O. Drake); In Old
        Monterey (G. Geraghty); Rovin' Tumbleweeds
        (alt. Washington Cowboy; B. Burbridge);
        South of the Border; Jeepers Creepers;
        Smashing the Spy Ring*
1940:   Barnyard Follies; Friendly Neighbors; Grand
        Ole Opry; In Old Missouri; Village Barn
        Dance
1941:   Arkansas Judge; Country Fair; Mountain
        Moonlight*; Tuxedo Junction
1942:   Hi, Neighbors; Mountain Rhythm; The Old
        Homestead; Shepherd of the Ozarks
1943:   Hoosier Holiday; O, My Darling Clementine;
        Swing Your Partner
1944:   San Fernando Valley; Sing, Neighbor, Sing
1945:   Don't Fence Me In (J. Butler); The Big
        Bonanza (P. Gangelin)
1946:   The Inner Circle; Night Train to Memphis;

Valley of the Zombies
1947: Twilight on the Rio Grande; The Trespasser
1949: Hellfire
1950: Singing Guns; The Showdown*
1951: Tokyo File 212
1958: Snowfire; The Littlest Hobo
1962: The Bashful Elephant (Germ.)

JOHN P. McGOWAN (1880-1952) director, producer

1929: Nothing but the Truth
1930: Pioneers of the West; Heads Up (J. Kirkland)
1936: Secret Patrol (R. Watson)
1937: What Price Vengeance; Broadway Melody of
      1938
1945: The Stork Club (B. G. DeSylva)

ROBERT F. McGOWAN

1938: Sons of the Legion*

STUART McGOWAN (see also DORRELL McGOWAN)

1978: The Billion Dollar Hobo*

T. J. McGOWAN

1951: The Man With My Face (S. W. Taylor)

WILLIAM McGRATH

1932: Secrets of Wu Sin; 70,000 Witnesses*
1933: Ladies They Talk About*

JOHN McGREEVEY

1956: Hot Rod Girl
1957: Death in Small Doses
1958: The Beast of Budapest
1959: Cast a Long Shadow (M. Goldsmith)
1969: Hello Down There (F. Telford)

THOMAS McGUANE

1975: Rancho DeLuxe; 92 in the Shade
1976: The Missouri Breaks
1980: Tom Horn (B. Shrake)

JAMES KEVIN McGUINNESS (-1950)

1930: The Three Sisters (G. Brooks)
1931: Men on Call
1933: Solitaire Man; When Strangers Marry
1934: Tarzan and His Mate*
1935: China Seas (J. Furthman)
1938: Arsene Lupin Returns*; Lord Jeff
1940: Florian*; I Take This Woman
1941: Men of Boys Town
1950: Rio Grande

DENNIS McGUIRE

1970: End of the Road*
1974: Shoot It: Black, Shoot It: Blue

DON McGUIRE (1919-   ) actor, director

1952: Back at the Front*; Meet Danny Wilson
1953: Walking My Baby Back Home (O. Brodney)
1954: Three Ring Circus
1956: Johnny Concho (D. Harmon); Artists and
       Models
1957: The Delicate Delinquent; Hear Me Good
1970: Suppose They Gave a War and Nobody Came? (H.
       Captain)

WILLIAM ANTHONY McGUIRE

1932: Disorderly Conduct; The Kid from Spain*;
       Okay America (S. Pembroke); She Wanted a
       Millionaire
1933: The Kiss Before the Mirror; Out All Night;
       Roman Scandals*
1934: Little Man, What Now?
1936: The Great Ziegfeld

1937:   Rosalie
1940:   Lillian Russell

CHARLES McGUIRK

1929:   Hot for Paris

TOM McINTYRE

1978:   Buckstone County Prison
1980:   Living Legend

BRIAN McKAY

1971:   McCabe and Mrs. Miller (R. Altman)

ST. CLAIR McKELWAY

1948:   The Mating of Millie (L. MacFarlane); Sleep
        My Love (L. Rosten)

DUDLEY McKENNA

1929:   Courtin' Wildcats

C. A. McKNIGHT

1971:   Mrs. Pollifax -- Spy

JOHN McLAID

1941:   The Wild Man of Borneo (W. Salt)

DON McLEMORE

1975:   The Great Lester Boggs

NORMAN McLEOD (1898-1964) director

1931: Newly Rich*; Skippy (J. Mankiewicz); Sooky
       (J. Mankiewicz)
1932: Finn and Hattie*
1939: Remember? (C. Ford)
1940: Law and Order (S. Lowe)
1943: The Batman (ser.)*

VICTOR McLEOD

1941: Boss of Bullion City (A. St. Claire); Bury
       Me Not on the Lone Prairie (S. Lowe); The
       Masked Rider (S. Lowe); Horror Island (M.
       Tombragel); Mutiny in the Arctic (M.
       Tombragel); Raiders of the Desert (M.
       Tombragel)
1942: Girls' Town (G. Kerr)
1943: The Phantom (ser.)*
1947: Little Miss Broadway*; Two Blondes and a
       Redhead (J. Brewer); Gang Busters (ser.)*

LEO McMAHON

1970: Madron (E. Chappell)

THOMAS McMAHON

1977: Sidewinder One (N. Crawford)
1978: Caravans*

R. G. McMULLEN

1969: Hell's Belles (J. G. White)

LARRY McMURTRY

1971: The Last Picture Show (P. Bogdanovich)

SUE McNAIR

1971: Horror of the Blood Monsters

TERRENCE McNALLY

1976:   The Ritz

PATRICK McNAMARA

1971:   Cycles South

TOM McNAMARA

1932:   Little Orphan Annie (W. Tuchock)
1933:   Crossfire

STEVE McNEIL

1964:   Man's Favorite Sport? (J. F. Murray)

JOHN McNULTY

1947:   Easy Come, Easy Go*

PATTERSON McNUTT

1935:   Curly Top (A. Beckhard); George White's 1935
        Scandals (J. Yellen); Spring Tonic*
1936:   Everybody's Old Man (A. Thomas); The Return
        of Sophie Lang (B. Marlow)
1938:   Vacation from Love (H. Ware)
1941:   Come Live with Me
1942:   A Gentleman After Dark (G. Bruce)

WILLIAM SLAVENS McNUTT

1929:   The Mighty (G. Jones)
1930:   The Light of the Westen Stars (G. Jones);
        Young Eagles (ser.; G. Jones)
1931:   The Conquering Horde (G. Jones); Gun Smoke
        (G. Jones); Huckleberry Finn (G. Jones);
        Touchdown*
1932:   Broken Wing (G. Jones); If I Had a Million*;
        Lady and Gent (G. Jones); Night of June 13*;

Strangers in Love (G. Jones)
1933: Hell and High Water*; One Sunday Afternoon
       (G. Jones)
1934: Mrs. Wiggs of the Cabbage Patch (J. Storm);
       Ready for Love (J. McEvoy); You Belong to
       Me*
1935: Annapolis Farewell*; Lives of a Bengal
       Lancer*
1942: Mrs. Wiggs of the Cabbage Patch*

JOHN McPARTLAND

1956: The Wild Party
1957: No Time to Be Young (R. Hayes); Street of
       Sinners
1958: The Lost Missile (J. Bixby)

HERB MEADOW

1946: The Strange Woman
1952: The Redhead from Wyoming (P. James); Sally
       and Saint Anne (J. O'Hanlon)
1953: The Master of Ballantrae
1954: Highway Dragnet (J. Odlum)
1955: Count Three and Pray; Stranger on Horseback
       (D. Martin)
1956: Everything But the Truth; The Lone Ranger;
       The Unguarded Moment (L. Marcus)
1957: Man Afraid

ED MEDARD

1973: Savage

JOHN R. MEDBURY

1935: Love in Bloom*

HAROLD MEDFORD

1948: Berlin Express
1950: The Damned Don't Cry (J. Weidman)
1951: Target Unknown

```
1954:   Phantom of the Rue Morgue (J. Webb)
1956:   The Killer Is Loose
1958:   South Seas Adventure*
1961:   Brainwashed (Fr.; G. Oswald)
1962:   Incident in an Alley (O. Harris)
1964:   Fate Is the Hunter
1966:   Smoky
```

B. B. MEDLIN

```
1980:   Roadie
```

MARK MEDOFF

```
1978:   Good Guys Wear Black (B. Cohn)
1979:   When You Comin' Back, Red Ryder?
```

ELIZABETH MEEHAN

```
1930:   The Case of Sergeant Grischa; Lummox
1931:   Beau Ideal; Transgression
1933:   Oliver Twist
1935:   Harmony Lane (J. Santley)
1936:   The Harvester*
1940:   Girl from God's Country (R. Lee); The Hidden
        Menace
1943:   Headin' for God's Country (H. Branch)
1947:   Northwest Outpost (R. Sale)
```

JOHN MEEHAN, JR. (1890-   ) Can.

```
1929:   The Lady Lies (G. Fort); The Rescue
1930:   The Divorcee (N. Grinde)
1931:   A Free Soul; Strangers May Kiss; This Modern
        Age
1932:   Letty Lynton (W. Tuchock); Washington
        Masquerade (S. Blythe); The Wet Parade (J.
        Mahin); Girl of the Rio
1933:   The Prizefighter and the Lady*; Stage Mother
        (B. Ropes); When Ladies Meet (Leon Gordon);
        Hell Below*
1934:   Let's Talk It Over; The Painted Veil*; Sadie
        McKee; Wake Up and Dream; What Every Woman
        Knows (M. Hoffe)
```

```
1935:  I've Been Around; Peter Ibbetson*
1936:  His Brother's Wife (Leon Gordon)
1937:  Madame X; When Thief Meets Thief (Brit.)
1938:  Boys Town (D. Schary); He Loved an Actress
1940:  Seven Sinners (H. Tugend)
1941:  Missing Ten Days (Brit.; J. Curtis)
1942:  Destination Unknown (L. Riggs); Nazi Agent
       (P. Gangelin)
1944:  Kismet
1945:  The Valley of Decision (S. Levien)
1948:  Three Daring Daughters*
1953:  That Man from Tangier
```

HELEN MEINARDI

```
1938:  Next Time I Marry (J. Twist)
```

MYRIN MEISEL

```
1974: I'm a Stranger Here Myself (doc.)*
```

ADOLFAS MEKAS

```
1968:  Windflowers
```

JONAS MEKAS

```
1964:  Guns of the Trees
```

IB MELCHIOR (1917-   ) Den.

```
1958:  Live Fast, Die Young*
1960:  The Angry Red Planet (S. Pink)
1962:  Journey to the Seventh Planet (S. Pink);
       Reptilicus (U.S/Den.)*
1964:  Robinson Crusoe on Mars (J. C. Higgins); The
       Time Travelers
1965:  Planet of the Vampires
1966:  Ambush Bay (M. Feinberg)
```

GEORGE MELFORD

```
1937:  Jungle Menace (ser. )*
```

WELDON MELICK

1939:   Escape to Paradise

WILLIAM BROWN MELONEY

1936:   Beloved Enemy*
1946:   Claudia and David (R. Franken)

CHARLES MELSON

1938:   Flirting with Fate*; The Gladiator*; Swiss
        Miss*

JOHN MELSON

1965:   Battle of the Bulge*

LEWIS MELTZER

1939:   Golden Boy*; Those High Grey Walls
1940:   Lady in Question
1941:   Texas*; New York Town (J. Swerling)
1942:   The Tuttles of Tahiti*
1943:   Destroyer*; First Comes Courage (M. Levy)
1944:   Once Upon a Time (O. Saul)
1947:   Ladies' Man*
1948:   Man-Eater of Kumaon (J. Bartlett); Texas,
        Brooklyn and Heaven
1950:   Comanche Territory (O. Brodney)
1951:   Along the Great Divide (W. Doniger)
1953:   The Jazz Singer*; Desert Legion (I.
        Wallace); Shark River (Joseph Carpenter)
1955:   The Man with the Golden Arm (W. Newman); New
        Orleans Uncensored (O. Hampton)
1956:   Autumn Leaves*
1957:   The Brothers Rico (B. Perry)
1958:   High School Confidential! (R. Blees)
1959:   The Beat Generation (R. Matheson)

GEORGE MENDELUK

1981: Stone Cold Dead

FERNANDO MENDEZ

1966: Rage (T. Sherman)

W. H. MENGER

1966: Blindfold (P. Dunne)

GIAN-CARLO MENOTTI

1951: The Medium

WILLIAM CAMERON MENZIES (1896-1957) director, art
        director, producer

1933: Alice in Wonderland (J. Mankiewicz)

BURGESS MEREDITH (1908-   ) actor, director

1946: The Diary of a Chambermaid

BESS MEREDYTH (1890-1969) actress

1929: Wonder of Women*
1930: Chasing Rainbows (alt. Road Show); In Gay
      Madrid*; The Sea Bat (J. Lawson); Our
      Blushing Brides (J. Lawson); Romance (E.
      Mayer)
1931: Laughing Sinners; Phantom of Paris; The
      Prodigal (W. Root); Cuban Love Song (J.
      Lynch)
1932: Strange Interlude (C. Sullivan); West of
      Broadway (G. Markey)
1933: Looking Forward (H. Harwood)
1934: The Affairs of Cellini; The Mighty Barnum
      (G. Fowler)
1935: Folies Bergere (H. Long); Metropolitan (G.
      Marion)
1936: Half Angel*; Under Two Flags*

1937: The Great Hospital Mystery*
1940: The Mark of Zorro (Garret Fort)
1941: That Night in Rio*
1947: The Unsuspected (Ranald MacDougall)

JOHN MEREDYTH

1950: Dark City*

RON MARK

1979: Pinocchio's Storybook Adventure

MILTON MERLIN

1939: Burn 'Em Up O'Connor (B. Morgan)
1940: Henry Goes Arizona (F. Ryerson)

GEORGE M. MERRICK

1935: Cyclone of the Saddle (E. Clifton); Pals of
       the Range (E. Clifton); Fighting Caballero
       (E. Clifton); Rough Riding Ranger (E.
       Clifton)
1937: The Mysterious Pilot (ser.)*
1938: The Secret of Treasure Island (ser.)*

BOB MERRILL

1976: W. C. Fields and Me

KEITH MERRILL

1979: Take Down (E. Hendershot); Rivals
1981: Harry's War

JACK MERSEREAU

1940: Hidden Gold (G. Geraghty)

ROGER MERTON

1939:   Down the Wyoming Trail (P. Dixon); Roll,
        Wagons, Roll*
1940:   The Golden Trail*; Rainbow over the Range*
1947:   Queen of the Amazons

SAM MERWIN, JR.

1958:   Manhunt in the Jungle (O. Crump)

KEN METCALF

1975:   TNT Jackson (D. Miller)

RADLEY METZGER

1982:   The Cat and the Canary (Brit.)

ROBERT METZLER

1941:   Riders of the Purple Sage (W. Buckner)
1942:   Sundown Jim (W. Buckner); Dr. Renault's
        Secret (W. Buckner)
1945:   Circumstantial Evidence

ANDREW MEYER

1970:   The Sky Pirate
1974:   Night of the Cobra Woman (K. Magnus)

NICHOLAS MEYER

1973:   Invasion of the Bee Girls
1976:   The Seven-Per-Cent Solution
1979:   Time After Time

RUSS MEYER (1924-   ) director

1966:   Faster Pussycat! Kill! Kill! (Jack Moran)
1969:   Cherry, Harry and Raquel (T. Wolfe)

1973:   Sweet Suzy (L. Neubauer)

SAM MEYER

1952:   Storm over Tibet (I. Tors)

BILLY MEYERS

1939:   One Dark Night

NANCY MEYERS

1980:   Private Benjamin*

SIDNEY MEYERS (1906-1969) director

1949:   The Quiet One (doc.)*
1960:   The Savage Eye (doc.)*

SIDNEY MICHAELS

1960:   Key Witness (A. Brenner)
1968:   The Night They Raided Minsky's*

STEVE MICHAELS

1975:   Panorama Blue
1979:   Racquet (E. Doud)

OSCAR MICHEAUX (-1951)

1930:   A Daughter of the Congo; Easy Street
1931:   The Exile
1932:   The Girl from Chicago (alt. The Spider's
        Web); Ten Minutes to Live; Veiled
        Aristocrats
1934:   Harlem After Midnight
1935:   Lem Hawkins' Confession
1936:   Temptation; Underworld
1937:   God's Stepchildren (alt. All God's
        Stepchildren)

1948:   The Betrayal

EDGAR MIDDLETON

1931:   Captivation

EDWARD MIDDLETON

1968:   Someone
1975:   Drifter

GEORGE MIDDLETON

1931:   Once a Sinner

TED V. MIKELS

1969:   The Astro-Zombies (W. Rogers)
1982:   Ten Violent Women (J. G. White)

RICHARD MILES

1964:   Madmen of Mandoras (S. Bennett)

LEWIS MILESTONE (1895-1980) director

1948:   Arch of Triumph (H. Brown)

JOHN MILIUS

1969:   The Devil's Eight*
1971:   Evel Knievel (A. Caillou)
1972:   Jeremiah Johnson (Edward Anhalt); The Life
        and Times of Judge Roy Bean
1973:   Magnum Force (M. Cimino); Dillinger
1975:   The Wind and the Lion
1978:   Big Wednesday (D. Aaberg)
1979:   Apocalypse Now (F. Coppola)
1982:   Conan the Barbarian (O. Stone)

RONALD MILLAR

1950: The Miniver Story (G. Froeschel)
1951: The Unknown Man (G. Froeschel)
1952: Scaramouche (G. Froeschel)
1954: Rose Marie (G. Froeschel); Betrayed (G. Froeschel)

OSCAR MILLARD

1949: Come to the Stable (S. Benson)
1951: No Highway in the Sky (Brit.)*
1952: Angel Face (F. Nugent)
1953: Second Chance (S. Boehm)
1956: The Conqueror
1960: Song Without End
1964: Dead Ringer (A. Beich)
1965: The Reward (Serge Bourguignon)
1972: The Salzburg Connection

JAMES KNOX MILLEN

1935: The Healer*

ALICE D.G. MILLER

1929: The Bridge of San Luis Rey
1933: Disgraced (F. Martin)
1936: Girl on the Front Page*; Rose Marie*; Wife Versus Secretary*
1939: On Borrowed Time*
1940: Irene
1943: Forever and a Day*

ARTHUR MILLER (1915-   ) playwright

1961: The Misfits

ASHLEY AYRE MILLER

1931: Alice in Wonderland (J. Godson)

CHARLOTTE MILLER

1933: Sailor's Luck (M. Roberts)

CHRIS MILLER

1978: National Lampoon's Animal House*

DICK MILLER

1975: TNT Jackson (K. Metcalf)

FLOURNEY E. MILLER

1939: Harlem Rides the Range (S. Williams); Double
       Deal (A. Hoerl)

HARVEY MILLER

1980: Private Benjamin*
1982: Jekyll and Hyde Together Again*

HERMAN MILLER

1968: Coogan's Bluff*

J. P. MILLER

1959: The Rabbit Trap
1961: The Young Savages (Ed. Anhalt)
1962: Days of Wine and Roses
1964: Behold a Pale Horse
1970: The People Next Door

JASON MILLER

1982: That Championship Season

MARK MILLER

1982: Savannah Smiles

MELISSA MILLER

1980: Oh, God! Book II*

MERLE MILLER

1955: The Rains of Ranchipur
1958: Kings Go Forth

ROBERT ALAN MILLER

1948: The Westward Trail

ROBIN MILLER

1964: Psychomania

RONALD MILLER

1953: Never Let Me Go (G. Froeschel)

SETON I. MILLER (1902-1974) producer

1928: Air Circus*
1929: The Far Call
1930: The Lone Star Ranger; The Dawn Patrol (H.
       Hawks); Today
1931: The Criminal Code (F. Niblo)
1932: Hot Saturday*; If I Had a Million*; The Last
       Mile; Once in a Lifetime; Scarface*; The
       Crowd Roars*
1933: Eagle and the Hawk (B. Rogers); Gambling
       Ship*; Master of Men (E. Paramore); Midnight
       Club (L. Charteris); Murders in the Zoo (P.
       Wylie)
1934: Charlie Chan's Courage; Murder in Trinidad;
       St. Louis Kid (W. Duff)
1935: The Frisco Kid (W. Duff); The G-Men; It
       Happened in New York (R. James); Murder on a
       Honeymoon (R. Benchley)

1936: Bullets or Ballots; The Leathernecks Have
       Landed; Two in the Dark
1937: Kid Galahad
1938: The Adventures of Robin Hood (N. R. Raine);
       The Dawn Patrol (D. Totheroh); Penitentiary
       (F. Niblo); Valley of the Giants (M.
       Fessier)
1940: Castle on the Hudson (Brown Holmes); The Sea
       Hawk (H. Koch)
1941: Here Comes Mr. Jordan (S. Buchman); This
       Woman Is Mine (F. Jackson)
1942: The Black Swan (B. Hecht); My Gal Sal*
1944: Ministry of Fear
1946: Two Years Before the Mast (G. Bruce)
1947: Calcutta; Singapore
1948: Fighter Squadron
1950: Convicted*; The Man Who Cheated Himself (P.
       MacDonald)
1951: Queen for a Day
1953: The Mississippi Gambler
1954: The Shanghai Story; Bengal Brigade
1957: Istanbul*
1959: The Last Mile (M. Subotsky)

VICTOR MILLER

1977: The Black Pearl (R. Sheldon)
1980: Friday the 13th
1982: A Stranger Is Watching (E. MacRauch)

WILLIAM F. MILLER

1976: In Search of Bigfoot

WINSTON MILLER

1937: The Painted Stallion (ser.)*; Dick Tracy
       (ser.)*
1940: Carolina Moon; Ride, Tenderfoot, Ride
1941: The Medico of Painted Springs; Prairie
       Stranger; The Royal Mounted Patrol
1942: Man from Cheyenne; Heart of the Rio Grande
       (L. Haywood); Song of Texas
1944: Home in Indiana; One Body Too Many (M.
       Shane); Double Exposure (M. Shane)

1945:   Follow That Woman (M. Shane)
1946:   My Darling Clementine (S. Engel); They Made
        Me a Killer*
1947:   Danger Street*
1948:   Relentless; Station West (F. Fenton)
1950:   Rocky Mountain (A. LeMay); Tripoli
1951:   The Last Outpost*; Hong Kong
1952:   The Blazing Forest (L. Foster); Carson City
        (S. Nibley)
1953:   The Vanquished*
1954:   The Boy from Oklahoma (F. Davis); The Bounty
        Hunter
1955:   The Far Horizons (E. North); Lucy Gallant
        (J. Mahin); Run for Cover
1956:   Tension at Table Rock
1957:   Escapade in Japan; April Love
1958:   Mardi Gras (H. Kanter)
1959:   A Private's Affair; Hound-Dog Man (F.
        Gipson)

BERTRAM MILLHAUSER

1932:   Sherlock Holmes
1933:   Ever in My Heart; Storm at Daybreak
1934:   Jimmy the Gent
1936:   The Garden Murder Case; The Magnificent
        Brute*
1937:   The Crime Nobody Saw; Ebb Tide; Under Cover
        of Night
1938:   The Texans*; Scandal Sheet (E. Welch)
1939:   Nick Carter -- Master Detective; 6,000
        Enemies
1940:   River's End (B. Trivers); An Angel from
        Texas (F. Niblo)
1942:   The Big Shot*
1943:   The Purple V (C. Siodmak); Sherlock Holmes
        Faces Death; Sherlock Holmes in Washington
        (L. Riggs)
1944:   Sherlock Holmes and the Spider Woman; The
        Invisible Man's Revenge; The Pearl of Death;
        Enter Arsene Lupin; The Suspect (A. Horman)
1945:   Patrick the Great (D. Bennett); The Woman in
        Green
1946:   White Tie and Tails
1947:   The Web*
1949:   Tokyo Joe*

HUGH MILLS

1937:   Personal Property (E. Vajda)
1954:   Lovers, Happy Lovers

PETER MILNE

1929:   Come Across
1933:   Kennel Murder Case (R. Lee); From
        Headquarters (R.N. Lee)
1934:   Registered Nurse (L. Hayward); Return of the
        Terror (E. Solow)
1935:   Gold Diggers of 1935 (M. Seff); Mary Jane's
        Pa (T. Reed); Miss Pacific Fleet (L.
        Newmark); Woman in Red (M. McCall)
1936:   Colleen*; The Murder of Dr. Harrigan*; Polo
        Joe (H. Cummings); The Walking Dead*
1937:   San Quentin (H. Cobb)
1939:   The House of Fear; Mr. Moto in Danger Island
1940:   Rancho Grande*; Private Affairs*
1941:   They Meet Again (M. Leo)
1944:   Lady, Let's Dance (M. Panaieff); Step Lively
        (W. Duff)
1945:   God Is My Co-Pilot
1946:   The Verdict
1947:   My Wild Irish Rose
1948:   April Showers
1950:   The Daughter of Rosie O'Grady
1952:   About Face; She's Workng Her Way Through
        College
1953:   Geraldine (F. Gill)
1956:   Glory

DAVID SCOTT MILTON

1971:   Born to Win

GEORGE MILTON (also GEORGE SAYRE, MILTON RAISON)

1933:   Air Hostess (K. Thompson); Reform Girl
1934:   Strictly Dynamite*
1935:   Code of the Mounted; Racing Luck (Jack
        O'Donnell)
1936:   Song of the Trail*; Go-Get-'Em Haines

1939:   The Girl from Rio (J. Neville); Undercover
        Agent
1940:   Murder on the Yukon; West of Carson City*
1941:   Tumbledown Ranch in Arizona' Double Cross
        (R. Ferguson)
1942:   Jungle Siren*; Queen of Broadway (R.
        McCullough); Secrets of a Co-Ed; Rolling
        Down the Great Divide; Billy the Kid's
        Smoking Guns; Sheriff of Sage Valley; Bombs
        over Burma (J. Lewis)
1943:   Fugitive of the Plains; Nearly Eighteen; The
        Sultan's Daughter (T. Ryan); Where Are Your
        Children? (H. Lynn)
1944:   Wild Horse Phantom; Alaska*; The Contender
1945:   Border Badmen; High Powered (M. Shane); His
        Brother's Ghost (G. Plympton); The Phantom
        of 42nd Street; The Shanghai Cobra (G.
        Callahan); They Shall Have Faith (alt.
        Forever Yours)*
1946:   Terrors on Horseback; The Mysterious Mr.
        Valentine; Secrets of a Sirority Girl
1947:   Spoilers of the North; The Web of Danger (D.
        Lang)
1948:   Big Town Scandal; Mr. Reckless (M. Shane);
        Speed to Spare; Stage Struck (A. Johnston)
1949:   Dynamite; State Department File 649
1950:   A Modern Marriage (S. Roeca)
1951:   Street Bandits; The Prince of Peace (M.
        Horn)
1952:   Old Oklahoma Plains
1953:   Topeka; The Homesteaders (S. Theil); Old
        Overland Trail

JO MILWARD

1937:   The Devil Is Driving (R. Blake)

ALLEN H. MINER

1968:   Chubasco

WORTHINGTON MINER

1934:   Let's Try Again (A. Scott)

R. J. MINNEY

1935:   Clive of India (W. Lipscomb)

SAM MINTZ

1930:   Santa Fe Trail; Only Saps Work*
1931:   Fin and Hattie
1932:   Handle with Care (F. Craven); Make Me a
        Star*
1933:   Gallant Lady; Man Hunt (L. Praskins); No
        Marriage Ties (A. Caesar)
1934:   Anne of Green Gables; Rafter Romance*
1935:   Roberta*
1936:   Chatterbox; The Farmer in the Dell (J.
        Grey); Crack-Up (Charles Kenyon)
1948:   Music Man

TIM MIRANDA

1930:   Mamba (Winifred Dunn)

JOSEF MISCHEL

1944:   Mademoiselle Fifi (P. Ruric)
1945:   Prison Ship (B. Markson); Isle of the Dead
        (A. Wray)
1946:   Danger Woman; Live Wires (T. Ryan)
1948:   Isn't It Romantic?*; My Own True Love (T.
        Strauss)

WILLIAM PAUL MISHKIN

1953:   Violated

MICHAEL MISLOVE

1976:   Tunnelvision (N. Israel)
1979:   Americathon*

BROWNIE MITCHELL

1931:   Sheer Luck

CRAIG MITCHELL

1976:   Jim -- the World's Greatest (D. Coscarelli)

DON MITCHELL

1972:   Thumb Tripping

HELEN MITCHELL

1933:   Her Secret

JULIAN MITCHELL

1966:   Arabesque*

SIDNEY MITCHELL

1933:   Smoke Lightning (G. Rigby)

THOMAS MITCHELL (1892-1962) actor

1934:   All of Me (S. Buchman)

WILSON MIZNER

1932:   Dark Horse (J. Jackson); One Way Passage (J.
        Jackson); Winner Take All
1933:   Frisco Jenny (R. Lord); Hard to Handle (R.
        Lord); Heroes for Sale (R. Lord); The Little
        Giant (R. Lord); The Mind Reader (R. Lord)

HY MIZRAHI

1971:   The Animals

DAVID MOESSINGER

1967:   The Caper of the Golden Bulls (E. Waters)
1969:   Number One

IVAN MOFFAT

1956:   Bhowani Junction (S. Levien); D-Day, the
        Sixth of June (H. Brown); Giant (F. Guiol)
1957:   Boy on a Dolphin (Dwight Taylor); The
        Wayward Bus
1959:   They Came to Cordura (R. Rossen)
1962:   Tender Is the Night
1965:   The Heroes of Telemark
1977:   Black Sunday*

JEFF MOFFIT

1935:   Bonnie Scotland (F. Butler)
1936:   Kelly the Second*

JACK MOFFITT

1955:   The African Lion (doc.)*

JOHN C. MOFFITT

1936:   Rhythm on the Range*; Murder with Pictures
        (S. Salkow)
1937:   Double or Nothing*; Mountain Music*;
        Exclusive*; Night Key (T. Tupper)
1938:   Ride a Crooked Mile (F. Reyher)
1939:   I'm from Missouri (D. Atterberry); Our
        Leading Citizen; St. Louis Blues (M. Boylan)
1940:   Melody Ranch*
1944:   Passage to Marseille (C. Robinson)
1947:   Ramrod*

JOE REB MOFFLY

1974:   Chosen Survivors (H. B. Cross)

ELICK MOLL

1946: Wake Up and Dream
1948: You Were Meant for Me (V. Davies)
1951: House on Telegraph Hill (F. Partos)
1952: Night Without Sleep (F. Partos)
1956: Storm Center (D. Taradash)
1957: Spring Reunion (R. Pirosh)

FERENC MOLNAR

1942: Tales of Manhattan*

ANTHONY MONACO

1975: Win, Place or Steal (R. Bailey)

PAUL MONASH

1954: Operation Manhunt
1957: Bailout at 43,000
1958: The Safecracker; The Gun Runners (G. Homes)

B. MONASTER

1965: Goldstein (P. Kaufman)

NATE MONASTER

1957: The Sad Sack (E. Beloin)
1962: That Touch of Mink (S. Shapiro)
1963: Call Me Bwana (J. Harwood)
1965: A Very Special Favor (S. Shapiro)
1968: How to Save a Marriage -- and Ruin Your Life
      (S. Shapiro)

JOHN MONKS, JR. (1910-   ) playwright

1940: Strike Up the Band (F. Finklehoffe)
1945: The House on 92nd Street*
1946: 13 Rue Madeleine (S. Bartlett)
1957: Wild Harvest

```
1949:   Knock on Any Door (D. Taradash)
1950:   Dial 1119; The West Point Story*
1951:   The People Against O'Hara
1952:   Where's Charley?
1953:   So This Is Love
1962:   No Man Is an Island (R. Goldstone)
```

CAROL MONPERE

```
1978:   The Mouse and His Child (anim.)
```

THOMAS MONROE

```
1945: The Affairs of Susan*
```

ERIC MONTE

```
1974:   Nine Lives of Fritz the Cat (anim.)*
1975:   Cooley High
```

GEORGE MONTGOMERY (1916-   ) actor

```
1961:   The Steel Claw*
1962:   Samar (F. Grofe)
```

H. FRANK MOON

```
1974:   Savage Sisters (H. Corner)
```

Q. MOONBLOOD

```
1982:   First Blood*
```

MARTIN MOONEY

```
1936:   Missing Girls (J. Krafft)
1937:   You Can't Buy Luck (A. Horman)
1941:   Emergency Landing; Federal Fugitives; Mr.
        Celebrity; Paper Bullets; The Blonde Comet
1942:   The Broadway Big Shot; Foreign Agent (J.
        Krafft); The Panther's Claw
```

1943:   Danger! Women at Work
1944:   The Monster Maker; Waterfront (I. Franklyn)

BETTY MOORE

1929:   Bachelor's Club; The Heroic Lover; Back from
        Shanghai

DANIEL MOORE

1936:   The Last of the Mohicans*
1938:   The Storm*

McELBERT MOORE

1944:   Ever Since Venus (A. Dreifuss)
1948:   An Old-Fashioned Girl (A. Dreifuss)
1949:   Shamrock Hill (A. Hoerl)

ROBIN MOORE

1981:   Inchon (L. Koenig)

VIN MOORE

1934:   The Red Rider (ser.)*; Tailspin Tommy (ser)*
1935:   Rustlers of Red Dog (ser.)*

WILLIAM MOORE

1979:   Five Days from Home

CHARLES MORAN

1947:   Exposed (R. Cole)

E. EDWARD MORAN

1935:   Two Fisted*
1937:   Topper*

1938: Merrily We Live (J. Jevne); There Goes My
       Heart (J. Jevne)
1939: Topper Takes a Trip*
1941: The Man Who Lost Himself
1942: Twin Beds*
1943: Wintertime*
1945: Eve Knew Her Apples; Hold That Blonde*

JACK MORAN

1966: Faster Pussycat! Kill! Kill! (R. Meyer)

JOHN E. MORAN

1967: Good Morning and Goodbye!

STEPHEN MOREHOUSE

1948: The Woman in White

WARD MOREHOUSE

1932: Big City Blues (L. Hayward); Central Park
       (E. Baldwin)

AINSWORTH MORGAN

1934: Man of Two Worlds (H. Green)
1935: A Dog of Flanders (D. Yost)
1936: The Gorgeous Hussy (S. Avery)
1937: Espionage*

AL MORGAN

1956: The Great Man (J. Ferrer)

ANDRE MORGAN

1982: Megaforce*

BYRON MORGAN

1929: All at Sea (A. Price)
1931: Five Star Final; Upper Underworld (R. Lord)
1932: Fast Life (R. Spence)
1933: Flying Devils (Louis Stevens)
1934: Come On, Marines (J. Sayre); Hell in the
      Heavens*; Sons of the Desert (F. Craven)
1935: It's in the Air*
1936: The Sky Parade*
1937: High Flyers*
1939: Burn 'Em Up O'Connor (M. Merlin); Danger
      Flight (E. Parsons)
1942: Wings for the Eagle (B. Orkow); The Powers
      Girl (H. Segall)
1946: Gallant Journey (W. Wellman)

GENE MORGAN

1932: Sin's Pay Day (B. Burbridge)

GEORGE MORGAN

1931: The Avenger (J. Townley); Headin' for
      Trouble; The Cyclone Kid; Quick Trigger Lee;
      Fingerprints (ser.)*
1932: Human Targets; The Devil Horse (ser.)*;
      Airmail Mystery (ser.)*; Jungle Mystery
      (ser.)*; The Lost Special (ser.)*
1933: Her Forgotten Past; The Whispering Shadow
      (ser.)*
1934: The Red Rider (ser.)*; Badge of Honor; The
      Fighting Rookie; The Oil Raider; Heroes of
      the Flames (ser.)*
1935: The Silent Code; Rescue Squad (B.
      Burbridge); Calling All Cars (B. Burbridge)
1940: Deadwood Dick (ser.)*

JOHN MORGAN

1933: Trailing North

JOSEPH MORHAIM

1957: The Happy Road*

LOUIS MORHEIM

1948: Larceny*; Smart Woman*
1949: Ma and Pa Kettle*
1952: For Men Only
1953: The Beast from 20,000 Fathoms (F.
       Freiberger)
1956: Rumble on the Docks (J. DeWitt)
1957: The Tijuana Story
1958: The Last Blitzkrieg

HENRY K. MORITZ

1947: Cigarette Girl

DAVID B. MORRIS

1975: Loose Ends (V. Wozniak)

EDMUND MORRIS

1962: The Savage Guns; Walk on the Wild Side (J.
       Fante)
1968: Project X

GOUVERNEUR MORRIS

1936: The Jungle Princess*

MICHAEL MORRIS

1963: For Love or Money (L. Markes)
1964: Wild and Wonderful*

RICHARD MORRIS

1951: Finders Keepers
1952: Ma and Pa Kettle at the Fair (John Grant)
1953: Take Me to Town

```
1962:   If a Man Answers
1967:   Thoroughly Modern Millie
```

QUINN MORRISON

```
1969:   The Hooked Generation*
```

T. J. MORRISON

```
1954:   Duel in the Jungle (S. Marx)
```

PAUL MORRISSEY (1939-   ) director

```
1968:   Flesh
1970:   Trash
1972:   Heat
1973:   L'Amour
1974:   Andy Warhol's Frankenstein; Andy Warhol's
        Dracula
```

DOUGLAS MORROW

```
1949:   The Stratton Story (G. Trosper)
1951:   Jim Thorpe -- All American (E. Freeman)
1956:   Beyond a Reasonable Doubt
1973:   Maurie
```

VIC MORROW

```
1967:   Deathwatch (B Turner)
1971:   A Man Called Sledge (F. Kowalski)
```

WILLIAM MORROW

```
1940:   Buck Benny Rides Again (E. Beloin); Love Thy
        Neighbor*
1952:   Road to Bali*
```

N. BREWSTER MORSE

```
1932:   The Savage Girl
```

1937:   The Perfect Specimen*

CHAPMAN MORTIMER

1967:   Reflections in a Golden Eye (Gladys Hill)

JOHN MORTIMER

1969:   John and Mary

GUY MORTON

1935:   Secrets of Chinatown (Can.)

JOHN MORTON

1962:   Panic in the Year Zero (J. Simms)

TAD MOSEL

1964:   Dear Heart
1967:   Up the Down Staircase

JAMES E. MOSER

1953:   Wings of the Hawk

ANDREW MOSES

1934:   Green Eyes; Murder on the Campus

RICHARD MOSES

1981:   On the Right Track*

BOB MOSHER

1966:   Munster, Go Home*

LOUIS MOSHER

1935:   Tarzan Escapes*

BERENICE MOSK

1958:   The Buccaneer*

GEORGE MOSKOV

1960:   Three Blondes in His Life

CHARLES MOSS

1972:   Dirty Little Billy (S. Dragoti)

FRANK L. MOSS

1951:   The Whip Hand (G. Bricker)
1952:   Caribbean (E. Ludwig)
1953:   The Vanquished*; Sangaree (D. Duncan)

OSCAR MUGGE

1947:   Heading for Heaven (L. Collins)

FLORABELL MUIR

1935:   Fighting Youth*

JAMES MULHAUSER (-1939)

1932:   Hidden Gold (J. Natteford)
1935:   Strange Wives (G. Unger)
1936:   The Dragnet; Love Letters of a Star*
1937:   Love in a Bungalow*; Prescription for a
        Romance*; Carnival Queen (H. Buckley)
1938:   The Gladiator*

574

DONN MULLALLY

1959: The Flying Fontaines (L. Erwin)

DON MULLALY

1933: Girl Missing (C. Erickson); Mystery of the
       Wax Museum (C. Erickson); She Had to Say Yes
       (R. James)

ROMEO MULLER

1974: Marco

CLAUDE MULOT

1982: Contract: Kill (A. Kantof)

LEWIS MUMFORD (1895-   ) writer, historian,
        philosopher, teacher

1939: The City (doc.; H. Rodakiewicz)

CYNTHIA MUNROE

1969: The Wedding Party*

JOEL MURCOTT

1956: Manfish

JANE MURFIN (1893-1955) playwright

1929: Street Girl; Dance Hall (J. Ruben)
1930: Seven Keys to Baldpate; The Pay Off;
       Leathernecking (A. Jackson); Lawful Larceny;
       The Runaway Bride
1931: Friends and Lovers (W. Smith); Too Many
       Crooks
1932: What Price Hollywood*; Young Bride (G.
       Fort); Rockabye (K. Glasmon); Way Back Home

1933: After Tonight (A. LeVino); Ann Vickers;
      Double Harness; Our Betters (H. Gribble);
      The Silver Cord
1934: Crime Doctor; The Fountain (S. Hoffenstein);
      Life of Vergie Winters; The Little
      Minister*; Romance in Manhattan (E.
      Kaufman); Spitfire (L. Vollmer); This Man Is
      Mine
1935: Alice Adams*; Roberta*
1936: Come and Get It (J. Furthman)
1937: I'll Take Romance (G. Oppenheimer)
1938: The Shining Hour (O. Nash)
1939: Stand Up and Fight*; The Women*
1940: Pride and Prejudice (A. Huxley)
1941: Andy Hardy's Private Secretary (H. Ruskin)
1943: Flight for Freedom*
1944: Dragon Seed (Marguerite Roberts)

MARY MURILLO

1931: The Parisian

DENNIS MURPHY

1967: Eye of the Devil (R. Estridge)
1968: The Sergeant
1971: The Todd Killings (J. Oliansky)

DUDLEY MURPHY (1897-   ) director, producer

1939: One Third of a Nation (O. Garrett)
1944: Alma del Bronce (Mex.)

EDWARD MURPHY

1982: Raw Force

EMMETT MURPHY

1955: Canyon Crossroads (L. Heideman)
1957: Valerie (L. Heideman)

JOSEPH MURPHY

1941: Law of the Wolf

RALPH MURPHY (1895–1967) director

1945: Sunbonnet Sue (R. Carroll)
1955: Mystery of the Black Jungle (J. Callegari)

RICHARD MURPHY (1912–   ) director

1941: Back in the Saddle (J. Lasky); The Apache
       Kid (E. Gibbons); Flying Blind (M. Shane)
1942: Jesse James, Jr.*; Cyclone Kid; I Live on
       Danger*; Wildcat (M. Shane); Wrecking Crew
       (M. Shane); X Marks the Spot (S. Palmer)
1947: Boomerang
1948: Cry of the City; Deep Waters
1949: Slattery's Hurricane (H. Wouk)
1950: Panic in the Streets*
1951: You're in the Navy Now (orig. U.S.S.
       Teakettle)
1952: Les Miserables
1953: The Desert Rats
1954: Broken Lance
1955: Three Stripes in the Sun
1959: Compulsion; The Last Angry Man (Gerald
       Green)
1960: The Wackiest Ship in the Army
1980: The Kidnapping of the President

WARREN MURPHY

1975: The Eiger Sanction*

DON MURRAY (1929–   )

1969: Childish Things
1970: The Cross and the Switchblade*
1977: Damien

JOHN FENTON MURRAY

1954: The Atomic Kid (B. Freedman)

```
1956:   Jaguar (B. Freedman)
1961:   Everything's Ducky (B. Freedman)
1962:   It's Only Money
1964:   Man's Favorite Sport? (S. McNeil)
1965:   McHale's Navy Joins the Air Force
1968:   Did You Hear the One About the Traveling
        Saleslady?
1970:   Puffnstuff (Si Rose)
1973:   Arnold (J. Brewer)
```

LARRY MURRAY

```
1973:   The Gospel Road (J. Cash)
```

CLARENCE MUSE (1889–1979) actor

```
1939:   Way Down South (L. Hughes)
1940:   Broken Strings*
```

ROBERT MUSEL

```
1961:   Circle of Deception (N. Balchin)
```

M. M. MUSSELMAN

```
1938:   Straight, Place and Show*; Kentucky
        Moonshine*
1939:   The Three Musketeers*
1943:   Rhythm of the Islands (O. Brodney)
1945:   Shady Lady*
1946:   Tangier (M. Collins)
```

FLOYD MUTRUX

```
1971:   Dusty and Sweets McGee; The Christian
        Licorice Store
1975:   Aloha, Bobby and Rose
1980:   The Hollywood Knights
```

HARRY MYERS

```
1930:   Her Wedding Night
```

1939: Destry Rides Again*

HENRY MYERS

1931: Murder by the Clock
1932: Million Dollar Legs*
1933: The Diplomaniacs
1935: The Black Room (A. Strawn); Father Brown,
       Detective (C. Sullivan)
1936: College Holiday*; The Luckiest Girl in the
       World (H. Fields)
1944: Hey, Rookie*
1951: Alice in Wonderland (Fr.)*

JOHN MYERS

1979: The Prize Fighter (Tim Conway)
1980: The Private Eyes (Tim Conway)

SIDNEY MYERS (1894-   ) psychiatrist, filmmaker

1948: The Quiet One (doc.)*
1960: The Savage Eye (doc.)*

ZION MYERS

1933: Lucky Dog
1940: Love Thy Neighbors*
1944: Here Come the Waves*

ALAN MYERSON

1976: It's Showtime (doc.)

FRED MYTON

1930: The Great Divide*; The Other Tomorrow
1932: White Eagle
1933: King of the Wild Horses
1937: The Gambling Terror (G. Plympton); Trail of
       Vengeance (G. Plympton); The Trusted Outlaw
       (G. Plympton); Gun Lords of Stirrup Basin

579

	(G. Plympton); Border Phantom; Moonlight on the Range; The Roaming Cowboy
1938:	Two Gun Justice; Knight of the Plains; Gunsmoke Trail; Desert Patrol; Terror of Tiny Town; Harlem on the Prairie
1939:	Six-Gun Rhythm; Code of the Fearless; Rollin' Westward
1940:	Two-Fisted Rangers; Pioneers of the Frontier; Texas Stagecoach; The Return of Wild Bill (R. Lees); Prairie Schooners (R. Lee); Wildcat of Tucson
1941:	The Pinto Kid; The Lone Rider in Frontier Fury; Billy the Kid Wanted; Billy the Kid's Roundup; Gentleman from Dixie
1942:	Tumbleweed Trail; Prairie Gunsmoke; The Lone Prairie; The Mad Monster
1943:	The Kid Rides Again; Riders of the Northwest Mounties; Law of the Saddle; Dead Men Walk; The Black Raven
1944:	Thundering Gun Slingers; Wyoming Hurricane; Oath of Vengeance; Nabonga
1945:	Shadows of Death; Stagecoach Outlaws; Prairie Rustlers; Kid Sister; Apology for Murder
1946:	Gentlemen with Guns; Prairie Badmen; Blonde for a Day; Murder Is My Business
1947:	Lady Chasers; Three on a Ticket
1948:	The Counterfeiters (B. Worth); Miraculous Journey
1950:	Hi-Jacked (O. Hampton); Western Pacific Agent
1951:	Whistling Hills
1952:	The Gunman

N

IVAN NAGY

1973: Bad Charleston Charlie*

MICHAEL NAHAY

1976: The Thursday Morning Murders

DESMOND NAKANO

1973: Boulevard Nights

ARTHUR A. NAMES

1966: The Black Klansman (J. T. Wilson)

ARTHUR & JO NAPOLEON

1957: Man on the Prowl
1958: Too Much Too Soon
1964: Ride the Wild Surf
1969: The Activist

ALDEN NASH

1958: Unwed Mother (A. Bond)

OGDEN NASH (1902-1971) poet

1937: The Firefly*

1938:   The Shining Hour (J. Murfin)
1941:   The Feminine Touch*

N. RICHARD NASH

1947:   Nora Prentiss
1949:   Dear Wife (A. Sheekman)
1950:   The Goldbergs (G. Berg); The Vicious Years
1952:   Mara Maru
1955:   Top of the World (J. Klorer)
1956:   The Rainmaker
1959:   Porgy and Bess
1976:   One Summer Love

ROBERT NATHAN

1945:   The Clock (J. Schrank)
1950:   Pagan Love Song (J. Davis)

RICH NATKIN

1978:   The Boys in Company C (S. Furie)
1980:   Night of the Juggler (W. Norton)

JOHN FRANCIS NATTEFORD

1929:   Dark Skies; Flying Marine; Light Fingers;
        New Orleans
1930:   Border Romance; Fightin' Thru; The
        Thoroughbred; Troopers Three
1931:   Clearing the Range; The Two Gun Man; Wild
        Horse; The Arizona Terror; Hard Hombre;
        Private Scandal; Women Men Marry
1932:   The Last of the Mohicans (ser.)*; The Cowboy
        Counsellor; Hidden Gold (J. Millhauser);
        Bachelor Mother*; File 113; My Pal, the King
        (T. Crizer); Out of Singapore (alt.
        Gangsters of the Sea)
1933:   His Private Secretary; Neighbors' Wives; The
        Dude Bandit; Fighting with Kit Carson
        (ser.)*; Riot Squad (B. Sarecky)
1934:   A Demon for Trouble; Brand of Hate; House of
        Danger; The Mystic Hour
1935:   The Crimson Trail*; The Rider of the Law;

Fighting Lady; The Headline Woman (B.
Church); Never Too Late (C. Krusada); $1,000
a Minute*

1936: The Lonely Trail (B. McConville); The Three
Mesquiteers; Roaring Lead (O. Drake); The
Millionaire Kid (B. Church); Ticket to
Paradise (N. West); The Oregon Trail*; ; The
Return of Jimmy Valentine (O. Cooper)

1937: Rootin' Tootin' Rhythm; Yodelin' Kid from
Pine Ridge*; Heart of the Rockies (O.
Drake); Paradise Express (B. Burbridge)

1938: Rawhide (D. Jarrett); Gold Mine in the Sky
(B. Burbridge); Billy the Kid Returns; Come
On, Rangers! (G. Geraghty); Shine On,
Harvest Moon; International Crime

1939: Rough Riders Round-Up; Southward Ho! (J.
Rathmell); Wyoming Outlaw (B. Burbridge);
The Kansas Terrors (B. Burbridge)

1940: Heroes of the Saddle; Pioneers of the West*;
One Man's Law (B. Cohen)

1941: Dangerous Lady; Double Trouble; Law of the
Timber

1942: Inside the Law; They Raid by Night

1945: Trail of Kit Carson (A. DeMond)

1946: Badman's Territory (L. Ward); Rustler's
Roundup

1947: Trail to San Antone (L. Ward)

1948: Black Bart*; Return of the Badmen*

1949: Rustlers (L. Ward)

1950: The Return of Jesse James

1951: Cattle Drive (L. Hayward)

1955: Blackjack Ketchum, Desperado (L. Ward)

1957: The Night the World Exploded (L. Ward)

1966: Kid Rodelo

1967: The Ride to Hangman's Tree*

WILLIAM T. NAUD

1972: Wild in the Sky (D. Gautier)

GREGORY NAVA

1982: The End of August*

LEX NEAL

1940: Mr. Washington Goes to Town (W. Weems)

RICHARD NEAL

1967: Valley of Mystery (L. Barrington)

HAROLD NEBENZAL

1954: Miss Robin Crusoe
1975: The Wilby Conspiracy (R. Amateau)

HAL NEEDHAM

1982: Megaforce*

JEAN NEGULESCO (1900-   ) director

1937: Expensive Husbands*

DAVID NEIBEL

1971: Chrome and Hot Leather*

ROY WILLIAM NEILL (1886-1946) director

1939: Murder Will Out (Brit.)*; Hoots Man (Brit.)*
1944: The Scarlet Claw (E. Hartmann)

ALVIN J. NEITZ (also ALAN JAMES)

1930: Canyon Hawks (H. Taylor); Breed of the West
       (H. Taylor); Trails of Peril
1931: Red Fork Range (H. Taylor); Hell's Valley;
       Flying Lariats; Lariats and Sixshooters;
       Come On, Tarzan
1932: Fargo Express (E. Snell)
1933: Drum Taps; The Phantom Thunderbolt*; The
       Lone Avenger; King of the Arena
1934: When a Man Sees Red
1936: Lucky Terror

584

1945: Manhunt of Mystery Island (ser.)*

DAVID NELSON

1971: Right On!*

DICK NELSON

1971: One More Train to Rob (D. Tait)

DON NELSON

1976: No Deposiit, No Return (A. Alsberg); Gus (A.
       A. Alsberg)
1977: Herbie Goes to Monte Carlo (A. Alsberg)
1978: Hot Lead and Cold Feet*

DONALD NELSON

1952: Here Come the Nelsons*

GRANT NELSON

1943: Captain America (ser.)*; The Masked Marvel
       (ser.)*
1944: Zorro's Black Whip (ser.)*; Haunted Harbor
       (ser.)*; The Tiger Woman (ser.)*
1945: Manhunt of Mystery Island (ser.)*

JACK NELSON

1931: Two Gun Caballero
1934: The Rawhide Terror; Pirate Treasure (ser.)*

OZZIE NELSON

1952: Here Come the Nelsons*
1965: Love and Kisses

RALPH NELSON (1916-   ) director

1971: Flight of the Doves (Brit.; F. Gabrielson)
1972: The Wrath of God

RUDY & SHIRLEY NELSON

1966: Way Out (J. Yeaworth)

LEN NEUBAUER

1973: Sweet Suzy (R. Meyer)
1981: New Year's Evil

E. JACK NEUMAN

1967: The Venetian Affair
1972: Company of Killers

SAM NEUMAN (also SAM NEWMAN)

1943: Career Girl; Hitler -- Dead or Alive (K.
       Brown)
1944: Dixie Jamboree; Machine Gun Mama
1946: Down Missouri Way
1948: The Shanghai Chest (W. Darling)
1949: The Judge*
1950: I Killed Geronimo (N. Tanchuck); Federal Man
       (N. Tuchock)
1951: The Hoodlum (N. Tanchuck)
1952: Buffalo Bill in Tomahawk Territory (N.
       Tanchuck)
1962: Hitler

ALFRED NEUMANN

1946: The Return of Monte Cristo (G. Bruce)

KURT NEUMANN (1906-1958) director

1950: Rocketship X-M
1954: Carnival Story*
1955: They Were So Young (F. Luetzkendorf)

```
1956:   The Desperadoes Are in Town (E. Snell)
1957:   She-Devil (Carroll Young); Apache Warrior*;
        The Deerslayer (Carroll Young)
1958:   Circus of Love (Germ.; H. Jacoby); Machete
        (Carroll Young)
```

GRACE NEVILLE

```
1935:   Air Hawks (G. Jay)
1936:   Dangerous Intrigue; Shakedown
1937:   Counsel for Crime*; Find the Witness (F.
        Niblo); The Game That Kills (F. Niblo);
        Motor Madness (F. Niblo)
1938:   All-American Sweetheart*; Little Miss
        Roughneck*
```

JOHN THOMAS NEVILLE

```
1930:   The Dawn Trail
1931:   The Flood; Homicide Squad; Trader Horn*
1932:   Heart Punch; Her Mad Night; Honor of the
        Press; Malay Nights; Midnight Warning
1933:   Alimony Madness; Behind Jury Doors; Her
        Resale Value; Justice Takes a Holiday;
        Revenge at Monte Carlo; Sister to Judas
1934:   Hollywood Hoodlum
1935:   Outlawed Guns; The Ivory-Handled Gun;
        Atlantic Adventure (N. Dorfman); The
        Midnight Phantom
1936:   Ridin' On; The Lion's Den; The Glory Trail;
        Rebellion
1937:   Battle of Greed; Blazing Sixes; Drums of
        Destiny (R. Whatley); Raw Timber (B. Cohen);
        Empty Holsters; County Fair; Tough to Handle
        (S. Lowe); Valley of Terror (S. Lowe)
1938:   Barefoot Boy (K. Brown); Female Fugitive (B.
        Cohen); Gang Bullets; My Old Kentucky Home;
        Numbered Woman (K. Brown)
1939:   The Girl from Rio (G. Milton)
1941:   Devil Bat; Never Give a Sucker an Even Break
        (P. Chaplin)
1944:   Shake Hands with Murder; Rogues' Gallery
1946:   The Flying Serpent
```

ROBERT NEVILLE

1938:   Peck's Bad Boy with the Circus*
1941:   The Black Cat*

GAYL NEWBURY

1939:   Should a Girl Marry (D. Silverstein)

SAM NEWFIELD

1942:   The Lone Rider in Border Roundup (alt.
        Border Roundup)
1952:   The Gambler and the Lady

DAVID NEWHOUSE

1967:   Point Blank*

RAFE NEWHOUSE

1967:   Point Blank*

GORDON NEWILL

1937:   The Californian (G. Wright)

DAVID NEWMAN (1937-   )

1967:   Bonnie and Clyde (R. Benton)
1970:   There Was a Crooked Man*
1972:   What's Up, Doc?*; Bad Company (R. Benton)
1974:   Money's Tight
1978:   Superman*
1981:   Superman II*
1982:   Jinxed (B. Blessing)

SAM NEWMAN (see SAM NEUMAN)

LESLIE NEWMAN

1978:   Superman*
1981:   Superman II*

SAMUEL NEWMAN

1951:   Jungle Manhunt; Tarzan's Peril (F. Swann)
1952:   Jungle Jim in the Forbidden Land; Voodoo
        Tiger; A Yank in Indo-China
1953:   Valley of the Headhunters; Prince of Pirates
        (J. O'Dea); Sky Commando*
1954:   Jungle Man-Eaters
1957:   The Giant Claw (P. Gangelin)
1959:   Invisible Invaders

WALTER NEWMAN

1951:   The Big Carnival (orig. Ace in the Hole)
1955:   The Man with the Golden Arm (L. Meltzer);
        Underwater!
1957:   The True Story of Jesse James
1959:   Crime and Punishment U.S.A.
1962:   The Interns (D. Swift)
1965:   Cat Ballou (F. Pierson)
1978:   Bloodbrothers
1979:   The Champ

LUCILLE NEWMARK

1935:   Miss Pacific Fleet (P. Milne)

SLOAN NIBLEY

1947:   Bells of San Angelo; Springtime in the
        Sierras; On the Old Spanish Trail
1948:   The Gay Ranchero; Under California Stars (P.
        Gangelin); Eyes of Texas; Night Time in
        Nevada; The Far Frontier; Nightmare in
        Nevada
1949:   Susanna Pass (J. Butler); Down Dakota Way
        (J. Butler); The Golden Stallion
1950:   Bells of Coronado; Twilight in the Sierras;
        Surrender (J. E. Grant)
1951:   Spoilers of the Plains; In Old Amarillo
1952:   Carson City (W. Miller)

1956:   Thunder over Arizona
1967:   Hostile Guns (S. Fisher)

FRED NIBLO, JR. (1903-1973)

1931:   The Criminal Code (S. Miller)
1933:   King of the Jungle*
1934:   Among the Missing*; The Hell Cat; Name the
        Woman (H. Asbury); Whom the Gods Destroy (S.
        Buchman); Fugitive Lady (H. Asbury)
1935:   Death Flies East (A. DeMond); Escape from
        Devil's Island (E. Snell); Unknown Woman (A.
        DeMond)
1936:   Lady from Nowhere*; The Man Who Lived
        Twice*; Roaming Lady (E. Snell); You May Be
        Next (F. Reyher)
1937:   Counsel for Crime*; Find the Witness (G.
        Neville); The Game That Kills (G. Neville);
        Motor Madness (G. Neville)
1938:   All-American Sweetheart*; City Streets (L.
        Breslow); Little Miss Roughneck*;
        Penitentiary (S. Miller)
1939:   Hell's Kitchen (C. Wilbur); No Place to Go*;
        Cowboy Quarterback
1940:   An Angel from Texas (B. Millhauser); East of
        the River; The Fighting 69th*
1941:   Father's Son; Nine Lives Are Not Enough;
        Passage from Hong Kong; Three Sons o' Guns;
        The Wagons Roll at Night (B. Trivers)
1942:   You Can't Escape Forever (H. Chevigny)
1943:   The Falcon in Danger (C. Rice)
1944:   Tampico*
1948:   Bodyguard (H. Essex); In This Corner (B.
        Symon); Incident (S. Roeca)
1950:   Convicted*

HERBERT NICCOLLS

1957:   Journey to Freedom

ALLAN NICHOLLS

1978:   A Wedding*
1979:   A Perfect Couple (R. Altman)

ANNE NICHOLS

1946:   Abie's Irish Rose

DUDLEY NICHOLS (1895-1960) director

1930:   Men Without Women; On the Level; Born
        Reckless; One Mad Kiss; A Devil with Women
        (H.M. Johnson)
1931:   Not Exactly Gentlemen (W. Counselman); The
        Seas Beneath; Skyline; Hush Money*
1932:   This Sporting Age
1933:   Robbers' Roost; The Man Who Dared (L.
        Trotti)
1934:   Call It Luck*; Hold That Girl (L. Trotti);
        Judge Priest (L. Trotti); The Lost Patrol
        (G. Fort); Marie Galante (unc.)
1935:   The Arizonian; The Crusades*; The Informer;
        Steamboat 'Round the Bend (L. Trotti); The
        Three Musketeers; Life Begins at 40 (unc.)*;
        She (unc.; Ruth Rose)
1936:   Mary of Scotland; The Plough and the Stars
1937:   The Hurricane*; The Toast of New York*
1938:   Bringing Up Baby (H. Wilde)
1939:   Stagecoach; The Four Hundred Million (doc.)
1940:   The Long Voyage Home
1941:   Man Hunt; Swamp Water
1943:   Air Force; For Whom the Bell Tolls;
        Government Girl; This Land Is Mine
1944:   It Happened Tomorrow (R. Clair)
1945:   The Bells of St. Mary's; And Then There Were
        None; Scarlet Street
1946:   Sister Kenny*
1947:   The Fugitive; Mourning Becomes Electra
1949:   Pinky (P. Dunne)
1951:   Rawhide
1952:   The Big Sky; Return of the Texan
1954:   Prince Valiant
1956:   Run for the Sun (R. Boulting)
1957:   The Tin Star
1959:   The Hangman
1960:   Heller in Pink Tights (W. Bernstein)

PETER NICHOLS

1965: Having a Wild Weekend

JACK NICHOLSON (1937-   ) actor

1963: Thunder Island (D. Devlin)
1966: Ride the Whirlwind; Flight to Fury
1967: The Trip
1968: Head (B. Rafelson)
1971: Drive, He Said (J. Lerner); Ride in the
       Whirlwind

KENYON NICHOLSON

1931: Wicked (K. Scola)
1932: Union Depot (W. DeLeon)
1936: Thirteen Hours by Air (B. Rogers)

NICK NICIPHOR

1978: Our Winning Season

D. JAMES NIELSON

1979: Cry to the Wind

JOSEFINA NIGGLI

1953: Sombrero (N. Foster)

WILLIAM NIGH (1881-   ) director

1931: The Sea Ghost (J. Von Ronbeo)
1944: They Shall Have Faith*

ROBERT NILES

1933: The Mysterious Rider (H. Gates)

BRENT NIMROD

1969: The Female Bunch (J. Lockwood)

STANLEY NISS

1964: FBI Code 98
1969: Pendulum

ANN NOBLE

1975: The Sins of Rachel

BILL NOBLE

1943: Young Ideas (I. Hunter)

WILLIAM F. NOLAN

1976: Burnt Offerings (D. Curtis)

WILLIAM L. NOLTE

1935: Gun Play (alt. Lucky Boots); Big Boy Rides
       Again
1939: Sundown on the Prairie (E. Kelso)
1947: Law of the Lash

THOMAS NOONAN (1922-1968) actor

1959: The Rookie (G. O'Hanlon)
1963: Promises! Promises!
1964: Three Nuts in Search of a Bolt*

VAN NORCROSS

1943: Behind Prison Walls; Revenge of the Zombies
       (E. Kelso)

DENNIS NORDEN

1968: Buona Sera, Mrs. Campbell*; The Bliss of

593

Mrs. Blossom (A. Coppel)

ERIC NORDEN

1956:   Stagecoach to Fury
1957:   The Quiet Gun; Apache Warriors*; Copper Sky;
        Ride a Violent Mile
1958:   Cattle Empire (A. Bohem)
1959:   The Little Savage
1973:   A Scream in the Streets

STEPHEN NORDI

1951:   Journey into Light
1952:   Island of Desire

MARC NORMAN

1973:   Oklahoma Crude
1974:   Zandy's Bride
1975:   Breakout*

STEPHEN NORRIS

1936:   Born to Fight; Racing Blood; Phantom Patrol

CARRINGTON NORTH

1938:   The Headleys at Home (N. Bela)

EDMUND H. NORTH (1911-   )

1934:   One Night of Love (S. Lauren)
1935:   I Dream Too Much (J. Gow); All the King's
        Horses*
1936:   Bunker Bean*; Murder on a Bridle Path*
1937:   The Outcasts of Poker Flat*
1940:   I'm Still Alive
1947:   Dishonored Lady (B. Hecht)
1949:   Colorado Territory (J. Twist)
1950:   Young Man with a Horn (C. Foreman); In a
        Lonely Place (A. Solt)

1951: Only the Valiant (H. Brown); The Day the
       Earth Stood Still
1952: The Outcasts of Poker Flat
1954: Destry
1955: The Far Country (W. Miller)
1956: The Proud Ones
1958: Cowboy (D. Trumbo)
1960: Sink the Bismarck! (Brit.)
1961: The Fiercest Heart
1962: Damn the Defiant (Brit.; N. Kneale)
1970: Patton (F. Coppola)
1979: Meteor (S. Mann)

ROBERT G. NORTH

1946: Dangerous Millions (I. Cummings)
1947: Jewels of Brandenburg*
1948: Night Wind (A. Belgard)

KAYE NORTHROP

1935: The Outlaw Tamer

B. W. L. NORTON

1977: Outlaw Blues
1978: Convoy
1979: More American Graffiti

ELEANOR NORTON

1977: Day of the Animals (W. Norton)
1981: Dirty Tricks*

GRACE KEEL NORTON

1931: Sky Spider
1942: Deep in the Heart of Texas

WILLIAM NORTON

1968: The Scalphunters

595

1969:   Sam Whiskey
1970:   The McKenzie Break
1972:   Cisco Pike
1973:   White Lightning; Trader Horn (E. Harper)
1974:   I Disremember Mama; Big Bad Mama (F. Doel)
1975:   Brannigan*
1976:   Gator; A Small Town in Texas; Moving
        Violation (D. Osterhout)
1977:   Day of the Animals (E. Norton)
1980:   Night of the Juggler (R. Natkin)
1981:   Dirty Tricks*

MAX NOSSECK (1902-1972) director   Germ.

1940:   Overture to Glory (doc.; O. Dymov)
1945:   The Brighton Strangler (A. Phillips)
1950:   Kill or Be Killed*
1957:   Garden of Eden*

KARL NOTO

1939:   The Girl Downstairs*

MICKELL NOVACK

1940:   One Million B.C.*; Turnabout*
1941:   Road Show*

IVOR NOVELLO (1893-1951) actor, playwright   Brit.

(American films only)
1932:   But the Flesh Is Weak

WILFRED NOY

1929:   Linda

SIMON NUCHTERN

1970:   The Cowards
1972:   What Do I Tell the Boys at the Station? (W.
        Reilly)

ELLIOT NUGENT (1899-1980) actor, director,
        playwright

1929:   Wise Girls*
1930:   The Unholy Three
1933:   Whistling in the Dark

FRANK S. NUGENT (1908-1965) film critic

1948:   Three Godfathers (L. Stallings); Fort Apache
1949:   She Wore a Yellow Ribbon (L. Stallings);
        Tulsa (Curtis Kenyon)
1950:   Wagonmaster (P. Ford); Two Flags West (C.
        Robinson)
1952:   Angel Face (O. Millard); The Quiet Man
1954:   The Paratrooper (R. Maibaum); Trouble in the
        Glen; They Rode West (D. Scott)
1955:   Mister Roberts (J. Logan); The Tall Men (S.
        Boehm)
1956:   The Searchers
1957:   The Rising of the Moon
1958:   Gunman's Walk; The Last Hurrah
1961:   Two Rode Together
1963:   Donovan's Reef (J. E. Grant)
1966:   Incident at Phantom Hill

BOB NUNESS

1950:   I Shot Billy the Kid*

RALPH NUSSBAUM

1976:   The Amorous Adventures of Don Quixote and
        Sancho Panza*

CARL NYSTROM

1954:   Twist of Fate

RON NYSTWANER

1982:   Smithereens (S. Seidelman)

O

DAN O' BANNON

1974:   Dark Star (John Carpenter)
1979:   Alien
1981:   Dead and Buried (R. Shusett)

ARCH OBOLER (1909-   ) director, producer

1940:   Escape (M. Roberts)
1943:   Gangway for Tomorrow
1945:   Bewitched; Strange Holiday
1947:   The Arnelo Affair
1951:   Five
1952:   Bwana Devil
1953:   The Twonky
1961:   1+1 (Exploring the Kinsey Reports)
1966:   The Bubble

EDNA O' BRIEN

1972:   X Y and Zee

LIAM O' BRIEN

1950:   Chain Lightning (V. Evans); Of Men and
        Music*
1951:   the Redhead and the Cowboy (J. Latimer);
        Here Comes the Groom*
1952:   Diplomatic Courier (C. Robinson)
1953:   The Stars Are Singing
1960:   The Great Impostor
1961:   The Devil at Four O'Clock

RICHARD O' BRIEN

1981:   Shock Treatment (J. Sharman)

ROBERT O'BRIEN

1950:   Fancy Pants (E. Hartmann)
1951:   The Lemon Drop Kid*
1952:   The Belle of New York (I. Elinson)
1953:   By the Light of the Silvery Moon (I.
        Elinson)
1954:   Lucky Me*
1959:   Say One for Me

JEFFREY OBROW

1982:   Pranks*

EDWARD O'CALLAGHAN

1955:   This Island Earth (F. Coen)
1956:   Flight to Hong Kong (L. Townsend)

JACK O'CONNELL

1963:   Greenwich Village Story

FRANK O'CONNOR

1938:   Religious Racketeers
1939:   Mystic Circle Murders

MANNING O'CONNOR

1940:   Michael Shayne, Private Detective (S. Rauh)
1941:   Dressed to Kill (S. Rauh)

VINCENT O'CONNOR

1949:   Jigsaw (F. Markle)

JOHN O'DEA

1947: Killer Dill
1950: The Admiral Was a Lady (S. Salkow)
1951: Fugitive Lady
1953: Prince of Pirates (S. Newman); Raiders of
       the Seven Seas (S. Salkow); Jack McCall,
       Desperado
1955: Robber's Roost*
1956: Wiretappers

DAVID ODELL

1971: Cry Uncle
1972: Dealing: or the Berkeley-to-Boston 40-Brick
       Lost-Bag Blues (P. Williams)
1975: Foreplay*
1981: The President's Women*
1982: The Dark Crystal

CLIFFORD ODETS (1906-1963) director, playwright

1936: The General Died at Dawn
1944: None but the Lonely Heart
1946: Deadline at Dawn; Humoresque (Z. Gold)
1957: Sweet Smell of Success (E. Lehman)
1959: The Story on Page One
1961: Wild in the Country

JEROME ODLUM

1944: Strange Affair (E. Greene)
1949: Cover Up (J. Rix)
1951: Never Trust a Gambler (J. Lasky)
1954: Highway Dragnet (H. Meadow); The Fast and
       the Furious (J. Howell)

JACK O'DONNELL

1935: Racing Luck (G. Sayre)
1937: North of the Rio Grande; The Texas Trail
1939: The Gentleman from Arizona (E. Haley)

JOSEPH O'DONNELL

1934:   Public Stenographer; The Moth
1935:   Trails of the Wild; His Fighting Blood;
        Timber War; Bulldog Courage (F. Guihan);
        Murder by Television
1936:   Roarin' Guns; Border Caballero; Lightnin'
        Bill Carson; Wildcat Trooper; The Traitor;
        Vengeance of Rannah
1937:   Whistling Bullets; The Fighting Texan;
        Anything for a Thrill (S. Lowenstein); Young
        Dynamite*
1938:   Land of Fighting Men; Songs and Bullets (G.
        Plympton); Phantom Ranger; Lightning Carson
        Rides Again; Six-Gun Trail
1939:   The Adventures of the Masked Phantom (C.
        Sanforth); Flaming Lead; The Gentleman from
        Oklahoma (E. Haley); Straight Shooter (B.
        Dickey); Port of Hate; Reform School (H.
        Jamieson); The Invisible Killer
1940:   Texas Renegades; Gun Code; Arizona
        Gangbusters; Billy the Kid in Texas; Riders
        of Black Mountain; The Shadow (ser.)*
1941:   The Lone Rider Rides On; Billy the Kid in
        Santa Fe; King of the Texas Rangers (ser.)*;
        The Lone Rider Fights Back; Dick Tracy vs.
        Crime, Inc. (ser.)*; Jungle Girl (ser.)*
1942:   King of the Mounties (ser.)*; Perils of
        Nyoka (ser.)*; Spy Smasher (ser.)*
1943:   Wild Horse Rustlers; Daredevils of the West
        (ser.)*; Death Riders of the Plains; Wolves
        of the Range; Cattle Stampede; The Renegade;
        Raiders of Red Gap; Devil Riders; G-Men vs.
        the Black Dragon (ser.)*; Secret Service in
        Darkest Africa (ser.)*
1944:   Frontier Outlaws; Valley of Vengeance;
        Rustlers' Hideout; Land of the Outlaws; Law
        of the Valley
1945:   The Royal Mounted Rides Again (ser.)*; The
        Master Key (ser.)*; Secret Agent X-9 (ser.)*
1946:   The Scarlet Horseman (ser.)*
1947:   Border Feud (P. Harper); Return of the Lash
1948:   Check Your Guns
1949:   Coyote Canyon
1950:   Tales of the West 1; Tales of the West 2;
        Tales of the West 3
1951:   Prairie Roundup; Tales of the West 4; Nevada
        Badmen; Stagecoach Driver; Oklahoma Justice

1952: Man from the Black Hills

JAMES T. O'DONOHUE

1928: Show Girl

MORTIMER OFFNER

1935: Alice Adams*; Sylvia Scarlett*
1937: Quality Street (Allan Scott); The Soldier
       and the Lady*
1938: Little Tough Guys in Society (E. Eliscu);
       Radio City Revels; The Saint in New York (C.
       Kaufman)
1939: The Family Next Door

DENNIS O'FLAHERTY

1982: Hammett (Ross Thomas)

LIAM O'FLAHERTY

1937: Devil's Playground*
1957: Jacqueline

GEORGE O'HANLON

1964: For Those Who Think Young*

JAMES O'HANLON

1947: Three Wise Fools (J. McDermott)
1950: Destination Moon*
1952: The Miracle of Our Lady of Fatima (C
       Wilbur); Sally and Saint Anne (H. Meadow);
       Stop, You're Killing Me
1953: Calamity Jane
1954: Lucky Me*
1955: Conquest of Space (P. Yordan)
1958: Johnny Rocco (S. Roeca)
1959: The Rookie (T. Noonan0
1964: For Those Who Think Young*

1965:   Murieta

JOHN O'HARA (1905-1970) novelist

1940:   He Married His Wife*; I Was an Adventuress*
1942:   Moontide

HARVEY O'HIGGINS

1936:   I Married a Doctor*

HENRY OLEK

1978:   A Different Story

JOEL OLIANSKY

1968:   Counterpoint (J. Lee)
1971:   The Todd Killings (Dennis Murphy)
1980:   The Competition

JAMES OLIVER

1946:   Thunder Town

STEPHEN OLIVER

1979:   Sunburn*

ED OLMSTEAD

1935:   The Crime of Dr. Crespi (K. Graham)

DANA OLSEN

1982:   It Came from Hollywood (doc.)

MARY OLSON

1972:   It Ain't Easy

DAVID O'MALLEY

1976:   The Adventures of Frontier Fremont
1982:   The Boogens (B. Hunt)

CHARLES O'NEAL

1943:   The Seventh Victim (D. Bodeen)
1944:   Cry of the Werewolf (G. Jay); The Missing
        Juror
1945:   I Love a Mystery
1946:   The Devil's Mask
1948:   Return of the Badmen*
1950:   Montana*
1951:   Golden Girl*
1957:   Johnny Trouble (D. Lord)
1963:   Lassie's Greatest Adventure (M. Manning)

ROBERT VINCENT O'NEIL

1980:   The Baltimore Bullet (J. Brascia)
1982:   Vice Squad*

ELLA O'NEILL

1931:   Battling with Buffalo Bill (ser.; G.
        Plympton); Heroes of the Flames (ser.)*
1932:   Airmail Mystery (ser.)*; Detective Lloyd
        (ser.); Heroes of the West (ser.)*; Jungle
        Mystery (ser.)*; The Lost Special (ser.)*
1933:   Clancy of the Mounted (ser.)*; Gordon of
        Ghost City (ser.)*
1934:   The Red Rider (ser.)*; Danger Island
        (ser.)*; Perils of Pauline (ser.)*; Tailspin
        Tommy (ser.)*
1935:   Rustlers of Red Dog (ser.)*; The Roaring
        West (ser.)*; Tailspin Tommy and the Great
        Air Mystery (ser.)*
1936:   The Phantom Rider (ser.)*; Adventures of
        Frank Merriwell (ser.)*; Flash Gordon
        (ser.)*
1938:   Flaming Frontiers (ser.)*

FRANK O'NEILL

1939: On Borrowed Time*

GEORGE O'NEILL

1933: Only Yesterday (A. Richman)
1934: Beloved (P. Gangelin)
1935: Magnificent Obsession*
1936: Sutter's Gold*; I'd Give My Life
1939: Intermezzo

DAVID OPATOSHU (1918-   )

1971: Romance of a Horsethief (A. Polonsky)

MARCEL OPHULS (1927-   ) director Fr.

(American films only)
1972: A Sense of Loss (U.S./Swit.)

GEORGE OPPENHEIMER

1933: Roman Scandals*
1935: Rendezvous*
1936: Libeled Lady*
1937: A Day at the Races*; I'll Take Romance (J.
       Murfin); London by Night; Married Before
       Breakfast (E. Freeman)
1938: The Crowd Roars*; Man-Proof*; Paradise for
       Three (H. Ruskin); Three Loves Has Nancy*; A
       Yank at Oxford*
1940: Broadway Melody of 1940*; I Love You Again*
1941: The Feminine Touch*; Two-Faced Woman*
1942: Pacific Rendezvous*; The War Against Mrs.
       Hadley; A Yank at Eton*
1943: The Youngest Profession*
1947: Killer McCoy*
1948: Adventures of Don Juan (H. Kurnitz)
1952: Anything Can Happen (G. Seaton)
1953: Tonight We Sing (H. Kurnitz)

PEER J. OPPENHEIMER

1965: Operation C.I.A. (B. Ballinger)
1976: Nashville Girl
1977: New Girl in Town

DON OPPER

1982: Android (J. Reigle)

THOMAS ORCHARD

1959: Behind the Great Wall (S. Kaufman)

WYOTT ORDUNG

1953: Combat Squad; Robot Monster (G. Ritchie)
1956: Walk the Dark Street

RUTH ORKIN

1953: Little Fugitive*
1956: Lovers and Lollipops (M. Engel)

BEN ORKOW

1939: Boy Slaves (A. Bein)
1942: Wings for the Eagle (B. Morgan)

HARRISON ORKOW

1930: The Truth About Youth
1932: Hell's House*
1944: Alaska*; Army Wives

HAROLD ORLOB

1948: Citizen Saint

ARTHUR A. ORLOFF

1947: Wild Country; Cheyenne Takes Over; The Lone Wolf in London
1950: Code of the Silver Sage; The Missourians; Beauty on Parade (G. Bricker)
1951: Thunder in God's Country; Buckaroo Sheriff of Texas
1952: Desperadoes Outpost (A. DeMond); The Last Musketeer; South Pacific Trail
1953: Sky Commando*; El Paso Stampede
1954: Red River Shore (G. Geraghty)

GIL ORLOVITZ

1956: Over-Exposed (J. Gunn)

.

RON ORMOND

1948: Dead Man's Gold (I. Webb); Mark of the Lash (I. Webb)
1949: Outlaw Country (I. Webb); Son of Billy the Kid (I. Webb); Son of a Badman (I. Webb); Square Dance Jubilee (D.Ullman); Red Desert (D. Ullman); Rimfire*
1950: The Daltons' Women (M. Tombragel); Marshal of Heldorado (M. Tombragel); Colorado Ranger (M. Tombragel); West of the Brazos (M. Tombragel); Crooked River (M. Tombragel); Fast on the Draw (M. Tombragel); Hostile Country (M. Tombragel)
1951: The Vanishing Outpost; Kentucky Jubilee (M. Tombragel); Varieties on Parade; Yes Sir, Mr. Bones

CZENZI ORMONDE

1951: Strangers on a Train (R. Chandler)
1958: Step Down to Terror*
1959: 1,001 Arabian Nights

ALAN ORMSBY

1974: Deranged

1980: My Bodyguard; The Little Dragons*
1982: Cat People

SAMUEL ORNITZ   (1891-1957)

1930: Richest Man in the World (alt. Sins of the
      Children)
1932: Hell's Highway*; Men of America (J.
      Jungmeyer); Secrets of the French Police (R.
      Trasker)
1933: One Man's Journey (L. Cohen)
1934: One Exciting Adventure (W. Hurlbut)
1935: Three Kids and a Queen*
1936: Fatal Lady (H. McCoy); Follow Your Heart*
1937: The Hit Parade (B. Ropes); It Could Happen
      to You (N. West); Portia on Trial; Two Wise
      Maids
1938: Army Girl (B. Trivers); Little Orphan Annie
      (B. Schulberg)
1940: Three Faces West*
1944: They Live in Fear (M. Simmons)
1945: China's Little Devils

GERTRUDE ORR

1931: The Mad Parade*
1932: Silver Lining
1934: Little Men; Without Children
1936: The Harvester*; Penthouse Party; Country
      Gentlemen (J. Hoffman)
1937: The Mandarin Mystery*
1938: Call of the Yukon (W. Bartlett); Slander
      House (J. Krafft)

MARION ORTH

1929: Romance of the Rio Grande; Cameo Kirby; The
      One Woman Idea; Christina; Not Quite Decent
1930: Crazy That Way (H. MacFadden); The Golden
      Calf; Man Trouble (G. Watters)
1933: Charlie Chan's Greatest Case (L. Cole)
1934: Sing Sing Nights (C. Logue); A Successful
      Failure
1935: Welcome Home (A. Horman)
1937: A Bride for Henry; Paradise Isle

1938: Romance of the Limberlost; Saleslady; Under
the Big Top (Karl Brown)
1940: Son of the Navy (J. West); Tomboy (D.
Davenport); Dr. Christian Meets the Women
1941: Sing Another Chorus*

DAVID OSBORN

1962: Malaga (D.O. Stewart)
1963: Follow the Boys (D. Chantler)
1968: Maroc 7
1971: Some Girls Do
1974: Open Season

PAUL OSBORN (1901-   ) playwright

1938: The Young in Heart (Charles Bennett)
1943: Cry Havoc; Madame Curie (P. Rameau)
1946: The Yearling
1948: The Homecoming; Portrait of Jenny (P.
Berneis)
1952: Invitation
1955: East of Eden
1957: Sayonara
1958: South Pacific
1960: Wild River

DAVID OSTERHOUT

1972: Women in Cages (J. Watkins)
1976: Moving Violation (W. Norton)

HOWARD OSTROFF

1974: Black Starlet

GERD OSWALD

1961: Brainwashed (Fr.; H. Medford)

RICHARD OSWALD

1949:   The Lovable Cheat (E. Lewis)

JEEDS O'TILBURY

1972:   The Only Way Home

JOHN O'TOOLE

1971:   Who Killed Mary What's'ername?

DORIAN OTVOS

1937:   Merry- Go-Round of 1938 (M. Brice)
1938:   Goodbye Broadway (R. Chanslor)

WILLIAM OVERGARD

1981:   The Bushido Blade

SEENA OWEN (1894-1966) actress

1934:   The Lemon Drop Kid*
1935:   McFadden's Flats*
1937:   Clarence (G. Garrett); This Way Please*;
        Thrill of a Lifetime*
1941:   Aloma of the South Seas*

611

p

PETER PACKER

1956:   Seventh Cavalry

ERNEST PAGANO

1933:   Son of a Sailor (H. Walker)
1935:   Old Man Rhythm (S. Herzig)
1937:   A Damsel in Distress*; Fight for Your Lady*;
        Shall We Dance*; Super Sleuth (G. Purcell)
1938:   Carefree*; Vivacious Lady (P. Wolfson)
1939:   The Flying Irishman (D. Trumbo)
1940:   Forty Little Mothers (D. Yost); Love Thy
        Neighbor*
1941:   Las Vegas Nights (H. Clork); You'll Never
        Get Rich (M. Fessier)
1942:   You Were Never Lovelier*
1943:   Fired Wife (M. Fessier)
1944:   Her Primitive Man (M. Fessier); San Diego, I
        Love You (M. Fessier); The Merry Monahans
        (M. Fessier)
1945:   That Night with You (M. Fessier); Frontier
        Gal (M.Fessier); That's the Spirit
        (M.Fessier)
1946:   Lover Come Back (M. Fessier)
1947:   Slave Girl (M. Fessier)

JO PAGANO

1938:   Tarnished Angel (S. Elkins)
1939:   They Made Her a Spy*; Almost a Gentleman (D.
        Silverstein)
1943:   The Leather Burners
1945:   Hotel Berlin (A. Bessie); Too Young to Know
1948:   Adventure in Silverado*; Jungle Goddess

612

```
1950:  The Sound of Fury
1953:  Murder Without Tears (W. Raynor)
1954:  Security Risk (F. McDonald)
1955:  Jungle Moon Men (D. Babcock)
1956:  Yaqui Drums (D. Beauchamp)
```

ADRIAN PAGE

```
1947:  Pioneer Justice
```

MARCO PAGE

```
1938:  Fast Company (H. Tarshis)
```

THOMAS PAGE

```
1975:  Bug (W. Castle)
```

ALAN J. PAKULA (1928-   )

```
1982:  Sophie's Choice
```

GEORGE PAL (1908-1980) director, producer

```
1975:  Doc Savage -- Man of Bronze
```

ALFRED PALCA

```
1951:  The Harlem Globe Trotters
```

STANLEY PALEY

```
1945:  An Angel Comes to Brooklyn (J. Carroll)
```

CHARLES PALMER

```
1951:  The Sellout
```

JOHN PALMER

1973:   Ciao! Manhattan (D. Weisman)

STUART PALMER

1938:   Bulldog Drummond's Peril; Hollywood Stadium
        Mystery (alt. The Stadium Murders)*
1939:   Arrest Bulldog Drummond; Bulldog Drummond's
        Bride (G. Weston); Death of a Champion (C.
        Fitzsimmons)
1940:   Emergency Squad (G. Weston); Opened by
        Mistake*; Seventeen (A. Johnson); Who Killed
        Aunt Maggie?
1941:   Secrets of the Lone Wolf
1942:   The Falcon's Brother (C. Rice); Pardon My
        Stripes (L. Kimble); X Marks the Spot (R.
        Murphy); Half Way to Shanghai
1943:   Petticoat Larceny (J. Townley)
1946:   Step by Step

DENNIS PALUMBO

1982:   My Favorite Year (N. Steinberg)

MICHAEL PANAIEFF

1944:   Lady, Let's Dance (P. Milne)

NORMAN PANAMA (1914-   ) director, producer

1943:   Happy Go Lucky*; Thank Your Lucky Stars*
1944:   And the Angels Sing (M. Frank)
1945:   Duffy's Tavern (M. Frank); Road to Utopia
        (M. Frank)
1946:   Monsieur Beaucaire (M. Frank); Our Hearts
        Were Growing Up (M. Frank)
1947:   It Had to Be You*
1948:   Mr. Blandings Builds His Dream House (M.
        Frank)
1949:   The Return of October (M. Frank)
1950:   The Reformer and the Redhead (M. Frank)
1951:   Callaway Went Thataway (M. Frank); Strictly
        Dishonorable (M. Frank)
1952:   Above and Beyond*

1954: Knock on Wood (M. Frank); White Christmas*
1956: The Court Jester (M. Frank); That Certain
      Feeling*
1959: The Trap (R. Simmons); Li'l Abner (M.
      Frank); The Jayhawkers*
1960: The Facts of Life (M. Frank)
1962: The Road to Hong Kong (M. Frank)
1966: Not with My Wife, You Don't*
1976: I Will, I Will...for Now (A. Lewin)

EDWARD E. PARAMORE (-1956)

1931: Fighting Caravans*; Newly Rich*; Rich Man's
      Folly (G. Jones)
1933: The Bitter Tea of General Yen; Master of Men
      (S. Miller)
1934: Baby Take a Bow (P. Klein)
1935: Rock Mountain Mystery (A. Doherty)
1936: Three Godfathers (M. Seff); Trouble for Two
      (M. Seff)
1938: Three Comrades (F. S. Fitzgerald)
1939: Oklahoma Kid*; Man of Conquest*
1940: Twenty Mule Team*; Mystery Sea Raider
1942: Tombstone -- The Town Too Tough to Die (A.
      LeVine)
1946: The Virginian*

GAIL PARENT

1975: Sheila Levine Is Dead and Living in New York
      (K. Solms)
1979: The Main Event (Andrew Smith)

MILDRED PARES

1974: The House on Skull Mountain

IDA MAY PARK

1930: Chiselers of Hollywood
1931: Playthings of Hollywood

ALAN PARKER

615

1976:   Bugsy Malone

AUSTIN PARKER

1931:   Honor Among Lovers
1932:   The Rich Are Always with Us; The Successful
        Calamity*
1933:   House on 56th Street (S. Gibney); Shanghai
        Madness (G. Wellesley)
1934:   Mandalay (C. Kenyon)
1936:   Girl on the Front Page*
1937:   Love in a Bungalow*; Something to Sing
        About; Three Smart Girls (A. Comandini)

BEN PARKER

1953:   Guerrilla Girl (J. Byrne)

DOROTHY PARKER (1893-1967) writer

1934:   Here Is My Heart (unc.)*
1935:   One Hour Late*
1936:   Lady Be Careful*; The Moon's Our Home*;
        Suzy*; Three Married Men (A. Campbell)
1937:   A Star Is Born*; Woman Chases Man*
1938:   Sweethearts (A. Campbell); Trade Winds*
1941:   Week-End for Three (A. Campbell)
1942:   Saboteur*
1949:   The Fan*

HAMM PARKER

1974:   Blood Couple (A. Condrey)

JEFFERSON PARKER

1935:   Great God Gold (N. Houston); Two Sinners
1936:   Human Cargo (D. Malloy); Yellowstone
1937:   Mysterious Crossing (J. Grey); Under
        Suspicion (J. Hoffman)
1938:   Crime Takes a Holiday*; Flight into Nowhere
        (G. Rigby); The House of Mystery (H. Green);

616

Making the Headlines (H. Green)
1939: Five Little Peppers and How They Grew (N. Bucknall)
1943: A Gentle Gangster

JIM PARKER

1971: Star Spangled Girl (A. Margolin)
1972: Snowball Express*

JOHN PARKER

1955: Dementia

LOUISE M. PARKER

1933: The Monkey's Paw (G. John)

NORTON S. PARKER

1931: Ten Nights in a Barroom
1932: Hell's Headquarters; Sinister Hands
1936: Tundra (C. Royal)
1937: Courage of the West
1938: Border Wolves; The Last Stand (H. Hoyt); Outlaw Express; Prison Break (D. Reid)
1939: Sky Patrol (J. West)
1940: Young Bill Hickok (O. Cooper); Three Men from Texas
1941: In Old Colorado*; Cyclone on Horseback; Six Gun Gold; The Bandit Trail
1942: Come On, Danger!
1943: Fighting Frontier (J. Cheney)
1946: Rio Grande Raiders

SCOTT PARKER

1980: He Knows You're Alone; Die Laughing*

FORBES PARKHILL

1935: Alias John Law; Blazing Guns; No Man's Range

1936:   Brand of the Outlaws

GORDON PARKS (1912-   ) author, director

1969:   The Learning Tree

JOHNSON PARKS

1939:   In Old Montana*

CLAIRE PARRISH

1940:   Misbehaving Husbands (V. Smith)

JAMES PARROTT (-1939)

1937:   Way Out West*
1938:   Block-Heads*; Swiss Miss*

H.M. PARSHLEY

1931:   Mystery of Life

MARION PARSONNET

1937:   Beg, Borrow or Steal*; Between Two Women (F.
         Stephani); The Thirteenth Chair
1938:   Love Is a Headache*
1939:   Miracles for Sale*; These Glamour Girls (J.
         Hall)
1940:   Gallant Sons (W. Lipman)
1941:   Blonde Inspiration; Washington Melodrama (R.
         Chanslor); Dangerously They Live
1944:   I'll Be Seeing You
1945:   Dangerous Partners
1946:   Gilda (B. Hecht)
1951:   My Forbidden Past

EDWIN C. PARSONS

1937:   Blazing Barriers

1939:   Danger Flight (B. Morgan)

E. M. PARSONS

1960:   Squad Car (S. Flohr)
1962:   Ready for the People (S. Salkowitz)

JOHN PARSONS

1974:   Watched

LINDSLEY PARSONS

1933:   Sagebrush Trail
1934:   The Man from Utah; Randy Rides Alone; The
        Trail Beyond
1935:   Rainbow Valley; The Desert Trail; Paradise
        Canyon (R. Tansey); Westward Ho*; Lawless
        Range
1936:   The Oregon Trail*
1938:   Rollin' Plains (E. Kelso)

MICHAEL PARSONS

1977:   High Velocity (Remi Kramer)

TED PARSONS

1934:   Hell in the Heavens*
1936:   Darkest Africa (ser.)*
1949:   King of the Jungleland (ser.)*

FRANK PARTOS (1901-   )

1932:   Heritage of the Desert (H. Shumate); Guilty
        as Hell (A. Kober)
1933:   Cradle Song*; Her Bodyguard (F. Martin);
        Jennie Gerhardt*
1934:   Good Dame*; 30-Day Princess*; Wharf Angel*
1935:   College Scandal*; The Last Outpost*; Wings
        in the Dark (J. Kirkland)
1936:   Rose of the Rancho*

1937:   The Great Gambini*; Night of Mystery (G.
        Unger); She's No Lady (G. Bruce)
1938:   Romance in the Dark (A. Chapin)
1939:   Honolulu (H. Fields); Rio*
1940:   Stranger on the Third Floor
1944:   The Uninvited (D. Smith); And Now Tomorrow
        (H. Chandler)
1948:   The Snake Pit*
1951:   House on Telegraph Hill (E. Moll)
1952:   Night Without Sleep (E. Moll)
1956:   Port Afrique (J. Cresswell)

ERNEST PASCAL (1896-   ) novelist

1928:   Interference
1930:   Last of the Duanes
1931:   Fair Warning; Age for Love (F. Lloyd); Born
        to Love; Husband's Holiday (V. Shore); The
        Spy
1933   The King's Vacation (M. Howell)
1934:   As the Earth Turns; Grand Canary; The Human
        Side (F. Craven); the White Parade (S.
        Levien)
1935:   Here's to Romance (S. Levien); Under the
        Pampas Moon (B. King)
1936:   Lloyds of London (W. Ferris)
1937:   Love Under Fire*; Wee Willie Winkie (J.
        Josephson)
1938:   Kidnapped*
1939:   Hollywood Cavalcade; The Hound of the
        Baskervilles
1940:   The Blue Bird
1943:   Flesh and Fantasy*; Jack London
1944:   Destiny (R. Chanslor)
1946:   Canyon Passage; A Night in Paradise

JEFFERSON PASCAL

1963:   Sword of Lancelot (R. Schayer)
1967:   Beach Red*

IVAN PASSER

1974:   Law and Disorder*

LOUIS PASTORE

1976:   The Premonition*

TOM PATCHETT

1980:   Up the Academy (J. Tarses)
1981:   The Great Muppet Caper*

NEIL PATTERSON

1962:   The Spiral Road (J. Mahin)

JACK PATRICK

1956:   Daniel Boone, Trail Blazer (T. Hubbard)

JOHN PATRICK (1905-   ) playwright

1936:   Educating Father*; 15 Maiden Lane*; High
        Tension*; 36 Hours to Kill (L. Breslow)
1937:   Big Town Girl*; Born Reckless*; Dangerously
        Yours (L. Breslow); The Holy Terror (L.
        Breslow); Midnight Taxi (L. Breslow); Sing
        and Be Happy*; Time Out for Romance (L.
        Breslow); One Mile from Heaven (L. Breslow)
1938:   The Battle of Broadway (L. Breslow); Five of
        a Kind (L. Breslow); International
        Settlement (L. Breslow); Mr. Moto Takes a
        Chance*; Up the River (L. Breslow)
1948:   Enchantment
1953:   The President's Lady
1954:   Three Coins in the Fountain
1955:   Love Is a Many Splendored Thing
1956:   High Society; The Teahouse of the August
        Moon
1957:   Les Girls
1958:   Some Came Running (A. Sheekman)
1960:   The World of Suzie Wong
1962:   Gigot
1963:   The Main Attraction
1968:   The Shoes of the Fisherman (J. Kennaway)

621

ELLIOT PAUL

1941:   A Woman's Face (D. Stewart)
1945:   It's a Pleasure! (L. Starling)
1945:   Rhapsody in Blue (H. Koch)
1947:   New Orleans*
1953:   My Heart Goes Crazy (S. Herzig)

OSCAR PAUL

1951:   The Secret of Convict Lake (V. Trivas)

STEVEN PAUL

1980:   Falling in Love Again*

JOHN PAXTON (1911-   )

1944:   My Pal Wolf*; Murder, My Sweet
1945:   Cornered
1946:   Crack-Up*
1947:   Crossfire; So Well Remembered
1950:   Of Men and Music*
1951:   14 Hours
1954:   The Wild One
1955:   The Cobweb; A Prize of Gold (R. Buckner)
1957:   Pickup Alley; How to Murder a Rich Uncle
1959:   On the Beach
1971:   Kotch

JOHN PAYNE (1912-   ) actor

1956:   The Boss*

JACK PEABODY

1930:   The Big Trail*

STEVE PEACE

1978:   Attack of the Killer Tomatoes*

DONN PEARCE

1967: Cool Hand Luke (F. Pierson)

HUMPHREY PEARSON

1929: Broadway Babies (M. Katterjohn)
1930: Sunny (H. McCarthy); Top Speed (H. McCarthy)
1931: Bright Lights (H. McCarthy); Consolation
      Marriage; Going Wild (H. McCarthy);
      Traveling Husbands
1933: Aggie Appleby, Maker of Men (E. Kaufman);
      Face in the Sky
1934: Elmer and Elsie; The Great Flirtation
1935: Red Salute (M. Seff); Ruggles of Red Gap*

JAMES PEATMAN

1968: A Man Called Dagger (R. Weekley)

CHARLES K. PECK, JR.

1951: The Basketball Fix (P. Brooke)
1952: Yankee Buccaneer
1953: Seminole

KIMI PECK

1980: Little Darlings (D. Young)

SAM PECKINPAH (1925-   ) director

1965: The Glory Guys; Major Dundee*
1968: Villa Rides (R. Towne)
1969: The Wild Bunch (W. Green)
1971: Straw Dogs (D. Z. Goodman)
1974: Bring Me the Head of Alfredo Garcia (G.
      Dawson)

SAMUEL A. PEEPLES

```
1964:   Advance to the Rear (W. Bowers)
1977:   Final Chapter -- Walking Tall (H. Kreitsek)
```

BILL PEET

```
1953:   Peter Pan (anim.)*
1959:   Sleeping Beauty (anim.)*
1961:   One Hundred and One Dalmations
1963:   The Sword in the Stone (anim.)
```

BOB PEETE

```
1976:   Drive-In
```

BARBARA PEETERS

```
1970:   The Dark Side of Tomorrow
1972:   Bury Me an Angel
1975:   Summer School Teachers
```

PAUL LESLIE PEIL

```
1958:   Gunsmoke in Tucson (R. Joseph)
```

HAIM PEKELIS

```
1979:   Squeeze Play
```

JEAN-MARIE PELISSIE

```
1973:   The House That Cried Murder (J. Grissmer)
```

LOUIS PELLETIER

```
1962:   Big Red
1964:   Those Callaways
1966:   Follow Me, Boys!
1968:   The Horse in the Gray Flannel Suit
1969:   Smith!
```

SCOTT PEMBROKE

1932: Okay, America (W. McGuire)
1933: King for a Night

ERNEST PENDRELL

1957: The Violators

ARTHUR PENN (1922-   ) director

1969: Alice's Restaurant (V. Herndon)

ERDMAN PENNER

1953: Peter Pan (anim.)*
1955: Lady and the Tramp (anim)*
1959: Sleeping Beauty (anim.)*

EDMUND PENNEY

1970: The Ballad of Cable Hogue (J. Crawford)

DAVID PEOPLES

1982: Blade Runner (H. Fancher)

DAN PEPPER

1957: Hold That Hypnotist
1960: The Enemy General

PAUL PEPPERMAN

1982: The Beastmaster (D. Coscarelli)

PAUL PERCY

1929: Love in the Desert (H. Thew)

625

LAURA PERELMAN

1936:   Florida Special*
1939:   Ambush (S. J. Perelman)
1940:   The Golden Fleecing (S. J. Perelman)

S. J. PERELMAN (1904-1979) humorist

1931:   Monkey Business*
1932:   Hold 'Em, Jail*; Horse Feathers*
1933:   Sitting Pretty*
1936:   Florida Special*; Early to Bed*
1939:   Ambush (L. Perelman); Boy Trouble*
1940:   The Golden Fleecing (L. Perelman)
1956:   Around the World in 80 Days*

PAUL PEREZ

1930:   The Great Divide*
1931:   Goldie (G. Towne); Kiss Me Again (J.
        Josephson)
1932:   Doomed Battalion*; Hotel Continental*
1933:   Smoky (S. Anthony); It's Great to Be Alive
1935:   East of Java (J. Creelman); Radio Parade of
        1935 (Brit.)
1936:   August Week-End; Brilliant Marriage; Last of
        the Mohicans*; Little Red Schoolhouse; Ring
        Around the Moon
1937:   Two-Fisted Sheriff; One Man Justice
1938:   Flaming Frontiers (ser.)*; The Missing Guest
        (C. Martin)

ARNOLD PERI

1960:   Jazz on a Summer's Day (doc.; A. D'Anniable)

FRANK RAY PERILLI

1973:   Little Cigars (L. Garfinkle)
1977:   End of the World; Mansion of the Doomed
1978:   Laserblast (F. Schacht); Dracula's Dog
1979:   She Came to the Valley (A. Band); Fairy

626

```
        Tales (F. Schacht)
1981:   The Land of No Return (K. Bateman)


ALBERT R. PERKINS

1936:   Girl on the Front Page*
1937:   The Mighty Treve*; Prescription for
        Romance*; She's Dangerous*
1941:   The Reluctant Dragon (anim.)*


ANTHONY PERKINS (1932-    ) actor

1973:   The Last of Sheila (S. Sondheim)


GRACE PERKINS

1934:   Social Register


KENNETH PERKINS

1949:   The Song of India (A. Arthur)


LYNN PERKINS

1945:   The Phantom Rider (ser.)*; The Purple
        Monster Strikes (ser.)*
1946:   Daughter of Don Q (ser.)*; King of the
        Forest Rangers (ser. )*


ARNOLD PERL

1969:   Cotton Comes to Harlem (O. Davis)
1972:   Malcolm X (doc.)


B. J. PERLA

1976:   Sweet Revenge (M. Goldin)


NAT PERRIN
```

1934:   Kid Millions*
1936:   Rose of the Rancho*; Dimples (A. Sheekman);
        Stowaway*
1937:   Don't Tell the Wife; New Faces of 1937*;
        On-Again Off-Again (B. Rubin)
1939:   The Gracie Allen Murder Case
1940:   Alias The Deacon (C. Grayson); Hullabaloo
1941:   Hellzapoppin (W. Wilson); Keep 'Em Flying
        (John Grant)
1942:   Pardon My Sarong*; Whistling in Dixie
1943:   Swing Fever (W. Wilson); Whistling in
        Brooklyn
1945:   Abbott and Costello in Hollywood (L.
        Breslow)
1947:   Song of the Thin Man (S. Fisher)
1949:   Miss Grant Takes Richmond*; Tell It to the
        Judge
1950:   Emergency Wedding (C. Binyon); The Petty
        Girl
1965:   I'll Take Sweden*
1968:   The Wicked Dreams of Paula Schultz*

BEN L. PERRY

1956:   The Boss*
1957:   The Brothers Rico (L. Metzger)
1958:   Terror in a Texas Town

CHARLES PERRY

1939:   Each Dawn I Die*

ELAINE PERRY

1972:   The Deadly Trap (S. Buchman)

ELEANOR PERRY

1963:   David and Lisa; Ladybug Ladybug
1968:   The Swimmer
1969:   Last Summer; Trilogy (T. Capote)
1970:   Diary of a Mad Housewife; The Lady in the
        Car with Glasses and a Gun
1973:   The Man Who Loved Cat Dancing

FRANK PERRY (1930-   ) director

1981: Mommie Dearest*

GEORGE SESSIONS PERRY

1938: The Arkansas Traveler (V. Shore)

MICHAEL PERTWEE (1916-   ) playwright Brit.

(American films only)
1964: Strange Bedfellows (M. Frank)
1965: The Cavern (J. Davies)
1966: A Funny Thing Happened on the Way to The
       Forum (M. Frank)
1968: Salt and Pepper (U.S./Brit.)
1970: One More Time (U.S./Brit.)

RONALD PERTWEE

1932: Illegal

CHARLIE PETERS

1981: Paternity
1982: Kiss Me Goodbye

DON PETERS

1966: The Naked Prey (C. Johnston)
1967: Beach Red*

KENNETH PETERS

1982: Vice Squad*

MARTHA PETERS

1982: Mark of the Witch (Mary Davis)

DON PETERSON

1979:   An Almost Perfect Affair (W. Bernstein)

H. G. PETERSON

1965:   Apache Gold; Treasure of Silver Lake
1966:   Desperado Trail (J. Bartsch)

MAURICE PETERSON

1982:   Homework (D. Saffran)

ROD PETERSON

1960:   Chartroose Caboose

DENNE BART PETITCLERC

1977:   Islands in the Stream

BERNICE PETKERE

1942:   Sabotage Squad*

JOSEPH PETRACCA

1958:   The Proud Rebel (L. Hayward)
1959:   The Jayhawkers*
1960:   Guns of the Timberland (A. Spelling)
1962:   The Reluctant Saint (It.; J. Fante)

HARRY MARK PETRAKIS

1969:   A Dream of Kings (I. Hunter)

WILFRED H. PETTITT

```
1945:   A Thousand and One Nights (R. English);
        Voice of the Whistler (W. Castle)
1946:   The Bandit of Sherwood Forest (M. Levy); The
        Walls Came Tumbling Down
1947:   The Swordsman
```

ARNOLD & LOIS PEYSER

```
1969:   The Trouble with Girls
```

MARJORIE L. PFAELZER

```
1944:   Three Is a Family (H. Chandlee)
1945:   Tarzan and the Mermaids (H. Jacoby)
```

FRANK PHARES

```
1958:   New Orleans After Dark
```

ARNOLD PHILLIPS

```
1941:   Gambling Daughters (J. Kaye)
1945:   Jealousy (G. Machaty)
1950:   Kill or Be Killed*
1951:   The Girl on the Bridge (H. Haas); Pickup
        (H. Haas)
```

ARTHUR PHILLIPS

```
1934:   Limehouse Blues*
1943:   Riding High*
1944:   Rainbow Island (W. DeLeon)
1945:   The Brighton Strangler (M. Nosseck);
        Delightfully Dangerous (W. DeLeon); Love,
        Honor and Goodbye*; Out of This World (W.
        DeLeon)
```

GORDON PHILLIPS

```
1936:   Desert Justice (L. Kingdon); Gun Grit (Allen
        Hall)
```

HERBERT O. PHILLIPS

1944: Enemy of Women (A. Zeisler)

IRVING PHILLIPS

1944: Seven Days Ashore*

JAMES ATLEE PHILLIPS

1958: Thunder Road (W. Wise)

KATE PHILLIPS

1958: The Blob (T. Simonson)

PEGGY PHILLIPS

1945: The Crimson Canary (H. Blankfort)

THOMAS HAL PHILLIPS

1958: Tarzan's Fight for Life

ROBERT PHIPPENY

1971: Simon, King of the Witches

THOMAS PHIPPS

1942: A Yank at Eton*

IRVING PICHEL (1891-1954) actor, director

1951: Santa Fe (K. Gamet)

LEONARD PICKER

1949: Apache Chief (G. Green)

ELIZABETH PICKETT

1929: Redskin

DOROTHY JUNE PIDGEON

1975: The Astrologer

ARTHUR C. PIERCE

1959: The Cosmic Man
1960: Beyond the Time Barrier
1965: The Human Duplicators; Mutiny in Outer Space
1966: Cyborg 2087; Dimiension Five
1968: The Destructors (L. Jackson)
1978: The Astral Factor (Earle Lyon)

CHARLES B. PIERCE

1975: Winter Hawk
1977: Grayeagle
1978: The Norseman
1979: The Evictors*

NOEL PIERCE

1935: Under Pressure*

TED PIERCE

1939: Gulliver's Travels (anim.)*

ARTHUR PIERSON (1902-1975)

1951: Home Town Story

FRANK R. PIERSON

1965:   Cat Ballou (W. Newman)
1967:   Cool Hand Luke (D. Pearce); The Happening*
1970:   The Looking Glass War
1971:   The Anderson Tapes
1975:   Dog Day Afternoon
1976:   A Star Is Born*
1978:   King of the Gypsies

LOUISE RANDALL PIERSON

1945:   Roughly Speaking

SAMUEL M. PIKE

1937:   When's Your Birthday?*

DAVE PINCUS

1934:   These Thirty Years

LES PINE

1965:   Wild Seed
1966:   A Man Called Adam (T. Rome)
1969:   Popi (T. Rome)
1974:   Claudine (T. Rome)

PHILLIP PINE

1970:   Don't Just Lay There
1972:   The Cat Ate the Parakeet
1975:   Pot! Parents! Police!
1976:   Posse from Heaven (W. Wood)

TINA PINE (also TINA ROME)

1966:   A Man Called Adam (L. Pine)
1969:   Popi (L. Pine)
1974:   Claudine (L. Pine)
1981:   On the Right Track*

MIGUEL PINERO

1977:   Short Eyes

SIDNEY W. PINK

1959:   The Angry Red Planet (I. Melchior)
1962:   Journey to the Seventh Planet (I. Melchior)
1963:   The Castilian
1964:   Pyro (L. De Los Arcos)
1965:   Finger on the Trigger (L. De Los Arcos)

HAROLD PINTER (1930-   ) playwright Brit.

(American films only)
1966:   The Quiller Memorandum (U.S./Brit.)
1976:   The Last Tycoon

ERNEST PINTOFF (1931-   ) animator, director

1965:   Harvey Middleman, Fireman
1973:   Blade (J. Lieberman)

ROBERT PIROSH (1910-   ) director

1935:   The Winning Ticket*
1937:   A Day at the Races*
1940:   The Quarterback
1941:   Night of January 16th*
1942:   I Married a Witch (M. Connelly); Song of the
        Islands*
1944:   Up in Arms (D. Hartman)
1949:   Battleground
1951:   Go for Broke
1952:   Washington Story
1954:   Valley of the Kings (K. Tunberg)
1955:   The Girl Rush (J. Davis)
1957:   Spring Reunion (E. Moll)
1962:   Hell Is for Heroes (R. Carr)
1963:   A Gathering of Eagles
1968:   What's So Bad About Feeling Good? (G.
        Seaton)

MONTGOMERY PITTMAN

1956:   Come Next Spring
1957:   Tarzan and the Lost Safari (L. Hayward);
        Slim Carter
1958:   Money, Women and Guns

ALAN PLATER

1979:   All Things Bright and Beautiful

JONATHAN PLATNICK

1977:   Looking Up

POLLY PLATT

1978:   Pretty Baby
1979:   Good Luck, Miss Wyckoff

GEORGE H. PLYMPTON

1930:   The Indians Are Coming (F. Beebe); The One
        Way Trail; Battling with Buffalo Bill (ser.;
        E. O'Neil)
1931:   Fingerprints (ser.)*; Heroes of the Flames
        (ser.)*; Range Feud (M. Krims)
1932:   The Last Frontier (ser.)*; Love Bound;
        Airmail Mystery (ser.)*; Heroes of the West
        (ser.)*; Jungle Mystery (ser.)*; The Lost
        Special (ser.)*
1933:   Gordon of Ghost City (ser.)*; Tarzan the
        Fearless (ser.; B. Dickey); Phantom of the
        Air (ser.; B. Dickey)
1934:   The Red Rider (ser.)*; Perils of Pauline
        (ser.)*; Pirate Treasure (ser.)*
1935:   Rustlers of Red Dog (ser.)*; The Roaring
        West (ser.)*; Stormy (B. Cohen); Call of the
        Savage (ser.)*; Tailspin Tommy in the Great
        Air Mystery (ser.)*
1936:   The Phantom Rider (ser.)*; The Crooked
        Trail; The Idaho Kid; Cavalry; Adventures of
        Frank Merriwell (ser.)*; Flash Gordon
        (ser.)*

1937:   The Gun Ranger; The Gambling Terror (F.
        Myton); Trail of Vengeance (F. Myton); Bar Z
        Bad Men; The Trusted Outlaw (F. Myton); Gun
        Lords of Stirrup Basin (F. Myton); A Lawman
        Is Born; Doomed at Sundown; The Red Rope;
        Boothill Brigade; Arizona Gunfighter
1938:   Paroled to Die; The Rangers' Roundup;
        Thunder in the Desert; The Feud Maker;
        Whirlwind Horseman; Songs and Bullets (J.
        O'Donnell); Flaming Frontiers (ser.)*;
        Durango Valley Raiders; The Spider's Web
        (ser.)*; Paroled from the Big House
1939:   Trigger Pals; The Phantom Creeps (ser.)*;
        Smoky Trails; Texas Wildcats; Mesquite
        Buckaroo; The Oregon Trail (ser.)*; Daughter
        of the Tong; Scouts to the Rescue (ser.)*;
        The Green Hornet (ser.)*
1940:   Flash Gordon Conquers the Universe (ser.)*;
        Winners of the West (ser.)*; The Green
        Hornet Strikes Again (ser.)*; Junior G-Men
        (ser.)*
1941:   Pride of the Bowery; Holt of the Secret
        Service (ser.)*; The Iron Claw (ser.)*; The
        Spider Returns (ser.)*; Outlaws of the Rio
        Grande; Billy the Kid's Fighting Pals;
        Riders of Death Valley (ser.)*
1942:   Captain Midnight (ser.)*; Gang Busters
        (ser.)*; Junior G-Men of the Air (ser.)*
1943:   Adventures of the Flying Cadets (ser.)*; Don
        Winslow of the Coast Guard (ser.)*; The
        Masked Marvel (ser.)*
1944:   The Great Alaskan Mystery (ser.; M.
        Tombragel)
1945:   His Brother's Ghost (G. Milton); Gangster's
        Den; Jungle Queen (ser.)*; Jungle Raiders
        (ser.)*; The Master Key (ser.)*; Who's
        Guilty? (ser.)*; Trouble Chasers (A. Lamb)
1946:   Betty Co-Ed (A. Dreifuss); Brenda Starr,
        Reporter (A. Lamb); Chick Carter, Detective
        (ser.)*; Hop Harrigan (ser.)*; Son of the
        Guardsman (ser.)*
1947:   The Vigilante (ser.)*; Last of the Redmen
        (H. Dalmas); Brick Bradford (ser.)*; The Sea
        Hound (ser.)*
1948:   Congo Bill (ser.)*
1949:   Adventures of Sir Galahad (ser.)*; Batman
        and Robin (ser.)*; Bruce Gentry — Daredevil
        of the Skies (Ser.)*

1950:   Atom Man vs. Superman (ser.)*; Cody of the
        Pony Express (ser.)*; Pirates of the High
        Seas (ser.)*
1951:   Roar of the Iron Horse (ser.)*; Captain
        Video (ser.)*; Gunfighters of the Northwest
        (ser.)*; Mysterious Island (ser.)*
1952:   Blackhawk (ser.)*; Son of Geronimo (ser.)*;
        King of the Congo (ser.)*
1953:   The Great Adventures of Captain Kidd
        (ser.)*; The Lost Planet (ser.)*
1954:   Riding with Buffalo Bill (ser.)*
1955:   Devil Goddess; Adventures of Captain Africa
        (ser.)*
1956:   Blazing the Overland Trail (ser.); Perils of
        the Wilderness (ser.)

JAMES POE (1921-1980)

1949:   Without Honor
1952:   Paula (W. Sackheim); Scandal Sheet*
1955:   The Big Knife
1956:   Around the World in 80 Days*; Attack!
1958:   Hot Spell; Cat on a Hot Tin Roof (R. Brooks)
1959:   Last Train from Gun Hill
1961:   Sanctuary; Summer and Smoke (M. Roberts)
1963:   Lilies of the Field; Toys in the Attic
1965:   The Bedford Incident
1969:   The Riot; They Shoot Horses, Don't They?

S. LEE POGOSTIN

1962:   Pressure Point (H. Cornfield)
1965:   Synanon (I. Bernard)
1969:   Hard Contract
1974:   Deadly Honeymoon; Golden Needles (Sylvia
        Schneble)

EUGENE POINC

1978:   Olly Olly Oxen Free

CLAUDE POLA

1978:   Avalanche (C. Allen)

JAMES POLAKOFF

1977:   Love and the Midnight Auto Supply
1982:   Satan's Mistress (Beverly Johnson)

JOSEPH POLAND

1929:   The Sophomore; Two Weeks Off (F. Wills)
1935:   The Sagebrush Troubador (O. Drake)
1936:   Silver Spurs; The Lawless Nineties; Winds of
        the Wasteland; The Old Corral (S. Lowe)
1937:   Range Defenders; The Trigger Trio (O. Drake)
1938:   Cattle Raiders (E. Repp)
1939:   Overland with Kit Carson (ser.)*; Mandrake
        the Magician (ser.)*; Scouts to the Rescue
        (ser.)*
1940:   The Mysterious Dr. Satan (ser.)*; King of
        the Royal Mounted (ser.)*; The Shadow
        (ser.)*
1941:   Dick Tracy vs. Crime, Inc. (ser.)*; Jungle
        Girl (ser.)*; King of the Texas Rangers
        (ser.)*; Adventures of Captain Marvel
        (ser.)*
1942:   King of the Mounties (ser.)*; Perils of
        Nyoka (ser.)*; Spy Smasher (ser.)*; Yukon
        Patrol*
1943:   Daredevils of the West (ser.)*; Captain
        America (ser.)*; G-Men vs. the Black Dragon
        (ser.)*; The Masked Marvel (ser.)*; Secret
        Service in Darkest Africa (ser.)*
1944:   Zorro's Black Whip (ser.)*; Haunted Harbor
        (ser.)*; The Tiger Woman (ser.)*
1945:   Federal Operator 99 (ser.)*; Manhunt of
        Mystery Island (ser.)*; The Purple Monster
        Strikes (ser.)*
1946:   Lost City of the Jungle (ser.)*; Mysterious
        Mr. M (ser.)*
1947:   Stage to Mesa City; Black Hills
1949:   Batman and Robin (ser.)*; Bruce Gentry -
        Daredevil of the Skies (ser.)*
1950:   Law of the Panhandle; Atom Man vs. Superman
        (ser.)*; Pirates of the High Seas (ser.)*
1951:   Texas Lawmen; Stage from Blue River; Captain
        Video (ser.)*
1952:   Canyon Ambush; Dead Man's Trail; Fargo (J.

639

DeWitt); Texas City
1953:   Texas Badman

ROMAN POLANSKI (1933-   ) director   Fr./Pol.

(American films only)
1968:   Rosemary's Baby

BARRY POLLACK

1972:   Cool Breeze

GENE POLLACK

1965:   The Incredibly Strange Creatures Who Stopped
        Living and Became Mixed Up Zombies (R.
        Silliphant); The Thrill Killers (R.
        Steckler)

 MAX POLLACK

1928:   On Trial (R. Lord)

BUD POLLARD

1930:   Danger Man

JACK POLLEXFEN

1943:   Mister Big (D. Bennett)
1950:   The Desert Hawk*
1951:   The Man from Planet X (A. Wisberg); The Son
        of Dr. Jekyll (M. Braus)
1952:   At Sword's Point*; Captive Women (A.
        Wisberg); Lady in the Iron Mask (A. Wisberg)
1953:   Sword of Venus (A. Wisberg); Port Sinister
        (A. Wisberg); Problem Girls (A. Wisberg);
        The Neanderthal Man (A. Wisberg); Captain
        John Smith and Pocahontas (A. Wisberg)
1954:   Dragon's Gold (A. Wisberg); Captain Kidd and
        the Slave Girl (A. Wisberg); Return to
        Treasure Island (A. Wisberg)

```
1955:  Son of Sinbad (A. Wisberg)
1957:  Daughter of Dr. Jekyll
```

VICKI POLON

```
1978:  Girlfriends
```

ABRAHAM POLONSKY (1910-   ) director, novelist

```
1947:  Body and Soul; Golden Earrings*
1948:  Force of Evil (I. Wolfert)
1951:  I Can Get It for You Wholesale
1968:  Madigan (H. Simoun)
1969:  Tell Them Willie Boy Is Here
1971:  Romance of a Horsethief (D. Opatoshu)
1979:  Avalanche Express
1982:  Monsignor (W. Mayes)
```

ABE POLSKY

```
1970:  Rebel Rousers*
1973:  The Baby
```

JOHN POMEROY

```
1982:  The Secret of N.I.M.H. (anim.)*
```

DARRYL PONICSAN

```
1973:  Cinderella Liberty
1981:  Taps (R. M. Kamen)
```

SAL PONTI

```
1973:  Doctor Death -- Seeker of Souls
```

ROBERT J. POOLE

```
1973:  The Mack
```

TOM POPE

1978: The Manitou*

TIM POPE

1973: Don't Look in the Basement

RALPH PORTER

1961: After Mein Kampf (doc.)

VLADIMIR POSNER

1944: The Conspirators
1948: Another Part of the Forest

CHARLES A. POST

1932: Single-Handed Sanders

FLORENCE POSTAL

1930: The Big Trail*

DICK POSTON

1971: The Jesus Trip
1972: Blood of Ghastly Horror (C. Martino)

VICTOR POTEL

1935: Hot off the Press (G. Griffith)

DENNIS POTTER

1981: Pennies from Heaven

RALPH B. POTTS

1975:   The Specialist*

AMOS POWELL

1962:   Tower of London*

CHARLES ARTHUR POWELL

1938:   The Great Adventures of Wild Bill Hickok
        (ser.)*; Panamint's Bad Man (L. Ward)
1939:   Home on the Prairie (P. Franklin)

PETER POWELL

1975:   The Human Factor (Tom Hunter)
1980:   The Final Countdown*

RICHARD POWELL

1957:   My Gun Is Quick (R. Collins)

BEULAH POYNTER

1934:   Dancing Man

STANLEY PRAGER

1949:   Joe Palooka in the Big Fight

LEONARD PRASKINS

1930:   Temptation
1931:   The Champ (F. Marion); Gentleman's Fate
1932:   Emma; Flesh (E. Woolf)
1933:   Advice to the Lovelorn; Man Hunt (S. Mintz)
1934:   Here Comes the Groom (C. Robinson); The Last
        Gentleman; Looking for Trouble (E. Harris);
        We Live Again*
1935:   Call of the Wild (G. Fowler);
        O'Shaughnessy's Boy*

```
1936:   One in a Million (M. Kelly)
1938:   Stablemates (R. Maibaum)
1939:   The Ice Follies of 1939*
1943:   So This Is Washington (R. Rogers)
1944:   My Pal Wolf*
1945:   The Caribbean Mystery (J. Andrews); Doll
        Face; Molly and Me
1952:   It Grows on Trees (B. Slater)
1953:   Mr. Scoutmaster (B. Slater)
1954:   Gorilla at Large (B. Slater)
```

GILBERT PRATT

```
1936:   Timothy's Quest*
1940:   Saps at Sea*
```

JOHN PREBBLE

```
1961:   Mysterious Island*
```

ERIC LEE PREMINGER

```
1975:   Rosebud
```

CHRIS PRENTISS

```
1976:   Goin' Home
```

DAVID PRENTISS

```
1967:   Journey to the Center of Time
```

G. PRENTISS

```
1972:   The Culpepper Cattle Company (E. Bercovici)
```

NORMAN PRESCOTT

```
1974:   Journey Back to Oz (F. Ladd)
```

ROBERT PRESNELL, JR.

1930: Young Man of Manhattan
1931: The Bargain; Leftover Ladies
1932: The Man Called Back
1933: Bureau of Missing Persons; Employees'
       Entrance; The Keyhole; The Narrow Corner
1939: Disbarred (L. Hayward); The Real Glory (J.
       Swerling)
1940: Money and the Woman; Thou Shalt Not Kill;
       Money and the Woman
1941: Hurricane Smith
1946: Cuban Pete
1947: For You I Die; The Guilty; High Tide; Ambush
1948: Open Secret*
1954: Man in the Attic (B. Lyndon)
1955: A Life in the Balance (L. Townsend)
1956: Screaming Eagles (D. Lang)
1957: Legend of the Lost (B. Hecht)
1958: Wink of an Eye*
1960: Cnspiracy of Hearts (Brit.); Let No Man
       Write My Epitaph
1962: 13 West Street (B. Schoenfeld)
1965: The Third Day (B. Wohl)

RUSSELL PRESNELL

1950: Second Chance

RAY PRESTON

1969: The Hooked Generation*

ANN PRICE

1929: All at Sea (Byron Morgan)

EUGENE PRICE

1970: Guess What We Learned in School Today? (J.
       Avildsen)
1972: Corky; The Stoolie*

645

OLGA PRINTZLAU

1933: Marriage on Approval

LEO PROCHNIK

1972: Child's Play

JAMES PROCTOR

1979: Dreamer (L. Bischof)

RICHARD PRYOR (1940-   ) actor

1974: Blazing Saddles*

WILLIAM PUGSLEY

1973: Dracula vs. Frankenstein (S. M. Sherman)

GERTRUDE PURCELL

1930: Follow the Leader (S. Silvers)
1931: Girl Habit (O. Davis); Royal Family of
       Broadway (H. Mankiewicz)
1932: Night Mayor; No More Orchids; Vanity Street
1933: Another Language (H. Mankiewicz); Child of
       Manhattan; Cocktail Hour (R. Schayer)
1934: Palooka*; She Was a Lady
1935: The Girl Friend (B. Rubin); If You Could
       Only Cook (H. Green)
1936: Make Way for a Lady; Witness Chair (R.
       James)
1937: Hitting a New High (J. Twist); Music for
       Madame (R. Harari); Super Sleuth (E. Pagano)
1938: Mother Carey's Chickens (S.Lauren); Service
       de Luxe (L. Spigelgass)
1939: Destry Rides Again*; The Lady and the Mob
       (R. Maibaum)
1940: A Little Bit of Heaven (D. Taradash); One
       Night in the Tropics (C. Grayson)
1941: Ellery Queen and the Murder Ring (E.
       Taylor); The Invisible Woman*

```
1942:   In Old California (F. Hyland); Ice Capades
        Revue (B. Ropes)
1944:   Follow the Boys (L. Breslow); Reckless Age
        (H. Blankfort)
1945:   Paris Underground (B. Ingster)
1947:   Winter Wonderland*
```

PAUL PURCELL

```
1959:   Gangster Story
```

HERBERT PURDUM

```
1952:   Target Hong Kong
1953:   El Alemein (H. McCoy)
```

DAVID PURSALL

```
1966:   The Blue Max*
```

MARIO PUZO

```
1972:   The Godfather (F. Coppola)
1974:   Earthquake (G. Fox); The Godfather, Part II
        (F. Coppola)
1978:   Superman*
1981:   Superman II*
```

ALBERT PYUN

```
1982:   The Sword and the Sorcerer*
```

Q

MOHY QUANDOR

1974:   The Spectre of Edgar Allan Poe

ROBERT QUIGLEY

1930:   The Land of Missing Men (J. P. McCarthy)
1931:   Shotgun Pass
1932:   Fighting for Justice
1933:   Man of Action; Rusty Rides Alone; Gun
        Justice; Before Midnight

JOSEPH QUILLAN

1944:   Show Business (D. Bennett)
1948:   Variety Time*
1952:   Son of Paleface*
1956:   Our Miss Brooks (Al Lewis)

ROBERT QUILLAN

1935:   Life Begins at 40*

RICHARD QUINE (1920–   ) director, actor

1952:   Sound Off (B. Edwards); Rainbow 'Round My
        Shoulder (B. Edwards)
1953:   Cruisin' Down the River (B. Edwards)
1954:   Drive a Crooked Road*
1955:   My Sister Eileen (B. Edwards)

DON QUINN

1944: Heavenly Days (H. Estabrook)

DAVID RABE

1982:   I'm Dancing As Fast As I Can

MARTIN RACKIN (1918-1976) producer

1943:   Air Raid Wardens*
1947:   Riffraff
1948:   Fighting Father Dunne (F. Davis); Race
        Street
1949:   A Dangerous Profession (W. Duff)
1950:   Three Secrets
1951:   Distant Drums (N. Busch); The Enforcer;
        Sailor Beware (J. Allardice)
1952:   The Stooge (F. Finkelhoffe); Loan Shark
1953:   The Clown; The Great Diamond Robbery (L.
        Vadnay)
1955:   Hell on Frisco Bay (S. Boehm); Long John
        Silver
1956:   Santiago (J. Twist)
1957:   The Big Land (D. Dortort)
1958:   The Deep Six*
1959:   The Horse Soldiers (J. Mahin)
1960:   North to Alaska*

ROBERT RADNITZ (1925-   ) producer

1958:   Wink of an Eye*

BOB RAFELSON (1934-   ) director

1968:   Head (J. Nicholson)
1972:   The King of Marvin Gardens (J. Brackman)
1976:   Stay Hungry (C. Gaines)

STEWART RAFFILL

1971: The Tender Warrior (D. Dalie)
1972: Napoleon and Samantha
1975: The Adventures of the Wilderness Family
1976: Across the Great Divide
1978: The Sea Gypsies
1981: High Risk

MARTIN RAGAWAY

1949: Abbott and Costello in the Foreign Legion
       (John Grant)
1950: Ma and Pa Kettle Go to Town (L. Stern); The
       Milkman*
1952: Lost in Alaska (L. Stern)

NORMAN REILLY RAINE (1895-1971)

1936: God's Country and the Woman; The Life of
       Emile Zola*
1937: Mountain Justice (L. Ward); The Perfect
       Specimen*
1938: The Adventures of Robin Hood (S. Miller);
       Men Are Such Fools (Horace Jackson)
1939: Each Dawn I Die*; The Private Lives of
       Elizabeth and Essex (A. MacKenzie)
1940: The Fighting 69th*
1942: Captains of the Clouds*; Eagle Squadron
1943: We've Never Been Licked (N. Grinde)
1944: Ladies Courageous (Doris Gilbert)
1945: A Bell for Adano (L. Trotti); Captain Kidd;
       Nob Hill (W. Tuchock)
1951: M (Leo Katcher)
1952: Woman of the North Country

PETER RAINER

1977: Joyride (J. Ruben)

DOROTHY RAISON

1958: Girls on the Loose*

MILTON RAISON (see GEORGE MILTON)

GIL RALSTON

1968:   Kona Coast
1971:   Willard
1972:   Ben

HANS RAMBEAU

1940:   Waterloo Bridge*
1942:   We Were Dancing*

PAUL H. RAMEAU

1943:   Madame Curie (P. Osborn)

HAROLD RAMIS

1978:   National Lampoon's Animal House*
1980:   Caddyshack*
1981:   Stripes*

AL RAMRUS

1970:   Halls of Anger (J. Shaner)
1977:   The Island of Dr. Moreau (J. Shaner)
1978:   Goin' South*

MARTIE RAMSON

1938:   The Spider's Web (ser.)*

AYN RAND

1945:   You Came Along (R. Smith); Love Letters
1949:   The Fountainhead

ARTHUR RANKIN, JR.

1966: The Daydreamer

W. RANKIN

1936: Counterfeit (B. Manning)

MATTHEW RAPF

1948: Adventures of Gallant Bess

MAURICE RAPF

1936: We Went to College (R. Maibaum)
1937: They Gave Him a Gun*
1939: Winter Carnival*; North of Shanghai (H.
       Buchman)
1941: Dancing on a Dime*; Jennie
1946: Song of the South*

FREDERIC RAPHAEL (1931-   )

1958: Bachelor of Hearts (Brit.)*
1964: Nothing but the Best (Brit.)
1965: Darling (Brit.)
1967: Two for the Road (Brit.); Far from the
       Madding Crowd (Brit.)
1970: Guilt (Brit.)
1971: A Severed Head (Brit.)
1974: Daisy Miller
1975: Carmela (Brit.)

SAMSON RAPHAELSON (1896-   )

1930: Boudoir Diplomat (unc.)*
1931: The Magnificent Lie; The Smiling Lieutenant
       (E. Vajda)
1932: Broken Lullaby (alt. The Man I Killed; E.
       Vajda); One Hour with You; Trouble in
       Paradise (G. Jones)
1934: Caravan; The Merry Widow (E. Vajda);
       Servants' Entrance

1935: Dressed to Thrill; Ladies Love Danger*; The
       Runaway Queen (M. Hoffe)
1937: Angel; The Last of Mrs. Cheyney*
1940: The Shop Around the Corner (B. Hecht)
1941: Suspicion*
1943: Heaven Can Wait
1946: The Harvey Girls*
1947: Green Dolphin Street
1948: That Lady in Ermine
1949: In the Good Old Summertime*
1953: Main Street to Broadway

I. C. RAPOPORT

1972: To Kill a Clown (G. Bloomfield)

JOEL M. RAPP

1959: High School Big Shot
1961: Battle of Blood Island

NELL RAPP

1976: Go for It (doc.)

PHILIP RAPP

1938: Start Cheering*
1945: Wonder Man*
1949: The Inspector General (H. Kurnitz)
1955: Ain't Misbehavin'*

MARK RAPPAPORT

1978: Scenic Route

JUDITH RASCOE

1974: Road Movie
1981: Endless Love

FRED RATH

1944: Sing a Jingle*

JOHN RATHMELL

1935: The Phantom Empire (ser.)*; The Miracle
Rider (ser.)*; Adventures of Rex and Rinty
(ser.; B. Sarecky)
1936: Ghost Town Gold (O. Drake); The Vigilantes
Are Coming (ser.)*; Darkest Africa (ser.)*;
Undersea Kingdom (ser.)*
1937: Riders of the Whistling Skull*; Trapped; Two
Gun Law; Zorro Rides Again (ser.)*
1938: The Painted Desert (O. Drake); Starlight
over Texas
1939: Song of the Buckaroo; Southward Ho! (J.
Natteford); Renegade Trail (H. Jacobs);
Fighting Mad (G. Rosener)
1940: Bullets for Rustlers; The Range Busters
1949: King of the Jungleland (ser.)*

TERENCE RATTIGAN (1911-1977) playwright Brit.

(American films only)
1944: Uncensored (R. Ackland)
1958: Separate Tables (J. Gay)
1969: Goodbye Mr. Chips (U.S./Brit.)

NEIL RAU

1945: They Shall Have Faith (alt. Forever Yours)*

HERMAN RAUCHER

1968: Sweet November
1970: Watermelon Man
1971: Summer of '42
1973: Class of '44
1976: Ode to Billy Joe
1977: The Other Side of Midnight (D. Taradash)

STANLEY RAUH

1934:   Cross Country Cruise (E. Harris)
1936:   Laughing Irish Eyes*
1938:   Hold That Kiss
1939:   Quick Millions (J. Hoffman); Too Busy to
        Work*
1940:   Charter Pilot (L. Ziffren); Michael Shayne,
        Private Detective (M. O'Connor); Pier 13 (C.
        Andrews); Young As You Feel (J. Hoffman)
1941:   Cadet Girl (H. Hanemann); Dance Hall (E.
        Hill); Dressed to Kill (M. O'Connor);
        Sleepers West (L. Breslow)

IRVING RAVETCH (1915-   )   (also JAMES P. BONNER)

1947:   Living in a Big Way (G. LaCava)
1950:   The Outriders
1951:   Vengeance Valley
1955:   Ten Wanted Men (K. Gamet)
1958:   The Long Hot Summer (H. Frank)
1959:   The Sound and the Fury (H. Frank)
1960:   The Dark at the Top of the Stairs (H.
        Frank); Home from the Hill (H. Frank)
1963:   Hud (H. Frank)
1967:   Hombre (H. Frank)
1969:   House of Cards (H. Frank); The Reivers
1972:   The Cowboys*
1974:   Conrack (H. Frank); The Spikes Gang (H.
        Frank)
1979:   Norma Rae (H. Frank)

ALBERT RAY

1932:   Hold 'Em, Jail*
1937:   45 Fathers (F. Hyland)
1938:   Change of Heart (F. Hyland); Island in the
        Sky (F. Hyland); Keep Smiling (F. Hyland)
1939:   Charlie Chan in Reno*; Winner Take All (F.
        Hyland); Everybody's Baby*; While New York
        Sleeps (F. Hyland)
1945:   The Cheaters (F. Hyland)

BERNARD B. RAY

1938:   It's All in Your Mind

656

```
1940:   Broken Strings (C. Krusada)
1960:   Spring Affair


MARC B. RAY

1972:   The Stoolie*


NICHOLAS RAY (1911-1979) director

1958:   Bitter Victory (Fr.)*
1960:   The Savage Innocents


DAVID RAYFIEL

1969:   Castle Keep (D. Taradash)
1971:   Valdez Is Coming (R. Kibbee)
1975:   Three Days of the Condor (L. Semple)
1976:   Lipstick


DALTON RAYMOND

1946:   Song of the South*


WILLIAM RAYNOR

1950:   Snow Dog
1951:   Yukon Manhunt; Northwest Territory; Casa
        Manana; Rhythm Inn
1952:   Without Warning; Yukon Gold
1953:   Phantom from Space (M. Wilder); Murder
        Without Tears (J. Pagano); Border City
        Rustlers; Son of Belle Starr (D. Beauchamp)
1954:   Killers from Space; Yukon Vengeance; Target
        Earth
1956:   Francis in the Haunted House (H. Margolis);
        Rock, Pretty Baby (H. Margolis)
1957:   The Kettles on Old MacDonald's Farm (H.
        Margolis)
1958:   Summer Love (H. Margolis)


GENNARO REA
```

1938: West of Rainbow's End (S. Roberts); Where
the West Begins (S. Roberts)

HARRY REBUAS (see HARRY SAUBER)

JAY REDACK

1978: Rabbit Test (J. Rivers)

WILLIAM REDLIN

1966: The Cat (L. Koenig)

JOEL REED

1981: Night of the Zombies

LUTHER REED

1930: Dixiana; Hit the Deck
1932: Bachelor Mother*
1933: Sweetheart of Sigma Chi*

TOM REED

1928: Lonesome
1929: Hell's Heroes
1930: Boudoir Diplomat; East is West
1931: Bad Sister (R. Schrock); Waterloo Bridge (B.
Levy)
1932: Law and Order (J. Huston); Afraid to Talk;
Laughter in Hell; Murders in the Rue Morgue
(D. Van Every) Radio Patrol
1933: S.O.S. Iceberg
1934: Babbitt*; Bombay Mail; Man with Two Faces
(N. Busch)
1935: Case of the Curious Bride (B. Holmes); The
Florentine Dagger (B. Holmes); Mary Jane's
Pa (P. Milne)
1936: The Captain's Kid; The Case of the Velvet
Claws; Love Begins at Twenty (D. Trumbo)
1937: The Great O'Malley (M. Krims); Marry the

```
                Girl*
1939:   On Dress Parade (C. Belden); The Dead End
                Kids on Dress Parade
1940:   Calling Philo Vance; The Man Who Talked Too
                Much (W. DeLeon)
1942:   The Spoilers*; Hello, Annapolis (D. Davis);
                The Loves of Edgar Allan Poe (S.
                Hoffenstein); Pittsburgh (K. Gamet)
1943:   Two Tickets to London
1944:   Up in Mabel's Room
1947:   Moss Rose (J. Furthman); Spirit of West
                Point
1948:   The Untamed Breed
1949:   Red Stallion in the Rockies (F. Rosenwald)
1950:   David Harding, Counterspy (C. Johnston)
1951:   Soldiers 3*
1953:   Back to God's Country
```

WINIFRED REEVE

```
1930:   Young Desire (M. Taylor)
1931:   Undertow
```

THEODORE REEVES (1911-1973)

```
1937:   Blossoms on Broadway; Internes Can't Take
                Money (R. James); She Asked for It*
1938:   The Storm*
1941:   Doctors Don't Tell (I. Dawn)
1943:   Night Plane from Chungking*
1944:   National Velvet (H. Deutch
1949:   The Doctor and the Girl
1957:   Bernardine
```

BILL REGA

```
1971:   The Late Liz
```

JAYNE REGAN

```
1934:   Terror of the Plains (C. Krusada)
```

PATRICK REGAN

1977:   The Farmer*

RICHARD REICH

1974:   Pets

MARK REICHERT

1980:   Union City

DOROTHY REID (pseud. of DOROTHY DAVENPORT)
         (1895-1977) actress, director

1934:   Road to Ruin*; Woman Condemned
1935:   Honeymoon Limited (B. Burbridge); Women Must
         Dress (E. Joseph)
1938:   Prison Break (N. Parker)
1940:   Drums of the Desert (J. West); The Haunted
         House; The Old Swimmin' Hole; On the Spot
         (J. West); Tomboy (M. Orth)
1941:   Redhead (C. Seiler)
1947:   The Hal Roach Comedy Carnival*; Curly
1948:   Who Killed "Doc" Robbin? (M. Geraghty)
1949:   Impact (J. Dratler)
1951:   Rhubarb (F. Cockrell)
1955:   Footsteps in the Fog (Brit.; L. Coffee)

JAMES REIGLE

1982:   Android (D. Opper)

WILLIAM C. REILLY

1972:   The Broad Coalition; What Do I Tell the Boys
         at the Station? (S. Nuchtern)

CARL REINER (1922-   ) actor, director, pruducer

1963:   The Thrill of It All
1965:   The Art of Love
1967:   Enter Laughing (J. Stein); The Comic (A.

        Ruben)
1982:   Dead Men Don't Wear Plaid*

ELIZABETH (BETTY) REINHARDT

1940:   Gold Rush Maisie (M. McCall)
1941:   Maisie Was a Lady (M. McCall)
1942:   Maisie Gets Her Man (M. McCall)
1943:   His Butler's Sister (S. Hoffenstein)
1944:   Laura*
1946:   Cluny Brown (S. Hoffenstein); Sentimental
        Journey (S. Hoffenstein)
1947:   Carnival in Costa Rica*
1948:   Give My Regards to Broadway (S. Hoffenstein)
1950:   Hit Parade of 1951*

GOTTFRIED REINHARDT (1911-   ) director, producer
        Germ.

(American films only)
1935:   I Live My Life*
1938:   The Great Waltz*
1939:   Bridal Suite (S. Hoffenstein)

JOHN REINHARDT

1951:   Chicago Calling

SYLVIA REINHARDT

1965:   Situation Hopeless -- but Not Serious

WOLFGANG REINHARDT

1939:   Juarez*
1962:   Freud (C. Kaufman)

IRVING REIS (1906-1953) director

1938:   King of Alcatraz
1939:   Grand Jury Secrets (R. Yost); King of
        Chinatown*

1944:   Gambler's Choice (M. Shane)

WALTER REISCH (1903-   ) director   Austr.

(American films only)
1938:   The Great Waltz*
1939:   Ninotchka*
1941:   That Hamilton Woman (R. C. Sheriff); That
        Uncertain Feeling (D.O. Stewart)
1942:   Seven Sweethearts (L. Townsend); Somewhere
        I'll Find You (Marguerite Roberts)
1943:   The Heavenly Body*
1944:   Gaslight*
1947:   Song of Scheherazade
1949:   The Fan*
1951:   The Mating Season*; The Model and the
        Marriage Broker*
1953:   Niagara*; Titanic*
1954:   The Girl in the Red Velvet Swing (C.
        Brackett)
1956:   Teenage Rebel (C. Brackett)
1957:   Stopover Tokyo (R. Breen)
1959:   The Remarkable Mr. Pennypacker; Journey to
        the Center of the Earth (C. Brackett)

ARNIE REISMAN

1973:   Hollywood on Trial (doc.)

DEL REISMAN

1974:   The Take

PHILIP REISMAN, JR.

1950:   The Tattooed Stranger
1955:   Special Delivery (D. Taylor)
1963:   All the Way Home
1968:   P. J.

CHARLES F. REISNER (1887-1962)

1931:   Flying High (A. Younger)

662

DEAN REISNER

1947: Bill and Coo (R. Foster)
1950: Operation Haylift (J. Sawyer)
1951: Skipalong Rosenbloom (E. Forman)
1957: The Helen Morgan Story*
1958: Paris Holiday (E. Beloin)
1964: The Man from Galveston (M. Zagor)
1968: Coogan's Bluff*
1971: Play Misty for Me (J. Heims); Dirty Harry*
1973: Charley Varrick (H. Rodman)
1976: The Enforcer (S. Silliphant)

HARRY RELIS

1963: Captain Sinbad (S. West)

DUNCAN RENALDO (also RENAULT DUNCAN) (1904-1980)

1947: The Bells of San Fernando (J. DeWitt); Don
       Ricardo Returns (J. DeWitt)

LES RENDELSTEIN

1972: Private Parts (P. Kearney)

JEAN RENOIR (1894-1979) director Fr.

(American films only)
1945: The Southerner (H. Butler)
1947: Woman on the Beach (F. Davis)

ED EARL REPP

1937: Devil's Saddle Legion; Prairie Thunder; The
       Old Wyoming Trail; Outlaws of the Prairie
1938: Cattle Raiders (J. Poland); Call of the
       Rockies; West of Cheyenne
1941: Rawhide Rangers
1943: Saddles and Sagebrush; Six Gun Gospel (A.
       Buffington); Silver City Raiders;

Wagonwheels West; Oklahoma Outlaws
1944: The Vigilantes Ride; The Last Horseman;
Trigger Trail (P. Harper); Roaring Guns
1945: Texas Panhandle
1946: Gunning for Vengeance (L. Rousseau);
Galloping Thunder; Heading West; Terror
Trail; The Fighting Frontiersman
1947: The Lone Hand Texan; Prairie Raiders; The
Stranger from Ponca City
1948: Guns of Hate (N. Houston); The Tioga Kid
1949: Challenge of the Range
1950: Storm over Wyoming; Rider from Tucson
1951: Law of the Badlands; Saddle Legion; Gunplay;
Cyclone Fury (B. Shipman)

LAWRENCE RESNER

1957: Gun Battle at Monterey (J. Leonard)

PATRICIA RESNICK

1978: A Wedding*
1979: Quintet*
1980: Nine to Five (C. Higgins)

NORMAN RETCHIN

1956: Uranium Boom*; The Leather Saint (A. Ganzer)
1957: Ride Out for Revenge

ALMA REVILLE (1900-   ) Brit.

(American films only)
1935: Strauss' Great Waltz (G. Bolton)
1936: The Passing of the Thrird Floor Back (M.
Hogan)
1941: Suspicion*
1943: Shadow of a Doubt*
1945: It's in the Bag (J. Dratler)
1948: The Paradine Case*
1950: Stage Fright (W. Cook)

FERDINAND REYHER

1932:   The All-American (F. Wead)
1933:   The Big Cage (E. Anthony)
1935:   Rendezvous at Midnight (G. Unger)
1936:   Two in Revolt*; Special Investigator*; You
        May Be Next (F. Niblo)
1938:   Ride a Crooked Mile (J. Moffitt)
1943:   The Boy from Stalingrad

CLARK E. REYNOLDS

1951:   Disc Jockey
1955:   Shotgun (R. Calhoun)
1959:   Gunmen from Laredo
1965:   Gunfighters of Casa Grande*; Genghis Kahn
        (B. Cross)
1966:   Son of a Gunfighter
1967:   The Viking Queen; The Viscount

QUENTIN REYNOLDS (1902-   ) writer, journalist

1948:   The Miracle of the Bells (B. Hecht)

SHELDON REYNOLDS

1956:   Foreign Intrigue
1969:   Assignment to Kill

V. J. RHEMS

1958:   Dragstrip Riot (G. Hodgins)

LARRY RHINE

1939:   Chip of the Flying U (A. Bennison)
1940:   The Devil's Pipeline*; The Leather Pushers*
1941:   A Dangerous Game*; Six Lessons from Madame
        La Zonga*

O'LETA RHINEHART

1946:   Crime of the Century*; Passkey to Danger (W.

Hagens)

RONALD RIBMAN

1970:   The Angel Levine (B. Gunn)

RUDOLPH J. RICCI

1972:   There's Always Vanilla

CRAIG RICE

1942:   The Falcon's Brother (S. Palmer)
1943:   The Falcon in Danger (F. Niblo)

ELMER RICE (1892-1967) playwright

1931:   Street Scene
1933:   Counsellor at Law

RON RICE

1962:   The Flower Thief

JOHN RICH

1953:   The Golden Blade

RUSSELL RICHARD

1957:   The Pajama Game*

ALEXANDER RICHARDS

1960:   Thunder in Carolina

HAL RICHARDS

1953:   Man of Conflict

1956:   The Peacemaker (J. Ingram)

JACKSON RICHARDS

1932:   Trailing the Killer

ROBERT L. RICHARDS

1940:   The Ramparts We Watch (doc.; C. Worth)
1947:   Act of Violence
1948:   One Sunday Afternoon
1949:   Johnny Stool Pigeon
1950:   Winchester '73 (B. Chase); Kansas Raiders
1951:   Air Cadet

SILVIA RICHARDS

1947:   Possessed (R. MacDougall)
1948:   Secret Beyond the Door
1951:   Tomahawk (M. Geraghty)
1952:   Ruby Gentry

ANNA STEESE RICHARDSON

1934:   Big-Hearted Herbert*

JACK RICHARDSON

1975:   Foreplay*
1981:   The President's Women*

W. LYLE RICHARDSON

1978:   Zero to Sixty

WILLIAM RICHERT

1975:   The Happy Hooker (D. Goldenberg)
1979:   Winter Kills
1980:   The American Success Company (L. Cohen)

MORDECAI RICHLER

1977: Fun with Dick and Jane*

MAURICE RICHLIN

1959: Pillow Talk (S. Shapiro); Operation
       Petticoat (S. Shapiro)
1961: All in a Night's Work*; Come September (S.
       Shapiro)
1963: Soldier in the Rain (B. Edwards)
1964: The Pink Panther (B. Edwards)
1974: For Pete's Sake (S. Shapiro)

ARTHUR RICHMAN

1933: Only Yesterday (G. O'Neill)

BILL RICHMOND

1961: The Ladies' Man (J. Lewis)
1962: The Errand Boy (J. Lewis)
1963: The Nutty Professor (J. Lewis)
1964: The Patsy (J. Lewis)
1967: The Big Mouth (J. Lewis)

HANS RICHTER (1888-1976) filmmaker, painter Germ.

(American films only)
1957: 8 X 8

W. D. RICHTER

1973: Slither
1976: Nickelodeon (P. Bogdanovich); Peeper
1978: Invasion of the Body Snatchers
1979: Dracula
1980: Brubaker
1981: All Night Long

BRUCE RICKER

1980: The Last of the Blue Devils (J. Arnoldy)

THOMAS RICKMAN

1972: Kansas City Bomber (C. Clements)
1973: The Laughing Policeman
1974: The White Dawn (J. Houston)
1975: W. W. and the Dixie Dancekings
1978: Hooper
1980: Coal Miner's Daughter

CHARLES F. RIESNER (see CHARLES F. REISNER)

DEAN RIESNER (see DEAN REISNER)

GORDON RIGBY

1929: Skin Deep; Tiger Rose (H. Thew)
1930: Under a Texas Moon; Mammy (J. Jackson)
1931: Captain Thunder; Command Performance (M.
       Fulton)
1932: The Golden West
1933: Smoke Lightning (S. Mitchell)
1935: Hitch Hike Lady (L. Cole)
1936: The Gentleman from Louisiana (J. Fields)
1937: The Wrong Road (E. Taylor)
1938: Flight into Nowhere (J. Parker); The Strange
       Case of Dr. Meade (C. Sand); Outside the
       Law; Reformatory
1939: Hidden Power; Trapped in the Sky (E.
       Taylor); Whispering Enemies (T. Kilpatrick)
1940: Sing, Dance, Plenty Hot (B. Ropes)
1941: Naval Academy (D. Silverstein)
1942: The Man Who Returned to Life

RAY RIGBY

1965: The Hill (Brit.)
1969: The Bridge at Remagen*

LYNN RIGGS

1936:   The Plainsman*; the Garden of Allah*
1942:   Destination Unknown (J. Meehan); Sherlock
        Holmes and the Voice of Terror*
1943:   Sherlock Holmes in Washington (B.
        Millhauser)

SARA RIGGS

1972:   Quadroon

LAWRENCE RILEY

1937:   Ever Since Eve*; The Perfect Specimen*
1943:   You're a Lucky Fellow, Mr. Smith*

WOLF RILLA

1960:   Village of the Damned (Brit.)*

JOE RINALDI

1953:   Peter Pan (anim.)*
1955:   Lady and the Tramp (anim.)*
1959:   Sleeping Beauty (anim.)*
1961:   Babes in Toyland*

FREDERIC I. RINALDO

1940:   Street of Memories (R. Lees)
1941:   Bachelor Daddy (R. Lees); The Black Cat*;
        Hold That Ghost*; The Invisible Woman*
1942:   Juke Box Jenny*
1943:   Crazy House (R. Lees); Hit the Ice*
1947:   The Wistful Widow of Wagon Gap (J. Grant);
        Buck Privates Come Home*
1948:   Abbott and Costello Meet Frankenstein*
1949:   Holiday in Havana*
1951:   Abbott and Costello Meet the Invisible Man*;
        Comin' Round the Mountain (R. Lees)
1952:   Jumping Jacks*

DAVID W. RINTELS

1973:   Scorpio

ARTHUR RIPLEY (1895-1961) director

1929:   Barnum Was Right (E. Adamson)
1930:   Captain of the Guard (H. Branch); The
        Hide-Out (L. Hillyer)
1939:   Waterfront (L. Katz)
1942:   Prisoner of Japan (R. Chapin)

CLEMENTS RIPLEY

1938:   Jezebel*; Love, Honor and Behave*
1944:   Buffalo Bill*
1948:   Old Los Angeles (ret. California Outpost; G.
        Adams)

ROBERT RISKIN (1897-1955) playwright

1929:   Men Are Like That*
1931:   Arizona (D. Howell); The Men in Her Life (D.
        Howell)
1932:   American Madness; Big Timer (D. Howell);
        Night Club Lady; Virtue
1933:   Ann Carver's Profession; Lady for a Day
1934:   Broadway Bill (S. Buchman); It Happened One
        Night
1935:   Carnival; The Whole Town's Talking (J.
        Swerling)
1936:   Mr. Deeds Goes to Town
1937:   Lost Horizon (S. Buchman); When You're in
        Love
1938:   You Can't Take It With You
1941:   Meet John Doe
1944:   The Thin Man Goes Home (Dwight Taylor)
1947:   Magic Town
1950:   Mister 880; Riding High (Jack Rose)
1951:   Half Angel
1956:   You Can't Run Away from It (C. Binyon)

CLAUDE RISTER

1932:   Tombstone Canyon

STEVEN RITCH

1957:   Plunder Road; Hell on Devil's Island
1959:   City of Fear (R. Dillon)

GUY R. RITCHIE

1953:   Robot Monster (W. Ordung)

LLOYD RITTER

1956:   Secrets of the Reef (doc.)*

ROSEMARY RITVO

1978:   Alice, Sweet Alice (A. Sole)

JAMES RITZ

1981:   Leo and Loree

W. L. RIVER

1941:   Reaching for the Sun
1942:   The Great Man's Lady; The Adventures of
         Martin Eden
1943:   City Without Men (B. Schulberg)

JOAN RIVERS

1978:   Rabbit Test (J. Redack)

ALLEN RIVKIN

1932:   The Devil Is Driving*; Madison Square Garden
         (P. Wolfson)
1933:   Dancing Lady (P. Wolfson); Girl in 419*;
         Meet the Baron (P. Wolfson); Picture

```
              Snatcher (P. Wolfson); Headline Shooter
              (A.C. Johnston)
1935:    Bad Boy; Black Sheep; Our Little Girl*
1936:    Champagne Charlie; Half Angel*
1937:    Love Under Fire*; This Is My Affair (L.
              Trotti)
1938:    Straight, Place and Show*
1939:    It Could Happen to You (L. Breslow); Let Us
              Live (A. Veiller)
1940:    Typhoon
1941:    Dancing on a Dime*; Highway West*; Singapore
              Woman (M. Webster)
1942:    Joe Smith, American; Kid Glove Killer (J.
              Higgins); Sunday Punch*
1946:    The Thrill of Brazil*; 'Til the End of Time
1947:    The Farmer's Daughter (L. Kerr); The Guilt
              of Janet Ames*
1949:    Tension
1950:    Gambling House (M. Borowsky); Grounds for
              Marriage (L. Kerr)
1951:    It's a Big Country*; The Strip
1954:    Prisoner of War
1955:    The Eternal Sea; The Road to Denver (H.
              McCoy); Timberjack
1958:    Girls on the Loose*; Live Fast, Die Young*
1959:    The Big Operator (R. Smith)
```

JONATHAN RIX

```
1949:    Cover Up (J. Odlum)
```

JOSEPH ANTHONY ROACH

```
1932:    Heroes of the West (ser.)*
1933:    Somewhere in Sonora; Jaws of Justice
1934:    The Ferocious Pal
```

HAROLD ROBBINS

```
1958:    Never Love a Stranger (R. Day)
1960:    The Pusher
```

MATTHEW ROBBINS

```
1974:   The Sugarland Express (H. Barwood)
1976:   The Bingo Long Traveling All-Stars and Motor
        Kings (H. Barwood)
1977:   MacArthur (H. Barwood)
1978:   Corvette Summer (H. Barwood)
1981:   Dragonslayer (H. Barwood)
```

JACQUES ROBERT

```
1971:   Someone Behind the Door (M. Behm)
```

ALAN ROBERTS

```
1970:   The Zodiac Couples (doc.; B. Stein)
```

BEN ROBERTS

```
1941:   Mr. District Attorney in the Carter Case (S.
        Sheldon); South of Panama (S. Sheldon)
1949:   Prejudice*; White Heat (I. Goff)
1951:   Captain Horatio Hornblower*; Come Fill the
        Cup (I. Goff); Goodbye, My Fancy (I. Goff)
1952:   O. Henry's Full House*
1953:   White Witch Doctor (I. Goff); King of the
        Khyber Rifles (I. Goff)
1954:   Green  Fire*
1956:   Serenade*
1957:   Man of a Thousand Faces*; Band of Angels*
1959:   Shake Hands with the Devil (I.Goff)
1960:   Midnight Lace (I. Goff); Portrait in Black
        (I. Goff)
1961:   The Legend of the Lone Ranger*
```

CHARLES EDWARD ROBERTS (-1953)

```
1932:   Western Limited
1933:   The Fighting Texans (W. Totman); Corruption;
        The Flaming Signal (T. Hughes)
1935:   Fighting Pioneers (H. Fraser); Adventurous
        Knights; Skybound
1936:   Mummy's Boys*
1937:   Rhythm Wranglers (E. Adamson)
1939:   Mexican Spitfire (J. Fields)
1940:   Mexican Spitfire Out West (J. Townley);
```

Millionaire Playboy (B. Granet); Pop Always Pays
1941: Mexican Spitfire's Baby (J. Cady)
1942: Mexican Spitfire at Sea (J. Cady); Mexican Spitfire Sees a Ghost (M. Brice); Mexican Spitfire's Elephant
1943: Ladies' Day (D. Lussier); Mexican Spitfire's Blessed Event (D. Lussier)
1944: Goin' to Town (C. Marion)
1945: Mama Loves Papa (M. Brice); What a Blonde
1946: Partners in Time; Riverboat Rhythm; Vacation in Reno (A. Ross)
1951: Honeychile (J. Townley); Cuban Fireball (J. Townley); Havana Rose (J. Townley)
1952: The Fabulous Senorita (J. Townley)

JACK ROBERTS

1942: A Man's World (E. Lowe)

JOHN R. ROBERTS

1950: When You're Smiling (K. DeWolfe)

MARGUERITE ROBERTS

1933: Jimmy and Sally (P. Schofield); Sailor's Luck (G. Miller)
1934: Peck's Bad Boy (B. Schubert)
1935: College Scandal*
1936: Florida Special*; Forgotten Faces*; Hollywood Boulevard; Rose Bowl
1937: Turn Off the Moon*; Wild Money*
1938: Meet the Girls
1940: Escape (A. Oboler)
1941: Honky Tonk (J. Sanford); Ziegfeld Girl (S. Levien)
1942: Somewhere I'll Find You (W. Reisch)
1944: Dragon Seed (J. Murfin)
1947: Desire Me (Z. Akins); If Winter Comes (A. Wimperis); The Sea of Grass (V. Lawrence)
1949: Ambush; The Bribe
1951: Soldiers Three*
1962: Diamond Head
1963: Rampage (R. Holt)

```
1965:   Loretta's Many Faces
1968:   Five Card Stud
1969:   True Grit
1970:   Norwood
1971:   Red Sky at Morning; Shoot Out
```

MEADE ROBERTS

```
1959:   The Fugitive Kind (Tennessee Williams)
1961:   Summer and Smoke (J. Poe)
1963:   In the Cool of the Day; The Stripper
1968:   Danger Route; Blue (R. M. Cohen)
```

STANLEY ROBERTS

```
1937:   Young Dynamite*
1938:   West of Rainbow's End (G. Rea); Where the
        West Begins (G. Rea); Code of the Rangers;
        Heroes of the Hills (B. Burbridge); Pals of
        the Saddle (B. Burbridge); Prairie Moon (B.
        Burbridge); Red River Range*
1939:   The Night Riders (B. Burbridge); Three Texas
        Steers (B. Burbridge); Colorado Sunset (B.
        Burbridge)
1942:   Behind the Eight Ball (M. Ronson); What's
        Cooking? (J. Cady); Who Done It?*
1943:   Hi Ya Sailor; Never a Dull Moment (M.
        Roberts)
1945:   Under Western Skies (C. Bruckman); Penthouse
        Rhythm (H. Dimsdale)
1950:   Louisa
1951:   Death of a Salesman; Up Front
1952:   The Story of Will Rogers (F. Davis)
1954:   The Caine Mutiny
1966:   Made in Paris
```

WILLIAM ROBERTS

```
1952:   You for Me
1953:   Fast Company; Easy to Love (L. Vadnay)
1954:   Her Twelve Men (L. Hobson)
1955:   The Private War of Major Benson (R. A.
        Simmons)
1959:   The Mating Game
1960:   The Magnificent Seven
```

```
1962:  The Wonderful World of the Brothers Grimm*
1963:  Come Fly with Me
1968:  The Devil's Brigade
1969:  The Bridge at Remagen*
1972:  Red Sun*
1973:  The Last American Hero
1975:  Posse (C. Knopf)
1981:  The Legend of the Lone Ranger*
```

BLAIR ROBERTSON

```
1966:  Agent for H.A.R.M.
```

CLIFF ROBERTSON (1925-   ) actor

```
1972:  J. W. Coop
1981:  The Pilot (Robert P. Davis)
```

E. C. ROBERTSON

```
1940:  Buzzy Rides the Range (ret. Western Terror)
1941:  Buzzy and the Phantom Pinto
```

SAM ROBINS (see STEVE BRAXTON)

BUDD ROBINSON

```
1972:  Where Does It Hurt? (R. Amateau)
```

CASEY ROBINSON (1903-1979)

```
1930:  The Squealer (D. Howell)
1932:  Is My Face Red? (B. Cormack)
1933:  Golden Harvest; Song of the Eagle (W. Mask)
1934:  Eight Girls in a Boat (L. Foster); Here
       Comes the Groom (L. Praskins); She Made Her
       Bed (F. Adams)
1935:  Captain Blood; I Found Stella Parish;
       McFadden's Flats*
1936:  Give Me Your Heart; Hearts Divided (L.
       Doyle); I Married a Doctor*; Stolen Holiday
1937:  Call It a Day; It's Love I'm After; Tovarich
```

```
1938:    Four's a Crowd (S. Herzig)
1939:    Dark Victory; The Old Maid; Yes, My Darling
         Daughter
1940:    All This and Heaven Too
1941:    Kings Row; Million Dollar Baby*; One Foot in
         Heaven
1942:    Now, Voyager
1943:    This Is the Army (C. Binyon)
1944:    Passage to Marseille (J. Moffitt); Days of
         Glory; The Racket Man*
1945:    Saratoga Trunk; The Corn Is Green (F.
         Cavett)
1947:    The Macomber Affair (S. Bennett)
1949:    Father Was a Fullback*
1950:    Two Flags West (F. Nugent); Under My Skin
1952:    Diplomatic Courier (L. O'Brien); The Snows
         of Kilimanjaro
1954:    A Bullet Is Waiting (Thames Williams); The
         Egyptian (P. Dunne)
1956:    While the City Sleeps
1959:    This Earth Is Mine
1964:    The Son of Captain Blood (It./U.S./Sp.)
```

CHRIS ROBINSON

```
1979:    Sunshine Run
```

DAVID ROBINSON

```
1953:    Monsoon*
```

GEORGE ROBINSON

```
1940:    If I Had My Way*
```

JACK A. ROBINSON

```
1970:    Tarzan's Deadly Silence*
```

JOHN ROBINSON

```
1956:    The Sharkfighters (L. Roman)
1957:    The Midnight Story (E. Blum)
```

MATT ROBINSON

1972: The Possession of Joel Delaney (G. Grice)
1973: Save the Children (doc.)
1974: Amazing Grace

R. D. ROBINSON

1971: The World Is Just a "B" Movie

RICHARD ROBINSON

1977: Kingdom of the Spiders (A. Caillou)

THELMA ROBINSON

1946: Up Goes Maisie
1947: Undercover Maisie

CHARLES ROBISON

1943: Follies Girl (M. Klauber)

WILLIAM ROBSON

1933: Private Jones (P. Chaplin)

PHILLIP ROCK

1961: Most Dangerous Man Alive
1969: The Extraordinary Seaman (H. Dresner)

HENWAR RODAKIEWICZ

1939: The City (doc.; L. Mumford)

GENE RODDENBERRY

1971:   Pretty Maids All in a Row

MARK RODGERS

1969:   Flareup

MARY RODGERS

1977:   Freaky Friday
1981:   The Devil and Max Devlin

RICHARD RODGERS (1902–1979) composer

1931:   Hot Heiress*

HOWARD RODMAN

1968:   Coogan's Bluff*
1969:   Winning
1973:   Charley Varrick (D. Riesner)

EARL RODNEY

1932:   Hypnotized*

STEPHEN ROE

1932:   By Whose Hand? (I. Bernstein)

JOHN ROEBURT

1951:   St. Benny the Dip
1962:   Dead to the World

SAMUEL ROECA

1948:   Incident (F. Niblo)
1950:   A Modern Marriage (G. Sayre); Sideshow
1951:   Sea Tiger; Navy Bound; I Was an American Spy
1953:   Trail Blazers (J. Marks); The Tall Texan;

```
         Torpedo Alley (W. Douglas)
1954:  The Outlaw's Daughter
1956:  Hidden Guns (A. Gannaway)
1957:  Sabu and the Magic Ring; Raiders of Old
         California (T. Hubbard)
1958:  Johnny Rocco (J. O'Hanlon)
1961:  Angel Baby*
1965:  Fluffy
```

MICHAEL ROEMER

```
1965:  Nothing but a Man (R. Young)
```

JULIAN ROFFMAN

```
1981:  The Glove (Hugh Smith)
```

BOGART ROGERS

```
1933:  Eagle and the Hawk (S. Miller)
1936:  13 Hours by Air (K. Nicholson)
```

CAMERON ROGERS

```
1935:  Cardinal Richelieu*
1938:  White Banners*
```

CHARLES ROGERS

```
1936:  Our Relations*
1937:  Way Out West*
1938:  Block-Heads*
1939:  The Flying Deuces*
1940:  A Chump at Oxford*; Saps at Sea*
1943:  Air Raid Wardens*
1944:  Abroad with Two Yanks*
1945:  Brewster's Millions*
```

HOWARD EMMETT ROGERS

```
1929:  The Forward Pass
1930:  No, No Nanette
```

```
1932:   Dancers in the Dark*
1933:   Don't Bet on Love (M. Roth); Hold Your Man
        (A. Loos)
1934:   Mystery of Mr. X*; Tarzan and His Mate*
1935:   Whipsaw
1936:   Libeled Lady*; The Unguarded Hour (Leon
        Gordon)
1938:   Arsène Lupin Returns*
1942:   Eyes in the Night (G. Troper)
1943:   Assignment in Brittany*
1950:   The Whipped (alt. The Underground Story)
1951:   Calling Bulldog Drummond (G. Fairlie); Two
        Dollar Bettor
1952:   The Hour of 13 (Leon Gordon)
```

JOE ROGERS

```
1971:   Brain of Blood (K. Lynn)
```

LELA E. ROGERS

```
1932:   Women Won't Tell
1953:   Tanga-Tika
```

ROSWELL ROGERS

```
1943:   So This Is Washington (L. Praskins); Two
        Weeks to Live (M. Simmons)
1952:   Just Across the Street (J. Malone)
1971:   The Million Dollar Duck
1973:   Charley and the Angel
```

WAYNE ROGERS

```
1969:   The Astro-Zombies (T. Mikels)
```

GILBERT ROLAND (1905-   ) actor

```
1947:   King of the Bandits (B. Cohen)
```

TOM ROLF

1971:   The Resurrection of Zachary Wheeler (J.
        Simms)

SAM ROLFE

1953:   The Naked Spur (H.J. Bloom)
1955:   The McConnell Story (T. Sherdeman); Target
        Zero
1956:   Pillars of the Sky (H. Bloom)
1966:   To Trap a Spy

LAWRENCE ROMAN

1953:   Vice Squad
1954:   Naked Alibi
1955:   The Man from Bitter Ridge; One Desire (R.
        Blees)
1956:   A Kiss Before Dying; The Sharkfighters (J.
        Robinson)
1957:   Slaughter on Tenth Avenue
1958:   Day of the Bad Men
1963:   Under the Yum Yum Tree (D. Swift)
1966:   The Swinger
1968:   Paper Lion
1972:   Red Sun*
1973:   A Warm December
1974:   McQ

SIGMUND ROMBERG (1887-1951) composer

1931:   Children of Dreams (O. Hammerstein II)

TINA ROME (see TINA PINE)

RACHEL ROMEN

1965:   The Desert Raven (A. Lee)

EDDIE ROMERO

1963:   Cavalry Command
1972:   Twilight People (J. Small)

GEORGE A. ROMERO

1973: Hungry Wives; The Crazies
1978: Martin
1979: Dawn of the Dead
1981: Knightriders

RAMON ROMERO

1953: City Beneath the Sea (J. Harvey)

MEL RONSON

1941: Behind the Eight Ball (S. Roberts)
1943: Always a Bridesmaid (O. Brodney); How's
      About It?; Never a Dull Moment (S. Roberts)

CONRAD ROOKS

1968: Chappaqua*

LYNN ROOT

1937: Wild and Woolly (F. Fenton); Angel's Holiday
      (F. Fenton); Step Lively, Jeeves! (F.
      Fenton)
1939: The Saint in London (F. Fenton)
1940: Little Orvie*; Millionaires in Prison (F.
      Fenton); The Saint Takes Over (F. Fenton)
1941: A Date with the Falcon (F. Fenton); The Gay
      Falcon (F. Fenton)
1942: The Falcon Takes Over (F. Fenton); Highways
      by Night (F. Fenton)
1943: The Sky's the Limit (F. Fenton)
1946: Lady Luck (F. Fenton)

WELLS ROOT

1928: Varsity
1930: The Storm
1931: Politics; The Prodigal (B. Meredyth)

```
1932:   Bird of Paradise; Tiger Shark
1933:   I Cover the Waterfront
1934:   Black Moon; Paris Interlude
1935:   Public Hero Number One (J.W. Ruben);
        Pursuit; Shadow of Doubt
1936:   The Bold Caballero; Sworn Enemy
1937:   The Prisoner of Zenda*
1939:   Man of Conquest*; Sergeant Madden; Thunder
        Afloat (H. Haislip)
1940:   Flight Command (H. Haislip)
1941:   The Bad Man; The Get-a-Way (W. Burnett)
1942:   Mokey (J. Fortune); Tennessee Johnson (J.
        Balderston)
1943:   The Man from Down Under (T. Seller)
1952:   Stronghold
1957:   Hell Ship Mutiny (D. Scott)
1961:   Secret of Deep Harbor (O. Harris)
1966:   Texas Across the River*
```

BRADFORD ROPES

```
1933:   Stage Mother  (J. Meehan)
1937:   Circus Girl (A. Buffington); The Hit Parade
        (S. Ornitz); Meet the Boyfriend
1940:   Melody and Moonlight; Sing, Dance, Plenty
        Hot (G. Rigby); Rancho Grande*; Gaucho
        Serenade (B. Burbridge); The Hit Parade of
        1941*
1941:   Ridin' on a Rainbow (D. Malloy); Angels with
        Broken Wings (George Brown); Glamour Boy (V.
        Burton)
1942:   Ice Capades Revue (G. Purcell); True to the
        Army (A. Arthur)
1943:   Man from Music Mountain (J. Cheney)
1944:   Hands Across the Border (J. Cheney); Swing
        in the Saddle*; Hi, Good Lookin'*
1945:   Steppin' in Society; Why Girls Leave Home
        (L. Ropes)
1946:   The Time of Their Lives*
1949:   Flame of Youth*
1950:   Belle of Old Mexico (F. Swan); The Arizona
        Cowboy; Redwood Forest Trail
```

LAWRENCE ROPES

```
1945:   Why Girls Leave Home (B. Ropes)
```

JUDITH ROSCOE

1978: Who'll Stop the Rain? (R. Stone)

HENRY ROSE

1954: Genevieve

JACK ROSE (1911–   ) producer

1947: Ladies' Man*; My Favorite Brunette (E.
       Beloin); Road to Rio (E. Beloin)
1948: The Paleface*
1949: Always Leave Them Laughing (M. Shavelson);
       The Great Lover*; It's a Great Feeling (M.
       Shavelson); Sorrowful Jones
1950: The Daughter of Rosie O'Grady*; Riding High
       (R. Riskin)
1951: I'll See You in My Dreams (M. Shavelson); On
       Moonlight Bay (M. Shavelson)
1952: April in Paris (M. Shavelson); Room for One
       More (M. Shavelson)
1953: Trouble Along the Way (M. Shavelson)
1954: Living It Up (M. Shavelson)
1955: The Seven Little Foys (M. Shavelson)
1957: Beau James (M. Shavelson)
1958: Houseboat (M. Shavelson)
1959: The Five Pennies (M. Shavelson)
1960: It Started in Naples*
1961: On the Double (M. Shavelson)
1962: Who's Got the Action?
1963: Papa's Delicate Condition; Who's Been
       Sleeping in My Bed?
1964: The Incredible Mr. Limpet (J. Brewer)
1973: A Touch of Class (M. Frank)
1976: The Duchess and the Dirtwater Fox*
1979: Lost and Found (M. Frank)
1981: The Great Muppet Caper*

LOUISA ROSE

1973: Sisters (B. De Palma)

MICKEY ROSE

1966: What's Up, Tiger Lily?*
1969: Take the Money and Run (W. Allen)
1971: Bananas (W. Allen)
1981: Student Bodies

RALPH ROSE

1971: Let's Scare Jessica to Death (N. Jonas)

REGINALD ROSE

1956: Crime in the Streets
1957: Twelve Angry Men
1958: Man of the West
1959: The Man in the Net
1978: Somebody Killed Her Husband; The Wild Geese
1981: Whose Life Is It Anyway? (Brian Clark); The
       Sea Wolves

RUTH ROSE

1933: King Kong*; Son of Kong; Blind Adventure
1935: Last Days of Pompeii (B. Ingster); She (D.
       Nichols)
1949: Mighty Joe Young

SI ROSE

1963: It Happened at the World's Fair (S. Jacobs)
1970: Puffnstuff (J. Murray)

STEPHEN BRUCE ROSE

1978: Coach (Nancy Larson)

TANIA ROSE

1963: It's a Mad, Mad, Mad, Mad World (W. Rose)

WILLIAM ROSE

1951: Lucky Nick Cain (G. Callahan); Operation X
(R. Thoeren)
1957: Decision Against Time; The Smallest Show on
Earth
1963: It's A Mad, Mad, Mad, Mad World (T. Rose)
1966: The Russians Are Coming, the Russians Are
Coming
1967: The Flim-Flam Man; Guess Who's Coming to
Dinner
1968: Pamela, Pamela, You Are... (R. Shull)
1969: The Secret of Santa Vittoria (B. Maddow)

JEB ROSEBROOK

1972: Junior Bonner
1979: The Black Hole (G. Day)

CHIPS ROSEN

1973: Ace Eli and Roger of the Skies

MARTIN J. ROSEN

1979: Burnout

MILT ROSEN

1965: Do Not Disturb (R. Breen)

PHIL ROSEN

1930: Extravagance*

SAM ROSEN

1970: The Phantom Tollbooth (Chuck Jones)

HENRY ROSENBAUM

1970: A Bullet for Pretty Boy; The Dunwich Horror*
1982: Hanky Panky (David Taylor)

C. A. ROSENBERG

1980: Maniac (J. Spinell)

JEANNE ROSENBERG

1979: The Black Stallion*

GEORGE ROSENER

1930: The Doorway to Hell; She Got What She Wanted
1933: Goodbye Love (H. Del Ruth)
1937: Jungle Menace (ser.)*; The Mysterious Pilot
       (ser.)*
1938: The Great Adventures of Wild Bill Hickok
       (ser.)*; The Secret of Treasure Island
       (ser.)*
1939: Fighting Mad (J. Rathmell)
1941: City of Missing Girls (O. Drake); I'll Sell
       My Life (E. Clifton)

ROBERT J. ROSENTHAL

1982: Zapped! (Bruce Rubin)

FRANCIS ROSENWALD

1947: In Self Defense (R. Wormser)
1948: The Dead Don't Dream; Perilous Waters (R.
       Wormser); Strike It Rich
1949: Red Stallion in the Rockies (T. Reed)

ARTHUR A. ROSS

1946: San Quentin*; Vacation in Reno (C. Roberts)
1948: Rusty Leads the Way
1949: Kazan
1950: Revenue Agent (W. Sackheim)

```
1952:   Okinawa (J. Brewer)
1953:   The Stand at Apache River
1954:   Creature from the Black Lagoon (H. Essex)
1956:   The Creature Walks Among Us
1959:   The Thirty-Foot Bride of Candy Rock (R.
        Barber)
1960:   The Three Worlds of Gulliver (J. Sher)
1965:   The Great Race
```

BOB ROSS

```
1966:   Three on a Couch (S.W. Taylor)
```

DICK ROSS

```
1957:   The Persuader (Curtis Kenyon)
```

FRANK ROSS

```
1943:   The More the Merrier*
```

GENE ROSS

```
1976:   Poor White Trash Part 2 (orig. Scum of the
        Earth; M. Davis)
```

JUDITH ROSS

```
1979:   Rich Kids
```

KENNETH ROSS

```
1977:   Black Sunday
```

RITA ROSS

```
1948:   Fighting Mustang
```

STANLEY RALPH ROSS

1969:   Follow Me

ROBERT ROSSEN (1908-1966) director, producer

1937:   Marked Woman (A. Finkel); They Won't Forget
        (A. Kandel)
1938:   Racket Busters (L. Bercovici)
1939:   Dust Be My Destiny; The Roaring Twenties*
1940:   A Child Is Born
1941:   Blues in the Night; Out of the Fog*; The Sea
        Wolf
1942:   Edge of Darkness
1945:   A Walk in the Sun
1946:   The Strange Love of Martha Ivers
1947:   Desert Fury; Johnny O'Clock
1948:   The Treasure of Sierra Madre (unc.; J.
        Huston)
1949:   All the King's Men
1955:   Mambo (It.)*
1956:   Alexander the Great
1959:   They Came to Cordura (I. Moffat)
1961:   The Hustler (S. Carroll)
1962:   Billy Budd (unc.)*
1964:   Lilith*

ARTHUR ROSSON (1889-1960) director

1930:   The Mounted Stranger

LEO ROSTEN (1908-   ) author

1944:   The Conspirators*
1947:   Lured
1948:   Sleep, My Love (S. McKelway); The Velvet
        Touch
1952:   Walk East on Beacon

NORMAN ROSTEN

1962:   A View from the Bridge

TED ROTER

1979:   One Page of Love

BOBBY ROTH

1981:   Independence Day
1982:   The Boss' Son

CY ROTH

1955:   Air Strike
1956:   Fire Maidens from Outer Space

ERIC ROTH

1974:   The Nickel Ride
1979:   The Concorde -- Airport '79

MURRAY ROTH

1928:   Lights of New York (F. Herbert)
1933:   Don't Bet on Love (H. Rogers)
1934:   Palooka*

ARTHUR ROTHAFEL

1932:   The Last Frontier (ser.)*

ROBERT C. ROTHAFEL

1935:   The Roaring West (ser.)*

JOSEPH ROTHMAN

1938:   Dynamite Delaney (C. Beahan)

STEPHANIE ROTHMAN

1967:   It's a Bikini World (C. Swartz)
1971:   The Velvet Vampire*
1974:   The Working Girls

1978: Starhops

RICHARD ROTHSTEIN

1982: Death Valley

RUSSELL ROUSE

1944: Nothing but Trouble (R. Golden); The Town
       Went Wild (C. Greene)
1949: D.O.A. (C. Greene)
1951: The Well (C. Greene)
1952: The Thief (C. Greene)
1953: Wicked Woman (C. Greene)
1955: New York Confidential (C. Greene)
1956: The Fastest Gun Alive (F. Gilroy)
1957: House of Numbers (D. Mankiewicz)
1959: Thunder in the Sun
1964: A House Is Not a Home (C. Greene)
1966: The Oscar*
1969: Color Me Dead

LOUISE ROUSSEAU

1944: Fuzzy Settles Down; Swing Hostess (G.
       Davenport)
1945: Riders of the Dawn; Fighting Bill Carson;
       Lonesome Trail
1946: Moon over Montana (A. Lamb); Lone Star
       Moonlight; Gunning for Vengeance (E. Repp);
       West of the Alamo (O. Drake)
1947: Over the Santa Fe Trail; Under Colorado
       Skies
1949: Prince of the Plains (A. DeMond)

JEAN ROUVEROL

1950: So Young, So Bad
1952: The First Time*
1963: A Face in the Rain (H. Butler)
1968: The Legend of Lylah Clare (H. Butler)

ARTHUR ROWE

1972:   The Magnificent Seven Ride

TOM ROWE

1971:   The Light at the End of the World
1981:   Tarzan, the Ape Man (G. Goddard)

ROY ROWLAND (1910-   ) director

1963:   The Girl Hunters*

CHARLES FRANCIS ROYAL

1935:   Between Men; The Courageous Avenger; The
        Firetrap
1936:   The New Adventures of Tarzan (ser.; E.
        Blum); Tundra (N. Parker)
1937:   Lightnin' Crandall; Guns in the Dark; Ridin'
        the Lone Trail; The Colorado Kid; Outlaws of
        the Orient (P. Franklin); Shadows of the
        Orient; Phantom of Santa Fe
1938:   The Old Barn Dance (B. McConville); The
        Colorado Trail; Rio Grande; Gangs of New
        York*; Tarzan and the Green Goddess
1939:   Texas Stampede; Taming of the West (R. L.
        Johnson); Outpost of the Mounties
1940:   The Man from Tumbleweeds
1941:   North from the Lone Star
1942:   A Tornado in the Saddle
1949:   Arctic Fury
1951:   All That I Have
1957:   God Is My Partner

MARC RUBEL

1980:   Xanadu*

AARON RUBEN

1969:   The Comic (C. Reiner)

ALBERT RUBEN

1972:   Journey Through Rosebud
1973:   The Seven Ups (A. Jacobs)
1974:   Visit to a Chief's Son

JOSEPH RUBEN

1975:   The Sister-in-Law
1976:   The Pom Pom Girls
1977:   Joyride (P. Rainer)

J. WALTER RUBEN (1889-1942) director, producer

1929:   The Marriage Playground (D. Anderson); Jazz
        Heaven (P. Forney); Dance Hall (J. Murfin)
1930:   Lovin' the Ladies; Shooting Straight; Check
        and Double Check; She's My Weakness
1931:   Bachelor Apartment; High Stakes; Royal Bed;
        White Shoulders; Young Donovan's Kid
1932:   Roadhouse Murder; Symphony of Six Million
        (B. Shubert); The Phantom of Crestwood*
1935:   Public Hero No. 1 (W. Root)

BENNY RUBIN (1899-   ) actor

1935:   Bright Lights*; The Girl Friend (G.
        Purcell); Traveling Saleslady*
1937:   High Flyers*; On Again off Again (N. Perrin)

BRUCE RUBIN

1970:   Dionysus in 69*
1982:   Zapped! (R. J. Rosenthal)

DANIEL N. RUBIN

1930:   The Texan (O. Garrett)
1931:   Dishonored

JACK RUBIN

1942:   Baby Face Morgan (E. Dein)
1948:   French Leave (J. Brewer)

MANN RUBIN

1959:   The Best of Everything (E. Sommer)
1964:   Walk a Tightrope
1965:   Brainstorm
1966:   An American Dream
1967:   Warning Shot
1980:   The First Deadly Sin

STANLEY RUBIN

1940:   Diamond Frontier (E. Hartmann); South to
        Karanga (E. Hartmann)
1941:   Burma Convoy (R. Chanslor); Mr. Dynamite;
        San Fancisco Docks (E. Hartmann); Six
        Lessons from Madame La Zonga*; Where Did You
        Get That Girl?*; Flying Cadets*
1942:   Bombay Clipper (R. Chanslor); Unseen Enemy
        (R. Chanslor)
1943:   Two Senoritas from Chicago (M. Tombragel)
1947:   Violence (L. Lantz)
1948:   Joe Palooka in Winner Take All
1952:   Macao (B. Schoenfeld)

HARRY RUBY

1931:   Broad-Minded (B. Kalmar)
1932:   The Kid from Spain*; Horse Feathers*
1933:   Duck Soup (B. Kalmar)
1934:   Hips, Hips, Hooray*; Kentucky Kernels (B.
        Kalmar)
1935:   Bright Lights*
1936:   Walking on Air*
1937:   Life of the Party*
1952:   Lovely to Look At (G. Wells)

ALBERT S. RUDDY

1978:   Matilda (T. Galfas)
1982:   Megaforce*

ROBERT RUDELSON

1969: Russ Meyer's Vixen
1970: Fools

ALAN RUDOLPH

1972: Premonition
1976: Buffalo Bill and the Indians (R. Altman)
1977: Welcome to L. A.
1979: Remember My Name
1982: Endangered Species (John Binder)

WESLEY RUGGLES (1889-1972) director, producer

1931: Are These Our Children? (H. Estabrook)

RUTH RUNNELL

1935: Racketeer Round-Up (alt. Gunners and Guns)

PETER RURIC

1934: Affairs of a Gentleman (C. Hume); The Black
       Cat
1942: Grand Central Murder
1944: Mademoiselle Fifi (J. Mischel)

PHILLIP RUSH (pseud. for IAN M. HUNTER & RING
         LARDNER, JR.)

RICHARD RUSH (1930-   ) director, producer

1960: Too Soon to Love (L. Gorog)
1963: Of Love and Desire (L. Gorog)

BUDDY RUSKIN

1971: Clay Pigeon (R. Buck)

HARRY RUSKIN

1934: Six of a Kind (W. DeLeon)
1935: The Glass Key*; Stolen Harmony*
1936: Great Guy*; Lady Be Careful*
1937: Bad Guy (E. Felton); Beg, Borrow or Steal*;
       23 1/2 Hours Leave*; Women Men Marry*
1938: The Chaser*; Love Is a Headache*; Paradise
       for Three (G. Oppenheimer); Young Dr.
       Kildare (W. Goldbeck)
1939: Calling Dr. Kildare (W. Goldbeck); Miracles
       for Sale*; Secret of Dr. Kildare (W.
       Goldbeck)
1940: Dr. Kildare Goes Home; Dr. Kildare's Crisis
       (W. Goldbeck); Dr. Kildare's Strange Case
       (W. Goldbeck); The Ghost Goes Home (R.
       Maibaum)
1941: Andy Hardy's Private Secretary (J. Murfin);
       Dr. Kildare's Victory (W. Goldbeck); Dr.
       Kildare's Wedding Day (W. Goldbeck); Keeping
       Company*; The Penalty (J. Higgins); The
       People vs. Dr. Kildare (W. Goldbeck)
1942: Calling Dr. Gillespie (W. Goldbeck); Dr.
       Gillespie's New Assistant*; This Time for
       Keeps; Tish
1943: Dr. Gillespie's Criminal Case*
1944: Rationing*; Three Men in White (M.
       Berkeley); Andy Hardy's Blonde Trouble; Lost
       in a Harem*; Between Two Women; Barbary
       Coast Gent*
1945: The Hidden Eye (G. Coxe)
1946: Love Laughs at Andy Hardy (W. Ludwig); The
       Postman Always Rings Twice (N. Busch)
1947: Dark Delusion (J. Andrews)
1948: Julia Misbehaves*; Tenth Avenue Angel (E.
       Griffin)
1950: The Happy Years; Watch the Birdie*
1955: Lady Godiva (O. Brodney)

GARY RUSOFF

1979: The Evictors*

LOU RUSOFF

1950: Girls in Prison
1956: The Oklahoma Woman; Runaway Daughters; The
       She-Creature; Shake, Rattle and Rock
1957: Cat Girl; Motorcycle Gang
1958: Suicide Battalion; Hot Rod Gang
1959: The Ghost of Dragstrip Hollow; Submarine
       Seahawk (O. Harris)
1963: Beach Party

A. J. RUSSELL

1968: A Lovely Way to Die
1969: Stiletto

BING RUSSELL

1966: An Eye for an Eye (S. Williams)

CHARLIE L. RUSSELL

1973: Five on the Black Hand Side

GORDON RUSSELL

1970: House of Dark Shadows (S. Hall)

RAY RUSSELL

1961: Mr. Sardonicus
1962: Premature Burial (C. Beaumont); Zotz!
1963: X -- the Man with the X-Ray Eyes (R. Dillon)
1964: The Horror of It All

ROBERT RUSSELL

1943: The More the Merrier*
1946: The Well-Groomed Bride (C. Binyon)
1951: The Lady Says No

VI RUSSELL

1956:   The Indestructable Man (S. Bradford)

JOHN A. RUSSO

1968:   Night of the Living Dead
1982:   Midnight

MADELEINE RUTHVEN

1934:   Dangerous Corner (A. Chapin); Shock
1936:   The Accusing Finger*; Straight from the
         Shoulder

BEN RYAN

1933:   My Weakness (D. Butler)
1934:   Million Dollar Ransom (W. Lipman); Palooka*
1935:   Chinatown Squad (D. Schary)
1936:   Laughing Irish Eyes*

CORNELIUS RYAN

1962:   The Longest Day

DON RYAN

1933:   Nagana (D. Van Every)
1936:   Smart Blonde (K. Gamet)
1937:   The Case of the Stuttering Bishop (K.
         Gamet); Fly-Away Baby (K. Gamet); Midnight
         Court (K. Gamet); Missing Witness (K. Gamet)
1938:   Broadway Musketeers (K. Gamet)
1939:   On Trial; You Can't Get Away with Murder*
1940:   Devil's Island (K. Gamet); Tear Gas Squad*
1941:   Death Valley Outlaws (J. Lait); West of
         Cimarron (A. DeMond); Citadel of Crime

ELAINE RYAN

1937:   Mr. Dodd Takes the Air (W. Haines)
1938:   Listen, Darling (A. Chapin)
1940:   Second Chorus*

1941:   Babes on Broadway (F. Finklehoffe); A Very
        Young Lady (L. Fodor)

FRANK RYAN (1907-1947) director

1941:   A Girl, a Guy and a Gob (B. Granet);
        Obliging Young Lady (B. Granet)
1942:   Call Out the Marines (W. Hamilton); The
        Mayor of 44th Street (L. Foster)
1943:   The Amazing Mrs. Holliday (J. Jacoby)
1944:   Can't Help Singing (L. Foster)

THOMAS C. RYAN

1966:   The Pad (and How to Use It) (B. Starr)
1967:   Hurry Sundown (H. Foote)
1968:   The Heart Is a Lonely Hunter

TIM RYAN

1943:   Melody Parade (C. Marion); Mystery of the
        13th Guest*; The Sultan's Daughter (G.
        Milton)
1944:   Hot Rhythm (C. Marion); Detective Kitty
        O'Day (V. Hammond); Leave It to the Irish
        (E. Davis); Crazy Knights
1945:   Adventures of Kitty O'Day*; Fashion Model
        (V. Hammond)
1946:   In Fast Company*; Live Wires (J. Mischel);
        Swing Parade of 1946; Spook Busters (E.
        Seward)
1947:   Bowery Buckaroos (E. Seward); News Hounds
        (E. Seward)
1948:   Angel's Alley*; Smuggler's Cove (E. Seward);
        Trouble Makers*
1952:   Feudin' Fools (B. Lawrence); Here Come the
        Marines*; Hold That Line (C. Marion); No
        Holds Barred*
1953:   Jalopy (J. Cruther)

FLORENCE RYERSON

1929:   Pointed Heels (J. Weaver)
1930:   Call of the West (C. Clements)

701

1931: Drums of Jeopardy; The Reckless Hour (R. Lord)
1933: The Crime of the Century (B. Marlow)
1934: Have a Heart*; This Side of Heaven*; A Wicked Woman (Z. Sears)
1935: Casino Murder Case (E. Woolf)
1936: Mad Holiday (E. Woolf); Moonlight Murder (E. Woolf); Tough Guy (E. Woolf)
1938: Everybody Sing (E. Woolf)
1939: The Ice Follies of 1939*; The Kid from Texas*; The Wizard of Oz*
1940: Henry Goes Arizona (M. Merlin)

MORRIE RYSKIND (1895-   ) playwright

1929: The Cocoanuts*
1930: Animal Crackers (P. Collings)
1931: Palmy Days*
1935: A Night at the Opera (G. Kaufman); Ceiling Zero (unc.; F. Wead); Anything Goes
1936: My Man Godfrey*
1937: Stage Door (A. Veiller)
1938: Room Service; There's Always a Woman (G. Lehman)
1939: Man About Town
1941: Penny Serenade
1943: Claudia
1945: Where Do We Go from Here?

S

ROBERT SABAROFF

1968:   The Split

BERYL SACHS

1943:   What a Man (W. Crowley); Spotlight Scandals
        (W. Crowley)
1944:   Follow the Leader (W. Crowley)
1950:   Radar Secret Service

WILLIAM SACHS

1976:   Secrets of the Gods (D. Davison)
1977:   There Is No Thirteen; The Incredible Melting
        Man
1979:   Van Nuys Boulevard
1980:   Galaxina

BARNARD L. SACKETT

1965:   All Men Are Apes (C. Mazin)

JERRY SACKHEIM

1941:   The Richest Man in Town (F. Foss)
1942:   The Night Before the Divorce
1945:   Road to Alcatraz (D. Babcock); The Fatal
        Witness
1946:   Saddle Pals (R. Williams); The Undercover
        Woman (S. Lowe); The Last Crooked Mile
1948:   Heart of Virginia; The Main Street Kid

```
1950:   Rookie Fireman
1951:   The Strange Door
1952:   The Black Castle
1960:   The Boy and the Pirates (L. Hayward); Young
        Jesse James (O. Hampton)
1962:   The Clown and the Kid (H. Spiro)
```

WILLIAM SACKHEIM

```
1946:   The Return of Rusty (L. Herman)
1948:   Smart Girls Don't Talk
1949:   One Last Fling (R. Flournoy); Homicide
1950:   Barricade; Revenue Agent (A. Ross)
1951:   Purple Heart Diary; A Yank in Korea
1952:   Paula (J. Poe)
1953:   Column South; Sky Commando*; Forbidden
1954:   Border River (Louis Stevens); Tanganyika (R.
        Simmons); The Human Jungle (D. Fuchs)
1982:   First Blood*
```

HOWARD SACKLER

```
1953:   Fear and Desire
1970:   The Great White Hope
1978:   Jaws 2 (C. Gottlieb); Gray Lady Down (J.
        Whittaker)
1979:   Saint Jack*
```

EZRA SACKS

```
1978:   FM
1980:   A Small Circle of Friends
```

DON SAFFRAN

```
1982:   Homework (M. Peterson)
```

HENRI SAFRAN

```
1982:   Norman Loves Rose
```

LEE SAGE

1932:   Without Honors (H. Fraser)

FRED SAIDY

1943:   I Dood It (S. Herzig)
1944:   Meet the People (S. Herzig)
1963:   The Sound of Laughter (doc.)
1968:   Finian's Rainbow (E. Harburg)

MALCOLM ST. CLAIR (1897-1952) director

1929:   Side Street

MICHAEL ST. CLAIR

1968:   Mission Mars

ROBERT ST. CLAIR

1936:   Doughnuts and Society*
1937:   Swing It, Professor (N. Barrows)
1938:   I'm from the City*
1948:   Women in the Night

ARTHUR ST. CLAIRE

1940:   Secrets of a Model (S. Lowe)
1941:   Boss of Bullion City (V. McLeod)
1942:   A Yank in Libya (S. Lowe); The Yanks Are
        Coming (S. Lowe); King of the Stallions (S.
        Lowe); Along the Sundown Trail; A Night for
        Crime (S. Lowe); Prison Girls; Gallant Lady
1943:   Man of Courage*; Miss V from Moscow (S.
        Lowe); Submarine Base; Tiger Fangs
1944:   Sweethearts of the U.S.A.*; Delinquent
        Daughters
1945:   Arson Squad; Shadow of Terror
1946:   The Mask of Diijon (G. Jay)
1947:   The Prairie; Philo Vance's Gamble (E.
        Conrad)
1949:   Rimfire*

GEORGE ST. GEORGE

1963:   Seven Seas to Calais*

CYRIL ST. JAMES

1976:   The Muthers

ADELA ROGERS ST. JOHN

1934:   Miss Fane's Baby Is Stolen

CHRISTOPHER ST. JOHN

1972:   Top of the Heap

THEODORE ST. JOHN

1952:   The Greatest Show on Earth*
1953:   Fort Algiers

ELLIS ST. JOSEPH

1942:   Joan of Paris (C. Bennett)
1943:   Flesh and Fantasy*
1944:   In Our Time (H. Koch)
1946:   Thieves' Holiday; A Scandal in Paris
1970:   The Christine Jorgensen Story (R.E. Kent)

SOL SAKS

1966:   Walk, Don't Run

RICHARD SALE (1911-   ) director

1946:   Rendezvous with Annie (M. Loos)
1947:   Calendar Girl*; Driftwood (M. Loos);
        Northwest Outpost (E. Meehan)
1948:   The Dude Goes West (M. Loos); Campus
        Honeymoon; The Inside Story (M. Loos); Lady

```
           at Midnight
1949:  Mother Is a Freshman; Mr. Belvedere Goes to
       College
1950:  Ticket to Tomahawk (M. Loos); I'll Get By
       (M. Loos); When Willie Comes Marching Home
       (M. Loos); Meet Me After the Show (M. Loos)
1953:  Let's Do It Again (M. Loos)
1954:  The French Line (M. Loos); Suddenly; Woman's
       World*
1955:  Gentlemen Marry Brunettes (M. Loos)
1956:  Around the World in 80 Days*
1957:  Abandon Ship! (Brit.)
1958:  Torpedo Run (W. Haines)
1977:  The White Buffalo
```

HARRISON E. SALISBURY

```
1972:  Russia (doc.)
```

KAE SALKOW

```
1946:  They Made Me a Killer*
1947:  Danger Street*
```

SIDNEY SALKOW (1909–   ) director

```
1936:  Rhythm on the Range*; Murder with Pictures
       (J. Moffitt)
1937:  Exclusive*
1938:  Come On, Leathernecks*; Prison Nurse (E.
       Felton)
1941:  The Lone Wolf Keeps a Date (E. Felton); The
       Lone Wolf Takes a Chance (E. Felton)
1950:  The Admiral Was a Lady (J. O'Dea)
1953:  Raiders of the Seven Seas (J. O'Dea)
1954:  Sitting Bull (J. DeWitt)
1955:  Robber's Roost*
```

SY SALKOWITZ

```
1964:  Ready for the People (E. M. Parsons)
1967:  Thunder Alley
1968:  The Biggest Bundle of Them All*
```

MICHAEL SALLE

1949:   Riders of the Pony Express

WALDO SALT (1914-   )

1938:   The Shopworn Angel
1941:   The Wild Man of Borneo (J. McLaid)
1943:   Tonight We Raid Calais
1944:   Mr. Winkle Goes to War*
1948:   Rachel and the Stranger
1950:   The Flame and the Arrow
1962:   Taras Bulba (K. Tunberg)
1964:   Flight from Ashiya (E. Arnold); Wild and
        Wonderful*
1969:   Midnight Cowboy
1971:   The Gang That Couldn't Shoot Straight
1973:   Serpico (N. Wexler)
1975:   The Day of the Locust
1978:   Coming Home (R.C. Jones)

JAMES SALTER

1969:   Downhill Racer; Three

LESSER SAMUELS

1940:   Bitter Sweet; The Earl of Chicago
1941:   Unholy Partners*
1945:   Tonight and Every Night (A. Finkel)
1950:   No Way Out (J. Mankiewicz)
1951:   The Big Carnival (orig. Ace in the Hole)*;
        Darling, How Could You (D. Smith)
1954:   The Long Night; The Silver Chalice
1956:   Great Day in the Morning

G. B. SAMUELSON

1931:   Should a Doctor Tell?

CARLTON SAND

1938: She Loved a Fireman (M. Grant); The Strange
      Case of Dr. Meade (G. Rigby)

B. W. SANDEFUR

1975: Poor Pretty Eddie
1979: Redneck County

DENNIS SANDERS

1958: The Naked and the Dead (T. Sanders)

TERRY SANDERS

1958: The Naked and the Dead (D. Sanders)

BARRY SANDLER

1972: The Loners (J. Lawrence)
1976: The Duchess and the Dirtwater Fox*; Gable
      and Lombard
1982: Making Love

ROBERT SANDLER

1973: Cannibal Girls

SALLY SANDLIN

1934: Love Time*

MARK SANDRICH (1900-1945) director

1932: Hold 'Em, Jail*
1933: Melody Cruise (B. Holmes)

LEE SANDS

1944: Sing a Jingle*

DONALD S. SANFORD

1969:   The Thousand Plane Raid
1976:   Midway
1979:   Ravagers

GERALD SANFORD

1975:   Aaron Loves Angela

HARRY SANFORD

1966:   Apache Uprising (M. Lamb)

JOHN SANFORD

1941:   Honky Tonk (M. Roberts)

CLIFFORD SANFORTH

1939:   The Adventures of the Masked Phantom (J.
        O'Donnell)

FILIPPO SANJUST

1963:   Seven Seas to Calais*

ANTONIO SANTEAN

1964:   The Glass Cage (ret. Den of Doom; J. Hoyt)
1974:   Dirty Mary Crazy Larry (L. Chapman)

ANTONIO SANTILLAN

1977:   Viva Knievel! (N. Katkov)

JOSEPH SANTLEY (1889-1971) director

1934:   I Like It That Way (C. Sprague)

1935: Harmony Lane (E. Meehan); Million Dollar
      Baby (J. Krafft)

RICHARD C. SARAFIAN (1925-   ) director

1958: The Notorious Mr. Monks; The Cool and the
      Crazy; The Man Who Died Twice
1962: Terror at Black Falls
1965: Andy
1976: The Next Man*

LANE SARASOHN

1974: The Groove Tube (K. Shapiro)

BARNEY A. SARECKY

1931: Honeymoon Lane (J. Levine); The Runaround
      (A. Jackson)
1932: The Devil Horse (ser.)*; The Hurricane
      Express (ser.)*
1933: Fighting with Kit Carson (ser.)*; Mystery
      Squadron (ser.)*; The Three Musketeers
      (ser.)*; The Whispering Shadow (ser.)*; Riot
      Squad (J. Natteford)
1934: Burn 'Em Up Barnes (ser.)*; The Lost Jungle
      (ser.)*
1935: Darkest Africa (ser.)*; Adventures of Rex
      and Rinty (ser.; J. Rathmell); Fighting
      Marines (ser.; S. Lowe)
1939: Zorro's Fighting Legion (ser.)*
1940: Adventures of Red Ryder (ser.)*; King of the
      Royal Mounted (ser.)*; Drums of Fu Manchu
      (ser.)*
1942: Yukon Patrol*
1943: The Ape Man (Karl Brown)
1945: The Phantom Rider (ser.)*; The Purple
      Monster Strikes (ser.)*
1947: Buffalo Bill Rides Again (F. Gilbert)
1949: King of the Jungleland (ser.)*

LOU SARECKY

1942: North of the Klondike*

711

ALVIN SARGENT

1966: Gambit
1969: The Stalking Moon; The Sterile Cuckoo
1970: I Walk the Line
1972: The Effect of Gamma Rays on Man-in-the-Moon Marigolds
1973: Paper Moon; Love and Pain and the Whole Damn Thing
1977: Bobby Deerfield; Julia
1978: Straight Time*
1979: The Electric Horseman (R. Garland)
1980: Ordinary People

HERBERT SARGENT

1968: Bye Bye Braverman

MICHAEL SARNE (1939-   ) director, actor Brit.

(American films only)
1970: Myra Breckinridge (D. Giler)

JOE SARNO

1968: Moonlight Wives
1976: Misty
1981: The Kirlian Witness

HARRY SAUBER

1932: Beauty Parlor
1933: Forgotten
1934: Happiness Ahead (B. Marlow); Let's Be Ritzy (E. Snell); 20 Million Sweethearts (W. Duff)
1935: Dinky; Maybe It's Love*
1936: Her Master's Voice (D. Schary)
1937: Manhattan Merry-Go-Round; Racketeers in Exile (R. Shannon); Youth on Parole
1938: Outside of Paradise
1940: Five Little Peppers at Home; Five Little Peppers in Trouble; Out West with the

```
          Peppers
1941:   Sing for Your Supper
1942:   Tramp, Tramp, Tramp (N. Dandy); Laugh Your
          Blues Away
1943:   Let's Have Fun; What's Buzzin', Cousin?
1945:   How Do You Do? (J. Carole)
1949:   Ladies of the Chorus (J. Carole)
```

OSCAR SAUL

```
1944:   Once Upon a Time (L. Meltzer)
1949:   Woman in Hiding
1951:   Thunder on the Hill (A. Solt)
1952:   Affair in Trinidad (J. Gunn)
1957:   The Joker Is Wild; The Helen Morgan Story*
1961:   The Second Time Around (C. Hansen)
1965:   Major Dundee*
1966:   The Silencers
1972:   Man and Boy (H. Essex)
1973:   Deaf Smith and Johnny Ears (H. Essex)
```

JOHN MONK SAUNDERS (1897-1940) author

```
1931:   The Last Flight; The Finger Points*
1933:   Ace of Aces (H. Hanemann)
```

CHARLES E. SAVAGE

```
1968:   Panic in the City (E. Davis)
1969:   It Takes All Kinds (E. Davis)
```

LES SAVAGE, JR.

```
1956:   The White Squaw
1958:   Return to Warbow
```

PAUL SAVAGE

```
1971:   The Wild Country (C. Clements)
1975:   Mackintosh and T. J.
```

JOE SAWYER

1950:   Operation Haylift (D. Reisner)

TONY SAWYER

1978:   Die Sister, Die!

MARY ANN SAXON

1972:   Squares

CHARLES SAXTON

1933:   High Gear*

JOHN SAXTON

1982:   Class of 1984*; Title Shot

JOHN SAYLES

1978:   Piranha
1979:   The Lady in Red
1980:   The Return of the Secaucus Seven; Battle
        Beyond the Stars; Alligator
1981:   The Howling (T. Winkless)
1982:   The Challenge (R. Maxwell)

GEORGE SAYRE (also see GEORGE MILTON)

1935:   Code of the Mounted
1936:   Song of the Trail*
1939:   Torture Ship
1943:   Wings over the Pacific
1945:   Black Market Babies
1948:   Stage Struck (A. Johnston)
1950:   A Modern Marriage (S. Roeca)
1952:   Untamed Women

JOEL SAYRE

```
1934:   Come On, Marines (B. Morgan)
1935:   Annie Oakley (J. Twist); His Family Tree (J.
        Twist); The Pay-Off (G. Brickner)
1936:   The Road to Glory (W. Faulkner)
1937:   Meet the Missus*; The Toast of New York*
1939:   Gunga Din*
```

ALMA SIOUX SCARBERRY

```
1934:   Hired Wife
```

GEORGE SCARBOROUGH

```
1928:   Lady of the Pavements
```

FRAN SCHACHT

```
1978:   Laserblast (F. Perilli)
1979:   Fairy Tales (F. Perilli)
```

ARMAND SCHAEFER

```
1934:   Mystery Mountain (ser.)*; Burn 'Em Up Barnes
        (ser.)*; The Lost Jungle (ser.)*
1935:   The Phantom Empire (ser.)*
```

ROBERT SCHAEFER

```
1958:   The Lone Ranger and the Lost City of Gold
        (E. Freiwald)
```

DON SCHAIN

```
1972:   A Place Called Today
1973:   Girls Are for Loving
```

DORE SCHARY (1905-1980) director, producer,
        playwright

```
1933:   He Couldn't Take It; Fog (E. Hill)
1934:   Fury of the Jungle (E. Hill); The Most
```

```
              Precious Thing (E. Hill); Murder in the
              Clouds (R. Chanslor); Young and Beautiful*
1935:         Chinatown Squad (B. Ryan); Silk Hat Kid*;
              Your Uncle Dudley (J. Hoffman);
              Mississippi*; The Raven*
1936:         Her Master's Voice (H. Sauber); Mind Your
              Own Business; Timothy's Quest*
1937:         The Big City (H. Butler); Girl from Scotland
              Yard (D. Anderson); Outcast (D. Malloy)
1938:         Boys Town (J. Meehan)
1940:         Young Tom Edison*
1941:         Married Bachelor
1952:         It's a Big Country*
1956:         The Battle of Gettysburg (doc.)
1958:         Lonelyhearts
1960:         Sunrise at Campobello
1963:         Act One
```

RICHARD SCHAYER

```
1928:         The Actress (A. Lewin); Circus Rookies
1929:         The Flying Fleet (F. Wead); Spite Marriage;
              Wild Orchids*
1930:         Free and Easy (P. Dickey); Children of
              Pleasure; Doughboys; Men of the North
1931:         Dance, Fools, Dance; Just a Gigolo*; Parlor,
              Bedroom and Bath; Private Lives*; Trader
              Horn*
1932:         Destry Rides Again (I. Bernstein); Impatient
              Maiden (W. Dunn); Night World
1933:         Cocktail Hour (G. Purcell)
1934:         Meanest Gal in Town*
1935:         The Winning Ticket*
1936:         Dangerous Waters*; The Devil Is a Sissy (J.
              Mahin)
1948:         The Black Arrow*
1950:         Kim*; Davy Crockett, Indian Scout; The
              Iroquois Trail
1951:         The Texas Rangers; Lorna Doone*
1952:         Cripple Creek; Indian Uprising (K. Gamet)
1953:         The Bandits of Corsica; The Steel Lady; Gun
              Belt
1954:         The Lone Gun (D. Martin)
1955:         Top Gun (S. Fisher)
1956:         Gun Brothers (G. Adams)
1961:         Five Guns to Tombstone (J. DeWitt); Gun
              Fight (G. Adams)
```

1963:   Sword of Lancelot (Brit.; J. Pascal)

MICHAEL SCHEFF

1977:   Airport '77 (D. Spector)

GEORGE SCHENCK

1967:   Kill a Dragon (W. Marks)
1969:   More Dead Than Alive
1970:   Barquero (W. Marks)
1972:   Superbeast
1976:   Futureworld (M. Simon)

HARRY SCHENCK

1934:   Beyond Bengal (doc.)

TOM SCHEUER

1974:   Gosh

FRED SCHILLER

1939:   The Flying Deuces*
1943:   The Heat's On*; Pistol Packin' Mamma (E.
        Dein)

WILTON SCHILLER

1964:   The New Interns

MURRAY SCHISGAL

1967:   The Tiger Makes Out
1982:   Tootsie (L. Gelbart)

SIG SCHLAGER

1932:   The Girl from Calgary (L. D'Usseau)

GEORGE SCHLATTER

1976:   Norman...Is That You?

ROBERT SCHLITT

1971:   Been Down So Long It Looks Like Up to Me
1973:   The Pyx

MARLENE SCHMIDT

1975:   The Specialist*

WALTER ROEBER SCHMIDT

1960:   Hell to Eternity (T. Sherdeman)

WAYNE SCHMIDT

1980:   The Day Time Ended*

DAVID SCHMOELLER

1979:   Tourist Trap (J. Larry Carroll)
1980:   The Day Time Ended*
1982:   The Seduction

SYLVIA SCHNEBLE

1974:   Golden Needles (S. Pogostin)

CHARLES SCHNEE (also JOHN DENNIS) (1916-1963)
        producer

1946:   From This Day Forward (H. Butler)
1947:   I Walk Alone
1948:   Red River (B. Chase); The Twisted Road
1949:   Easy Living; Scene of the Crime; They Live
        by Night

1950: The Furies; The Next Voice You Hear; Paid in
       Full (R. Blees); Right Cross
1951: Bannerline; Westward the Women
1952: The Bad and the Beautiful; When in Rome (D.
       Kingsley)
1960: Butterfield 8 (J. Hayes); The Crowded Sky
1961: By Love Possessed*
1962: Two Weeks in Another Town

THELMA SCHNEE

1954: The Detective (R. Hames)
1958: The Colossus of New York

BARRY SCHNEIDER

1977: Ruby (G. Edwards)
1978: Harper Valley P.T.A. (G. Edwards)
1979: Roller Boogie
1981: Take This Job and Shove It

HERMAN & NINA SCHNEIDER

1955: The Naked Dawn

PAUL SCHNEIDER

1966: That Tennessee Beat

STANLEY SCHNEIDER

1966: Hot Rod Hullabaloo

S. L. SCHNEIDERMAN

1966: The Last Chapter (doc.)

ARRUMIE SCHNITZER

1979: Summer Camp

GERALD SCHNITZER

1942: Bowery at Midnight
1943: Kid Dynamite; A Scream in the Dark (A. Coldeway)
1948: Angel's Alley*; Trouble Makers*
1949: Angels in Disguise*; Fighting Fools*; Hold That Baby (C. Marion)
1955: Naked Sea (doc.)

ROBERT ALLEN SCHNITZER

1975: No Place to Hide
1976: The Premonition*

BERNARD C. SCHOENFELD

1944: Phantom Lady
1946: The Dark Corner (J. Dratler)
1950: Caged (V. Kellogg)
1952: Macao (S. Rubin)
1954: Down Three Dark Streets (L. Gordon)
1956: There's Always Tomorrow
1958: The Space Children
1959: Pier 5, Havana
1962: The Magic Sword; 13 West Street (R. Presnell)

PAUL SCHOFIELD

1929: Scandal
1930: Framed
1933: Jimmy and Sally (M. Roberts); Sensation Hunters (A. DeMond)
1935: Sunset Range
1937: Wells Fargo*
1939: Mystery Plane (J. West)

JACK SCHOLL

1945: Law of the Badlands

LEONARD SCHRADER

1978:   Blue Collar (P. Schrader)
1979:   Old Boyfriends (P. Schrader)

PAUL SCHRADER (1946-   ) director

1975:   The Yakuza (R. Towne)
1976:   Taxi Driver; Obsession
1977:   Rolling Thunder (H. Gold)
1978:   Blue Collar (L. Schrader)
1979:   Hardcore; Old Boyfriends (L. Schrader)
1980:   American Gigolo; Raging Bull (M. Martin)

JOSEPH SCHRANK

1938:   He Couldn't Say No*; A Slight Case of Murder
        (E. Baldwin); Swing Your Lady (M. Leo)
1942:   Song of the Islands*
1943:   Cabin in the Sky
1945:   The Clock (R. Nathan)

EDWARD SCHREIBER

1961:   Mad Dog Coll

OTTO SCHREIBER

1950:   It's a Small World (W. Castle)

MYRL A. SCHREIBMAN

1979:   The Clonus Horror (R. Fiveson)

RAYMOND L. SCHROCK

1929:   The Duke Steps Out (D. Van Every)
1931:   Bad Sister (T. Reed); Shipmates*
1933:   Hell Below*
1935:   Hard Rock Harrigan (D. Jarrett)
1936:   Happy Go Lucky (O. Cooper); Sitting on the
        Moon*

1939:   Kid Nightingale (C. Belden); Secret Service
        of the Air; Smashing the Money Ring (A.
        Coldeway)
1940:   Murder in the Air
1941:   Bullets for O'Hara
1942:   Wild Bill Hickok Rides*; Escape from Crime;
        Murder in the Big House; Secret Enemies
1943:   Isle of Forgotten Sins; Truck Busters (R.
        Kent)
1944:   Men on Her Mind; The Contender*; The Last
        Ride; The Great Mike
1945:   Club Havana; Crime, Inc.; The Missing
        Corpse; White Pongo
1946:   Danny Boy; Larceny in Her Heart; Secret of
        the Whistler; Shadows over Chinatown
1947:   The Millerson Case; The Thirteenth Hour (E.
        Bock)
1949:   Daughter of the West (I. Franklyn)

DORIS SCHROEDER

1934:   Crimson Romance (M. Krims)
1935:   Hop-a-Long Cassidy; The Eagle's Brood (H.
        Jacobs); Bar 20 Rides Again (G. Geraghty)
1936:   Call of the Prairie (V. Smith); Three on the
        Trail (V. Smith); Heart of the West
1940:   Legion of the Lawless; Bullet Code; Prairie
        Law (A. Jones); Oklahoma Renegades (E.
        Snell); Texas Terrors (A. Coldeway)
1941:   The Phantom Cowboy; Two-Gun Sheriff; Kansas
        Cyclone (O. Drake); Gangs of Sonora (A.
        DeMond); A Missouri Outlaw (J. Lait)
1942:   Arizona Terrors (T. Cavan); Jesse James,
        Jr.*; Westward Ho (M. Grant); Pirates of the
        Prairie (J. Cheney)
1945:   Bandits of the Badlands
1946:   Fool's Gold; Days of Buffalo Bill (W.
        Lively); Death Valley
1947:   Dangerous Venture
1948:   Sinister Journey; False Paradise (H.
        Jacobs); Strange Gamble*
1949:   The Gay Amigo

BERNARD SCHUBERT

1931:   Public Defender; Secret Service (G. Lloyd)

```
1932:   Symphony of Six Million (J. Ruben)
1933:   No Other Woman (W. Tuchock)
1934:   The Band Plays On*; Peck's Bad Boy (M.
        Roberts); Straight Is the Way
1935:   Kind Lady; Mark of the Vampire (G. Endore)
1936:   Hearts in Bondage (O. Cooper)
1937:   The Barrier*; Make a Wish*
1938:   Breaking the Ice*
1939:   Fisherman's Wharf*
1941:   Scattergood Pulls the Strings (C. Cabanne)
1942:   Silver Queen (C. Kramer)
1944:   Jungle Woman; The Mummy's Curse
1945:   The Frozen Ghost (L. Ward)
```

LYNN SCHUBERT

```
1976   Goodbye, Norma Jean (L. Buchanan)
1978:  Hughes and Harlow: Angels in Hell (L.
       Buchanan)
```

BUDD SCHULBERG (1914–   ) novelist

```
1937:   A Star Is Born (unc.)*
1938:   Little Orphan Annie (S. Ornitz)
1939:   Winter Carnival*
1943:   City Without Men (W. River)
1954:   On the Waterfront
1957:   A Face in the Crowd
1958:   Wind Across the Everglades
```

ARNOLD SCHULMAN

```
1957:   Wild Is the Wind
1959:   A Hole in the Head
1960:   Cimarron
1963:   Love with the Proper Stranger
1968:   The Night They Raided Minsky's*
1969:   Goodbye, Columbus
1972:   To Find a Man
1975:   Funny Lady (J. Allen)
1976:   Won Ton Ton, the Dog Who Saved Hollywood (Cy
        Howard)
1979:   Players
```

CHARLES M. SCHULZ

1969:   A Boy Named Charlie Brown (anim.)
1972:   Snoopy, Come Home (anim.)
1977:   Race for Your Life, Charlie Brown (anim.)
1980:   Bon Voyage, Charlie Brown (anim.)

FRANZ SCHULZ

1935:   The Lottery Lover (B. Wilder); The Night Is
        Young (E. Woolf); Paris in Spring*
1936:   April Romance*
1940:   Adventure in Diamonds (L. Lee)

JOEL SCHUMACHER

1976:   Car Wash; Sparkle
1978:   The Wiz

LAURENCE SCHWAB (-1951)

1933:   Take a Chance*

AL SCHWARTZ

1982:   Lookin' to Get Out (J. Voight)

DAVID R. SCHWARTZ

1963:   Island of Desire
1964:   Robin and the Seven Hoods; Sex and the
        Single Girl (J. Heller)
1965:   That Funny Feeling
1967:   The Bobo

IRWIN SCHWARTZ

1958:   Stakeout on Dope Street*

S. L. SCHWEITZER

1969:   Change of Habit*

RICHARD SCHWEIZER

1948:   The Search (Germ./Switz.; D. Wechsler)
1950:   Four Days' Leave (C. Siodmak)
1951:   Four in a Jeep (Aust.)
1954:   Heidi and Peter

DON SCIOLI

1975:   Mysteries from Beyond the Earth (doc.)*

KATHRYN SCOLA

1931:   The Lady Who Dared (F. Halsey); Wicked (K.
        Nicholson)
1933:   Baby Face (G. Markey); Female (G. Markey);
        Lady of the Night (G. Markey); Lilly Turner
        (G. Markey); Luxury Liner (G. Markey);
        Midnight Mary (G. Markey)
1934:   Fashions of 1934*; A Lost Lady (G. Markey);
        The Merry Frinks (G. Markey); A Modern Hero
        (G. Markey)
1935:   The Glass Key*; One Hour Late*
1936:   It Had to Happen (H. E. Smith)
1937:   Second Honeymoon (D. Ware); Wife, Doctor and
        Nurse*
1938:   Alexander's Ragtime Band*; Always Goodbye
        (E. Skouras); The Baroness and the Butler*
1939:   Hotel for Women (D. Ware)
1940:   The House Across the Bay
1941:   Lady from Cheyenne (W. Duff)
1943:   The Constant Nymph; Happy Land (J.
        Josephson)
1945:   Colonel Effinham's Raid
1949:   Night unto Night

MARTIN SCORSESE (1942-   ) director

1968:   Who's That Knocking at My Door?
1973:   Mean Streets (M. Martin)

725

ADRIAN SCOTT (1912-1973) producer

1941:   Keeping Company*; The Parson of Panamint (H.
        Shumate); We Go Fast*
1943:   Mr. Lucky (M. Holmes)

ALLAN SCOTT

1934:   By Your Leave; Let's Try Again (W. Miner)
1935:   In Person; Roberta*; Top Hat (D. Taylor);
        Village Tale
1936:   Swing Time (H. Lindsay)
1937:   Quality Street (M. Offner); Shall We Dance*;
        Wise Girl
1938:   Carefree*; Joy of Living*
1939:   Fifth Avenue Girl
1940:   Lucky Partners (J. Van Druten); The Primrose
        Path (G. LaCava)
1941:   Remember the Day*; Skylark
1943:   So Proudly We Hail!
1944:   I Love a Soldier; Here Come the Waves*
1950:   Let's Dance
1951:   The Guy Who Came Back
1952:   The Four Poster; Wait 'Til the Sun Shines,
        Nellie
1953:   The Five Thousand Fingers of Dr. T (Dr.
        Seuss)
1957:   Top Secret Affair (R. Kibbee)
1959:   Imitation of Life (E. Griffin)
1974:   The Girl from Petrovka (C. Bryant)
1980:   The Awakening

BILL SCOTT

1967:   The Crazy World of Laurel and Hardy (doc.)

DE VALLON SCOTT

1945:   A Letter for Evie (A. Friedman)
1950:   Hunt the Man Down
1952:   The Pace That Thrills
1953:   Conquest of Cochise (A. Lewis); Slaves of
        Babylon; Prisoners of the Casbah
1954:   The Saracen Blade (G. Yates); They Rode West
        (F. Nugent); The Black Dakotas; The Iron

Glove (J. Lasky)
1956: The Maverick Queen (K. Gamet)
1957: Hell Ship Mutiny (W. Root)

EWING SCOTT

1937: Park Avenue Logger (D. Jarrett); Hollywood
       Cowboy (D. Jarrett)
1948: Harpoon (P. Smith)

PETER SCOTT

1974: Vanishing Wilderness (doc.; Lee Chaney)

EDWARD F. SEABROOK

1941: Tanks a Million*; Miss Polly (E. Conrad)
1942: About Face (E. Conrad); Fall In (E. Conrad);
       Yanks Ahoy (E. Conrad); Hay Foot (E. Conrad)
1944: Abroad with Two Yanks*
1948: Here Comes Trouble (G. C. Brown)
1951: As You Were

JACK SEAMAN

1953: Project Moonbase (R. Heinlein)

TED SEARS

1941: The Reluctant Dragon (anim.)*
1953: Peter Pan (anim.)*; The Living Desert
       (doc.)*
1954: The African Lion (doc.)*
1959: Sleeping Beauty*

ZELDA SEARS

1931: Daybreak (R. Cummings)
1932: New Morals for Old (W. Tuchock); Prosperity*
1933: Beauty for Sale (E. Greene); Day of
       Reckoning (E. Greene); Tugboat Annie (E.
       Greene)

1934:   Operator 13*; This Side of Heaven*; A Wicked
        Woman (F. Ryerson); You Can't Buy Everything
        (E. Greene)

EULA SEATON

1982:   The End of August*

GEORGE SEATON (1911-1979) director, producer

1937:   A Day at the Races*
1940:   The Doctor Takes a Wife (K. Englund)
1941:   Charley's Aunt; That Night in Rio*; This
        Thing Called Love*
1942:   The Magnificent Dope
1943:   Coney Island; The Meanest Man in the World
        (A. House); The Song of Bernadette
1944:   The Eve of St. Mark
1945:   Diamond Horseshoe; Junior Miss
1947:   Miracle on 34th Streeet; The Shocking Miss
        Pilgrim
1948:   Apartment for Peggy; Chicken Every Sunday
        (V. Davies)
1950:   The Big Lift; For Heaven's Sake
1952:   Anything Can Happen (G. Oppenheimer)
1953:   Little Boy Lost
1955:   The Country Girl
1956:   The Proud and the Profane
1962:   The Counterfeit Traitor
1964:   36 Hours
1968:   What's So Bad About Feeling Good? (R.
        Pirosh)
1970:   Airport

BEVERLY & FRED SEBASTIAN

1973:   The Hitchhikers
1974:   Gator Bait
1976:   Flash and Firecat
1979:   Delta Fox; On the Air with Captain Midnight

JACK SEDDON

1966:   The Blue Max*

HAL SEEGER

1947: Killer Diller

SUSAN SEIDELMAN

1982: Smithereens (R. Nystwaner)

MANUEL SEFF

1933: The College Coach (N. Busch); Footlight
       Parade (J. Seymour); Girl in 419*; Terror
       Aboard (H. Thew)
1934: Easy to Love (C. Erickson); Housewife (L.
       Hayward); Kansas City Princess (C.
       Bartlett); Side Streets
1935: Gold Diggers of 1935 (P. Milne); A Night at
       the Ritz*; Red Salute (H. Pearson);
       Traveling Saleslady*
1936: Three Godfathers (E. Paramore); Love on the
       Run*; Trouble for Two (E. Paramore)
1937: Espionage*; Let's Make a Million (R. Yost);
       Woman Chases Man*
1938: Breaking the Ice*
1944: Sailor's Holiday; Jam Session; Kansas City
       Kitty

ERICH SEGAL

1968: The Yellow Submarine (anim.)*
1970: R.P.M.; Love Story; The Games
1971: Jennifer on My Mind
1978: Oliver's Story (J. Korty)
1980: A Change of Seasons*

FRED SEGAL

1972: A Separate Peace
1980: A Change of Seasons*

JERRY SEGAL

```
1977:    One on One (R. Benson)
1980:    Die Laughing*


MARVIN SEGAL

1959:    Tokyo After Dark (N. Herman)


STUART A. SEGAL

1978:    Speed Trap (W. Spear)


HARRY SEGALL (1897-1975)

1936:    Don't Turn 'Em Loose
1937:    Fight for Your Lady*; The Outcasts of Poker
         Flat*; There Goes My Girl
1938:    Everybody's Doing It*; Blonde Cheat*
1939:    Blind Alibi*; Coast Guard*
1940:    The Lone Wolf Strikes (A. Duffy)
1941:    She Knew All the Answers*
1942:    Two Yanks in Trinidad*; The Powers Girl (E.
         Moran)
1946:    Angel on My Shoulder (R. Kibbee)


CONRAD SEILER

1941:    Redhead (D. Reid)


GEORGE B. SEITZ (1888-1944) director

1932:    Behind Stone Walls; Love in High Gear; Sally
         of the Subway; Passport to Paradise
1934:    Fugitive Lovers*


CHARLES E. SELLER

1976:    In Search of Noah's Ark (doc.; J. Conway)


THOMAS SELLER
```

```
1940:   Andy Hardy Meets Debutante (A. Whitmore)
1943:   The Man from Down Under (W. Root)
1948:   The Black Arrow*
```

ARTHUR SELLERS

```
1981:   Modern Problems*
```

WILLIAM SELLERS

```
1950:   The Gunfighter (W. Bowers)
```

DAVID SELTZER

```
1971:   The Hellstrom Chronicle (doc.)
1972:   One Is a Lonely Number
1975:   The Other Side of the Mountain
1976:   The Omen
1977:   King, Queen, Knave (David Shaw)
1979:   Prophecy
1982:   Six Weeks
```

TERREL SELTZER

```
1982:   Chan Is Missing*
```

EDGAR SELWYN (1875-1944) director, producer

```
1929:   The Girl in the Show
```

DAVID O. SELZNICK (1902-1965) producer

```
1944:   Since You Went Away
1946:   Duel in the Sun
1948:   The Paradine Case*
```

LORENZO SEMPLE, JR.

```
1966:   Batman
1967:   Fathom
1968:   Pretty Poison
```

1969: Daddy's Gone A-Hunting (L. Cohen)
1971: The Sporting Club; The Marriage of a Young
       Stockbroker
1973: Papillon (D. Trumbo)
1974: The Super Cops; The Parallax View (D. Giler)
1975: The Drowning Pool*; Three Days of the Condor
       (D. Rayfiel)
1976: King Kong
1979: Hurricane
1980: Flash Gordon

ROD SERLING (1924-1975)
1956: Patterns
1958: Saddle the Wind
1962: Requiem for a Heavyweight
1963: The Yellow Canary
1964: Seven Days in May
1966: Assault on a Queen
1968: Planet of the Apes (M. Wilson)
1972: The Man

EDMOND SEWARD

1933: Walls of Gold (W. Sullivan)
1937: The Duke Comes Back (A. Buffington); Wild
       Innocence
1939: Gulliver's Travels (anim.)*
1946: Bowery Bombshell; In Fast Company*; Spook
       Busters (T. Ryan)
1947: Bowery Buckaroos (T. Ryan); News Hounds (T.
       Ryan)
1948: Angel's Alley*; Jinx Money; Smuggler's Cove
       (T. Ryan); Trouble Makers*
1949: Fighting Fools*

JAMES SEYMOUR

1932: Carnival Boat; Lawyer Man (R. James)
1933: Central Airport (R. James); Footlight Parade
       (M. Seff); Forty-Second Street (R. James);
       Gold Diggers of 1933 (E. Gelsey)
1935: King of Burlesque*
1948: Meet Me at Dawn (L. Storm); Springtime
       (Brit.; Montgomery Tully)

DAVID SHABER

1979:   Last Embrace; The Warriors (W. Hill)
1980:   Those Lips, Those Eyes
1981:   Nighthawks; Rollover

MONROE SHAFF

1937:   Hollywood Roundup (J. Hoffman)
1938:   The Overland Express; The Stranger from
        Arizona; Law of the Texan (A. Hoerl);
        California Frontier (A. Hoerl); She's Got
        Everything (J. Hoffman)

LOUIS SHAFFNER

1976:   The Commitment*

JOSEF SHAFTEL

1956:   The Naked Hills
1958:   The Biggest Bundle of Them All*

STEVE SHAGAN

1973:   Save the Tiger
1975:   Hustle
1976:   Voyage of the Damned (D. Butler)
1979:   Nightwing*
1980:   The Formula

KRISHNA SHAH

1972:   Rivals

MORDAUNT SHAIRP

1935:   The Dark Angel (L. Hellman)
1936:   The White Angel (M. Jacoby)
1937:   The Barrier*

BERNARD SHAKEY

1982:   Human Highway*

VIRGINIA SHALER

1949:   Lost Boundaries
1951:   The Whistle at Eaton Falls (L. Esler)
1960:   Man on a String (J. Kafka)

MAXWELL SHANE (1905-   ) director

1937:   You Can't Beat Love (D. Silverstein)
1938:   Adventure in Sahara; Tip-Off Girls*
1939:   Federal Man-Hunt; S.O.S. Tidal Wave (G.
        Kahn)
1940:   Comin 'Round the Mountain*; Golden Gloves
        (L. Foster); The Leather Pushers*; The
        Mummy's Hand (G. Jay)
1941:   A Dangerous Game*; Flying Blind (R. Murphy);
        Forced Landing (E. Churchill); No Hands on
        the Clock; Power Dive (E. Churchill); Too
        Many Blondes (L. S. Kaye)
1942:   I Live on Danger*; Top Sergeant (G. Jay);
        Torpedo Boat; Wildcat (R. Murphy); Wrecking
        Crew (R. Murphy)
1943:   Aerial Gunner; Alaska Highway; Cowboy in
        Manhattan (W. Wilson); High Explosive (H.
        Green); Minesweeper (E. Lowe); Submarine
        Alert; Tornado
1944:   Dark Mountain; One Body Too Many (W.
        Miller); Timber Queen (E. Lowe); The Navy
        Way; Gambler's Choice (I. Reis); Double
        Exposure (W. Miller)
1945:   Follow That Woman (W. Miller); High Powered
        (G. Milton); Scared Stiff (G. Homes); Tokyo
        Rose (D. Mainwaring)
1946:   People Are Funny (D. Lang)
1947:   Adventure Island; Big Town (D. Mainwaring);
        Danger Street*; Fear in the Night; Seven
        Were Saved
1948:   Mr. Reckless (G. Milton); Shaggy
1949:   City Across the River (D. Cooper)
1953:   The Glass Wall (I. Tors)
1955:   Hell's Island; The Naked Street (L. Katcher)

1956:   Nightmare

JOHN SHANER

1970:   Halls of Anger (A. Ramrus)
1977:   The Island of Dr. Moreau (A. Ramrus)
1978:   Goin' South*
1980:   The Last Married Couple in America

RON SHANIN

1961:   All Hands on Deck*
1969:   African Safari (doc.)

ROBERT T. SHANNON

1931:   Lover Come Back
1935:   King Solomon of Broadway*; A Night at the
        Ritz*; Times Square Lady (A. Cohen)
1937:   A Girl with Ideas (B. Manning); The Lady
        Fights Back (Brown Holmes); Prescription for
        Romance*; Racketeers in Exile (H. Sauber)
1941:   The Great Train Robbery*
1942:   Sons of the Pioneers*
1948:   Unknown Island (J. Harvey)

KEN SHAPIRO

1974:   The Groove Tube (L. Sarasohn)
1981:   Modern Problems*

RICHARD SHAPIRO

1976:   The Great Scout and Cathouse Thursday

STANLEY SHAPIRO (1925-   ) producer

1953:   South Sea Woman (E. Blum)
1958:   The Perfect Furlough
1959:   Pillow Talk (M. Richlin); Operation
        Petticoat (M. Richlin)
1961:   Come September (M. Richlin); Lover Come Back

735

        (P. Henning)
```
1962:   That Touch of Mink (N. Monaster)
1964:   Bedtime Story (P. Henning)
1965:   A Very Special Favor (N. Monaster)
1968:   How to Save a Marriage -- and Ruin Your Life
        (N. Monaster)
1974:   For Pete's Sake (M. Richlin)
1978:   The Seniors
1981:   Carbon Copy
```

JIM SHARMAN

```
1981:   Shock Treatment (Richard O'Brien)
```

ALAN SHARP

```
1971:   The Last Run; The Hired Hand
1972:   Ulzana's Raid
1974:   Billy Two Hats
1975:   Night Moves
1977:   Damnation Alley (L. Heller)
```

ALFRED SHAUGHNESSY

```
1956:   High Terrace (N. Hudis)
1972:   Crescendo
```

MELVILLE SHAVELSON (1917-   ) director, producer

```
1944:   The Princess and the Pirate*
1945:   Wonder Man*
1946:   The Kid from Brooklyn*
1947:   Where There's Life (A. Boretz)
1949:   Sorrowful Jones*; Always Leave Them Laughing
        (J. Rose); The Great Lover*; It's a Great
        Feeling (J. Rose)
1950:   The Daughter of Rosie O'Grady*
1951:   Double Dynamite; I'll See You in My Dreams
        (J. Rose); On Moonlight Bay (J. Rose)
1952:   April in Paris (J. Rose); Room for One More
        (J. Rose)
1953:   Trouble Along the Way (J. Rose)
1954:   Living It Up (J. Rose)
1955:   The Seven Little Foys (J. Rose)
```

```
1957:  Beau James (J. Rose)
1958:  Houseboat (J. Rose)
1959:  The Five Pennies (J. Rose)
1960:  It Started in Naples*
1961:  On the Double (Jack Rose)
1962:  The Pigeon That Took Rome
1963:  A New Kind of Love
1966:  Cast a Giant Shadow
1968:  Yours, Mine and Ours (M. Lachman)
1972:  The War Between Men and Women (D. Arnold)
1974:  Mixed Company (M. Lachman)
```

DAVID SHAW

```
1969:  If It's Tuesday, This Must Be Belgium
1977:  King, Queen, Knave (D. Seltzer)
```

FRANK SHAW

```
1979:  The Frisco Kid (M. Elias)
```

IRWIN SHAW (1913-   ) author, playwright

```
1936:  The Big Game
1942:  The Talk of the Town (S. Buchman)
1943:  The Commandos Strike at Dawn
1949:  Take One False Step (C. Erskine)
1951:  I Want You
1953:  Act of Love
1955:  Ulysses (It.; I. Berilli)
1957:  Fire Down Below
1958:  This Angry Age (It.; R. Clement); Desire
       Under the Elms
1961:  The Big Gamble
1963:  In the French Style
1968:  Survival (doc.)
```

KERRY SHAW

```
1946:  Smooth as Silk (D. Lussier)
```

LOU SHAW

```
1973:   Crypt of the Living Dead
1974:   The Bat People
```

PHILIP SHAW

```
1973:   Tarzana, the Wild Girl
```

JAMES SHAWKEY

```
1934:   Frontier Days
```

HARRY SHEARER

```
1979:   Real Life*
```

PERLEY POORE SHEEHAN

```
1935:   The Lost City (ser.)*
```

ARTHUR SHEEKMAN (1901-1978)

```
1931:   Monkey Business*
1933:   Roman Scandals*
1934:   Kid Millions*
1936:   Rose of the Rancho*; Dimples (N. Perrin);
        Stowaway*; Pigskin Parade
1938:   The Gladiator*
1946:   Blue Skies
1947:   Blaze of Noon (F. Wead); Dear Ruth; The
        Trouble with Women; Welcome Stranger
1948:   Dream Girl; Hazard (R. Chanslor); Saigon (P.
        Wolfson)
1949:   Dear Wife (R. Nash)
1950:   Mr. Music
1952:   Young Man with Ideas
1953:   Call Me Madam
1956:   Bundle of Joy*
1958:   Some Came Running (John Patrick)
1961:   Ada (W. Driskill)
```

DAVID SHELDON

1976: Grizzly (H. Flaxman)

E. LLOYD SHELDON

1929: Illusion

FORREST SHELDON

1930: The Lone Rider
1931: The Texas Ranger; Between Fighting Men (B.
       Burbridge)
1932: Hell Fire Austin (B. Burbridge); Dynamite
       Ranch (B. Barringer)
1933: Phantom Thunderbolt*
1934: The Fighting Trooper
1935: Men of Action*

MARY SHELDON

1944: Sweethearts of the U.S.A.

NORMAN SHELDON

1946: The El Paso Kid
1949: Rio Grande
1951: Border Fence

RODNEY SHELDON

1977: The Black Pearl (V. Miller)

SIDNEY SHELDON (1917-   ) novelist

1941: Mr. District Attorney in the Carter Case (B.
       Roberts); South of Panama (B. Roberts)
1942: She's in the Army
1947: The Bachelor and the Bobby-Soxer
1948: Easter Parade*
1950: Annie Get Your Gun; Nancy Goes to Rio
1951: No Questions Asked; Rich, Young and Pretty
       (D. Cooper); Three Guys Named Mike
1952: Just This Once

1953:   Dream Wife*; Remains to Be Seen
1955:   You're Never Too Young
1956:   Anytning Goes; The Birds and the Bees (P.
        Sturges); Pardners
1957:   The Buster Keaton Story (Robert Smith)
1961:   All in a Night's Work*
1962:   Billy Rose's Jumbo

WALTER SHENSON

1951:   Korea Patrol (Kenneth Brown)

SAM SHEPARD

1969:   Me and My Brother (R. Frank)
1970:   Zabriskie Point*

ANTONIO SHEPHERD

1979:   Chorus Call

DAVID P. SHEPPARD

1948:   The Black Arrow*

JACK SHER (1913-   ) director

1951:   My Favorite Spy (E. Hartmann)
1953:   Off Limits (H. Kantor); The Kid from Left
        Field
1956:   Four Girls in Town; Walk the Proud Land (G.
        Doud); World in My Corner
1957:   Joe Butterfly*
1958:   Kathy O' (S. Gomberg)
1959:   The Wild and the Innocent (S. Gomberg)
1960:   The Three Worlds of Gulliver (A. Ross)
1961:   Love in a Goldfish Bowl; Paris Blues*
1963:   Critic's Choice; Move Over, Darling (H.
        Kanter)

TED SHERDEMAN

```
1949:   Lust for Gold (R. English)
1950:   Breakthrough (B. Girard)
1952:   Retreat, Hell! (M. Sperling); Scandal
        Sheet*; The Winning Team*
1953:   The Eddie Cantor Story*
1954:   Them
1955:   The McConnell Story (S. Rolfe)
1956:   Away All Boats; Toy Tiger
1958:   St. Louis Blues (R. Smith); Maracaibo
1959:   A Dog of Flanders
1960:   Hell to Eternity (W. Schmidt)
1961:   The Big Show; Misty
1964:   Island of the Blue Dolphins (J. Klove)
1966:   ...And Now Miguel (J. Klove)
1969:   My Side of the Mountain*
1970:   Latitude Zero (Jap.)
```

JAY J. SHERIDAN

1966:   Nashville Rebel (I. Kerns)

OSCAR M. SHERIDAN

1934:   Such Women Are Dangerous*

ALIDA SHERMAN

1969:   Slaves*

ARTHUR SHERMAN

1947:   Shadow Valley

ERIC SHERMAN

1968:   Charles Lloyd: Journey Within

GEORGE L. SHERMAN

1971:   The Pursuit of Happiness (J. Boothe)

HAROLD SHERMAN

1934:   Are We Civilized?

JOSEPH SHERMAN

1934:   Death on the Diamond*
1935:   Murder in the Fleet (F. Wead)

RICHARD SHERMAN

1936:   To Mary -- with Love (Howard Smith)
1938:   Alexander's Ragtime Band*; Four Men and a
        Prayer*; Girls' School (T. Slesinger)
1939:   In Name Only; The Story of Vernon and Irene
        Castle*
1942:   For Me and My Gal*

RICHARD M. SHERMAN

1973:   Tom Sawyer (Robert Sherman)
1974:   Huckleberry Finn (Robert Sherman)
1976:   The Slipper and the Rose (Brit.)
1978:   The Magic of Lassie*

ROBERT SHERMAN

1966:   Picture Mommy Dead
1973:   Tom Sawyer (R. M. Sherman)
1974:   Huckleberry Finn (R. M. Sherman)
1978:   The Magic of Lassie*

SAMUEL M. SHERMAN

1973:   Dracula vs. Frankenstein (W. Pugsley)

STANFORD SHERMAN

1980:   Any Which Way You Can

TEDDI SHERMAN

1948: Four Faces West (G. Baker)
1959: Ten Seconds to Hell (R. Aldrich)
1963: Four for Texas (R. Aldrich)
1966: Rage (F. Mendez)

VINCENT SHERMAN

1938: Crime School (C. Wilbur); Heart of the North
       (L. Katz); My Bill (R. White)
1939: King of the Underworld (G. Bricker); Pride
       of Bluegrass; Adventures of Jane Arden*

TOM SHEROHMAN

1981: Modern Problems*

R. C. SHERRIFF (1896-1975) novelist, playwright
       Brit.

(American films only)
1933: The Invisible Man
1934: One More River
1937: The Road Back (Charles Kenyon)
1939: Goodbye, Mr. Chips (Brit./U.S.)
1941: That Hamilton Woman (W. Reisch)
1942: This Above All
1943: Forever and a Day*

JOHN SHERRY

1967: The Last Challenge (R. Ginna)
1971: The Beguiled (G. Grice)
1974: Hangup

ROBERT E. SHERWOOD (1896-1955) playwright

1931: Around the World in 80 Minutes (D.
       Fairbanks)
1932: Cock of the Air (C. Lederer)
1935: The Scarlet Pimpernel (Brit.; A. Wimperis)
1936: The Gost Goes West (Brit.)
1937: Thunder in the City (A. Kandel)

743

1938:   The Adventures of Marco Polo; The Divorce of
        Lady X (Brit.)
1939:   Idiot's Delight
1940:   Abe Lincoln in Illinois (G. Jones); Rebecca
        (J. Harrison)
1946:   The Best Years of Our Lives
1947:   The Bishop's Wife (L. Bercovici)
1953:   Man on a Tightrope

RUSSELL SHIELDS

1934:   Devil Tiger*

ALAN SHILLIN

1951:   A Wonderful LIfe

BARRY SHIPMAN

1936:   Robinson Crusoe of Clipper Island (ser.)*
1937:   Dick Tracy (ser.)*; S.O.S. Coast Guard
        (ser.)*; The Painted Stallion (ser.)*; Zorro
        Rides Again (ser.)*
1938:   The Lone Ranger (ser.)*; Dick Tracy Returns
        (ser.)*; The Fighting Devil Dogs (ser.)*;
        Hawk of the Wilderness (ser.)*
1939:   The Lone Ranger Rides Again (ser.)*;
        Daredevils of the Red Circle (ser.)*; Dick
        Tracy's G-Men (ser.)*
1940:   Hi-Yo Silver (edited from serial The Lone
        Ranger); Rocky Mountain Rangers (E. Snell);
        Frontier Vengeance (B. Cohen); The Trail
        Blazers; Lone Star Raiders (J. Marsh); Flash
        Gordon Conquers the Universe (ser.)*
1941:   Prairie Pioneers
1942:   Code of the Outlaw; Raiders of the Range;
        The Phantom Plainsmen (R. Yost); City of
        Silent Men
1944:   Lumberjack (N. Houston)
1946:   Roaring Rangers; Mysterious Mr. M (ser.)*
1947:   Swing the Western Way; Riders of the Lone
        Star; Smoky River Serenade; Rose of Santa
        Rosa
1948:   Six Gun Law; West of Sonora; Song of Idaho;
        Trail to Laredo; Singing Spurs; Smoky

Mountain Melody
1949: Home in San Antone; Laramie; The Blazing
Trail; Bandits of Eldorado; Horsemen of the
Sierras; Feudin' Rhythm; Frontier Outpost
1950: Outcasts of Black Mesa; Texas Dynamo;
Streets of Ghost Town; Across the Badlands;
Raiders of Tomahawk Creek; Hoedown
1951: Fort Savage Raider; Snake River Desperadoes;
Bonanza Town (B. Horswell); Cyclone Fury (E.
Repp); The Kid from Amarillo; Pecos River
1952: Junction City; The Kid from Broken Gun;
Laramie Mountains; Montana Territory; Smoky
Canyon
1953: Eyes of the Jungle (S. Lowe)
1954: Untamed Heiress
1955: Carolina Cannonball; Lay That Rifle Down
1956: Stranger at My Door
1957: Hell's Crossroads (J. Butler); Last
Stagecoach West; Gunfire at Indian Gap

ADAM HULL SHIRK

1931: Ingagi (doc.)

MICHAEL SHOOB

1982: Parasite*

SOL SHOR

1938: Dick Tracy Returns (ser.)*; The Fighting
Devil Dogs (ser.)*
1939: The Lone Ranger Rides Again (ser.)*; Zorro's
Fighting Legion (ser.)*; Daredevils of the
Red Circle (ser.)*; Dick Tracy's G-Men
(ser.)*
1940: Adventures of Red Ryder (ser.)*; King of the
Royal Mounted (ser.)*; Drums of Fu Manchu
(ser.)*; The Mysterious Dr. Satan (ser.)*
1941: Adventures of Captain Marvel (ser.)*
1942: Yukon Patrol*
1946: The Crimson Ghost (ser.)*
1947: The Black Widow (ser.)*; Son of Zorro
(ser.)*; Jesse James Rides Again (ser.)*
1948: Dangers of the Canadian Mounted (ser.)*;

```
                 Adventures of Frank and Jesse James (ser.)*;
                 Sons of Adventure (F. Adreon); G-Men Never
                 Forget (ser.)*
       1949:    Ghost of Zorro (ser.)*; Federal Agents vs.
                 Underworld, Inc. (ser.)*; King of the Rocket
                 Men (ser.)*
       1950:    The James Brothers of Missouri (ser.)*
       1953:    Savage Mutiny
```

VIOLA BROTHERS SHORE

```
1931:    Husband's Holiday (E. Pascal); No Limit (S.
         Field)
1933:    Men Are Such Fools (E. Doherty); Sailor Be
         Good (E. Doherty)
1936:    Smartest Girl in Town; Walking on Air*
1937:    Breakfast for Two*; Life of the Party*
1938:    The Arkansas Traveler (G. Perry); Blonde
         Cheat*
1939:    Chicken Wagon Family
```

LUKE SHORT

```
1948:    Blood on the Moon*
```

STAN SHPETNER

```
1958:    The Bonnie Parker Story
1959:    The Legend of Tom Dooley; Paratroop Command
```

BUD SHRAKE

```
1979:    Nightwing*
1980:    Tom Horn (T. McGuane)
```

EDWIN SHRAKE

```
1973:    Kid Blue
```

DENNIS SHRYACK

```
1969:    The Good Guys and the Bad Guys (R. M. Cohen)
```

1977:   The Car*; The Gauntlet (M. Butler)

PHIL SHUKEN

1959:   Plunderers of Painted Flats (John Greene)
1967:   Doctor, You've Got to Be Kidding!

RICHARD B. SHULL

1968:   Pamela, Pamela You Are...(W. Rose)

IRVING SHULMAN

1952:   The Ring
1953:   Champ for a Day
1957:   Baby Face Nelson (G. Homes)
1960:   College Confidential

MAX SHULMAN

1953:   The Affairs of Dobie Gillis; Confidentially
        Connie; Half a Hero
1978:   House Calls*

HAROLD SHUMATE

1928:   River Woman (A. Buffington)
1929:   The Careless Age; Hold Your Man
1930:   The Love Trader
1932:   Ridin' for Justice; Heritage of the Desert
        (F. Partes); Wild Horse Mesa (F. Clark)
1933:   Scarlet River; Son of the Border (W.
        Totman); Man of the Forest (J. Cunningham)
1934:   Beyond the Law; The Westerner; Crime of
        Helen Stanley; Girl in Danger; Hell Bent for
        Love; A Man's Game; A Voice in the Night;
        White Lies; Against the Law; One Is Guilty
1935:   Square Shooter; Home on the Range*; After
        the Dance (B. Manning); Behind the Evidence;
        Superspeed
1936:   End of the Trail; Dodge City Trail; The
        Final Hour; Hell-Ship Morgan; Killer at
        Large; Panic on the Air; Pride of the

747

            Marines
1937: Escape by Night; A Fight to the Finish; The
       Frame-Up; Parole Racket
1939: Charlie McCarthy, Detective*
1940: Konga, the Wild Stallion; When the Daltons
       Rode; Trail of the Vigilantes; Cafe Hostess;
       My Son Is Guilty (J. Carole)
1941: Romance of the Rio Grande (S. Engel); The
       Round Up; The Parson of Panamint (A. Scott);
       Under Fiesta Stars (E. Gibbons)
1942: Men of Texas (R. Brooks); The Forest Rangers
1943: The Kansan
1946: Abilene Town
1948: Blood on the Moon*
1950: Saddle Tramp; Buccaneer's Girl (J. Hoffman)
1951: Little Big Horn (C. Warren)
1952: The Half-Breed (R. Wormser)
1954: Pride of the Blue Grass

RONALD SHUSETT

1981: Dead and Buried (D. O'Bannon)

JAMES SHUTE

1958: Windjammer (doc.; A. Villiers)

CHARLES SHYER

1977: Smokey and the Bandit*
1978: House Calls*; Goin' South*
1980: Private Benjamin*

MELVILLE SHYER

1934: The Man from Hell

J. DONALD SIDDON

1978: Their Only Chance

BARRY SIEGEL

1980:   Windows

MARC SIEGLER

1971:   The Ski Bum (Bruce Clark)
1981:   Galaxy of Terror (Bruce Clark)

MARJORIE L. SIGLEY

1982:   Never Never Land

RONALD SILKOSKY

1970:   The Dunwich Horror*
1977:   Maniac (J. Broderick)

ALF SILLIMAN, JR.

1970:   The Stewardesses

ROBERT SILLIPHANT

1965:   Incredibly Strange Creatures Who Stopped
        Living and Became Mixed Up Zombies (G.
        Pollack)

STIRLING SILLIPHANT (1918-   ) producer

1955:   Five Against the House (W. Bowers)
1956:   Huk; Nightfall
1958:   Damn Citizen; The Line-Up
1960:   The Village of the Damned (Brit.)*
1965:   The Slender Thread
1967:   In the Heat of the Night
1968:   Charly
1969:   Marlowe
1970:   The Liberation of L. B. Jones (J. Hillford);
        A Walk in the Spring Rain
1971:   Murphy's War
1972:   The New Centurions; The Poseidon Adventure
        (W. Mayes)

749

```
1973:   Shaft in Africa
1974:   The Towering Inferno
1975:   The Killer Elite
1976:   The Enforcer (D. Riesner)
1977:   Telefon (P. Hyams)
1978:   The Swarm
1979:   Circle of Iron (S. Mann); The Day the World
        Ended
1980:   When Time Ran Out (C. Foreman)
```

TED SILLS

```
1944:   Abroad with Two Yanks*
```

JOAN MICKLIN SILVER

```
1972:   Limbo (J. Bridges)
1975:   Hester Street
1979:   Head over Heels
1982:   Chilly Scenes of Winter (alt. Head over
        Heels)
```

PAT SILVER

```
1960:   The Wizard of Baghdad (J. Lasky)
1961:   Pirates of Tortuga*; Seven Women from Hell
        (J. Lasky)
1976:   Crime and Passion (J. Lasky)
```

STANLEY H. SILVERMAN

```
1958:   Gun Fever (M. Stevens)
```

SID SILVERS

```
1930:   Follow the Leader (G. Purcell)
1934:   Bottoms Up*
1935:   Broadway Melody of 1936*
1936:   Born to Dance (Jack MacGowan)
1939:   The Gorilla (R. James)
1942:   The Fleet's In (W. DeLeon); For Me and My
        Gal*
1951:   Two Tickets to Broadway (H. Kanter)
```

DAVID SILVERSTEIN

1933:   Devil's Mate (L. Fields)
1934:   King Kelly of the U.S.A. (L. Fields);
        Manhattan Love Song (L. Fields); The Scarlet
        Letter (L. Fields); Uncertain Blonde (L.
        Fields)
1935:   Streamline Express (L. Fields); Woman Wanted
        (L. Fields)
1936:   Song of the Trail*; 15 Maiden Lane*
1937:   Flight from Glory (J. Twist); Saturday's
        Heroes*; You Can't Beat Love (M. Shane)
1939:   Should a Girl Marry? (G. Newbury); Almost a
        Gentleman (J. Pagano)
1940:   Military Academy (K. Brown)
1941:   The Kid from Kansas (G. Jay); Mystery Ship
        (H. Branch); Naval Academy (G. Rigby)
1942:   Sabotage Squad*

BEN SIMCOE

1958:   Murder by Contract

LESLIE SIMMONDS

1933:   The Important Witness (D. Doty)

MICHAEL L. SIMMONS

1931:   First Aid
1935:   Awakening of Jim Burke
1936:   Girl of the Ozarks (S. Anthony)
1937:   Murder in Greenwich Village; Venus Makes
        Trouble
1938:   All-American Sweetheart*; Flight to Fame;
        Juvenile Court*; The Little Adventuress;
        Little Miss Roughneck*; Squadron of Honor
1939:   Missing Daughters (G. Bricker); Mutiny on
        the Blackhawk; Romance of the Redwoods;
        Tropic Fury
1941:   Scattergood Baines (E. Lowe); Scattergood
        Meets Broadway (E. Stone)
1942:   Scattergood Rides High; Scattergood Survives

751

          a Murder
1943:   Cinderella Swings It; Cosmo Jones, Crime
        Smasher (W. Gering); Eyes of the Underworld
        (A. Strawn); Two Weeks to Live (R. Rogers)
1944:   They Live in Fear (S. Ornitz)
1946:   Landrush
1947:   South of the Chisholm Trail

RICHARD ALAN SIMMONS

1953:   The Lady Wants Mink (D. Lussier); War Paint
        (M. Berkeley)
1954:   Beachhead; Tanganyika (W. Sackheim); The
        Yellow Tomahawk; Shield for Murder (J.
        Higgins); Three Hours to Kill (R. Huggins)
1955:   Female on the Beach (R. Hill); The Looters;
        The Private War of Major Benson (W. Roberts)
1956:   Congo Crossing; The King and Four Queens (M.
        Fitts)
1957:   Istanbul*; Outlaw's Son; The Fuzzy Pink
        Nightgown
1958:   Tarawa Beachhead
1959:   The Trap (N. Panama)
1962:   Belle Sommers

JAY SIMMS

1959:   The Giant Gila Monster; The Killer Shrews
1962:   Panic in the Year Zero (J. Morton)
1971:   The Resurrection of Zachary Wheeler (T.
        Rolf)

MAYO SIMON

1969:   Marooned
1974:   Phase IV
1976:   Futureworld (G. Schenck)

NEIL SIMON (1927-   ) playwright

1966:   After the Fox (Ital./Brit./U.S.)
1967:   Barefoot in the Park
1968:   The Odd Couple
1970:   The Out-of-Towners

```
1971:   Plaza Suite
1972:   Last of the Red Hot Lovers; The Heartbreak
        Kid
1975:   The Prisoner of Second Avenue; The Sunshine
        Boys
1976:   Murder by Death
1977:   The Goodbye Girl
1978:   The Cheap Detective; California Suite
1979:   Chapter Two
1980:   Seems Like Old Times
1981:   Only When I Laugh
1982:   I Ought to Be in Pictures
```

PAUL SIMON

```
1980:   One-Trick Pony
```

ROGER SIMON

```
1978:   The Big Fix
1981:   Bustin' Loose
```

George Simonelli

```
1966:   That Man in Istanbul
```

THEODORE SIMONSON

```
1958:   The Blob (K.Phillips)
1959:   The 4-D Man (C. Chermak)
```

HENRI SIMOUN

```
1968:   Madigan (A. Polonsky)
```

DONALD SIMPSON

```
1976:   Cannonball (P. Bartel)
```

CHARLES SINCLAIR

1976:   Track of the Moonbeast (W. Finger)

EDWARD SINCLAIR

1933:   Marriage on Approval (H. Higgin)

GERALD & ROGER SINDELL

1968:   Doublestop

ALEXANDER SINGER (1932–   ) director

1972:   Glass Houses (J. Singer)

JUDITH SINGER

1972:   Glass Houses (A. Singer)

RAY SINGER

1969:   The Maltese Bippy (E. Freeman)

TOM SINGER

1979:   Malibu High (J. Buckley)

CURT SIODMAK (1902–   ) director   Germ.

(American films only)
1940:   The Ape (R. Carroll); Black Friday (E.
        Taylor); The Invisible Man Returns (L. Cole)
1941:   The Wolf Man
1942:   Invisible Agent; London Blackout Murders
1943:   Frankenstein Meets the Wolfman; I Walked
        with a Zombie (A. Wray); The Mantrap; The
        Purple V (B. Millhauser); False Faces
1944:   The Climax (L. Starling)
1945:   Frisco Sal (G. Geraghty); Shady Lady*
1946:   The Beast with Five Fingers
1949:   Tarzan's Magic Fountain (H. Chandlee)
1951:   Bride of the Gorilla; Four Days' Leave

```
                (U.S./Sw.; R. Schweizer)
1953:   The Magnetic Monster (I. Tors)
1954:   Riders to the Stars
1955:   Creature with the Atomic Brain
1956:   Curucu, Beast of the Amazon; Earth vs. the
        Flying Saucers*
1957:   Love Slaves of the Amazon
1969:   Ski Fever (Aust./Czech./U.S.; R. Joseph)
```

DOUGLAS SIRK (1900-   ) director Den.

(American films only)
1944:   Summer Storm (R. Leigh)

ROSEMARY ANNE SISSON

1976:   Ride a Wild Pony
1978:   Candleshoe (D. Swift)
1980:   The Watcher in the Woods*

VANCE SKARSTEDT

1958:   Man or Gun (J. Cassity); No Place to Land
1963:   The Slime People
1967:   Once Before I Die

SIDNEY SKOLSKY

1953:   The Eddie Cantor Story*

EDITH SKOURAS

1938:   Always Goodbye (K. Scola)
1940:   High School*; Manhattan Heartbeat*

BERNARD SLADE

1972:   Stand Up and Be Counted
1978:   Same Time, Next Year
1980:   Tribute

                        755

LANE SLATE

1972:　They Only Kill Their Masters
1977:　The Car*

BARNEY SLATER

1952:　It Grows on Trees (L. Praskins)
1953:　Mr. Scoutmaster (L. Praskins)
1954:　Gorilla at Large (L. Praskins)

ROBERT F. SLATZER

1969:　The Hellcats (T. Huston)
1973:　Big Foot (J. G. White)

FRANK G. SLAUGHTER (1908-　　) novelist

1957:　Naked in the Sun (J. Hugh)

GEORGE F. SLAVIN

1947:　Intrigue (B. Trivers)
1950:　The Nevadan (G.W. George); The Fighting
　　　　Stallion (F. Kavanaugh); Peggy (G. George)
1951:　Red Mountain*
1953:　City of Bad Men (G. W. George)
1955:　Desert Sands*; Smoke Signal (G. W. George)
1956:　Uranium Boom*
1957:　The Halliday Brand (G. W. George)
1959:　The Son of Robin Hood (G. W. George)

HENRY SLESAR

1965:　Two on a Guillotine (J. Kneubuhl)
1971:　Murders in the Rue Morgue (C. Wicking)

TESS SLESINGER (　　-1945)

1937:　The Bride Wore Red (B. Foote); The Good
　　　　Earth*
1938:　Girls' School (R. Sherman)

```
1940:   Dance, Girl, Dance (Frank Davis)
1941:   Remember the Day*
1942:   Are Husbands Necessary? (Frank Davis)
1945:   A Tree Grows in Brooklyn (Frank Davis)
```

ALLAN SLOANE

```
1961:   Question 7
1975:   The Hiding Place (L. Holben)
```

PAUL H. SLOANE (1893-   ) director

```
1935:   Here Comes the Band*
1938:   The Texans*
1940:   Geronimo
1950:   The Sun Sets at Dawn
```

JEROME SMALL

```
1972:   Twilight People (E. Romero)
```

AL AUSTIN SMITH

```
1933:   The Cohens and Kellys in Trouble (F. Guiol)
```

ANDREW SMITH

```
1979:   The Main Event (G. Parent)
```

CHARLES B. SMITH

```
1964:   Apache Rifles
```

DODIE SMITH

```
1944:   The Uninvited (D. Smith)
1951:   Darling, How Could You (L. Samuels)
```

EARLE E. SMITH

```
1973:  The Legend of Boggie Creek
1974:  Bootleggers
1976:  The Winds of Autumn
1977:  The Town That Dreaded Sundown
1978:  Wishbone Cutter
```

GEORGE SMITH

```
1948:  The Hawk of Powder River
```

HAL SMITH

```
1946:  Dangerous Business; Night Editor
1948:  Thunderhoof; Black Eagle (E. Huebsch)
1955:  It Came from Beneath the Sea (G. Yates)
```

HAROLD JACOB SMITH

```
1957:  The River's Edge (J. Leicester)
1958:  The Defiant Ones (N. Douglas); Enchanted
       Island (J. Leicester)
1960:  Inherit the Wind (N. Douglas)
1970:  The McMasters
```

HARRY G. SMITH

```
1930:  The Love Kiss
```

HINTON SMITH

```
1936:  In His Steps (K. Brown)
```

HOWARD ELLIS SMITH

```
1928:  Land of the Silver Fox
1935:  The Man Who Broke the Bank at Monte Carlo
       (H. Jonson); Professional Soldier (G.
       Fowler)
1936:  It Had to Happen (K. Scola); To Mary -- with
       Love (R. Sherman)
1937:  Think Fast, Mr. Moto (N. Foster)
```

HUBERT SMITH

1978: Night Creature

HUGH SMITH

1977: Black Oak Conspiracy (J. Vint); Moonshine
      County Express (D. Ansley)
1978: Out of the Darkness
1981: The Glove (J. Roffman)

J. AUGUSTUS SMITH

1934: Drums o' Voodoo (alt. She Devil; A. Hoerl)

JOSHUA SMITH

1976: Super Seal (V. Lundin)

MARTIN C. SMITH

1979: Nightwing*
1981: Under the Rainbow*

MAURA SMITH

1978: Towing

PAUL GERARD SMITH

1930: Dangerous Nan McGrew (P. Collings)
1931: Sidewalks of New York (G. Landy)
1934: Harold Teen (Al Cohn); Son of the Gods;
      Circus Clown; Eyes of the Eagle
1935: Hold 'Em Yale (E. Welch); One Hour Late*
1936: F-Man*; It's a Great Life (H. Thompson)
1937: Mama Runs Wild*; Thrill of a Lifetime*; Turn
      off the Moon*
1938: The Higgins Family (J. Townley)
1940: I Can't Give You Anything but Love, Baby (A.

                     Horman); La Conga Nights*; Margie*
        1941:   Steel Against the Sky; Tanks a Million*;
                You're in the Army Now (G. Beatty); Wild
                Bill Hickok Rides*; Give Out, Sisters (W.
                Wilson); Here We Go Again (J. Bigelow); Jail
                House Blues (H. Tarshis); Niagara Falls*;
                Hello Sucker (Maurice Leo); Sing Another
                Chorus*
        1943:   Moonlight and Cactus (E. Conrad)
        1944:   Hi, Good Lookin'*; Oh, What a Night
        1947:   Untamed Fury (T. Caven)
        1948:   Harpoon (E. Scott)

ROBERT SMITH

        1945:   You Came Along (A. Rand)
        1949:   The Big Wheel
        1950:   Quicksand
        1951:   The Second Woman; The Magic Face (M.
                Briskin)
        1952:   Invasion U.S.A.; Sudden Fear (L. Coffee)
        1953:   99 River Street; Paris Model; Perils of the
                Jungle (F. Taussig)
        1957:   The Buster Keaton Story (S. Sheldon); The
                Lonely Man (H. Essex)
        1958:   St. Louis Blues (T. Sherdeman)
        1959:   The Big Operator (A. Rivkin); Girls' Town
        1960:   Platinum High School
        1969:   The First Time (J. Heims)

ROGER SMITH

        1970:   C.C. and Company

SHIRLEY SMITH

        1949:   It Happens Every Spring (V. Davies)

STEVEN P. SMITH

        1980:   The Long Riders*

VERNON SMITH

1936:   Call of the Prairie (D. Schroeder); Three on
        the Trail (D. Schroeder)
1940:   Misbehaving Husbands (C. Parrish)

WALLACE SMITH

1929:   Bulldog Drummond (S. Howard); Delightful
        Rogue
1930:   Beau Bandit; The Silver Horde; Love Comes
        Along
1931:   Friends and Lovers (J. Murfin); The Lady
        Refuses (G. Bolton)
1932:   Almost Married; The Lost Squadron (H.
        Mankiewicz); Men of Chance (L. Stevens); The
        Woman Decides (alt. The Delightful Rogue)
1934:   The Captain Hates the Sea; The Trumpet Blows
        (B. Cormack)
1935:   Bordertown (L. Doyle); Seven Keys to
        Baldpate (A. Veiller)
1936:   The Gay Desperado
1937:   Her Husband Lies (E. Greene)

EARLE SNELL

1929:   The Cohens and the Kellys in Atlantic City;
        One Hysterical Night
1930:   Sunny Skies; Embarrassing Moments (G.
        Lehman)
1931:   Alias the Bad Man; Range Law; Branded Men;
        Subway Express
1932:   Fargo Express (A. Neitz); Fast Companions;
        Information Kid; Racing Youth; Steady
        Company
1933:   Her First Mate*
1934:   Half a Sinner (C. Marks); Let's Be Ritzy (H.
        Sauber); Love Past Thirty; Night Alarm;
        Tomorrow's Youth
1935:   Stone of Silver Creek; Branded a Coward;
        Escape from Devil's Island (F. Niblo)
1936:   Sunset of Power; Desert Phantom; Rogue of
        the Range; Everyman's Law; King of the Royal
        Mounted; Wild Brian Kent*; Burning Gold;
        Rainbow on the River*; Roaming Lady (F.
        Niblo); Two in a Crowd
1937:   Secret Valley*; It Happened Out West*; Make

761

a Wish*
1938:   The Gladiator*; Wide Open Faces*
1939:   Days of Jesse James; Homicide Bureau; Torchy
         Plays with Dynamite (C. Belden
1940:   Covered Wagon Days; Rocky Mountain Rangers
         (B. Shipman); Oklahoma Renegades (D.
         Schroeder); West of Pinto Basin
1941:   Trail of the Silver Spurs; The Kid's Last
         Ride; Saddle Mountain Roundup (J. Vlahos);
         Gauchos of Eldorado (A. DeMond); Borrowed
         Hero
1942:   Brooklyn Orchid (C. Marks); Thunder River
         Feud (J. Vlahos); Riding the Wind (M.
         Grant); Rock River Renegades (J. Vlahos);
         The McGuerins from Brooklyn (C. Marks)
1943:   Prairie Chickens (A. Belgard); Taxi, Mister
         (C. Marks); That Nazty Nuisance (C. Marks)
1944:   Three of a Kind (A. Caesar); Shadow of
         Suspicion (A. DeMond); Bowery Champs
1945:   Phantom of the Plains (Charles Kenyon);
         Colorado Pioneers; Wagon Wheels Westward;
         Come Out Fighting
1946:   Alias Billy the Kid (B. Burbridge); Sun
         Valley Cyclone; Conquest of Cheyenne;
         Sheriff of Redwood Valley; Santa Fe
         Uprising; Stagecoach to Denver
1947:   Vigilantes of Boomtown; Homesteaders of
         Paradise Valley; Oregon Trail Scouts;
         Rustlers of Devil's Canyon; Robin Hood of
         Texas (J. Butler); Marshal of Cripple Creek;
         Along the Oregon Trail; The Last Round-Up
         (J. Townley)
1948:   Carson City Raiders; El Dorado Pass·
1949:   South of Death Valley; Desert Vigilante;
         Renegades of the Sage
1951:   Valley of Fire (G. Geraghty)
1956:   The Desperadoes Are in Town (K. Neumann)

HOWARD SNYDER

1941:   Melody Lane*; San Antonio Rose*
1942:   Almost Married (H. Wedlock); Don't Get
         Personal (H. Wedlock)
1943:   All by Myself (H. Wedlock); The Good Fellows
         (H. Wedlock); Salute for Three*
1945:   George White's Scandals*
1949:   Abbott and Costello Meet the Killer Boris

Karloff*

CAROL SOBIESKI

1978: Casey's Shadow
1980: Honeysuckle Rose*
1982: Annie; The Toy

JERRY SOHL

1960: Twelve Hours to Kill
1965: Die, Monster, Die

ROBERT W. SOLDERBERG

1949: The Reckless Moment (H. Gardon)

ALFRED SOLE

1978: Alice, Sweet Alice (R. Ritvo)

PETER J. SOLMO

1976: Jack and the Beanstalk (anim.)

KENNY SOLMS

1975: Sheila Levine Is Dead and Living in New York
(G. Parent)

LEO SOLOMON

1946: The Dark Horse (C. Marion)

LOUIS SOLOMON

1944: Mr. Winkle Goes to War*
1945: Snafu (H. Buchanan)
1948: Variety Time*
1951: Mark of the Renegade (R. H. Andrews)

EUGENE SOLOW

1934: Fog over Frisco (R. N. Lee); Gentlemen Are
      Born (R. N. Lee); Return of the Terror (P.
      Milne)
1935: Thunder in the Night (F. Hyland); While the
      Patient Slept*
1936: Crash Donovan*
1937: The League of Frightened Men (G. Endore)
1938: The Patient in Room 18 (R. White); Start
      Cheering*
1939: Of Mice and Men
1940: Bowery Boy*

ANDREW SOLT

1943: My Kingdom for a Cook (H. Goldman)
1946: The Jolson Story*; Without Reservations
1948: Joan of Arc (M. Anderson)
1949: Little Women*
1950: In a Lonely Place (E. North)
1951: The Family Secret (F. Cockrell); Thunder on
      the Hill (O. Saul)
1959: For the First Time; Whirlpool (B. Hecht)
1981: This Is Elvis (M. Leo)

ARNOLD SOMKIN

1975: Best Friends

EDITH SOMMER

1950: Born to Be Bad; Perfect Strangers
1959: The Best of Everything (M. Rubin); Blue
      Denim (P. Dunne)
1962: Jessica
1964: The Pleasure Seekers
1966: This Property Is Condemned*

JAY SOMMERS

1961: All Hands on Deck*

STEPHEN SONDHEIM

1973: The Last of Sheila (A. Perkins)

TERRY SOUTHERN

1964: Dr. Strangelove (S. Kubrick)
1965: The Cincinnati Kid (R. Lardner); The Loved
       One (C. Isherwood)
1968: Barbarella*; Candy (B. Henry)
1969: Easy Rider*
1970: End of the Road*; The Magic Christian

JACK B. SOWARDS

1982: Star Trek II: The Wrath of Khan

ROBERT SPAFFORD

1960: Heaven on Earth (Ital.)

HARRY SPALDING

1960: Freckles
1962: The Firebrand
1963: The Day Mars Invaded Earth; House of the
       Damned; Police Nurse
1964: Surf Party; Witchcraft; The Young Swingers
1965: The Curse of the Fly; Raiders from Beneath
       the Sea; Space Flight IC-I; Wild on the
       Beach
1966: The Murder Game
1973: One Little Indian
1980: The Watcher in the Woods*

LARRY G. SPANGLER

1972: The Legend of Nigger Charley (M. Goldman)

NICHOLAS SPANOS

1977:   Whiskey Mountain

IZZY SPARBER

1939:   Gulliver's Travels (anim.)*

ROBERT SPARKS

1933:   Cradle Song*

WALTER M. SPEAR

1978:   Speedtrap (S. Segal)

JAMES SPEARING

1934:   Devil Tiger*

JAN SPEARS

1979:   Game of Death

KATHERINE SPECKTOR

1982:   Love Child (A. Gerard)

DAVID SPECTOR

1977:   Airport '77 (M. Scheff)

JACK SPEIRS

1968:   Charlie, the Lonesome Cougar
1970:   King of the Grizzlies

AARON SPELLING

1960:   Guns of the Timberland (J. Petracca); One

Foot in Hell (S. Boehm)

RALPH SPENCE

1930: Hook, Line and Sinker (T. Whelan)
1931: Caught Plastered (D. MacLean); The Gorilla
1932: The Crooked Circle; Fast Life (B. Morgan);
       Peach O'Reno; Speak Easily (L. Johnson)
1933: Mr. Skitch (S. Levien); Tomorrow at Seven;
       Warrior's Husband*
1934: The Band Plays On*; Death on the Diamond*;
       I'll Tell the World (D. Van Every); Murder
       in the Private Car*; Strictly Dynamite*;
       Student Tour (P. Dunne); Stand Up and Cheer
1935: The Big Broadcast of 1936*; Here Comes the
       Band*; The Winning Ticket*
1936: Everybody Dance (Leslie Arliss)
1937: King Solomon's Mines (Brit.)*
1939: The Flying Deuces*
1941: Larceny Street (Brit.)
1942: Seven Days' Leave*
1943: Around the World; Higher and Higher*

DON SPENCER

1970: The Student Nurses
1973: Sweet Sugar

FRANZ G. SPENCER

1941: Down in San Diego
1942: Born to Sing (H. Clork)
1945: Fighting Guardsman (E. Dein)

RAY SPENCER

1946: Crack-Up*

SCOTT SPENCER

1982: Split Image*

KAREN SPERLING

1971:   Make a Face (B. Connell)

MILTON SPERLING (1912–   ) producer

1936:   Sing, Baby, Sing*
1937:   Thin Ice (B. Ingster)
1938:   Happy Landing (B. Ingster); I'll Give a
        Million (B. Ingster)
1939:   The Return of the Cisco Kid; Here I Am a
        Stranger (S. Hollman)
1940:   The Great Profile (H. Lynn)
1952:   Retreat, Hell! (T. Sherdeman)
1955:   The Court Martial of Billy Mitchell*
1960:   The Bramble Bush (P. Yordan)
1962:   Merrill's Marauders (S. Fuller)
1965:   Battle of the Bulge*
1971:   Captain Apache (P. Yordan)

BELLA SPEWACK

1933:   The Cat and the Fiddle (S. Spewack); Clear
        All Wires (S. Spewack); The Nuisance (S.
        Spewack); Should Ladies Behave (S. Spewack)
1934:   The Gay Bride (S. Spewack)
1935:   Rendezvous*
1937:   Vogues of 1938 (S. Spewack)
1938:   Boy Meets Girl (S. Spewack); The Chaser*;
        Three Loves Has Nancy*
1940:   My Favorite Wife (S. Spewack)
1945:   Weekend at the Waldorf (S. Spewack)

SAMUEL SPEWACK (1899–1971)

1931:   The Secret Witness (alt. Terror by Night)
1933:   The Cat and the Fiddle (B. Spewack); Clear
        All Wires (B. Spewack); The Nuisance (B.
        Spewack); Should Ladies Behave (B. Spewack)
1934:   The Gay Bride (B. Spewack)
1935:   Rendezvous*
1937:   Vogues of 1938 (B. Spewack)
1938:   Boy Meets Girl (B. Spewack); The Chaser*;
        Three Loves Has Nancy*
1940:   My Favorite Wife (B. Spewack)
1942:   The World at War (doc.)

768

1945: Weekend at the Waldorf (B. Spewack)
1963: Move Over, Darling

LARRY SPIEGEL

1973: Book of Numbers; Hail to the Chief (P.
      Dusenberry)
1977: God Bless Mr. Shegetz (Richard Benson)
1979: Washington B. C. (P. Dusenberry)
1980: Survival Run (G. M. Cahill)

STEVEN SPIELBERG (1947-   ) director

1977: Close Encounters of the Third Kind
1982: Poltergeist*

ED SPIELMAN

1973: Gordon's War (H. Friedlander)

WILLIAM SPIER

1972: The Devil's Widow

LEONARD SPIGELGASS

1932: Walking Down Broadway (alt. Hello, Sister;
      E. von Stroheim)
1934: I'll Fix It
1938: Letter of Introduction (S. Gibney); Service
      de Luxe (G. Purcell)
1939: Unexpected Father (C. Grayson)
1940: The Boys from Syracuse (C. Grayson); Private
      Affairs*
1941: Tight Shoes (A. Arthur)
1942: All Through the Night (E. Gilbert); The Big
      Street; Butch Minds the Baby
1943: The Youngest Profession*
1946: The Perfect Marriage
1948: So Evil My Love
1949: I Was a Male War Bride*
1951: The Law and the Lady (K. Tunberg); Night
      into Morning (K. Tunberg)

1952: Because You're Mine (K. Tunberg)
1954: Deep in My Heart
1957: Ten Thousand Bedrooms*; Silk Stockings (L. Gershe)
1961: A Majority of One
1962: Gypsy

MICKEY SPILLANE

1963: The Girl Hunters*

JOE SPINELL

1980: Maniac (A. Rosenberg)

HERBERT ABBOTT SPIRO

1958: The World Was His Jury
1960: The Music Box Kid
1962: The Clown and the Kid (J. Sackheim)

MARIAN SPITZER

1945: The Dolly Sisters (J. Larkin)

ROGER SPOTTISWOODE

1982: Forty-Eight Hours*

CHANDLER SPRAGUE

1934: I Like It That Way (J. Santley); Menace (A. Veiller)
1942: The Bashful Bachelor

NORMAN SPRINGER

1932: Stowaway
1935: The Shadow of Silk Lennox; Scream in the Night (alt. Murder in Morocco)

LANGSTON STAFFORD

1976:   Ilsa, Harem Keeper of the Oil Sheiks

RAY STAHL

1954:   The Scarlet Spear (G. Breakston)

HILDEGARDE STADIE

1934:   Maniac

LAURENCE STALLINGS (1894-1968) playwright,
        novelist, critic

1930:   Way for a Sailor (C. MacArthur); Billy the
        Kid*
1933:   The Big Executive
1935:   So Red the Rose*
1938:   Too Hot to Handle (J. Mahin)
1940:   The Man from Dakota; Northwest Passage (T.
        Jennings)
1942:   The Jungle Book*
1945:   Salome, Where She Danced
1947:   Christmas Eve (B. Bogeaus)
1948:   Three Godfathers (F. Nugent); A Miracle Can
        Happen; On Our Merry Way
1949:   She Wore a Yellow Ribbon (F. Nugent)
1953:   The Sun Shines Bright (I. Cobb)

SYLVESTER STALLONE (1946-   ) actor, director

1976:   Rocky
1978:   F.I.S.T. (J. Eszterhas); Paradise Alley
1979:   Rocky II
1982:   Rocky III

DONALD STANFORD

1967:   A Taste of Blood

HUGH STANGE

1931:   Black Camel*

JACK STANLEY

1941:   The Iron Claw (ser.)*
1942:   Captain Midnight (ser.)*
1944:   Black Arrow (ser.)*; The Desert Hawk (ser.)*

JOHN STANLEY

1976:   Nightmare in Blood (Kenn Davis)

JANE C. STANTON (see also JANE STANTON HITCHCOCK)

1974:   Our Time (P. Hyams)

JAISON STARKES

1976:   J. D.'s Revenge
1979:   The Fish That Saved Pittsburgh (E. Stevens)

LYNN STARLING

1930:   Oh, for a Man (P. Klein)
1931:   Always Goodbye; Don't Bet on Women (Leon
        Gordon)
1932:   Cynara (F. Marion); First Year
1933:   Torch Singer (L. Coffee)
1934:   Down to Their Last Yacht*; Love Time*; The
        President Vanishes*
1935:   Private Worlds (G. La Cava); Shanghai*
1936:   Give Us This Night (E. Mayer); More Than a
        Secretary (D. Van Every)
1937:   As Good As Married (F. Herbert); Women of
        Glamour (M. McCall)
1938:   Thanks for the Memory; Three Blind Mice
        (Brown Holmes)
1939:   The Cat and the Canary (W. DeLeon)
1940:   He Married His Wife*; A Night at Earl
        Carroll's
1942:   Footlight Serenade*

```
1943:   Wintertime*
1944:   The Climax (C. Siodmak)
1945:   It's a Pleasure! (E. Paul)
1946:   The Time, the Place and the Girl*
```

BEN STARR

```
1966:   Our Man Flint (H. Fimberg); The Pad and How
        to Use It (T. C. Ryan); Texas Across the
        River*
1967:   The Busy Body; The Spirit Is Willing
1969:   How to Commit Marriage (M. Kanin)
```

JAMES A. STARR

```
1930:   The Man Hunter; Rough Waters
```

JUNE STARR

```
1967:   C'mon, Let's Live a Little
```

JOSEPH T. STECK

```
1967:   Waterhole #3 (R. R. Young)
```

RAY D. STECKLER

```
1965:   The Thrill Killers (G. Pollack)
```

JOSEPH STEFANO

```
1959:   The Black Orchid
1960:   Psycho
1961:   The Naked Edge
1969:   Eye of the Cat; Futz
```

BOB STEIN

```
1970:   The Zodiac Couples (doc.; A. Roberts)
```

JEFF STEIN

1979:   The Kids Are Alright

JOSEPH STEIN

1967:   Enter Laughing (C. Reiner)
1971:   Fiddler on the Roof

JOHN STEINBECK (1902-1968) novelist

1941:   The Forgotten Village (doc.; Mex.)
1948:   The Pearl (Mex.; Emilio Fernandez, Jack
        Wagner)
1949:   The Red Pony
1952:   Viva Zapata!

NORMAN STEINBERG

1982:   My Favorite Year (D. Palumbo); Yes, Giorgio

JOHN W. STEINER

1958:   The Incredible Petrified World

FREDERICK STEPHANI

1935:   All the King's Horses*
1936:   Flash Gordon (ser.)*
1937:   Between Two Women (M. Parsonnet)
1948:   Sofia
1949:   Johnny Holiday*
1957:   Two Grooms for a Bride

ROBERT STEPHEN

1947:   Dick Tracy's Dilemma

STEWART STERLING

1945:   Having Wonderful Crime*

DAVID STERN

1949:   Francis
1956:   Swamp Women

LEONARD STERN

1950:   Ma and Pa Kettle Go to Town (M. Ragaway);
        The Milkman*
1952:   Lost in Alaska (M. Ragaway)
1953:   The Jazz Singer*
1955:   Three for the Show (E. Hope)
1979:   Just You and Me, Kid (O. Hailey)
1980:   The Nude Bomb*

SANDOR STERN

1979:   Fast Break; The Amityville Horror

STEVEN H. STERN

1971:   B.S. I Love You
1979:   Running

STEWART STERN

1951:   Teresa
1955:   Rebel Without a Cause
1956:   The Rack
1957:   The James Dean Story
1961:   The Outsider
1963:   The Ugly American
1968:   Rachel, Rachel
1971:   The Last Movie
1973:   Summer Wishes, Winter Dreams

JOSEF VON STERNBERG (see VON STERNBERG, JOSEPH)

WALTER STERRET

1929:   The Invaders

EDMOND STEVENS

1979:   The Fish That Saved Pittsburgh (J. Starkes)

GEORGE STEVENS (1904-1975) director, producer

1965:   The Greatest Story Ever Told (J. C. Barrett)

LESLIE STEVENS (1924-   ) director, playwright,
        producer

1958:   The Left Handed Gun
1960:   The Marriage-Go-Round; Private Property
1962:   Hero's Island
1979:   Buck Rogers in the 25th Century

LOUIS STEVENS

1932:   Men of Chance (W. Smith)
1933:   Flying Devils (B. Morgan)
1935:   Mary Burns, Fugitive*
1936:   The Texas Rangers; Special Investigator*
1937:   The Last Train from Madrid (R. Wyler)
1938:   Sinners in Paradise*
1940:   Colorado (H. Jacobs); The Border Legion (O.
        Cooper)
1949:   Massacre River
1951:   The Cimarron Kid
1952:   Horizons West
1954:   Border River (W. Sackheim)
1957:   Gun Duel in Durango; Cartouche
1958:   Wolf Dog; Flaming Frontier
1959:   The Widow

MARK STEVENS   (1915-   ) actor, producer

1958:   Gun Fever (S. Silverstein)
1965:   Sunscorched (Sp./Ger.)*

JANET STEVENSON

1953:   The Man from Cairo*

PHILIP STEVENSON

1945:   The Story of G.I. Joe*
1952:   The Girl in White (I. Von Cube)
1953:   The Man from Cairo*

ROBERT STEVENSON (1905-   ) director   Brit.

(American films only)
1944:   Jane Eyre*

DONALD STEWART

1976:   Jackson County Jail
1978:   Deathsport (H. Suso)
1982:   Missing (Costa-Gavras)

DONALD OGDEN STEWART (1894-1980) novelist,
        playwright   (also GILBERT HOLLAND)

1931:   Tarnished Lady
1933:   Going Hollywood; The White Sister
1934:   The Barretts of Wimpole Street*
1935:   No More Ladies (H. Jackson)
1937:   The Prisoner of Zenda*
1938:   Holiday (S. Buchman); Marie Antoinette*
1939:   Love Affair (D. Daves); The Women (unc.)*
1940:   Kitty Foyle (D. Trumbo); The Night of
         Nights; The Philadelphia Story
1941:   Smilin' Through (J. Balderston); That
         Uncertain Feeling (W. Reisch); A Woman's
         Face (E. Paul)
1942:   Keeper of the Flame; Tales of Manhattan*
1943:   Forever and a Day*
1945:   Without Love
1947:   Cass Timberlane; Life with Father
1949:   Edward, My Son (Brit.)
1955:   Escapade (Brit.)
1962:   Malaga (Brit.)*

DOUGLAS STEWART

1974: Where the Red Fern Grows (E. Lamb)
1975: Seven Alone (E. Lamb); Against a Crooked Sky
       (E. Lamb)
1978: The Other Side of the Mountain Part 2
1980: The Blue Lagoon
1982: An Officer and a Gentleman

MILAN STITT

1979: The Runner Stumbles

DEAN STOCKWELL

1982: Human Highway*

VICTOR STOLOFF

1953: Volcano
1958: The She-Gods of Shark Reef (R. Hill)
1959: Desert Desperadoes
1971: Three Hundred Year Weekend

ANDREW L. STONE (1902-   ) director, producer

1941: There's Magic in Music (R. Lively)
1944: Sensations of 1945 (D. Bennett)
1946: The Bachelor's Daughters
1947: Fun on a Weekend
1950: Highway 301
1952: Confidence Girl; The Steel Trap
1953: A Blueprint for Murder
1955: The Night Holds Terror
1956: Julie
1958: Cry Terror; The Decks Ran Red
1960: The Last Voyage
1961: Ring of Fire
1963: The Password Is Courage (Brit.)
1964: Never Put It in Writing (Brit.)
1965: The Secret of My Success (Brit.)
1970: Song of Norway
1972: The Great Waltz

778

ETHEL B. STONE

1941: Scattergood Meets Broadway (M. Simmons)

HAROLD STONE

1973: The Soul of Nigger Charley

IRVING STONE (1903-   ) novelist, playwright

1946: Magnificent Doll

JOHN STONE

1929: Fugitives; The Girl from Havana; The Black
      Watch; Blue Skies; Captain Lash (A.
      Bennison); Chasing Through Europe (A.
      Bennison)
1943: Passport to Suez
1948: Fighting Back

JOSEPH STONE

1958: Wild Heritage (doc.; P. King)

MICHAEL STONE

1982: Waitress (C. Kaufman)

N. B. STONE, JR.

1955: Man with the Gun (R. Wilson)
1962: Ride the High Country

OLIVER STONE

1974: Seizure (E. Mann)
1978: Midnight Express
1981: The Hand
1982: Conan the Barbarian (J. Milius)

779

PETER STONE (1930–   ) playwright (also Pierre
        Marton, Quentin Werty)

1963:   Charade
1964:   Father Goose (F. Tarloff)
1965:   Mirage
1966:   Arabesque*
1968:   The Secret War of Harry Frigg (F. Tarloff);
        Jigsaw; Dark of the Sun
1969:   Sweet Charity
1971:   Skin Game
1972:   1776
1973:   That Man Bolt (C. Johnson)
1974:   The Taking of Pelham One Two Three
1978:   Silver Bears; Someone Is Killing the Great
        Chefs of Europe
1980:   Why Would I Lie?

ROBERT STONE

1970:   WUSA
1978:   Who'll Stop the Rain? (J. Roscoe)

ROGER STONE

1982:   Goin' All the Way (J. Cooper)

PHIL STONG

1933:   The Stranger's Return (B. Holmes)

GEORGE C. STONY

1952:   Birthright (doc.)

TOM SAWYER STOREY

1935:   Man's Best Friend

JANE STORM

                        780

1933:   Adorable (G. Marion); My Lips Betray (H.
        Kraly)
1934:   Mrs. Wiggs of the Cabbage Patch (W. McNutt);
        Such Women Are Dangerous*
1935:   Millions in the Air (S. Herzig)
1938:   Love on Toast*
1940:   Sandy Gets Her Man (S. Bartlett)
1942:   Mrs. Wiggs of the Cabbage Patch*

LESLEY STORM

1948:   Meet Me at Dawn (J. Seymour)
1954:   Personal Affair
1957:   The Spanish Gardener (J. Bryan)

LOUIS CLYDE STOUMEN

1957:   The Naked Eye (doc.)
1963:   The Black Fox (doc.)
1965:   The Image of Love (doc.)

PAUL STRAND

1942:   Native Land (doc.)*

RICHARD STRAUBB

1953:   Run for the Hills

THEODORE STRAUSS

1946:   California (F. Butler)
1948:   Isn't It Romantic?*; My Own True Love (J.
        Mischel)
1964:   Four Days in November (doc.)
1969:   The Bridge at Remagen*

ARTHUR STRAWN

1935:   The Black Room (H. Myers)
1936:   Lady from Nowhere*; The Man Who Lived Twice*

```
1941:   Road Agent (ret. Texas Road Agent; M. Cox)
1943:   Eyes of the Underworld (M. Simmons)
1948:   Bad Men of Tombstone (P. Yordan)
1951:   Flight to Mars
1952:   Hiawatha (D. Ullman)
```

FRANK STRAYER (1891-1964) director

```
1931:   Murder at Midnight (W. Darling)
```

JOSEPH STRICK (1923-   ) director, producer

```
1960:   The Savage Eye*
1967:   Ulysses (F. Haines)
1970:   Tropic of Cancer (B. Botley)
```

HERBERT STROCK

```
1964:   The Crawling Hand (W. Edelson)
1973:   Brother on the Run
```

ERICH VON STROHEIM (see VON STROHEIM, ERIC)

WILLIAM STROMBERG

```
1977:   The Crater Lake Monster (R. Cardella)
```

AUSTIN STRONG

```
1936:   Along Came Love
```

MALCOLM STUART

```
1950:   Customs Agent (R. Hughes)
```

JOHN STUCKMEYER

```
1982:   The Sword and the Sorcerer
```

JOHN STURDY

1943:   Corvette K-225

PRESTON STURGES (1898-1959) director, playwright

1933:   The Power and the Glory
1934:   30-Day Princess*; We Live Again*; Imitation
        of Life (unc.)*
1935:   The Good Fairy; Diamond Jim*
1936:   Next Time We Love (unc.; M. Baker)
1937:   Easy Living; Hotel Haywire
1938:   If I Were King; Port of Seven Seas
1939:   Never Say Die*
1940:   Christmas in July; The Great McGinty;
        Remember the Night
1941:   The Lady Eve; Sullivan's Travels
1942:   Palm Beach Story
1944:   The Miracle of Morgan's Creek; The Great
        Moment; Hail the Conquering Hero
1946:   The Sin of Harold Diddlebock
1947:   I'll Be Yours
1948:   Unfaithfully Yours
1949:   The Beautiful Blonde from Bashful Bend
1950:   Mad Wednesday
1956:   The Birds and the Bees (S. Sheldon)
1957:   The French They Are a Funny Race

BURT STYLER

1951:   Call Me Mister (A. Lewin)
1953:   Down Among the Sheltering Palms*
1966:   Boy, Did I Get the Wrong Number*
1967:   Eight on the Lam*
1968:   The Wicked Dreams of Paula Schultz*

ROBERT A. SUBOSKY

1982:   The House Where Evil Dwells

MILTON SUBOTSKY

1958:   Lost Lagoon (J. Lynn)
1959:   The Last Mile (S. I. Miller)
1962:   Ring-A-Ding Rhythm (Brit.)

1963:   Just for Fun! (Brit.)
1965:   Dr. Terror's House of Horrors; The Skull

HENRY SUCHER

1942:   The Miracle Kid*; The Mummy's Tomb (G. Jay)
1943:   Captive Wild Woman (G. Jay); Mug Town*
1944:   Jungle Woman; The Mummy's Ghost*

MARK SUFRIN

1957:   On the Bowery

PHILLIP SUKEN

1968:   Speedway

C. GARDNER SULLIVAN (1879—1965)

1929:   Alibi (R. West); The Locked Door
1932:   Skyscraper Souls; Strange Interlude (B.
        Meredyth)
1933:   Men Must Fight
1935:   Car 99 (K. Detzer); Father Brown, Detective
        (Henry Myers); Three Live Ghosts
1938:   The Buccaneer*
1939:   Union Pacific*; Tumbleweeds (1925 reissue)
1940:   North West Mounted Police*
1958:   The Buccaneer*

ED SULLIVAN

1933:   Mr. Broadway

EDWARD DEAN SULLIVAN

1935:   The People's Enemy (G. Kahn)

FRED G. SULLIVAN

1982:   Cold River

T. SULLIVAN

1979: Cocaine Cowboys*

WALLACE SULLIVAN

1933: Walls of Gold (E. Seward)
1935: Just My Luck (S. Cleethorpe)
1942: Sabotage Squad*
1943: I Escaped from the Gestapo (H. Blankfort);
       Spy Train*

ARNE SULTAN

1980: The Nude Bomb*

A. M. SURGAL

1965: Mickey One

HENRY SUSO

1978: Deathsport (D. Stewart)

EDWARD SUTHERLAND (1895-1974) director

1932: Sky Devils (J. March)

JOHN SUTHERLAND

1947: Too Many Winners

SIDNEY SUTHERLAND

1932: The Match King (H. Branch)
1933: I Loved a Woman (C. Kenyon); Ladies They
       Talk About*
1934: Friends of Mr. Sweeney*; Hi Nellie (A.
       Finkel); I Sell Anything (B. Holmes); I've

785

Got Your Number (W. Duff)
1936: The Leavenworth Case (A. DeMond); Sitting on the Moon*
1945: Divorce (H. Gates)
1946: Wife Wanted (C. Coleman)

BILL SVANOE

1982: Waltz Across Texas

LESLIE SWABACKER

1936: The Vigilantes Are Coming (ser.)*
1937: Secret Agent X-9 (ser.)*
1943: The Batman (ser.)*; The Phantom (ser.)*; Spy Train*
1944: The Desert Hawk (ser.)*
1945: Northwest Trail (H. Gates)
1947: Where the North Begins (B. Burbridge); Jack Armstrong (ser.)*

FRANCIS SWANN

1944: Shine On, Harvest Moon; Make Your Own Bed (E. Joseph)
1946: The Time, the Place and the Girl*
1947: Love and Learn*
1948: Jungle Patrol; The Gay Intruders
1950: Belle of Old Mexico (B. Ropes); 711 Ocean Drive (R. English)
1951: The Barefoot Mailman (J. Gunn); Tarzan's Peril (S. Newman)

LOGAN SWANSON

1964: The Last Man on Earth (U.S./Ital.; W. Leicester)

HAROLD SWANTON

1968: The Ballad of Josie
1969: Rascal

786

MILES HOOD SWARTHOUT

1976:   The Shootist (S. Hale)

BERMAN SWARTZ

1954:   Duffy of San Quentin (W. Doniger); The Steel
        Cage*

CHARLES SWARTZ

1967:   It's a Bikini World (S. Rothman)
1971:   The Velvet Vampire*

CHARLES SWENSON

1977:   Dirty Duck (anim.)

KNUT SWENSON

1959:   Edge of Eternity (R. Collins)

JO SWERLING (1897-   ) playwright

1930:   Madonna of the Streets; Ladies of Leisure;
        Sisters; Rain or Shine (D. Howell); Hell's
        Island; Around the Corner
1931:   Dirigible (D. Howell); Good Bad Girl;
        Miracle Woman (D. Howell); Platinum Blonde
        (D. Howell); Ten Cents a Dance; The Last
        Parade
1932:   Attorney for the Defense; Behind the Mask
        (D. Howell); Forbidden; Hollywood Speaks (N.
        Krasna); Love Affair (D. Howell); Man
        Against Woman; War Correspondent; Washington
        Merry-Go-Round
1933:   As the Devil Commands; Below the Sea; Circus
        Queen Murder; East of Fifth Avenue; A Man's
        Castle; The Woman I Stole; The Wrecker
1934:   The Defense Rests; Lady by Choice; No
        Greater Glory; Once to Every Woman; Sisters
        Under the Skin

1935: Love Me Forever (S. Buchman); The Whole
      Town's Talking (R. Riskin)
1936: The Music Goes 'Round; Pennies from Heaven
1937: Double Wedding
1938: Dr. Rhythm (R. Connell); I Am the Law
1939: Made for Each Other; The Real Glory (R.
      Presnell)
1940: The Westerner (N. Busch)
1941: Blood and Sand; Confirm or Deny; New York
      Town (L. Meltzer)
1942: The Pride of the Yankees (H. Mankiewicz)
1943: Crash Dive
1944: Lifeboat
1945: Leave Her to Heaven
1946: It's a Wonderful Life
1953: Thunder in the East
1961: King of the Roaring Twenties

DAVID SWIFT (1919-   ) director, producer

1960: Pollyanna
1961: The Parent Trap
1962: The Interns (W. Newman)
1963: Love Is a Ball*; Under the Yum Yum Tree (L.
      Roman)
1964: Good Neighbor Sam*
1967: How to Succeed in Business Without Really
      Trying
1978: Candleshoe (R. Sisson)
1980: Foolin' Around (M. Kane)

DON SWIFT

1935: Thunder Mountain (D. Jarrett); Calling of
      Dan Matthews*; Whispering Smith Speaks (D.
      Jarrett)
1936: Wild Brian Kent*; Let's Sing Again (D.
      Jarrett); The Mine with the Iron Door (D.
      Jarrett)

PAUL SYLBERT

1971: The Steagle

ROBERT SYLVESTER

1953: The Joe Louis Story

BURKE SYMON

1938: Birth of a Baby (doc.; A. Jarrett)
1948: In This Corner (F. Niblo)

T

GEORGE TABORI

1953: I Confess (W. Archibald)
1959: The Journey
1972: Parades

BESS TAFFEL

1947: A Likely Story
1951: Elopement

TOM TAGGART

1954: Gog

DON TAIT

1969: Hell's Angels '69
1971: Chrome and Hot Leather*; One More Train to
       Rob (D. Nelson)
1972: Snowball Express*
1974: The Castaway Cowboys
1975: The Apple Dumpling Gang
1976: The Shaggy D.A.; Treasure of Matacumbe
1979: The North Avenue Irregulars; The Apple
       Dumplng Gang Rides Again; Unidentified
       Flying Oddball
1980: Herbie Goes Bananas

MONROE TALBOT

1935: Wagon Trail

1936:   Ghost Town; Hair-Trigger Casey; Wildcat
        Saunders; Aces Wild
1939:   Lure of the Wasteland

GREGG TALLAS

1951:   Prehistoric Women (S. Abarbanel)

ROBERT TALLMAN

1940:   Slightly Honorable
1956:   The Price of Fear

WILLIAM TALMAN

1956:   I've Lived Before (N. Jolley)
1957:   Joe Dakota (N. Jolley)

DANIEL TAMKUS

1970:   The Way We Live Now (B. Brown)

HARRY TAMPA

1979:   Nocturna - Granddaughter of Dracula

NAT TANCHUCK

1950:   I Killed Geronimo (S. Neuman); Federal Man
        (S. Neuman)
1951:   The Hoodlum (S. Neuman)
1952:   Buffalo Bill in Tomahawk Territory (S.
        Neuman)
1957:   Garden of Eden

JOHN TANSEY

1930:   Romance of the West (R. Tansey)

ROBERT E. TANSEY (-1951) also ROBERT EMMET

1929: Pals of the Prairie (F. Clark)
1930: Romance of the West (J. Tansey)
1931: Riders of Rio
1932: The Galloping Kid
1935: Paradise Canyon (L. Parsons); Westward Ho*;
       The New Frontier; Law of the 45's; Courage
       of the North; Timber Terrors
1936: The Oregon Trail*; Pinto Rustlers; Men of
       the Plains; Song of the Gringo*; Headin' for
       the Rio Grande
1937: Trouble in Texas; Hittin' the Trail; Sing,
       Cowboy, Sing; Riders of the Rockies; Riders
       of the Dawn; God's Country and the Man;
       Stars over Arizona (E. Adams); Where Trails
       Divide; Danger Valley; Romance of the
       Rockies
1938: The Painted Trail; Man's Country; Mexicali
       Kid; Where the Buffalo Roam; Gun Packer;
       Wild Horse Canyon
1939: Drifting Westward; Trigger Smith; Man from
       Texas; Across the Plains; Overland Mail;
       Westward Stage
1940: Rhythm of the Rio Grande; The Cowboy from
       Sundown (R. Lynch); The Golden Trail*;
       Rainbow over the Range*; Arizona Frontier;
       Take Me Back to Oklahoma; Rollin' Home to
       Texas; Westbound Stage
1941: Silver Stallion; Wanderers of the West;
       Dynamite Canyon (F. Kavanaugh); The Driftin'
       Kid (F. Kavanaugh); Riding the Sunset Trail
       (F. Kavanaugh); Lone Star Lawmen (F.
       Kavanaugh)
1942: Western Mail (F. Kavanaugh); Arizona
       Roundup; Where Trails End (F. Kavanaugh)
1943: Two Fisted Justice; Death Valley Rangers*;
       Thundering Trails*
1949: Riders of the Dusk (A. Buffington)
1951: Badman's Gold (A. Lockwood)

DANIEL TARADASH (1913-   )

1939: Golden Boy*
1940: A Little Bit of Heaven (G. Purcell)
1949: Knock on Any Door (J. Monks)
1952: Don't Bother to Knock; Rancho Notorious

```
1953:   From Here to Eternity
1954:   Desiree
1955:   Picnic
1956:   Storm Center (E. Moll)
1958:   Bell, Book and Candle
1965:   Morituri (alt. Saboteur, Code Name-Morituri)
1966:   Hawaii (D. Trumbo)
1969:   Castle Keep (D. Rayfiel)
1971:   Doctors' Wives
1977:   The Other Side of the Mountain (H. Raucher)
```

ARNE TARKAS

```
1957:   Will Success Spoil Rock Hunter? (F. Tashlin)
```

FRANK TARLOFF

```
1964:   Father Goose (P. Stone)
1967:   A Guide for the Married Man
1968:   The Secret War of Harry Frigg (P. Stone);
        The Double Man (A. Hayes)
1969:   Once You Kiss a Stranger (N. Katov)
```

JAY TARSES

```
1980:   Up the Academy (T. Patchett)
1981:   The Great Muppet Caper*
```

HAROLD TARSHIS

```
1930:   The Concentratin' Kid
1932:   The Hurrican Express (ser.)*
1933:   Deception
1938:   Fast Company (M. Page)
1939:   Stop, Look and Love (S. Cowan)
1940:   High School*
1942:   Jail House Blues (P. Smith)
1943:   Mug Town*
1947:   The Adventures of Don Coyote*
```

FRANK TASHLIN (1913-1972) director

```
1947:   Variety Girl*; Ladies' Man (unc.)*
```

```
1948:  The Paleface*; The Fuller Brush Man (D.
       Freeman); One Touch of Venus (H. Kurnitz)
1949:  Love Happy*; Miss Grant Takes Richmond*
1950:  The Fuller Brush Girl; The Good Humor Man;
       Kill the Umpire
1951:  The Lemon Drop Kid (unc.)*
1952:  The First Time*; Son of Paleface*
1953:  Marry Me Again
1955:  Artists and Models*
1956:  The Girl Can't Help It (H. Baker); The
       Lieutenant Wore Skirts (A. Beich); The
       Scarlet Hour*; Hollywood or Bust (unc.; E.
       Lazarus)
1957:  Will Success Spoil Rock Hunter? (A. Tarkas)
1958:  Rock-A-Bye Baby; The Geisha Boy
1960:  Cinderfella
1961:  Bachelor Flat (B. Grossman)
1963:  Who's Minding the Store? (H. Tugend)
1964:  The Disorderly Orderly
1966:  Caprice (J. Jason)
1968:  The Private Navy of Sgt. O'Farrell; The
       Shakiest Gun in the West (E. Hartmann)
```

ROBERT TASKER

```
1932:  Doctor X (E. Baldwin); Hell's Highway*
1933:  The Great Jasper (H. Hannemann)
1935:  A Notorious Gentleman (L. Atlas)
1936:  The Accusing Finger*
1939:  Back Door to Heaven*
1940:  The Secret Seven
1942:  Secrets of the Underground (G. Homes)
```

FRANK H. TAUSSIG

```
1953:  Perils of the Jungle (R. Smith)
```

CURTIS BROWN TAYLOR

```
1974:  Like a Crow on a June Bug
```

DAVID TAYLOR

```
1982:  Hanky Panky (H. Rosenbaum)
```

DELORES TAYLOR

1978:   Billy Jack Goes to Washington (T. Laughlin)

DWIGHT TAYLOR

1931:   Secrets of a Secretary (G. Abbott)
1932:   Are You Listening?
1933:   If I Were Free; Today We Live (E.
        Fitzgerald)
1934:   Long Lost Father
1935:   Top Hat (Allan Scott)
1936:   Follow the Fleet
1939:   The Amazing Mr. Williams*; When Tomorrow
        Comes
1940:   Rhythm on the River
1941:   I Wake Up Screaming; Kiss the Boys Goodbye
        (H. Tugend)
1942:   Nightmare
1944:   The Thin Man Goes Home (R. Riskin)
1945:   Conflict (A. Horman)
1952:   Something to Live For
1953:   Vicki
1955:   Special Delivery (R. Reisman)
1957:   Boy on a Dolphin (I. Moffat)

ERIC TAYLOR

1937:   Navy Blues (G. Kahn); The Wrong Road (G.
        Rigby)
1938:   Lady in the Morgue (R. White); Orphans of
        the Street*
1939:   Fugitive at Large (H. Gates); Trapped in the
        Sky (G. Rigby)
1940:   Black Friday (C. Siodmak); Ellery Queen,
        Master Detective
1941:   The Black Cat*; Ellery Queen and the Murder
        Ring (G. Purcell); Ellery Queen and the
        Perfect Crime; Ellery Queen's Penthouse
        Mystery
1942:   Enemy Agents Meet Ellery Queen; Close Call
        for Ellery Queen; Desperate Chance for
        Ellery Queen
1943:   Crime Doctor's Strangest Case; No Place for

a Lady; The Phantom of the Opera (S.
Hoffenstein); Son of Dracula
1944:   The Whistler
1945:   The Crime Doctor's Courage; Shadows of the
        Night; The Crime Doctor's Warning; Dick
        Tracy
1946:   Just Before Dawn (A. Wisberg); The
        Mysterious Intruder; The Spider Woman
        Strikes Back; The Truth About Murder*
1947:   Dick Tracy Meets Gruesome (R. White)
1949:   The Devil's Henchman; Prison Warden; The
        Secret of St. Ives
1950:   North of the Great Divide; Destination Big
        House
1951:   Heart of the Rockies; South of Caliente;
        Pals of the Golden West (A. DeMond)
1952:   Colorado Sundown (W. Lively)

HENRY TAYLOR

1930:   Canyon Hawk (A. J. Neitz); Breed of the West
        (A. J. Neitz)
1931:   Red Fork Range (A. Neitz)
1938:   Juvenile Court*; Who Killed Gail Preston?
        (R. Kent)

LAWRENCE TAYLOR

1941:   White Eagle (ser.)*
1947:   Devil Ship; Philo Vance's Secret Mission
1950:   The Jackie Robinson Story (Arthur Mann)

MATT TAYLOR

1929:   Red Hot Speed (G. Lehman); Skinner Steps
        Out; Tonight at Twelve
1930:   Dames Ahoy!; Young Desire (W. Reeve)
1931:   The Lion and the Lamb

RAY TAYLOR

1948:   Frontier Revenge

RENEE TAYLOR

1970: Lovers and Other Strangers*
1971: Made for Each Other (James Bologna)

REX TAYLOR

1930: Big Boy (W. Wells)
1931: Sit Tight
1933: High Gear*
1936: Sitting on the Moon*
1937: The Mandarin Mystery*
1938: Dick Tracy Returns (ser.)*; Hawk of the
      Wilderness (ser.)*
1939: Daredevils of the Red Circle (ser.)*; Dick
      Tracy's G-Men (ser.)*

RICHARD C. TAYLOR

1958: Ambush at Cimarron Pass (J. Butler)
1978: Stingray

ROBERT TAYLOR

1974: Nine Lives of Fritz the Cat (anim.)*
1982: Heidi's Song (anim.)*

ROBERT LEWIS TAYLOR

1957: The Silken Affair

SAM TAYLOR (1895-1958) director

1930: DuBarry, Woman of Passion
1931: Kiki
1934: The Cat's Paw

SAMUEL W. TAYLOR

1951: The Man with My Face (T. J. McGowan)
1954: Bait
1956: The Eddy Duchin Story

```
1957:   The Monte Carlo Story
1958:   Vertigo (A. Coppel)
1961:   Goodbye Again; The Pleasure of His Company
1966:   Three on a Couch (B. Ross)
1967:   Rosie!
1969:   Topaz
1971:   The Love Machine
```

STEPHEN TAYLOR

```
1975:   The Man Who Would Not Die*
```

THEODORE TAYLOR

```
1973:   Showdown
```

ZARA TAZIL

```
1935:   Lawless Borders; The Reckless Buckaroo
1936:   Blazing Justice; Outlaws of the Range
```

CHARLES TEDFORD (-1954)

```
1941:   Here Comes Happiness
1955:   Wakamba
```

FRANK TELFORD

```
1968:   Bamboo Saucer
1969:   Hello Down There (J. McGreevey)
```

GEORGE TEMPLETON

```
1942:   On the Sunny Side (L. Hayward)
```

WILLIAM TENNANT

```
1975:   Cleopatra Jones and the Casino of Gold
```

DEL TENNEY

1964: The Curse of the Living Corpse

BERT TENZER

1969: Two Thousand Years Later
1973: Free (doc.)
1977: The Day the Music Died

WILLIAM TERHUNE

1936: Kelly the Second*

COURTNEY TERRETT

1931: Hush Money*; Quick Millions (R. Brown);
       Reckless Living
1932: The Famous Ferguson Case (H. Thew); Love Is
       a Racket
1933: Made on Broadway; 20,000 Years in Sing Sing
       (R. Lord)

GEORGE TERWILLIGER

1935: Ouango (alt. Crime of Voodoo)

STEVE TESICH

1979: Breaking Away
1981: Eyewitness; Four Friends
1982: The World According to Garp

JOAN TEWKESBURY

1974: Thieves Like Us*
1975: Nashville

EUGENE THACKERY

1941: Unfinished Business
1942: Lady in a Jam*

799

PATRICIA THACKERY

1977:   Raggedy Ann and Andy (anim.)

SYLVIA THALBERG

1930:   Montana Moon
1931:   New Moon (F. Butler); This Modern Age*
1932:   When a Feller Needs a Friend (F. Butler)
1933:   Christopher Bean (L. Johnson)
1934:   Now and Forever (V. Lawrence)
1936:   A Son Comes Home

JOSEPH THAN

1946:   Deception (J. Collier)

MORTH THAW

1974:   The Harrad Summer (S. Zacharias)

TIFFANY THAYER

1932:   If I Had a Million*

SID THEIL

1952:   The Maverick
1953:   Rebel City; The Homesteaders (G. Milton);
        Vigilante Terror

GEORGE THEOKIS

1974:   The Black Six
1975:   The Candy Tangerine Man; Lady Cocoa

PAUL THEROUX

1979:   Saint Jack*

JACQUES THERY

1946:   To Each His Own*

HARVEY THEW

1929:   The Hottentot; Love in the Desert (P.
        Percy); The Sacred Flame; Tiger Rose (G.
        Rigby)
1930:   Song of the West; Dumbbells in Ermine; Show
        Girl in Hollywood; Sinners' Holiday
1931:   Expensive Women; Illicit; Mad Genius (J.
        Alexander); Public Enemy
1932:   The Famous Ferguson Case (C. Terrett);
        Silver Dollar (G. Erickson); Stranger in
        Town (C. Erickson); Two Seconds; Woman from
        Monte Carlo
1933:   She Done Him Wrong (J. Bright); Supernatural
        (B. Marlow); Terror Aboard (M. Seff)
1934:   Death on the Diamond*; Murder in the Private
        Car*; Operator 13*
1935:   Transient Lady (A. Caesar)
1936:   Trail of the Lonesome Pine*
1937:   Four Days' Wonder (M. Uris)

WILLIAM THIELE (1890-1975) director   Aust.

(American films only)
1946:   The Madonna's Secret (B. Foote)

JOE THIRTY

1972:   J.C. (W. McGaha)

THOMAS THITELEY

1932:   Pleasure (J. Von Ronkel)

ROBERT THOEREN

1939:   Hotel Imperial (G. Gabriel)

801

```
1941:   Rage in Heaven (C. Isherwood)
1944:   Mrs. Parkington (P. James)
1946:   Temptation
1948:   An Act of Murder (M. Blankfort)
1949:   The Fighting O'Flynn (D. Fairbanks, Jr.)
1950:   Captain Carey, U.S.A.; September Affair
1951:   Operation X (W. Rose)
1960:   Between Time and Eternity (Germ.)
```

ROBERT THOM

```
1966:   All the Fine Young Cannibals; The
        Subterraneans
1968:   Wild in the Streets
1969:   Angel, Angel, Down We Go
1970:   Bloody Mama
1975:   Crazy Mama; Death Race 2000 (C. Griffith)
1976:   The Witch Who Came from the Sea
```

A. E. THOMAS

```
1936:   Everybody's Old Man (P. McNutt)
1937:   Good Old Soak
```

ANNA THOMAS

```
1982:   The End of August*
```

FAITH THOMAS

```
1934:   I Can't Escape
```

GUY THOMAS

```
1980:   Wholly Moses!
```

JACK THOMAS

```
1959:   The Lone Texan (J. Landis)
1960:   Thirteen Fighting Men (R. Hammer)
1961:   20,000 Eyes
1962:   We'll Bury You! (doc.)
```

1976: Embryo (A. Doohan)

JAMES THOMAS

1968: Suburban Roulette

JERRY THOMAS

1949: The Fighting Redhead (P. Franklin); Cowboy
      and the Prizefighter

LOWELL THOMAS (1892-   ) journalist, news
      commentator

1957: Search for Paradise (doc.)*

MICHAEL THOMAS

1975: Truckin'

R. L. THOMAS

1981: Ticket to Heaven (A. Cameron)

ROSS THOMAS

1982: Hammett (D. O'Flaherty)

TED THOMAS

1945: Out of the Depths (M. Berkeley)
1946: Talk About a Lady (R. Weil)
1965: Nightmare in the Sun (F. Lawrence)

WILLIAM C. THOMAS

1976: Cat Murkil and the Silks

BOB THOMPSON

1975:   Hearts of the West

DONALD G. THOMPSON

1976:   Project: Kill
1978:   The Evil

ERNEST THOMPSON

1981:   On Golden Pond

FRANKLIN THOMPSON

1982:   Forced Vengeance

HARLAN THOMPSON

1930:   The Big Party
1931:   Girls Demand Excitement
1932:   He Learned About Women (R. Harris); The
        Phantom President (W. DeLeon)
1933:   I'm No Angel (M. West)
1934:   Here Is My Heart*; Kiss and Make Up*
1935:   Ruggles of Red Gap*; Ship Cafe (H. Fields)
1936:   It's a Great Life (P. Smith)

JIM THOMPSON

1957:   Paths of Glory*

KEENE THOMPSON

1930:   True to the Navy (D. Anderson)
1931:   Fighting Caravans*; Caught (A. Leahy); June
        Moon (J. Mankiewicz); Palmy Days*
1932:   The Last Man (F. Faragoh)
1933:   The Cheyenne Kid; Air Hostess (G. Milton)
1934:   Many Happy Returns*; Springtime for Henry
        (F. Tuttle)
1935:   Love in Bloom*; Paris in Spring*

MORTON THOMPSON

1941: Two in a Taxi*
1946: My Brother Talks to Horses

PEGGY THOMPSON

1938: King of the Newsboys (L. Weitzenkorn)

THOMAS THOMPSON

1963: Cattle King

ALAN THORNHILL

1960: The Crowning Experience (doc.)

STEVEN THORNLEY

1980: Hangar 18

E. J. THORNTON

1935: The Judgment Book; Riddle Ranch (L.
       Jefferson)

RALPH THORNTON

1957: I Was a Teen-Age Werewolf; Blood of Dracula

RICHARD THORPE (1896-   ) director

1931: The Lawless Woman*

WALLACE THURMAN

1934: Tomorrow's Children (C. Wilbur)
1935: High School Girl

GEORGE TIBBLES

1966:   Munster, Go Home*
1967:   Tammy and the Millionaire
1971:   How to Frame a Figg

ERNEST TIDYMAN

1971:   Shaft (J. Black); The French Connection
1972:   Shaft's Big Score!
1973:   High Plains Drifter
1975:   Report to the Commissioner (A. Mann)
1976:   Street People (R. Kleiser)
1979;   A Force of One

JAMES TOBACK

1974:   The Gambler
1978:   Fingers
1982:   Love and Money

SARETT TOBIAS

1945:   She Wouldn't Say Yes*
1946:   Tars and Spars*

JEROME TODD

1948:   Inner Sanctum

RUTH TODD

1933:   Cornered

MEL TOLKIN

1966:   Last of the Secret Agents?

MAURICE TOMBRAGEL

```
1939:   Legion of Lost Flyers
1940:   Danger on Wheels; Zanzibar (M. Wright)
1941:   Men of the Timberland (G. Jay); Horror
        Island (V. McLeod); Mutiny in the Arctic (V.
        McLeod); Raiders of the Desert (V. McLeod)
1942:   Danger in the Pacific (W. Doniger);
        Sweetheart of the Fleet (A. Duffy); Stand By
        All Networks*
1943:   Two Senoritas from Chicago (S. Rubin)
1944:   The Great Alaskan Mystery (ser.; G.
        Plympton); Mystery of the River Boat (ser.)
1947:   The Lone Wolf in Mexico (M. Goldsmith)
1948:   The Return of the Whistler (E. Bock); The
        Creeper; Highway 13; The Prince of Thieves;
        Trapped by Boston Blackie; Thunder in the
        Pines
1949:   Arson, Inc.; Boston Blackie's Chinese
        Venture; Sky Liner
1950:   Motor Patrol (O. Hampton); The Daltons'
        Women (R. Ormond); Hostile Country (R.
        Ormond); Marshal of Heldorado (R. Ormond);
        Colorado Ranger (R. Ormond); West of the
        Brazos (R. Ormond); Crooked River (R.
        Ormond); Fast on the Draw (R. Ormond)
1951:   Man from Sonora; Lawless Cowboys; Kentucky
        Jubilee (R. Ormond)
1952:   Night Raiders
1957:   The Dalton Girls
1958:   Fort Bowie; Street of Darkness (M. Wald)
1962:   Moon Pilot
1967:   Monkeys, Go Home!
```

JOHN TOMERLIN

```
1963:   Operation Bikini
```

PETER TOMPKINS

```
1978:   The Secret Life of Plants*
```

BURT TOPPER

```
1958:   Hell Squad
1959:   The Diary of a High School Bride*; Tank
        Commandos
```

1964:   War Is Hell
1971:   The Hard Ride
1976:   The Day the Lord Got Busted

FREDERICK TORBERG

1944:   Voice in the Wind

JOAN TORRES

1972:   Blacula (R. Koenig)
1973:   Scream, Blacula, Scream*

MIGUEL G. TORRES

1939:   The Mad Empress*

IVAN TORS (1916–   ) director, producer

1947:   Song of Love*
1949:   That Forsyte Woman*; In the Good Old
        Summertime*
1950:   Watch the Birdie*
1952:   Storm over Tibet (S. Meyer)
1953:   The Magnetic Monster (C. Siodmak); The Glass
        Wall (M. Shane); The Mask of the Himalayas

DAN TOTHEROH

1933:   The Zoo in Budapest*
1934:   Count of Monte Cristo*
1935:   Remember the Night*
1938:   The Dawn Patrol (S. Miller)
1941:   All That Money Can Buy (S. V. Benet)
1954:   Roogie's Bump (J. Hanley)

WELLYN TOTMAN

1931:   Sunrise Trail; God's Country and the Man;
        Rider of the Plains; The Ridin' Fool; The
        Nevada Buckaroo; Mother and Son; Ships of
        Hate

1932:   Forgotten Women (A. Buffington); Ghost City
        (H. Fraser); Vanishing Men; Riders of the
        West; Texas Pioneers (H. Fraser); From
        Broadway to Cheyenne; Hidden Valley; The Man
        from Arizona; Young Blood; Lucky Larrigan;
        Galloping Thru; The Fighting Champ; Riders
        of the Desert
1933:   Son of the Border (H. Shumate); Crashing
        Broadway; The Fighting Texans (C. Roberts);
        Carnival Lady
1934:   Mystery Liner
1935:   Confidential (O. Cooper); Ladies Crave
        Excitement; One Frightened Night; Waterfront
        Lady
1936:   Dancing Feet*; Down to the Sea (R. Johnson);
        Girl from Mandalay (A. Bohem)
1937:   Exiled to Shanghai
1938:   Gangs of New York*; Wanted by the Police
1939:   Boys' Reformatory (R. Trampe); Fighting
        Thoroughbreds; Tough Kid
1941:   The Deadly Game

ARTHUR B. TOURTELLOT

1964:   The Guns of August (doc.)

GENE TOWNE

1930:   The Czar of Broadway; Loose Ankles
1931:   Goldie (P. Perez)
1932:   Business and Pleasure (W. Counselman);
        Hypnotized*
1933:   The Billion Dollar Scandal (G. Baker);
        Broadway Thru a Keyhole (G. Baker); I Love
        That Man (G. Baker)
1935:   Every Night at Eight (G. Baker); Mary Burns,
        Fugitive*; Shanghai*
1936:   The Case Against Mrs. Ames (G. Baker)
1937:   History Is Made at Night (G. Baker);
        Stand-In (G. Baker); You Only Live Once (G.
        Baker)
1938:   Joy of Living*
1939:   Eternally Yours (G. Baker)
1940:   Swiss Family Robinson*; Tom Brown's School
        Days*
1954:   Top Banana

ROBERT TOWNE

1960: The Last Woman on Earth (alt. World Without
       Women)
1965: The Tomb of Ligeia)
1968: Villa Rides (S. Peckinpah)
1973: The Last Detail
1974: Chinatown
1975: Shampoo (W. Beatty); The Yakuza (P.
       Schrader)
1982: Personal Best

SPENCER TOWNE

1938: Prison Train (Shepard Traube)

JACK TOWNLEY

1929: The Bachelor Girl; Father and Son
1930: The Call of the Circus; The Last Dance
1931: The Avenger (G. Morgan)
1932: Bachelor Mother*
1933: Strange People
1936: The Last Outlaw (J. Twist); Mummy's Boys*;
       Silly Billies (A. Boasberg)
1937: All over Town (J. Chodorov); Meet the
       Missus*
1938: The Higgins Family (P. Smith); Orphans of
       the Street*; Romance on the Run
1939: The Covered Trailer; My Wife's Relatives;
       Should Husbands Work? (T. Caven)
1940: Mexican Spitfire Out West (C. Roberts);
       Grandpa Goes to Town; Money to Burn;
       Scatterbrain (V. Burton)
1941: Ice- Capades*; Puddin'head (M. Gross);
       Rookies on Parade*; Sis Hopkins*
1942: The Great Gildersleeve (J. Josephson); Joan
       of Ozark*; The Traitor Within
1943: Gildersleeve's Bad Day; Here Comes Elmer (S.
       Davis); Petticoat Larceny (S. Palmer)
1944: Yellow Rose of Texas; Rosie, the Riveter (A.
       Leslie); Jamboree; Goodnight, Sweetheart (I.
       Dawn); Faces in the Fog
1945: Utah (J. Butler); Bells of Rosarita; The

Chicago Kid; Hitchhike to Happiness
1946:   My Pal Trigger (J. Butler); One Exciting
        Week (J. Butler)
1947:   The Last Round-Up (E. Snell)
1949:   Riders of the Whistling Pines
1950:   The Blazing Sun
1951:   Honeychile (C. E. Roberts); Havana Rose (C.
        Roberts); Cuban Fireball (C. E. Roberts);
        Oklahoma Annie
1952:   The Fabulous Senorita (C. Roberts)
1956:   Crashing Las Vegas; Hot Shots (E. Ullman)
1957:   The Disembodied; The Crooked Circle; Up in
        Smoke

LEO TOWNSEND

1941:   It Started with Eve (N. Krasna)
1942:   Seven Sweethearts (W. Reisch)
1944:   Chip off the Old Block (E. Conrad)
1946:   Night and Day*
1947:   That Way with Women
1950:   Southside 1-1000 (B. Ingster)
1952:   One Big Affair
1953:   Dangerous Crossing
1954:   The Siege at Red River (S. Boehm)
1955:   A Life in the Balance (R. Presnell); Running
        Wild; White Feather (D. Daves)
1956:   Flight to Hong Kong (E. O'Callaghan)
1957:   Four Boys and a Gun (P. Yordan); Shadow on
        the Window (D. Harmon)
1958:   Fraulein
1964:   Bikini Beach*
1965:   Beach Blanket Bingo (W. Asher); How to Stuff
        a Wild Bikini (W. Asher)
1966:   Fireball 500 (W. Asher)

RAY TRAMPE

1936:   Ace Drummond (ser.)*
1937:   Wild West Days (ser.)*; Jungle Jim (ser.)*;
        Radio Patrol (ser.)*; Secret Agent X-9
        (ser.)*; Tim Tyler's Luck (ser.)*
1938:   Mars Attacks the World (edited Flash Gordon
        Serial)*; Flash Gordon's Trip to Mars
        (ser.)*; Red Barry (ser.)*
1939:   Boys' Reformatory (W. Totman); Buck Rogers

811

(ser.; N. Hall)

ROBERT TRASKER

1932: Secrets of the French Police (S. Ornitz)

JOE TRAUB

1936: Earthworm Tractors*

SHEPARD TRAUBE

1938: Prison Train (Spencer Towne)
1939: Goose Step (alt. Beasts of Berlin)

JOHN-MICHAEL TREBELAK

1973: Godspell (D. Greene)

RICHARD TREGASKIS

1951: The Wild Blue Yonder
1953: Fair Wind to Java

MAX TRELL

1947: High Conquest
1948: Sixteen Fathoms Deep
1951: New Mexico
1954: Hell Below Zero (A. Coppel)
1956: The Last Man to Hang (Brit.; I. Montague)

LUIS TRENKER

1932: Doomed Battalion*; The Rebel (E. Knopf)

MICHAEL TREVELYAN

1932: Daring Danger

PAUL TRIPP

1966:   The Christmas That Almost Wasn't

VICTOR TRIVAS (1896-1970) director   Rus.

(American films only)
1950:   Where the Sidewalk Ends (B. Hecht)
1951:   The Secret of Convict Lake (O. Paul)

BARRY TRIVERS

1934:   Romance in the Rain*
1935:   Lady Tubbs (N. Busch); Manhattan Moon*;
        Night Life of the Gods; Three Kids and a
        Queen*
1936:   Here Comes Trouble*; Three Cheers for Love
1937:   Behind the Mike
1938:   Army Girl (S. Ornitz); That's My Story
1939:   The Arizona Wildcat (J. Cady); Boy Friend
        (J. Hoffman)
1940:   River's End (B. Millhauser); Dreaming Out
        Loud*; Girl in 313 (C. Adams); South of Suez
1941:   Flight from Destiny; International Squadron;
        The Men in Her Life*; The Wagons Roll at
        Night (F. Niblo)
1942:   Army Surgeon (E. Lavery); Flying Tigers (K.
        Gamet)
1943:   There's Something About a Soldier (Horace
        McCoy); What a Woman! (T. Lewis)
1947:   Intrigue (G. Slavin)

GUY TROSPER

1941:   I'll Wait for You
1942:   Crossroads; Eyes in the Night (H. Rogers)
1949:   The Stratton Story (D. Morrow)
1950:   Devil's Doorway
1951:   Inside Straight
1954:   The Steel Cage*
1955:   The Americano; Many Rivers to Cross (H.
        Brown)
1956:   The Girl He Left Behind
1957:   Jailhouse Rock

1958:   Darby's Rangers
1961:   One-Eyed Jacks (C. Willingham)
1962:   Bird Man of Alcatraz
1965:   The Spy Who Came in from the Cold (Paul
        Dehn)

LAMAR TROTTI (1900-1952) producer

1933:   The Man Who Dared (D. Nichols)
1934:   Bachelor of Arts; Call It Luck*; Hold That
        Girl (D. Nichols); Judge Priest (D. Nichols)
1935:   Life Begins at 40*; Steamboat 'Round the
        Bend (D. Nichols); This Is the Life (A.
        Horman)
1936:   The Country Beyond (A. Commandini); Can This
        Be Dixie?; Career Woman; The First Baby;
        Gentle Julia; Pepper; Ramona
1937:   Slave Ship*; This Is My Affair (A. Rivkin);
        Wife, Doctor and Nurse*
1938:   Alexander's Ragtime Band*; The Baroness and
        the Butler*; Gateway; In Old Chicago (S.
        Levien); Kentucky (J. Foote)
1939:   Drums Along the Mohawk (S. Levien); The
        Story of Alexander Graham Bell; Young Mr.
        Lincoln
1940:   Brigham Young -- Frontiersman
1941:   Hudson's Bay; Belle Starr
1942:   Tales of Manhattan*; Thunder Birds; To the
        Shores of Tripoli
1943:   The Ox-Bow Incident; Guadalcanal Diary; The
        Immortal Sergeant
1944:   Wilson
1945:   A Bell for Adano (N. Raine)
1946:   The Razor's Edge
1947:   Captain from Castile; Mother Wore Tights
1948:   The Walls of Jericho; Yellow Sky; When My
        Baby Smiles at Me
1949:   You're My Everything (W. Hays)
1950:   American Guerrilla in the Philippines;
        Cheaper by the Dozen; My Blue Heaven (C.
        Binyon)
1951:   As Young As You Feel; I'd Climb the Highest
        Mountain
1952:   O. Henry's Full House*; Stars and Stripes
        Forever; With a Song in My Heart

814

GUERDON TRUEBLOOD

1972:   Welcome Home, Soldier Boys
1976:   The Last Hard Man

CHRISTOPHER TRUMBO

1975:   Brannigan*

DALTON TRUMBO (1905-1976) novelist (pseudonyms:
        Marcel Klauber, Sally Stubblefield, Robert
        Rich, Les Crutchfield)

1936:   Love Begins at 20 (T. Reed); Road Gang
1937:   Devil's Playground*
1938:   A Man to Remember; Fugitive for a Night
1939:   Career (B. Granet); Five Came Back*; The
        Flying Irishman (E. Pagano); Sorority House
1940:   A Bill of Divorcement; Curtain Call; Heaven
        with a Barbed Wire Fence*; Kitty Foyle (D.
        Stewart); We Who Are Young
1942:   The Remarkable Andrew
1943:   A Guy Named Joe; Tender Comrade
1944:   Thirty Seconds over Tokyo
1945:   Our Vines Have Tender Grapes
1951:   The Prowler (unc.; H. Butler)
1954:   Carnival Story (unc.)*
1956:   The Boss (unc.)*; The Brave One (unc.; H.
        Franklin)
1957:   The Green-Eyed Blonde (unc.)
1958:   Cowboy (unc.)*
1960:   Exodus; Spartacus
1961:   The Last Sunset
1962:   Lonely Are the Brave
1965:   The Sandpiper (M. Wilson)
1966:   Hawaii (D. Taradash)
1968:   The Fixer
1971:   Johnny Got His Gun; The Horsemen
1972:   F.T.A.
1973:   Executive Action; Papillon (L. Semple)

ALAN R. TRUSTMAN

1968:   The Thomas Crown Affair; Bullitt (H.
        Kleiner)

815

```
1970:   They Call Me Mr. Tibbs (J. R. Webb)
1973:   Hit! (D. Wolf); Lady Ice (H. Clemens)
1976:   The Next Man*
```

GLENN TRYON (1894-1970) actor, director

```
1934:   Bachelor Bait; Gridiron Flash; Rafter
        Romance*; The Richest Girl in the World (N.
        Krasna)
1935:   Orchids to You*
1937:   Small Town Boy
1944:   Law Men
1950:   Messenger of Peace
```

TOM TRYON

```
1972:   The Other
```

WANDA TUCHOCK

```
1929:   Hallelujah
1930:   Billy the Kid*; Not So Dumb
1931:   Sporting Blood (W. Mack); Susan Lenox, Her
        Fall and Rise
1932:   Letty Lynton (J. Meehan); Little Orphan
        Annie (T. McNamara); New Morals for Old (Z.
        Sears)
1933:   Bed of Roses; No Other Woman (B. Schubert)
1934:   Finishing School (L. Doyle)
1935:   O'Shaughnessy's Boy*
1938:   Hawaii Calls
1939:   The Llano Kid
1940:   Youth Will Be Served
1941:   For Beauty's Sake*
1944:   This Is the Life; Ladies of Washington;
        Sunday Dinner for a Soldier (M. Levy)
1945:   Nob Hill (N. Raine); Within These Walls (E.
        Ling)
1947:   The Foxes of Harrow; The Homestretch
```

LARRY TUCKER

```
1968:   I Love You, Alice B. Toklas! (P. Mazursky)
1969:   Bob and Carol and Ted and Alice (P.
```

Mazursky)
1970: 'Alex in Wonderland (P. Mazursky)

HARRY TUGEND (1898-   ) producer

1935: King of Burlesque*; The Littlest Rebel (E.
Burke); Thanks a Million (N. Johnson)
1936: Captain January*; Pigskin Parade*; The Poor
Little Rich Girl*; Sing, Baby, Sing*
1937: Ali Baba Goes to Town (J. Yellen); Love Is
News (J. Yellen); Wake Up and Live (J.
Yellen); You Can't Have Everything*; Thanks
for Listening
1938: Little Miss Broadway (J. Yellen); My Lucky
Star (J. Yellen); Sally, Irene and Mary (J.
Yellen); Thanks for Everything (C. Kenyon)
1939: Second Fiddle
1940: Little Old New York; Seven Sinners (J.
Meehan)
1941: Birth of the Blues (W. DeLeon); Caught in
the Draft; Kiss the Boys Goodbye (D. Taylor)
1942: The Lady Has Plans; Star Spangled Rhythm
1943: Let's Face It; True to Life (D. Hartman)
1946: Cross My Heart
1948: A Southern Yankee; A Song Is Born
1949: Take Me Out to the Ball Game (G. Wells)
1950: Wabash Avenue (C. Lederer)
1957: Public Pigeon No. 1
1961: Pocketful of Miracles (H. Kanter)
1963: Who's Minding the Store? (F. Tashlin)

RICHARD TUGGLE

1979: Escape from Alcatraz

KARL TUNBERG (1907-   )

1937: Life Begins in College (D. Ettinger); You
Can't Have Everything*
1938: Hold That Co-ed*; Rebecca of Sunnybrook Farm
(D. Ettinger)
1940: Down Argentine Way (D. Ware); I Was an
Adventuress*; Public Deb No. 1 (D. Ware)
1941: Tall, Dark and Handsome (D. Ware); Week-End
in Havana (D. Ware); A Yank in the R.A.F.

(D. Ware)
1942: Lucky Jordan (D. Ware); My Gal Sal*;
      Orchestra Wives (D. Ware)
1943: Dixie*
1944: Standing Room Only (D. Ware)
1945: Bring on the Girls (D. Ware); Masquerade in
      Mexico (E.J. Mayer) Kitty (D. Ware)
1947: The Imperfect Lady
1948: Up in Central Park; You Gotta Stay Happy
1950: Love That Brute*
1951: The Law and the Lady (L. Spigelgass); Night
      into Morning (L. Spigelgass)
1952: Because You're Mine (L. Spigelgass)
1954: Beau Brummel; Valley of the Kings (R.
      Pirosh)
1955: The Scarlet Coat
1957: The Seventh Sin
1959: Count Your Blessings; Libel*; Ben-Hur
1962: Taras Bulba (W. Salt); I Thank a Fool
1964: The Seventh Dawn
1965: Harlow
1968: Where Were You When the Lights Went Out? (E.
      Freeman)
1970: How Do I Love Thee? (E. Freeman)

WILLIAM TUNBERG

1944: That's My Baby! (N.T. Barrows)
1957: Old Yeller (F. Gipson)
1963: Savage Sam (F. Gipson)

IRVE TUNICK

1957: Lady of Vengeance
1958: High Hell
1960: Murder, Inc. (M. Barr)

TRISTRAM TUPPER (1886-   )

1932: Klondike
1933: The Phantom Broadcast; Self Defense
1934: Beggars in Ermine
1935: Red Hot Tires
1937: Girl Overboard; Night Key (J. Moffitt)

RON TURBEVILLE

1974:   Buster and Billie

SAUL TURELL

1963:   The Great Chase (doc.)*
1965:   The Love Goddesses (doc.; Graeme Ferguson)

JACK TURLEY

1977:   Empire of the Ants

BARBARA TURNER

1967:   Deathwatch (V. Morrow)

HELENE TURNER

1958:   Hong Kong Affair*

TERRY TURNER

1929:   Should a Girl Marry?

CATHERINE TURNEY

1945:   Mildred Pierce (R. MacDougall)
1946:   The Man I Love; My Reputation; Of Human
        Bondage; One More Tomorrow (C. Hoffman); A
        Stolen Life
1947:   Cry Wolf
1948:   Winter Meeting
1950:   No Man of Her Own (S. Benson)
1952:   Japanese War Bride
1957:   Back from the Dead

BETTY TUSHER

1968:   Psych-Out (B. Ulius)

BUD TUTTLE

1941:   Underground Rustlers*

BURL R. TUTTLE

1932:   Son of Oklahoma (G. Hull)
1934:   'Neath the Arizona Skies; Circle Canyon

FRANK TUTTLE (1892-1963) director

1934:   Springtime for Henry (K. Thompson)
1935:   All the King's Horses (E. Stephani); Two for
        Tonight

GENE TUTTLE

1942:   Rodeo Rhythm (E. Allen)

W. C. TUTTLE

1940:   The Fargo Kid

JOHN STUART TWIST (1898-1976)

1929:   The Big Diamond Robbery
1934:   West of the Pecos (M. Krims)
1935:   Annie Oakley (J. Sayre); Grand Old Girl*;
        His Family Tree (J. Sayre); Red Morning (W.
        Fox)
1936:   Yellow Dust (C. Hume); The Last Outlaw (J.
        Townley); Wanted -- Jane Turner; We Who Are
        About to Die
1937:   Annapolis Salute; Flight from Glory (D.
        Silverstein); Hitting a New High (G.
        Purcell); The Outcasts of Poker Flat*; Sea
        Devils*; The Toast of New York*
1938:   The Law West of Tombstone (C. Young); Next
        Time I Marry (H. Meinardi)
1939:   Reno; The Great Man Votes; Pacific Liner;
        The Saint Strikes Back; Three Sons; Twelve

```
          Crooked Hours
1940:  Too Many Girls
1941:  Four Jacks and a Jill; Parachute Battalion
          (Hugh Fite)
1942:  The Navy Comes Through*
1943:  Bombardier
1947:  Sinbad the Sailor; Tycoon (B. Chase)
1948:  Colorado Territory (E. North)
1950:  Dallas
1951:  Best of the Badmen (R. Andrews); Fort Worth
1952:  The Big Trees (J. Webb); The Man Behind the
          Gun (R. Buckner)
1953:  So Big
1954:  King Richard and the Crusaders
1955:  Helen of Troy (H. Gray); The Sea Chase (J.
          Bellah)
1956:  Santiago (M. Rackin); Serenade*
1957:  Band of Angels*
1958:  The Deep Six*
1959:  The FBI Story (R. Breen)
1961:  Marines, Let's Go
1964:  A Distant Trumpet
1965:  None but the Brave (Katsua Susaki)
```

JAMES TYNAN

1933: Olsen's Big Moment (H. Johnson)

U

BETTY ULIUS

1968:   Psych-Out (B. Tusher)

DAN ULLMAN

1945:   Honeymoon Ahead (V. Burton); Men in Her
         Diary (F. Herbert)
1946:   Susie Steps Out
1949:   Square Dance Jubilee (R. Ormond); Red Desert
         (R. Ormond)
1950:   Silver Raiders; Cherokee Uprising; Outlaws
         of Texas; Hot Rod
1951:   Cavalry Scout (E. Blackburn); Montana
         Desperado; Gold Raiders (E. Ullman); The
         Longhorn; The Big Gusher; Flame of Stamboul;
         Smuggler's Gold
1952:   Waco; Wild Stallion; Wyoming Roundup; Fort
         Osage; Hiawatha (A. Strawn); Kansas
         Territory; Montana Incident; Wagons West
1953:   Loose in London (E. Bernds); Hot News (C.
         Marion); The Star of Texas; The Fighting
         Lawman
1954:   The Forty-Niners; Paris Playboys*; Two Guns
         and a Badge
1955:   At Gunpoint; An Annapolis Story (G. Holmes);
         Bobby Ware Is Missing; Dial Red O; Seven
         Angry Men; Sudden Danger (E. Ullman); The
         Warriors; Wichita
1956:   Canyon River; The First Texan
1957:   Badlands of Montana; The Oklahoman
1958:   Good Day for a Hanging (M. Zimm)
1959:   The Gunfight at Dodge City (M. Goldsmith);
         Face of a Fugitive (D. Chandler); Battle of
         the Coral Sea (S. Kandel)

1961:   Mysterious Island*

ELWOOD ULLMAN

1951:   Gold Raiders (D. Ullman)
1952:   Harem Girl (E. Bernds)
1953:   The Maze; The Royal African Rifles; The
        Marksman; Kansas Pacific; Fort Vengeance;
        Clipped Wings (C. Marion)
1954:   The Bowery Boys Meet the Monster (E.
        Bernds); Jungle Gents (E. Bernds); Paris
        Playboys*
1955:   Bowery to Bagdad (E. Bernds); Jail Busters
        (E. Bernds); Ma and Pa Kettle at Waikiki (H.
        Clork); Sudden Danger (D. Ullman)
1956:   Dig That Uranium (B. Lawrence); Fighting
        Trouble; Hot Shots (J. Townley)
1957:   Spook Chasers; Chain of Evidence; Footsteps
        in the Night (A. Band); Looking for Danger
1958:   In the Money (R. Matin)
1959:   Battle Flame
1961:   Snow White and the Three Stooges (N.
        Langley)
1962:   The Three Stooges in Orbit; The Three
        Stooges Meet Hercules
1963:   The Three Stooges Go Around the World in a
        Daze
1965:   Dr. Goldfoot and the Bikini Machine (R.
        Kaufman); The Outlaws Is Coming!; Tickle Me
        (E. Bernds)
1966:   Ghost in the Invisible Bikini (L. Heyword)

EDGAR G. ULMER (1904-1972) director

1933:   Damaged Lives (Don Davis)
1943:   Corregidor (D. Malloy); My Son the Hero (D.
        Malloy)

GLADYS UNGER (-1940)

1932:   Wayward (W. Day)
1934:   Cheating Cheaters; Coming Out Party (J.
        Lasky); Countess of Monte Cristo (D.
        deWolfe); Embarrassing Moments (C. Logue);
        Glamour (D. Anderson); Great Expectations;

Romance in the Rain*
1935: Alias Mary Dow (R. Franken); Mystery of
Edwin Drood*; Rendezvous at Midnight (F.
Reyher); Strange Wives (J. Mulhauser);
Sylvia Scarlett*
1937: Daughter of Shanghai (G. Weston); Night of
Mystery (F. Partos)

EVE UNSELL

1931: Secret Call (A. Kober); Unfaithful; Up Pops
the Devil (A. Kober)

GABRIELLE UPTON

1959: Gidget
1962: Escape from East Berlin*

LEON M. URIS (1924-   ) novelist

1955: Battle Cry
1957: Gunfight at the O.K. Corral

MICHAEL H. URIS (-1967)

1937: Four Days' Wonder (H. Thew)
1944: In the Meantime, Darling (A. Kober)

PETER USTINOV (1924-   ) actor, Brit.

(American films only)
1961: Romanoff and Juliet
1962: Billy Budd (D. Bodeen)
1966: Lady L
1968: Hot Millions (I. Wallach)

V

LASZLO VADNAY

1942:   Tales of Manhattan*
1944:   Uncertain Glory (Max Brand)
1945:   The Big Show-off (R. Weil)
1947:   Copacabana*
1950:   The Great Rupert; South Sea Sinner*
1952:   No Time for Flowers (Aust.; H. Wilhelm)
1953:   Easy to Love (W. Roberts); The Great Diamond
        Robbery (M. Rackin)
1957:   Ten Thousand Bedrooms*
1962:   It Happened in Athens
1963:   Dime with a Halo (H. Wilhelm)
1966:   Way...Way Out (W. Bowers)

STEVEN A. VAIL

1979:   Scavenger Hunt (H. Harper)

ERNEST VAJDA (1887-1954) novelist, playwright

(American films only)
1929:   Marquis Preferred*
1930:   Monte Carlo; Such Men Are Dangerous
1931:   The Guardsman (C. West); The Smiling
        Lieutenant (S. Raphaelson); Son of India;
        Tonight or Never
1932:   Broken Lullaby (alt. The Man I Killed; S.
        Raphaelson); Payment Deferred (C. West);
        Smilin' Through (C. West)
1933:   Reunion in Vienna (C. West)
1934:   The Barretts of Wimpole Street*; The Merry
        Widow (S. Raphaelson)
1936:   A Woman Rebels (A. Veiller)

825

1937:   The Great Garrick; Personal Property (H.
        Mills)
1938:   Dramatic School (M. McCall); Marie
        Antoinette*
1940:   He Stayed for Breakfast*
1941:   They Dare Not Love (C. Bennett)

LUIS VALDEZ

1982:   Zoot Suit

EUGENE VALE

1950:   The Second Face
1961:   Francis of Assisi (J. Forsyth)

LESLIE VALE

1947:   Linda Be Good (G. Halasz)

ROMAN VALENTI

1974:   Terror Circus (R. Harolde)

VINCENT VALENTINI

1948:   Miracle in Harlem

BEATRICE VAN

1929:   Modern Love
1930:   Take the Heir
1933:   Night of Terror (W. Jacobs)

JOHN VAN DRUTEN

1937:   Night Must Fall; Parnell (S. Behrman)
1940:   Lucky Partners (Allan Scott); Raffles (S.
        Howard)
1941:   My Life with Caroline (A. Belgard)
1943:   Forever and a Day*; Johnny Come Lately; Old

826

Acquaintance (L. Coffee)
1944: Gaslight*
1947: Voice of the Turtle

TOM VAN DYCKE

1936: Alibi for Murder; The Man Who Lived Twice*;
Two Fisted Gentleman
1937: Counterfeit Lady

DALE VAN EVERY

1929: The Duke Steps Out (R. Schrock); Marianne
1930: Navy Blues
1931: East of Borneo; Ex-Bad Boy; A House Divided
(J. Clymer); Trader Horn*; Virtuous Husband
1932: Air Mail (F. Wead); Murders in the Rue
Morgue (T. Reed); The Unexpected Father (R.
Keith)
1933: Nagana (D. Ryan); Saturday's Millions
1934: I'll Tell the World (R. Spence); The Poor
Rich (E. Havez)
1936: More Than a Secretary (L. Starling)
1937: Captains Courageous*; Souls at Sea (G.
Jones)
1951: Sealed Cargo (R. Huggins)

OSSO VAN EYES

1949: Big Jack*

J. VAN HEARN

1969: The Hanging of Jake Ellis

H. H. VAN LOAN

1932: Docks of San Francisco

GEORGE VAN MARTER

1954: Four Guns to the Border

GEORGE VAN NOY

1976:   Freewheelin'

MELVIN VAN PEEBLES (1932-   ) director, producer

1968:   The Story of a Three-Day Pass (Fr.)
1971:   Sweet Sweetback's Baadasssss Song
1977:   Greased Lightning*

KAY VAN RIPER

1937:   A Family Affair
1938:   Judge Hardy's Children; Out West with the
        Hardys*; You're Only Young Once
1939:   Andy Hardy Gets Spring Fever; Babes in Arms
        (Jack MacGowan); The Hardys Ride High*
1941:   Lady Be Good*

RIP VAN RONKEL

1950:   Destination Moon*
1956:   The Scarlet Hour*
1958:   The High Cost of Loving

RAYMOND VAN SICKLE

1934:   Three on a Honeymoon*

VIRGINIA VAN UPP (1902-1970) producer

1934:   Pursuit of Happiness*
1935:   So Red the Rose*
1936:   Easy to Take; My American Wife; Poppy (W.
        Young); Timothy's Quest*; Too Many Parents
        (D. Malloy)
1937:   Swing High, Swing Low (O. Hammerstein)
1938:   You and Me
1939:   Cafe Society; Honeymoon in Bali
1941:   Bahama Passage; One Night in Lisbon;
        Virginia

1943:   The Crystal Ball; Young and Willing
1944:   Cover Girl; The Impatient Years; Together
        Again (F. Herbert)
1945:   She Wouldn't Say Yes*
1951:   Here Comes the Groom*

JOSEPH VAN WINKLE

1973:   The Gatling Gun (M. Hanna)
1981:   The Woman Inside

NORMAN T. VANE

1976:   Shadow of the Hawk (H.J. Wright)

JAY VANN

1938:   Tarzan's Revenge (R. Lee)

AGNES VARDA

1969:   Lions Love

MARTIN VARNO

1958:   Night of the Blood Beast

FRANCIS VEBER

1982:   Partners

ANTHONY VEILLER (1903-1965) producer

1934:   Menace (C. Sprague); The Notorious Sophie
        Lang; The Witching Hour (S. Field)
1935:   Jalna*; Seven Keys to Baldpate (W. Smith);
        Star of Midnight*; Break of Hearts*
1936:   The Ex-Mrs. Bradford; The Lady Consents (P.
        Wolfson); Winterset; A Woman Rebels (E.
        Vajda)
1937:   The Soldier and the Lady*; Stage Door (M.

```
              Ryskind)
1938:   Radio City Revels*
1939:   Disputed Passage (S. Gibney); Let Us Live
        (A. Rivkin)
1942:   Her Cardboard Lover*; Divide and Conquer
        (doc.; R. Heller)
1943:   Assignment in Brittany*; The Battle of
        Russia (doc.; R. Heller); The Battle of
        Britain (doc.); Prelude to War (doc.; E.
        Knight)
1944:   Tunisian Victory (doc.); The Battle of China
        (doc.; R. Heller)
1945:   War Comes to America (doc.); Adventure
1946:   The Stranger; The Killers (J. Huston)
1948:   State of the Union (M. Connolly)
1952:   Moulin Rouge; Red Ball Express*; Red Planet
        Mars (J. Balderston)
1955:   That Lady (Sy Bartlett)
1956:   Safari (Brit.; R. Buckner)
1957:   Monkey on My Back*
1959:   Timbuktu (P. Dudley); Solomon and Sheba
1963:   The List of Adrian Messenger
1964:   The Night of the Iguana (J. Huston)
```

BAYARD VEILLER

```
1931:   Guilty Hands
1932:   Night Court (L. Coffee); Unashamed; Arsene
        Lupin*
1933:   The Woman Accused
1941:   The Trial of Mary Dugan
```

ED VERDIER

```
1941:   The Bride Wore Crutches
1944:   Seven Days Ashore*
```

BOBBY VERNON

```
1934:   The Lone Cowboy (A. Leahy)
```

STEPHEN F. VERONA

```
1974:   The Lords of Flatbush*
```

```
1976:   Pipe Dreams
1979:   Boardwalk (L. Chapman)


BEN VERSCHLEISER

1932:   Breach of Promise (J. Goodrich)


DAVID VICTOR

1957:   Trooper Hook*


JAY VICTOR

1950:   Sarumba (Cuba)


MARK VICTOR

1981:   Death Hunt (M. Grais)
1982:   Poltergeist*


GORE VIDAL (1925-    ) novelist, playwright

1956:   The Catered Affair
1958:   I Accuse!
1959:   The Scapegoat*; Suddenly, Last Summer*
1964:   The Best Man
1966:   Is Paris Burning?*
1970:   Last of the Mobile Hot-Shots
1977:   Caligula


JOHN VIDETTE

1972:   Doomsday Voyage


KING VIDOR (1894-    ) director

1934:   Our Daily Bread*
1941:   H. M. Pulham, Esq. (Elizabeth Hill)
1956:   War and Peace*
```

JAMES VIDOS

1979: A Matter of Love (C. Vincent)

JACK VIERTEL

1981: Delusion
1982: The House Where Death Lives

PETER VIERTEL

1942: The Hard Way (D. Fuchs); Saboteur*
1949: We Were Strangers (J. Huston)
1951: Decision Before Dawn
1957: The Sun Also Rises
1958: The Old Man and the Sea
1963: Five Miles to Midnight (H. Wheeler)

SALKA VIERTEL

1933: Queen Christina*
1934: The Painted Veil*
1935: Anna Karenina*
1937: Conquest*
1941: Two-Faced Woman*
1947: Deep Valley (S. Avery)

ALAN VILLIERS

1958: Windjammer (doc.; J. Shute)

ALLEN VINCENT

1941: The Face Behind the Mask (P. Jarrico)
1947: Song of Love*
1948: Johnny Belinda (I. Von Cube)

CHUCK VINCENT

1978: Cheerleaders' Beach Party
1979: A Matter of Love (James Vidos)
1980: Hot T-Shirts (Bill Slobodian)

JESSE VINT

1977: Black Oak Conspiracy (Hugh Smith)
1979: Hometown, U.S.A.

JOE VIOLA

1971: Angels Hard As They Come (J. Demme)

LOUIS VITTES

1957: Pawnee*
1958: Gang War; Showdown at Boot Hill; Villa!; I
       Married a Monster from Outer Space
1959: Here Come the Jets; The Rebel Set (B.
       Girard); The Oregon Trail (G. Fowler)
1964: The Eyes of Annie Jones

JOHN VLAHOS

1941: Wrangler's Roost (R. Finkle); Fugitive
       Valley (R. Finkle); Saddle Mountain Roundup
       (E. Snell); Tonto Basin Outlaws; Underground
       Rustlers*
1942: Thunder River Feud (E. Snell); War Dogs
       (ret. Pride of the Army); Rock River
       Renegades (E. Snell)
1943: Man of Courage*

JESSE VOGEL

1967: Carmen, Baby

VIRGIL VOGEL

1958: Terror in the Midnight Sun (alt. Invasion of
       the Animal People; J. Warren)

JON VOIGHT

1982:   Lookin' to Get Out (A. Schwartz)

LULU VOLLMER

1934:   Spitfire (J. Murfin)

KARL VOLLMOELLER

1941:   The Shanghai Gesture*

IRMEGARD VON CUBE

1947:   Song of Love*
1948:   Johnny Belinda (A. Vincent)
1952:   The Girl in White (P. Stevenson)

JO VON RONBEO

1931:   The Sea Ghost (W. Nigh)

JO VON RONKEL

1931:   Convicted
1932:   Pleasure (T. Thiteley)

JOSEF VON STERNBERG (1894-1969) director   Aust.

(American films only)
1931:   An American Tragedy (S. Hoffenstein)
1937:   I, Claudius (unfinished)
1941:   The Shanghai Gesture*

ERICH VON STROHEIM (1885-1957) actor, director

1932:   Walking down Broadway (L. Spigelgass)
1934:   Fugitive Road*
1936:   The Devil-Doll*

KURT VONNEGUT, JR. (1922-   ) novelist

1971: Happy Birthday, Wanda June

BERNARD VORHAUS (1898-   ) director

(American films only)
1950: So Young, So Bad (J. Rouverrol)

KENNETH VOSE

1977: Greased Lightning*

V.I. VOSS

1957: Voodoo Woman (R. Bender)

W

MICHAEL WADLEIGH

1981:   Wolfen (D. Eyre)

RICHARD H. WADSACK

1979:   Screams of a Winter Night

GEORGE WAGGNER (1894-   ) director

1932:   Gorilla Ship
1933:   Sweetheart of Sigma Chi*
1934:   Girl o' My Dreams; The Line-Up; Once to
        Every Bachelor; City Limits; Among the
        Missing*
1935:   The Cowboy Millionaire (D. Jarrett); Cappy
        Ricks Returns; Champagne for Breakfast;
        Cheers of the Crowd; Dizzy Dames; The
        Healer*; Keeper of the Bees (A. Buffington);
        The Nut Farm; Spring Tonic*
1936:   Don't Get Personal*; Sea Spoilers
1937:   I Cover the War; Idol of the Crowds (H.
        Buckley); The Three Legionnaires (C
        Harbaugh)
1938:   Air Devils (H. Buckley); Midnight Intruder
        (L. Cole); The Spy Ring; State Police
1941:   Sealed Lips
1949:   The Fighting Kentuckian
1951:   Operation Pacific
1954:   Bitter Creek; Return from the Sea
1957:   Destination 60,000; Pawnee*; New Day at
        Sundown
1958:   Man from God's Country

JACK WAGNER

```
1936:   Dancing Pirate*
1948:   The Pearl (Mex.)*


JANE WAGNER

1978:   Moment by Moment
1981:   The Incredible Shrinking Woman


LEE WAINER

1950:   Holiday Rhythm


RALPH WAITE

1980:   On the Nickel


GILBERT WAKEFIELD

1932:   Aren't We All? (B. Mason)


JERRY WALD (1911-1962) producer

1934:   Gift of Gab*
1935:   Broadway Gondolier*; I Live for Love*; In
        Caliente (J. Epstein); Little Big Shot*;
        Living on Velvet (J. Epstein); Maybe It's
        Love*; Stars over Broadway (J. Epstein);
        Sweet Music*
1936:   Sing Me a Love Song (S. Herzog); Sons o'
        Guns (J. Epstein)
1937:   Hollywood Hotel*; Ready, Willing and Able*;
        Varsity Show*
1938:   Brother Rat (R. Macaulay); Garden of the
        Moon (R. Macaulay); Going Places*; Hard to
        Get*
1939:   The Kid from Kokomo (R. Macaulay); Naughty
        but Nice (R. Macaulay); On Your Toes (R.
        Macaulay); The Roaring Twenties*
1940:   Brother Rat and a Baby*; They Drive by Night
        (R. Macaulay); Three Cheers for the Irish
        (R. Macaulay); Torrid Zone (R. Macaulay)
1941:   Manpower (R. Macaulay); Million Dollar Baby;
```

Navy Blues*; Out of the Fog*; Two in a Taxi*

MALVIN WALD

1943:   Jive Junction*
1948:   Behind Locked Doors (E. Ling); The Naked
        City (A. Maltz)
1950:   Outrage*
1955:   Battle Taxi
1958:   Street of Darkness (M. Tombragel)
1959:   Al Capone (H. Greenberg)
1961:   The Steel Claw*
1979:   In Search of Historic Jesus (Jack Jacobs);
        Legend of Sleepy Hollow (Jack Jacobs)

JOE WALDERS

1976:   Death Machines (P. Kyriazi)

FRANK WALDMAN

1944:   Bathing Beauty*
1960:   High Time (T. Waldman)
1963:   Love Is a Ball*
1968:   The Party*; Inspector Clouseau (T. Waldman)
1970:   Dirty Dingus Magee*
1975:   The Return of the Pink Panther (B. Edwards)
1976:   The Pink Panther Strikes Again (B. Edwards)
1978:   Revenge of the Pink Panther*
1982:   Trail of the Pink Panther*

TOM WALDMAN

1960:   High Time (F. Waldman)
1963:   Love Is a Ball*
1968:   The Party*; Inspector Clouseau (F. Waldman)
1970:   Dirty Dingus Magee*
1982:   Trail of the Pink Panther*

GY WALDRON

1974:   Moonrunners

JOHN A. WALDRON

1932: Hypnotized*

GRANVILLE WALKER

1939: Barricade

GERTRUDE WALKER

1943: Whispering Footsteps
1944: Silent Partner; End of the Road (D. Clift)
1946: Crime of the Century*
1951: Insurance Investigator

H. M. WALKER

1931: Pardon Us
1932: Pack Up Your Troubles; They Just Had to Get
       Married (G. Lehman)
1933: Her First Mate*; Son of a Sailor (E. Pagano)
1935: The Affair of Susan*

JOSEPH A. WALKER

1976: The River Niger

ROBERT G. WALKER

1931: The Kid from Arizona
1932: Tex Takes a Holiday

TURNLEY WALKER

1958: Wolf Larsen (J. DeWitt)

CHARLES WALLACE

1964: Stage to Thunder Rock
1967: Castle of Evil

1968:   The Money Jungle
1969:   The Girl Who Knew Too Much

IRVING WALLACE (1916-   ) novelist

1943:   Jive Junction*
1950:   The West Point Story*
1952:   Meet Me at the Fair
1953:   Split Second (W. Bowers); Desert Legion (L.
        Meltzer); Bad for Each Other (H. McCoy); Gun
        Fury (R. Huggins)
1954:   The Gambler from Natchez (G. Adams)
1955:   Jump into Hell; Sincerely Yours
1956:   The Burning Hills
1957:   Bombers B-52
1959:   The Big Circus*

ROBERT WALLACE

1957:   That Night (J. Bowles)

TOMMY LEE WALLACE

1982:   Amityville II: the Possession; Halloween
        III: Season of the Witch

IRA WALLACH

1962:   Boys' Night Out
1963:   The Wheeler Dealers (G. Goodman)
1967:   Don't Make Waves (G. Kirgo)
1968:   Hot Millions (P. Ustinov)

HUGH WALPOLE

1935:   David Copperfield (H. Estabrook); Vanessa,
        Her Love Story (L. Coffee)
1936:   Little Lord Fauntleroy

BILL WALSH (1914-1975) producer

1954:   Stormy, the Thoroughbred

```
1955:  The Littlest Outlaw
1959:  The Shaggy Dog (L. Hayward)
1960:  Toby Tyler (L. Hayward)
1961:  The Absent-Minded Professor
1962:  Bon Voyage!
1963:  Son of Flubber
1964:  Mary Poppins (D. DaGradi)
1965:  That Darn Cat*
1966:  Lt. Robin Crusoe, U.S.N. (D. DaGradi)
1968:  Blackbeard's Ghost (D. DaGradi)
1969:  The Love Bug (D. DaGradi)
1971:  Scandalous John (D.DaGradi); Bedknobs and
       Broomsticks (D. DaGradi)
1974:  Herbie Rides Again
1975:  One of Our Dinosaurs Is Missing
```

BOB WALSH

```
1978:  Smokey and the Goodtime Outlaws (Frank
       Dobbs)
```

CHRISTY WALSH

```
1931:  Spirit of Notre Dame
```

GABRIEL WALSH

```
1970:  Quackser Fortune Has a Cousin in the Bronx
```

JOSEPH WALSH

```
1974:  California Split
```

RAOUL WALSH (1887-1980) director

```
1929:  The Cock-Eyed World
1936:  Big Brown Eyes (B. Hanlon); Spendthrift (B.
       Hanlon)
1960:  Esther and the King (M. Elkins)
```

ROBERT E. WALSH

1938: Booloo

EUGENE WALTER (-1941)

1928: Mother Knows Best
1929: Jealousy
1936: Woman Trap (B. Marlow)

FRED WALTON

1979: When a Stranger Calls (S. Feke)

JAMES WAMBAUGH

1979: The Onion Field
1980: The Black Marble

WARREN D. WANDBERG

1951: Sierra Passage (T. Blackburn); Yellow Fin
       (C. Johnston)

RAY WANDER

1957: The Abductors

WAYNE WANG

1982: Chan Is Missing*

LOU WANGER

1937: One Mile from Heaven

AL C. WARD

1956: Please Murder Me (D. Hyde)

DAVID S. WARD

```
1973:   The Sting; Steelyard Blues
1982:   Cannery Row


LUCI WARD

1936:   The Law in Her Hands (G. Bricker); Murder by
        an Aristocrat (R. Chanslor)
1937:   Land Beyond the Law (J. Watson); Cherokee
        Strip (J. Watson); Melody for Two*; Mountain
        Justice (N. Raines)
1938:   Call the Mesquiteers; Panamint's Bad Man (C.
        Powell); Man from Music Mountain (B.
        Burbridge); Overland Stage Raiders; Santa Fe
        Stampede (B. Burbridge); Red River Range*
1939:   New Frontier (B. Burbridge); The Arizona Kid
        (G. Geraghty); Beyond the Sacramento
1942:   The Lone Star Vigilantes; Lawless Plainsmen;
        Bad Men of the Hills; Vengeance of the West
1943:   The Fighting Buckaroo; Law of the Northwest
1944:   Sundown Valley; Riding West; Raiders of
        Ghost City (ser.; M. Cox); Cowboy from
        Lonsesome River; Sagebrush Heroes
1945:   The Frozen Ghost (B. Schubert)
1946:   Badman's Territory (J. Natteford)
1947:   Trail to San Antone (J. Natteford)
1948:   Black Bart*; Return of the Badmen*
1949:   Six Gun Music; Rustlers (J. Natteford)
1956:   Blackjack Ketchum, Desperado (J. Natteford)
1957:   The Night the World Exploded (J. Natteford)
1967:   The Ride to Hangman's Tree*


ROBERT WARD

1981:   Cattle Annie and Little Britches (D. Eyre)


ROLLO WARD

1935:   Rainbow's End


JANE WARDELL

1964:   A Yank in Viet-Nam (Jack Lewis)
```

CLYDE WARE

1966:   The Spy with My Face
1971:   No Drums, No Bugles

DARRELL WARE (-1945)

1937:   Second Honeymoon (K. Scola); Wife, Doctor
        and Nurse*
1938:   Just Around the Corner*; Submarine Patrol*
1939:   Hotel for Women (K. Scola)
1940:   Down Argentine Way (K. Tunberg); He Married
        His Wife*; Public Deb No. 1 (K. Tunberg)
1941:   Tall, Dark and Handsome (K. Tunberg);
        Week-End in Havana (K. Tunberg); A Yank in
        the R.A.F. (K. Tunberg)
1942:   Lucky Jordan (K. Tunberg); My Gal Sal*;
        Orchestra Wives (K. Tunberg)
1943:   Dixie*
1944:   Standing Room Only (K. Tunberg)
1945:   Bring on the Girls (K. Tunberg); Kitty (K.
        Tunberg)
1950:   Love That Brute

HARLAN WARE

1936:   College Holiday*; Yours for the Asking*
1937:   Turn Off the Moon*
1938:   Vacation from Love (P. McNutt)

ANDY WARHOL (1928-   )

1966:   The Chelsea Girls
1967:   Bike Boy; I, a Man; The Nude Restaurant
1973:   L'Amour (P. Morrissey)

JERRY WARNER

1946:   Bringing Up Father; The Cat Creeps (E.
        Dein); Girl on the Spot (D. Cochran); Her
        Adventurous Night; Inside Job (G. Bricker)
1947:   Fall Guy

844

CHARLES MARQUIS WARREN (1912–   ) director,
        playwright, producer

1948:   Beyond Glory*
1949:   Streets of Laredo
1951:   Oh Susanna; Little Big Horn (H. Shumate);
        Hellgate
1952:   Springfield Rifle (F. Davis)
1953:   Pony Express; Arrowhead; Flight to Tangier
1957:   Trooper Hook*
1968:   Day of the Evil Gun (E. Bercovici)
1969:   Charro!

EDGAR WARREN

1977:   Her Last Fling

JERRY WARREN

1958:   Terror in the Midnight Sun (alt. Invasion of
        the Animal People; V. Vogel)

MICHAEL WARREN

1976:   Hawmps (W. Bickley)

SAMUEL J. WARSHAWSKY

1937:   23 1/2 Hours Leave*

FRED WARSHOFSKY

1975:   The Outer Space Connection (doc.)

DEREC WASHBURN

1972:   Silent Running*
1978:   The Deer Hunter
1982:   The Border*

DALE WASSERMAN

1964: Quick, Before It Melts
1966: Mr. Buddwing
1969: A Walk with Love and Death
1972: Man of La Mancha

DUDLEY WATERS

1938: Storm over Bengal

ED WATERS

1957: Sorority Girl
1961: Man-Trap
1967: The Caper of the Golden Bulls (D.
       Moessinger)
1970: Darker Than Amber

GEORGE WATERS

1959: Speed Crazy (R. Bernstein)

JOHN WATERS

1981: Polyester

LAWRENCE E. WATKIN

1947: Keeper of the Bees (M. Boylan)
1950: Treasure Island
1953: The Sword and the Stone; Rob Roy; The
       Highland Rogue
1956: The Great Locomotive Chase
1958: The Light in the Forest
1959: Darby O'Gill and the Little People
1960: Ten Who Dared
1972: The Biscuit Eater

EDITH WATKINS

1945: Hollywood and Vine (C. Williams)

HATTIE WATKINS

1931: Hell's Alley (Jean Webb)

JIM WATKINS

1972: Women in Cages (D. Osterbout)

MAURICE WATKINS

1930: Up the River
1931: Doctors' Wives
1932: No Man of Her Own (M. Gropper); Play Girl
1933: Professional Sweetheart
1934: Search for Beauty*; Strictly Dynamite*
1936: Libeled Lady*

GEORGE M. WATTERS

1930: Good Intentions; Man Trouble (M. Orth)

CAROL WATSON

1982: Friday the 13th (M. Kitrosser)

JOSEPH K. WATSON

1937: Land Beyond the Law (L. Ward); Cherokee
       Strip (L. Ward); Melody for Two*

ROBERT WATSON

1936: Secret Patrol (J. P. McGowan); Stampede;
       Tugboat Princess

W. W. WATSON

1939: The Oregon Trail (ser.)*

NATE WATT

1938:   Pride of the West

LARUE WATTS

1973:   Checkmate

SAL WATTS

1974:   Solomon King

DENNIS WAYNE

1970:   Satan's Sadists

PAUL WAYNE

1967:   The King's Pirate*

FRANK WEAD (1895-1947)

1929:   The Flying Fleet (R. Schayer)
1931:   Shipmates
1932:   Air Mail (D. Van Every); The All-American
        (R. Reyher)
1933:   Midshipman Jack
1935:   Ceiling Zero (M. Ryskind); The Great
        Impersonation (E. Greene); Murder in the
        Fleet (J. Sherman); Storm over the Andes*;
        West Point of the Air (A. Beckhard)
1936:   China Clipper
1937:   Sea Devils*; Submarine D-1*
1938:   The Citadel (Brit.)*
1939:   Tail Spin
1940:   Moon over Burma*
1941:   Dive Bomber (R. Buckner)
1943:   Destroyer*
1945:   They Were Expendable
1946:   The Hoodlum Saint (J. Hill)
1947:   The Beginning or the End; Blaze of Noon (A.
        Sheekman)

848

TED WEAR

1952: If Moscow Strikes (doc.)

JOHN V. A. WEAVER

1929: Pointed Heels (F. Ryerson)
1930: A Man from Wyoming (A. LeVino)
1934: Romance in the Rain*
1935: Sweet Surrender*
1938: The Adventures of Tom Sawyer

IRA WEBB

1948: Dead Man's Gold (R. Ormond); Mark of the
       Lash (R. Ormond)
1949: Outlaw Country (R. Ormond); Son of Billy the
       Kid (R. Ormond); Son of a Badman (R. Ormond)
1951: King of the Bullwhip (Jack Lewis)

JAMES R. WEBB (1909-1974)

1941: Nevada City; Bad Man of Deadwood; Jesse
       James at Bay; Rags to Riches
1942: South of Santa Fe
1949: South of St. Louis (Z. Gold)
1950: Montana*
1951: Raton Pass (T. Blackburn)
1952: The Big Trees (J. Twist); The Iron Mistress;
       Operation Secret
1953: The Charge at Feather River
1954: Apache; Phantom of the Rue Morgue (H.
       Medford); Vera Cruz (R. Kibbee)
1955: Illegal (W. Burnett)
1956: Trapeze
1958: The Big Country*
1959: Pork Chop Hill
1962: Cape Fear; How the West Was Won
1963: Kings of the Sun (E. Arnold)
1968: Guns for San Sebastian
1969: Alfred the Great (Ken Taylor); Sinful Davey
1970: The Hawaiians; They Call Me Mr. Tibbs (A.
       Trustman)

1971: The Organization

JEAN WEBB

1931: Hell's Alley (H. Watkins)

JOSEPH R. WEBB

1964: Cheyenne Autumn

ROBERT D. WEBB (1903-   ) director

1957: The Way to the Gold (W. Mayes)

LOIS WEBER

1934: White Heat (J. Bodrero)

CAROL WEBSTER

1933: Notorious but Nice

M. COATES WEBSTER

1938: A Desperate Adventure (H. Kraly)
1940: Isle of Destiny*
1941: Knockout; A Shot in the Dark; Singapore
      Woman (A. Rivkin)
1942: Home in Wyomin' (R. Tasker); Sons of the
      Pioneers*; Flying with Music (L. S. Kaye)
1943: Klondike Kate (H. Branch); He's My Guy (G.
      Garrett)
1945: Blonde Ransom; I'll Remember April; Jungle
      Captive (D. Babcock); Strange Confession
1946: Song of Arizona; Ding Dong Williams (B.
      Weisberg)
1947: The Brute Man (G. Bricker)
1948: Renegades of Sonora; Glamour Girl (L. Gold);
      I Surrender Dear; Mary Lou
1949: The Wyoming Bandit; Navajo Trail Raiders
1950: Gunmen of Abilene; Salt Lake Raiders;
      Covered Wagon Raiders; Frisco Tornado

```
1951:    Rough Riders of Durango; Night Riders of
         Montana; Wells Fargo Gunmaster; Desert of
         Lost Men
1952:    Black Hills Ambush (R. Davidson); Captive of
         Billy the Kid (R. Wormser); Leadville
         Gunslinger; Thundering Caravans
```

DAVID WECHSLER

```
1948:    The Search (Germ./Sw.; R. Schweizer)
1953:    The Village
```

HUGH WEDLOCK, JR.

```
1941:    Melody Lane*; San Antonio Rose*
1942:    Almost Married (H. Snyder); Don't Get
         Personal (H. Snyder)
1943:    All by Myself (H. Snyder); The Good Fellows
         (H. Snyder); Salute for Three*
1945:    George White's Scandals*
1949:    Abbott and Costello Meet the Killer, Boris
         Karloff*
```

MARLENE WEED

```
1972:    Soul Soldier
```

ROBERT S. WEEKLEY

```
1968:    A Man Called Dagger (J. Peatman)
```

WALTER WEEMS

```
1936:    Conflict (C. Logue)
1940:    Mr. Washington Goes to Town (L. Neal)
```

ROBERT O. WEHLING

```
1960:    Get Out of Town
```

JEROME WEIDMAN

```
1950:   The Damned Don't Cry (H. Medford)
1953:   The Eddie Cantor Story*
1956:   Slander
```

RICHARD WEIL

```
1931:   Naughty Flirt (E. Baldwin)
1943:   The Mysterious Doctor
1944:   Shine On, Harvest Moon*; Crime by Night (J.
        Malone)
1945:   Hit the Hay (C. Marion); Identity Unknown;
        Behind City Lights; The Big Show-Off (L.
        Vadnay); G.I. Honeymoon; The Great
        Flamarion*
1946:   The Gentleman Misbehaves (R. Wyler); The
        Phantom Thief (R. Wormser); Talk About a
        Lady (T. Thomas)
```

HERSCHEL WEINGROD

```
1980:   Cheaper to Keep Her (T. Harris)
```

BOB WEINSTEIN

```
1982:   The Burning (P. Lawrence)
```

MARVIN WEINSTEIN

```
1956:   Running Target*
```

BRENDA WEISBERG

```
1938:   Little Tough Guy (G. Brown)
1941:   Hit The Road (R. Lee); Mob Town (W.
        Doniger); Sing Another Chorus*
1942:   Tough As They Come (L. Amster); There's One
        Born Every Minute (R. Hunt); You're Telling
        Me (F. Hyland)
1943:   Keep 'Em Slugging; Mug Town*
1944:   The Mummy's Ghost*; Weird Woman
1945:   China Sky (J. Hoffman)
1946:   Alias Mr. Twilight; Ding Dong Williams (M.
```

Webster); Shadowed
1947: King of the Wild Horses; When a Girl's Beautiful
1948: My Dog Rusty; Port Said
1949: Rusty Saves a Life; Rusty's Birthday
1950: Girls' School; On the Isle of Samoa (H. Greene)

DAN WEISBURD

1960: Dinosaurus! (J. Yeaworth)

STANLEY WEISER

1980: Coast to Coast

SUSAN WEISER-FINLEY

1982: The First Time*

DAVID WEISMAN

1973: Ciao! Manhattan (J. Palmer)

STRAW WEISMAN

1979: Staying Alive

ALLAN WEISS

1962: Girls! Girls! Girls! (Edward Anhalt)
1963: Fun in Acapulco
1964: Roustabout (A. Lawrence)
1965: The Sons of Katie Elder*
1966: Paradise, Hawaiian Style (A. Lawrence)
1967: Easy Come, Easy Go (A. Lawrence)

ARTHUR WEISS

1963: Flipper
1964: Rhino (A. Arthur)

1966:   Around the World Under the Sea (A. Arthur);
        Namu, the Killer Whale

LOUIS WEITZENKORN

1931:   Ladies of the Big House; 24 Hours
1932:   The Devil Is Driving*
1938:   King of the Newsboys (P. Thompson)

PETER WELBECK

1965:   City of Fear; Ten Little Indians (P.
        Yeldham)

EDDIE WELCH

1935:   Hold 'Em Yale (P. Smith)
1936:   F-Man*
1937:   Murder Goes to College*; Wild Money*
1938:   Her Jungle Love*; Prison Farm*; Scandal
        Sheet (B. Millhauser)

ROBERT WELCH

1947:   Variety Girl*
1952:   Son of Paleface*

WILLIAM WELCH

1971:   The Brotherhood of Satan

MICHAEL WELLER

1979:   Hair
1981:   Ragtime

HALSTED WELLES

1957:   3:10 to Yuma
1959:   The Hanging Tree (W. Mayes)
1968:   A Time for Killing; The Hell with Heroes (H.

Livingston)

ORSON WELLES (1915-   ) actor, director, producer

1941: Citizen Kane (H. Mankiewicz)
1942: Journey into Fear (J. Cotten); The
       Magnificent Ambersons
1946: The Stranger*
1948: The Lady from Shanghai; Macbeth
1952: Othello ((Ital.)
1958: Touch of Evil
1962: Mr. Arkadin
1963: The Trial
1966: Chimes at Midnight
1967: Falstaff (Sp.; alt. Chimes at Midnight)
1969: The Immortal Story
1972: Treasure Island (Brit.; Wolf Mankowitz)
1977: F for Fake (doc.)

GORDON WONG WELLESLEY

1933: Shanghai Madness (A. Parker)
1935: Java Head (Brit.; M. Brown)

WENDELL WELLMAN

1982: Firefox (A. Lasker)

WILLIAM A. WELLMAN (1896-1975) director

1936: Robin Hood of Eldorado*
1946: Gallant Journey (B. Morgan)

ALEXANDER WELLS

1958: The Rawhide Trail

GEORGE WELLS (1909-   )

1946: The Show-Off (H. Mankiewicz); Till the
       Clouds Roll By*
1947: Merton of the Movies (L. Breslow); The

Hucksters (L. Davis)
1949: Take Me Out to the Ball Game (H. Tugend)
1950: Summer Stock (S. Gomberg); Three Little
      Words; The Toast of New Orleans (S. Gomberg)
1951: Angels in the Outfield (D. Kingsley); Excuse
      My Dust; It's a Big Country*
1952: Everything I have Is Yours; Lovely to Look
      At (H. Ruby)
1953: I Love Melvin
1957: Designing Woman; Don't Go Near the Water (D.
      Kingsley)
1958: Party Girl
1959: Ask Any Girl; The Gazebo
1960: Where the Boys Are
1961: The Honeymoon Machine
1962: The Horizontal Lieutenant
1966: Penelope
1967: Three Bites of the Apple
1968: The Impossible Years
1970: Cover Me Babe

WILLIAM K. WELLS

1929: Fox Movietone Follies of 1929
1930: Big Boy (Rex Taylor); Cohens and Kellys in
      Africa; Let's Go Places
1931: Gold Dust Gertie (R. Enright); Side Show

TOM WENNING

1932: The Sport Parade*

RUBY WENTZ

1937: Heroes of the Alamo

MICHAEL WERNER

1973: The Harrad Experiment (T. Cassedy)

SNAG WERRIS

1944: Four Jills in a Jeep*; Take It or Leave It*

1946:   If I'm Lucky*

QUENTIN WERTY (see PETER STONE)

RICHARD WESLEY

1974:   Uptown Saturday Night
1975:   Let's Do It Again

RICHARD WESSON

1969:   Change of Mind (S. Lester)

CLAUDINE WEST (—1945)

1930:   The Soul Kiss (ret. A Lady's Morals; H.
        Kraly)
1931:   The Guardsman (E. Vajda); Just a Gigolo*;
        Private Lives*
1932:   Payment Deferred (E. Vajda); Smilin' Through
        (E. Vajda); The Son-Daughter (J. Goodrich)
1933:   Reunion in Vienna (E. Vajda)
1934:   The Barretts of Wimpole Street*
1937:   The Good Earth*
1938:   Marie Antoinette*
1939:   Goodbye, Mr. Chips (Brit.)*; On Borrowed
        Time*
1940:   The Mortal Storm*
1942:   Mrs. Miniver*; Random Harvest*; We Were
        Dancing*
1943:   Forever and a Day*
1944:   The White Cliffs of Dover*

ELLIOT WEST

1958:   The Fearmakers (C. Appley)

JAMES WEST

1959:   Hey Boy! Hey Girl! (R. Hayes)

JESSAMYN WEST

1963:   Stolen Hours

JOHN WEST   (see JACK JEVNE)

JOSEPH WEST

1938:   Western Trails; Black Bandit; Guilty Trail;
         Prairie Justice; Ghost Town Riders
1939:   Honor of the West; The Phantom Stage; Wolf
         Call; Oklahoma Terror; Mystery Plane (P.
         Schofield); Sky Patrol (N. Parker); Stunt
         Pilot (W. Darling)
1940:   Queen of the Yukon; Drums of the Desert (D.
         Davenport); Laughing at Danger (J. Krafft);
         On the Spot (D. Davenport); Son of the Navy
         (M. Orth); Phantom of Chinatown
1941:   City Limits; Father Steps Out; Man Made
         Monster; Flying Cadets*

MAE WEST (1892-   ) actress

1933:   I'm No Angel (H. Thompson)
1934:   Belle of the Nineties
1935:   Goin' to Town
1936:   Go West, Young Man; Klondike Annie
1937:   Every Day's a Holiday
1940:   My Little Chickadee (W. C. Fields)

NATHANAEL WEST

1936:   Follow Your Heart*; The President's Mystery
         (L. Cole); Ticket to Paradise (J. Natteford)
1937:   It Could Happen to You (S. Ornitz)
1938:   Born to Be Wild
1939:   Five Came Back*; I Stole a Million; Spirit
         of Culver (W. Bolton)
1940:   Let's Make Music; Men Against the Sky

ROLAND WEST

1929:   Alibi (C. G. Sullivan)

1931:   The Bat Whispers

SAMUEL B. WEST

1963:   Captain Sinbad (H. Relis)

VICTOR WEST

1950:   Gunfire (W. Berke); Train to Tombstone (O.
         Hampton); Border Rangers (W. Berke); Bandit
         Queen (B. Lesser)
1951:   Pier 23 (J. Harmon); Roaring City (J.
         Harmon)

ROBERT J. WESTBROOK

1970:   The Magic Garden of Stanley Sweetheart

ROBERT WESTERBY

1954:   Fire over Africa
1966:   The Fighting Prince of Donegal

DONALD E. WESTLAKE

1973:   Cops and Robbers
1979:   Hot Stuff (M. Kane)

ERIC WESTON

1982:   Evilspeak (J. Garofolo)

GARNETT WESTON

1931:   The Viking
1932:   White Zombie
1934:   The Ninth Guest; The Old Fashioned Way (J.
         Cunningham)
1935:   Nevada (S. Anthony)
1937:   Daughter of Shanghai (G. Unger); Partners in
         Crime

```
1938:   Bulldog Drummond in Africa
1939:   Bulldog Drummond's Bride (S. Palmer);
        Bulldog Drummond's Secret Police; Mill on
        the Floss (Brit.)
1940:   The Crooked Road (J. Krumgold); Emergency
        Squad (S. Palmer); Opened by Mistake*
1941:   The Great Train Robbery*
```

EDWIN K. WESTRATE

```
1946:   Renegade Girl; Rolling Home
```

HASKELL WEXLER (1926-   ) director of photography

```
1965:   The Bus (doc.)*
1969:   Medium Cool
1974:   Introduction to the Enemy*
```

NORMAN WEXLER

```
1970:   Joe
1973:   Serpico (W. Salt)
1975:   Mandingo
1976:   Drum
1977:   Saturday Night Fever
```

JOHN WEXLEY

```
1938:   Angels with Dirty Faces (W. Duff); The
        Amazing Dr. Clitterhouse (J. Huston)
1939:   Confessions of a Nazi Spy (M. Krims)
1940:   City for Conquest
1941:   Footsteps in the Dark (L. Cole)
1943:   Hangmen Also Die*
1947:   The Long Night
```

JAMES WHARTON

```
1934:   Bedside*
```

ROGER WHATELY

1934: Silver Streak (H. Hanemann)
1936: We're in the Legion Now
1937: Drums of Destiny (J. Neville)

KEN & JIM WHEAT

1979: Silent Scream (W. C. Bennett)

JOHN WHEDON

1974: The Island at the Top of the World; The
       Bears and I

HUGH WHEELER

1963: Five Miles to Midnight (P. Viertel)
1970: Something for Everyone
1978: A Little Night Music

RALPH WHEELWRIGHT

1933: Fast Workers (K. Brown)

TIM WHELAN (1893-1957) director

1930: Hook, Line and Sinker (R. Spence)
1931: Everything's Rosie
1932: Girl Crazy (H. Mankiewicz)
1934: Along Came Sally (Brit.)
1935: The Murder Man*
1937: The Mill on the Floss (Brit.)

ROD WHIPPLE

1975: Teenage Hitchhikers

JAMES WHITAKER

1931: Up for Murder

ROD WHITAKER

1975:   The Eiger Sanction*

ALEXANDER WHITE

1951:   The Thundering Trail

ANDY WHITE

1966:   Africa -- Texas Style
1967:   Gentle Giant (E. Lakso)
1968:   Daring Game

GARY MICHAEL WHITE

1973:   Scarecrow
1976:   Sky Riders*
1979:   The Promise

JAMES GORDON WHITE

1968:   The Glory Stompers (J. Lawrence); The
        Mini-Skirt Mob; The Young Animals; Born Wild
1969:   The Devil's Eight*;
1970:   Hell's Belles (R. McMullen)
1971:   The Incredible Two-Headed Transplant (J.
        Lawrence)
1972:   The Thing with Two Heads*
1973:   Big Foot (R. Slater)
1982:   Ten Violent Women (T. Mikels)

JOHN MANCHIP WHITE

1965:   Crack in the World (J. Halvey)

LESLIE T. WHITE

1939:   Behind Prison Gates (A. Horman)
1944:   Two-Man Submarine (G. Jay); The Unwritten
        Code (Charles Kenyon)

862

PHILIP GRAHAM WHITE

1932:   The Local Bad Man; The Gay Buckaroo; Spirit
        of the West
1937:   Boots of Destiny; Trailing Trouble

ROBERTSON WHITE

1937:   The Adventurous Blonde (D. Diamond); The
        Footloose Heiress; Once a Doctor (B. Kahn);
        The Westland Case
1938:   He Couldn't Say No*; Lady in the Morgue (E.
        Taylor); My Bill (V. Sherman); Mystery House
        (S. Lowe); The Patient in Room 18 (E. Solow)
1939:   The Witness Vanishes
1940:   Charlie Chan's Murder Cruise (L. Ziffren)
1947:   Dick Tracy Meets Gruesome (E. Taylor)

ROBB WHITE

1958:   Macabre; House on Haunted Hill
1959:   The Tingler
1960:   Thirteen Ghosts
1961:   Homicidal

SHIRLEY WHITE

1951:   Reunion in Reno (H. Jacoby)
1952:   Tarzan's Savage Fury*

LOU WHITEHILL

1973:   Wonder Women

RICHARD WHITLEY

1979:   Rock 'n' Roll High School*
1982:   Pandemonium (Jaime Klein)

HARRY WHITLINGTON

1969:   Fireball Jungle

ANNALEE WHITMORE

1940:   Andy Hardy Meets Debutante (T. Seller)

STANFORD WHITMORE

1962:   War Hunt
1964:   Your Cheatin' Heart
1971:   My Old Man's Place (alt. Glory Boy)
1972:   Hammersmith Is Out
1976:   Baby Blue Marine
1979:   The Dark

DAVID WHITNEY

1974:   Gravy Train (B. Kerby)

JAMES WHITTAKER

1978:   Gray Lady Down (H. Sackler)
1982:   Megaforce*

RON WHYTE

1970:   Pigeons
1972:   The Happiness Cage

CHRISTOPHER WICKING

1970:   Cry of the Banshee (Tim Kelly)
1971:   Murders in the Rue Morgue (H. Slesar)

ANNE WIGHTON

1945:   The Great Flamarion*

CRANE WILBUR (1889-1973) actor, director

1930: Lord Byron of Broadway
1934: Tomorrow's Children (W. Thurman)
1935: Unwelcome Stranger
1936: Captain Calamity; The Devil on Horseback;
Yellow Cargo
1937: Dance, Charlie, Dance (W. Jacobs); Navy Spy;
West of Shanghai
1938: Alcatraz Island; Crime School (V. Sherman);
Girls on Probation; The Invisible Menace;
Over the Wall (G. Bricker); Penrod's Double
Trouble (E. Booth)
1939: Blackwell's Island; Hell's Kitchen (F.
Niblo)
1940: King of the Lumberjacks
1944: Roger Touhy, Gangster (J. Cady); A Night of
Adventure
1947: Born to Speed*; The Devil on Wheels; The Red
Stallion (R. Kent)
1948: Adventures of Casanova*; Canon City; He
Walked by Night (J. Higgins)
1949: The Story of Molly X
1950: Outside the Wall
1951: I Was a Communist for the FBI; Inside the
Walls of Folsom Prison
1952: The Lion and the Horse; The Miracle of Our
Lady of Fatima (J. O'Hanlon)
1953: House of Wax
1954: Crime Wave; The Mad Magician
1955: The Phenix City Story (G. Homes); Women's
Prison (J. DeWitt)
1956: Battle Stations
1957: Monkey on My Back*
1959: The Bat
1961: The George Raft Story ; Mysterious Island*

1962: House of Women

FRED M. WILCOX (1905-1964)

1960: I Passed for White

CORNEL WILDE (1915-   ) actor, director

1957: The Devil's Hairpin (J. Edmiston)
1975: Shark's Treasure

865

HAGAR WILDE

1938:   Bringing Up Baby (D. Nichols)
1945:   The Unseen*
1949:   I Was a Male War Bride*; Red, Hot and Blue
        (J. Farrow)
1954:   This Is My Love (H. Brooke)

BILLY WILDER (1906-   ) director, producer Aust.

(American films only)
1934:   Music in the Air (H. Young)
1935:   The Lottery Lover (F. Schulz)
1938:   Bluebeard's Eighth Wife (C. Brackett)
1939:   Midnight (C. Brackett); Ninotchka*; What a
        Life (C. Brackett)
1940:   Arise, My Love (C. Brackett)
1941:   Ball of Fire (C. Brackett); Hold Back the
        Dawn (C. Brackett)
1942:   The Major and the Minor (C. Brackett)
1943:   Five Graves to Cairo (C. Brackett)
1944:   Double Indemnity*
1945:   The Lost Weekend (C. Brackett)
1946:   To Each His Own*
1948:   The Emperor Waltz (C. Brackett); A Foreign
        Affair*
1950:   Sunset Boulevard*
1951:   The Big Carnival (orig. Ace in the Hole)*
1953:   Stalag 17
1954:   Sabrina (E. Lehman)
1955:   The Seven Year Itch (G. Axelrod)
1957:   Witness for the Prosecution*; The Spirit of
        St. Louis*; Love in the Afternoon (I.
        Diamond)
1959:   Some Like It Hot (I. Diamond)
1960:   The Apartment (I. Diamond)
1961:   One, Two, Three (I. Diamond)
1963:   Irma La Douce (I. Diamond)
1964:   Kiss Me, Stupid (I. Diamond)
1966:   The Fortune Cookie (I. Diamond)
1970:   The Private Life of Sherlock Holmes (I.
        Diamond)
1972:   Avanti! (I. Diamond)
1974:   The Front Page (I. Diamond)
1979:   Fedora (I. Diamond)
1981:   Buddy Buddy (I. Diamond)

GENE WILDER (1935-   ) actor

1974: Young Frankenstein (M. Brooks)
1975: The Adventure of Sherlock Holmes' Smarter
       Brother
1977: The World's Greatest Lover

MARGARET BUELL WILDER

1946: Young Widow (R. Macaulay)
1947: Pirates of Monterey (S. Hellman)

MYLES WILDER

1953: Phantom from Space (W. Raynor)
1954: The Snow Creature
1958: Seven Guns to Mesa*; Spy in the Sky
1960: Bluebeard's Ten Honeymoons

ROBERT WILDER

1949: Flamingo Road
1958: The Big Country*

THORNTON WILDER (1897-1975) playwright

1940: Our Town*
1943: Shadow of a Doubt*

YVONNE WILDER

1971: The Return of Count Yorga (B. Kelljan)

DWIGHT MITCHELL WILEY

1946: The Bride Wore Boots

HANS WILHELM

```
1946:   Heartbeat*
1948:   On an Island with You*
1952:   No Time for Flowers (Aust.; E. Vadnay)
1961:   Five Golden Hours
1963:   Dime with a Halo (L. Vadnay)
```

MAX WILK

```
1948:   Close-Up (J. Bright); Open Secret*
1968:   Don't Raise the Bridge, Lower the Water
```

MARTHA WILKERSON

```
1951:   Hard, Fast and Beautiful
```

NAT WILKES

```
1957:   The Big Fun Carnival (L. Heyword)
```

JOHN WILLARD

```
1929:   Black Waters
1932:   The Mask of Fu Manchu*
```

CHARLES WILLEFORD

```
1974:   Cock Fighter
```

JOHN WILLIAM

```
1971:   The Omega Man (J. Corrington)
```

BOB WILLIAMS

```
1942:   Treat 'Em Rough (R. Chanslor)
1943:   Dead Man's Gulch (N. Hall); Overland Mail
        Robbery (R. Yost)
1944:   Pride of the Plains (J. Butler); Beneath
        Western Skies (A. DeMond); Hidden Valley
        Outlaws (J. Butler); Call of the Rockies;
        Bordertown Trail (J. Duffy); Lights of Old
```

```
              Santa Fe (G. Kahn)
1945:   Lone Texas Ranger; Marshal of Laredo; Trail
        to Vengeance
1946:   California Gold Rush; Lawless Breed
1947:   The Adventures of Don Coyote*; Saddle Pals
        (J. Sackheim); Bandits of Dark Canyon
1948:   Oklahoma Badlands; The Bold Frontiersman;
        The Timber Trail; Marshal of Amarillo;
        Desperadoes of Dodge City; The Denver Kid
1949:   Sheriff of Wichita; Death Valley Gunfighter;
        Frontier Investigator; Rangers of Cherokee
        Strip; Pioneer Marshal
1950:   The Old Frontier; Under Mexicali Skies; The
        Vanishing Westerner
1951:   Stage to Tucson*; Silver City Bonanza
1956:   Accused of Murder (W. Burnett)
1957:   Duel at Apache Wells; Twenty Million Miles
        to Earth (C. Knopf)
1958:   The Saga of Hemp Brown
```

C. B. WILLIAMS

```
1939:   Heroes in Blue
1940:   Midnight Limited (H. Carter)
```

CHARLES WILLIAMS

```
1934:   Woman in the Dark*
1945:   Hollywood and Vine (E. Watkins)
1964:   Joy House*
1968:   The Pink Jungle; Don't Just Stand There
```

DON WILLIAMS

```
1972:   Slaughter (M. Hanna)
```

GEORGE WILLIAMS

```
1965:   War Party (W. Marks)
```

HUGH WILLIAMS (1904-1969) actor, playwright Brit.

(American films only)

1960: The Grass Is Greener*

JAMES B. WILLIAMS

1949: That Forsyte Woman*

JOHN T. WILLIAMS

1954: The Law vs. Billy the Kid

LORRAINE WILLIAMS

1954: The Cowboy

1978: Caravans*

OSCAR WILLIAMS

1972: The Final Comedown
1974: Black Belt Jones; Truck Turner (M. Allin)
1976: Hot Potato
1977: Sudden Death

PAUL WILLIAMS (1944-   ) director

1969: Out of It
1972: Dealing: or the Berkeley-to-Boston 40-Brick
      Lost-Bag Blues (D. Odell)

ROBERT WILLIAMS (see BOB WILLIAMS)

ROBERT CREIGHTON WILLIAMS

1964: He Rides Tall (C. Irwin); Taggart

SPENCER WILLIAMS, JR.

1939: Harlem Rides the Range (F. E. Miller)
1940: Son of Ingagi
1946: Dirty Gertie from Harlem, U.S.A.

SUMNER WILLIAMS

1966:   An Eye for an Eye (B. Russell)

TENNESSEE WILLIAMS (1914–1983) playwright

1950:   The Glass Menagerie (P. Berneis)
1951:   A Streetcar Named Desire (E. Kazan)
1955:   The Rose Tattoo (H. Kantor)
1956:   Baby Doll
1959:   Suddenly, Last Summer*
1960:   The Fugitive Kind (Meade Roberts)
1968:   Boom!

THAMES WILLIAMS

1949:   Brimstone
1954:   A Bullet Is Waiting (C. Robinson)

FRED WILLIAMSON (1938–   ) actor, director

1975:   Boss Nigger
1976:   Adios Amigo; No Way Back; Joshua

JEFF WILLIAMSON

1977:   Mr. Mean
1982:   One Down Two to Go

THOMAS WILLIAMSON

1947:   Cheyenne (A. LeMay); Escape Me Never (L.
         Coffee)
1949:   The Last Bandit
1956:   Taming Sutton's Gal (F.L. Fox)

CALDER WILLINGHAM

1957:   The Strange One; Paths of Glory*
1958:   The Vikings

1961:   One-Eyed Jacks (G. Trosper)
1967:   The Graduate (B. Henry)
1970:   Little Big Horn
1974:   Thieves Like Us*

MARY WILLINGHAM

1964:   Bullet for a Badman (W. Willingham)
1965:   Arizona Raiders*
1966:   Gunpoint (W. Willingham)
1967:   Forty Guns to Apache Pass (W. Willingham)

WILLARD WILLINGHAM

1961:   Battle at Bloody Beach (R. Maibaum)
1964:   Bullet for a Badman (M. Willingham)
1965:   Arizona Raiders*
1966:   Gunpoint (M. Willingham)
1967:   Forty Guns to Apache Pass (M. Willingham)

F. McGREW WILLIS

1929:   Two Weeks Off (J. Poland)
1930:   Charley's Aunt; The Costello Case
1931:   The Big Gamble (W. DeLeon); Meet the Wife
         (W. DeLeon)
1932:   The Forty-Niners; The Fighting Gentleman;
         Gambling Sex
1933:   Secret Sinners
1934:   Back Page
1935:   Manhattan Butterfly
1938:   Let's Make a Night of It (Brit.; H. Brooke)
1940:   One Night in Paris (Brit.)

LES WILLIS

1945:   The Woman Who Came Back (D. Cooper)

ANTHONY WILSON

1974:   Newman's Law

872

CAREY WILSON (1889-   ) producer

1929:   Why Be Good?; His Captive Woman
1930:   The Bad One*
1931:   Behind Closed Doors; Fanny Foley Herself;
        The Flying Fool
1932:   Arsene Lupin*; Faithless; Polly of the
        Circus
1933:   Gabriel over the White House; What! No Beer?
1934:   Murder at the Vanities*; The President
        Vanishes*; Sequoia*
1935:   Mutiny on the Bounty*
1937:   Dangerous Number
1939:   Judge Hardy and Son

DOUG WILSON

1967:   The Violated Ones (C. Davis)

ELIZABETH WILSON

1951:   Cave of Outlaws
1958:   Raw Wind in Eden (R. Wilson)
1964:   Invitation to a Gunfighter (R. Wilson)

FRANK ARTHUR WILSON

1976:   Blast

GERALD WILSON

1971:   Lawman
1972:   Chato's Land
1973:   The Stone Killer
1979:   Firepower

JOHN T. WILSON

1966:   The Black Klansman (A. Names)

MICHAEL WILSON (1914-1978)

```
1941:   The Men in Her Life*
1942:   Border Patrol
1943:   Colt Comrades; Bar 20*
1944:   Forty Thieves (B. Kamins)
1951:   A Place in the Sun (H. Brown)
1952:   Five Fingers
1954:   Salt of the Earth
1956:   Friendly Persuasion (unc.)
1957:   The Bridge on the River Kwai (unc.; C.
        Foreman)
1962:   Lawrence of Arabia (unc.)
1965:   The Sandpiper (D. Trumbo)
1968:   Planet of the Apes (R. Serling)
1969;   Che! (S. Bartlett)
```

RICHARD WILSON (1915-   ) director, producer

```
1955:   Man with the Gun (N. B. Stone)
1958:   Raw Wind in Eden (E. Wilson)
1964:   Invitation to a Gunfighter (E. Wilson)
```

TED WILSON

```
1946:   The Devil's Playground
```

WARREN WILSON

```
1941:   Helzapoppin (N. Perrin); Tanks a Million*
1942:   Give Out, Sisters (P. Smith)
1943:   Cowboy in Manhattan (M. Shane); Follow the
        Band (D. Bennett); Get Going; Good Morning,
        Judge (M. Geraghty); Strictly in the Groove
        (K. Higgins); Swing Fever (N. Perrin); Hi,
        Buddy!
1944:   Allergic to Love
1945:   On Stage Everybody (O. Brodney); She Gets
        Her Man (C. Bruckman)
1946:   She Wrote the Book (O. Brodney)
1948:   If You Knew Susie (O. Brodney)
1950:   Square Dance Katy; Tall Timber
```

DAVID WILTSE

```
1973:   Hurry Up, or I'll Be 30 (J. Jacoby)
```

ARTHUR WIMPERIS (1874-1953) Brit.

(American films only)
1942: Mrs. Miniver*; Random Harvest*
1947: If Winter Comes (M. Roberts)
1948: Julia Misbehaves*
1949: The Red Danube (G. Kaus)
1951: Calling Bulldog Drummond
1953: Young Bess (S. Lustig)

SIMON WINCELBERG

1953: Fighter Attack
1956: On the Threshold of Space (F. Cockrell)

IRWIN WINEHOUSE

1961: Blueprint for Robbery (A. Sanford Wolf)

HARRY WINER

1976: The Legend of Bigfoot (P. Labrot)

TERENCE H. WINKLESS

1981: The Howling (J. Sayles)

MICHAEL WINNER (1935-   ) director, producer,
        Brit.

(American films only)
1977: The Sentinel (J. Konvitz)

RON WINSTON

1970: The Gamblers

KEITH WINTER

```
1941:   The Chocolate Soldier (L. Lee)
1943:   Above Suspicion*; Forever and a Day*
1946:   Devotion
```

NICHOLAS WINTER

```
1950:   Cry Murder (J. Carthart)
```

SALLY WINTERS

```
1929:   Riders of the Rio Grande
1930:   Covered Wagon Trails; The Cowboy and the
        Outlaw; The Canyon of Missing Men; Near the
        Rainbow's End; 'Neath the Western Skies;
        Call of the Desert; The Parting of the
        Trails; Western Honor (alt. The Man from
        Nowhere)
```

HAROLD C. WIRE

```
1945:   The Royal Mounted Rides Again (ser.)*
```

FRANK WISBAR

```
1945:   Strangler of the Swamp
1949:   Rimfire*
```

AUBREY WISBERG

```
1942:   Counter-Espionage; Submarine Raider
1943:   Bomber's Moon (K. Gamet); They Came to Blow
        Up America
1944:   U-Boat Prisoner
1945:   The Power of the Whistler; The Adventures of
        Rusty; Betrayal from the East (K. Gamet);
        Escape in the Fog
1946:   The Falcon's Adventure; Just Before Dawn (E.
        Taylor); Rendezvous 24
1947:   The Big Fix (G. Bricker); The Burning Cross;
        Road to the Big House
1948:   The Wreck of the Hesperus
1950:   The Desert Hawk*; Hit Parade of 1951*
1951:   The Man from Planet X (J. Pollexfen)
```

```
1952:   At Sword's Point*; Captive Women (J.
        Pollexfen); Lady in the Iron Mask (J.
        Pollexfen)
1953:   Sword of Venus (J. Pollexfen); Port Sinister
        (J. Pollexfen); Problem Girls (J.
        Pollexfen); Neanderthal Man (J. Pollexfen);
        Captain John Smith and Pocahontas (J.
        Pollexfen)
1954:   Casanova's Big Night; Dragon's Gold (J.
        Pollexfen); Captain Kidd and the Slave Girl
        (J. Pollexfen); Return to Treasure Island
        (J. Pollexfen)
1955:   Murder Is My Beat (M. Field); Son of Sinbad
        (J. Pollexfen)
1956:   The Women of Pitcairn Island
```

WALTER WISE

```
1936:   Sinner Take All (L. Lee)
1939:   First Offenders
1958:   Thunder Road (J. Phillips)
```

FRED WISEMAN

```
1969:   High School (doc.)
```

JERRY WISH

```
1968:   Angel from Hell
1969:   Run, Angel, Run (V. A. Furlong); The Gay
        Deceivers
```

MORTON WISHINGRAD

```
1953:   The Hidden Heart
```

GEORGE WISLOCKI

```
1976:   Deadly Hero
```

JANE WITHERSPOON

1974:   The Swinging Cheerleaders (B. Conklin)

WILLIAM D. WITTLIFF

1979:   The Black Stallion*
1980:   Honeysuckle Rose*
1981:   Raggedy Man
1982:   Barbarosa

P. G. WODEHOUSE (1881-1975)

1937:   A Damsel in Distress*

BURTON WOHL

1961:   A Cold Wind in August
1965:   The Third Day (R. Presnell)
1966:   Blues for Lovers
1970:   Rio Lobo (L. Brackett)

A. SANFORD WOLF

1961:   Blueprint for Robbery (I. Winehouse)
1965:   The Naked Brigade (A. J. Cohen)

DAVID M. WOLF

1973:   Hit! (A. Trustman)
1976:   The Next Man*
1979:   The American Game (Jay Freund)

RICHARD A. WOLF

1978:   Skateboard (G. Gage)

TOM WOLFE

1969:   Cherry, Harry and Raquel (R. Meyer)
1970:   Wilbur and the Baby Factory

IRA WOLFERT

1948:   Force of Evil (A. Polonsky)

P. J. WOLFSON

1932:   The Devil Is Driving*; Madison Square Garden
        (A. Rivkin)
1933:   Dancing Lady (A. Rivkin); The Girl in 419*;
        Meet the Baron (A. Rivkin); Picture Snatcher
        (A. Rivkin)
1935:   Mad Love*; Reckless; Rendezvous*
1936:   The Bride Walks Out (P. Epstein); The Lady
        Consents (A. Veiller); Love on a Bet (P.
        Epstein); That Girl from Paris*
1937:   Sea Devils*; Shall We Dance?*
1938:   Vivacious Lady (E. Pagano)
1939:   Allegheny Uprising
1940:   He Stayed for Breakfast*; Vigil in the
        Night*
1941:   Our Wife; Submarine Zone (alt. Escape to
        Glory); This Thing Called Love*
1942:   Pacific Rendezvous*; They All Kissed the
        Bride
1947:   Suddenly It's Spring (C. Binyon)
1948:   Saigon (A. Sheekman)
1955:   The Twinkle in God's Eye

VICTOR WOLFSON

1966:   Rings Around the World (doc.)

CLEMENT C. WOOD

1971:   Welcome to the Club

CYRUS WOOD

1930:   The Cuckoos

EDWARD D. WOOD, JR.

1953:   Glen or Glenda (alt. I Led Two Lives)

879

1956:   Bride of the Monster (Alex Gordon)
1958:   The Bride and the Beast
1959:   Night of the Ghouls (unr.); Plan Nine from
        Outer Space

MORRISON C. WOOD

1940:   The Green Hornet (ser.)*

WARD WOOD

1976:   Posse from Heaven (P. Pine)

WILLIAM WOOD

1963:   My Six Loves*
1964:   The Lively Set (M. Goldberg)

ROBERT WOODBURN

1975:   God's Bloody Acre (W. Crawford)

GITTA & WILLIAM WOODFIELD

1960:   The Hypnotic Eye

RUTH WOODMAN

1953:   Last of the Pony Riders

JACK WOODS

1970:   Equinox
1972:   Beware! the Blob (A. Harris)

LOTTA WOODS

1929:   The Iron Mask

WALTER WOODS

1930: The Big Fight; Once a Gentleman
1931: Salvation Nell
1934: David Harum
1936: Sutter's Gold*

BRONTE WOODWARD

1978: Grease
1980: Can't Stop the Music (A. Carr)

ED WOODWORTH

1976: The Amorous Adventures of Don Quixote and
       Sancho Panza*

EDGAR ALLAN WOOLF

1931: The Great Lover (G. Markey); A Tailor Made
       Man
1932: Flesh (L. Praskins); The Mask of Fu Manchu*
1933: Broadway to Hollywood (W. Mack)
1934: Have a Heart*; Murder in the Private Car*;
       This Side of Heaven*
1935: Casino Murder Case (F. Ryerson); The Night
       Is Young (F. Schulz); Tough Guy (F. Ryerson)
1936: Mad Holiday (F. Ryerson); Moonlight Murder
       (F. Ryerson)
1938: Everybody Sing (F. Ryerson)
1939: The Ice Follies of 1939*; The Kid from
       Texas*; The Wizard of Oz*

BASIL WOON

1932: While Paris Sleeps

CHUCK (CHARLES) WORKMAN

1976: The Money
1981: Sweet Dirty Tony

RICHARD WORMSER

1938: Fugitives for a Night; Start Cheering*
1946: The Plainsman and the Lady; The Phantom
       Thief (R. Weil)
1948: Perilous Waters (F. Rosenwald)
1949: Powder River Rustlers
1950: Vigilante Hideout; Rustlers on Horseback;
       The Showdown*
1951: Fort Dodge Stampede
1952: Captive of Billy the Kid (M. Webster); The
       Half-Breed (H. Shumate)
1953: A Perilous Journey
1954: The Outcast (J. Butler)

BARBARA WORTH

1947: Dragnet (H. Essex)
1948: The Counterfeiters (F. Myton)
1949: Zamba

CEDRIC WORTH

1934: The President Vanishes*
1940: The Ramparts We Watch (doc.; R. Richards)

STEPHEN WORTH

1943: Border Roundup

HERMAN WOUK (1915-   ) novelist

1949: Slattery's Hurricane (R. Murphy)

VICTORIA WOZNIAK

1975: Loose Ends (D. Morris)

ARDEL WRAY

1943: The Falcon and the Co-Eds (G. Geraghty); I
       Walked with a Zombie (C. Siodmak); The

Leopard Man
1945:   Isle of the Dead (J. Mischel)

BETTY WRIGHT

1947:   Little Miss Broadway*

GEORGE WRIGHT

1934:   Three on a Honeymoon*

GILBERT WRIGHT

1937:   The Californian (G. Newill); Springtime in
        the Rockies (B. Burbridge)
1938:   Wild Horse Rodeo*

HERBERT J. WRIGHT

1976:   Shadow of the Hawk (N. Vane)

JOSEPH WRIGHT

1930:   The Arizona Kid (R. Brock)

LENORE WRIGHT

1981:   Underground Aces*

MAURICE WRIGHT

1940:   Zanzibar (M. Tombragel)

RALPH WRIGHT

1953:   Peter Pan*
1955:   Lady and the Tramp (anim.)*
1957:   Perri*
1959:   Sleeping Beauty*
1961:   Nikki, Wild Dog of the North (W. Hibler)

1967:   The Jungle Book (anim.)*

RICHARD WRIGHT (1908-1960) novelist

1951:   Native Son (P. Chenal)

SIDNEY FOWLER WRIGHT

1933:   The Deluge*

WILLIAM H. WRIGHT

1942:   Her Cardboard Lover*
1943:   Assignment in Brittany*
1965:   The Sons of Katie Elder*

WILLIAM L. WRIGHT

1936:   Blake of Scotland Yard (ser.; R.F. Hill)

DONALD WRYE

1978:   Ice Castles (G. Baim)

RUDOLPH WURLITZER

1971:   Two Lane Blacktop (W. Corry)
1973:   Pat Garrett and Billy the Kid

ROBERT WYLER

1937:   The Last Train from Madrid (L. Stevens);
        Murder Goes to College*; Sophie Lang Goes
        West*
1946:   The Gentleman Misbehaves (R. Weil)
1951:   Detective Story (P. Yordan)

WILLIAM WYLER (1902-   ) director

1944:   The Memphis Belle (doc.)

PHILIP WYLIE (1902-1971) novelist

1932:   Island of Lost Souls (W. Young)
1933:   King of the Jungle*; Murders in the Zoo (S.
        Miller)

NED WYNN

1979:   California Dreaming

TRACY KEENAN WYNN

1974:   The Longest Yard
1975:   The Drowning Pool*
1977:   The Deep (P. Benchley)

Y

FRANK YABLANS

1979:   North Dallas Forty*
1981:   Mommie Dearest*

HAROLD YABLONSKY

1960:   The Secret of the Purple Reef (G. Corman)

YABO YABLONSKY

1971:   B. J. Presents
1979:   Jaguar Lives
1981:   Victory (Evan Jones)

STEPHEN YAFA

1968:   Three in the Attic
1971:   Summertree (E. Hume)

LEONARD YAKIR

1982:   Out of the Blue (G. Jouvenat)

RICHARD YALEM

1979:   Delirium

NEIL YAREMA

1973:   A Taste of Hell

BROCK YATES

1980:   Smokey and the Bandit II (J. Belson)
1981:   The Cannonball Run

GEORGE WORTHING YATES

1938:   The Lone Ranger (ser.)*
1940:   Hi-Yo Silver (edit. from above serial)
1944:   The Falcon in Mexico (G. Geraghty)
1945:   The Spanish Main (H. Mankiewicz)
1951:   The Last Outpost*; The Tall Target*
1952:   This Woman Is Dangerous (G. Homes)
1953:   China Venture (R. Collins); Those Redheads
        from Seattle*
1954:   The Saracen Blade (D. Scott)
1955:   It Came from Beneath the Sea (Hal Smith)
1956:   Earth vs. the Flying Saucers*
1958:   The Flame Barrier (P. Fielder); Space Master
        X-7 (G. Homes); Frankenstein -- 1970 (R.
        Landau); Attack of the Puppet People; The
        Spider (L. Gorog); War of the Colossal Beast
1960:   Tormented

HAL YATES

1936:   General Spanky*
1937:   Mama Runs Wild*; Nobody's Baby*
1941:   Niagara Falls*

PAUL YAWITZ

1937:   Breakfast for Two*; Saturday's Heroes*; They
        Wanted to Marry (E. Borden)
1938:   Affairs of Annabel (B. Granet); Crashing
        Hollywood (G. Atwater); Go Chase Yourself
        (B. Granet); Blonde Cheat*
1939:   Fixer Dugan (B. Granet); Little Accident (E.
        Greene)
1941:   Confessions of Boston Blackie; Honolulu Lu
        (E. Gibbons)
1942:   Alias Boston Blackie; Boston Blackie Goes

```
             Hollywood
1943:    The Chance of a Lifetime; She Has What It
         Takes
1944:    The Racket Man*; Louisiana Hayride; One
         Mysterious Night
1945:    Boston Blackie Booked on Suspicion; I Love a
         Bandleader
1946:    The Falcon's Alibi
1952:    Models, Inc. (H. Essex)
```

JEAN YEAWORTH

```
1960:    Dinosaurus! (D. Weisburd)
1966:    Way Out*
```

JACK YELLEN

```
1934:    George White's Scandals; Hell in the
         Heavens*
1935:    George White's 1935 Scandals (P. McNutt);
         Our Little Girl*
1936:    Pigskin Parade*; Sing, Baby, Sing*
1937:    Ali Baba Goes to Town (H. Tugend); Love Is
         News (H. Tugend); Wake Up and Live (H.
         Tugend); You Can't Have Everything*
1938:    Hold That Co-Ed*; Little Miss Broadway (H.
         Tugend); My Lucky Star (H. Tugend); Sally,
         Irene and Mary (H. Tugend); Submarine
         Patrol*
```

DUKE YELTON

```
1967:    Hillbillys in a Haunted House
```

LOREES YERBY

```
1972:    Richard (H. Hurwitz)
```

PHILIP YORDAN (1913-   ) novelist, producer

```
1942:    Syncopation (F. Cavett)
1943:    The Unknown Guest
1944:    When Strangers Marry (Dennis Cooper); Johnny
```

```
         Doesn't Live Here Any More  (J. Kafka)
1945:  Dillinger
1946:  The Chase; Suspense; Whistle Stop
1948:  Bad Men of Tombstone (A. Strawn)
1949:  Anna Lucasta (A. Laurents); House of
       Strangers; Reign of Terror (alt. The Black
       Book; A. MacKenzie)
1950:  Edge of Doom
1951:  Drums in the Deep South (S. Harmon);
       Detective Story (R. Wyler)
1952:  Mutiny (S. Harmon)
1953:  Houdini; Blowing Wild
1954:  Man Crazy (S. Harmon); The Naked Jungle*;
       Johnny Guitar (B. Maddow)
1955:  The Big Combo; The Last Frontier (R. S.
       Hughes); The Man from Laramie (F. Burt);
       Conquest of Space (J. O'Hanlon)
1956:  The Harder They Fall; Joe Macbeth
1957:  Four Boys and a Gun (L. Townsend); Men in
       War (B. Maddow); No Down Payment
1958:  Island Women; God's Little Acre (B. Maddow);
       The Bravados; The Fiend Who Walked the West
       (H. Brown); Anna Lucasta
1959:  Day of the Outlaw
1960:  The Bramble Bush (M. Sperling); Studs
       Lonigan
1961:  El Cid (F. Frank); King of Kings
1963:  The Day of the Triffids; 55 Days at Peking
       (Bernard Gordon)
1964:  The Fall of the Roman Empire*
1965:  Battle of the Bulge*
1969:  The Royal Hunt of the Sun
1971:  Captain Apache (M. Sperling)


DOROTHY YOST

1933:  Hello Everybody (L. Hazard)
1934:  The Gay Divorcee*
1935:  Alice Adams*; A Dog of Flanders (A. Morgan);
       Freckles; Laddie (R. Harris)
1936:  Bunker Bean*; M'Liss; Murder on a Bridle
       Path*; That Girl from Paris*
1937:  Racing Lady (T. Lennon); There Goes the
       Groom*; Too Many Wives*
1939:  Bad Little Angel; Four Girls in White; The
       Story of Vernon and Irene Castle*
1940:  Forty Little Mothers (E. Pagano); Sporting
```

Blood (A. Mannheimer)
1945: Thunderhead -- Son of Flicka (D. Cummings)
1946: Smoky*
1948: The Strawberry Roan (D. Cummings)
1949: Loaded Pistols (D. Cummings); The Cowboy and
the Indians (D. Cummings); The Big Cat (M.
Grant)
1953: Saginaw Trail

ROBERT M. YOST

1935: Dante's Inferno (P. Klein)
1936: Drift Fence (alt. Texas Desperadoes; S.
Anthony); Desert Gold (S. Anthony); The
Arizona Raiders (J. Krafft); Arizona Mahoney
(S. Anthony); Forgotten Faces*; Preview
Murder Mystery (B. Marlowe)
1937: Forlorn River (S. Anthony); Thunder Trail
(S. Anthony); Born to the West (S. Anthony);
Let's Make a Million (M. Seff)
1938: Illegal Traffic*; Prison Farm*; Tip-Off
Girls*
1939: Grand Jury Secrets (I. Reis)
1940: Young Buffalo Bill*; The Carson City Kid (G.
Geraghty)
1942: The Phantom Plainsmen (B. Shipman)
1943: Thundering Trails*; Overland Mail Robbery
(B. Williams); Canyon City

BURT YOUNG

1978: Uncle Joe Shannon

CARROLL YOUNG

1943: Tarzan Triumphs (R. Chanslor)
1946: Tarzan and the Leopard Woman
1948: Jungle Jim; Tarzan and the Mermaids
1950: Bamba and the Hidden City; Mark of the
Gorilla; Pygmy Island; Captive Girl
1951: Fury of the Congo
1952: The Jungle (Ind.)
1953: Tarzan and the She-Devil (K. Lamb); Killer
Ape (A. Hoerl)
1954: Cannibal Attack

1957:   She—Devil (K. Neumann); Apache Warrior*; The
        Deerslayer (K. Neumann)
1958:   Machete (K. Neumann)

CLARENCE UPSON YOUNG

1936:   The Plot Thickens
1938:   The Law West of Tombstone (J. Twist)
1939:   The Girl and the Gambler (J. Fields); Bad
        Lands
1940:   Son of Roaring Dan; Black Diamonds (S.
        Rubins); The Devil's Pipeline*; Hot Steel;
        Love, Honor and Oh Baby!
1941:   Sea Raiders (ser.)*; Sky Raiders (ser.)*
1942:   Time to Kill; North to the Klondike*; Night
        Monster; The Strange Case of Dr. Rx; Madame
        Spy (L. Riggs)
1944:   The Black Parachute; The Ghost That Walks
        Alone
1947:   Riding the California Trail
1948:   Albuquerque (G. Lewis)

COLLIER YOUNG

1950:   Never Fear (I. Lupino); Outrage*
1953:   The Bigamist
1954:   Private Hell 36 (I. Lupino)

DALENE YOUNG

1980:   Little Darlings (K. Peck)

FRANK H. YOUNG

1944:   Partners of the Trail; Range Law; Ghost
        Guns; Million Dollar Kid
1945:   Gun Smoke; Stranger from Santa Fe
1946:   Border Bandits; The Haunted Mine; Trigger
        Fingers
1947:   Flashing Guns
1948:   Song of the Drifter

HILDA MAY YOUNG

```
1938:   Topa Topa (A. Hoerl)
1940:   Killers of the Wild


HOWARD IRVING YOUNG

1934:   Music in the Air (B. Wilder)
1937:   The Great Gambini*; She Asked for It*
1945:   You Can't Do Without Love


JOHN SACRET YOUNG

1972:   Chandler


NED YOUNG

1946:   Decoy
1947:   Joe Palooka in the Knockout


R. R. Young

1967:   Waterhole #3 (J. Steck)


ROBERT YOUNG

1956:   Secrets of the Reef (doc.)*
1965:   Nothing but a Man (M. Roemer)


ROBERT MALCOLM YOUNG

1962:   Trauma
1975:   Escape to Witch Mountain
1979:   Alambrista!


STARK YOUNG

1958:   Uncle Vanya


TERENCE YOUNG

1958:   Tank Force (R. Maibaum)
```

1969:   The Christmas Tree

WALDEMAR YOUNG (1890-1938)

1929:   Trail of '98; Tide of Empire; Where East Is
        East; Sally
1930:   The Girl of the Golden West
1931:   Chances; Compromised; Penrod and Sam
1932:   Island of Lost Souls (P. Wylie); Love Me
        Tonight*; The Miracle Man; The Sign of the
        Cross (S. Buchman); Sinners in the Sun*
1933:   A Bedtime Story*
1934:   Cleopatra*; Men in White
1935:   The Crusades*; Lives of a Bengal Lancer*;
        Peter Ibbetson*
1936:   The Plainsman*; Desire*; Poppy (V. Van Upp)
1938:   Man-Proof*; Test Pilot (V. Lawrence)

A. P. YOUNGER

1928:   Alias Jimmy Valentine (S. Y. Mason); Lady of
        Chance
1931:   Five and Ten; Flying High (C. Reisner)

ROBERT YOUNGSON (1917-1974) producer

1960:   When Comedy Was King (doc.)
1961:   Days of Thrills and Laughter (doc.)
1963:   Thirty Years of Fun (doc.)
1965:   Laurel and Hardy's Laughing '20s (doc.)
1968:   The Further Perils of Laurel and Hardy
        (doc.)
1970:   Four Clowns (doc.)

RICHARD YRIONDO

1954:   Miss Robin Crusoe*

LARRY YUST

1973:   Trick Babies
1974:   Homebodies*

Z

ALFREDO ZACHARIAS

1978: The Bees

RICHARD ZACHARY

1968: Finders Keepers, Lovers Weepers

MICHAEL ZAGOR

1964: The Man from Galveston (D. Riesner)

LEROY H. ZEHREN

1951: Tales of Robin Hood

ALFRED ZEISLER

1944: Enemy of Women (H. Phillips)
1946: Fear (D. Cooper)

ROBERT ZEMECKIS

1978: I Wanna Hold Your Hand (B. Gale)
1979: 1941 (Bob Gale)
1980: Used Cars (B. Gale)

LESTER ZIFFREN

1937: City Girl*

```
1940:   Charlie Chan's Murder Cruise (R. White);
        Charter Pilot (S. Rauh); The Man Who
        Wouldn't Talk*; Murder over New York
1941:   Charlie Chan in Rio (S. Engel)
```

DON ZIMBALIST

```
1965:   Young Dillinger
```

JULIAN ZIMET

```
1941:   Sierra Sue (E. Felton)
1946:   Heldorado (G. Geraghty)
```

MAURICE ZIMM

```
1955:   The Prodigal
1957:   Affair in Havana (B. Lane)
1958:   Good Day for a Hanging (D. Ullman)
```

VERNON ZIMMERMAN

```
1976:   Bobbie Jo and the Outlaw
1980:   Fade to Black
```

PAUL ZINDEL

```
1972:   Up the Sandbox
1974:   Mame
```

STEPHEN ZITO

```
1982:   The Escape Artist (R. Mathison)
```

JOHN W. ZODROW

```
1974:   The Ultimate Thrill
```

DAVID ZUCKER

```
1977:   The Kentucky Fried Movie*
1980:   Airplane!*
```

JERRY ZUCKER

```
1977:   The Kentucky Fried Movie*
1980:   Airplane!*
```

GEORGE ZUCKERMAN

```
1949:   Trapped (E. Felton)
1950:   Spy Hunt (L. Lee); Under the Gun
1951:   Iron Man (B. Chase)
1954:   Ride Clear of Diablo; Dawn at Socorro; The
        Yellow Mountain*; Taza, Son of Cochise
1955:   The Square Jungle
1956:   Written on the Wind
1957:   The Tattered Dress; The Tarnished Angels
```

ALBERT ZUGSMITH (1910-   ) director, producer

```
1961:   Dondi (Gus Edson)
1965:   The Incredible Sex Revolution (doc.)
1966:   Movie Star American Style or LSD -- I Hate
        You*; On Her Bed of Roses
1969:   Sappho, Darling; The Very Friendly
        Neighbors; Two Roses and a Golden-Rod
```

RALPH ZUKOR

```
1973:   The Devil's Wedding Night (Alan Harris)
```

A. MARTIN ZWEIBACK

```
1969:   Me, Natalie
1971:   Cactus in the Snow
```